MOTOCOURSE™

THE WORLD'S LEADING GRAND PRIX & SUPERBIKE ANNUAL

icon
PUBLISHING LIMITED

THE OFFICIAL WEBSITE
FIM-MOTO.COM
FIMLive
FIM_live
fimlive
tvfim
FIM

CONTENTS

MOTOCOURSE
2022–2023
is published by:
Icon Publishing Limited
4 Suffolk Villas
Suffolk Road,
Cheltenham
Gloucestershire
GL50 2AX
United Kingdom

Tel: +44 (0)1242 245329

Email: info@motocourse.com
Website: www.motocourse.com

Printed in the United Kingdom by
Gomer Press Ltd
Llandysul Enterprise Park
Llandysul
Ceredigion
SA44 4JL
Tel: 01559 362371
email: sales@gomer.co.uk

© Icon Publishing Limited 2022.
No part of this publication may be reproduced, stored in a retrieval system or transmitted, in any form or by any means, electronic, mechanical, photocopying, recording or otherwise, without prior permission in writing from Icon Publishing Limited.

ISBN: 978-1910584-51-4

DISTRIBUTORS
Gardners Books
1 Whittle Drive, Eastbourne,
East Sussex, BN23 6QH
Tel: +44 (0)1323 521555
email: sales@gardners.com

Chaters Wholesale Ltd
25/26 Murrell Green Business Park,
Hook, Hampshire, RG27 9GR
Tel: +44 (0)1256 765443
Fax: +44 (0)1256 769900
email: books@chaters.co.uk

NORTH AMERICA
NATIONAL BOOK NETWORK
NBN
4501 Forbes Boulevard
Suite 200
Lanham, MD 20706
Tel: (301) 459-3366
Fax: (301) 429-5746

Dust jacket: Pecco Bagnaia became Ducati's first MotoGP world champion since 2007.
Photo: Whit Bazemore

Title page: Alvaro Bautista, Ducati's 2022 World Superbike champion.
Photo: Gold & Goose

Acknowledgements

The Editor and staff of MOTOCOURSE wish to thank the following for their assistance and support: Matt Birt, Peter Clifford, Simon Crafar, Matt Dunn, Michael Guy, Isabelle Lariviere, Hector Martin, Neil Morrison, Mat Oxley, David Pato, Ignacio Sagnier, Paolo Scalera, Federico Tonelli, Mike Trimby, Frine Vellila, Artur Vilalta, Mike Webb and Gunther Wiesinger, as well as numerous others. The usual apologies to colleagues if I ignored their helpful comments and advice.

Photographs published in MOTOCOURSE 2022–2023 have been contributed by:
Chief photographers: Gold & Goose.
Other photographs contributed by: Whit Bazemore, Clive Challinor Motorsport Photography, David Collister, Photography, Double Red Photography, Ducati Corse, HRC, Repsol Honda, Lou Martin, John Morris/MPix, MotoAmerica/Brian J. Nelson, Monster Energy Yamaha MotoGP, Pramac Ducati, David Purves, Red Bull KTM, Rennie Scaysbrook, www.suzuki-racing.com, Mark Walters, Bryn Williams.

publisher
STEVE SMALL
steve.small@iconpublishinglimited.com

commercial director
BRYN WILLIAMS
bryn.williams@iconpublishinglimited.com

editor
MICHAEL SCOTT

text editor
IAN PENBERTHY

results and statistics
PETER McLAREN

chief photographers
GOLD & GOOSE
David Goldman
Gareth Harford
David 'Chippy' Wood
www.goldandgoose.com
Tel: +44 (0)208 444 2448

MotoGP bike and circuit illustrations
ADRIAN DEAN
f1artwork@blueyonder.co.uk

MOTOCOURSE
www.motocourse.com

Ducati.com

Developed with Shell Advance Technical partner Pirelli

New Ducati Panigale V4 R

This is Racing

The closest production model to a competition bike – ever. Every technical detail has been thought out and designed to enhance the pure racing feel of the bike, from the newly refined Desmosedici Stradale R engine to race orientated electronics and beyond. The track soul of the new Panigale V4 R makes it perfect for your track days. The new livery is inspired by MotoGP in its graphics and conveys a racing spirit from the very first glance, incorporating white number plates with the number "1" prominently displayed. Available in Standard* and Racing configurations, the latter able to produce an incredible 240.5 hp.**

Contact your local Ducati Dealership for more details

DUCATI

* **Displacement** 998cc (61 cu in) | **Power** 218 hp (160.4 kW) @ 15,500 rpm | **Torque** 111.3 Nm (82 lb ft) @ 12,000 rpm | **Dry weight** 172 kg (379 lb)

** In combination with the full titanium racing exhaust and new performance oil developed by Shell in collaboration with Ducati Corse.

FOREWORD
by PECCO BAGNAIA

Photo: Ducati Corse

IT is every racer's dream to become World Champion. It is the target that drives us to work hard and race hard through a gruelling season. In 2022, we won it. And it tastes good!

Anyone can see that the year was not straightforward.

Ducati made me a super motorcycle. It was strong in everything: acceleration, braking, top speed, cornering... But, as well as the usual rivals from other manufacturers, I had to race also some very, very fast riders who were also riding the excellent Desmosedici GP. They had the same potential as I did.

To tell the truth, I enjoyed that challenge. I never expected or wanted any help or support from anyone. I wanted to fight for the title, to achieve what I could achieve by my own efforts only – and that is what I did.

I had to have faith in myself. After the German Grand Prix, I was 91 points behind and in sixth place. I knew I was fast, but I knew my weak point was inconsistency. I had to work on myself, and to change.

After that, I was able to improve my position race by race, and after the Thai GP, I knew the title was possible.

I'm proud of fulfilling an ambition that has driven me since my childhood.

I want to thank Ducati, my team, my family and all my fans for their support. And all the people at the VR46 Academy who work so hard to support all of us.

Also my rivals for making me work so hard. Your fighting made this title worthwhile.

MOTOCOURSE has been the classic racing annual since before I was born. Seeing my image on the cover and writing this Foreword are among the proud privileges of being World Champion.

Now I want to do it again.

EDITOR'S INTRODUCTION

FAST FORWARD!

Above: Ducati and Pecco Bagnaia ruled MotoGP for the first time since 2007.
Photo: Ducati Corse

Top right: Five hundred podiums, but soon just memories for departing Suzuki. Alex Rins's second at CoTA brought past marque champions, winners and stars together: Capirossi, Uncini, Mamola, Rins, Mir, Schwantz, (and kneeling) Hopkins and Vinales.
Photo: www.suzuki-racing.com

Top far right: The TT returned after a two-year hiatus.
Photo: David Collister Photography

Above right: Marquez rides again. Magic Marc came back with a vengeance.
Photo: Gold & Goose

Above centre right: Europe met the USA In MotoAmerica. Jake Gagne fought off a strong challenge from Danilo Petrucci.
Photo: MotoAmerica/Brian J. Nelson

Above far right: BSB continued to thrill as Bradley Ray came good.
Photo: Bryn Williams

Right: World Superbike was a three-horse race, but an entertaining one.
Photo: Ducati Corse

THE trouble with surveys is two-fold: the people who frame the questions, and the people who answer them. The first can lead the answers in a certain direction – deliberately or not. The second risk accusations of being over-keen on their own opinions. Like the club bore.

Dorna commissioned a massive 109,000-strong fan survey in 2022, which revealed, among not much else, that bike racing fans love bike racing, attend tracks or watch on TV, and use social media.

MOTOCOURSE prefers to make its own assumptions: that our readers have a deep and lasting passion for world-level motorcycling and all its supporting structures, a well-informed appreciation of the technical aspects and developments, a desire to learn more about the remarkable men (and now and again women) whose skill and obsession take them to the pinnacle of the sport, and an intelligent interest in the nuances of history, current racing affairs and future prospects.

Plus the desire to preserve on their bookshelves the memories of yet another epic racing season, the longest in more than seven decades, illustrated with superlative photographs and illuminated with insider insights.

This edition celebrates a year when racing came back, the tracks came back and the fans came back, after the strictures of Covid. Excitement and tension were preserved throughout.

Two out of three MotoGP titles went to the final race, and if WorldSBK was settled slightly earlier, it was hardly less absorbing.

In both major series, Ducati led the way in a resurgence of European manufacturers, who for so long have lagged behind Japan; and while great riding genius Marc Marquez finally made a belated return at full strength, new faces and fast rookies confirmed the essential renewal that drives the sport ever forward.

In 2023, MotoGP turns 75, with an even longer season spanning even more countries, and (with Saturday sprints) more than double the number of races.

Until then, let's continue to appreciate the last one.

MICHAEL SCOTT
West Sussex
November, 2022

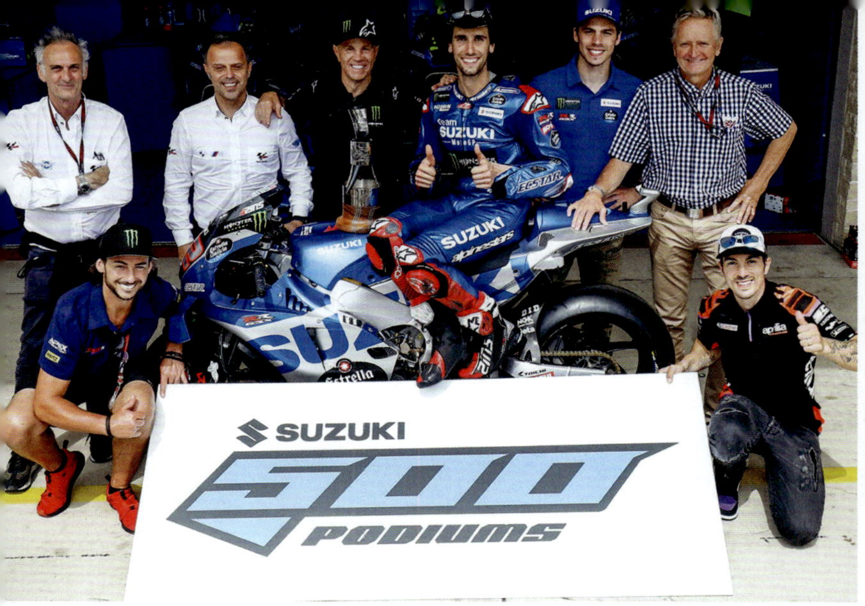
SUZUKI
500
PODIUMS

BRANDS

MOTOAMERICA
YAMAHA
KATO

Circuit de Barcelona
CATALUNYA
Barcelona
ACERBIS

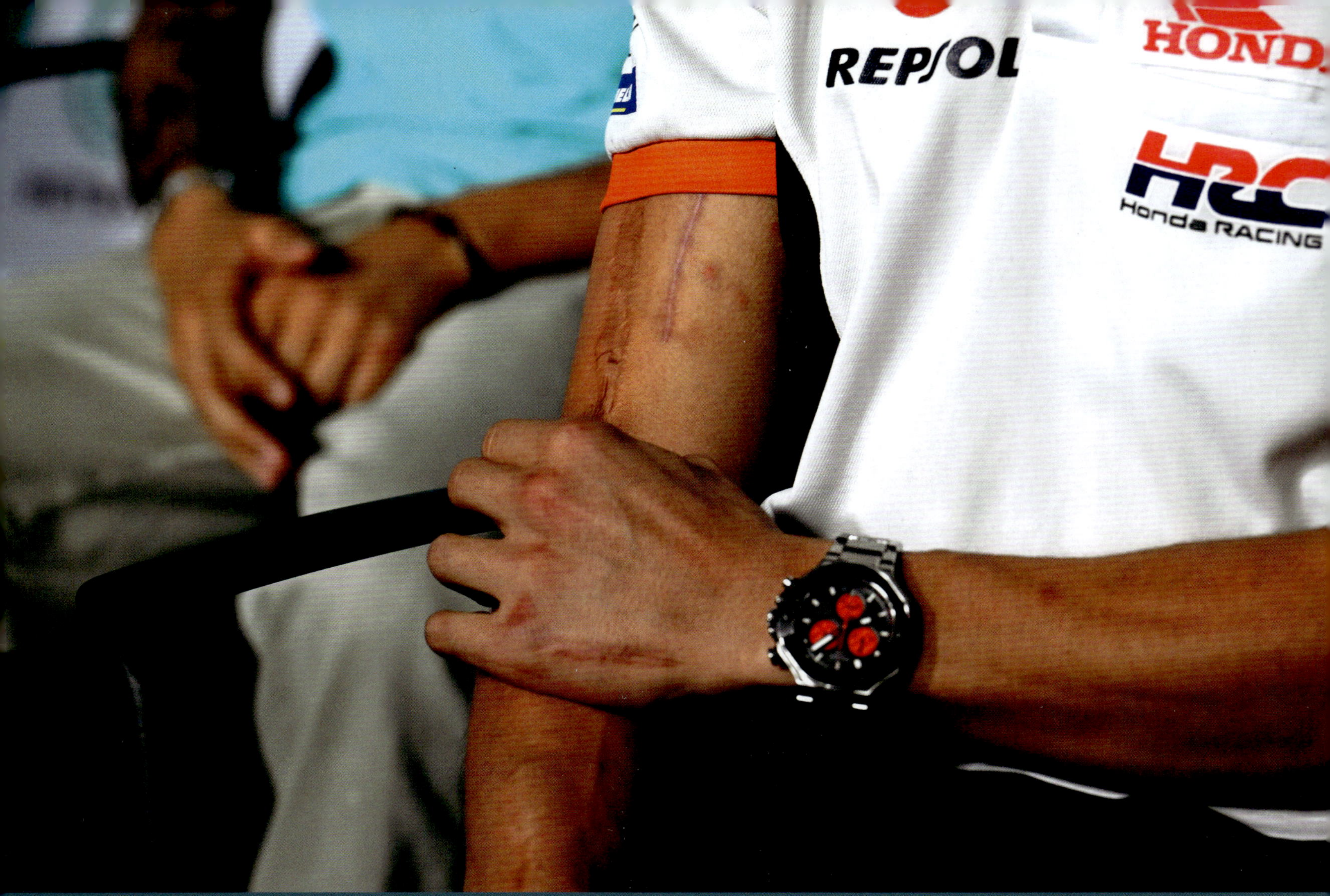

FIM WORLD CHAMPIONSHIP 2022

TOP TEN RIDERS

THE EDITOR'S CHOICE

Rider Portraits by Gold & Goose

1 MARC MARQUEZ

MARC MARQUEZ didn't need to be there all season, nor to win a race, to stamp his authority on the class.

Riding a Honda that, in his fitful two-season absence, had become so recalcitrant that its other riders could barely stay on it, let alone claim strong results, Marc was awe-inspiring.

A fourth major surgery on the broken humerus in his right arm, correcting an accumulated torsional distortion of an astonishing 30-plus degrees, meant that he was neither physically fully fit nor race-fit when he returned to round 15 at Aragon.

Undaunted, revelling in that again he could "ride as I like", he was immediately testing the limits. In the first two corners, he had surged from 13th on the grid to sixth when he collided (innocently) with Quartararo, triggering further disasters for himself and Nakagami further around the same lap.

Thereafter, he was simply brilliant: on pole at Motegi, a sliver away from the win in Australia, and aiming for the podium on a clearly inadequate bike at Valencia when he crashed.

Brilliance undimmed, he was the best rider in a field with many exceptionally talented rivals.

2 FABIO QUARTARARO

AS with Marquez, Quartararo had to exploit exceptional talent to overcome technical mediocrity. He did so repeatedly, but not even his herculean efforts could withstand the Ducati steamroller and Bagnaia's growing challenge.

It could have been a devastating experience, but most of the time, the defending champion remained cheerful and kept trying anyway. Without doubt, his lowest moment was when he was knocked off for zero points at Aragon, but once more he came back fighting.

Not that he didn't make his disappointment with the Yamaha known, especially earlier in the season, as the size of the disadvantage of its relatively sluggish acceleration and top speed became increasingly clear. In spite of this, he was still leading on points until after the Australian GP, with just two races to go.

Lips remained sealed, but it was obvious that Yamaha had made a misstep in development, possibly because the intended power-up 2022 engine ran into development problems. Equally, it was clear that they were able to convince Quartararo that in 2023, the picture would be different, for he signed a new two-year contract before the summer break.

He'll be back...

3 PECCO BAGNAIA

IS it fair not to put the new World Champion at the top? Pecco himself acknowledged, after the final race, that overall Quartararo had been the better rider.

This was becomingly modest, for while it was clearly true over the first half of the season, by the end of it, the Italian had undergone a sea change.

Historically, the numbers favour Bagnaia. He had won a Moto3 race when Quartararo's best had been second; and then had added a championship and eight more wins in two Moto2 seasons, to Quartararo's single win.

Pecco, however, took longer to find his feet in MotoGP, echoed in a championship season that took half the year before it could be taken seriously. At the halfway point, he wasn't even top Ducati, lying sixth overall, with both Zarco and Bastianini ahead.

More significantly, after four no-scores in ten races, he was 91 points behind Quartararo.

In the second half of the year, he made only one more error, falling in Japan. Instead, often under huge pressure, he racked up a record number of consecutive Ducati wins, and took a well-deserved title in an unprecedented comeback.

If he is that strong through 2023, he will be hard to beat.

4 ENEA BASTIANINI

BASTIANINI was on fire in 2022. The suave Italian, whose self-chosen 'Beast' nickname is only apposite when he is actually on the bike, had been one of the revelations of 2021. In his second MotoGP season, he compounded that reputation, finishing third overall, and with a full factory contract with Ducati to follow.

He started his tally of four wins (only Bagnaia had more) at the opening round; and whether adding three more wins or mercilessly harrying his 2023 team-mate to the flag before taking second, they were all achieved thanks to an impressive gift for preserving tyres and speeding up at the end of races, when other riders were perforce slowing down. An impressive and precocious maturity.

There were a couple of missteps, not always his own fault and including a puncture after taking a maiden pole at the Red Bull Ring. The others were forgivable in a second-year rider, still finding his feet in the premier class.

It is impossible not to expect that he will get even better in 2023, which is something the established riders will have to worry about. Especially new team-mate Bagnaia.

5 BRAD BINDER

IT wasn't a strong season for KTM. There were two race wins, true, but both were in the wet, and in more normal conditions, the Austrian bikes failed to continue the strong progress of recent years.

Yet with the same capacity to impose willpower over technical weakness shown by Marquez and Quartararo, former Moto3 champion Brad Binder moved reliably forward from poor qualifying positions, especially strong in the later stages of the race. This further reinforced his reputation as an ever reliable 'Sunday man'.

Race after race, his finishing spot was much higher than his starting position, with a best of ten places at Le Mans – from 18th to eighth.

This in a season when many riders complained that a combination of factors had made overtaking more difficult than ever. If anybody told Brad, he wasn't listening.

Disappointingly, this was the first season since 2017 when Binder did not claim at least one race win. Consider it an aberration. At the final race, KTM produced a chassis that solved some of the bike's issues. Another little step, and Binder should be right up at the front.

6 ALEX RINS

A strong finish to a season always creates a good impression, and Rins excelled. Add a solid dose of empathy for misfortunes beyond his control to his two convincing late wins, and his reputation was given a welcome boost.

The biggest misfortune was the unexpected withdrawal of Suzuki, which took the team and riders as much by surprise as the whole of racing. The news came shortly after the start of the European season, casting a pall over the ensuing races.

Rins's other disaster was as innocent victim of a nasty first-corner crash at Catalunya, knocked off by Nakagami. It left him nursing an injured wrist, which had a major impact on mid-season results.

Rins is a smooth rider, and capable of very fast and consistent race pace. The sweet-natured Suzuki suited him well, and a tendency to try too hard and fall off was less in evidence in the later races.

In 2023, he takes on a different challenge – switching to Honda with LCR. The RC213V is the direct opposite of the Suzuki, with a mean streak to go with its obvious strength in speed. It will be interesting to watch Alex adapt.

7 ALEIX ESPARGARO

OH, what might have been. The elder Espargaro brother had waited so long to achieve success, had watched his younger sibling win the Moto2 championship, and felt undervalued and (by Suzuki) discarded, his ability and dedication ignored.

It all came together at last in 2022, with an Aprilia that had improved hugely, if somewhat unobtrusively, for a rider who had helped it every step of the way.

A first race win at his 200th attempt came in only the third round in Argentina, and it was assured and accomplished. Espargaro even led the championship charts briefly, maintaining his position through the first part of the season.

The first blunder was his own, celebrating second position at home in Catalunya one lap too early. It lost valuable points.

The second was by Quartararo, who knocked Aleix off-track at Assen, only for him to follow with a magnificent ride back through to fourth. But it was a race he might easily have won; and likewise the Japanese GP, had his team not made a desperate mistake with the electronic settings.

Will the oldest rider on the grid ever be presented with as good a chance again?

8 JACK MILLER

IN spite of a return to pole position and (just once) the winner's circle, it wasn't a great year for the popular Australian. Too many crashes out of top positions robbed him of results.

When he did win, in Japan, it was magnificently bold and daring in the sort of tricky conditions in which he has so often excelled.

It surely didn't help that he was just one of a number of very fast Ducati riders, and often the only one who seemed always willing to wholeheartedly support the title chances of his factory team-mate, Bagnaia.

Added to this was the burden that he was going to lose his factory seat, and while Ducati valued his talent, loyalty and development skills enough to offer him a seat in the Pramac satellite squad, instead he opted for a new adventure with KTM, joining Binder in the factory team.

MotoGP would be a poorer place without the affable and amusing Australian, and everyone would be delighted if the change in motorcycle reinvigorates him.

9 MIGUEL OLIVEIRA

PORTUGAL'S first and still only grand prix winner has a mature, self-contained personality, and he manages to be equally unobtrusive on the track.

In this way, two resounding wins in the wet were as surprising as each other. Yet this should not be the case, given Oliveira's all-round ability.

But 2022 was a season in which the KTM did little to help its riders in a very competitive midfield, and Oliveira's other secondary results did not flatter his talent. Although very reliable, only failing to finish twice and always in the points, he was too often mired at the wrong end of the top ten.

Nor did those too-average placings do enough for him to keep his ride in the factory team. At the same time, Oliveira's self-belief prevented him from accepting relegation to the satellite KTM squad (name change to GasGas and 'factory team' status notwithstanding.

For 2023, he joins the new Aprilia satellite team, for another chance to demonstrate his depth.

10 IZAN GUEVARA

NOBODY in Moto2 really excited in 2022. Ogura and Fernandez fought for the title; rookie Pedro Acosta shone from time to time when not injured.

The raw excitement came from the smallest class, where reliably huge and frighteningly volatile gangs of front-runners tore chunks out of one another.

It takes a special talent to rise above this maelstrom repeatedly, and that is what Izan Guevara did, winning seven races and claiming five more top-three positions.

It wasn't only in the races that the 2020 CEV 'Junior World Champion' excelled. Ten front-row starts, five of them from pole, were achieved not by the usual means of canny slipstreaming at the end of Q2, but by running alone, supremely confident and working on race pace. A pace that his rivals too often found impossible to match.

One never knows how these precocious teenagers will adapt to bigger bikes, but examples like Marc Marquez, Maverick Vinales and Jorge Martin map out an encouraging future for most of them.

BOOM AND BUST?

MotoGP's growing strength showed some cracks in 2022. How can the ship be righted? MICHAEL SCOTT reports...

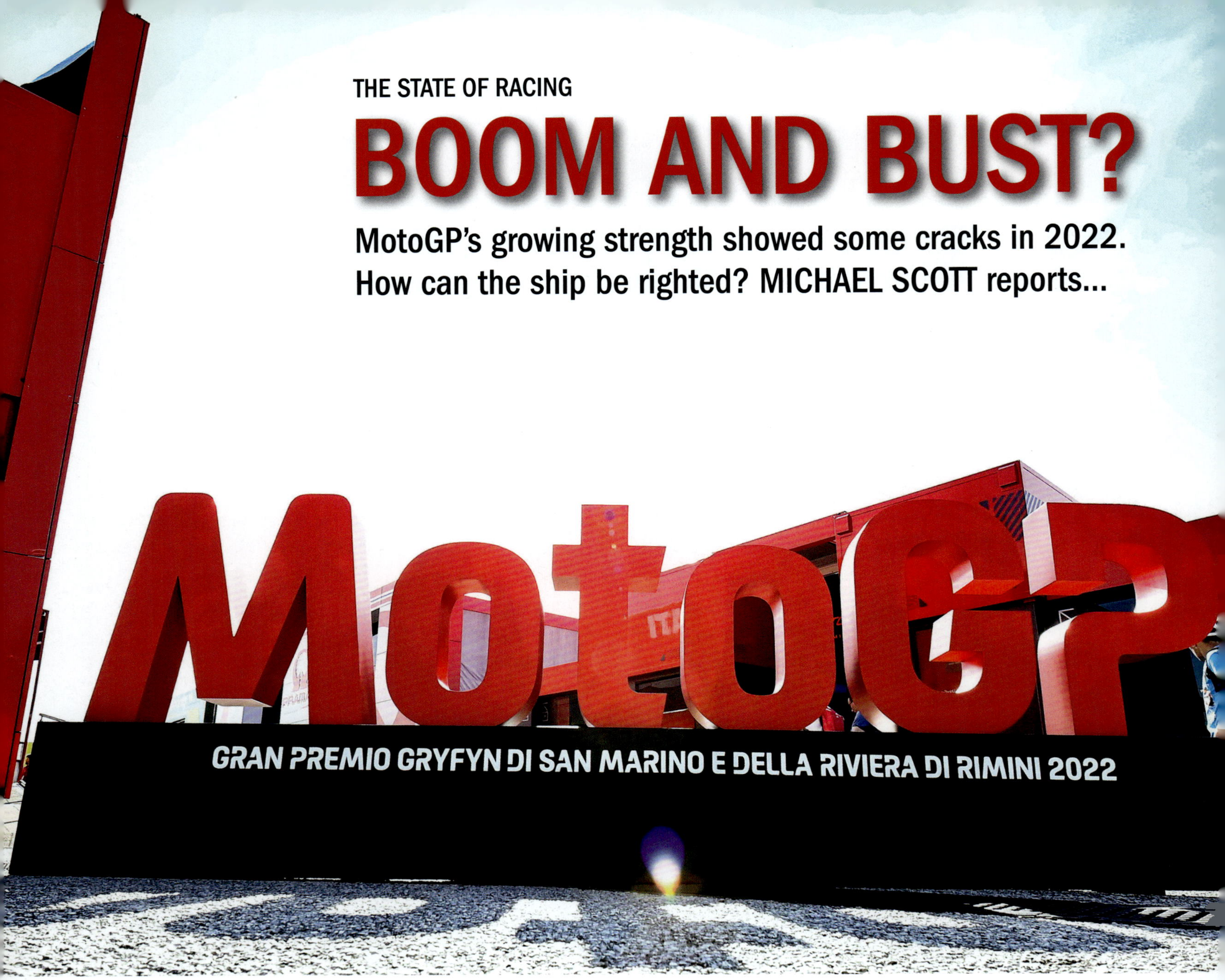

Above: **Grandiose presentation – but where do Dorna take MotoGP next?**

Top right: **Remote-control TV cameras were trialled in Valencia – remote-control viewers needed to pay to watch the result.**

Above right: **On the grid, but not on a bike. Valentino Rossi's absence was sorely felt...**

Right: **...no more so than at Misano, where previously packed grandstands were a distant memory.**

Photos: Gold & Goose

ON the face of it, MotoGP was booming in 2022. If you looked in the right places. A record crowd at Le Mans, grandstands packed at Assen, the Covid bounce-back in full swing...

It was not like that everywhere. A different kind of bounce-back might have been responsible for the opposite in Italy, both at Mugello and Misano, where crowd numbers slumped. Was it the elevated ticket prices or just because of the absence of Rossi? As one fan poster at the Italian GP had it, "Mugello without Rossi is like a nightclub without girls."

Or was there a greater malaise? Falling TV viewing figures, with the increasing introduction of pay walls, were mirrored in the flop of the Amazon streaming video *MotoGP Unlimited*, intended to replicate the huge success of Formula 1's *Drive to Survive*, which has recruited legions of younger fans.

Then followed the seemingly abrupt decision to liven up the weekend by introducing a Saturday afternoon sprint race – looking very much like another knee-jerk imitation of Formula 1, and far from popular throughout the paddock. Many were the calls for a more considered strategy. Likewise, many the mutterings that the blatant nepotism of Dorna, treated like a family firm, seemed more like a corner-shop dynasty than an international sports marketing exercise.

It is perhaps not too far fetched to assume that MotoGP's past decade and more of burgeoning success has reached an impasse, and that without a reasoned rethink, a decline in popularity only partly (although quite a large part) triggered by the departure of Rossi will take some stopping.

Is the Rossi factor overrated? Not if you take heed of social media figures, where media titan Valentino individually has more followers than MotoGP, the series. There is not much to be done about that, except to rely on the truth that no man is bigger than the sport, and another star may already be in the paddock. Cometh the hour, cometh the man.

The other factors?

The taint of nepotism is uncomfortably pronounced, although at this point it's difficult to point to any specific failings as a result. Carmelo Ezpeleta's son, Carlos, has had a meteoric rise to the senior levels of Dorna management, but has made the climb without making enemies or attracting exceptional criticism. Likewise daughter Ana, in charge of talent development, which, with lively junior series thriving in all major areas, has kept up a good flow of youngsters into the Junior and then real Moto3 World Championship – and increasingly not all of them from Spain. Now, nephew Bartolome 'Tome' Alfonso Ezpeleta has taken over the role of safety officer, and his partner has a place on the FIM Stewards Panel. Also, there have been allegations of cronyism in the replacement of the long-standing Italian-founded Clinica Mobile (effectively a paddock GP service supplementing the official circuit medical facilities) with a Spanish substitute.

It goes further. Ezpeleta's long-term right-hand man, Manel Arroyo, chief commercial officer, negotiates TV rights. He and his son, Alex, were named as 'executive producers' of the *MotoGP Unlimited* flop, while son David left Dorna at the end of 2020 after seven years with the company.

This is not a direct concern for fans, and in the absence of any comment or action, one must assume that Dorna's owners – venture capital company Bridgepoint Capital and the Canada pensions board, CPP – are similarly not concerned.

What does affect fans, as well as the previously reported loss of TV viewers due to retreating behind a pay wall, now almost everywhere except Indonesia, is the opportunity that was lost in the unsuccessful Amazon series. This was bodged

from its launch in several different ways. An English-language version featured clumsy dubbing by actors of the riders speaking, hastily replaced with equally clumsily written subtitles, which were ill suited to the quick-cuts style. This offered hardly enough time to read them, let alone absorb the visuals, before the next scene. Availability was also puzzlingly restricted. It was unavailable in India and as crucially South-east Asia, key markets for motorcycles and MotoGP, with Indonesia having rejoined the calendar in 2022 and India scheduled for 2023.

That was probably more Amazon's fault than Dorna's, but there needs to be a major rethink of directing and marketing if a 2023 relaunch is to regain lost ground. Given how close and exciting the racing has been, it is some kind of tragedy for it to be so badly undersold.

Too Close For Comfort?

"Close and exciting" was a long-term target for Dorna from before the short-lived, but salutary production-based CRT bikes a decade ago – the last step in kerbing the dominance of elite factory teams and giving independent teams a greater chance.

This has certainly been achieved, with 'closest-ever' records continually broken. In 2022, for example, Silverstone's top ten within 6.646 seconds was the second closest in history (to the Qatar GP's 5.365 in 2021) – only to be deposed a couple of months later by Phillip Island's 5.940.

It certainly makes thrilling viewing, although tempered by the fact that at some venues (Jerez in particular), the racing has been tediously processional. Technical regulations, and the freezing of engine and aero development have resulted in a generation of MotoGP bikes so similar in performance that overtaking has become increasingly difficult. Many, though not all, riders complained about this in 2022, blaming a front tyre that was over-sensitive to pressure caused by heat build-up, an aspect that was exaggerated not only when following closely in another bike's hot air, but also by the extra loads from front-aero downforce, and the harder braking allowed by dropping rear ride heights. Michelin have promised a revised front tyre for 2023 to address this issue.

Above: **MotoGP's premier class – close at the start and often close at the finish, too.**
Photo: Monster Energy Yamaha

Top right: **Long-lap penalties were unfairly inconsistent. Jack Miller takes his in Germany, losing 1.7 seconds, which dropped him from third to sixth.**

Top far right: **Red Bull KTM have added GasGas as a new factory, but without actually having to make any new bikes.**
Photos: Gold & Goose

Above right: **Peril in the pack. Close racing meant big risks. Here at Catalunya, the inverted Rins got away with a broken wrist. Thankfully, lucky escapes were the common denominator in 2022.**
Photo: www.suzuki-racing.com

Right: **Yamaha's Fabio Quartararo felt particularly put upon by erratic stewards' decisions.**
Photo: Monster Energy Yamaha

Even riding techniques have been smoothed so that every rider and every bike tackle every corner in more or less the same way, with only small differences. This makes finding any advantage very difficult indeed.

Some argue that reducing everything to a median level is the antithesis of the pinnacle of motorcycle racing – that this should be an arena of excellence rather than a one-size-fits-all brawl. That racing was better when it was contested by an elite of four or five obviously superior riders on obviously superior bikes, with the others there not exactly to make up the numbers, but to make their pitch to join the cream.

This might seem a begrudging cavil. But there is another aspect that carries more weight – safety. It is undeniably true that motorcycle racing is on the one hand a dangerous sport, and on the other immeasurably safer than in its early days, and becoming safer still, at least in objective safety – track design, medical attention, riding equipment. Yet the grim statistics have taken a turn for the worse. In a spell of 21 years, between 1989 and 2010, there were only two fatalities in MotoGP (sidecar racing apart) – Nobuyuki Wakai, after a collision with a pedestrian in the pit lane in 1993, and Daijiro Kato in 2003, after running off track at high speed at Suzuka (the circuit has not hosted a GP since).

However, a different type of crash claimed the lives of Shoya Tomizawa at Misano in 2010, Marco Simoncelli in Malaysia in 2011 and Jason Dupasquier at Mugello in 2021. In each case, the rider had fallen among a pack of bikes and been fatally injured by being struck or run over. One other death, of Luis Salom in 2016, was in a single-bike accident. More distressingly, ultra-close racing and consequent collisions in crowded packs in 'Road to MotoGP' events and feeder classes have also cost the lives of three teenagers since 2018 – Andreas Perez (14), Hugo Millan (14) and Dean Berta Vinales (15). Afridza Munandar (20) was another victim, as was Victor Steeman (22) in 2022. Increased minimum age limits introduced in 2022 and 2023, and smaller grid sizes, are welcome, but no real solution.

It is remarkable, in fact, that MotoGP, across all classes, has got away with it as the racing has become ever closer. This is especially true in Moto3, where packs of 15 or more hotheads circulate within touching distance for lap after lap, but also in the larger classes. In MotoGP in 2022, for example, there were miraculously lucky escapes for a number of riders who had fallen and been missed only narrowly, including Quartararo at Aragon and Nakagami twice, in Catalunya and Aragon.

We can only hope that we continue to get away with it.

Punishment To Fit The Crime

The FIM Stewards Panel took the usual amount of stick during 2022 for a lack of consistency in their decisions. One case in point involved Quartararo at Assen and at the next event at Silverstone.

The points leader was given a long-lap penalty for his indiscreet attempt to pass Aleix Espargaro at the Strubben hairpin. He fell, but remounted; Espargaro stayed on board, but dropped from second to 15th before making a heroic comeback ride. After the race, Quartararo (who had fallen off again) was given a long-lap penalty, carried over to the next race at Silverstone. (This in itself was somewhat inconsistent: other riders penalised in this way, who had fallen off before taking the penalty, did not have to serve it at the next race – but since it was awarded post-race, the case wasn't quite the same.)

This was just two races after Nakagami had made a not dissimilar error at Catalunya, knocking off Bagnaia and Rins, who was injured. He had escaped sanction. So what was the difference? In Portugal, Miller had lost it under braking inside Mir, taking both down – very similar to Quartararo's mistake; in Qatar, Bagnaia had done it to Martin.

Weasel-word explanations had it that Nakagami's error had been an honest mistake, sucked into the corner faster than usual in Bagnaia's slipstream, whereas Quartararo's lunge had been "overambitious".

This occasioned fury from Yamaha. The rider posted an ironic comment on social media, suggesting that if trying to overtake was considered too ambitious, then he wouldn't be trying it any more. Yamaha Racing MD Lin Jarvis followed with a stern statement two days later: "We are disappointed to see the inequality with which penalties are applied by the FIM MotoGP Stewards panel." A reasonable attitude, considering the precedents.

There was another inconsistency in the penalty itself. Obviously, different circuit layouts lend themselves to different long-lap loops, and the time lost in them can vary considerably from one circuit to another. Likewise, the circumstances in which the rider takes the penalty – if he is on his own, it can be accomplished quicker and with less loss of position than if he needs to rejoin in heavy traffic.

One extreme example came in Australia, where Alonso Lopez had grabbed an early lead with a couple of sizzling laps, lost almost two seconds taking the penalty, but emerged still in front to win the race. At Silverstone, Quartararo lost around 1.5 seconds, but three positions. At Assen, Miller's penalty cost him 1.8 seconds, but Nakagami's later in the race almost three. At Misano, a much costlier loop covers two corners and ends in a slower exit on to a fast section: Oliveira lost 3.4 seconds there, Moto2's Marcel Schrotter, 3.7 seconds.

In other words, inconsistent in the extreme.

It is understood that sometimes penalties are appropriate, and that you will almost always find disagreement about whether they are correctly applied – the role of the stewards is not to make friends with the riders. It is also understood that a point of principle is to have race results that match the order in which people pass the chequered flag, although this is often undermined by one-position penalties when riders stray over track limits on the last lap.

It would be more consistent, however, if instead of highly variable long-laps, punishments of losing one or perhaps more positions were applied.

What's In A Name?

When is a factory team not a factory team? And how much difference does it make?

Dorna's big push after the turn of the century to level the difference between factory and privateer squads, nowadays with the official status of Independent teams, has achieved a new equality. This was demonstrated by the announcement of the advent in MotoGP of a new factory team for Spanish manufacturer GasGas in 2023.

In fact, the 'new factory team' is simply an old Independent team with a new nomenclature – the long established

Above: **Quitting while ahead. Insiders found Suzuki's departure hard to explain.**
Photo: www.suzuki-racing.com

Above right: **Emotional Armada. Wayne Rainey and his title-winning Yamaha lead Doohan, Schwantz and Roberts up the Goodwood hill.**

Top far right: **Champions all – Kenny Roberts, Wayne Rainey, Kevin Schwantz and Mick Doohan won a dozen titles between them.**
Photos: Lou Martin

Above far right: **Just like 1993. MOTOCOURSE editor Scott gets the lowdown after Rainey's run.**
Photo: Clice Challinor Motorsport Photography

French Tech3 squad, for many years Yamaha's satellite team before switching to KTM in 2019.

After losing Red Bull sponsorship, Tech3 continued in the same role with KTM's support, running nominally factory-level machines, although in practice at the back of the queue for the latest updates. For 2023, however, Tech3 will be an official factory squad for an official new factory entrant, which (by replacing Suzuki) maintains the ability of Dorna to claim the participation of six factories.

GasGas is a small Spanish company founded in 1985, which made its name with specialised trials bikes. In 2019, after a merger with OSSA, the company was acquired by KTM owner Stefan Pierer to add to the company's growing portfolio, which by 2022 also included Husqvarna and Chinese company CFMoto, brands that were racing rebadged KTMs in Moto3. GasGas joined that gang in 2022, and won the championship to boot.

Pierer clearly has ambitions to expand the GasGas name into the street-bike market, hence the new 'factory' MotoGP team bearing its name.

Smoke and mirrors, of course. But illustrative of how the distinction between works and privateer teams has been all but completely eliminated.

Suzuki Slip Away – Who Next?

In a year when Honda failed to win a single race, when Yamaha had to rely on superhuman riding to compete, when KTM struggled to consolidate its gains and when Aprilia blazed brightly only to slip back out of the limelight, Suzuki closed the season on a high.

Two wins in the last three races showed a bike and a team that had found superb form. The much-admired GSX-RR, finely balanced, well rounded and sleekly handsome in a way that its aero-bedecked rivals had long since abandoned, was the bike to outrace even the dominant Ducatis.

All the more shocking that this was the swan song. Suzuki quit, at least while they were ahead.

Suzuki astonished everyone when they decided that the MotoGP game was not worth the candle. Or any other flammable fuel. Citing difficult economic times, and the need to concentrate on alternative power and their new electric car enterprise, they pulled the plug.

This shocked their entire factory racing department (endurance and off-road as well as MotoGP), their flabbergasted riders and grand prix team, but also the whole of racing.

Suzuki's original DNA was based on the racing success of their adventurous two-strokes of the 1960s, using advanced technology acquired (with some skulduggery) from the East German MZ pioneering work of Walter Kaaden. Now senior management far removed from the race-department shop floor, where engineering prowess bordering on genius might help build better motorbikes, have decided that it has little relevance to the balance sheet.

This is not the first time it's happened, even apart from the mass withdrawal of Japanese factories towards the end of the 1960s.

Suzuki had done it again in the 1980s, after the square-four RG500 had achieved serial success with Barry Sheene and many others. Suzuki GB soldiered on, however, using hand-me-down parts and their own experimental chassis, until a factory U-turn delivered a new V4 in 1987 – the bike that took Kevin Schwantz and Kenny Roberts Junior to the championship.

The second surprise withdrawal was in 2011. They managed to square the breach of contract with Dorna by promising that it would be only temporary, and they returned in 2015. The all-new in-line four GSX-RR, despite Suzuki's relatively tiny racing department and meagre budget compared with Honda and Yamaha, became a race- and championship-winning machine in 2020.

The riders loved it. Phillip Island and Valencia winner Alex Rins was in tears both before and after the final race.

Why did Suzuki kill it off, leaving staff and fans dismayed, and doubtless customers, too? What wins on Sunday sells on Monday. And you have to be in it to win it.

One answer might be found in a surprise end-of-season action that demonstrated a strange management disconnection. After the Malaysian GP, with only one race left, the race department commissioned a test of new parts. Rins for one was dumbfounded. Why spend money testing things that will never be used?

A former Suzuki insider explained: "The engineers had a budget, so they spent it. Senior management probably wouldn't even notice."

No details have emerged of the financial cost of leaving, but having just signed a new Dorna contract until the end of 2026, Suzuki's bail-out fee is likely to be considerable. They obviously consider it worthwhile.

But if Suzuki can turn their back on MotoGP so easily, what about other long-standing competitors? Honda have endured an embarrassing spell of poor results, and they pulled out themselves in 1967. A year later, Yamaha followed suit. With European factories looking set to take over, who'll be next to leave?

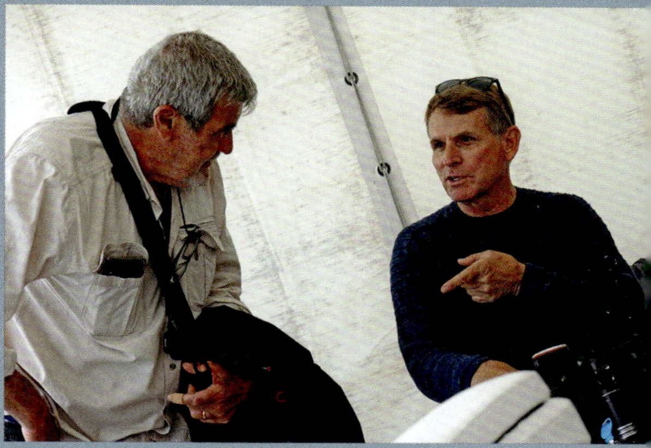

RAINEY RIDES AGAIN

THIRTY years ago, Wayne Rainey won a third straight World Championship, his dayglo-and-white Marlboro Yamaha YZR500 king of the thrilling generation of 500cc two-strokes. It was an era when a rider's courage and determination were at a premium.

The following year, 1993, on course for a classic fourth straight title, the beast bit him. A crash at Misano left him paralysed from the chest down.

"Early on in hospital, I don't know if it was the drugs I was on or what, but my goal was to try to ride my grand prix bike again, the next year.

"As time went on, things changed and my reality came real. That was not going to happen, But it got me through the first weeks. That was a goal – just to ride it round."

It took 30 years.

"Goodwood actually asked me in 2020, but I didn't have anything I could ride at that point. Then the pandemic hit… They started thinking about the 30-year anniversary.

"Yamaha had that bike sitting in a museum. We asked if it would be possible to prepare it."

Worries about cost and safety caused initial doubts. "They were concerned about the bike being so old, no parts, and if something was to happen … how would that look?"

Yamaha were also concerned about how Shea, Wayne's wife, felt. "Everybody that had to be in the loop to make this work all had the same concern. But I was thinking, 'I'm okay with it. I understand they're asking these questions,' but I thought, 'Y'know, if I felt like this, I wouldn't get out of bed every day.'"

Goodwood owner the Duke of Richmond was a prime mover, Yamaha Racing boss Lin Jarvis also "a big help organising it".

At Yamaha, Masahiko Nakajima took control. He had been Wayne's engineer and since had become president of Yamaha Racing. "Nakajima-San took the bike apart, and said, 'It's in much better shape than we thought.'"

Some detuning modifications were required for the YZR's role as demonstrator rather than fighter – "steel brakes and Michelin rain tyres." Plus a gear-shifting mechanism. Lacking electronic aids, this proved difficult.

A system was devised to trigger upshifts by means of the kill button, downshifts by declutching, but it proved troublesome during tests before the event and was abandoned. First gear was workable to tackle the hill – "It was a pretty tall first, good for something like 85mph."

In 2019, Rainey had ridden a modified Yamaha R1 in an emotional public gallop at Suzuka. As a street bike, however, its control was less daunting, with electronics enabling a push-button gearchange and a flexible engine offering smooth running at lower revs. And an electric start should it stall. The 500cc racing two-stroke was more of a challenge.

"The difficult part is going to be taking off, and stopping. I have to get a bit of a roll … as long as I'm moving already, then the momentum gets you going," Wayne explained in the weeks before the ride.

"It is so different riding a bike now. The only thing I feel is the handlebars … nothing else. I rode a minibike back in March, and you catch everything late, because you only know that you're making a mistake when you see it, not when you feel it in your feet or your butt or through the bike. It's a whole different experience."

That was when visiting Kenny Roberts: "Kenny zip-tied my feet on to the pegs, and I rode it for 20 minutes. He was a little nervous, but it all worked out."

Later, Wayne practised at home in Monterey: "I was riding an Ohvale GP2. It's got an electric start and it's an automatic … but it's less than 200cc, so it is real calm. Doug Chandler put on [clip-on] bicycle footpegs, and some buddies helped me get on and off the bike, and I just rode it in my local church parking lot."

Wayne was reunited with his title-winning bike only days before the Goodwood ride, for shake-down tests at the venue. It was a nervy occasion, with apprehension as to how a feisty GP two-stroke might co-operate when tasked with going slowly for starting and stopping. Helpers were on hand for a push-start and a catch-stop.

At one point, Wayne did topple over at low speed. This was no setback compared with his thrill at opening the throttle of a racing two-stroke again, leaving a cloud of nostalgic exhaust smoke.

The mixture was set rich for safety. Wayne asked for it to be leaned off, and now a blip of throttle would lift the front wheel. That was a bit more like it.

Come the weekend, with two runs scheduled for each of three days, Wayne received a hero's welcome from a capacity crowd. More important than the adulation was the pleasure of winding on the throttle and feeling the bike fly.

Dressed in his classic Marlboro leathers, he was joined by grand prix racing royalty. Kenny Roberts, and contemporary rivals Mick Doohan and Kevin Schwantz escorted him up the hill to wild applause. Roberts rode his own Proton KR3 and later a factory Yamaha, Doohan and Schwantz their victorious Honda NSR and Suzuki RGV.

"I've waited 30 years for this," he beamed after the first of five runs.

It was a thrill for his companions, too. "I'm not an emotional guy, but that was very special," said triple-champion Roberts, who had brought Wayne from US racing to Europe and had owned the Marlboro team he rode for. He added, "I think I could have beat him if there'd been another lap."

He ran twice each on Friday and Saturday. There would have been two more runs on Sunday, but for a scare on the first one. "After the finish line, after the other guys took off [on the run to the post-climb *parc fermé*], I thought, 'I'll do that, too' … but the bike just felt like it ran out of fuel. Just quit. I was coasting in a place where nobody could see me. I was looking for some sturdy hay bales to stop next to. I found some, but I wasn't sure if they could support me, or even if I'd fall over the other side."

Fortunately, they held his weight and rescue was soon at hand.

Would he do it again? Months later, he said, "After 30 years, it was so much fun. A real thrill, like going into the unknown. On the run, seeing the line and feeling how to ride it fast … there was no way I could do it, but it was a real nice vision.

"Again? No plans at the present time."

THE COMEBACK CHAMPION

Pecco Bagnaia's season got off to a shaky start. Then, as rivals ran into their own problems, he became stronger and stronger, to emerge as the last man standing. By NEIL MORRISON...

Above: Bagnaia and Ducati came back to control the second half of the season.

Top right: Swamped by his team after his ride in Malaysia had put him within touching distance of the title.
Photos: Ducati Corse

Above right: Pecco in calm and reflective mood.
Photo: Whit Bazemore

Right: Experienced crew chief Cristian Gabarrini had filled the same role with Casey Stoner when he won Ducati's last championship (and then one more with Honda).
Photo: Ducati Corse

ACCORDING to some, just who was the world's fastest rider in 2022 is still up for discussion. A glance at the MotoGP World Championship table shows Francesco Bagnaia's name at number one after 20 races run. Yet even when his hair was still matted from the victory champagne sprayed after securing Italy's first premier-class crown in 13 years, the 25-year-old openly admitted that there were more complete riders than him on the grid.

After the longest season in GP history, there could be no doubting that Bagnaia had won aboard the grid's best bike. In the second half of 2022, the premier class hadn't witnessed such dominance from one manufacturer – 12 wins, 32 podiums, 16 poles spread among Ducati's fleet of eight riders – since Honda's brilliant five-cylinder RC211V had laid waste to the opposition in 2003. In crunch moments, Bagnaia could call upon able back-up when his chief rival was battling alone.

And there remains the argument that Fabio Quartararo's refusal to give in, despite the drastic shortcomings of his underpowered Yamaha M1, was worthy of greater admiration. Bagnaia's points average scored per race (13.25) was the second lowest since the current points-scoring system was introduced in 1993 (only Joan Mir in 2020 was lower). Indeed, he didn't even make the number-one spot in this publication's fabled list of the year's ten best riders, with Marc Marquez and Quartararo edging him out of places one and two.

Yet that's not to say Bagnaia isn't a worthy champion – far from it. The rider from Turin, in the north of Italy, didn't just outscore Quartararo in terms of points (265 to 248), he did so in all the other metrics that matter: wins (seven to three), podiums (ten to eight), pole positions (five to one) and front-row starts (ten to five). Plus he took the title despite not finishing a quarter of the year's 20 races – a new first.

More impressive still was the manner in which he won six of his seven victories. A stroll at Assen aside, his biggest winning margin all year long was 0.7 of a second. Not once was he afforded a smooth ending, with intense last-lap pressure at Jerez, Silverstone, Misano and Sepang – as intense a scrutiny as any champion could imagine. On each occasion, he held his nerve. And when it was starlet Enea Bastianini sniping from behind, it was hard to argue that all of Ducati was united behind him.

"This year, I was always with a lot of pressure from behind," Bagnaia said after securing his second world championship. "Enea was fast behind me, trying to overtake, and I was trying to manage the situation. It's one where you can easily lose your concentration. But I think we worked well. At [Valentino's] ranch, we are always together, fighting like this, putting a lot of pressure on each other. So, this helps in these situations."

After his last major blunder in Japan, the following outings in Thailand, Australia and Malaysia, replete with strange conditions and unpredictable forecasts, offered opportunities aplenty for a crucial mistake. Yet Bagnaia tackled each of these rounds like a champion. Even Marc Marquez was moved to commend his win-it-or-bust approach at Sepang. "Believe me, it's not easy when you are fighting for a championship. [But] He took a risk and did it," said the Catalan.

Most impressive was where he found himself after Germany. A fourth crash in ten races left him 91 points adrift of a swashbuckling Quartararo. He took stock. From then on, his form was devastating. In ten races, he amassed 197 points from an available 250. Six wins and eight podiums gave him an average of 19.7 points per race – Marquez levels of dominance.

In 74 years of premier-class competition, no rider had recovered from so far back.

"I just lost faith in the championship for like one hour after the race at the Sachsenring," he said. "But from that moment, I knew there was still a chance. We tried to analyse everything at home: what to improve, why I was crashing, why I was committing so many mistakes. But from that moment, we did something incredible."

Bagnaia had cut a largely exasperated figure through the first five grands prix. His polite, patient demeanour was replaced by irritability when dealing with the media. The reason for this less-than-perky Pecco was glaringly clear: Ducati had ended 2021 in a tremendous position of strength, having dominated the final race by locking out the front row and podium for the first time in history. They had followed that with a positive test at Jerez, where Bagnaia had proclaimed, "The old bike was perfect already and we are improving this perfect bike."

But what arrived at the Sepang test in February was far from his liking – or that of any of the four other GP22 riders. The engine was too peaky and aggressive, it offered little of its predecessor's front-end stability under braking. It seemed that the incessant tinkering of Gigi Dall'Igna, Ducati Corse's general manager, had gone too far. While the ride-height device (introduced in 2019), which lowered the rear on corner exit, had been quickly adopted by all the grid's other bikes, a new device that lowered the front (eventually abandoned for all but test rider Zarco) required a complete change in riding technique.

Front feel is what Bagnaia depends on. "He uses 100 per cent of the front tyre," said Dall'Igna in 2021. Bagnaia offered, "I'm braking harder than the others, I can stop the bike more. When I enter the corners, I'm in a better direction. I don't need to let it turn with the rear sliding. I make it turn in braking, and they do it on the exit."

His sharpest tool had been blunted. And it didn't end there. He was so unhappy with Ducati's 2022 engine that he requested a dramatic change before the first race – he and team-mate Jack Miller would revert to "a slightly hybrid version between the '21 and '22 engine," according to sporting director Paolo Ciabatti. But still it wasn't done. Bagnaia and Ducati went to the first race chopping and changing parts and set-up. The lead rider was not amused. It underlined a weakness to which many could relate. "He wants to come up with a base set-up and then make very little changes to it," admitted Ciabatti.

Still it got worse: Bagnaia was all over the place on Saturday in Argentina, repeatedly throwing his hands in the air, before Miller put a caring arm around his shoulder. That was before a painful qualifying crash in Portugal made his participation in that GP doubtful.

Their issues were exacerbated by the state of the grid: Yamaha was running the same underpowered bike as the previous year, while Honda and KTM were miles off. Ducati was standing in front of an open goal. The speed of the GP21 in Bastianini's hands was an added insult. Free of testing responsibilities, aboard a fully sorted bike, the Italian swept to three wins in the first seven races, a galling sight for those grappling to find a base setting with new hardware.

Alessio 'Uccio' Salucci, Rossi's right-hand man through a 25-year stint in racing and currently sporting director of the VR46 Academy, did not think that this was all Ducati's doing, however. "Sometimes one of Pecco's problems is he is too optimistic," he explained. "When he first rode the '22 bike at Jerez last November, he came to me and said, 'Wow, it's the best bike I've ever ridden!' He started speaking to newspapers. I told him, 'Pecco, no! I don't like this. Keep a low profile.' This isn't good for Ducati because when a rider arrives and says, 'The new bike was fantastic,' the engineers say, 'Perfect!'

"The mistake of the first part of this year was last November. Then, when we arrived in Malaysia in February, he tried the new bike and said, 'In November, it was the best

Above: **Back in the groove. Fist clenched after his battle with Bastianini at Aragon.**

Top right: **Crisis point. After this unforced error at the Sachsenring, Bagnaia changed his approach and turned his luck around.**
Photos: Ducati Corse

Above centre right: **Bezzecchi, Uccio and Pecco. The Rossi clan larks around.**
Photo: Gold & Goose

Above right: **Bagnaia is Ducati's second champion, and the first since 2007.**
Photo: Ducati Corse

Above far right: **Rossi was at Valencia to watch his protégé take the Academy's first premier-class championship.**
Photo: Gold & Goose

bike, now it's shit!' He realised that the first five races would be really tough. But Pecco always remained focused. He's a clever rider also."

By Jerez, the Ducati engineers had found a base setting that returned Bagnaia's confidence when braking robustly, where much of his work is done. But crashes at Le Mans, when chasing Bastianini, and Barcelona, when taken out, negated those gains. Then came the season's nadir at Sachsenring, when another careless fall left him really up against it.

At this point, members of the VR46 Academy rallied around and told him a few home truths. "In my situation, I love when some people around me say what they think about me," Bagnaia said of that moment. "I'm a difficult guy because at the start, I say, 'No, it's not like that.' Then I try to change my mindset, to change myself, taking that advice on board." Salucci agreed: "[After Germany] He said he was stupid, but he understood why he crashed. When a rider understands why he crashes, it's easier to recover, to restart. Pecco stayed calm, and the guys in the Academy were together. The Academy grouped around him in that moment."

"The most difficult moment was at the Sachsenring because I was very competitive," Bagnaia explained. "Like in Le Mans, I was there with a possibility to win, but I crashed. In that moment, I recognised that my weak point was there, that I was a rider with a lot of ups and downs." The French and German GP crashes were of a similar kind: when settling in behind the bike ahead, thinking too much of the final laps. "In those two moments, I had said, 'I will be calmer, breathe and then come back.' But right away, I crashed," he acknowledged at Assen. "Maybe with our bike, my feeling is that when you are not pushing on the tyres, maybe it's easier to crash." From then on, the only focus was the immediate job at hand.

By then, the GP22's teething problems had become a thing of the past, and Ducati felt that a run of victories was possible. Crew chief Cristian Gabarrini said, "It's easy to be happy when everything is fine. But the trick is to be strong when everything goes wrong. Every person in this project never lost our focus, which was to win this championship. Pecco felt that, and this was some additional momentum for him."

The advice and support worked. The four races that followed demonstrated his strongest attributes, namely tyre management and an exceptional late-braking ability. Quartararo, meanwhile, had lost all of that mid-season assurance. He was missing out on the front row, and misfortune stalked him at Aragon and Thailand. The wet encounter at Buriram told Bagnaia that the championship was his: "Thailand was a very difficult race for me. I struggled a lot in the wet, but I tried everything to be on the podium and recovered a lot of points. In that moment, I recognised we could win it."

Two races later, he had 23 points in hand, a reversal of 114 in just nine outings: "That gave me the margin to control the gap."

It wasn't just on-track where Bagnaia endured a tumultuous time. During the summer break, he had crashed his car in Ibiza while driving over the limit. Unwise. But more perplexing was the reaction: both he and Ducati felt attacked when journalists had the temerity to quiz him about this misdemeanor at the next race. And then there was his tribute helmet to basketball legend Dennis Rodman at his home race in Misano. The American might have won serial NBA titles, but now he's better known for a close relationship with North Ko-

rean dictator Kim Jong Un. Again, Bagnaia's response when quizzed on this didn't point to a great deal of thought beyond the sporting sphere.

There was also the impression that he wasn't the most independent of spirits. The figure of Rossi often loomed large, with pre-race pep talks by him, ex-factory test rider Casey Stoner (at Silverstone) and team-mate Miller (in Thailand) all needed at certain moments to maintain the momentum of his fight-back. Rossi's comments after Bagnaia's maiden premier-class success at Aragon in 2021 – "I tried yesterday to hypnotise him, 'hard-soft, hard-soft', because sometimes Pecco makes some strange decisions for the tyres" – suggested that occasionally his protégé needed to be talked out of his maverick instincts.

There is no doubt that his mettle will be tested like never before in 2023. Not only should Quartararo have faster equipment, but also Marquez should be back in strength; and what Bastianini did in the second half of 2022 made it perfectly clear that he will do everything within his power to unseat his countryman from the position of factory number-one.

But that fails to take into account Bagnaia's own margin for improvement. He is only the second rider to have triumphed in both Moto2 and the MotoGP classes, after Marquez. And just imagine what he can do from the start of the new season, provided Ducati doesn't try to reinvent the wheel over the winter. "I don't think his growth is at an end, he's only halfway," said Gabarrini. "He's growing every race and showing us this by controlling the pressure, the other competitors or making a super-explosive lap in qualifying. He doesn't know where his limit is, which is good because we can look toward the future with a positive trend."

THE ACADEMY AWARDS

BAGNAIA'S championship win wasn't just a triumph for himself, Ducati and Italy; it also marked the first occasion that a rider from Valentino Rossi's fabled VR46 Academy claimed the sport's highest honour.

Established in 2014, the school for the next generation of Italian talent grew out of Rossi's desire to put Italy back on the racing map – even to find a successor. The country's prospects were falling short in the junior classes. Take 2013, for example. Italy's intermediate-class hopes fell on experienced riders Mattia Pasini and Simone Corsi. The best-placed Italian in Moto3 was tenth. And Spain was cleaning up across the board.

Bagnaia's thoughts on the merits of the Academy verge on elements of fantasy. "For me, it's like the island of Peter Pan," he said in 2019. For those in this game, the benefits are second to none. As if regular access to Rossi's experience isn't enough, participants can compete against him and other members morning and afternoon – then repeat it all the following day.

Your English not up to scratch? Well, come down and take these free language classes so that you can communicate with technicians and the media in a savvier way. No aspect of the modern rider's life is left to chance: advice on diet, physical preparation and training are available. Members have access to flat-track, dirt-track and mini-bikes in training rituals between world championship races. On occasion, they can follow Rossi around Misano or Mugello aboard a Yamaha R6. "They give us everything," Bagnaia said.

Contracts are taken care of, and a rider's own merchandise and branding will be provided. Essentially, a space here commands a worldwide audience and guarantees an allegiance of fans. In short, a ticket to the big time.

Franco Morbidelli won the Academy's first world title in 2017 in Moto2; Bagnaia's crown followed on in 2018. By 2020, they had become genuine challengers to Rossi, both denying him a final career podium at Misano. A wryly amused Valentino commented, "At one point in the race, I wondered, 'Whose f*cking idea was it to start this academy?'"

Rossi's retirement laid down a challenge for Bagnaia, Morbidelli, Luca Marini and Marco Bezzecchi, the Academy's MotoGP representatives. Until 2021, he'd been ever present on track to offer advice. He only attended three GPs in 2022. "Without Vale, we passed through tough moments," said half-brother Marini. "When we were training, we had a key point, like an idol, to follow every day. Without him, it's been a bit more difficult."

Yet Salucci maintains that Rossi is as interested in his fledglings as ever. "Vale is always present," he said during the season's finale at Valencia. "When we did the four races outside Europe, he was always sending me messages. Pecco would come to me and say, 'Okay, now I'll speak to Vale.' Morbidelli the same. He'd put his alarm early to watch, wake up for one hour, then go back to sleep!

"His presence is very important for everybody, and for me especially. After 25 years together, this year was the first year alone. Also [at Valencia], he's in the box, checking the data with the Ducati engineers. He'll be in the box for three hours: one hour-and-a-half with Marini, one-and-a-half with Bezzecchi. He was out on track, telling the guys, 'The first corner is not good, the second one, yes.' But this is Valentino."

Bagnaia heaped praise on the Academy after his championship triumph. "It's not just the influence of Valentino, but all the guys working for us at home," he said. "At the start, it was a totally different academy ... a big help for sure, but now we are very professional. We can say, 'Today, I want to go to a track with the pocket bikes.' And they organise everything to do it. We say, 'We want to go to Portimao to have a test before the season.' They organise it. They are giving all the possibilities, all the passion to us, and this is incredible.

"At home, we work together. We push each other. This helped me a lot to improve myself."

MOTOGP'S CONQUISTADOR!

Bombastic Dorna boss Carmelo Ezpeleta has been at the controls of MotoGP since 1992 and has rebuilt the sport to his own model. Spanish journalist JUAN PEDRO DE LA TORRE looks behind the bluster and the bullying façade to find a skilled negotiator, a diplomatic problem solver, a clear-sighted planner and a dedicated motorcycle racing fan who hasn't missed a single race in more than 30 years...

I HAD been working for the magazine *Motociclismo* for just over a year, after two seasons at the sports newspaper *Marca* in Madrid, when the editor, Javier Herrero, an old-school journalist seasoned by years behind the straw bales of the Spanish urban circuits, commissioned me to interview Carmelo Ezpeleta. It was just days after Dorna's chaotic debut at the 1991 Spanish Grand Prix at Jerez.

This was the first public experience of the Spanish company to which the FIM had awarded the commercial rights of the World Championship. It is likely that by giving me the job, Javier was looking for a fresh approach, a different vision of someone who had not had previous dealings with Ezpeleta.

Of course, I knew who Ezpeleta was. If you were an avid reader of motorcycle magazines since the age of 13, more interested in knowing every story from the motorcycle world than in learning the Pythagorean theorem, you had to know who he was, but I had never dealt with him. And Javier warned, "Don't worry if he raises his voice a lot. He's not angry with you, he just talks like that."

More than 30 years after that first meeting, Ezpeleta remains energetic and vibrant. He speaks in a resounding way, always, with vehemence and confidence, with total conviction in what he says. Now he modulates his tone of voice at times, and although he no longer bangs the table as much as he did, he continues to fix you with a piercing gaze with each answer.

I know that he is not exactly a popular figure among the international press. Italian journalists were especially cutting in respect of Dorna and Ezpeleta, from the first minute of their connection with the grands prix, perhaps because they never forgave Jos Vaessen, then president of the FIM, for awarding the commercial-rights contract to the Spanish company, rather than to the glamorous and high-profile Italian Flammini Group.

In spite of the passage of many years, and an important and positive transformation in motorcycle racing recognisably wrought by Dorna, the Italian press is still the first to agitate and aim its arrows at Ezpeleta. The English-language press is hardly less scathing, because it blames all the evils of motorcycling on Dorna, and personalises them in the figure of Ezpeleta. He is the boss, he has to carry that burden.

How fair is this view of Dorna and Ezpeleta as the reincarnation of evil?

Because taking into account the heartbeat of social media (that, honestly, you always have to take with some reservation), the animosity is also seen among fans of other nationalities, many of them also Spanish, who ascribe all the evils in MotoGP to Dorna. Personally, I find this exaggerated, but we live in a time of hyperbole. These are difficult moments, caused above all by the environment that surrounds us rather than by failures in the management of the championship. While it is far from being perfect, I consider it remarkable.

But this is just the view of a Spanish journalist. In fact, I think that to discover the true character of Ezpeleta, and by extension of Dorna, it is best to forget everything that we journalists write and say, for sometimes we have very long tongues, especially on social media, and instead consider opinion within the paddock. What a few letters put together say matters little; the important thing is what people who depend directly on the decisions feel. Decisions that are made in Dorna's small, discreet headquarters in the long street called Principe de Vergara (Prince of Vergara) in the heart of Madrid. This location could not be more fitting, because we have to recognise in Ezpeleta motorcycle racing's own Prince of Vergara.

For those unfamiliar with the history of Spain, the Prince of Vergara was the title granted to General Baldomero Espartero, a notable military officer of the 19th century, in recognition of his negotiating skills, which ended the first Carlist War in 1839. This was one of many civil wars with which we Spaniards have been punishing ourselves in the course of our history.

At the end of the 1980s, the motorcycle World Championships were a battlefield, with a war being fought between the different factions of motorcycling: FIM, ROPA (association of promoters and organisers), AICP (association of circuits) and IRTA (association of teams), each claiming its own corresponding part of the cake. And among all this appeared Bernie Ecclestone, like a shark attracted to waters agitated by a shoal of fish.

The FIM stirred things up by awarding Steve McLaughlin and the Sports Marketing Company management of the new Superbike World Championship in 1988. Thus it was only a matter of time before this new concept, of private promoters taking over the championships, reached the GPs. This aroused much interest, and in the middle of that rough sea appeared Dorna.

Continuing with the analogies, it was logical that in a rough and unpredictable sea, Dorna would take the prey, because a *'dorna'* is a Galician fishing boat, characterised by its robustness. And Carlos Garcia Pardo, an engineer of Construcciones MOZV, who founded Dorna in 1974 as a real estate management company, is Galician.

But let's return to the Prince of Vergara. In this condition of open confrontation, Dorna arrives on the scene in 1991, and Ezpeleta, who has just joined the company, having launched the Circuit de Catalunya, is in a complicated situation. The entire cast of the motorcycle world is against him, distrusting those unknown Spaniards. Yet his ability to communicate, his dedicated involvement and his intelligence had a pacify-

ing effect on all the *indignados*, able even to put an end to the rebellion and sabre rattling, and an attempt to re-enliven the ghost of the failed 1980 breakaway World Series.

Carmelo (everyone calls him by his first name) managed one by one to get all of his opponents on side, starting with IRTA. And he did not do it with promises or flattery, but with action. The first of these was a collaboration with Flammini to replace the suspended Yugoslav Grand Prix in 1991. A substitute race, the European Grand Prix, held at Jarama outside Madrid, was launched in just three weeks. And it was a success.

I remember perfectly the words of Mike Trimby, secretary general of IRTA, after that race. "We have enjoyed the highest level of collaboration that has ever existed between an organiser and the major teams. It's been like the World Cup we've always dreamed of," he said. Dorna had won an important ally in the World Championship paddock, and today the teams' association remains a fundamental supporter.

Ezpeleta won over IRTA with the demonstration of organisational capacity that Dorna displayed at Jarama. Eventually, this modern Prince of Vergara convinced all the parties to share a common vision. This was not easy, because the FIM had created a conflict of interest through the poor management of its contracts with promoters, TV production com-

Above: **A rare tranquil moment for the architect of modern MotoGP.**

Photo: Gold & Goose

Left: **Dorna CEO Guimaraes and TV chief Roures flank Ezpeleta at the 'chaotic' 1991 press launch at Jarama.**

Photo: Motociclismo

Above: **Close allies. Dorna's Ezpeleta and IRTA's Mike Trimby.**
Photo: Gold & Goose

Above right: **Hobnobbing – Carmelo with FIM president Francesco Zerbi and former road-racing commission chief Luigi Brenni.**
Photo: FIM Pictures

Top: **Family affair: the Ezpeleta clan in Austria in 2018.**

Top right: **Carmelo has never missed a race. This is on the grid in Qatar in 2009.**

Top far right: **Carlos Ezpeleta.**
Photos: Gold & Goose

panies and other interested parties. On the one hand, the FIM had a contract with ISC, the Ecclestone company that managed television rights, and in turn, ISC had an agreement with IRTA. Then, at the Autumn Congress of the FIM in Budapest, in 1990, the management of the commercial and marketing rights was awarded to Dorna. Theoretically, no one would have been happy with this, but the Prince of Vergara got away with it. Even with Ecclestone, the shark.

The major, mainly Anglophone, sponsors did not want Dorna. When the new rights holder was introduced at Jerez in 1991, Leo de Graffenreid (Marlboro) and David Beck (Rothmans), sitting among the journalists, whipped them up with probing questions during a chaotic press conference, poorly organised by the FIM, which should never have been more than an informal meeting. In the following weeks, the tobacco companies spoke openly of their opinion of Dorna, in case anyone had not been clear about their position: "Dorna inspires us with so little confidence that we have frozen our plans for the immediate future. ISC is not a perfect company, but with Bernie Ecclestone we know where we are," David Beck said a week later at Misano.

When the people who invest the most money in a championship are turned against you, as we say in Spain, "*date por jodido*" (you are f**ked). That's what they thought. Of course, they didn't know Carmelo, but they discovered him very soon after. On 7th September, Dorna presented its plans to the teams and sponsors – minus Marlboro and Rothmans – and negotiations continued with other parties. On 21st September, the FIM was able to award not only the commercial rights, but also the crucial television rights. How was this possible, if ISC had the rights until 1992?

On 29th September, when the GP series was in Shah Alam, the first visit to Malaysia, Dorna's opposition was still on manoeuvres. Meanwhile, the Spanish Formula 1 Grand Prix was being held for the first time at the Circuit de Catalunya – the track that Ezpeleta had been in charge of building. There, he, Ecclestone and the FIM signed an agreement whereby Two Wheels Promotions (TWP), Ecclestone's new company dedicated to motorcycle racing, and Dorna took over the management of the championship for a period of ten years, with the FIM controlling the sporting decisions. The danger of a rupture had vanished; the Prince of Vergara had imposed peace.

This has been a constant in Ezpeleta's management style: he is able to turn the page. Recently, I had the opportunity to meet him again, taking advantage of the surprise announcement of Suzuki's departure from the championship. An hour of conversation with him is worth a lot because he never rambles; he is direct and does not conceal his arguments. I always have a long questionnaire prepared when I meet him because normally I am machine-gunned with his answers, fast and accurate. Not surprisingly, we look back – Dorna's 30 years of GP management gives us a chance to consider that difficult start.

"It's funny how good we are now with IRTA, and IRTA was the first one that was negative at that meeting, but that's one thing I think we've done well. But looking back is nonsense," he told me.

And it is true, because some of the people I have questioned about how Carmelo is seen from the inside have told me about his characteristic dialogue, about the outstretched hand, and about how in the GP paddock there were many second chances because he knew perfectly well that many of those who had turned against him were people of great capacity who could contribute to raising the championship to unimagined levels. As Dorna has done under his direction in those 30 years.

Even when the erstwhile IRTA chief, the late Michel Metraux, pushed for IRTA to betray Dorna in 1997 and embrace ISL, the Swiss sports marketing giant, keeping it all 'at home', Ezpeleta continued to rely on Mike Trimby and Paul Butler, another founding member of IRTA.

But let no one think that he is a friendly, cuddly character: he is a fierce negotiator. Someone close to the management told me, "He has an immense job." That is, he masters the subject and knows what he is talking about. He knew it in 1991, because long before Dorna took the GP reins, before that "company of unknowns" (a contempt as painful as it was ignorant) directed the championship, Carmelo had already experienced first hand the same situation. The Motorcycle World Championship's family feud had occurred

a decade earlier in F1. It was a kind of déjà vu.

The worst part of the battle between FISA (the FIM's automotive equivalent), Ecclestone's FOCA teams' assocation and ROPA (association of promoters) took place in 1980 at Jarama, which in those days had a 33-year-old dynamic director. It was Carmelo Ezpeleta, who witnessed the dispute between the incisive and dynamic Ecclestone and authoritarian Jean-Marie Balestre (a controversial figure with past links to the administration of Vichy France), using it as a masterclass. For a decade, he was in charge of organising both the Spanish F1 and motorcycle GPs at Jarama.

Ezpeleta treasures that experience, among many others, and it has helped him to rely on the strength of his convictions. To those who don't know him, his tone may seem abrupt, but the firmness he displays is a requisite for anyone charged with the responsibility of heading an organisation like Dorna. Ezpeleta is often authoritarian in his meetings with the press, especially in respect of what he calls, with much irony, "my classics", because the criticisms of his management surface regularly from this particular group.

But that's our job. Journalists represent an uncomfortable check on authority, in any aspect of life, and for Dorna, and by extension for Carmelo, we are surely a necessary evil, although today, with new forms of communication, we can become expendable. The pandemic made this clear, leaving the press isolated from the paddock, forced to establish a virtual relationship with the teams and riders. There is no doubt that for Dorna that was an ideal situation.

However, when Carmelo stands before the riders, the relationship is completely different. There is mutual respect and a relationship of trust, or at least that's how someone who often witnessed it for several seasons has described it to me. The Safety Commission meetings on the Friday afternoon of every grand prix have provided continuous contact between Ezpeleta and the riders for two decades, although in recent years his actual presence has become no longer essential. More usually, it is Carlos Ezpeleta, his son and managing director of MotoGP, who meets with Loris Capirossi and Franco Uncini. Carmelo attends when he knows that the matter to be dealt with is important or complex.

He is serious and commands respect, and in that position, he ceases to be the passionate follower of motorcycling to become the iron executive.

But he is not an ogre. He is demanding and rigorous, he is firm, and when he has absolute conviction about something, he defends it with an uncompromising vehemence. And the only thing that really makes him angry is Barca. Because, for a Barcelonan like him, FC Barcelona is almost a religion.

CARMELO AND HIS FAMILY

SOME media clamour for a change in the direction of Dorna because they consider that Ezpeleta's time has come to an end. "Dorna needs to keep up in a modern world," I've read. At our last meeting, I asked him when he would retire. "With the age I am, 76 years old, it may be tomorrow. There are certain functions that I can do for the benefit of the company, but in Dorna, a very consistent team has been created. I can disappear any day without much notice," he replied.

He has not missed a single championship race since 29th March, 1992. That was the day of the Japanese Grand Prix, the first race under Dorna's management. Since then, he has concentrated solely and exclusively on the championship, having to give up other commitments, even of a family nature. Fourteen or fifteen years ago, I witnessed one of those situations. In the middle of an interview, his mobile phone rang. He looked at me sideways, "It's my son." I turned off the tape recorder and he answered the call, in case it was an emergency. On the other end of the phone, Carlos asked his father a question. He replied, "It's the Italian Grand Prix. Well, I'm not going to be able to go, son. I'm so sorry." They said goodbye. I saw a quick grimace, and he noticed me. "I'm not going to be able to go to his graduation," he explained. And we continued with the questions.

Ezpeleta is a tremendous family man. Some detractors speak of nepotism because his son, Carlos, and also his daughter, Ana, are employees of the company, taking care of different areas. Carlos has been in various departments since he was very young. His title of managing director was changed to chief sporting officer in 2021, although the role was little altered: keeping in constant touch with all the entities involved in the championship, applying the same policy as his father – communication and rigour. Ana is in charge of talent promotion, which has led to the creation of the Asia Talent Cup, the European Talent Cup, the Northern Talent Cup and the British Talent Cup. Perhaps in other latitudes, it is understood that offering your children the opportunity to develop their professional career in the company you run is nepotistic, but if you had the opportunity to give your child a job, wouldn't you?

In any case, such comments don't cause Ezpeleta sleepless nights. He worries more about the MotoGP paddock continuing to progress, because he has made the paddock his home and the teams an extension of his family. The people in the championship know this.

In 2020, the pandemic could have cancelled the season, but Ezpeleta promised everyone that there would be both MotoGP and WorldSBK championships, and Dorna supported all the teams financially, and secured all the races with the help of those circuits that committed to run them. The result was a drop in revenue of almost 30 per cent and, as a result, Dorna lost more than 94 million euros. But all the teams survived.

The spontaneous applause that the directors, technicians, mechanics, riders and members of the teams dedicated to Ezpeleta at the final grand prix of 2020 was a sincere show of gratitude and a recognition of the enormous effort made by Dorna. The closeness between him and the teams, and also with the manufacturers, is absolute, so at present Dorna's decisions are not questioned.

The matter of whether his time has come is not an issue that Carmelo talks about. As much as this can be discussed, no one can imagine MotoGP without him. Surely, neither do Dorna's shareholders, the investment companies Bridgepoint and CCPIB, which have just received a juicy dividend. Moreover, the business is in a healthy position, since Dorna has extended its agreement on the rights to the FIM championships until 2041.

What is evident is that the future of the championship will be built around the legacy of Carmelo Ezpeleta.

TECHNICAL ESSAY

THE FAST ART OF COMPROMISE

Change one aspect of a motorcycle and it affects every other area of performance. In an era when increasingly sophisticated engineering solutions butt up against ever tightening 'cost-cutting' regulations, the quest for faster lap times must continue. KEVIN CAMERON puts it in perspective...

Above: **Follow my leader. Some riders blamed technology changes for making overtaking more difficult.**
Photo: Monster Energy Yamaha

Above right: **Tyre pressure changes became crucial. Could new systems remove the risks from pre-race guesswork?**
Photo: Gold & Goose

Right: **Triple 1960s world champion Hugh Anderson on the 125 Suzuki – a master of juggling ignition timing.**
Photo: Motocourse Archive

NEARLY every design choice made in the creation of a motorcycle is a compromise. As circumstances change and technologies advance, the nature of those compromises also changes. Yet useful advances can still be made by finding ways to break, or at least soften, those compromises.

Here are three such compromises that have long stood in the way of potentially quicker lap times:

1 The output of a four-stroke internal-combustion (IC) piston engine is basically that of an air pump – fairly smooth and free from large variations. But, as 'Mr Superbike' Rob Muzzy observed in the 1990s, "The harder you work to get power from a four-stroke, the more it begins to act like a two-stroke."

Superimposed on natural four-stroke smoothness are strongly rpm-dependent effects, such as wave action in intake and exhaust pipes, intake airbox pressure resonance and the ever-present temptation to extend cam timings to add peak power at the sacrifice of acceleration.

Should we tune these effects additively or should we offset them to broaden torque? In the pre-electronics era, it was up to the rider to compensate for zones of fast-changing torque, using rapid throttle movements to prevent wheelies or loss of rear grip. Combine the limited speed of human reactions and the small motorcycle tyre footprint with 'Muzzy's Law' and you severely limit the scope of engine tuning. This is why the earliest MotoGP engines made so little power – in the order of 220hp/litre, while at the same time, Formula 1's giant tyres could handle 300hp/litre. In MotoGP's first seasons, any more than that exceeded the ability of human riders to compensate by throttle movement for the torque curve 'mountains and valleys' resulting from higher states of tune.

MotoGP broke this compromise just as aerospace did – by assisting human control with electronics. This took the form of regarding the rider's throttle angle as a torque demand, then letting an on-board computer find the best way to create that torque (by rapidly varying throttle opening, ignition timing, etc). Today, as a rider exiting a turn feeds throttle to keep the rear tyre working at peak grip as the bike lifts from full lean, the engine's computer-controlled throttle butterflies are in constant fluttering motion as they send the desired torque to the rear tyre. This is throttle-by-wire.

2 Unlike a car, a motorcycle must lean over to go around corners. As tyres and their tread rubber evolve, maximum lean angle increases and will continue to do so. This process is effectively compressing the motorcycle between right and left ground planes. During the classic GP racing of the 1960s, maximum lean angle was just over 45 degrees, so the two ground planes added up to a 'motorcycle space' of, say, 85 degrees. Today, maximum lean has increased to 63 degrees, shrinking the 'motorcycle space' to a narrow 54 degrees. To

compensate, engines and footpegs have been made narrower or mounted higher.

The latter is a problem because the taller the bike, the lower the maximum rates of acceleration and deceleration (wheelie limit and stoppie limit) become. Riders have responded by radically offsetting their body weight to the inside in corners, to effectively push the motorcycle more upright, keeping it within the 'motorcycle space'. Engineers have lowered fuel cg height by moving much of it backward and down to the area beneath the rider's seat.

A way out of this compromise has long been known, but has been implemented only recently: by making chassis ride height variable while under way. Because the hardest braking and acceleration occur at small or zero lean angles, where the constraints of the 'motorcycle space' don't apply, the bike's ride height can be lowered at such times to significantly raise the wheelie/stoppie limits to acceleration and braking.

3 Because the MotoGP engine displacement limit is now at 1000cc, top speeds are very high, as is the ability to continue to accelerate at such speeds. Riders speak of a floaty feeling or loss of directional stability nearing top speed. This is caused by the aero drag force, acting on a lever equal to the height of the frontal aero centre-of-pressure above the track, causing progressive transfer of load off the front wheel and on to the rear as speed rises. Aero drag is literally trying to blow the motorcycle over backward.

This effect is boosted not only by the bike's continued acceleration, but also by the trend, driven by rising tyre grip, towards the taller ride heights required to preserve cornering clearance.

Anti-wheelie systems maintain control by keeping the front tyre on the track, but as they operate only by reducing power, they sacrifice acceleration.

Now breaking this compromise is the aerodynamic downforce of small inverted wings or winglets, presented to free-stream air near the front of the machine. Downforce devices are now receiving criticism for reasons as various as not looking like motorcycles, raising front tyre temperature and generating wakes that disturb following machines.

These compromises and approaches to compromise-breaking are not new to motorcycling, but in fact define the forces that have always driven its evolution.

Early motorcycles had clutchless single-speed belt drive and were started by the rider pedalling forcefully to spin the engine through its operating cycle until it fired. While clutches and multi-speed gearboxes had long been normal equipment for cars by 1910, motorcycle makers resisted their adoption on the ground that their added cost would reduce sales. The result was machines capable of perhaps 40km/h, whose engines had to be restarted after every stop.

In 1910, the organisers of the Isle of Man TT races decided that this was limiting the utility of motorcycles. Consequently, for 1911, they specified that TT competitors' machines had to have a free engine clutch, to allow halting without stopping the engine, and some means of varying the drive ratio between engine crankshaft and rear wheel to improve hill climbing, starting from rest and acceleration. The nonsense about clutches and multi-speed gearboxes being too expensive or complicated ceased.

A compromise with which the author had personal experience was that regarding engine spark timing. The early 250 Yamaha two-stroke production racers, on which many future champions would train, were sparked by magnetos having fixed timing. The engines actually needed different spark timing at different rpm levels, however – a lot different at lower rpm, less as the exhaust pipes began their pumping action and least of all at peak torque.

At the time, there was no way to provide this awkward variation, so a compromise was struck – to fix the timing at 20 degrees BTDC. This was too little at 6,500rpm, sacrificing acceleration, and too much at 10,000rpm, making the engine work against itself. The result was weaker torque at low revs and excess heat in the power band. To 'paper over' this compromise, very 'cold' spark plugs were fitted (to prevent electrode overheating and pre-ignition). Even colder plugs – today considered suitable only for Top Fuel dragsters – were specified for hot days.

The result? We tuned those engines rich to avoid detonation or possible seizure, making plug fouling a frequent problem.

A further problem of magnetos was that, being triggered mechanically, they were subject to spark scatter.

Technically savvy GP riders of the 1960s – Hugh Anderson of Suzuki comes to mind – had used the handlebar-mounted spark lever of that era to advantage, but at the cost of splitting attention between engine management and preparing for the next corner.

Attempts in 1969 to break this compromise with electronics were a step forward – non-contact trigger systems gave accurately timed sparks – but still at fixed timing. Not until the 1980s did the sophistication of low-cost computer memory appear in racing motorcycle ignitions – the ability to store and use the spark timing that gives best torque at every combination of rpm and throttle angle.

That timing was established by step-wise dynamometer testing and was recorded in digital form as a three-dimensional map, with rpm on the X-axis, throttle angle on the Y-axis and best timing on the Z-axis. This finally put an end to the waste of engine power inherent in fixed timing.

Electronic ignitions drew criticism in the 1970s and '80s, just as aero devices and variable ride height do today. An experienced rider would be helpless were an electronic 'black box' to fail, but would soon be on his way after simple adjustments

Above: **Hunkered down front and rear. Bagnaia practices his launch.**
Photo: Ducati Corse

Top right: **No fairings on the AJS of Les Graham in 1949.**
Photo: Motocourse Archive

Top far right: **Yamaha rider Kent Andersson in 1969. Note the hand hovering on the clutch in case the engine seizes.**
Bernd Fischer - motoarchive.com

Above right: **Extra controls were needed for experimental extra suspension functions.**

Above far right: **Seat-hump tail fins were the latest protuberances to appear in 2022, pioneered as always by Ducati.**
Photos: Gold & Goose

Right: **Stickier tyres allow ever greater angles of lean. Quartararo's weight shift reduces the angle for a given speed, making it possible for him to go faster.**
Photo: Monster Energy Yamaha

to a conventional ignition. Only gradually did such carping die away. Today, digital mapped ignitions have become the norm worldwide.

Carburettor fuel systems respond passively, in an analogue way, to the airflow passing through them. In a racing engine's power band, intake pulsing is strong, providing a useful 'signal' that decisively pulls fuel from the needle jet. But at lower engine speeds, where intake and exhaust waves are weakened or confused, the result was 'megaphonitis' – delivery of weak, incompletely evaporated mixtures that were hard to ignite, resulting in reduced torque or actual misfiring. Classic in this respect was the Manx Norton single-cylinder race engine, which for the foregoing reasons was unable to accept full throttle below 5,500 rpm.

Through the 1980s, various 'fixes' were added to carburettors to widen their capabilities, such as powerjets that sprayed fuel only at larger throttle openings (but that had to be shut off by solenoid valve above a certain rpm to prevent top-end over-richness); aircraft-style back-suction mixture control; or the use of a mechanical accelerator pump to prevent fuel from falling behind airflow during rapid throttle opening. The widely used CV carbs of the 1970–90s added a second throttle valve whose delayed opening assisted throttle response. Was this pile of patches easy to repair at the roadside?

The end came when government-imposed exhaust emissions limits could be met only by greater mixture accuracy than carburettors – complex as they had become – could deliver. Again, the objection was raised that fuel injection would add cost and be unrepairable at the roadside. In fact, fuel injection has not only proved highly reliable, but also has greatly improved upon the 'stutter-and-stall' running of emissions-compliant models with carburettors. Engines of today start and run obediently, and respond promptly to throttle while meeting emissions, thanks to digital fuel injection.

Present objections to such innovations as aero devices must be balanced by considering how in future we will manage without them. Production motorcycles lack winglets? Look in the showrooms – here they come. Motorcycle appearance has changed radically again and again, and riders have accepted it. In the late 1940s and early 1950s, AJS refused to put fairings on race bikes, even at the expense of a loss of top speed. Bodywork is normal today. Bikes of the 1960s placed the rider far back, with the seat stop directly above the rear axle. Bikes of today put the rider as far forward as possible. This change, and with it the forward placement of engines, has been made to allow bikes to accelerate harder before front wheel lift occurs.

If winglets are banned one day, shall we urge riders made nervous by floaty front-end lightness at 350km/h to man up and pin the throttle? Do we avoid the issue by slowing the entire field by means of reducing engine displacement and imposing rev limits?

In the case of variable ride height, as this is written, it appears that a partial ban will be adopted for 2023. As already stated, increases in tyre grip gradually force motorcycles to become narrower or taller. The taller their ride height, the greater the loss of front tyre load at high speed, with loss of directional stability – especially on straights with surface waviness, as at the US CoTA circuit.

Many other design compromises remain to be broken and new ones will be discovered. At present, there is much difficulty in maintaining front tyre grip when tyre temperature is driven upwards by winglet downforce or by close drafting in the hot slipstreams of other bikes. In the 1980s, a now-retired

2

111

OFF

BARDAHL
FASSI

YAMAHA
MICHELIN
alpinestars
MONSTER ENERGY
20

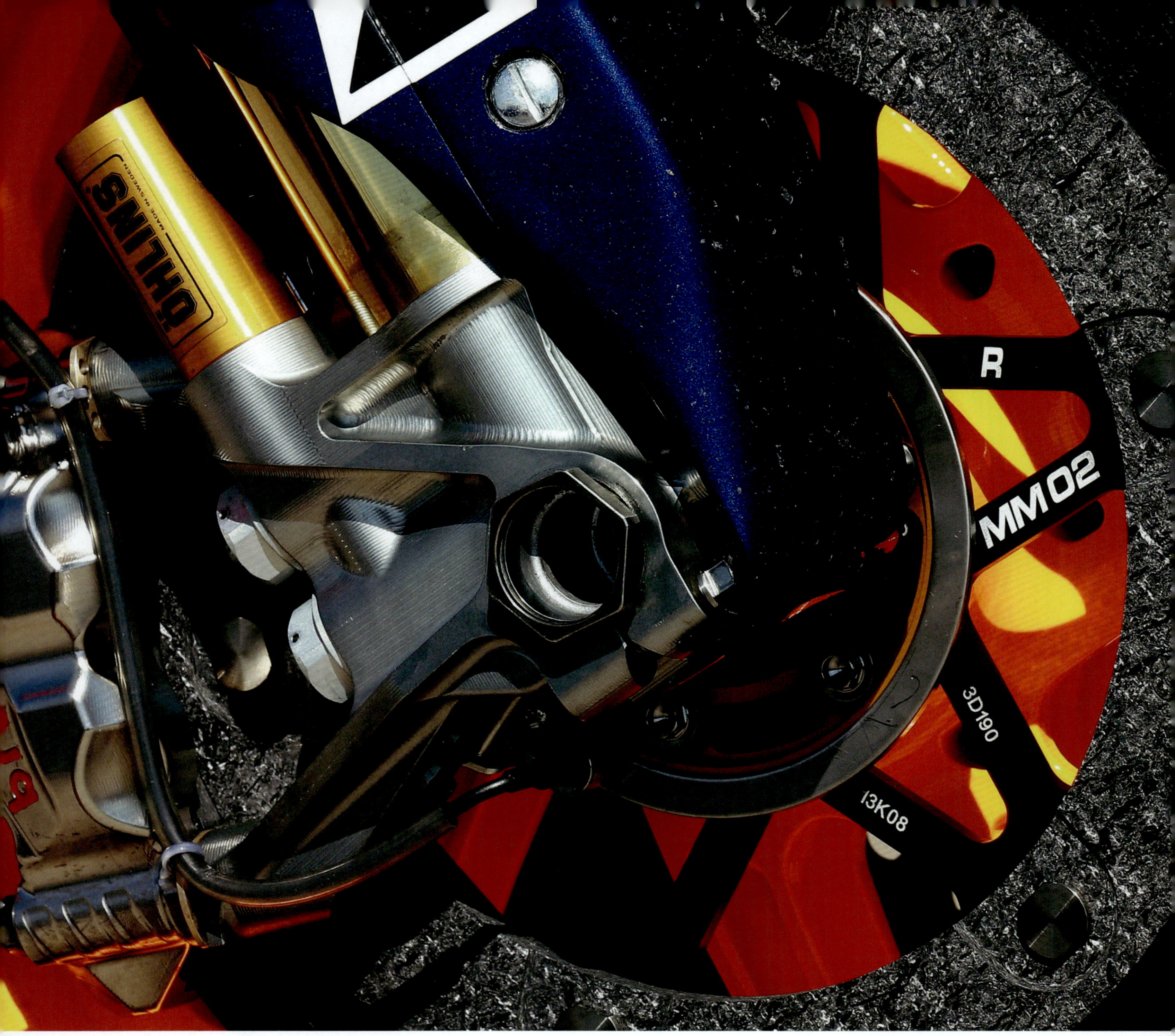

Above: **Brakes just keep on getting bigger and bigger.**

Top right: **Yamaha's shapely front wing: aero bodywork increases downforce, and sets street-bike fashions.**

Photos: Gold & Goose

Above centre right: **Swiss sidecar champion Rolf Biland pushed the limits of the regulations.**

Photo: Motocourse Archive

Centre far right: **Buttons, switches, knobs and levers ... KTM's left handlebar gives the rider plenty to do.**

Right: **Fine adjustments are never completed. Suzuki mechanics fiddle with the details..**

Photo: www.suzuki-racing.com

Dunlop tech proposed active control of tyre pressure as a possible future technology. I was told that this was inspired by the variable tyre-pressure system implemented on one of Dunlop's big drum test units.

In my first interview with Marc Marquez, he described the problem of coping with an overheating tyre. If the process is allowed to continue, footprint area diminishes as pressure rises, leading to increased tyre slip, generating yet more heat in a destructive spiral. He described the tyre (Bridgestone was the spec-tyre supplier then) becoming "hot and bouncy" unless the rider rested it for a lap or two (possibly leading to loss of position). Will riders and teams remain satisfied with the present system of having to guess the front tyre pressure that will finish the race with grip to spare?

MotoGP brakes are showing signs of distress, evidenced by successive increases in permitted disc diameter from 320 to 340mm, and now to 355mm. Part of this may come from the increased front grip created by winglet downforce (an effect proportional to vehicle speed, squared), but Ben Spies was able to virtually destroy his bike's carbon-carbon brakes in three hectic laps at Motegi a decade ago.

This suggests that even then, riders were being forced to manage brakes to some degree, just as they must manage tyres. To reduce disc temperature, they have already been spaced out further from the front wheel's central plane to expose them to faster moving air. Calipers have been redesigned to improve their cooling. Fork legs, in their turn, have been spaced more widely apart. Is MotoGP braking now fully under control, or might brake distress erupt in future at Motegi and Phillip Island?

MotoGP suspension is stiff because otherwise, with the great increase in suspension load as a bike leans over for a turn, its travel would be used up and the engine or exhaust pipes would contact the track. But stiff suspension is not best for grip, because of the high tyre forces generated. Another job for ride-height control could be to compensate for this loss of travel.

All the systems on a motorcycle are interrelated – change one detail here and it causes a cascade of effects elsewhere. This means that rule changes must be considered carefully for their broader effects. Engineers seek to improve lap time, reliability and rider control, but the sport is a business, the product of which is the excitement of close and unpredictable racing.

Are technical and business managers intelligible to each other? Why, for example, was the dual-clutch transmission banned, obliging teams to develop much more costly 'seamless' transmissions?

Because the racing motorcycle always has problems that limit its performance, engineers seek solutions. Remember the long duel between sidecar racer/constructor Rolf Biland and the FIM. Biland made sidecars unrecognisable by single-mindedly seeking to win championships, while the FIM countered with rules intended to maintain sidecar racing's continuity with its traditional past. Let's hope that engineers and business managers can seek their goals sensibly while retaining a sense of humour.

MONSTER ENERGY
YAMALUBE
A Liquid Engine Component

Gusto
2
DEVILLE
SIEBDRUCK AG BIEL
hostettler

ECSTAR
MOTUL
AKRAPOVIC
MICHELIN

REALISATION: APRILIA BURSTS OUT OF THE SHADOWS

From MotoGP's poor relation to serious title challenger in one easy move? NEIL MORRISON finds Aprilia's transformation didn't happen overnight...

Above: **You beauty. Espargaro kisses his Aprilia in *parc fermé* after his momentous win.**

Above right: **Aprilia stalwart Romano Albesiano has been there from bad times to good.**
Photos: Gold & Goose

Right: **Perfect harmony – man and machine gelled in 2022.**
Photo: Whit Bazemore

YOU wouldn't have known it from the long faces in the Aprilia box as the season drew to a close, but 2022 was a major highpoint in the history of the Noale factory, whose team, lead rider and much-improved RS-GP had carried out a campaign of pleasant surprise to so nearly shake up the MotoGP establishment. Only at the final hurdle did they fall.

Yes, Pecco Bagnaia mounted the biggest reversal in premier-class history. But it would be no grand overstatement to assert that the year's biggest surprise was Aprilia's rise from a project that had showed potential, although prone to trip over its own shoelaces, to flower into an unlikely challenger for the MotoGP title.

Forget the final five rounds, when Aleix Espargaro's title challenge dispersed with two non-scores, rendering the lively Catalan a ball of monosyllabic misery on Sunday at Valencia. The very fact that he and Aprilia had harboured realistic goals of winning the title with two races to go was a stunning achievement in itself. Aprilia Racing CEO Massimo Rivola had spoken of his hope for the factory to be "the sort of underdog, the little bastard" of the class in April. And it succeeded, ending the year in a stronger position than at any other time in its MotoGP history. Going into the off-season, it can now boast of a satellite team to bolster its position in 2023.

As a factory that has amassed 54 world championship victories in classes including 125cc, 250cc and World Superbike, Aprilia is no stranger to success. Yet its presence in MotoGP, since it returned in an official capacity in 2015, hadn't always given the impression that it was destined for the pinnacle of the sport. For a factory that had collected just five podiums and a best championship finish of eighth across 16 years of officially competing in the class of kings, the 20 races of 2022 make for standout reading.

Across the year, Espargaro notched up the factory's first premier-class win and pole position in the four-stroke era in Argentina. That same day, he became the first Aprilia rider ever to lead the championship. His 212 points accumulated by the end of the year were 92 more than any previous Aprilia-mounted rider had managed. And until the autumnal end of the European season, the RS-GP was considered to be among the grid's best bikes, even on a par with Ducati's awesome Desmosedici.

Quite the turnaround for the factory that had had as many blunders as successes in the four years following its official re-entry into MotoGP in 2015, after 11 years away. At the end of 2018, one wondered what Aprilia was achieving exactly in the class. Fielding a MotoGP bike obviously isn't cheap, and so often the operation had a ragtag element to it. Why were there so many engine blow-ups? And why did each of Espargaro's team-mates receive the cold shoulder so soon into their tenures? When Scott Redding's frustrations at events behind the scenes boiled over in Austria that year, his comment – "There are so many things that... in a team of this level should not be happening" – really stood out.

But the first shoots of recovery were evident prior to 2019, when the factory began to put its house in order. Recognising that technical director Romano Albesiano was totally stretched, Massimo Rivola – formerly of Minardi/Toro Rosso and Ferrari in Formula 1 – was brought in as Aprilia Racing CEO to look after team management. That proved pivotal. "In the past, Albesiano was in charge of almost everything," Espargaro said. "Massimo started to change the organisation in Noale and the way they work, while Romano started to be more focused on the development of the bike. The organisation by Massimo has been the key."

It's difficult to argue. Concentrating solely on technical details, Albesiano succeeded in developing the factory's 90-degree V4 engine from 2020 to the point where it was outrunning a Ducati in a straight line during the first races of 2022. "We have two or three seasons in front of us without major

changes on the bike," said the technical director in 2021. "We know performance comes from refinement, generally not from revolution."

Rivola used 2019 to assess the resources already at Aprilia's disposal before convincing the Piaggio Group, which had acquired the Italian factory in 2004, to plough more into its MotoGP project. "The company has invested a lot more in recent seasons," Albesiano told MOTOCOURSE. "This has allowed us to hire the people, to have more material, to make more engines for development. When we started, we had really a different approach, not probably a MotoGP-level approach. Now we have. The more you have, the more competitive you can be. Now it's sufficient to be at a good level.

"When we started this MotoGP adventure, we had some knowledge in the racing department which we believed was enough. It wasn't. So, we had to build a lot. Year by year, we learned and we improved, myself first, and all the guys with me. We got more material, more people. It's been an overall increase in the potential."

Soon it wasn't just the company's racing CEO who could boast of Formula 1 credentials; Rivola was able to convince a number of names from his previous paddock to try their hand at two wheels, a transition that had had limited success in the bike world previously. Former Ferrari engineer Luca Marmoni was one to collaborate on evolving the RS-GP's 90-degree V4 engine over the winter of 2020–21. Others formerly with Ferrari were brought in to understand and develop the complex aerodynamics that can aid acceleration and turning on two wheels. At times, Toyota's wind tunnel in Cologne, Germany, was used.

"In our team, we have people in the aerodynamic department who came from car racing," said Albesiano. "The level of development of aerodynamics in car racing is unbelievable. These people have been very clever to adapt to motorcycles. I've seen many people coming from the car industry to transit to the motorcycle industry, and for many, it has been difficult to change their minds. But our guys have worked well. For them, it's like when Christopher Columbus went to America, it's a new world, like nobody had gone there before. It's not just optimising something, but discovering something new. And it's really exciting."

Other working methods used effectively in Formula 1, and by Ducati in MotoGP, were implemented. Like more advanced means of analysing data by a number of specialised technicians, including a handful based in Noale. Also, an effective

test team, using a number of engineers previously employed in World Superbike, was established.

"When we started, we had a very classic approach," Albesiano admitted. "The analysis of the data was an average level, not the level you need here. Then, brick by brick, we've built something that has been, at times, too complex. But the level of analysis we do now is very high. Adding some people with the right experience, and getting back people that left Aprilia years before, and then rejoining in this new wave has been another kick. If you came to the garage four years ago, and now, you wouldn't realise you're in the same team.

"We also have people in Noale that check the data. We are continuously in contact with them, [saying], 'Please check this tyre behaviour…' They then answer back. It's like Formula 1's remote garage concept. Okay, they have dozens of people. We have two or three good guys that do a good job."

Covid-afflicted 2020 aside, when the factory was caught out by the aerodynamic freeze, the project has gone from strength to strength. As Rivola noted in Argentina in April, "Every year, we are reducing [the gap to] the leader. [It was a] 30-second average in '19 at the end of the race, 20 seconds in '20, ten seconds in '21. And now we are very close so the target was five seconds."

Another feather in Rivola's cap was attracting the rider alongside Espargaro. While the experienced Catalan has been a factory mainstay since 2017, so often the other side of the garage had fallen into disarray. The stays of GP winner and world champion Stefan Bradl, Sam Lowes and Scott Redding were deeply troubled, before Andrea Iannone eventually lost a place due to doping. Finding a rider to take over from the Italian at the end of 2020 was problematic. Three names in Moto2 – Marco Bezzecchi, Aron Canet and Joe Roberts – were offered the seat for the following year; all three turned it down.

Yet ultimately that worked in Aprilia's favour. It left them able to offer Maverick Vinales a lifeline in August, 2021, when his relationship with Yamaha disintegrated spectacularly.

Aware of the mercurial characteristics of the former Moto3 world champion and nine-times MotoGP race winner, Aprilia knew they needed to adopt a different approach when managing him. The human aspect of Rivola's approach could be seen when he welcomed Vinales to the Noale project for the first time. "How we make him feel is the key to everything," he told the gathered engineers, as seen in the *MotoGP Unlimited* series. "We must put him at the heart of the project, like we're integrating our own child."

It didn't take long for race manager Paolo Bonora to gain an understanding of how to approach his new rider. "When we met him, we immediately found a rider with an open mind. That showed to us he needed trust, to have each engineer and mechanic close to him, and they needed to give him the trust. When he feels the trust coming from the guys close to him, he gives his best. He's a very sensitive rider. But we need to keep him in a comfortable situation without pushing him so hard. He is a big talent. It's necessary to keep him calm to allow him to push to his limits."

Vinales was protected closely, put under little pressure. Let's not forget, 2021 wasn't just a nadir in his career, with all that went wrong at Yamaha; it was a low point on a personal level, too, after the death of cousin Dean Berta. Even at the start of that season, the Noale factory understood that it had to reduce the high expectations he already had. "We didn't put pressure on him," said Bonora. "It was the correct way because at the moment, he's without pressure. He's giving his best, thinking about podiums or winning, but with only positive [energy], much like what we did with Aleix earlier this year." This approach bore fruit mid-season, with Vinales not just backing up his team-mate, but also beating him. This was another first: *two* Aprilias fighting at the front.

Ultimately, Aprilia fell just short in the search for ultimate glory. It was rumoured that a shortage of new parts contributed to Espargaro's haul of just 18 points from the final five rounds, with crucial technical errors in Japan and Australia leading him to conclude, "We're not ready to fight for the title." Albesiano

admitted that the factory is still unable to explain poor performances in Thailand and Malaysia.

"We had this incident in Motegi which was just a trivial mistake," he said. (The fuel-saving sighting-lap electronics were not disengaged, and Espargaro had to switch bikes and start from the pit lane, for his first no-score of the season.) "This has been a hammer stroke on his championship. Then in Thailand, we had some troubles with grip for the very first time. This was surprising. It was one of the two races we still need to understand. In Phillip Island, we had quite a good race, except a detail in the traction control setting. A very small mistake, and nobody's perfect. And then we had Malaysia, which was the second race to understand. He expected more because we were so fast there in winter testing. So, we need to understand to be more solid in the performance in the future."

Even Espargaro, devastated at losing third place in the riders' championship at the final race, had previously admitted that 2022 will come to be viewed as a major success. "Our season has been incredible," he said. "Last year, we celebrated the podium of Silverstone like a victory, like historic, and this year, we won a race, took 5–6 podiums, took pole positions and fought for the title until the end, so it doesn't matter what happens in Valencia or in the championship. Our season has been a ten out of ten."

ALEIX ESPARGARO – PATIENCE REWARDED

For most of 2022, Aleix Espargaro couldn't wipe the smile off his face. Keeping company on track with names previously out of reach, fielding questions about race wins and championship fights – he couldn't get enough. "It's the best year of my life," he said at the end of the European season.

After Dovizioso retired, Espargaro, at 33, became the grid's oldest and most experienced rider. Often outspoken and unafraid to criticise his rivals, occasionally he had attracted their ridicule for his lack of success – only three podiums across 16 full seasons in all classes. His and Aprilia's first win came in his 200th premier-class race, displacing Danilo Petrucci (123 starts) for the longest wait for a win.

Yet twice Espargaro had been a champion of the much-loathed CRT championship, within MotoGP in 2012–13, and before he took Aprilia to a winning level, he had done the same at Suzuki.

Does he feel undervalued?

"I know in this paddock, the engineers that know me know how I work, how enthusiastic I am to develop the bikes. I was missing the fight for wins and podiums ... but every year, Aprilia brought me a new team-mate and said he would beat me. And every year, I beat them at almost every race. This gave me some credibility."

There was always the fear that a title shot might never come: "When I left Suzuki for Aprilia, I sometimes said to myself, 'You're moving from one of the biggest brands to the smallest factory, and the slowest bike on the grid. Maybe this is the end.'"

It has been far from plain sailing in Aprilia colours, with "really low moments in 2019. I was not happy, crashing and finishing outside the top ten in every race. I was very close to ending my career. But life is amazing, things changed a lot for 2020, and look where we are now."

The Aprilia-Espargaro synergy was reminiscent of Ducati's rise with Andrea Dovizioso. The Italian felt that 2022 had been an example of a rider being allowed to develop in tandem with a bike and factory, "like Marc with Honda, Fabio with Yamaha, what I was able to do with Ducati," Dovizioso told MOTOCOURSE. "It's about your riding style being good for the characteristics of the bike, and year by year, you can just use that potential more and not adapt. There is already a connection."

Above: A podium selfie captures the win in Argentina.

Top: Espargaro with Massimo Rivola – a winning combination.

Top right: Espargaro scored six podium finishes in 2022.

Right: Head-on shot shows Aprilia's trend-setting wind-tunnel-developed fairing-flank bulge. Ducati copied it at post-season tests.

Photos: Gold & Goose

Left: Maverick Vinales brought status and experience to Aprilia after his divorce from Yamaha.

Photo: Whit Bazemore

APPRECIATIONS

By Michael Scott

250cc Yamaha, 1964.

PHIL READ OBE 1939–2022

PHIL READ, who died on 6th October, was Britain's last link with the glory days of grand prix racing – the era when the new Japanese factories were flooding the grids with ever more adventurous technology, and riders who had cut their teeth on single-cylinder Velocettes and Nortons in the rain at Snetterton, Oulton Park and the Isle of Man came into their own on the world stage.

Read spearheaded Yamaha's near-decade of battles with Honda, a fearsome two-stroke versus four-stroke contest across the smaller classes, with riders usually competing in at least two and sometimes three classes at a GP meeting, across treacherous circuits – many on public roads – where the smallest error or (even more soberingly) a mechanical failure could mean serious injury or death. Later, Read admitted that sometimes he would vomit because of pre-race nerves, likening the experience to that of pilots in the Battle of Britain, never knowing whether you would survive or not.

Read was one of the foremost of the breed. In a world-class career spanning more than 20 years, he set one landmark after another, becoming Britain's second most decorated rider. He was only outstripped by his contemporary and perpetual rival, Mike Hailwood. He had seven world championships (plus a slightly off-beam Formula TT Championship in 1977) to Hailwood's nine and 52 grand prix wins to his 76.

Phil was the first rider to win titles in the 125, 250 and 500 class, a feat not repeated until Valentino Rossi won the last 500 title in 2001.

But while Hailwood left bike racing after the withdrawal of the Japanese factories at the end of the 1960s, Read never really gave up, winning another title as a privateer Yamaha rider in 1971 and then joining MV Agusta, where he won two premier-class titles, the second in 1974, which was the last in the 500cc category for a four-stroke.

Even after retiring abruptly from GPs mid-season in 1976, ceding the limelight to the fast-rising Barry Sheene, Phil continued to race more occasionally in (among other places) World Endurance, and later in classic series, well into his seventies.

Read, a fierce fighter and determined competitor, was nicknamed the Prince of Speed. But he was equally comfortable with the Rebel Read tag, earned through a series of independently-minded acts designed to further his career, sometimes at the expense of others.

Most notoriously, in 1968, after the withdrawal of Honda, Yamaha had an open goal. The factory decreed that Phil should win the 125 title, and his team-mate, Bill Ivy, the 250 crown. Cheeky Kentish lad Ivy made it obvious that he was letting Phil win at round three on the Isle of Man. But come the end of the year, by which point, it was clear that Yamaha was also about to withdraw from the championship, Phil declined to return to favour, winning the last race at Monza to finish equal on points. Better elapsed times gave him the double championship, and while Yamaha sacked him at once, it hardly mattered.

At MV Agusta, he was an equally troublesome team-mate to Agostini, who quit the firm after nine years as its favourite son and never forgave Phil. But modern fans might draw parallels with Valentino Rossi, who equally made certain that any team-mate able to threaten his results would find life very uncomfortable.

Another unpopular act is also open to re-evaluation, his boycott of the Isle of Man TT – a race he had won six times – in 1973, along with Agostini and other leading riders. Eventually, this led to the TT losing world championship status from 1977.

That same year, Phil went back, taking two more wins. He was dubbed a hypocrite, critics saying that he had killed the race and then returned for the money. But it was more true that he'd boycotted the race in the interest of other riders and returned to show his love of the classic event, now that it had become a matter of choice, not a championship obligation, for those (like him and Hailwood) willing to face the challenge.

Read was born in Luton in 1939, and his first racing exploits were encouraged and supported by his mother in the late 1950s. He came to prominence soon afterwards with strong results on short circuits and at the Isle of Man, where he won the 1961 Junior TT, and was perfectly placed when Yamaha was looking for riders for their part in the Japanese motorcycle arms race.

Both Read's personal and business lives could best be described as "colourful", the more so following the death of his second wife, Madeleine, in 1978. He remained a regular visitor to classic race meetings until shortly before his death at Canterbury. He is survived by four sons and a daughter.

Lightweight TT, Isle of Man 1961.

KUNIMITSU TAKAHASHI 1940–2022

KUNIMITSU TAKAHASHI was a genuine history man of Japanese racing. Having come to Europe in 1960, riding alongside Jim Redman and Tom Phillis, among others, in Honda's first full assault on grand prix racing, he found the level of competition sobering.

But it did not take long for the rider or the manufacturer to get up to speed, and in only his second year, he became the first Japanese rider to win a grand prix, taking victory in the West German round at Hockenheim, four seconds ahead of illustrious team-mate Jim Redman, both of them riding Honda's howling four-cylinder 250.

Takahashi won a 125 GP later that year and would go on to win the two opening rounds in 1962, a serious contender in the smaller class. But substantial injuries in round three, the Isle of Man TT, curtailed his motorcycling career.

Racing was in his blood, however, and he went on to a distinguished career on four wheels, winning four national championships in Japan in the sports prototype class, racing in Formula 3000 and even being given a Formula 1 outing. Subsequently, he became a successful team manager, adding a class win at the Le Mans 24-hour race to his CV.

Takahashi's remarkable car control earned him the title 'Father of Drift' in Japan, but his first love was for motorcycles, and he returned for an emotional demonstration ride at Assen in 2019, aboard Honda's RC142 – the original 125 of Honda's first 1959 visit to the TT.

He died of lymphoma in March, aged 82.

STEVE HARRIS 1940–2022

THE death of STEVE HARRIS marked the end of an era when a single or a small group of independent engineers could play a major part in motorcycling.

Essentially self-taught, working with younger brother Lester and schoolfriend Steve Bayford, Harris built racing and road chassis, designed and sold accessories, and played a significant role from street level to MotoGP and World Superbikes.

Having started out converting Yamaha TZ250/350 production racers to monoshock, later Harris made frames for Barry Sheene and others, and was selected (with French constructors ROC) to build replica Yamaha YZR500 chassis for private teams between 1992 and 1996.

An inspirational engineer at a time when independent chassis makers could often outdo the factories, Steve succumbed to Parkinson's disease in June.

DIETRICH MATESCHITZ 1944–2022

MOTORSPORT lost a fervent and generous benefactor when DIETRICH MATESCHITZ died in October, having succumbed to cancer, aged 78.

Over almost 30 years, the Red Bull boss and his drinks company supported every conceivable racing series on two and four wheels, sponsoring teams, the KTM factory squads, the Rookies Cup and scores of individual riders, as well as regenerating the former Osterreichring as the Red Bull Ring in 2011, reviving the Austrian car and motorcycle GPs.

Mateschitz discovered the energy drink on a business trip to Thailand in 1982 and founded Red Bull GmbH in 1984, holding 49 per cent, the balance belonging to the family of Thai originator Chaleo Yoovidhya.

By 2021, sales worldwide had reached almost ten billion cans annually, and budgets had grown exponentially. Mateschitz devoted a third of the income to sponsorship and promotion, rather than maximising profit, to the benefit of motorsport worldwide.

ONE MAN'S ISLAND

RENNIE SCAYSBROOK, US-based Australian journalist, racer and Pikes Peak winner, had a lifelong dream of taking on the challenge of the TT. Here is his story…

Above: **Rennie flies through the daunting Molyneux's right-hander on the final night of practice. It was starting to click.**
Photo: Chippy Wood

Top right: **Follow my leader. Rennie clings on to rookie guide 'Milky' Quayle on his Sunday-afternoon speed-controlled rookie lap.**

Above right: **Leathered-up and ready to take the plunge down Bray Hill.**
Photos: Double Red Photography

Right: **I'm coming past! Peter Hickman lines up Davey Todd out of Kate's Cottage on the run down to Creg-Ny-Baa.**
Photo: David Purves

QUARRY BENDS is a snaking series of switchbacks that holds one of the many keys to a fast lap of the Isle of Man TT Mountain Course. Approaching in sixth gear, I knock it back one to fifth and rail past the first right in anticipation of the upcoming left that Peter Hickman tells me is the most important corner on the course. If you get through it right, you'll be able to hold full throttle through the next right/left/right, clicking sixth before the final kink on to the fastest part of the track.

On this third lap of my final night of practice on Thursday, I know I've nailed it. The little Suzuki is wailing its brains out in fifth, I'm counter-steering so hard it feels like I'm rowing through drying cement, and as I click sixth, I tuck in and prepare for that last left kink and my entry once again on to the world's fastest roller coaster – the Sulby Straight might be straight, but it's far from smooth.

Then, in an instant, the PRF Suzuki is heading towards the trees at near top speed. I haven't hit anything and nothing has broken. It was simply Jamie Coward on his Superbike-spec Yamaha going around the outside of me so fast that his bow-wave literally knocked me off course.

That old racing expression, "came past so quickly it sucked the stickers off the bike" has never been more true.

Welcome to the Isle of Man, kid. As John McGuinness says, "The Nurburgring, Pikes Peak, those places are car parks. This is the daddy's circuit, right here."

Back after a two-year Covid hiatus, the world's oldest motorsports event is, after a century, still the ultimate place to test the mettle of man and machine. The dangers are undeniable. Six riders did not make it home in 2022, the deadliest year since 1970.

It's a common conundrum of the event that although they died, these racers all lined up, as did I, of their own free will, knowing that this indeed could be their last ride. The TT is unique in that it is one of the few places left in the world where a man or woman can make that choice, to be in command of their bodies and their ultimate destiny.

That destiny is controlled by a simple tap on the shoulder from the official race starter, letting you know that it's your turn to face the challenge of the Snaefell Mountain Course. In the increasingly digitised world we live in, the TT retains this beautifully simple tradition, one that provides what for some is a final human touch.

From personal experience, you hardly feel that touch because you're so focused on the starting control panel to the top right of your vision that your body almost goes numb.

Lap record holder Hickman describes varying levels of understanding about the TT that make it genuinely hard to explain the experience. "Unless you've been here and seen what the TT is all about, I really don't think it's describable," he said, mere hours after winning the 2022 Senior. "If you've been here as a spectator, you'll understand a little bit; if you've ridden your own bike around the track, you'll get it a bit more; and anyone who's lucky enough to have done a closed-roads lap will get a little bit more again.

"But the few that's raced here, they truly get it. That feeling is absolutely unlike anything else."

There are other road races, but the TT remains the grandfather. It is so ingrained in the Isle of Man's DNA that the place would be lost without it. The last time it had been run, in 2019, it had brought around £37 million to the local economy. The population of the island explodes for two weeks.

The people come to watch something extraordinary. Nowhere else can you get so close to riders doing 185mph, the rushing wind bringing a delayed cacophony of noise much like a fighter jet breaking the sound barrier. To sit at Hillberry and watch Hickman, McGuinness, Dunlop and Harrison whizz past so close that you could touch them is a surreal feeling. From the handlebars, however, it feels like you're the artist in a constantly evolving water painting. Colours blend from the trees to the fences and buildings, and you can see the look of exhilaration and terror on some spectators' faces as you sit up for braking – not because you're looking for them, but because they are so close that you can't help but notice.

This was my first foray to the Isle of Man. Having spent the previous three years getting match fit by racing as much as possible in Southern California, I felt that I was ready for the challenge. But I'll freely admit that I'd completely under-

estimated it. The battering my body took was far different from what I was used to on the short tracks of America. My shoulders, in particular, took such a hammering after the first night of practice that I could barely lift my left arm.

The constant jackhammering the circuit imparts, first to the motorcycle and then to the human body, cannot be overstated. You need to use your ankles, knees, hips, wrists, elbows and shoulders all as independent springs, constantly moving and adjusting your position on the motorcycle, with your butt rarely touching the seat.

At times, you need to ride your road racer like a dirt bike – butt off the seat, weight tilted towards the rear, allowing it to track where it wants and to let the suspension do its job. Places like the mile-long straight after the sixth-gear Ballacrye jump are dealt with by minimal handlebar inputs, the rider simply angling the motorcycle in the direction of travel and letting the mechanical forces take care of themselves.

The TT course really lets you know just how good you are, or aren't. Former 250 GP star Jamie Robinson once told me about being completely blown away by a rider nearly twice his size, because the TT course is all about carrying as much speed as possible out of the corner for the next long straight.

Speed multiplication has never been more apparent to me – a rider going 5mph faster on the exit of a corner will have gained seconds on you by the time you reach the end of a two-mile straight. It's a demoralising feeling being on the wrong side of that equation, and a beautiful one on the right side.

But the big thing you need to get used to is the sheer, brain-melting speed. My winning average speed at Pikes Peak in 2019 was 58mph. By the fourth night of practice, I'd doubled that to 117mph, and I was still not even in the top 20. The chronic speed means that your brain's synapses are firing harder than ever – from Union Mills to Greeba Castle, you only roll slightly for Ballagarey, but the rest is absolutely flat out. That section is nearly five miles long, and you're hardly ever going straight. It's no wonder that my eyes felt like they were going to pop out of my head each night.

Some sections make you truly glad to be alive. Plunging down over Ballig Bridge into Doran's Bend, through Laurel Bank and into the Glen Helen section is pure dopamine overload: you and your motorcycle surfing the smooth grey strip beneath you and the trees forming a glorious green tunnel.

On the flip side, exiting Ginger Hall into Kerrowmoar and then past the Glen Duff post office at top speed, with the motorcycle tying itself in knots underneath you, is truly terrifying for the first-timer, but a little trick I taught myself at Pikes Peak worked well here.

Back there, I'd always struggled from Devil's Playground to the Summit – the balls-to-the-wall section, the highest sustained top speed of the course, and the point where you really have to lay it on the line. One morning, I told myself, "You love this section, you love it," and I made myself repeat that until it was true. Sure enough, this became one of my best parts of the track, so I employed the same trick for Glen Duff and, despite it being categorically the most bumpy section of the track, I learned to love it.

However, my favourite part was the Mountain. After so much time in the trees, all of a sudden you're on a totally different racetrack. The dark of the overhanging branches gives way to enormous vision with no real blind corners, and when you crest the highest point, Hailwood Heights, suddenly gravity is working with you and the speed increases exponentially. You're throwing gears at the bike all the time as you roll down the mountain towards the Creg-Ny-Baa hotel – it's a glorious, other-worldly feeling.

Loved and feared in equal measure, the TT Mountain Course takes absolutely no prisoners and punishes those who make even the slightest transgression. Broken bikes and bodies are common sights at the TT, but you must tell yourself, "There's someone helping that guy," put it out of your mind and attack the next part of the course – or you could be next. In that sense, the TT Mountain Course is the absolute motorcycle equivalent of Mount Everest – this is the greatest challenge in racing.

The Isle of Man is near to my family's heart. I grew up with photos of my father racing his TT Ducati, Yamaha and AJS. I'd always hankered after doing it. My 'in' came via the Pikes Peak International Hill Climb, where I had won the final motorcycle event in 2019. A quick visit to the island at the end of that year confirmed that, yes, I did want to take on this greatest of challenges. The ensuing Covid hiatus meant that I had plenty of time to talk myself out of it. Not enough time, as it turned out.

My team for the event was PRF Racing, run by Paul Rennie in Skelmersdale, Lancashire, an outfit that has been around since 1995 and enjoyed success with team rider and Paul's brother, Carl. I figured that sharing a name was a good omen.

After arriving on the island a week before practice to get my bearings and, more importantly, into the time zone, Paul and I met face to face on the Thursday, for a quick shake-down test at the Jurby Airfield the next day. Our quick-shifter wasn't working, and neither was the gear position indicator, but I still felt optimistic.

My engine was a beast. Paul said it was good for 137hp, 18 up on my personal GSX-R back in California. It pulled hard even with the ultra-tall TT gearing, and the suspension felt near spot on. As it turned out, I didn't touch the front once for the full two weeks, save for two turns of preload, while the rear shock only required a slightly heavier 1.0kg spring and a bit less preload. Again, good omens.

I'd spent hours on the PlayStation, watched countless YouTube on-boards and spent a week doing car laps of the track with rookie liaison officers Richard 'Milky' Quale and Johnny Barton. I felt I was in a good position, knowledge-wise, as we walked up to the packed grid to complete my rookie speed-controlled lap on Sunday afternoon.

This is something every new TT rider has to do, from Honda Britain's Glenn Irwin right down to me. I wasn't even nervous. A little excited, a bit edgy, but just looking forward to getting this lap out of the way so that I could start my TT apprenticeship. However, my bike refused to play ball. When the moment came to fire up on Glencrutchery Road – crickets. With cameras pointing and onlookers onlooking, all I could do was sit there as Paul and Scott from PRF began stripping the bodywork on the grid in search of some hidden gremlin.

Johnny Barton waited and waited, but eventually, he and the three rookies in his care had to go, leaving me stranded on the grid, and the organisers telling Paul to take the bike and all its bits back to the pits. Thus we were informed that we would miss out on the whole day of practice, which, for a rookie like me, was devastating news.

Eventually, Paul found a fault in a throttle position sensor and the switch block on the left handlebar, and thanks to 'Milky' Quale, I managed to get in my rookie lap at the end of the day. Thus I was allowed to start Monday evening practice.

That first lap behind 'Milky' was an experience I will never, ever forget. Going down the Sulby Straight, pinned in sixth gear while trying like hell to keep him and his CBR1000 RR-R SP marshal bike in sight, I remember yelling in my helmet, "This is f**king nuts!"

And it was nuts.

How on earth was this legal? Not just legal, but actively encouraged? I came over the mountain from Hailwood Heights to Windy Corner totally aware of my own mortality, knowing that if I messed up here, it would be the last time. But the fear was balanced by unbridled exhilaration. I'd forgotten the Suzuki's electronic problem. The bike was going great. And I was living my oldest dream – pure, uncut adrenalin, I'd never felt anything like it.

Paul replaced the Suzuki's entire wiring loom and the switch block for Monday night, and the bike was beautiful for my first real practice. I went to 109.9mph average for the second lap – my first flying lap – but the session was cut short when Sam West lost control of his BMW through the Laurel Bank section of the course, his cartwheeling bike

splitting its fuel tank, exploding into flames and incinerating part of the hedge.

I was stopped at Parliament Square in Ramsay after two-and-a-half laps. It was almost welcome, as my shoulders felt like they'd done six rounds with a heavyweight UFC fighter. I had been told my upper body would take a beating at the TT, but I could hardly believe just how sore the muscles were around the front of my shoulders and on my neck. How was I going to do a full four-lapper?

My second night of practice was going brilliantly. Coming in after two laps to get a drink, a visor change and a tank of fuel, I headed out, completed lap three at 113.15mph and thought a fourth-lap flyer would put me at least into the 114mph bracket. Thoughts of improvement were quickly replaced with bewilderment as, going over the jump at Rhencullen, I felt a massive knock from the front end of the Suzuki. At first, I thought the steering head was loose, but then I pushed on my left handlebar and felt the knock again.

I pulled into a driveway of the Bishopscourt section of the track, a daunting, sixth-gear thread-the-needle section that for me is way more intimidating than Bray Hill or even Ballagarey. The marshal came up to me with a concerned look on his face: "What's the matter, lad?"

"I think my handlebar is loose."

"Really? No..."

He gave the left handlebar a slight tug, and out it popped from the clamp. I nearly fainted, and the disbelieving look on the few spectators' faces was all I needed. One of them found an Allen key so that I could retighten the bar. I triple checked everything else and cruised back to the pits, shot Paul a gnarly look and told him, rather loudly, "The f**king handlebar fell off!" He told me that this was the first time something like this had ever happened in the team's history, but it was still a major knock to my confidence. 'Milky' Quale was a good help: "Things break here that don't break anywhere else, mate. Don't let it get to you." He was right. I couldn't let that stuff play on my mind, but each time I got on the bike, my Metzeler USA sponsor, Oscar Solis, and I went over all the fasteners just to make sure...

We needed some good luck, and my third day started well. With two laps under my belt, I was 18th overall and feeling chuffed, having knocked out a 114.56mph run on lap two.

Earlier in that run, Mark Purslow and his sky-blue Yamaha YZF-R6 had passed me on the Cronk-y-Voddy straight, dragging me into the daunting right-hander faster than I'd ever gone. His line showed me the right way, but he was so quick that he was out of sight within five miles.

We crossed each other in the pits as we refuelled and Mark had trouble getting his bike turned around, so I'd leapfrogged him on the road. Setting off for lap three, I knew he was right behind me, so I put my head down and nailed my now beautifully-handling Suzuki as hard as I could to build a gap to Mark.

Coming through Greeba Castle and into Appledean, there

Above: **Snaefell sunset, and Rennie is on top of the world.**
Photo: Chippy Wood

Top left: **Rennie rounds one of the ten consecutive hairpins at Pikes Peak in 2019. America's greatest road race is no rival to the TT.**

Centre left: **Rookies together – BSB star Glenn Irwin and Rennie were both TT first-timers.**

Above left: **Home from home. The modest PRT workshop tent.**
Photos: Rennie Scaysbrook

Left: **'Rider and Machine Only' presages the moment of truth. Rennie, on bike 38, lines up ahead of Gary Vines (40) before the first Supersport race.**
Photo: Double Red Photography

in front of me flashed the red-flag light. I looked behind me, but Mark was nowhere to be seen. I thought he must have pulled off after the Crosby Jump.

I pulled into Ballacraine and was told that there had been an accident at Ballagarey – the daunting near-top-speed right-hander Guy Martin had made famous when miraculously he survived a fireball crash in 2010. After a little while, I realised that it was Mark who had gone down. It's rare for someone to survive a crash at Ballagarey, yet we all held out hope. But the longer we waited, the more apparent it became that this was a very grave accident indeed. The news filtered through a few hours later that Mark Purslow had lost his life. One of the fast TT up-and-comers, he was living his dream when it all came to an abrupt end. He was 29.

It was my first brush with death at the TT, and, sadly, it wouldn't be the last.

Qualifying night five will stay with me for the rest of my life. Four full laps, including two flyers, the little Suzuki and I gelling like dance partners. Lap four was pure ecstasy, catching and passing multiple riders from Union Mills to Governor's Bridge for the first time, and pulling away as they had done to me only the day before.

With no red flags, no crashes for anyone, I rocked out a 117.07mph lap to finish 22nd for the night, one place behind old sparring partner Chris Sarbora. I was beaming. That lap was, categorically, the most fun I've ever had on a bike. I started to feel like I belonged, that I could do this. I was capable of becoming a TT rider.

This euphoria was quashed the following night. I rode terribly, too full of myself, and I couldn't go as fast as the night before, when everyone else did. I had peaked too early, and the TT bitch-slapped me firmly into place.

Then on the final lap, coming into Joey's on the Mountain, I saw an explosion of hay bales. Bits of bike, too smashed to be recognisable, were strewn across the track, and I could vaguely make out the mangled figure of a rider on the side of the road. Thankfully, I couldn't see who it was, and with the medics attending, I put it out of my mind and got back on with the job of finishing the lap and the night.

On returning to the pits, my mate, Al Fagan, from 44 Teeth rushed up to me, concern written across his face: "Have you seen Boothy?" That figure on the ground was my colleague Mike Booth from 44teeth.com, the British bike review web site and YouTube channel, one of my favourites in this industry. "No, mate, I couldn't see it was him. All I could see was a rider and bits of bike everywhere."

It hadn't looked good, and it wasn't. Boothy, the man who just two days before had been hugging me, and giving me tips and pointers as a fellow journo and TT rider, had suffered very serious leg injuries. It took out whatever wind was in my sails.

The Suzuki had jumped out of gear a couple of times over that final lap. The team changed the height of the gear-shifter, and we decided on a preload and gearing change for the Saturday warm-up lap as a bit of a tester for the race. It was the only track time left before our race on Monday.

On Saturday morning, I dumped the clutch and sped through first gear, went for second gear and… nothing. With the revs below 8,000rpm, the Suzuki finally shifted into second. I went for third and… nothing. It was terminal. I coasted down Bray Hill and exited stage left, feeling rather embarrassed. It was another long afternoon for Paul and Scott, who not only had to replace the motor, but also weld the frame, which had cracked at the gearbox mount by the end of the day. A quick dyno run ensued: we were 10hp down on the old motor, but it was a fresh one after all and it would probably gain a few more ponies as it loosened up. At least we had a working motorcycle.

I used the time to play spectator, watching the real heroes of the TT do their thing in the Superbike race. Seeing the TT from this angle really brought home just what it means to the people who come to watch it. When you're racing, all that matters is you. But when you're spectating, the event takes on a new level, and you can't help but fall in love with the place, no matter the hardships it dishes out.

With a good night's sleep, I was ready to rock for race one on Monday. Paul and Scott had the bike running great, but going into a TT with an untested engine was a little off-putting.

It begins. The commotion of racing's most famous start-

Left: Gary Vines closes in on Rennie during their Supersport duel.
Photo: Double Red Photography

Right: Rennie with fellow racer and journalist Mike Booth. The injuries he suffered in practice hammered home the dangers of the TT.
Photo: Rennie Scaysbrook

Below: The fast men, like Dean Harrison, are awe-inspiring.
Photo: David Purves

Bottom: Enjoying a well-earned pint in Douglas.
Photo: Rennie Scaysbrook

line tapers down like the tip of an arrow as we line up, single file. The ambient noise of cheering spectators and frantic mechanics is slowly drowned out, replaced by the scream of four-cylinder engines ready for take-off. Like parachutists leaping into the airborne battlefield via a tap on the left shoulder, each rider releases the clutch and roars down the ever-increasing steepness of Bray Hill – like riding off the edge of the world at 160mph.

I've hardly had time to process what I'm about to do. The pace of the start procedure is rapid fire, at ten-second intervals. You're shuffled to the starting area with its board reading 'Rider and Machine Only'. That means it's now just you, with the greatest challenge in racing ahead.

This must be what it's like going to war, knowing that there's a possibility one of you or more won't make it back alive. Perhaps it'll be you. "No, it won't be me," I tell myself. "It won't be me."

But like anything that's truly difficult, the contemplation of the act is often more intimidating than the actual doing. Once the clutch is out and sixth gear is finally selected, there's no room for nerves, as I need every ounce of mental capacity to steer my wailing metallic horse down Bray Hill and up over Ago's Leap, the Suzuki chassis doing its best to flex itself in half with me, more or less, just a passenger.

Over the second jump at Ago's at close to top revs in sixth, I flash past the big white house on the left and dart into the shade. Then, it's hard on the brakes for Quarter Bridge, where the madness of the previous 15 seconds or so is replaced by a serene, first-gear right-hand cruise for three seconds or so, before I'm back on the throttle and pointing the motorcycle towards the left of Braddon Bridge.

The vast crowds lining each side of the track turn into a 3D artwork. All that matters is hitting my lines, staying on track and, most importantly, staying alive.

But by the end of the second lap, I'd been caught by Gary Vines, who had started directly behind me. I'd been cautious on the first lap as I got the feel of the engine and made sure everything was fine before being comfortable enough to really send it, and Gary's CBR had come roaring past into Schoolhouse Corner in Ramsay.

Here's where a characteristic of the TT shines through. I knew I was faster than Gary. I had been quicker in qualifying and my bike accelerated quicker than his, but the ultra-high-speed nature of the track means it's damn near impossible to get away, thanks to the slipstream.

Gary and I played cat and mouse for two-and-a-half laps, which dragged both our average speeds down. The race had been shortened to three laps. Then, coming into the 27th Milestone, once again there was devastation – hay bales blown out and yellow flags flying furiously. Gary and I slowed to a crawl and rode through on to the Mountain Mile, determined to put what we'd just seen out of our minds.

Coming into The Nook at the end of the lap, with two corners to go, the red flag was flown. To be honest, I was surprised that it had taken that long. Later that afternoon, it was confirmed that Davy Morgan, a 20-year veteran of the TT, had lost his life. In his famous pink helmet, he had been just in front of Gary and me, just out of sight, when it all had gone wrong.

Davy's crash cast a large shadow over the race. The paddock was sombre, and I have never been so happy to see my little boy, Harvey, on FaceTime that afternoon. A tough end to my first TT, but a reminder of what a knife-edge it can be. I was classified 44th, even though I did not cross the finish line, but it didn't matter. I just wanted a beer and a quiet evening.

Our second and final race was scheduled for Wednesday, but the Manx weather had other plans. We were rescheduled for Thursday and a full four-lap race, so I went to bed early, got the best sleep I'd had in two weeks and woke ready to give it absolute hell.

The weather looked good, but within an hour, fog had coated the mountain and once again we were informed that we wouldn't be racing that day – rescheduled again, for Friday and a two-lap race.

At this point, something rather interesting happened. Returning to the pits at about 11:00am, I thought I'd go see the team, just to say "Hi", as I was sure they'd be as down as I was that we weren't racing. You can imagine my surprise when I arrived to see my gear on the grass, the awning taken down and the bike strapped down in the truck.

Team boss Paul had an operation scheduled for Friday back in the UK, and he wasn't going to miss it, regardless of missing the race. I will spare you the details of the language used, but I told him that I'd run the bike myself. I'd done it before; the bike had a new rear tyre and full tank of fuel…

Thanks to Oscar Solis and fellow TT rider Shaun Anderson, I had some shelter for the bike and my gear, and we were good to go. Scott from PRF also came back to help us put the bike through tech inspection and run it the next day, which was gracious given the circumstances.

My second TT came and went in a blur. With no pit stops, it was effectively a sprint. The wind was incredible across the Mountain, and it was impossible to get sixth gear without a slipstream, which I received on lap two after Spaniard Raul Torras and his Yamaha came by at Ramsay Hairpin.

Following him out of the Creg-Ny-Baa right-hander on the last lap and through the glorious, fifth-gear sweeper of Brandish, I yelled at myself, "Remember this! Remember this!" Perhaps a little dramatic, but I will always remember those last five miles or so of the TT course.

I came out of the trees on to Glencrutchery Road and pinned the Suzuki for one final time. Seeing the chequered flag was the realisation of a dream I'd had since my earliest memories. I'd done it. I'd completed a TT race. No red flags, no accidents, no problems with the bike. It was done.

The relief in that moment was indescribable. Although I missed a bronze replica trophy by just 12 seconds, I'd improved to 37th and came away happy, given the two weeks we'd had. But the best thing, the thing that no one can ever take away, is that I can legitimately say I made the oldest dream I've ever had come true. I can call myself an Isle of Man TT racer.

2022 MOTOGP · BIKE BY BIKE by SIMON CRAFAR

CHASING DUCATI

DUCATI DESMOSEDICI GP22

SIMPLY put, Ducati's GP22 was their fantastic 2021 machine with a few updates: a new, smaller front fairing and wings, and a new more powerful engine.

All the GP22 riders liked the new fairing immediately, but unfortunately the new-spec engine delivered its extra torque in a manner that caused loss of traction on corner exit, a negative point that all of them could agree on. The teams and crew chiefs adjusted electronic settings and also chassis weight distribution settings to improve the situation, but never succeeded in fixing the problem completely.

Late in the day, under pressure from their two factory riders, Pecco Bagnaia and Jack Miller, Ducati homologated a 'hybrid' (mix of 2021 and '22) engine for them. At this late stage, however, it was not possible to change the engines of the remaining three GP22 riders (Johann Zarco, Jorge Martin and Luca Marini), who would have to persevere.

The GP22 was also fitted with a front ride-height device, which caused a collective sigh to resonate through the paddock, as the other manufacturers – who had just developed their own rear devices – now faced the prospect of having to develop a front device, too.

In practice, though, the front device was a bit more complicated. Riders are sensitive to changes in front geometry, by as little as two millimetres, let alone ten or 20 times that. The result was that some lost confidence, and in no time at all, only Johann Zarco – Ducati's development rider – persevered with it. Then, MotoGP officials banned front devices, except for use during the start, for 2023.

As in 2021, Ducati appeared to be two years ahead of others in the development of these devices and aero. Mid-season, they further updated their front fairing and wing. This was also made available to the GP21 riders, who had not received the GP22 fairing at the start of the season. All felt that it was another small step forward. In the latter half of the season, two pairs of tail-fin winglets on the seat were a further innovation.

Much like the previous season, rivals struggled to match all the Ducatis, GP22 and GP21, in braking and simply could not equal them in acceleration. To make matters worse for the opposition, it became clear that Ducati had improved or even eradicated all their weak points. The new, smaller fairing made the steering lighter, so less tiring over race distance. It was affected less by wind and also helped the bike turn well.

The GP22 was probably the best MotoGP machine to date. I was able to ride it at Misano, and it was every bit as wonderful as its recent racing results had proved.

Above: Mid-season Ducati – aero bodywork led the field.

Left: Tail fins appeared at Silverstone, being dubbed 'stegosaurus'.

Below left: Latest front aero presents a complex cross-section.
Photos: Gold & Goose

Far left: Desmosedici GP22 was the bike for the season.
Photo: Ducati Corse

Below: Pramac Ducatis used the less tractable engine.
Photo: Pramac Racing

New aerodynamics and variable ride heights combine with vaulting horsepower to make the Desmosedicis the class of 2022. SIMON CRAFAR explains...

TIMES are always changing, but the changes we've seen in MotoGP recently are in areas we've never seen before.

It has become clear that we are in an era that to be competitive, it's necessary not just to have a motorcycle with all the conventional strengths needed for motorcycle racing, but also the modern devices refined.

Conventional racing motorcycle technical strengths are:

- An engine with as much power as possible, which delivers that power and torque in a very smooth and linear way so that it does not break traction (rear tyre) and/or cause instability.
- A good chassis and set-up that allow the rider to change direction without the need for more strength than he has available over race distance.
- A machine that loses speed during the braking phase as quickly as possible without front tyre locking, or overloading the tyre's construction, causing it to deform excessively, destroying steering performance.
- Crucially, good turning performance both on and off the brakes, allowing the rider to spend as little time as necessary in the turning phase and to pick up the machine on to the drive area of the rear tyre sooner, starting the acceleration phase earlier.

Motorcycle racing has been mostly about all these things (and a few others) for decades, and still is very much so, but the recent advent of aero/wings/downforce and also ride-height devices has added another layer of complication. It is clear that Ducati have not only done a good job in all the traditional areas of motorcycle development, but also they are clearly leading the race in the new areas of development.

If you watch Ducati riders and machines running into and out of slow corners, it's obvious that they have an advantage in the braking and acceleration phases.

Slowing from high speed into a low-speed corner, they are so efficient that usually they prevent the opposition from launching an attack in this area. Then, after mid-turn, the Ducati has acceleration that is also superior. These two areas (hard acceleration and hard deceleration) are exactly what the new inventions were aimed at improving.

During the turning phase (mid-corner), the machine's geometry is crucial. One or two millimetres of change can make the difference between good turning and not good, but during the acceleration phase, the turning is mostly finished. At this point, the ride-height device is activated, lowering the rear of the machine by a substantial amount. This also lowers the centre of gravity and thus reduces the tendency to wheelie, in turn allowing the application of much more power and torque. The result is a significant increase in acceleration.

Riders describe the effect as feeling like the machine has an extra 30hp.

In 2022, Ducati experimented with extending the use of front ride-height adjustment. Previously, this had been used only off the start-line, but the experimental system allowed it to be engaged, like the rear system, during the lap as well. The GP Commission responded quickly, outlawing what it considered to be an additional and costly complication from 2023. Ducati persisted only with Pramac rider Johann Zarco.

Timing of ride-height engagement is important, as is the speed at which the rear drops. At the Red Bull Ring in Austria, I have watched some riders of machines with less-refined devices struggle with wheelspin and, in some cases, stability during the acceleration phase.

If the device is not activated at exactly the right moment, the rider will not gain the full advantage. If it does not drop at exactly the right speed, it will not keep a smooth, consistent amount of pressure on the rear tyre during the transition.

Pressure is needed to maintain traction. If traction is broken and spinning occurs, acceleration is lost and wear to the rear tyre is increased.

Wings added to the front and sides of machines assist still more by creating downforce, also helping among other things to prevent or delay wheelie and, in turn, allow more power and torque to be applied.

Furthermore, both of these incredible new devices also affect the braking phase. Because the machine arrives at the end of the acceleration phase (end of the straight) with the rear in a low position, initial braking can be harder because, just as wheelie is the limiting factor during hard acceleration, the rear lifting off the track is the limiting factor under hard braking. The rear being in a low position reduces the lifting tendency momentarily, until it rises back into position. Also, when the rear is low, the 'angle of attack' of the wings is reduced, helping to attain a better top speed.

Another effect has been noticed. In the bike's lowered position, the rider is also lower and, therefore, more sheltered behind the screen and fairing. This improves aerodynamics further and contributes to a higher top speed.

Then, as the rear ride-height device extends back to its original high position, the angle of attack of the wings is increased, creating both drag and downforce on the front tyre, helping to reduce the speed of the machine in the braking phase, which improves front contact and stability.

Now we are also seeing aero devices on the tail units of machines. I can only guess that they increase downforce and stability to the rear in this crucial braking phase.

Once these new technologies and the effects they produce are fully understood, it's easy to grasp that simply adding more power or bigger brakes will not necessarily produce the results they once did – especially if a rival already has not only an incredibly powerful machine, but also the most refined aero package and devices.

In 2022, we witnessed admirable efforts by riders trying to fight the Ducatis, none more regularly than Fabio Quartararo. At the Misano test, Yamaha arrived with what he had been requesting from them for more than two years – more power. We all knew that he would put it to good use in 2023, but will it be enough? Sadly, I don't think so because of the aero and device refinement I have described here.

YAMAHA YZR-M1

YAMAHA seemed to have made almost no changes at all from 2021 to 2022. They are an impressive manufacturer. For them to make no steps forward with their engine, when they so obviously wanted to and needed to, leads me to believe that the engine they had developed over the winter for the 2022 season, for some reason or other, could not be used. Your guess is as good as mine as to exactly why.

The possibilities range from what happened to Ducati's 2022 engine efforts (power and torque delivery were less smooth, causing too much wheelspin and loss of acceleration) to a reliability issue discovered too late to correct, forcing them to revert to the 2021 engine.

Whatever the reason, Monster Yamaha were forced to start the season with a machine that was essentially the same as the previous year's, apart from an aero and fairing update that gave more downforce. Although this downforce came at a price – a further loss of top speed – it proved repeatedly to be a step forward.

Yamaha tried more versions of the carbon-fibre swing-arm, but settled on aluminium. A chassis update arrived at the Misano test in early September, and although it did not prove to be faster, Fabio Quartararo liked the feel of it and used it for the remainder of the season.

Overall, the YZR-M1 is a good machine, but with its lack of improvement in recent years and its slow development aero-wise, other manufacturers have left Yamaha behind.

One other thing. Through till the end of 2019, everyone loved the Yamaha. It was known as a rookie-friendly machine that every rider got on with well. That all ended when the 2020 version arrived.

For that year, Yamaha had changed the chassis and engine to allow a larger air intake to pass through the steering head, creating a more direct route to the airbox. From that point on, it seemed that riders found it harder to make friends with the bike. Quartararo regularly lost his temper with the front-end feel and lack of turning in 2020. Eventually, he overcame these difficulties and was brilliant, but he seemed to be the only one able to ride with the confidence that once was shared by all YZR-M1 riders. I hope for Yamaha's sake that they look into this as well as engine performance for the coming season.

HONDA RC213V

FOR 2022, Honda arrived with an all-new machine that looked great and sounded the same as the old one, indicating that it was an evolution rather than a revolution. The chassis was new, and the bodywork and exhausts a very different shape.

The riders tested many parts, both old and new, before the season started. At that point, Honda appeared to be on the right path. A happy Pol Espargaro, having experienced good rear grip, and demonstrated competitive times and race simulations, made everyone believe this. As Marc Marquez subsequently pointed out, however, riding on a circuit where so much Michelin rubber has been laid down after days of MotoGP testing produces results that can be, and usually are, misleading, because never again during the season do riders experience such conditions. That is the best explanation I've heard for what happened to Honda in 2022.

Clearly in trouble, Honda introduced many chassis updates during the year. There were two distinctly different chassis and many variations based on these two. Some were modified in the swing-arm pivot area, others had different bracing/stiffness or steering-head areas. In fact, my estimate would be as high as eight chassis, possibly more.

They also came with aero packages old and new, and tried chassis set-ups from one extreme to the other, but when pressed for comments, Honda riders all complained about every aspect of the machines' performance: front feel on entry; lack of rear contact during braking, resulting in a floating feeling from the rear; a lack of turning, which also made the exit difficult; a lack of rear edge grip; a lack of rear grip on exit; and finally a lack of acceleration and outright speed.

Just when you thought things could not be worse, the RC213V's heavy handling sapped riders' strength over race distance. Honda had gone through difficult times in the past, but never have I struggled to recognise a single strong point in their machine. That was the case in 2022.

Late in the season, Marquez tested yet another couple of chassis updates: a new front wing that I first saw at Misano, which proved positive; an aluminium swing-arm made by German manufacturer Kalex; a lower fairing-mounted air duct like Ducati's; tail-mounted wings that looked like copies of Ducati's; and at the Misano test, a wide lower fairing similar to Aprilia's.

They were trying hard, and to me it was a sign of the depth of Honda's trouble that they were looking at what others were doing for direction in technical development, using the expertise of outside specialists. I think that it was arrogance that got them into this situation and that this humble approach eventually will turn things around for them.

I wish Honda luck. They have a great rider line-up for 2023. All they need is a competitive machine. Surely, this technological giant will fight back.

Above: Honda at the Sepang MotoGP test – full of promise.

Left: At the Thai GP, Marquez had an outsourced aluminium swing-arm.
Photos: Gold & Goose

Top: Honda's RCV213 looked the part, but failed to deliver.
Photo: Repsol Honda

Top far left: Yamahas in Thailand: lack of speed cost riders dear.
Photo: Gold & Goose

Above far left: The 2022 M1 was free of aerodynamic add-ons.

Far left: Quartararo's bike looked very similar to 2021's model.
Photos: Monster Energy Yamaha MotoGP

Above: The Aprilia was the most improved bike on the grid.

Left: Refinements and polish made the 2022 RS-GP a race winner.
Photos: Aprilia MotoGP

Below: KTM RC16 – a year of consolidation rather than innovation.
Photo: Red Bull KTM

APRILIA RS-GP

IN 2022, Aprilia used the 90-degree V4 engine that had been introduced in 2020. In the intervening period, it had had the development time needed to achieve both reliability and speed. They had moved away from their earlier, narrower-V engine design mainly because of engine-brake management. That engine had produced its best power curve with an exhaust that had balance pipes connecting the headers, making the exhaust-valve system ineffective.

The new 90-degree engine, Aprilia engineers believed, had been necessary to gain the best of both worlds in acceleration and deceleration. In 2022, this engine was fitted to a narrower updated chassis. Because of the different dimensions, everything that was bolted to the new RS-GP had to be redesigned. This small change had created a lot of work, but from the very first test, it showed potential.

The engine was closer in performance to the opposition and the riders were singing praises of the chassis, while a couple of redesigned front wings worked wonderfully. Aleix Espargaro went as far as to say that it was difficult to get the bike to understeer even when he entered a corner too fast.

During the year, there were small updates to the chassis (a lighter version that most likely had a different stiffness), a new, wider, aerodynamic lower fairing that apparently helped turning and stability, and a few updates to the rear ride-height device and its activation. All the time, Aprilia were developing another engine update for the future.

Aprilia's effort in 2022 was nothing short of inspired. Their engineers came together to achieve something so special that at Assen, Espargaro looked like he could do things that the opposition could not. The RS-GP might not get my 'best bike of the year' vote, but it came very close at some circuits, and Aprilia can be proud of their performances.

KTM RC16

I WAS surprised to see very few changes to the 2022 KTM RC16. Previously, their MotoGP efforts had made them the kings of new hardware, but in 2022, they seemed to be making an effort to get the most from what they already had, to find a clearer direction for future development.

In 2021, KTM had introduced a lot of new hardware, but seemed to become lost in a game of 'musical chassis', so they already had many parts to go back through and double check – not only chassis, but also many aero package combinations, chassis geometry set-ups and electronics.

At various circuits in 2022, we saw different aero wings and later in the year lengthened exhausts aimed at a smoother, traction-friendly power delivery. However, very little else on the RC16 was changed visibly.

Although it was not a particularly good year for KTM, I think that we saw them using everything they had to the best of their ability, the outcome being a clearer direction for the future. From early to mid-2022, it was uncanny how KTM's rider complaints were similar to those of Honda riders. Later in the year, they complained less of corner entry problems, the machine clearly having improved in this area, and simply complained of turning mid-corner and lack of drive grip on exit. At the last round at Valencia, a revised chassis addressed the drive issue, and Binder returned to the podium.

I believe KTM – much like the Japanese manufacturers – have been left behind by the Italian manufacturers when it comes to incorporating aero, and I think they know this because I saw Red Bull Formula 1 people in the Red Bull KTM garage in 2022. I look forward to seeing the aero packages they bring for 2023.

SUZUKI GSX-RR

SUZUKI brought two great riders to MotoGP from the smaller class. They nurtured and developed their talents, and reaped the rewards of their investment. Joan Mir and Alex Rins are very different riders with very different styles. Thus they have very different preferences for machine set-up and balance.

At the start of 2022, the GSX-RR appeared almost identical to the 2021 bike, but after a few races, it became apparent that Suzuki had changed the weight bias. Rins, who sits forward, got on well with these changes. Mir, who sits more to the rear, did not.

I began to see evidence for what Suzuki had done from looking at the changes that were being made to Mir's set-up. Moving the front wheel closer to the engine and the rear wheel further away, in an effort to regain the old feeling, was a clear indication that Suzuki had moved the engine rearwards in the chassis.

Mir's team were obviously trying to compensate for this with set-up. If you move the front and rear wheels towards the rear, you are effectively moving the engine forward. Although this does not have identical results, it's a step in the right direction. I believe that the modification Suzuki had made was the root of why the 2022 bike suited one rider more than the other. It also seemed that Rins coped better with the shocking news that Suzuki was pulling out of MotoGP, leaving both riders without a job.

Suzuki made much needed improvements to engine performance for 2022, and it showed in the top-speed traps and rider comments.

As the season progressed, at least two updates to their rear ride-height device allowed them to use the increase in power more efficiently, though it seemed to me that Suzuki's device was probably the least refined on the grid, making it more susceptible to rear tyre spinning and consumption, and also instability. This is not really surprising when you consider that Suzuki were the last manufacturer to introduce this now universal technology, giving them less development time.

Everyone noticed the increase in the Suzuki's top speed in 2022, and most put this down to their engine improvements. However, I believe that, at least in part, it was due to the rear ride-height device itself, because the low position the bike achieved allowed the riders to be hidden more efficiently behind the screen and fairing. An unexpected, but very welcome advantage, I imagine.

Speaking of aero, Suzuki arrived with two new aero-package updates, consisting of redesigned front and side-pod wings. Mir tried both at the Catalunya test and chose what he preferred. Rins, injured in the Catalunya T1 incident the day before, had to choose a package to homologate (only one upgrade per rider per season being allowed) without testing them. He and his crew made this choice using the feedback from Mir while taking into consideration their different styles and requirements. He chose the opposite package to his team-mate.

The Suzuki showed it strengths regularly: turning, corner speed and tyre management at the end of a race. It also regularly displayed its weakness in qualifying, when, regardless of rider, they struggled to obtain an advantage from a new soft rear tyre when the opposition did. Thus, despite the bikes regularly having podium race pace, they were buried deep on the grid.

I had always suspected that the Suzuki was a nice handling machine, but this was confirmed when Danilo Petrucci filled in for injured Mir in Thailand. He loved the bike so much that he could not say enough nice things about it, and also said he wanted to buy it.

Above: In its final season, the Suzuki's improvements were real, but mostly hidden from view.

Top: Rins won two races on the outwardly-modest GSX-RR.

Right: Like the Yamaha, the Suzuki made do with minimal aerodynamic protuberances.

Photos: www.suzuki-racing.com

Photo: www.suzuki-racing.com

TEAM-BY-TEAM

2022 MOTOGP REVIEW

Teams and Riders
MATTHEW BIRT

Bike Illustrations
ADRIAN DEAN

Bike Specifications
SIMON CRAFAR

DUCATI LENOVO TEAM

TEAM STAFF

Luigi DALL'IGNA: Ducati Corse General Manager
Paolo CIABATTI: Ducati Corse Sporting Director
Davide BARANA: Ducati Corse Technical Director
Davide TARDOZZI: Team Manager
Riccardo SAVIN: Chassis & Vehicle Dynamics Engineer
Gabriele CONTI: Electronic Systems Manager
Massimo BARTOLINI: Vehicle Performance Engineer
Leonardo SIMONCINI: Track Technical Co-ordinator
Andrea GIAVARINI: Data Analyst
Artur VILALTA: MotoGP Press Manager
Julie GIOVANOLA: MotoGP Press Officer
Mauro GRASSILLI: Marketing & Sponsorship Manager
Yuri DE CASSAN: Sponsor and Hospitality Manager
Paola BRAIATO: Operations Manager
Davide GIBERTINI: Team Co-ordinator
Davide BARALDINI: Warehouse

JACK MILLER PIT CREW

Cristian PUPULIN: Track Engineer
Andrea MATTIOLI: Electronics Engineer
Michele DUCOLI: Chief Mechanic
Marco POLASTRI, Fabio MORANDINI,
Pedro RIVERA CRESPO, Giuliano POLETTI: Mechanics
Rhys HOLMES: Öhlins Suspension Technician

FRANCESCO BAGNAIA PIT CREW

Cristian GABARRINI: Track Engineer
Tommaso PAGANO: Electronics Engineer
Marco VENTURA: Chief Mechanic
Ivan BRANDI, Massimo TOGNACCI,
Lorenzo CANESTRARI, Tommaso PELI: Mechanics
Giacomo MASSAROTTO: Öhlins Suspension Technician

FRANCESCO BAGNAIA

Born: 14 January, 1997 – Torino, Italy

GP Starts: 172 (67 MotoGP, 36 Moto2, 69 Moto3)

GP Wins: 21 (11 MotoGP, 8 Moto2, 2 Moto3)

World Championships: 1 MotoGP, 1 Moto2

JACK MILLER

Born: 18 January, 1995 – Townsville, Queensland, Australia

GP Starts: 192 (137 MotoGP, 55 Moto3/125cc)

GP Wins: 10 (4 MotoGP, 6 Moto3)

Photos: Gold & Goose

THE long wait, 15 years of hurt, was finally over. Australian legend Casey Stoner was no longer Ducati's stand-alone MotoGP world champion, after Pecco Bagnaia completed the greatest comeback in grand prix history to cap an utterly dominant season for the Bologna factory.

Seemingly dead and buried after falling 91 points behind Fabio Quartararo in the tenth round at the Sachsenring in Germany, Bagnaia's rousing recovery ended with him becoming Italy's first MotoGP world champion since Valentino Rossi had clinched the last of his seven premier-class titles in 2009.

In just his second season in the Lenovo-backed factory Ducati squad, Bagnaia's title glory was certainly accomplished the hard way. No other rider in history had ever managed to lift motorcycle racing's biggest prize after failing to score in five races.

When he remained upright on Ducati's flawless GP22, he was the cream of an exceptional crop of talent in MotoGP.

Bagnaia didn't win a race until round six at Jerez, as Ducati encountered early-season rear grip issues with the new machine. The matter was such a concern in the lead-up to the first race that Ducati homologated a hybrid 21/22 motor exclusively for its factory team.

DUCATI Desmosedici GP22

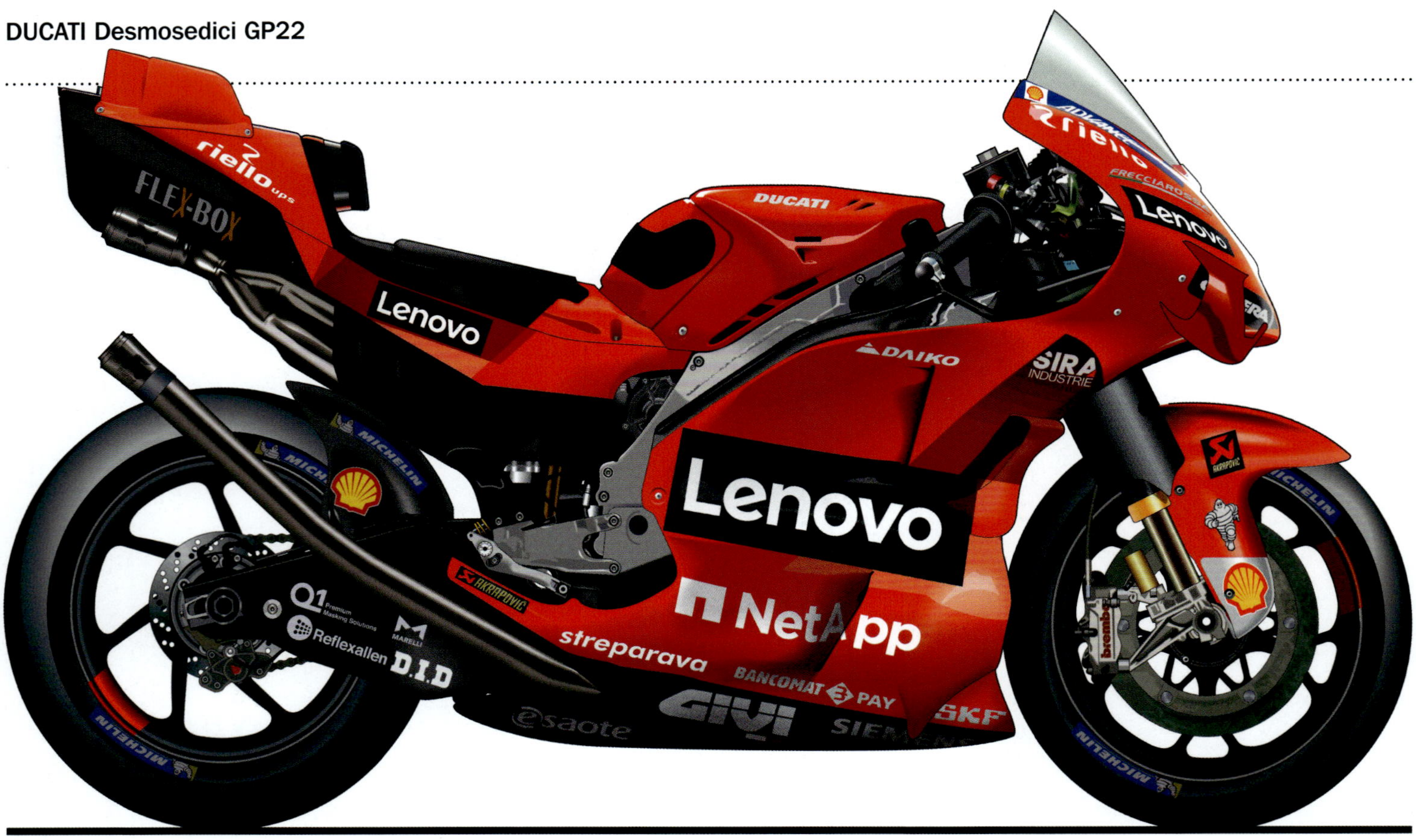

Engine: 1000cc liquid-cooled 90-degree V4, counter-rotating crankshaft, DOHC, 4-valves per cylinder, desmodromic valve gear

Power: More than 250bhp

Ancillaries: Magneti Marelli ECU, Dorna software, ride-by-wire fuel injection, active Akrapovic titanium 4-into-2 exhaust • *Lubrication:* Shell Advance

Transmission: Six-speed seamless-shift cassette-type gearbox, dry clutch, DID chain

Frame: Aluminium-alloy twin-spar chassis, carbon-fibre swing-arm, front and rear ride-height devices

Suspension: Öhlins inverted front fork, carbon outer tubes, Öhlins rear shock absorber

Tyres: Michelin • *Brakes:* Brembo 340mm carbon-fibre twin front discs, single stainless-steel rear disc, thumb and foot levers

Photo: Ducati Corse

MICHELE PIRRO

Born: 5 July, 1986 – San Giovanni Rotondo, Italy

GP Starts: 110 (63 MotoGP, 18 Moto2, 29 125cc)

GP Wins: 1 Moto2

Celebrating Bagnaia's win at Misano.

Photo: Ducati Corse

Davide Tardozzi

Luigi Dall'Igna

Paolo Ciabatti

Photos: Gold & Goose

Most of the momentum gained in Jerez was quickly surrendered, however, when Bagnaia suffered a disastrous run of three DNFs in the following four races, including being wiped out by Taka Nakagami in a shocking first-corner incident at the Circuit de Barcelona-Catalunya.

The third of that nightmare sequence came with an early tumble in Germany, which seemed to bring a premature end to his aspirations. But the former Moto2 world champion's reset was spectacular.

Successive wins at Assen, Silverstone, Red Bull Ring and Misano made him the first Ducati rider in history to win four MotoGP races in a row. Only Valentino Rossi, Marc Marquez and Jorge Lorenzo had done so.

It was so nearly five in Aragon, but he was beaten in a last-lap thriller by future factory Ducati teammate Enea Bastianini.

Bagnaia might have had the best machine at his disposal, but he was still a worthy world champion. Seven wins and three more podiums trumped anyone else in the class, and he was a huge reason why Ducati sealed only its second Triple Crown, with the constructors' and teams' prizes secured in advance of his personal triumph (with a safe ninth place) in the final-round decider in Valencia.

Bagnaia's brilliance had come to the fore towards the end of 2021, when he had won four of the last six races, and his entire crew remained unchanged for the new season. Track engineer duty went to the calming and knowledgeable Cristian Gabarrini, who had been at the helm of Stoner's crew when he had won the 2007 crown for Ducati and 2011 title with Repsol Honda. Leading the support cast was electronics engineer Tommaso Pagano and chief mechanic Marco Ventura.

Bagnaia's winning blitz at the end of the previous season meant that he was pre-season favourite ahead of 2022, and Ducati were eager to avoid any distractions. That's why he was the first big name to confirm his plans for 2023 and beyond, when he inked a two-year extension in late February.

Ducati's senior staff remained in place once again. Overall responsibility for the project went to Ducati Corse general manager Gigi Dall'Igna. The Italian had been headhunted by Ducati from Aprilia at the end of 2013 to restore the glory days of Borgo Panigale. It might have taken longer than anticipated, but it was mission accomplished for Dall'Igna, who arguably had built potential title-winning machines in recent history, but had always fallen just short.

Other prominent roles went to Paolo Ciabatti (sporting director) and Davide Tardozzi (team manager). And back again was technical director Davide Barana who, during a press conference in Aragon in mid-September, had confidently expressed that the GP22 had no obvious weaknesses.

Jack Miller at Motegi.

Photo: Ducati Corse

It's hard to argue with that statement. Ducati stacked the grid with eight bikes, but it also boasted an arsenal of hot, young talent.

The GP22 ended the season with 12 wins, 16 more podiums and 16 poles. Ducati had at least one bike on the front row of the grid and at least one bike on the podium in all 20 races.

As late as round 18, at the jaw-droppingly fast Phillip Island track in Australia, Ducati Lenovo still had two horses in the title race. Jack Miller was back for his fifth season on a Ducati and, as for Bagnaia, 2022 was his second crack in the official works squad.

Once again, Miller's crew was led by Ducati stalwart Cristian Pupulin, while Andrea Mattioli was back as electronics engineer. There was one change, and that was the arrival of Michele Ducoli as chief mechanic. He replaced Michele Perugini.

Miller enjoyed his best season so far in MotoGP, which ended with seven podiums. The best was undoubtedly his dominant win from the third row in Japan. He was also on pole for the first time in over four years at Ducati's home round in Misano, but he failed to capitalise on a stunning Q2 performance by falling out of the lead early on.

But Miller's slim title hopes were ended in painful fashion in front of his home crowd at Phillip Island when Alex Marquez careered into him at Turn Four. Ironically, only 24 hours earlier, that turn had been named after him as a wedding gift following his marriage to Ruby Mau. For 2023, he switched to KTM.

RED BULL KTM

TEAM STAFF

Stefan PIERER: KTM CEO
Hubert TRUNKENPOLZ: KTM CMO
Pit BEIRER: KTM Motorsport Director
Jens HAINBACH: KTM Head of Sports Management Road Racing
Francesco GUIDOTTI: Team Manager
Sebastian RISSE: Technical Manager MotoGP
Sebastian KUHN: Head of Motorsport Sponsorship & PR
Sarah KINRADE: PR Specialist
Zoe BOSCH: Marketing Project Manager
Beatriz GARCIA: Team Co-ordinator
Jeremy WILSON: Logistics Manager

MIGUEL OLIVEIRA PIT CREW

Paul TREVATHAN: Crew Chief
Alessio CAPUANO: Strategy Engineer
Peter SCHLAEGER: Data Recording Engineer
Christophe LEONCE: Chief Mechanic
Andreas RIEGER, Xavi QUEIXALOS,
Mark BARNETT: Mechanics
Stefano SIGNORETTI: Tyres
Manuel OLIVENZIA: WP Suspension Technician

BRAD BINDER PIT CREW

Andres MADRID: Crew Chief
Errki SIUKOLA: Strategy Engineer
Tex GEISSLER: Data Recording Engineer
Mark LLOYD: Chief Mechanic
Daniel PETAK, John EYRE,
Florian FERRACCI: Mechanics
Craig BURTON: Tyre Mechanic
Gerald PERDON: WP Suspension Technician

BRAD BINDER

Born: 11 August, 1995 – Potchefstroom, South Africa

GP Starts: 197 (52 MotoGP, 52 Moto2, 93 Moto3/125cc)

GP Wins: 17 (2 MotoGP, 8 Moto2, 7 Moto3)

World Championships: 1 Moto3

Photos: Gold & Goose

MIGUEL OLIVEIRA

Born: 4 January, 1995 – Pragal, Portugal

GP Starts: 197 (68 MotoGP, 50 Moto2, 79 Moto3/125cc)

GP Wins: 17 (5 MotoGP, 6 Moto2, 6 Moto3)

KTM'S sixth season in MotoGP seemed like a case of so near, yet so far. Undoubtedly the highlights were a stellar start to 2022, with Brad Binder a close second to Enea Bastianini in Qatar's curtain-raiser. And at round two, Miguel Oliveira splashed his way to success in a treacherously wet first Indonesian Grand Prix in 25 years at the new Mandalika track.

At that early stage, Red Bull-backed KTM led the constructors' and teams' championships for the very first time. But it proved something of a false dawn, with only three other podiums scored in the 18 races that followed, including another wet-weather masterclass in Southeast Asia from Oliveira when he won a rain-soaked Thai Grand Prix in Buriram.

Binder and Oliveira racked up top-ten finishes for fun without seriously threatening the podium, as the RC16 was plagued by a lack of turning, which in turn compromised corner exit performance.

The 2021 season had only just ended when KTM announced a surprise overhaul of its senior management structure. A disappointing failure to capitalise on a strong 2020 season resulted in Mike Leitner being removed from the post of MotoGP race manager. The Austrian had been an integral member of KTM's MotoGP project, hired in 2015 to help the Mattighofen factory build a premier-class empire from scratch.

Leitner moved to a consultancy role, with his position filled by Francesco Guidotti, who had caught the

KTM RC16

Engine: 1000cc liquid-cooled 86-degree V4, counter-rotating crankshaft, DOHC, 4 valves per cylinder, pneumatic valve return system

Ancillaries: Magneti Marelli ECU, Dorna software, ride-by-wire fuel injection, non-active Akropovic titanium 4-into-2 exhaust

Transmission: Six-speed seamless-shift cassette-type gearbox, dry clutch

Frame: Steel-tube chassis, carbon-fibre swing-arm, front and rear ride-height devices

Suspension: WP front and rear

Tyres: Michelin • *Brakes:* Brembo carbon-fibre twin front discs, single steel rear disc

Oliveira's second race win of the season came in Thailand.

eye helping to make Pramac Racing one of the most successful Independent teams on the grid. He had been team manager there since 2012, but effectively was returning home. He had started his grand prix management career with KTM in 2006, in charge of the Austrian factory's 125 and 250cc efforts. He was there until the end of 2009 before moving to work with Aprilia's World Superbike project.

Guidotti was the second senior figure whom KTM had enticed away from Ducati in the space of 12 months, after headhunting technical guru Fabiano Sterlacchini. He'd spent 17 years working with the Bologna manufacturer and was widely seen as Gigi Dall'Igna's right-hand man.

The rest of KTM's upper management structure remained untouched. Forthright KTM CEO Stefan Pierer remained at the helm. Other leading positions of authority were retained by Hubert Trunkenpolz, who continued as chief marketing officer; Pit Beirer, who was hugely influential again as KTM motorsport director; and Jens Hainbach, who was back in the role of KTM vice-president motorsports road racing.

Sebastian Risse also continued under the slightly tweaked job title that went from technical co-ordinator MotoGP to technical manager MotoGP.

South African Binder was in the first of a three-year contract extension with KTM, and once again he was the star performer on the RC16. Capable of riding around problems and extracting the maximum from a bike that clearly was not as competitive as some of its rivals, Binder was the only KTM rider to finish on the podium in dry conditions in 2022. His second podium came off his first MotoGP front-row start in Japan, and his third in Valencia.

Binder worked with the same tight-knit crew. His former Moto2 crew chief, Andres Madrid, was the lead figure again, with Mark Lloyd in the role of chief mechanic, and the vital electronics roles going to Errki Siukola and Tex Geissler.

Oliveira's crew also remained intact from 2021, with his side of the garage led by Kiwi crew chief Paul Trevathan. Chief mechanic duty was taken again by Christophe Leonce, with Alessio Capuano and Peter Schlaeger back in the roles of strategy engineer and date recording engineer respectively.

Oliveira established himself as MotoGP's undisputed rain-master after his wet-race wins in Indonesia and Thailand, but he managed only three top-six finishes in dry conditions. With five victories, he became the most successful rider in KTM's relatively short MotoGP career, but the Portuguese star's record wasn't enough to save him from expulsion from KTM's factory squad.

Oliveira knew his time was up in the official factory squad in early June, when KTM announced the signing of Jack Miller on a two-year deal. Those negotiations were certainly eased by the fact that Miller's personal manager was Aki Ajo, who ran KTM's official Moto3 and Moto2 projects. The Aussie was also well known to Guidotti, having worked closely with him at Pramac Ducati for three years. Miller had other previous connections with Red Bull and KTM. It was in that project that he had narrowly missed winning the 2014 Moto3 title, ahead of his bold leap straight into MotoGP the following year.

Miller confirmed months after his signing that he would move to KTM with his Ducati factory crew chief Cristian Pupulin for 2023. That was seen as another blow to Ducati. This fresh high-profile defector to KTM had been with Ducati since the Bologna factory had joined MotoGP in 2003. KTM also completed a successful raid on Ducati for Andrea Dovizioso's former and Enea Bastianini's current crew chief, Alberto Giribuola, who would take on a senior technical role in the following season.

Oliveira instantly rejected the chance to revert to the Tech3 Independent team, and was locked in discussions about switches to Gresini Racing on a Ducati GP22 and with the RNF squad about a move to ride a year-old Aprilia RS-GP. A potential late plot twist arose in early August when Beirer spoke during a press conference at the Red Bull Ring to confirm that Tech3 would be rebranded from KTM to GasGas, with full factory team status for the satellite squad.

He confirmed that KTM had made an 11th-hour bid to retain Oliveira, but again the rider had rejected an improved offer. Subsequently, he signed to join Aprilia's new independent team with current Yamaha runners RNF.

Pit Beirer

Francesco Guidotti

Binder leads Oliveira at Motegi.

Photos: Gold & Goose

APRILIA RACING TEAM

TEAM STAFF

Massimo RIVOLA: Aprilia Racing CEO
Paolo BONORA: Team Manager
Romano ALBESIANO: Aprilia Racing Technical Director
Dario RAIMONDI: Team Co-ordinator
Andrea ZOCCARATO: Press Officer
Mike WATT: Öhlins Technician
Stefano ROMEO: Electronics Engineer
Michele FANTINI: Engine Engineer
Elena DE CIA: Strategy Engineer
Michele BERTELLI: Chassis Engineer
Andrea ROSTAGNO: Performance Engineer
Massimo MENEGHIN: Spare Parts
Giuseppe BUSATO: Engine Technician

MAVERICK VINALES PIT CREW

Giovanni MATTAROLLO: Crew Chief
Luca CONTI: Electronics Engineer
Matteo FRISON: Data Engineer
Matteo FRIGO: Suspension
Roberto SIMIONATO, Gianluca PERETTI, Simone ALESSANDRINI, Davide CALVERT: Mechanics
Inigo GARCIA: Tyres & Fuel

ALEIX ESPARGARO PIT CREW

Antonio JIMINEZ: Crew Chief
Renato PENNACCHIO: Electronics Engineer
Guido FONTANA: Data Engineer
Oscar BOLZONELLA: Suspension
Carlo TOCCAFONDI, Franco SALVA, Roberto MARINONI, Barber JOSE: Mechanics
Oscar MARTINEZ: Tyres & Fuel

ALEIX ESPARGARO

Born: 30 July, 1989 – Granollers, Spain
GP Starts: 301 (217 MotoGP, 61 Moto2/250cc, 23 125cc)
GP Wins: 1 MotoGP

Photos: Gold & Goose

MAVERICK VINALES

Born: 12 January, 1995 – Figueres, Spain
GP Starts: 207 (140 MotoGP, 18 Moto2, 49 Moto3/125cc)
GP Wins: 25 (9 MotoGP, 4 Moto2, 12 Moto3/125cc)
World Championships: 1 Moto3

NOBOBY could have predicted that Aprilia would only lose the chance to be shock MotoGP world champions in 2022 after the penultimate round of an incredible season in Malaysia.

Without doubt, Aprilia's astonishing ascent from whipping boys to title contenders was one of the feel-good stories of the season. The unforgettable highlight was a career-first win in his 200th MotoGP start for perennial underdog Aleix Espargaro.

The Spaniard had nearly quit in 2019, when Aprilia had been beset by reliability issues and seemed to be making little headway in transforming the RS-GP into a machine that was capable of consistently challenging at the front. But his victory in dominant fashion at round three in Argentina was the first of his grand prix career, and Aprilia's first in MotoGP. In fact, the Noale factory had not won in any class since Maverick Vinales had taken victory in the last ever 125cc two-stroke GP at Valencia in 2011.

The win briefly put him into the lead of the World Championship, and Aprilia's startling early-season success was such that it became the last manufacturer to be robbed of the concessions that had helped make the RS-GP a bike that finally was universally admired.

Espargaro's third in Jerez was the result that lost

APRILIA RS-GP

Engine: 1000cc liquid-cooled 90-degree V4, counter-rotating crankshaft, DOHC, 4 valves per cylinder, pneumatic valve return system

Ancillaries: Magneti Marelli ECU, Dorna software, ride-by-wire fuel injection, active Akrapovic titanium 4-into-2 exhaust

Transmission: Six-speed seamless-shift cassette-type gearbox, dry clutch

Frame: Aluminium twin-spar chassis, aluminium swing-arm, front and rear ride-height devices

Suspension: Öhlins front and rear

Tyres: Michelin • *Brakes:* Brembo carbon-fibre twin front discs, single steel rear disc, thumb and foot levers

LORENZO SAVADORI

Born: 4 April, 1993 – Cesena, Italy

GP Starts: 48 (17 MotoGP, 31 125cc)

Aleix Espargaro

Aprilia its concession privileges for 2023. These included the availability of nine instead of seven engines, unlimited testing days and the possibility of six rather than three wild-card entries.

For 2022, Espargaro's backroom team was almost identical to the one he had worked with the year before. Antonio Jimenez was back in the role of crew chief, with key electronics and data roles once again taken by Renato Pennacchio and Guido Fontana. The only change was the arrival of mechanic Roberto Marinoni, who replaced Alberto Presutti.

Espargaro and his crew were the revelations of the first part of the season, with five podium finishes in the opening ten races. It should have been six, but Aleix suffered a blunder he'll never live down, dropping from second to fifth position in his home grand prix in Catalunya. Mistakenly thinking that the race was over and slowing, he embarked on a hugely embarrassing premature celebration, only to be passed by Martin, Zarco and Mir.

Ironically, his mechanic, Franco Salva, had suffered identical humiliation when Julian Simon had committed the same howler in a 125cc race at Catalunya in 2009.

Aprilia came a long way in 2022, but an end-of-season collapse showed that they still had a long way to go. Espargaro made only one more visit to the podium in the last ten races, and a late capitulation was triggered by another spectacular own goal in Japan. A fuel-saving mapping mode, designed to limit revs on the warm-up lap of such thirsty tracks as Motegi, was mistakenly left turned on. As a result, Espargaro was forced to change bikes and start from the pit lane. It turned out to be one of only two races all year in which he didn't score a point.

On the opposite side of the garage, Vinales was seeking to rebuild his career and reputation after his controversial early split from Yamaha during a woeful 2021. Three podiums in four races on favourite tracks – Assen, Silverstone and Misano – were followed by a nightmare end to the season, which mirrored the slump experienced by his team-mate.

Once again, Giovanni Mattarollo was the Spaniard's crew chief, but there were changes to the squad with whom Vinales had competed in the last five races of 2021. Matteo Frison came in to replace Niccolo Ceccato as data engineer, and Davide Calvert took over from Filippo Tognoni in one of the four mechanic roles.

One significant change to be implemented by Aprilia to help Vinales rediscover his form for 2023 would be the arrival of Jose Manuel Cazeaux as crew chief. Cazeaux was on the market following the disbanding of the factory Suzuki team. He had worked as Vinales's crew chief with that team in 2015 and 2016.

The senior management remained unchanged, as for the first time since Aprilia had returned to the MotoGP arena in 2015, it was as a fully-fledged factory effort rather than being aligned with the independent Gresini team.

CEO Massimo Rivola was very much the high-profile driving force behind the project, and since arriving in 2019, he had been a key contributor to Aprilia's rise to prominence.

Paolo Bonora was back again in the slightly altered role of team manager rather than race manager, while another vital member of Aprilia's hierarchy was Romano Albesiano, who returned in the prominent position of technical director.

Romano Albesiano

Massimo Rivola

Maverick Vinales

Photos: Gold & Goose

It was perhaps no coincidence that once freed to focus solely on development of the RS-GP after Rivola's arrival from F1 in 2019, Aprilia improved in leaps and bounds. Many predicted that they would be title contenders again in 2023.

Eager to retain continuity and stability to help guarantee future success, the team signed Espargaro and Vinales to two-year contracts for 2023 and 2024.

Aprilia's breakthrough success in 2022 helped to notch a landmark – a two-rider satellite Independent team for 2023, the RNF squad switching from Yamaha. Miguel Oliveira and Raul Fernandez, both ex-KTM, were recruited as riders.

PRIMA PRAMAC DUCATI

TEAM STAFF

Paolo CAMPINOTI: Team Principal
Claudio CALABRESI: Team Manager
Fonsi NIETO: Sporting Director
Felix RODRIGUEZ: Team Co-ordinator
Iacopo MICANGELI: Marketing & Sponsorship Manager
Rita SIMONINI: Media & Press Officer
Alex GHINI: Hospitality Manager
Luca DAVID: Warehouse Spare Parts

JOHANN ZARCO PIT CREW

Marco RIGAMONTI: Crew Chief
Erik CHIARVESIO: Data Engineer
Francesco GALINDO: Chief Mechanic
Carlo CORRADINI, Adriano CABRAS, Andrea ZAMPIERI, Ricardo PEPE: Mechanics
Moris GRASSI: Fuel & Tyres

JORGE MARTIN PIT CREW

Daniele ROMAGNOLI: Crew Chief
Cristian BATTAGLIA: Data Engineer
Nicola MANNA: Chief Mechanic
David GALACHO, Daniele PENZO, Jarno POLASTRI: Mechanics
Luca PARTIGLIANI: Fuel & Tyres

JOHANN ZARCO

Born: 16 July, 1990 – Cannes, France
GP Starts: 242 (104 MotoGP, 88 Moto2, 50 125cc)
GP Wins: 16 (15 Moto2, 1 125cc)
World Championships: 2 Moto2

Photos: Gold & Goose

JORGE MARTIN

Born: 29 January, 1998 – Madrid, Spain
GP Starts: 133 (34 MotoGP, 32 Moto2, 67 Moto3)
GP Wins: 11 (1 MotoGP, 2 Moto2, 8 Moto3)
World Championships: 1 Moto3

A WINLESS season and the emergence of a new enemy from within didn't drastically alter the perception that Prima Pramac Racing remained Ducati's top Independent Team in 2022, although the startling rise to prominence of the new Gresini Racing squad, which won more races in 2022 than Pramac had done in a 17-year collaboration with Ducati, certainly didn't go unnoticed.

Gresini's stock rose largely thanks to Bastianini's superlative season, overshadowing the Pramac duo of Jorge Martin and Johann Zarco, who had a steady rather than spectacular season.

It began with a new management line-up for the first time in a decade. Team principal Paolo Campinoti was still very much the public figurehead, but long-serving team manager Francesco Guidotti had been lured away by KTM's factory team. He was replaced by Claudio Calabresi, previously in charge of Pramac's MotoE World Cup project.

Calabresi had gained front-line managerial experience during a career as an executive vice-president and commercial director of oil and natural-gas giant ENI. He did not have the public profile of Guidotti, and Fonsi Nieto, a former 250cc Grand Prix winner and

DUCATI Desmosedici GP21

Engine: 1000cc liquid-cooled 90-degree V4, counter-rotating crankshaft, DOHC, 4-valves per cylinder, desmodromic valve gear
Power: More than 250bhp

Ancillaries: Magneti Marelli ECU, Dorna software, ride-by-wire fuel injection, active Akrapovic titanium 4-into-2 exhaust • *Lubrication:* Shell Advance

Transmission: Six-speed seamless-shift cassette-type gearbox, dry clutch, DID chain

Frame: Aluminium-alloy twin-spar chassis, carbon-fibre swing-arm, front and rear ride-height devices

Suspension: Öhlins inverted front fork, carbon outer tubes, Öhlins rear shock absorber

Tyres: Michelin • *Brakes:* Brembo 340mm carbon-fibre twin front discs, single stainless-steel rear disc, thumb and foot levers

The Pramac team celebrate their success as top Independent team in MotoGP.

Paolo Campinoti

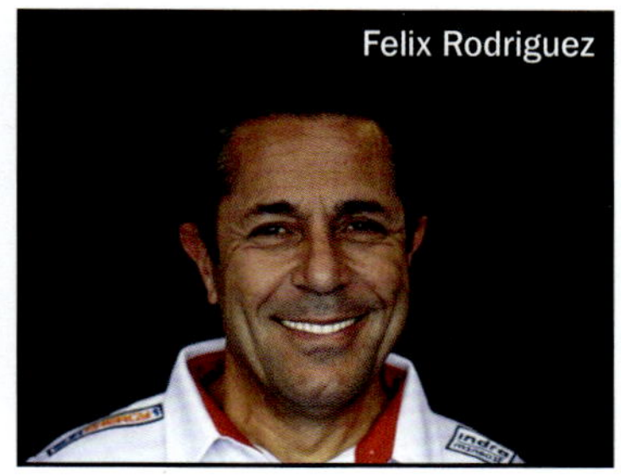
Felix Rodriguez

Photos: Pramac Racing

Jorge Martin

Photos: Gold & Goose

Johann Zarco

nephew of late Spanish legend Angel Nieto, became the team's new mouthpiece, after a significant promotion from rider coach to sporting director.

However, Calabresi's tenure was short. For 2023, it was confirmed that Campinoti was hiring another team manager, with a glowing reputation. Since 2006, Italian Gino Borsoi, an accomplished 125cc racer between 1997 and 2004, had been sporting director for the highly-respected Aspar outfit, owned and run by Spanish legend Jorge Martinez.

Borsoi had helped mastermind four 125cc titles for Aspar with Alvaro Bautista, Gabor Talmasci, Julian Simon and Nico Terol, and also had overseen the squad's Moto3 titles with Albert Arenas in 2020 and Izan Guevara in 2022. He was already well acquainted with Martin. They had worked together at Aspar during the Spaniard's first two seasons in Moto3.

At the team's home round at Mugello in late May, Campinoti unveiled a new title sponsorship deal with Italian insurance company Prima for the remainder of 2022 until the end of 2024. As a result, Martin and Zarco switched to a striking and predominantly purple livery.

Martin's second season in MotoGP didn't reach the heights of his outstanding rookie season in 2021. True to his word, he had treated all his crew and associated staff to a winter break in the Dominican Republic, following his maiden win at the Red Bull Ring in 2021. There would be no return to Punta Cana in 2022, but there were still flashes of brilliance from the former Moto3 world champion, with podium finishes in Argentina, Catalunya and Japan.

He also achieved the distinction of becoming the fastest rider in GP history with a new top-speed record of 363.6km/h on the fearsome start/finish straight at Mugello.

Once again, Martin's crew was headed by crew chief Daniele Romagnoli. Other top roles were filled again by Cristian Battaglia as data engineer and Nicola Manna as chief mechanic. The only newcomer was Luca Partigiani, who replaced Riccardo Pepe as fuel and tyres technician. Pepe moved to Zarco's crew to become a mechanic.

Martin's early-season charge was blunted somewhat by a lack of front-end confidence with the all-new GP22. He also struggled in the opening races with numbness in his right hand, caused by a lingering nerve issue, a legacy of his violent practice crash in Portimao at the beginning of 2021. Surgery in Modena immediately after his home round in Barcelona cured the problem.

Martin lost arguably the biggest contest of his career when he was beaten to the 2023 factory Ducati seat by Bastianini. He signed a one-year contract to stay with Pramac on a GP23 shortly before Ducati's home round in Misano.

Zarco's third season at Ducati had a similar theme to those before: he started extremely strongly, but struggled to maintain momentum after the summer break. In the first half of 2021, he had amassed four podiums, but no more in the second. In 2022, history repeated itself. Four podiums in the opening half made him a potential dark horse for the title.

Second in Portimao gained an unenviable distinction, however: gaining the most four-stroke podiums without a win. He took that dubious honour away from Texan Colin Edwards.

But in the second half of the season, the trophy cabinet was bare once again, and Zarco remained winless in MotoGP, despite having appeared in over 100 races. He might have had a podium or better in a wet Thailand Grand Prix at Buriram, but played the team game and sat behind title contender Pecco Bagnaia for fourth, when he was clearly faster. Ducati's instructions had been to choose discretion when fighting Bagnaia for anything other than a win. If anybody was going to toe the party line, it was Zarco. Ducati had saved his career after his controversial split from KTM halfway through 2019, and just weeks before Buriram, he'd been given a new one-year contract to reward his continuing loyalty.

He was paired again with crew chief Marco Rigamonti and Erik Chiarvesio as data engineer. Francesco Galindo took over from Fabrizio Malaguti as chief mechanic. Rigamonti would link up with Enea Bastianini in Ducati's factory squad in 2023, however, with Zarco reunited again with current Red Bull KTM Ajo crew chief Massimo Branchini, with whom he had won back-to-back Moto2 titles in 2015 and 2016.

MONSTER ENERGY YAMAHA MOTOGP

TEAM STAFF

Hiroshi ITO: President, Yamaha Motor Racing
Lin JARVIS: Managing Director, Yamaha Motor Racing & Team Principal
Takahiro SUMI: General Manager, Motorsports Development, Yamaha Motor Co
Kazutoshi SEKI: YZR-M1 Project Leader, Yamaha Motor Co
Massimo MEREGALLI: Team Director
William FAVERO: Marketing & Communications

FABIO QUARTARARO PIT CREW

Diego GUBELLINI: Crew Chief
Shinya YADA: Yamaha Engineer
Pablo GUILLIEM: Data Engineer
Bernard ANSIAU, Achim KARIGER, Daniele GRELLI, Mark ELDER: Mechanics
Julian SIMON: Rider Performance Analyst

FRANCO MORBIDELLI PIT CREW

Patrick PRIMMER: Crew Chief
Hitoshi HOSHINO: Yamaha Engineer
Davide MARELLI: Data Engineer
Ian GILPIN, Jurij PELLEGRINI, Julien ARMENGAUD, Juan MADURGA REVILLA: Mechanics

FABIO QUARTARARO

Born: 20 April, 1999 – Nice, France
GP Starts: 138 (71 MotoGP, 36 Moto2, 31 Moto3)
GP Wins: 12 (11 MotoGP, 1 Moto2)
World Championships: 1 MotoGP

FRANCO MORBIDELLI

Born: 4 December, 1994 – Rome, Italy
GP Starts: 153 (82 MotoGP, 71 Moto2)
GP Wins: 11 (3 MotoGP, 8 Moto2)
World Championships: 1 Moto2

Photos: Monster Energy Yamaha MotoGP

NOT since the halcyon days of Valentino Rossi, 13 years earlier, had a Yamaha rider successfully defended a MotoGP title.

They fell short once again in 2022, but it certainly wasn't through a lack of trying on the part of outgoing world champion Fabio Quartararo. The Frenchman was in a class apart on the YZR-M1 in 2022, and it was sobering for the Iwata factory to consider how different their season might have been without his brilliance.

Quartararo was the only Yamaha rider on the grid to score a top-six all season, and the most obvious sign of his importance and value to Yamaha was the fact that he outscored misfiring team-mate Franco Morbidelli by more than 200 points.

He pushed himself to the limit and beyond on a YZR-M1 that once again was severely outgunned in the speed charts, particularly against the brutal power of Ducati's Desmosedici. He was frequently the only rider on Japanese machinery capable of mixing it at the front, but at times even he was powerless to stave off the battering ram of Ducati's enormous talent pool.

Quartararo's defence of his title began in supreme fashion. He was first or second in six of the opening ten races. That impressive spell included wins at

YAMAHA YZR-M1

Engine: 1000cc liquid-cooled in-line 4, counter-rotating cross-plane crankshaft, DOHC, 4 valves per cylinder, pneumatic valve return system
Power: More than 240bhp

Ancillaries: Magneti Marelli ECU, Dorna software, ride-by-wire fuel injection, active Akrapovic titanium 4-into-2-into-1 exhaust

Transmission: Six-speed seamless-shift cassette-type gearbox, dry clutch

Frame: Aluminium twin-spar chassis, aluminium or carbon-fibre swing-arm, front and rear ride-height devices

Suspension: Öhlins inverted front fork, Öhlins rear shock absorber • *Wheels:* Forged magnesium, 17in diameter • *Tyres:* Michelin

Brakes: Brembo 320 or 340mm carbon-fibre twin front discs; single steel rear disc, thumb and foot levers

abio Quartararo wins in Portimao.

Photo: Gold & Goose

Franco Morbidelli

Photos: Monster Energy Yamaha MotoGP

Portimao, Catalunya and Sachsenring. After that, who would have expected him to score only two more podiums and not lead another lap in the whole campaign?

His once commanding lead began to evaporate at an alarming rate in the second half of the season. A first-lap collision with Marc Marquez in Aragon didn't help, and then disaster struck in Buriram, where he was a sitting duck in torrential rain because of incorrect front tyre pressure.

Phillip Island, where he crashed, was the third race in four where he failed to score a point at a critical phase of the title chase, and ultimately it proved to be a fatal blow to his championship campaign.

Unsurprisingly, as reigning champion, Quartararo didn't mess with a winning formula, retaining his complete crew for 2022. Once again, the most senior technical role went to crew chief Diego Gubellini, while Yamaha's engineer was Shinya Yada. Responsibility for data was in the hands of Pablo Guilliem who, with Gubellini, had worked with the Frenchman since his maiden season in MotoGP in 2019.

In the early part of the season, Quartararo had been publicly and heavily critical of the YZR-M1's lack of power and off-season improvements. However, that didn't deter him from signing a new two-year contract on the eve of the Catalunya round in early June. During the same weekend in Barcelona, Yamaha senior management confirmed a multi-year extension to its title sponsorship deal with Monster Energy. The US energy-drink giant had first collaborated with Yamaha's factory squad as an official partner in 2013 and had acquired naming rights in 2019.

The most senior roles at Yamaha were unchanged. Hiroshi Ito remained as president of Yamaha Motor Racing, while long-serving Lin Jarvis continued in the dual role of managing director of Yamaha Motor Racing and team principal of the Monster Energy Yamaha MotoGP Team.

Elsewhere, there was a significant reshuffle for 2022. Takahiro Sumi was promoted from YZR-M1 project leader to general manager of Yamaha's Motorsport Division, with Kazutoshi Seki taking over the vacated role. Massimo 'Maio' Meregalli continued as team director.

With a full factory bike and completely fit after a serious left-knee injury, which had wrecked the majority of his 2021 season, there was huge anticipation of what highly-rated Italian Morbidelli could deliver in 2022. He had narrowly missed capturing the Covid-delayed 2020 crown, but in truth, he endured a dreadful season.

The former Moto2 world champion was paired with new crew chief Patrick Primmer. He was well respected and well known to Yamaha, having previously been an Öhlins suspension technician for Jorge Lorenzo's three MotoGP titles, and his most recent engagement had been working with Maverick Vinales. Hitoshi Ashino came in as Yamaha engineer in place of Federico Giovannini.

Fabio Quartararo

Massimo Meregalli

Photo: Monster Energy Yamaha MotoGP

Lin Jarvis

Photo: Gold & Goose

Morbidelli appeared to be a shadow of the star who had run Joan Mir so close for the title just two years earlier, and he was nowhere near the level of Quartararo. It could be said that he was fortunate to have a 2023 contract tucked away in his pocket already, because normally his dismal results would have forced Yamaha into the rider market.

Seventh in round two at rain-lashed Mandalika in Indonesia and tenth at Valencia were his only top-tens of the season. Only once did he qualify inside the top ten, and that took him until round 19 at the Sepang International Circuit in Malaysia, where he launched from seventh. He also had the unwanted distinction of being MotoGP's most penalised rider in 2022, with indiscretions that included last-lap track limits, slow riding and irresponsible riding in a practice start zone.

TEAM SUZUKI ECSTAR

TEAM STAFF

Shinichi SAHARA: Project Leader
Ken KAWAUCHI: Technical Manager
Livio SUPPO: Team Manager
Atsushi KAWASAKI: Chassis Engineer
Jordi MELENDO: Parts Manager
Roberto BRIVIO, Mitia DOTTA: Team Co-ordinators
Alberto GOMEZ: Marketing & Communication Manager
Federico TONDELLI: Press Officer & Media Co-ordinator
Hatsumi TSUKAMOTO: Marketing & Relations
Adriana PINTO: Digital Co-ordinator
Georgia WELLS: Social Media
Emanuele MAZZINI: Test Team Co-ordinator
Massimo TOMASONI: Truck Driver

ALEX RINS PIT CREW

Jose Manuel CAZEAUX: Crew Chief
Yuta SHIMABUKURO: Engine Management Engineer
Davide MANFREDI, Kevin LOUSSOUARN,
'Paco' NOGUEIRA, Tiziano VERNIANI: Mechanics

JOAN MIR PIT CREW

Frankie CARCHEDI: Crew Chief
Claudio RAINATO: Engine Management Engineer
Tsutomu MATSUGANO, Jacques ROCA, Marco Rosa GASTALDO, Fernando MENDEZ PICON: Mechanics

JOAN MIR

Born: 1 September, 1997 – Palma de Mallorca, Spain
GP Starts: 120 (65 MotoGP, 18 Moto2, 37 Moto3)
GP Wins: 12 (1 MotoGP, 11 Moto3)
World Championships: 2 (1 MotoGP, 1 Moto3)

Photos: Gold & Goose

ALEX RINS

Born: 8 December, 1995 – Barcelona, Spain
GP Starts: 187 (99 MotoGP, 36 Moto2, 52 Moto3)
GP Wins: 17 (5 MotoGP, 4 Moto2, 8 Moto3)

WHEN Suzuki left Portimao five races into the 2022 season, Alex Rins was the joint World Championship leader. A second MotoGP title in three years appeared well within reach, thanks to a GSX-RR given a major power boost by winter engine upgrades.

Suzuki's challenge was bolstered by a more refined rear ride-height device, after the Hamamatsu factory had been the last to implement the latest must-have gadget halfway through 2021.

Just a week later, Suzuki dropped a bombshell.

A little over 12 months after signing a new five-year contract with Dorna – until the end of 2026 – Suzuki confirmed its intention to quit the World Championship. The news broke at the post-race test following the Spanish GP at Jerez, where project leader Shinichi Sahara had called an impromptu meeting to inform stunned team members. Almost two weeks later, on the eve of the French GP, Suzuki made a formal, but brief statement. It cited financial pressures resulting from the global pandemic and the Russian invasion of Ukraine.

Another major reason for Suzuki's second shock MotoGP exit in 11 years was the need to redistribute resources to focus more on sustainable technologies.

Suzuki's withdrawal blindsided everybody connected to the project. It had a competitive machine firmly

SUZUKI GSX-RR

Engine: 1000cc liquid-cooled in-line 4, cross-plane counter-rotating crankshaft, DOHC, 4 valves per cylinder, pneumatic valve return system
Power: More than 240bhp
Ancillaries: Magneti Marelli ECU, Dorna software, ride-by-wire fuel injection, active Akropovic titanium 4-into-2 exhaust
Transmission: Six-speed seamless-shift cassette-type gearbox, dry clutch
Frame: Aluminium twin-spar chassis, aluminium or carbon-fibre swing-arm, front and rear ride-height devices
Suspension: Öhlins inverted front fork, Öhlins rear shock absorber
Brakes: Brembo carbon-fibre twin front discs, single steel rear disc, thumb and foot levers

Photo: www.suzuki-racing.com

TAKUYA TSUDA

Born: 27 April, 1984 – Wakayama, Japan

GP Starts: 2 MotoGP

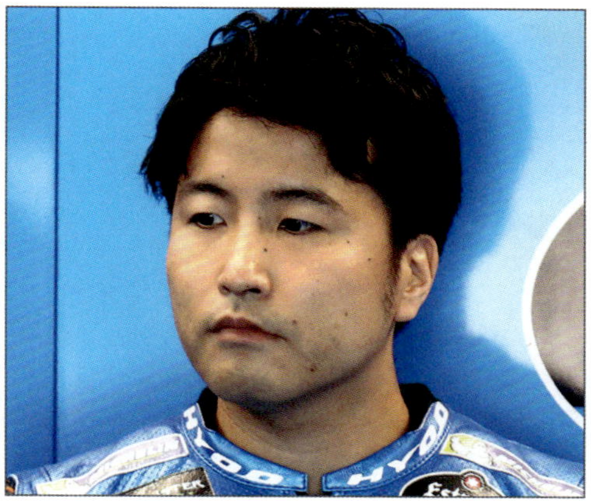

KAZUKI WATANABE

Born: 2 October, 1990 – Yamanashi, Japan

GP Starts: 6 (1 MotoGP, 5 Moto2/250cc)

Photos: Gold & Goose

DANILO PETRUCCI

Born: 24 October, 1990 – Terni, Italy

GP Starts: 170 MotoGP

GP Wins: 2 MotoGP

in title contention. And while senior management were plotting the team's closure in Japan, Rins and Joan Mir were locked in negotiations over contract extensions that were all but agreed when the pin was pulled. The team's mid-season demise was all the more staggering considering it had seemed on such a sound footing.

The withdrawal was confirmed in mid-July in a statement made by Toshihiro Suzuki, representative director and president.

Suzuki also confirmed that it was ending support for SERT, the official Suzuki Endurance Racing Team, which had won the EWC series in 2020 and 2021.

Two weeks prior to the first race, Sahara's long hunt for a replacement for former team manager Davide Brivio had reached a successful conclusion. Brivio had quit Suzuki in early 2021 for F1, and his stopgap replacement was a management committee featuring seven prominent team members, including Sahara and technical manager Ken Kawauchi. While the experiment wasn't a failure, it highlighted the value of a dedicated manager. This multi-task role was filled by Livio Suppo.

The Italian's impressive CV made him an ideal candidate. His paddock experience stretched back nearly 30 years to the Benetton Honda team in 125s and 250s. But he is perhaps best remembered for being a key figure in the shrewd signing of Casey Stoner for Ducati in 2007. They were reunited at Honda after Suppo had transferred to HRC in 2010 as marketing and communications director. Suppo had assumed the role of team principal in 2013, before he was replaced by Alberto Puig four years later. In the intervening years out of the paddock, he'd established a successful e-bike company.

Once again, Rins was under the guidance of crew chief Jose Manuel Cazeaux, with a crew that featured minimal tweaking in the shape of Tiziano Verniani, who replaced Massimo Mirano in the four-strong mechanic line-up.

Four top-five finishes in the opening five races, including podiums in Argentina and America, had elevated his status. The negative impact of Suzuki's withdrawal was laid bare post-Jerez, and Rins's decline was tough to watch. He admitted to "full crying" when learning of the plan to quit. His main concern – like that of his team-mate, Mir – was for the future prospects of his crew, whose seemingly safe jobs were no more.

Rins endured a mid-season slump, which was not helped by his innocent involvement in the horrible first-corner mêlée in Catalunya. He was left with a fractured left wrist and withdrew in agony after FP3 at the next round in Sachsenring.

He rebounded to victory, however, with a stunning display at Phillip Island and emerged victorious at the team's final race in Valencia.

Alex Rins took Suzuki's penultimate win in Australia.

Shinichi Sahara

Livio Suppo

Photos: Gold & Goose

Joan Mir's crew remained unchanged for a fourth season, with the senior roles held again by crew chief Frankie Carchedi and engine management engineer Claudio Rainato.

The 2020 world champion was his usual rock-solid self at the start of the season, with top-six finishes in five of the opening six races. After Jerez, though, came a nightmare collapse in form and fortune, and he ended a frustrating year without registering a single podium.

He suffered DNFs in five of the seven races after Jerez, with the worst a vicious high-side on the opening lap of the Austrian Grand Prix, which left him with ligament and bone damage to his right ankle. That ruled him out of the Misano round, but replacement options were severely restricted.

Official tester and substitute Sylvain Guintoli was injured, and Suzuki chose Kazuki Watanabe, who had made five 250cc/Moto2 appearances in 2009 and 2010. He had finished on the podium at the Suzuka 8-Hours, riding for the official SERT squad, and was contesting the All-Japan Superbike series, in a Suzuki squad run by popular former GP, British and World Superbike rider Yukio Kagayama.

Mir aborted an attempted return to action in Motorland Aragon, before his seat in Suzuki's final home grand prix in Japan went to veteran test rider Takuya Tsuda. The initial plan had been to run the Japanese as a wild-card, to thank fans as well as Tsuda, who had been test rider when Suzuki had returned to MotoGP in 2015. It was not the home goodbye Suzuki had craved, however, with Tsuda's machine suffering a spectacular engine blow-up and Rins ruled out with a puncture.

Mir was also absent from the Thai Grand Prix, which paved the way for a return to MotoGP for the popular Danilo Petrucci. The Italian had just finished runner-up in the MotoAmerica Superbike series, having created history at the beginning of the year by becoming the first ex-MotoGP rider to win a stage of the Dakar Rally. He finished 20th in a rain-lashed Buriram encounter.

Mir returned for the final three races, but arm-pump issues spoiled his results.

GRESINI RACING MOTOGP DUCATI

TEAM STAFF

Nadia PADOVANI: Team Owner & Team Principal
Michele MASINI: Team Manager
Carlo MERLINI: Commercial & Marketing Director
Sandra VILCHEZ: Team Co-ordinator
Manuel POGGIALI: Rider Coach
Cristian MASSA: Press Manager
Sergio VERBENA: Technical Co-ordinator
Davide BALLARINI: Electronics Co-ordinator
Mike WATT: Öhlins Suspension Technician
Gregory PARRA: Tyre Technician
Luca BELLOSI: Spare Parts
Claudio BRICCOLI: Facilities Co-ordinator

ENEA BASTIANINI PIT CREW

Alberto GIRIBUOLA: Track Engineer
Dario MASSARIN: Electronics Engineer
Rafa LOPEZ: Chief Mechanic
Alberto PRESUTTI, Claudio EUSEBI, Joan TORTOSA, Marco CARANCINI: Mechanics

FABIO DI GIANNANTONIO PIT CREW

Donatello GIOVANOTTI: Track Engineer
Stefano GUIDI: Electronics Engineer
Filippo TOGNONI: Chief Mechanic
Edoardo CIFERRI, David CASTANEDA. Mirco FIUZZI, Francesco SCIUSCO: Mechanics

ENEA BASTIANINI

Born: 30 December, 1997 – Rimini, Italy
GP Starts: 159 (38 MotoGP, 33 Moto2, 88 Moto3)
GP Wins: 10 (4 MotoGP, 3 Moto2, 3 Moto3)
World Championships: 1 Moto2

Photos: Gold & Goose

FABIO DI GIANNANTONIO

Born: 10 October, 1998 – Rome, Italy
GP Starts: 127 (20 MotoGP, 52 Moto2, 55 Moto3)
GP Wins: 3 (1 Moto2, 2 Moto3)

REGARDLESS of results, the 2022 season was always going to be an emotional and poignant campaign for the Gresini Racing squad. After a six-year collaboration with Aprilia that had begun when the Noale brand returned to MotoGP in 2015, Fausto Gresini had engineered a deal to return to Independent Team status for 2022, running Ducatis.

Gresini would never witness his dream fulfilled. The former 125cc world champion had succumbed to complications from Covid-19 just weeks prior to the 2021 season.

Immediate family and close colleagues had vowed to honour his legacy by keeping the show on the road. And so the show did roll on. Gresini's widow, Nadia Padovani, became the new team owner and principal, while prominent roles went to long-serving and loyal Gresini staff, including Carlo Merlini as commercial and marketing director and Michele Masini as sporting director.

Given the trauma and turmoil of the preceding 13 months, there was not a dry eye in the house when Enea Bastianini stormed to victory in the team's first

DUCATI Desmosedici GP21

Engine: 1000cc liquid-cooled in-line 4, cross-plane counter-rotating crankshaft, DOHC, 4 valves per cylinder, pneumatic valve return system
Power: More than 240bhp
Ancillaries: Magneti Marelli ECU, Dorna software, ride-by-wire fuel injection, active Akropovic titanium 4-into-2 exhaust
Transmission: Six-speed seamless-shift cassette-type gearbox, dry clutch
Frame: Aluminium twin-spar chassis, aluminium or carbon-fibre swing-arm, front and rear ride-height devices
Suspension: Öhlins inverted front fork, Öhlins rear shock absorber
Brakes: Brembo carbon-fibre twin front discs, single steel rear disc, thumb and foot levers

Enea Bastianini

Fabio Di Giannantonio

race in round one at Qatar. Remarkably, it was the first Gresini win in 5,621 days since Toni Elias had won a last-lap thriller against Valentino Rossi and Kenny Roberts Junior at Estoril in 2006.

That was just the start of a breakthrough season for Bastianini, who emerged as one of the big success stories of 2022.

The suave Italian had been given his big break in the World Championship when signed by Gresini for Moto3 in 2014. The self-styled 'Beast', a former Moto2 world champion, had shown immense potential with a series of giant-killing performances on a two-year-old Ducati in 2021. On more competitive machinery and in an environment he knew like the back of his hand, Bastianini won three of the opening seven races and eventually finished with four victories on the second-hand GP21. He had won only three races in a five-year Moto3 career!

Key to his success was an often unrivalled ability to manage fading grip on worn tyres, particularly evident when he hunted down and beat Bagnaia at Le Mans and Aragon.

Also fundamental to his success was the fact that crew chief Alberto Giribuola and electronics engineer Dario Massarin had followed him from the defunct Esponsorama Racing squad, in which he'd excelled during 2021. Mechanics Rafa Lopez and Joan Tortosa also had followed him to Gresini.

Ducati's eyes and ears in the garage came from new technical co-ordinator Sergio Verbena, whose most recent role had been as crew chief to Danilo Petrucci at Tech3 KTM during the Italian's farewell season.

Bastianini's eye-catching performances won him a crucial contest against highly-rated Spaniard Jorge Martin for a prized seat alongside Pecco Bagnaia in Ducati's factory squad for 2023. The dream move to the Ducati Lenovo team came at the end of August, in the build-up to his home round at Misano.

Gresini were resigned to losing their prized asset regardless. A contractual stipulation was that he would ride the latest-spec Desmosedici in 2023, but one would not be supplied to Gresini. Had Martin got the nod, Bastianini would simply have slotted into his seat next to Johann Zarco at Pramac Racing on the GP23. The only sour note was that he would no longer be in tandem with crew chief Giribuola, who was the latest Ducati tech whizz to be headhunted by KTM to take up a senior position in 2023. Bastianini would be paired with Johann Zarco's crew chief, Marco Rigamonti, for the following season.

Another rider given his big opportunity on the world stage by Gresini in 2016 was Fabio Di Giannantonio, so it was fitting that his move to the premier class also came courtesy of Gresini.

Di Giannantonio also raced a year-old GP21 in a team spearheaded by crew chief Donatello Giovanotti, former Moto2 crew chief to Luca Marini at Sky VR46 and previously with Tito Rabat in MotoGP at Ducati. In 2021, he had been a Gresini Moto2 crew chief with Nicola Bulega. Electronics engineer Stefano Guidi moved up from the same role with Di Giannantionio in Moto2 in 2021. Experienced Ducati mechanics David Castaneda and Edoardo Ciferri were also members of the squad.

It was a baptism of fire for Di Giannantonio, and it took him until round seven at Le Mans to score points. He returned to the top 15 in just five other races, with a slow finish with just one point in the last seven races. He claimed a singular top-ten with a season-best eighth at the Sachsenring.

The undisputed highlight was a sensational pole position in front of his home crowd in Mugello. He topped a damp Q1 before using knowledge of track conditions and grip levels to lead home the first all-Italian front row since the Austrian round in 2016 (Iannone, Rossi, Dovizioso). It was also the first time that two rookies had started in the top two since Jorge Lorenzo and James Toseland at Qatar in 2008.

Victory celebrations at Aragon.

Special Fausto Gresini livery for Bastianini at Misano.

Photos: Gold & Goose

MOONEY VR46 RACING TEAM

TEAM STAFF

Valentino ROSSI: Team Owner
Alessio SALUCCI: Team Director
Gianluca FALCIONI: Sponsor & Partner
Carlo Alberto TEBALDI: CFO
Pablo NIETO: Team Manager
Luca BRIVIO: Senior Co-ordinator
Giorgia FRATESI: Team Co-ordinator
Pol BERTRAN: Communications
Laura BERETTA: Press Officer
Alessandro BADALIN: Social Media Manager
Idalio GAVIRA: Coach

LUCA MARINI PIT CREW

David MUNOZ: Crew Chief
Daniel VILLAR: Electronics Engineer
Federico PECCI: Chief Mechanic
Christian DIONIGI, Federico PECCI, Giacomo SILVESTRI, Gianluca FALCONI: Mechanics
Guillem RODRICUEX: Tyres and Fuel

MARCO BEZZECCHI PIT CREW

Matteo FLAMIGNI: Crew Chief
Sergio MARTINEZ: Electronics Engineer
Miguel PERURENA: Chief Mechanic
Alex JOAQUIN, Robin SPIJKERS, Luca CASALI, Filippo BERTI: Tyres and Fuel

Luca FERRACCIOLI, Mattia SERENI, Giulio DE BLASI: Ducati Technicians

LUCA MARINI

Born: 10 August, 1997 – Urbino, Italy

GP Starts: 126 (38 MotoGP, 87 Moto2, 1 Moto3)

GP Wins: 6 Moto2

MARCO BEZZECCHI

Born: 12 November, 1998 – Rimini, Italy

GP Starts: 112 (20 MotoGP, 52 Moto2, 40 Moto3)

GP Wins: 6 (3 Moto2, 3 Moto3)

Photos: Gold & Goose

VALENTINO ROSSI was out of the premier class after more than 20 years, but his influence was still very much felt. Following a trail blazed by former Yamaha greats Giacomo Agostini, Kenny Roberts and Wayne Rainey, Rossi started a new chapter in his illustrious career, dabbling in premier-class team ownership for the first time, campaigning a fully-fledged, two-rider MotoGP squad.

'The Doctor' had dipped a toe into MotoGP management in 2021, when Sky Italy – the Italian arm of the leading media and entertainment company – had backed a VR46-inspired, one-rider effort for his half-brother, Luca Marini, as an independent part of the Esponsorama Racing project that ran Enea Bastianini in its last premier-class season.

As expected, Rossi took over the Esponsorama grid slots for 2022. He juggled MotoGP team ownership with a new four-wheeled adventure in the GT World Challenge Europe touring car series, while remaining the figurehead of the famed VR46 Academy.

Full team ownership completed a meteoric rise for his Tavullia enterprise. He had stepped into team management in 2014 with a Moto3 outfit that had featured the then unknown talent and potential of Pecco Bagnaia.

Not surprisingly, given the Academy's commitment

DUCATI Desmosedici GP22

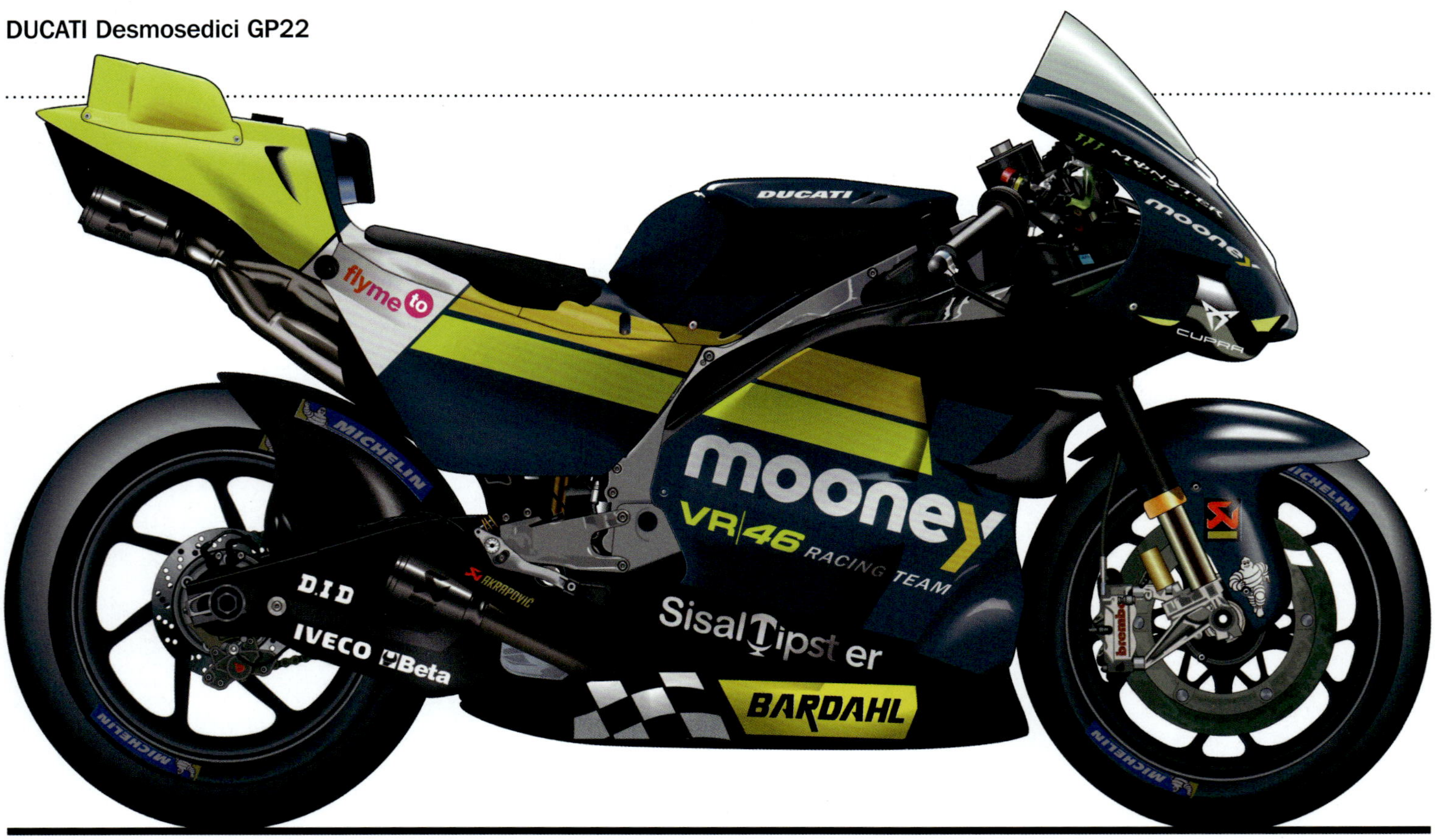

Engine: 1000cc liquid-cooled 90-degree V4, counter-rotating crankshaft, DOHC, 4 valves per cylinder, desmodromic valve gear
Power: More than 250bhp

Ancillaries: Magneti Marelli ECU, Dorna software, ride-by-wire fuel injection, active Akropovic titanium 4-into-2 exhaust

Transmission: Six-speed seamless-shift cassette-type gearbox, dry clutch

Frame: Aluminium-alloy twin-spar chassis, carbon-fibre swing-arm, front and rear ride-height devices

Suspension: Öhlins inverted front forks, Öhlins rear shock absorber

Tyres: Michelin • *Brakes:* Brembo carbon-fibre twin front discs, single steel rear disc, thumb and foot levers

Luca Marini

Bezzecchi, Di Giannantonio, Marini – the all-Italian front row at Mugello.

to unearthing and nurturing young Italian talent, Rossi selected an all-Italian line-up. Close family ties and Marini's 2021 experience meant that he was tasked with racing the team's only current-spec GP22 Desmosedici. Rookie team-mate Marco Bezzecchi would learn his craft on the year-old GP21.

After the controversy and chaos surrounding potential investment from Saudi state-owned oil giant Aramco, Italian support was found. It was announced in early January that Mooney (an alternative financial service for bill payments, cash withdrawals and transfers only previously possible through banks) would be naming-rights backers of the new team. The deal included title sponsorship rights to Rossi's Moto2 effort, running Academy graduates Celestino Vietti and Niccolo Antonelli.

Rossi was very much a behind-the-scenes team owner, hiring a trusted band of close allies to steer the ship in his absence trackside. Team director responsibility went to lifelong friend and close confidant Alessio 'Uccio' Salucci, while team manager duty went to Pablo Nieto, son of late Spanish racing legend Angel Nieto. Both had played prominent roles in overseeing Rossi's Moto2 effort, in its final year. Italian off-road specialist Fantic would assume control of the VR46 squad, and the Venice-based company would also work with the VR46 Academy on rider development in future.

Marco Bezzecchi

Marini's crew was staffed with most of those who had been at his side for his rookie season in 2021. The most obvious changes were in senior roles, with David Munoz, the last crew chief of Rossi's career, replacing Luca Ferraccioli. Munoz had begun working with Rossi in 2020 during his final season in Yamaha's official factory team, where he had replaced Silvano Galbusera.

Daniel Villar also replaced Mattia Sereni as electronics engineer. But Ferraccioli and Sereni were still very much part of the VR46 set-up, assigned to the team as official Ducati technicians. Mechanics Federico Pecci, Christian Dionigi and Gianluca Falconi had all worked with Marini in 2021.

Marini had an excellent second season in MotoGP, reeling off an impressive seven top-six finishes. But he had the unwanted distinction of being the only one of Ducati's eight-strong star-studded line-up not to score a pole or podium in 2022.

That aside, it was no surprise that shortly after his home round in Misano, he signed a one-year extension with the VR46 squad. One notable difference, though, would be the absence of a machinery upgrade for 2023. Ducati would only supply half of its eight-strong talent pool with the latest-spec GP23. That meant Marini would stay on board the GP22 for the following season, as would Bezzecchi and Gresini Racing duo Alex Marquez and Fabio Di Giannantonio.

Marini was expected to be the headline grabber in 2022, but it was unfancied rookie Bezzecchi who wrote history for Rossi. The accolade of scoring the team's first podium went to him when he ran Bagnaia close for second in Assen. And he grabbed the limelight again in Thailand to secure Rossi a first MotoGP pole position as team owner.

Rossi hired a crew chief he trusted implicitly to oversee Bezzecchi's launch into MotoGP. Although it was the first time he had occupied the role, Matteo Flamigni was blessed with an abundance of experience. The Italian had previously worked as an electronics and data specialist with the likes of Luca Cadalora, Alex Barros, Loris Capirossi, Max Biaggi and Marco Melandri, but since 2004 until his retirement in 2021, he had been ever present at Rossi's side, both at Yamaha and Ducati.

Bezzecchi was also provided with two other crew members who had been at Rossi's side for his 26th and farewell season in 2021, Miguel Perurena and Robin Spijkers having been recruited from the Petronas SRT team.

Pablo Nieto

Photos: Gold & Goose

REPSOL HONDA TEAM

TEAM STAFF

Tetsuhiro KUWATA: HRC Director, General Manager Race Operations

Alberto PUIG: Team Manager

Takeo YOKOYAMA: HRC Technical Manager

MARC MARQUEZ/STEFAN BRADL PIT CREW

Santi HERNANDEZ: Chief Engineer

Carlo LUZZI: Electronics Engineer

Jenny ANDERSON: Data Engineer

Carlos LINAN: Chief Mechanic

Roberto CLERICI, Jordi CASTELLA,

Javier ORTIZ, Koji KAMINAKABEPPU: Mechanics

POL ESPARGARO PIT CREW

Ramon AURIN: Chief Engineer

Ricardo CARRASCOSA: Electronics Engineer

Marco BARBIANI: Data Engineer

Masashi OGO: Chief Mechanic

Emanuel BUCHNER, Carles LURBE,

Felix KERTZSCHER, Juan LLANSA: Mechanics

MARC MARQUEZ

Born: 17 February, 1993 – Cervera, Spain

GP Starts: 232 (154 MotoGP, 32 Moto2, 46 125cc)

GP Wins: 85 (59 MotoGP, 16 Moto2, 10 125cc)

World Championships: 8 (6 MotoGP, 1 Moto2, 1 125cc)

POL ESPARGARO

Born: 10 June, 1991 – Granollers, Spain

GP Starts: 276 (154 MotoGP, 51 Moto2, 71 125cc)

GP Wins: 15 (10 Moto2; 5 125cc)

World Championships: 1 Moto2

Photos: Gold & Goose

IF Honda had thought its fall from grace couldn't get any worse, 2022 dished out another huge slap in the face for MotoGP's troubled giant.

Any factory robbed of a rider of the other-worldly talent of Marc Marquez would expect a drastic downturn in fortunes, but the supremely gifted Spaniard's absence for an extended injury spell for the third season in a row sent HRC and its once all-conquering Repsol squad crashing to an all-time low.

Once again, the eight-times world champion's season was severely compromised by the career-threatening crash he had suffered in an over-exuberant surge from last to podium contention in the Covid-19-delayed start to 2020 at Jerez. Riding in constant and debilitating pain, Marquez eventually learned that his right arm was 34 degrees out of alignment after three major operations to his fractured humerus.

By round eight in Mugello, not even his famed pain threshold and mental resilience could take it any longer. Racing was a battle, but so too was normal life. A fourth and final operation was the only option to save his career, so he flew to the Mayo Clinic in Minnesota in early June. It was there that world-renowned specialist Dr Joaquin Sanchez Sotelo spent three hours rotating his right humerus bone back into position.

Marquez missed the next six races, his seat once

HONDA RC213V – Repsol

Engine: 1000cc liquid-cooled 90-degree V4, counter-rotating crankshaft, DOHC, 4 valves per cylinder, pneumatic valve return system

Power: More than 240bhp

Ancillaries: Magneti Marelli ECU, Dorna software, ride-by-wire fuel injection, non-active Arrow 4-into-2 exhaust

Transmission: Six-speed seamless-shift cassette-type gearbox, dry clutch

Frame: Aluminium twin-spar chassis, carbon-fibre swing-arm, front and rear ride-height devices

Suspension: Öhlins front and rear

Tyres: Michelin • *Brakes:* Brembo twin carbon-fibre front discs, Yutaka single steel rear disc, thumb and foot levers

STEFAN BRADL

Born: 29 November, 1989 – Augsburg, Germany

GP Starts: 206 (119 MotoGP, 33 Moto2, 54 125cc)

GP Wins: 7 (5 Moto2, 2 125cc)

World Championships: 1 Moto2

TETSUTA NAGASHIMA

Born: 2 July, 1992 – Kanagawa, Japan

GP Starts: 206 (119 MotoGP, 33 Moto2, 54 125cc)

GP Wins: 1 Moto2

Marc Marquez

Photos8: Gold & Goose

again kept warm by Honda's German test rider, Stefan Bradl.

Marquez came back with a bang, when two first-lap collisions in Motorland Aragon inadvertently wiped out Fabio Quartararo and HRC stablemate Taka Nakagami, after a storming start from 13th to sixth in two corners, a reminder of how he had been missed.

Marc returned for 2022 with his eight-strong crew completely unchanged. Once again, Santi Hernandez was his trusted sidekick as crew chief, with Carlos Linan the chief mechanic, and Carlo Luzzi and Jenny Anderson dedicated to electronics and data.

There was one major surprise departure from his backroom team – former 125cc world champion Emilio Alzamora. He had worked with Marquez as manager and mentor since 2005, when he had been 12 and emerging as a big future star. At the end of August, it was revealed that he had been replaced by Jaime Martinez, former head of motorsport marketing at Red Bull, who would look after the affairs of both Marquez brothers.

How much did HRC miss Marquez? Actually he was absent from two other races – the first in Indonesia, when the last of four high-speed tumbles on Sunday morning had left him concussed, and then triggered a second case of diplopia (double vision) in six months. That meant he missed Argentina, too.

Eight races spent sidelined, yet he finished comfortably top Honda rider overall. But not even the mercurial Marquez could save Honda from a season of humiliation. It finished last in the coveted constructors' championship, the statistics telling a sorry tale.

A shocking Sachsenring was the first time Honda didn't score a point in 40 years. Just two races later at Silverstone, it suffered its worst qualifying performance since 1980, and 22 races without a win was its worst barren run since returning to premier-class competition in 1982.

These results increased the pressure on senior management, which was led again by Tetsuhiro Kuwata, HRC director and general manager race operations management division. He was senior in command over Repsol Honda team manager Alberto Puig and HRC technical manager Takeo Yokoyama, who perhaps felt the heat the most in his role as leader of RC213V development. Evidence of change became clear when Shinichi Kokubu, general manager technology development division, began attending selected European races in an attempt to get a grasp on Honda's woes.

Upon his return, Marquez suggested that the entire project needed a top-to-toe shake-up, as Japanese factories began to see their iron grip on MotoGP loosened by the bold and aggressive development strategies employed by the likes of Ducati, Aprilia and KTM.

It was fair to say that without Marquez, Honda resembled a rudderless ship. It was a stark contrast to early-season optimism. Pol Espargaro led more laps of the opening race in Qatar than he'd done in his previous 135 MotoGP starts, and he boldly boasted that he and a radically revised RC213V were title contenders in 2022.

Alberto Puig

Photo: Gold & Goose

Takeo Yokoyama

Tetsuhiro Kuwata

Photos: Honda Racing Corporation

Pol Espargaro and team celebrate their podium in Qatar.

Photo: Gold & Goose

That promise had been eroded completely by the time the season hit Europe. Much like predecessor Jorge Lorenzo, Espargaro was powerless to stop the destruction of his reputation by an RC213V that was plagued by a multitude of sins.

The former Moto2 world champion's HRC dream descended into a nightmare. He didn't score another top-six finish after Qatar and was victim of some sickening crashes, while he gave blood, sweat and tears to make the RC213V competitive.

Espargaro's pit crew remained unaltered from 2021, with Ramon Aurin operating as crew chief once more. Masashi Ogo was back as chief mechanic, while electronics roles went to Ricardo Carrascosa and Marco Barbiani.

It was no surprise that he was out at the end of 2022, while the loss of the Suzuki team was certainly Honda's gain. Big-name riders Joan Mir and Alex Rins were on the open market. More than three months after the initial news of Suzuki's departure, it was announced that 2020 MotoGP world champion Mir would take Espargaro's seat, the latest highly rated and respected Spaniard to put his reputation on the line with HRC. Espargaro returned to KTM, with the Tech3 satellite team.

Tetsuta Nagashima rode as a wild-card at Motegi.

LCR HONDA

TEAM STAFF

Lucio CECCHINELLO: Team Manager

Christophe BOURGUIGNON: Team Technical Director

ALEX MARQUEZ PIT CREW

David GARCIA: Crew Chief

Jaume CARRAU: Engine Mapping

Albert TALAMINO: Data Recording

Joan CASAS, Christopher RICHARDSON,

Michele ANDREINI: Mechanics

Sergi SANGRA LLUCH: Tyres

Jose CARRIO: Rider's Associate

Yuji KIKUCHI: HRC Technician

Katsuhiko IMAI: HRC Staff

TAKAAKI NAKAGAMI PIT CREW

Giacomo GUIDOTTI: Crew Chief

Eric PEREZ SALVA: Engine Mapping

Koen VAN LIEROP: Data Recording

Filippo BRUNETTI, Marc CANELLAS,

Federico VICINO: Mechanics

Willibrord KLEINE: Tyres

Enrique PINTOR: Rider's Associate

Yuichiro SEGAWA: HRC Technician

Dakota MAMOLA: Team Staff

ALEX MARQUEZ

Born: 23 April, 1996 – Cervera, Spain

GP Starts: 187 (52 MotoGP, 89 Moto2, 46 Moto3)

GP Wins: 12 (8 Moto2, 4 Moto3)

World Championships: 2 (1 Moto2, 1 Moto3)

TAKAAKI NAKAGAMI

Born: 9 February, 1992 – Chiba, Japan

GP Starts: 222 (83 MotoGP, 105 Moto2, 34 125cc)

GP Wins: 2 Moto2

Photos: Gold & Goose

HONDA'S abysmal 2022 was not exclusive to its underperforming factory squad. The decline had an inevitable impact on the fortunes of its independent team, operated by Lucio Cecchinello's dual-sponsored LCR squad for a 16th year in succession.

The Monaco-based LCR effort fielded former Moto2 and Moto3 world champion Alex Marquez for a second year, alongside Japan's Takaaki Nakagami, back for his fifth season with Cecchinello.

The recent manufacturers' strategy had been to strengthen the potential of their Independent teams by arming them with factory-spec machinery. Honda was no exception. But while the fortunes particularly of Ducati's Independent teams flourished, LCR Honda's prospects stagnated. For the third season in a row, the team failed to score a podium. Even more alarming, there wasn't even a single top-six finish, as Marquez and Nakagami were bamboozled by an RC213V that once again appeared only remotely competitive in the hands of Marc Marquez.

Once again, the younger Marquez raced in the livery of British oil company Castrol – a subsidiary of BP after a multi-billion-dollar acquisition in 2000.

LCR Honda's crew underwent one of its biggest shake-ups since it had joined MotoGP in 2006 as a one-bike outfit featuring rising Aussie star Casey Stoner. David Garcia had been crew chief to Alex Marquez when the Spaniard had captured a third Moto2

HONDA RC213V – LCR

Engine: 1000cc liquid-cooled 90-degree V4, counter-rotating crankshaft, DOHC, 4 valves per cylinder, pneumatic valve return system

Power: More than 240bhp

Ancillaries: Magneti Marelli ECU, Dorna software, ride-by-wire fuel injection, non-active Arrow 4-into-2 exhaust

Transmission: Six-speed seamless-shift cassette-type gearbox, dry clutch

Frame: Aluminium twin-spar chassis, carbon-fibre swing-arm, front and rear ride-height devices • *Suspension:* Öhlins front and rear

Tyres: Michelin • *Brakes:* Brembo carbon-fibre twin front discs, single steel rear disc, thumb and foot levers

TETSUTA NAGASHIMA

Born: 2 July, 1992 – Kanagawa, Japan

GP Starts: 91 (4 MotoGP, 87 Moto2)

GP Wins: 1 Moto2

Alex Marquez – Givi Honda 213CV

title for Marc VDS Racing in 2019. His most recent engagement had been data recording with the younger Marquez in 2021. For 2022, he was promoted to crew chief with the rider, Albert Talamino coming in to take his data role.

That meant a change for Christophe 'Beefy' Bourguignon, who was installed in the new capacity of team technical director. Bourguignon had been a crew chief with LCR since 2008, and had enjoyed notable success with current HRC test rider Stefan Bradl and current Yamaha test rider Cal Crutchlow. His new position meant that he oversaw both Marquez and Nakagami, and was the main path of communication between the two sides of the garage and HRC.

Marquez had a tough third year in MotoGP, scoring only four top-ten finishes. Inevitably, this triggered a search for fresh motivation. He found it on race-day morning of the historic Dutch TT at Assen in late June.

Gresini Racing had long been in the market for a replacement for Bastianini, with Alex Rins and Miguel Oliveira linked to the position. Eventually, it went to Marquez, who would race a year-old GP22 alongside Fabio Di Giannantonio in 2023. Next, during the five-week summer break, news broke that Rins had signed a two-year HRC contract to join LCR, the second ex-Suzuki rider undeterred by one of Honda's worst season's in its proud history.

Nakagami's crew had a familiar appearance. Giacomo Guidotti was back again as crew chief, though changes were made to the electronics support crew. Engine mapping engineer Alessandro Damia had moved to KTM in the role of track support strategy engineer for the Independent Tech3 squad. As a result, Eric Salva moved from his data recording position to engine mapping duty. Koen van Lierop took over Salva's role.

Nakagami's season was one of underachievement, controversy, bad luck and injury. Like Alex Marquez, he found his way into the top ten in only four races, with a season's best of seventh coming at Jerez and Le Mans.

He was also involved in two of the major talking points of the season. First, he drew stinging criticism for inadvertently wiping out Bagnaia and Rins in a scary first-corner clash in Catalunya. He was fortunate to escape serious injury when his visor was ripped off after his head struck the rear tyre of Bagnaia's Ducati.

Then Nakagami became the luckless victim of contact with Marc Marquez on the opening lap in Aragon. Fortunately, with more than half the field following closely, he wasn't struck. Unfortunately, his right hand was trapped under his RC213V, and he was left with severe tendon damage to the third and fourth fingers.

Just five days after surgery in Barcelona, he was back on track at his home round in Japan, where he rode heroically to 20th. He needed further reconstructive surgery for a torn tendon in his little finger.

Takaaki Nakagami

Alex Marquez

He was replaced in Thailand, Australia and Malaysia by HRC test rider and compatriot Tetsuta Nagashima, following his own wild-card ride at Motegi.

Nakagami spent most of 2022 with a cloud hanging over his MotoGP future. His team was bankrolled once again by Japanese petroleum giant Idemitsu, which had ploughed huge investment into developing South and East Asian talent. His seat was constantly linked to the highly rated Ai Ogura, a leading light of the Idemitsu youth system since his World Championship debut in 2018.

Ogura publicly distanced himself from the constant speculation, and at times even hinted that he had little or no interest in moving to MotoGP until 2024. So, it wasn't a startling revelation when LCR and Honda confirmed that Nakagami had signed a one-year extension shortly before the Aragon Grand Prix in mid-September.

Lucio Cecchinello

Photos: Gold & Goose

WITHU YAMAHA RNF TEAM

TEAM STAFF

Razlan Ahmad RAZALI: Team Principal

Wilco ZEELENBERG: Team Manager

Marzlyny RAZALI: Team Principal's Executive Assistant

Cyril FRANCIS: Head of Partnership & Hospitality

Maria POHLMANN: Press Officer

Torleif HARTELMAN: Rider Analyst

Carl MEAKIN: Logistics & Warehouse Co-ordinator

Mats MELANDER: Parts Manager

ANDREA DOVIZIOSO/CAL CRUTCHLOW PIT CREW

Ramon FORCADA/Silvano GALBUSERA: Crew Chief

Andy GRIFFITH: Data Engineer

Stewart MILLER, Matthew LLOYD,

Benjamin FRY: Mechanics

Calum WILLEY: Mechanic/Tyres

DARRYN BINDER PIT CREW

Noel HERRERA CRISPI: Crew Chief

Daniel BONMATI GALVEZ: Data Engineer

Jorge MORELL ESTELA, Martin ZABALA ORDONO,

Hibbatuulah FUAD: Mechanics

BRUNO ZEELENBERG: Mechanic/Tyres

ANDREA DOVIZIOSO

Born: 23 March, 1986 – Forlimpopoli, Forli, Italy

GP Starts: 346 (248 MotoGP, 49 250cc, 49 125cc)

GP Wins: 24 (15 MotoGP, 4 250cc, 5 125cc)

World Championships: 1 125cc

Photos: Gold & Goose

DARRYN BINDER

Born: January 21, 1998 – Potchefstroom, South Africa

GP Starts: 137 (20 MotoGP; 117 Moto3)

GP Wins: 1 Moto3

THE days of a stable and successful Independent team in MotoGP seemed a distant memory for Yamaha at the end of 2022. Four years out from a surprise split from Tech3, after almost two decades, Yamaha would enter 2023 with just its official factory team for the first time in the modern four-stroke era.

It was a tale of hero to zero.

When Tech3 had jumped ship to KTM for 2019, in stepped the Petronas SRT squad. In its first year, it had set Fabio Quartararo on his road to MotoGP stardom and had come close to winning the 2020 title with Franco Morbidelli. In 2019 and 2020, it had dominated the Independent teams' championship and appeared destined for several glory years in partnership with the Iwata factory.

It all came crashing down when Malaysian oil and gas giant Petronas announced a shock withdrawal at the end of a fruitless 2021 campaign with Morbidelli and retiring superstar Valentino Rossi. Team principal Malaysian Razlan Razali rescued the project from oblivion by setting up his own private UK-registered company under the RNF Racing banner. The former CEO of the Sepang International Circuit inked a one-year deal to remain with Yamaha for 2022, with an option to extend into 2023 and 2024.

Wilco Zeelenberg remained in the high-profile role

YAMAHA YZR-M1

Engine: 1000cc liquid-cooled in-line 4, counter-rotating cross-plane crankshaft, DOHC, 4 valves per cylinder, pneumatic valve return system

Power: More than 240bhp

Ancillaries: Magneti Marelli ECU, Dorna software, ride-by-wire fuel injection, active Akrapovic titanium 4-into-2-into-1 exhaust

Transmission: Six-speed seamless-shift cassette-type gearbox, dry clutch

Frame: Aluminium twin-spar chassis, aluminium or carbon-fibre swing-arm, front and rear ride-height devices

Suspension: Öhlins inverted front fork, Öhlins rear shock absorber • *Wheels:* Forged magnesium, 17in diameter • *Tyres:* Michelin

Brakes: Brembo 320 or 340mm carbon-fibre twin front discs, single steel rear disc, thumb and foot levers

CAL CRUTCHLOW

Born: 29 October, 1985 – Coventry, England

GP Starts: 178 MotoGP

GP Wins: 3 MotoGP

World Championships: 1 World Supersport

Darryn Binder

Razlan Razali

Wilko Zeelenberg

Andrea Dovizioso

Photos: Gold & Goose

of team manager, but there was one notable casualty of the reshuffle. Former 250cc GP racer Johan Stigefelt had been a vital member of the Petronas operation across all three classes as team director. The squad also had entries in Moto3 and Moto2, but they were shut down completely after the Petronas withdrawal. Rumours of a rift between Razali and Stigefelt showed substance when it was confirmed that the Swede would not be part of the new RNF Racing project.

Stigefelt was not left seeking alternative employment for long. Although a much less frequent visitor to the paddock, he was hired by Rossi's VR46 brand as business development manager, responsible for new partnerships and business for VR46 and Rossi's Mooney-backed Ducati squad.

Razali's rescue deal was bankrolled by Italian company WithU, part of the Europe Energy Group. WithU gives customers the chance to sign up for electricity, gas, phone and internet services from a single supplier. The company was tempted in when Razali signed Andrea Dovizioso for 2022, after the former Ducati title contender had taken a sabbatical the previous year. He had been a member of the Petronas squad for the final five races of 2021, when Yamaha had been playing musical chairs in response to the bitter and premature departure of Maverick Vinales from its factory squad.

Equipped with a factory-spec 2022 YZR-M1, Dovizioso was expected to slot immediately back into race-winning contention, having been the only rider to consistently threaten Marc Marquez before the pandemic. To put it mildly, his campaign was disastrous. Immense experience notwithstanding, the Italian still couldn't solve the puzzle of how to match Quartararo's blistering speed on the YZR-M1.

Dovizioso inherited the crew who had worked with Morbidelli in his injury-ravaged final season at Petronas. His crew chief was the knowledgeable Ramon Forcada, who had won three MotoGP titles with Jorge Lorenzo at Yamaha.

In 19 races aboard a Yamaha, Dovizioso didn't notch a single top-ten. He wasn't fast enough, and he certainly wasn't enjoying being in the unusual position of midfield mediocrity. It was still something of a surprise, though, when during the build-up to the British Grand Prix at Silverstone in early August, he confirmed that he wouldn't even complete the season. He retired with immediate effect after his home grand prix at Misano. His place for the final six rounds of the season went to Briton Cal Crutchlow, still on Yamaha's books as official test rider.

The ramifications were quickly felt. WithU had been feeling the financial strain after a global surge in energy prices following the Russian invasion of Ukraine. It was widely reported in September that the company's boss, Matteo Ballarin, had stated that his company would no longer be in partnership with RNF Racing beyond 2022.

By that stage, Razali was already committed to an exciting new venture. The increasingly competitive Aprilia made an Independent team collaboration with the Noale factory a very attractive proposition.

During their home round at Mugello, Aprilia inked a milestone deal with RNF to run an Independent team for 2023 and 2024, with the option of a further two-year extension. Razali would have access to the 2022 RS-GP, and later in the season, it was announced that Miguel Oliveira and Raul Fernandez would form the new line-up.

Dovizioso's decision also brought a premature end to Forcada's MotoGP career, which had spanned more than 500 races, beginning in 1989, when he had worked with Alex Criville. Crutchlow preferred to bring in Silvano Galbusera, with whom he was working closely on the test team. Galbusera had been retained by Yamaha to work on its development projects after Valentino Rossi had axed him as crew chief at the end of 2019.

Crutchlow partnered Darryn Binder, the South African having become only the second rider to bypass the Moto2 class, as Jack Miller had done with a daring switch directly to MotoGP in 2015. The younger sibling of former Moto3 world champion Brad, he rode a 2021-spec YZR-M1, and it was certainly a baptism of fire. He scored points in just three races, with an impressive best of tenth in a wet Mandalika battle in Indonesia.

Binder worked with an entirely new pit crew following Rossi's departure, although some of them had been absorbed from the defunct Moto2 and Moto3 Petronas efforts. His crew chief was Noel Herrera Crispi, the 2021 technical brains behind Red Bull KTM Ajo rider Raul Fernandez's best Moto2 rookie season since Marc Marquez in 2011. Herrera Crispi would be reunited with Fernandez in 2023. Previously, he had also worked with Johann Zarco, Brad Binder and Oliveira.

Binder's career was due to take the unconventional route of Moto3 to MotoGP and then to Moto2, after he was thrown a career lifeline by the German-based Liqui Moly Intact squad.

TECH3 KTM

TEAM STAFF

Herve PONCHARAL: Team Manager

Fabien ROPERS: Parts/Design Manager

Mathilde PONCHARAL: Press Officer/Communication

Amelie JOURDAIN: Social Media Co-ordinator

Laurence COTTIN: Secretary

RAUL FERNANDEZ PIT CREW

Nicolas GOYON: Crew Chief

Alessandro DAMIA: Strategy Engineer

Carles SALO BRAUT: Data Engineer

Eric LABORIE, Thomas RUBANTEL,

David LIEBERT: Mechanics

Jerome PORCHET: Fuel & Tyres Manager

REMY GARDNER PIT CREW

Alexandre MERHAND: Crew Chief

Flavio NAPOLI: Strategy Engineer

Guillaume DUMAS: Data Engineer

Steve BLACKBURN, Herve GOURCY, Brice GROSSIN:

Mechanics

Pascal AUBEROUX: Fuel & Tyres Manager

RAUL FERNANDEZ

Born: 23 October, 2000 – Madrid, Spain

GP Starts: 78 (18 MotoGP, 18 Moto2, 42 Moto3)

GP Wins: 10 (8 Moto2, 2 Moto3)

REMY GARDNER

Born: 24 February, 1998 – Sydney, Australia

GP Starts: 134 (20 MotoGP, 93 Moto2, 21 Moto3)

GP Wins: 6 Moto2

World Championships: 1 Moto2

Photos: Gold & Goose

THERE was a huge buzz of anticipation and expectation when KTM promoted Remy Gardner and Raul Fernandez into the Tech3 squad for 2022. The pair had destroyed the opposition in Moto2 the previous season, winning 13 of 18 races and taking 24 podiums, which included an astonishing seven 1-2s.

What looked like being a dream team of speed and youth, however, rapidly turned into a nightmare for Herve Poncharal's French-based squad. By the end of a turbulent season, both riders were out of Tech3.

And Gardner, son of 1987 500cc world champion Wayne, was out of the MotoGP paddock less than 12 months after capturing the Moto2 crown for Red Bull in 2021.

Australia's first intermediate-class world champion since Kel Carruthers in 1969 was certainly not helped by turning issues that dogged KTM's RC16 throughout the season. Gardner scored points in only six races. He didn't register a single top-ten and appeared to butt heads with KTM management on more than one occasion in an instantly forgettable season. Reluctant to make a rapid return to Moto2, he opted to follow in the tyre tracks of Iker Lecuona, who had bombed out of Tech3 at the end of 2021 to rebuild his career and

KTM RC16 – Tech3

Engine: 1000cc liquid-cooled 86-degree V4, counter-rotating cross-plane crankshaft, DOHC, 4 valves per cylinder, pneumatic valve return system

Power: Approximately 265bhp, rev limit 18,500rpm

Ancillaries: Magneti Marelli ECU, Dorna software, ride-by-wire throttle, Akrapovic exhaust • *Lubrication:* Elf

Transmission: Six-speed seamless-shift cassette-type gearbox, dry clutch

Frame: Steel-tube chassis, carbon-fibre swing-arm, front and rear ride-height devices

Suspension: WP front and rear

Tyres: Michelin • *Brakes:* Brembo carbon-fibre twin front discs, single steel rear disc

Raul Fernandez

Remy Gardner

reputation in Honda's official World Superbike squad alongside Xavi Vierge.

On the eve of the Aragon round in mid-September, Gardner confirmed that World Superbikes was his 2023 destination. He would replace Garrett Gerloff in the GRT Yamaha squad.

Gardner's lone season in MotoGP was under the guidance of crew chief Alexandre Merhand. He was a long-serving Tech3 employee, who had worked as a strategy engineer for Johann Zarco, Miguel Oliveira and, most recently, Danilo Petrucci before being given the crew-chief promotion.

In Merhand's place came KTM factory track support strategy engineer Flavio Napoli, while the only other change to the 2021 line-up was mechanic Herve Gourcy in place of Jerome Poncharal, who had retired at the end of the previous season.

Fortunes weren't any better for Fernandez. He was paired with the majority of Lecuona's staff, led by long-standing Tech3 crew chief Nicolas Goyon. Factory strategist Alessandro Damia came in to replace Maxime Reysz, while Carles Salo was drafted in as new data engineer in place of Kylian Sauvage.

The Spaniard scored points in just six races and finished no higher than 12th, although he had the consolation of being ahead of Gardner, reversing their Moto2 positions. He also missed the Iberian Peninsula double-header in Portimao and Jerez after injuring his right hand in a practice crash in Portugal.

During his stellar Moto2 campaign, Fernandez had been promoted by KTM to Tech3 to fend off potential pursuers, Yamaha being among a big list of admirers chasing his signature for 2022. He never seemed enamoured with that decision, and deep in the 2022 season, KTM motorsport director Pit Beirer revealed that Fernandez had informed the Austrian factory as early as round six in Jerez that he would not ride an RC16 in 2023.

Fernandez had been hotly pursued by Independent Yamaha team boss Razlan Razali for 2022, and the Malaysian finally got his man. The Spaniard would form one half of a new RNF Aprilia project in 2023.

Back at Tech3 for 2023 would be Pol Espargaro, following his dismal seasons at Repsol Honda. The Spaniard had cut his teeth in MotoGP at Tech3 on a Yamaha, between 2014 and 2016, before embarking on a four-year stint with the official Red Bull-backed KTM project.

Espargaro's signing was confirmed on the eve of the Austrian Grand Prix in early August as part of an unveiling of a major strategy shift for KTM. As part of the Pierer Mobility Group, the GasGas brand had become synonymous with success in Moto3 and Moto2, after making its name in the off-road sector.

In Moto3, GasGas, Husqvarna and CFMoto were all rebadged KTMs, and now that would be replicated in MotoGP. Poncharal's Tech3 project would race KTM

Tech3 garage in Japan.

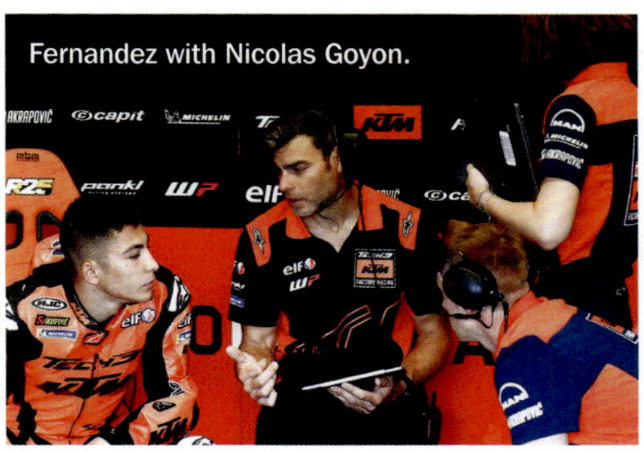
Fernandez with Nicolas Goyon.

Herve Poncharal

Photos: Gold & Goose

RC16 machinery badged as GasGas and be designated a factory team from 2023 onwards.

Espargaro's return would result in a major change in the Tech3 hierarchy for that year. He would be reunited with crew chief Paul Trevathan, with whom he had formed a close bond in the KTM works squad between 2017 and 2020.

The displaced Goyon would assume greater responsibility in 2023 as team manager, although not as a direct replacement for paddock devotee Herve Poncharal, but rather to help lessen the workload on the man who had created Tech3 in 1990. In addition to his team responsibilities, Poncharal would remain in the prominent role of International Race Teams Association president. And with a calendar extension to a record 21 races in 2023, it was possible that he would not attend all the rounds.

While KTM welcomed back the vast experience of Espargaro, he would be joined by another newbie hoping to avoid the same fate that had struck Gardner and Fernandez. Like Gardner, Spaniard Augusto Fernandez would arrive with a burgeoning reputation as Moto2 world champion in a move that was confirmed during the Aragon round in mid-September.

2022 TEAMS AND RIDERS

By PETER McLAREN

RED BULL KTM AJO made it back-to-back Moto2 World Championships, with Augusto Fernandez repeating Remy Gardner's path to glory during his debut season with the team.

The similarities continued, with Fernandez also partnering a rookie star (Pedro Acosta) and going on to seal a future MotoGP seat with Tech3 – at Gardner's expense.

But unlike the 2021 duel between Gardner and team-mate Raul Fernandez (no relation), Augusto's opposition came from Honda Team Asia's Ai Ogura, who took the fight to the final round.

Kalex cruised to its tenth successive constructors' and riders' titles by filling the top seven places. However, an unbeaten run of victories, stretching back to Silverstone in 2019, was finally broken by the Boscoscuro (ex-Speed Up) chassis, which celebrated its first wins since a certain Fabio Quartararo.

The rider on board, Alonso Lopez, wasn't even on the grid in Qatar. The 20-year-old was parachuted into Luca Boscoscuro's team at Romano Fenati's expense from Le Mans, but he still went on to challenge reigning Moto3 champion Acosta for Rookie of the Year.

A changing of the Moto2 guard was reflected by seven first-time winners. Celestino Vietti was among the new heroes in an unpredictable opening half, before collapsing from the title lead to seventh in the standings.

MV Agusta continued alongside Kalex and Boscoscuro as an official constructor, but was rarely in the points.

Technical development in the Triumph-powered class was limited to one in-season upgrade of the frame, swing-arm, main fairing and front fender.

Italian manufacturer Fantic will gain a foothold in Moto2 in 2023, after taking over the VR46 project, but is following KTM's example by running the Kalex chassis rather than its own frame.

A revised minimum age limit of 18 comes into effect for new riders from 2023, when Triumph has pledged to unleash an extra 400rpm and five more horsepower (over the current 140+) from the 765cc triple.

2022 MOTO 2 RIDERS

No.	Rider	Team
2	Gabriel Rodrigo	Pertamina Mandalika SAG Team - Kalex
4	Sean Dylan Kelly	American Racing - Kalex
5	Romano Fenati	Speed Up Racing - Boscoscuro
6	Cameron Beaubier	American Racing - Kalex
7	Barry Baltus	RW Racing GP - Kalex
8	Senna Agius	ELF Marc VDS Racing Team - Kalex
9	Jorge Navarro	Flexbox HP40 - Kalex
11	Mattia Pasini	GasGas Aspar Team - Kalex
12	Filip Salac	Gresini Racing Moto2 - Kalex
13	Celestino Vietti	Mooney VR46 Racing Team - Kalex
14	Tony Arbolino	ELF Marc VDS Racing Team - Kalex
16	Joe Roberts	Italrans Racing Team - Kalex
18	Manuel Gonzalez	Yamaha Master Camp Team - Kalex
19	Lorenzo Dalla Porta	Italtrans Racing Team - Kalex
20	Azroy Anuar	Petronas MIE Racing RW - Kalex
21	Alonso Lopez	Speed Up Racing - Boscoscuro
22	Sam Lowes	ELF Marc VDS Racing Team - Kalex
23	Marcel Schrotter	Liqui Moly Intact GP - Kalex
24	Simone Corsi	MV Agusta Forward Racing - MV Agusta
27	Kasma Daniel	Petronas MIE Racing RW - Kalex
28	Niccolo Antonelli	Mooney VR46 Racing Team - Kalex
29	Taiga Hada	Pertamina Mandalika SAG Team - Kalex
33	Rory Skinner	American Racing - Kalex
35	Somkiat Chantra	Idemitsu Honda Team Asia - Kalex
37	Augusto Fernandez	Red Bull KTM Ajo - Kalex
40	Aron Canet	Flexbox HP 40 - Kalex
42	Marcos Ramirez	MV Agusta Forward Racing - MV Agusta
51	Pedro Acosta	Red Bull KTM Ajo - Kalex
54	Fermin Aldeguer	Speed Up Racing - Boscoscuro
55	Alex Toledo	Pertamina Mandalika SAG Team - Kalex
61	Alessandro Zaccone	Gresini Racing Moto2 - Kalex
62	Stefano Manzi	Yamaha Master Camp Team - Kalex
64	Bo Bendsneyder	Pertamina Mandalika SAG Team - Kalex
72	Borja Gomez	Flexbox HP 40 - Kalex
74	Piotr Biesiekirski	Pertamina Mandalika SAG Team - Kalex
75	Albert Arenas	GasGas Aspar Team - Kalex
79	Ai Ogura	Idemitsu Honda Team Asia - Kalex
81	Keminth Kubo	VR46 Master Camp Team - Kalex
84	Zonta van den Goorbergh	RW Racing GP - Kalex
96	Jake Dixon	GasGas Aspar Team - Kalex
98	David Sanchis	MV Agusta Forward Racing - MV Agusta

Ai Ogura

Augusto Fernandez

Cameron Beaubier

Manuel Gonzalez

Lorenzo Dalla Porta

Marcos Ramirez

Bo Bendsneyder

Barry Baltus

Tony Arbolino

Aron Canet

Photos: Gold & Goose

Celestino Vietti

Jake Dixon

Fermin Aldeguer

Albert Arenas

Stefano Manzi

Sam Lowes

Alessandro Zaccone

Romano Fenati

Pedro Acosta

Joe Roberts

Somkiat Chantra

Alonso Lopez

Sean Dylan Kelly

Gabriel Rodrigo

Filip Salac

Jeremy Alcoba

Niccolo Antonelli

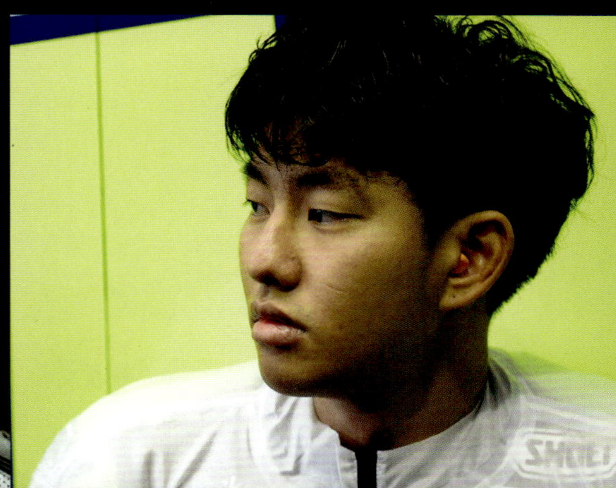

Keminth Kubo

Jorge Navarro

Marcel Schrotter

Photos: Gold & Goose

2022 TEAMS AND RIDERS

By PETER McLAREN

IZAN GUEVARA took the GasGas name to the top of the Moto3 World Championship during a dream one-two season for the Aspar Team. His success marked KTM's third riders' title in a row, after Albert Arenas and Pedro Acosta, but first for one of the factory's rebranded machines.

RC250s were entered under the KTM, GasGas, Husqvarna and (new for 2022) CFMoto banners, giving an artificially high impression of five Moto3 constructors for what, in reality, was again a KTM vs Honda technical contest.

Guevara had taken a race win in 2021, but he was overshadowed by Acosta, a rider he had beaten comfortably to the JuniorGP crown the previous year.

Team-mate Garcia had won twice by the time Guevara opened his 2022 tally, but the younger Spaniard went on to win almost half the races that followed. Impressively for the Moto3 class, Guevara's only non-scores were both out of his control.

Ayumu Sasaki was the only new grand prix winner of the season, while reigning runner-up Dennis Foggia, Jaume Masia, John McPhee and Andrea Migno joined Guevara and Garcia in adding to their victory tallies.

The world championship podium of Guevara, Garcia and top Honda rider Foggia won 14 of the 20 races between them, and all were set to move up to Moto2 for 2023.

Almost a quarter of the grid was comprised of rookies, a statistic set to be slashed in 2023 when the new minimum age limit of 18 (16 for the winner of the JuniorGP or Red Bull Rookies Cup) comes into force.

None of the newcomers came close to matching Acosta's 2021 heroics, with Diogo Moreira taking the Rookie title through consistency, while only Daniel Holgado and David Munoz featured on the podium.

Cost-saving initiatives introduced during the Covid pandemic mean that 2021's Moto3 machine specifications remain frozen until 2024.

2022 MOTO3 RIDERS

No.	Rider	Team
5	Jaume Masia	Red Bull KTM Ajo - KTM
6	Ryusei Yamanaka	MT Helmets-MSi - KTM
7	Dennis Foggia	Leopard Racing - Honda
9	Niccolo Carraro	QJmotor Avintia Racing Team - KTM
10	Diogo Moreira	MT Helmets-MSi - KTM
11	Sergio Garcia	GasGas Aspar Team - GasGas
16	Andrea Migno	Rivacold Snipers Team - Honda
17	John McPhee	Sterilgarda Husqvarna Max - Husqvarna
18	Matteo Bertelle	QJmotor Avintia Racing Team - KTM
19	Scott Ogden	Vision Track Racing - Honda
20	Lorenzo Fellon	SIC58 Squadra Corse - Honda
21	Vincente Perez	Rivacold Snipers Team - Honda
22	Ana Carrasco	BOE SKX - KTM
23	Elea Bertolini	QJmotor Avintia Racing Team - KTM
24	Tatsuki Suzuki	Leopard Racing - Honda
27	Kaito Toba	CIP Green Power - KTM
28	Izan Guevara	GasGas Aspar Team - GasGas
29	Harrison Voight	SIC58 Squadra Corse - Honda
31	Adrian Fernandez	Red Bull KTM Tech3 - KTM
34	Kanta Hamada	Rivacold Snipers Team - Honda
38	David Salvador	Sterilgarda Husqvarna Max - Husqvarna
41	Marc Garcia	CIP Green Power - KTM
43	Xavier Artigas	CFMoto Racing Pruestel GP - CFMoto
44	David Munoz	BOE SKX - KTM
48	Ivan Ortola	Angeluss MTA Team - KTM
53	Deniz Oncu	Red Bull KTM Tech3 - KTM
54	Riccardo Rossi	SIC58 Squadra Corse - Honda
63	Syarifuddin Azman	Rivacold Snipers Team - Honda
64	Mario Aji	Honda Team Asia - Honda
66	Joel Kelso	CIP Green Power - KTM
67	Alberto Surra	Rivacold Snipers Team - Honda
69	Maria Herrera	Angeluss MTA Team - KTM
70	Joshua Whatley	Vision Track Racing - Honda
71	Ayumu Sasaki	Sterilgarda Husqvarna Max - Husqvarna
72	Taiyo Furusato	Honda Team Asia - Honda
77	Filippo Farioli	GasGas Aspar Team – GasGas
80	David Alonso	GasGas Aspar Team - GasGas
82	Stefano Nepa	Angeluss MTA Team - KTM
85	Luca Lunetta	QJmotor Avintia Racing Team - KTM
87	Gerard Riu	BOE SKX - KTM
89	Marcos Uriate	Rivacold Snipers Team - Honda
91	Alessandro Morosi	MT Helmets-MSi - KTM
95	David Almansa	Finetwork Team BOE Motorsports – KTM
96	Daniel Holgado	Red Bull KTM Ajo – KTM
98	Jose Antonio Rueda	Rivacold Snipers Team - Honda
99	Carlos Tatay	CFMoto Racing Pruestel GP – CFMoto

Sergio Garcia

Izan Guevara

Andrea Migno

Riccardo Rossi

Daniel Holgado

John McPhee

Ryusei Yamanaka

David Munoz

Deniz Oncu

Dennis Foggia

Photos: Gold & Goose

Tatsuki Suzuki

Ayumu Sasaki

Xavier Artigas

Ivan Ortola

Carlos Tatay

Scott Ogden

Joel Kelso

Elia Bartolini

Taiyo Furusato

Syarifuddin Azman

David Salvador

Jaume Masia

Diogo Moreira

Adrian Fernandez

Kaito Toba

Stefano Nepa

Mario Aji

Lorenzo Fellon

Matteo Bertelle

Joshua Whatley

Ana Carrasco

Jose Antonio Rueda

MOTOGP · MOTO2 · MOTO3

GRANDS PRIX 2022

Reports by MICHAEL SCOTT & NEIL MORRISON

Statistics compiled by PETER McLAREN

Photo: Monster Energy Yamaha

Main: Bastianini managed to keep Binder's KTM at bay during a tense final lap.

Inset, right: Bastianini lofts Nadia Padovani, widow of Gresini team founder Fausto and first female MotoGP team principal winner, in an emotional moment on the podium.

Inset, centre: KTM's Brad Binder relishes the forthcoming fight.

Inset, top far right: Andrea Migno celebrates a long awaited second career win.

Inset, bottom far right: VR46 Racing's Celestino Vietti was a clear Moto2 winner.

Photos: Gold & Goose

FIM WORLD CHAMPIONSHIP · ROUND 1

QATAR GRAND PRIX

LOSAIL INTERNATIONAL CIRCUIT

Red Bull
KTM
33
KTM

DUNLOP
MONSTER
RIVACOLD
SNIPERS
JUSTSPEED

DUNLOP
QAT
moto2
mooney
VR 46

THE NEXT
23
33
KTM

Above: In the spotlight, but frustrated by Ducati's lack of direction, Pecco Bagnaia would end his race in the gravel.
Photo: Ducati Corse

Top right: Long day's journey into night. Dovi was back, but would not last the season.

Above right: Prematurely blonde, Quartararo looked apprehensive before the action.
Photos: Gold & Goose

Right: Pole-man Martin limbers up for an abbreviated race.
Photo: Pramac Ducati

RESTRICTED pre-season testing – just five days – had put up a few flags. Some would turn out to be meaningful, others possibly misleading. Although with a quartet of flyaway races that produced close finishes and very variable results, it would take time for the dust to clear.

The most portentous came from Enea Bastianini, after the strong finish to his rookie season. That had been on a 2019 Desmosedici; now he rode a GP21 – the bike on which Bagnaia had won four of the previous six races. Thus he was in the second tier of the expanded Ducati octet: factory teamsters Miller and Bagnaia, Pramac men Martin and Zarco, plus favoured satellite rider Luca Marini in the new Rossi/Mooney team had the latest GP22; while Bastianini, and rookies Marco Bezzecchi and Fabio Di Giannantonio had the previous year's model.

For now at least, this well-sorted hand-me-down was a blessing, fit for a perfectly judged victory, which made Bastianini the ninth maiden winner of the past two seasons. He would follow it up with another win in round four.

The new model was proving something of a handful, however, riders struggling to find the right balance, with none in the running for the podium. The usually phlegmatic Bagnaia railed at Ducati's pre-season strategy, prioritising testing over race preparation: "From his first day of test, Enea just put fuel in the bike and rode. We were too concentrated on developing ... I never rode the same bike for two days in a row. I was still discovering things during the race. You arrive to the race not ready, and this was the situation. This is something unacceptable. I need to focus more on my riding style, to adapt better and work for the track."

He and Miller had made a surprising engine-spec change ahead of the first race, to what Bagnaia described as "a mix of last year's engine and this new year's." Various Ducati riders had complained at the tests that the 2022 spec was too aggressive on the first touch of the throttle, but the other three GP22 riders stayed with it.

In the two test days at Sepang, the clearly much improved Aprilia also made a mark, with Aleix Espargaro second and Vinales fourth – not the first time that MotoGP's poor relation had made a strong showing early on, but somehow this time it was more suggestive; while third-fastest Rins on the power-up Suzuki demonstrated the upgrade. Defending champion Quartararo was sixth, continuing to complain that Yamaha was lagging on power and speed.

Three subsequent days at Mandalika were as much a test of the circuit (the surface was found somewhat wanting), but they gave Pol Espargaro the chance to lead, and speak encouragingly of the all-new Honda.

Team-mate Marc Marquez, after another winter of recuperation, this time from the troubling diplopia (double vision) that had cost him the end of the previous season and previously scuppered his 2011 Moto2 title bid, was short on training and preparation, and even doubtful for the first tests, a month before the first race. He was given the all-clear, however, and promised to play himself in gradually, placing eighth at the Sepang run and ninth in Indonesia. The new bike required some adaptation, he said.

KTM had left Sepang in a spin, with its riders 15th and 18th. But engineers pored over the data and worked on set-up improvements that made Brad Binder immediately competitive at Mandalika, and effectively reborn in Qatar. Such was his late-race speed that he came within three-tenths of

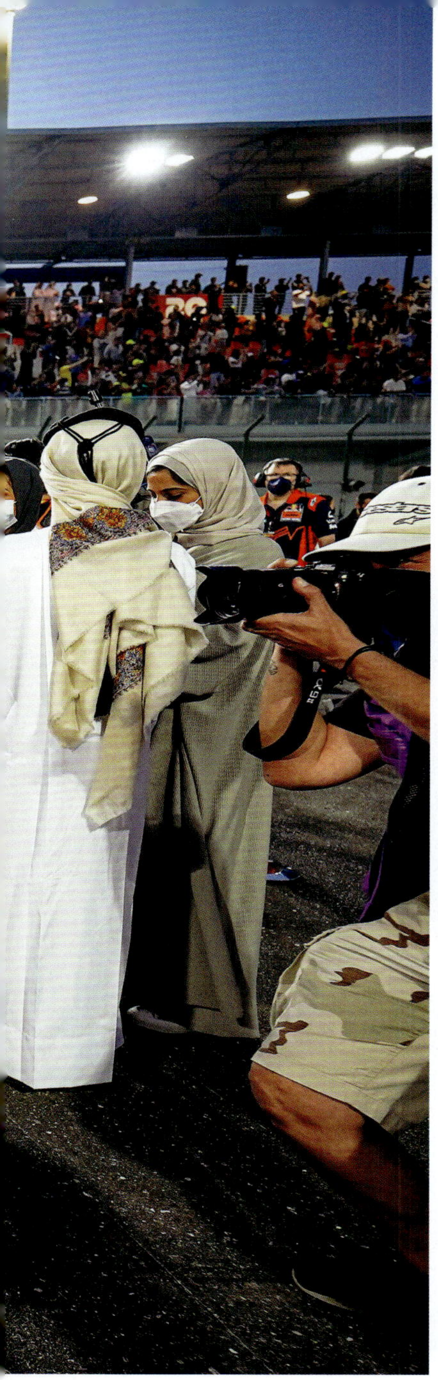

Bastianini. The improvement? "The bike turns! Normally, especially last year, unless we were braking really hard, we really struggled to get the front to start coming around on lean angle. Now I can release the front brake and just roll in with a lot more corner speed. You don't have to be completely on the limit of the brakes every corner."

There were important changes at Suzuki – first, a new team boss, after a year of management by committee following the departure of Davide Brivio to Formula 1. The Hamamatsu factory had recruited another Italian, Livio Suppo, already well travelled in the paddock, after fruitful years at Marlboro Ducati and Repsol Honda. Apart from introducing a hard-nosed management style, delaying suggested contract negotiations with the incumbent riders, this freed project leader Shinichi Sahara to focus on technical affairs.

The bike's improvement somewhat shamed the similarly in-line-four Yamaha. Mir spoke about better performance at high revs, and the speed gun proved the point. He was fastest all weekend, at 222.2mph, while Rins was second at 220.7. Bastianini's Ducati set an identical speed, and both Aprilias and both factory Hondas were next, at a whisker under 220.

For Yamaha, there was an uncomfortable reality check. Morbidelli placed 21st at 217.2mph, then Quartararo and Dovizioso, followed only by rookies Remy Gardner (KTM) and Darryn Binder (2021 Yamaha). At 216.4mph, the defending champion was giving away some 6mph, and it told, as he qualified 11th and raced to ninth, complaining once again of how being stuck in traffic overheated his front tyre. He finished 10.5 seconds off the winner: previously, the largest gap for the top Yamaha in the 1000cc era at this track had been 0.797 of a second. At this early stage, defending his crown successfully appeared a tall order.

With echoes of the furore caused by Ducati's introduction of the 'spoon' rear aero device in 2019, a row was brewing over another of Gigi Dall'Igna's innovations: a front ride-height device that riders could operate not only at the start line, but also during the race, had been seen on all the GP22s at pre-season testing. The rival factories in the MSMA put forward a condemnatory proposal to be discussed at the next GP Commission meeting, and before the end of March, the device had been banned from 2023 onwards.

The start of racing was a welcome distraction from the invasion of Ukraine a week before. Fears of a limp official reaction appeared to be confirmed on Thursday when the MotoGP field posed in front of the vapid, non-specific slogan 'United For Peace'. On Saturday, however, the FIM announced a series of tough sanctions, including the suspension of FIM licences to Russian and Belarusian federations, and suspension of their officials, effectively banning their riders and teams from all FIM activities. FIM President Jorge Viegas described the response as being "in line with the recommendations and statements made by the International Olympic Committee, adapted to suit our sport."

MOTOGP RACE – 22 laps

Martin's fifth pole in 15 races was a shade short of Bagnaia's 2021 record, but race time was fully 10.7 seconds inside the same year's fastest – one of a number of surprises. Among them, the fate of three fancied runners on the fancied Ducatis. Bagnaia and Martin went out after the former wiped out the latter, while Miller retired early with an electronics glitch.

Bastianini was alongside Martin, then Marc Marquez, with Miller, Aleix Espargaro and brother Pol behind them. Brad Binder and Quartararo were through from Q1, on the third and fourth rows respectively; Zarco missed the cut and started from 13th.

The first omen came at once, the Ducatis' potency off the line surprisingly dull. Martin dropped to seventh, Miller to tenth, Bagnaia to 14th. Instead, Honda's all-new RC213V showed the way. Espargaro led Marquez out of the first turn. Behind them, Binder and Mir made short work of Bastianini and Aleix Espargaro on lap one.

Rear tyre choice was open between Michelin's soft and medium, and Pol's choice of the soft required a plan to conserve rubber early on. Those thoughts were soon banished,

Above: **Moto3 champion Pedro Acosta found the move up to Moto2 harder than he and his fans had expected.**

Top: **Celestino Vietti led from pole to flag In Moto2.**

Above right: **Repsol's Pol Espargaro leads team-mate Marc Marquez early on. His podium finish flattered to deceive.**

Centre right: **Precocious Spanish teenager Izan Guevara's maiden pole was a powerful portent.**

Centre far right: **Another Spanish young gun, but Fermin Aldeguer's race went wrong.**

Below right: **Moto3 madness as Migno leads Sasaki, Toba, Oncu, Garcia, McPhee and the rest.**
Photos: Gold & Goose

however. After nipping under Marquez's Turn One overtaking attempt on the second lap, Espargaro laid down a ferocious pace at the front.

An early group of nine scrabbled to keep up, with Martin, Rins, Bagnaia and a feisty Quartararo joining the leaders.

It soon became clear that neither Marquez nor Mir could live with this rhythm, the Honda wide at Turn One, allowing Binder to nip by to second on lap six. Five turns later, and Bastianini was under Mir's Suzuki, before nabbing third at the final corner on lap seven. Suddenly, the top four had a gap in hand, with the Aprilia pushing to regain its place among them.

Rins had lost touch with the leaders by lap 12. Behind him, Bagnaia tucked the front at Turn One while attempting a pass on Martin. "I was a bit late on entry, but the braking was not too hard, so it was quite strange," said the Italian. Martin, meanwhile, had "feared for my life", caught between the two bikes when rolling through the gravel.

Up front, Pol was a second clear on lap 13. For Bastianini, it was time to react. He breezed by Binder on the run to Turn One a lap later and immediately started closing. By lap 19, he was within range, and as he charged past the Honda on the start/finish straight, Espargaro was sucked into the slipstream entering Turn One: "My speed increased so much I thought I would end in the gravel." He didn't go that far, rejoining behind Binder and ahead of brother Aleix, who had passed Marc Marquez on lap 17 with a fine move at Turn 15. Pol's early speed had exhausted his soft rear, and he had to work to hang on to third.

Quite suddenly, Bastianini had 1.3 seconds in hand, but Binder ensured that he couldn't rest. The last lap was a nervy affair, as the South African took tenths out of the lead in each sector. But the Italian just held on to claim the Gresini team's first premier-class win since Toni Elias had snitched the Portuguese GP in 2006. After Fausto Gresini's death from Covid in 2021, it was an emotional moment for the reconstituted outfit.

Pol just held off brother Aleix for third. Like Binder, he was enthused with his factory's efforts over the off-season; while Aleix rued time lost behind Mir, which had scuppered any podium hopes. "This is the first time I've felt I had the best pace of anyone," he said; 2.2 seconds off the winner was the closest Aprilia had been in the four-stroke era.

Marc Marquez, in fifth, admitted that he still needed to understand how to get the most from the new Honda; both Mir and Rins, sixth and seventh, were frustrated by a lack of front-end feel. Zarco pinched eighth from countryman Quartararo on the line, while Nakagami finished tenth, over a second clear of Morbidelli.

Vinales trailed in, then Marini and Dovizioso, after some to-and-fro. Finally, four rookies in a bunch, Gardner eventually getting the better of Darryn Binder, from Di Giannantonio and Fernandez. The fifth beginner, Bezzecchi, had crashed out early.

Also crashing out, Alex Marquez and Oliveira, while Miller retired on lap seven: "The bike was lost. I had 100 per cent power in some very strange points of the track: over the back of the track, it would give me a massive burst of throttle, then coming on to the front straight, no power. Everyone was passing me. It was better to pull in."

MOTO2 RACE – 20 laps

The departure of 2021's title top three – Gardner, Raoul Fernandez and Bezzecchi – was accompanied by some significant reshuffles.

Augusto Fernandez and title-winning Moto3 rookie Pedro Acosta had replaced the first two in the respected Red Bull Ajo team. Much was expected of both, especially Acosta, after having been fastest at pre-season tests in Portimao.

And the pre-eminence of Kalex was reinforced by the shrinkage of the Boscoscuro-chassis ranks to just two. Both Aron Canet and Jorge Navarro had moved to Kalex, but the Boscoscuro team did have a bright spot: the acquisition of 16-year-old Fermin Aldeguer, winner of the 2021 CEV Moto2 Junior World Championship. Eight impressive substitute rides

for the team in 2021 meant that he was not classified as a rookie – and nor would he perform like one.

Veteran Corsi and Marco Ramirez, on a pair of MV Agustas, were the only others not to use the German chassis.

But it was not one of the pre-season favourites who would shine in the desert. After a quietly efficient pre-season, second-year rider Celestino Vietti notched up a debut pole, while Fernandez, Canet and Acosta struggled in sixth, ninth and tenth respectively.

It was the precursor to a textbook ride and a massive victory. After getting the jump into Turn One, Vietti never looked back, using the added grip of Dunlop's softer rear tyre option and managing to make it last. The Rossi protégé ran riot for his first Moto2 win.

Canet took second from Arbolino on lap two, and as the Spaniard tried in vain to reel in Vietti, all eyes were on the fight for third, four seconds behind.

Double winner at the track in 2021, Sam Lowes shrugged off tendonitis in his left wrist to fight with Fernandez, Ai Ogura and Arbolino. The last named blew his chance when he hit a neutral at Turn Six, which dropped him to sixth. Fernandez thought third was sealed after neat moves on Lowes (Turn Ten, penultimate lap) and Ogura (Turn 15, last lap), but the Japanese rider's attempt at the final turn caused him to lose the front before barging Fernandez wide. Lowes got through for a 24th Moto2 podium, with Fernandez, Arbolino and Ogura just behind.

Navarro's first Kalex ride yielded a lonely seventh, ahead of American pair Roberts and Beaubier, who swapped places with three laps to go. Close behind, Marcel Schrotter saved tenth from Jake Dixon by a matter of hundredths. The Englishman, qualified seventh, had finished the first lap 20th after a tangle, but came through to hound the German for the latter half of the race.

Acosta's debut had been troubled. Pushed wide at the first turn by fellow white hope Aldeguer, he had finished lap one 24th, but had ridden through to 11th by the end, his last victim Albert Arenas, with two laps to go, and by less than a tenth. In turn, Aldeguer had come through from 21st to 16th, missing points by half a second.

MOTO3 RACE – 18 laps

The largest winning margin in the previous five Moto3 outings had been a meagre 0.053 of a second, so it was natural to expect a close contest. Yet for just over half of this race, Ayumu Sasaki made a mockery of that. The pole-starter's Husqvarna stretched the field seemingly at his whim, breaking clear to hold a three-second lead on the tenth lap, and still stretching.

The breakaway was helped by penalties for pre-race dawdling. Fastest qualifier Izan Guevara, pre-season favourite Dennis Foggia and new Leopard Honda team-mate Tatsuki Suzuki all started from the back of the grid, with a long-lap penalty for both Guevara and Suzuki, and a double long-lap for Foggia.

Sasaki's charge faltered on lap 11 when a near high-side at Turn Six threw him into the air. He landed back on the bike, but his fairing had broken loose and the chasing pack was soon upon him: Andrea Migno, Deniz Oncu, Kaito Toba and Sergio Garcia, the last recovering from a long-lap penalty after early contact with Carlos Tatay.

Starting the last lap, Migno had an edge that soon turned into a handy advantage as Toba and Garcia disputed second at Turns Four and Six. Then Garcia tried to chase down Migno, but it was too little, too late. Although he drew level on the run to the line, the top speed of the Snipers Honda was enough to hold off the GasGas by mere hundredths. Toba claimed third, Oncu was fourth, with John McPhee and impressive rookie Diogo Moreira completing a close top six. While not matching Acosta's 2021 win from the pit lane, Foggia and Guevara recovered impressively, coming home seventh and eighth.

FIM WORLD CHAMPIONSHIP: ROUND 1

GRAND PRIX OF QATAR

4-6 MARCH, 2022

LOSAIL INTERNATIONAL CIRCUIT

22 laps
Length: 5.380 km. / 3,343 miles
Width: 12m

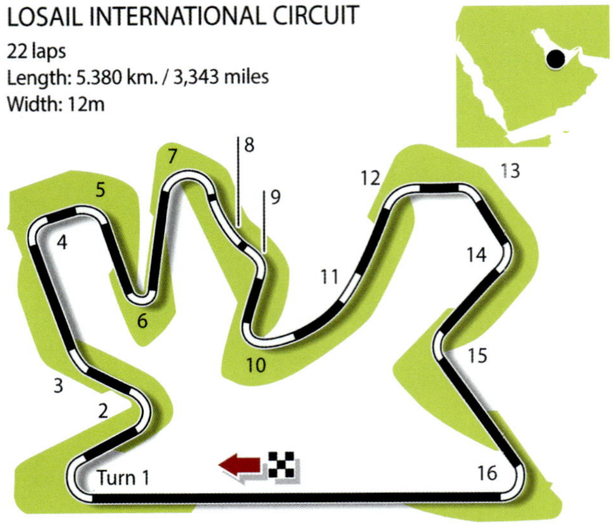

MotoGP

RACE DISTANCE: 22 laps, 73.545 miles/118.360km · RACE WEATHER: Dry (air 23°, humidity 53%, track 28°)

Pos.	Rider	Nat.	No.	Entrant	Machine	Tyres	Race tyre choice	Laps	Time & speed
1	**Enea Bastianini**	ITA	23	Gresini Racing MotoGP	Ducati Desmosedici	M	F: Soft/R: Medium	22	42m 13.198s 104.5mph/168.2km/h
2	**Brad Binder**	RSA	33	Red Bull KTM Factory Racing	KTM RC16	M	F: Medium/R: Medium	22	42m 13.544s
3	**Pol Espargaro**	SPA	44	Repsol Honda Team	Honda RC213V	M	F: Soft/R: Soft	22	42m 14.549s
4	**Aleix Espargaro**	SPA	41	Aprilia Racing	Aprilia RS-GP	M	F: Soft/R: Medium	22	42m 15.440s
5	**Marc Marquez**	SPA	93	Repsol Honda Team	Honda RC213V	M	F: Soft/R: Soft	22	42m 17.297s
6	**Joan Mir**	SPA	36	Team SUZUKI ECSTAR	Suzuki GSX-RR	M	F: Soft/R: Medium	22	42m 18.041s
7	**Alex Rins**	SPA	42	Team SUZUKI ECSTAR	Suzuki GSX-RR	M	F: Soft/R: Medium	22	42m 22.008s
8	**Johann Zarco**	FRA	5	Pramac Racing	Ducati Desmosedici	M	F: Soft/R: Soft	22	42m 23.734s
9	**Fabio Quartararo**	FRA	20	Monster Energy Yamaha MotoGP	Yamaha YZR-M1	M	F: Soft/R: Medium	22	42m 23.741s
10	**Takaaki Nakagami**	JPN	30	LCR Honda IDEMITSU	Honda RC213V	M	F: Medium/R: Soft	22	42m 28.165s
11	**Franco Morbidelli**	ITA	21	Monster Energy Yamaha MotoGP	Yamaha YZR-M1	M	F: Soft/R: Soft	22	42m 29.910s
12	**Maverick Vinales**	SPA	12	Aprilia Racing	Aprilia RS-GP	M	F: Soft/R: Medium	22	42m 36.414s
13	**Luca Marini**	ITA	10	Mooney VR46 Racing Team	Ducati Desmosedici	M	F: Soft/R: Soft	22	42m 40.481s
14	**Andrea Dovizioso**	ITA	4	WithU Yamaha RNF MotoGP Team	Yamaha YZR-M1	M	F: Soft/R: Medium	22	42m 40.572s
15	**Remy Gardner**	AUS	87	Tech3 KTM Factory Racing	KTM RC16	M	F: Medium/R: Medium	22	42m 54.305s
16	Darryn Binder	RSA	40	WithU Yamaha RNF MotoGP Team	Yamaha YZR-M1	M	F: Soft/R: Medium	22	42m 54.317s
17	Fabio Di Giannantonio	ITA	49	Gresini Racing MotoGP	Ducati Desmosedici	M	F: Soft/R: Medium	22	42m 54.547s
18	Raul Fernandez	SPA	25	Tech3 KTM Factory Racing	KTM RC16	M	F: Medium/R: Medium	22	42m 55.555s
	Jorge Martin	SPA	89	Pramac Racing	Ducati Desmosedici	M	F: Soft/R: Soft	11	DNF-crash
	Francesco Bagnaia	ITA	63	Ducati Lenovo Team	Ducati Desmosedici	M	F: Soft/R: Medium	11	DNF-crash
	Miguel Oliveira	POR	88	Red Bull KTM Factory Racing	KTM RC16	M	F: Medium/R: Medium	10	DNF-crash
	Alex Marquez	SPA	73	LCR Honda CASTROL	Honda RC213V	M	F: Soft/R: Soft	9	DNF-crash
	Marco Bezzecchi	ITA	72	Mooney VR46 Racing Team	Ducati Desmosedici	M	F: Soft/R: Soft	6	DNF-crash
	Jack Miller	AUS	43	Ducati Lenovo Team	Ducati Desmosedici	M	F: Soft/R: Soft	6	DNF-technical

Fastest lap: Enea Bastianini, on lap 17, 1m 54.338s, 105.2mph/169.3km/h.
Lap record: Francesco Bagnaia, 1m 54.491s, 105.1mph/169.1km/h (2021).
Event maximum speed: Joan Mir, 222.2mph/357.6km/h (race).

Qualifying

Weather: Dry
Air Temp: 21° **Humidity:** 75%
Track Temp: 24°

1	Martin	1m 53.011s
2	Bastianini	1m 53.158s
3	M. Marquez	1m 53.283s
4	Miller	1m 53.298s
5	A. Espargaro	1m 53.319s
6	P. Espargaro	1m 53.346s
7	B. Binder	1m 53.350s
8	Mir	1m 53.407s
9	Bagnaia	1m 53.411s
10	Rins	1m 53.481s
11	Quartararo	1m 53.635s
12	Morbidelli	1m 53.982s
	Q1	
13	Zarco	1m 53.780s
14	Oliveira	1m 53.819s
15	Bezzecchi	1m 53.915s
16	Nakagami	1m 54.038s
17	Marini	1m 54.222s
18	A. Marquez	1m 54.224s
19	Vinales	1m 54.228s
20	Dovizioso	1m 54.244s
21	Di Giannantonio	1m 54.276s
22	Gardner	1m 54.378s
23	Fernandez	1m 54.889s
24	D. Binder	1m 56.011s

Fastest race laps

1	Bastianini	1m 54.338s
2	A. Espargaro	1m 54.465s
3	B. Binder	1m 54.484s
4	P. Espargaro	1m 54.534s
5	Rins	1m 54.610s
6	M. Marquez	1m 54.643s
7	Bagnaia	1m 54.654s
8	Zarco	1m 54.671s
9	Mir	1m 54.689s
10	Martin	1m 54.771s
11	Oliveira	1m 54.831s
12	Morbidelli	1m 54.853s
13	Quartararo	1m 54.916s
14	Nakagami	1m 55.080s
15	A. Marquez	1m 55.205s
16	Vinales	1m 55.210s
17	Dovizioso	1m 55.415s
18	Bezzecchi	1m 55.446s
19	Marini	1m 55.480s
20	Miller	1m 55.520s
21	D. Binder	1m 55.591s
22	Fernandez	1m 55.954s
23	Gardner	1m 55.974s
24	Di Giannantonio	1m 55.982s

Championship Points

1	Bastianini	25
2	B. Binder	20
3	P. Espargaro	16
4	A. Espargaro	13
5	M. Marquez	11
6	Mir	10
7	Rins	9
8	Zarco	8
9	Quartararo	7
10	Nakagami	6
11	Morbidelli	5
12	Vinales	4
13	Marini	3
14	Dovizioso	2
15	Gardner	1

Constructor Points

1	Ducati	25
2	KTM	20
3	Honda	16
4	Aprilia	13
5	Suzuki	10
6	Yamaha	7

Grid order	1	2	3	4	5	6	7	8	9	10	11	12	13	14	15	16	17	18	19	20	21	22	
89 MARTIN	44	44	44	44	44	44	44	44	44	44	44	44	44	44	44	44	44	23	23	23	23	23	1
23 BASTIANINI	93	93	93	93	93	33	33	33	33	33	33	33	23	23	23	23	23	44	33	33	33	33	2
93 M. MARQUEZ	33	33	33	33	33	93	23	23	23	23	23	23	33	33	33	33	33	33	44	44	44	44	3
43 MILLER	36	36	36	36	36	23	93	93	93	93	93	93	93	93	93	93	41	41	41	41	41	41	4
41 A. ESPARGARO	23	23	23	23	23	36	41	41	41	41	41	41	41	41	41	41	93	93	93	93	93	93	5
44 P. ESPARGARO	41	41	41	41	41	41	36	36	36	36	36	36	36	36	36	36	36	36	36	36	36	36	6
33 B.BINDER	89	89	89	89	89	89	42	42	42	42	42	42	42	42	42	42	42	42	42	42	42	42	7
36 MIR	20	20	42	42	42	42	89	89	89	89	89	20	20	20	20	20	20	20	20	20	20	5	8
63 BAGNAIA	42	42	20	20	20	20	20	20	63	63	63	5	5	5	5	5	5	5	5	5	5	20	9
42 RINS	43	73	63	63	63	63	63	63	20	20	20	30	30	30	30	30	30	30	30	30	30	30	10
20 QUARTARARO	73	63	73	73	73	73	73	88	88	88	30	21	21	21	21	21	21	21	21	21	21	21	11
21 MORBIDELLI	88	43	43	88	88	88	88	73	73	30	5	12	12	12	12	12	12	12	12	12	12	12	12
5 ZARCO	30	30	88	72	72	72	30	30	30	5	21	10	10	10	10	10	4	4	4	10	10	10	13
88 OLIVEIRA	63	88	30	43	30	30	5	5	5	21	12	4	4	4	4	4	10	10	10	4	4	4	14
72 BEZZECCHI	72	72	72	30	43	5	21	21	21	10	10	87	87	87	87	87	40	40	40	87	87	87	15
30 NAKAGAMI	21	21	21	21	5	43	10	10	10	12	4	40	40	40	40	40	87	25	25	40	40	40	
10 MARINI	4	10	5	5	21	21	12	12	12	4	87	25	25	25	25	25	25	49	87	49	49	49	
73 A. MARQUEZ	10	5	10	10	10	10	40	4	4	40	40	49	49	49	49	49	49	87	49	25	25	25	
12 VINALES	5	4	4	4	12	40	4	40	40	87	25												
4 DOVIZIOSO	12	12	12	40	40	12	87	87	87	25	49												
49 DI GIANNANTONIO	40	87	40	12	87	4	49	25	25	49													
87 GARDNER	87	40	87	87	4	87	25	49	49														
25 FERNANDEZ	25	25	49	49	49	49																	
40 D.BINDER	49	49	25	25	25	25																	

43 Pit stop

Moto2

RACE DISTANCE: 20 laps, 66.860 miles/107.600km · RACE WEATHER: Dry (air 25°, humidity 52%, track 33°)

Pos.	Rider	Nat.	No.	Entrant	Machine	Laps	Time & Speed
1	**Celestino Vietti**	ITA	13	Mooney VR46 Racing Team	Kalex	20	39m 53.637s
							100.5mph/161.8km/h
2	**Aron Canet**	SPA	40	Flexbox HP40	Kalex	20	39m 59.791s
3	**Sam Lowes**	GBR	22	Elf Marc VDS Racing Team	Kalex	20	40m 03.818s
4	**Augusto Fernandez**	SPA	37	Red Bull KTM Ajo	Kalex	20	40m 03.896s
5	**Tony Arbolino**	ITA	14	Elf Marc VDS Racing Team	Kalex	20	40m 05.058s
6	**Ai Ogura**	JPN	79	IDEMITSU Honda Team Asia	Kalex	20	40m 05.968s
7	**Jorge Navarro**	SPA	9	Flexbox HP40	Kalex	20	40m 08.503s
8	**Joe Roberts**	USA	16	Italtrans Racing Team	Kalex	20	40m 09.008s
9	**Cameron Beaubier**	USA	6	American Racing	Kalex	20	40m 11.005s
10	**Marcel Schrotter**	GER	23	Liqui Moly Intact GP	Kalex	20	40m 12.545s
11	**Jake Dixon**	GBR	96	Inde GASGAS Aspar Team	Kalex	20	40m 12.595s
12	**Pedro Acosta**	SPA	51	Red Bull KTM Ajo	Kalex	20	40m 19.688s
13	**Albert Arenas**	SPA	75	Inde GASGAS Aspar Team	Kalex	20	40m 19.776s
14	**Jeremy Alcoba**	SPA	52	Liqui Moly Intact GP	Kalex	20	40m 25.392s
15	**Romano Fenati**	ITA	5	MB Conveyors Speed Up	Boscoscuro	20	40m 27.276s
16	Fermin Aldeguer	SPA	54	MB Conveyors Speed Up	Boscoscuro	20	40m 27.792s
17	Marcos Ramirez	SPA	42	MV Agusta Forward Racing	MV Agusta	20	40m 29.919s
18	Simone Corsi	ITA	24	MV Agusta Forward Racing	MV Agusta	20	40m 31.336s
19	Bo Bendsneyder	NED	64	Pertamina Mandalika SAG Team	Kalex	20	40m 34.231s
20	Manuel Gonzalez	SPA	18	Yamaha VR46 Master Camp Team	Kalex	20	40m 37.583s
21	Gabriel Rodrigo	ARG	2	Pertamina Mandalika SAG Team	Kalex	20	40m 37.984s
22	Alessandro Zaccone	ITA	61	Gresini Racing Moto2	Kalex	20	40m 42.817s
23	Keminth Kubo	THA	81	Yamaha VR46 Master Camp Team	Kalex	20	40m 43.840s
24	Zonta van den Goorbergh	NED	84	RW Racing GP	Kalex	20	40m 49.831s
25	Sean Dylan Kelly	USA	4	American Racing	Kalex	20	40m 49.973s
26	Niccolo Antonelli	ITA	28	Mooney VR46 Racing Team	Kalex	20	40m 49.994s
	Barry Baltus	BEL	7	RW Racing GP	Kalex	19	DNF-crash
	Lorenzo Dalla Porta	ITA	19	Italtrans Racing Team	Kalex	15	DNF-crash
	Filip Salac	CZE	12	Gresini Racing Moto2	Kalex	2	DNF-crash

Fastest lap: Celestino Vietti, on lap 6, 1m 59.053s, 101.0mph/162.6km/h.

Lap record: Thomas Luthi, 1m 58.711s, 101.3mph/163.1km/h (2019).

Event maximum speed: Fermin Aldeguer, 183.8mph/295.8km/h (race).

Qualifying

Weather: Dry

Air: 23° **Humidity:** 64%

Track: 30°

1	Vietti	1m 59.082s
2	Arbolino	1m 59.194s
3	Lowes	1m 59.226s
4	Salac	1m 59.287s
5	Ogura	1m 59.302s
6	Fernandez	1m 59.339s
7	Dixon	1m 59.357s
8	Aldeguer	1m 59.359s
9	Canet	1m 59.480s
10	Acosta	1m 59.528s
11	Beaubier	1m 59.551s
12	Navarro	1m 59.626s
13	Schrotter	1m 59.670s
14	Roberts	1m 59.671s
15	Arenas	1m 59.779s
16	Baltus	1m 59.833s
17	Bendsneyder	1m 59.971s
18	Chantra	2m 00.213s
	Q1	
19	Corsi	2m 00.063s
20	Dalla Porta	2m 00.151s
21	Ramirez	2m 00.151s
22	Alcoba	2m 00.270s
23	Rodrigo	2m 00.542s
24	Gonzalez	2m 00.551s
25	Zaccone	2m 00.957s
26	Kubo	2m 01.033s
27	Fenati	2m 01.137s
28	Kelly	2m 01.201s
29	V D Goorbergh	2m 01.327s
30	Antonelli	2m 01.874s

Fastest race laps

1	Vietti	1m 59.053s
2	Lowes	1m 59.062s
3	Canet	1m 59.107s
4	Ogura	1m 59.208s
5	Fernandez	1m 59.241s
6	Beaubier	1m 59.369s
7	Arbolino	1m 59.422s
8	Salac	1m 59.596s
9	Roberts	1m 59.635s
10	Dixon	1m 59.692s
11	Acosta	1m 59.714s
12	Navarro	1m 59.819s
13	Arenas	1m 59.960s
14	Schrotter	2m 00.005s
15	Aldeguer	2m 00.272s
16	Ramirez	2m 00.297s
17	Fenati	2m 00.306s
18	Corsi	2m 00.319s
19	Bendsneyder	2m 00.495s
20	Alcoba	2m 00.518s
21	Baltus	2m 00.538s
22	Dalla Porta	2m 00.909s
23	Gonzalez	2m 00.925s
24	Zaccone	2m 00.975s
25	Rodrigo	2m 00.988s
26	Kubo	2m 01.138s
27	Antonelli	2m 01.397s
28	Kelly	2m 01.501s
29	V D Goorbergh	2m 01.520s

Championship Points

1	Vietti	25
2	Canet	20
3	Lowes	16
4	Fernandez	13
5	Arbolino	11
6	Ogura	10
7	Navarro	9
8	Roberts	8
9	Beaubier	7
10	Schrotter	6
11	Dixon	5
12	Acosta	4
13	Arenas	3
14	Alcoba	2
15	Fenati	1

Constructor Points

1	Kalex	25
2	Boscoscuro	1

Moto3

RACE DISTANCE: 18 laps, 60.174 miles/96.840km · RACE WEATHER: Dry (air 27°, humidity 36%, track 41°)

Pos.	Rider	Nat.	No.	Entrant	Machine	Laps	Time & Speed
1	**Andrea Migno**	ITA	16	Rivacold Snipers Team	Honda	18	37m 59.522s
							95.0mph/152.9km/h
2	**Sergio Garcia**	SPA	11	Gaviota GASGAS Aspar Team	GASGAS	18	37m 59.559s
3	**Kaito Toba**	JPN	27	CIP Green Power	KTM	18	38m 00.095s
4	**Deniz Oncu**	TUR	53	Red Bull KTM Tech3	KTM	18	38m 00.116s
5	**John McPhee**	GBR	17	Sterilgarda Husqvarna Max	Husqvarna	18	38m 00.586s
6	**Diogo Moreira**	BRA	10	MT Helmets - MSI	KTM	18	38m 01.003s
7	**Dennis Foggia**	ITA	7	Leopard Racing	Honda	18	38m 01.473s
8	**Izan Guevara**	SPA	28	Gaviota GASGAS Aspar Team	GASGAS	18	38m 02.067s
9	**Ryusei Yamanaka**	JPN	6	MT Helmets - MSI	KTM	18	38m 02.264s
10	**Xavier Artigas**	SPA	43	CFMOTO Racing PruestelGP	CFMOTO	18	38m 05.577s
11	**Ivan Ortola**	SPA	48	Angeluss MTA Team	KTM	18	38m 05.602s
12	**Riccardo Rossi**	ITA	54	SIC58 Squadra Corse	Honda	18	38m 12.455s
13	**Stefano Nepa**	ITA	82	Angeluss MTA Team	KTM	18	38m 12.496s
14	**Adrian Fernandez**	SPA	31	Red Bull KTM Tech3	KTM	18	38m 12.511s
15	**Joel Kelso**	AUS	66	CIP Green Power	KTM	18	38m 12.606s
16	Daniel Holgado	SPA	96	Red Bull KTM Ajo	KTM	18	38m 12.521s
17	Matteo Bertelle	ITA	18	QJMotor Avintia Racing Team	KTM	18	38m 28.620s
18	Elia Bartolini	ITA	23	QJMotor Avintia Racing Team	KTM	18	38m 28.650s
19	Mario Aji	INA	64	Honda Team Asia	Honda	18	38m 29.019s
20	Ana Carrasco	SPA	22	BOE SKX	KTM	18	38m 42.630s
21	Gerard Riu Male	SPA	87	BOE SKX	KTM	18	38m 47.486s
22	Joshua Whatley	GBR	70	VisionTrack Racing Team	Honda	18	38m 47.794s
	Ayumu Sasaki	JPN	71	Sterilgarda Husqvarna Max	Husqvarna	12	DNF-crash
	Jaume Masia	SPA	5	Red Bull KTM Ajo	KTM	9	DNF-crash
	Alberto Surra	ITA	67	Rivacold Snipers Team	Honda	9	DNF-crash
	Scott Ogden	GBR	19	VisionTrack Racing Team	Honda	6	DNF-crash
	Lorenzo Fellon	FRA	20	SIC58 Squadra Corse	Honda	3	DNF-crash
	Tatsuki Suzuki	JPN	24	Leopard Racing	Honda	3	DNF-crash
	Carlos Tatay	SPA	99	CFMOTO Racing PruestelGP	CFMOTO	3	DNF-crash

Fastest lap: Dennis Foggia, on lap 12, 2m 5.561s, 95.8mph/154.2km/h.

Lap record: Romano Fenati, 2m 5.403s, 95.9mph/154.4km/h (2019).

Event maximum speed: Sergio Garcia, 153.2mph/246.5km/h (race).

Qualifying:

Weather: Dry

Air: 25° **Humidity:** 63%

Track: 32°

1	Guevara	2m 04.811s
2	Sasaki	2m 04.896s
3	Masia	2m 05.023s
4	Migno	2m 05.174s
5	Foggia	2m 05.189s
6	Yamanaka	2m 05.536s
7	McPhee	2m 05.549s
8	Garcia	2m 05.658s
9	Suzuki	2m 05.683s
10	Ortolá	2m 05.763s
11	Tatay	2m 05.900s
12	Oncu	2m 06.173s
13	Artigas	2m 06.384s
14	Toba	2m 06.400s
15	Holgado	2m 06.445s
16	Rossi	2m 06.631s
17	Kelso	2m 06.720s
18	Bertelle	2m 10.067s
	Q1	
19	Nepa	2m 06.391s
20	Ogden	2m 06.394s
21	Moreira	2m 06.705s
22	Surra	2m 06.907s
23	Fernandez	2m 06.997s
24	Fellon	2m 07.075s
25	Aji	2m 07.889s
26	Carrasco	2m 08.013s
27	Bartolini	2m 08.270s
28	Riu Male	2m 08.779s
29	Whatley	2m 09.679s

Fastest race laps

1	Foggia	2m 05.561s
2	McPhee	2m 05.623s
3	Artigas	2m 05.636s
4	Sasaki	2m 05.689s
5	Toba	2m 05.697s
6	Suzuki	2m 05.739s
7	Garcia	2m 05.770s
8	Oncu	2m 05.771s
9	Guevara	2m 05.844s
10	Yamanaka	2m 05.849s
11	Moreira	2m 05.849s
12	Rossi	2m 05.933s
13	Migno	2m 05.980s
14	Masia	2m 05.997s
15	Ortolá	2m 06.022s
16	Holgado	2m 06.050s
17	Fernandez	2m 06.065s
18	Kelso	2m 06.148s
19	Bertelle	2m 06.199s
20	Nepa	2m 06.285s
21	Aji	2m 06.300s
22	Fellon	2m 06.333s
23	Bartolini	2m 06.495s
24	Ogden	2m 06.497s
25	Surra	2m 06.778s
26	Tatay	2m 07.278s
27	Carrasco	2m 07.731s
28	Riu Male	2m 08.017s
29	Whatley	2m 08.143s

Championship Points

1	Migno	25
2	Garcia	20
3	Toba	16
4	Oncu	13
5	McPhee	11
6	Moreira	10
7	Foggia	9
8	Guevara	8
9	Yamanaka	7
10	Artigas	6
11	Ortolá	5
12	Rossi	4
13	Nepa	3
14	Fernandez	2
15	Kelso	1

Constructor Points

1	Honda	25
2	GASGAS	20
3	KTM	16
4	Husqvarna	11
5	CFMOTO	6

Main: Quartararo and Oliveira dispute the lead on the soaked surface at the end of lap one, chased by Miller and Rins. They would not be this close again.
Photo: Monster Energy Yamaha

Insets, left to right: That winning feeling. Oliveira, Foggia and first-timer Chantra enjoy the moment.
Photos: Gold & Goose

FIM WORLD CHAMPIONSHIP · ROUND 2

INDONESIAN GRAND PRIX

MANDALIKA CIRCUIT

INTERNATIONALE
Honda
Asia
Arai

KTM

Above: **Brothers at odds. Brad Binder forces his KTM inside inspired younger sibling Darryn.**

Above right: **Under pressure. Michelin's Piero Taramasso had to explain an unconventional tyre solution.**

Right: **Another miserable crash-strewn weekend for Marc Marquez, his season starting to unravel.**

Centre far right: **Mr Muscle-Man Miller just missed the podium.**

Below far right: **Quartararo and Yamaha were back on form for a first pole in 13 races.**

Photos: Gold & Goose

THE return to Indonesia, reviving a short-lived event of 25 years before, was a skin-of-the-teeth exercise. An example of getting away with it. The event itself came under threat when the track surface – having already undergone one emergency repair following the tests four weeks before – started to break up again. A rescue package was devised, with severely shortened races – and then the weather struck. For a while on Sunday, cancellation of the main event became a real possibility.

The layout of the new Mandalika circuit, planned as part of an as-yet unbuilt beachside resort on the island of Lombok, was instantly popular, with 17 corners offering a varying challenge. Problems surfaced, literally, at the tests. Thanks partly to blazing heat, the track began to break up. A hasty resurfacing job was carried out between the 17th corner and Turn Five.

However, the weaknesses resurfaced. On Thursday, several of those walking the track noticed that in some places, it was breaking up underfoot. Friday rain and cooler temperatures brought some relief, although riders observed that straying even slightly off line was perilous.

Sunday started with the Moto3 race, which revealed serious worries, the asphalt in Turns Two, Three and 17 coming to bits. Emergency measures were implemented: the Moto2 race shortened from 25 laps to 16, MotoGP down to 20 from 27, the official reason being the heat, with track temperatures threatening to exceed 50 degrees.

After the Moto2 race, Sam Lowes said, "The only place I could notice was T17, but if the MotoGP race is dry… it's very bad. They won't get back. Bad."

Light rain had started, offering relief both for comfort and the track surface – until it intensified, to the point where standing water and minimal visibility forced the start to be deferred, not once, but twice. With the majority of the paddock booked on flights out of Lombok on Sunday evening, there was a real fear that the main event wouldn't go ahead. This was hardly allayed when a *pawang hujan* (rain whisperer) was deployed in the pit lane, smiling and beating a gong to clear the clouds. But this seemed to work, and eventually the race went ahead, 75 minutes late, with rain still falling, but in conditions that at least were acceptable.

Extreme heat had triggered another curve ball. After the tests, when tyres had suffered blistering, Michelin had elected to change the rear tyre allocation, bringing back a stiffer construction, last used in 2018 at the Thai GP, albeit with 2022 compounds. That forced everyone to revise their settings, with Suzuki riders among those complaining. Honda, fastest at pre-season tests, were the worst affected, with all riders struggling for rear grip on a bike that, compared with its predecessor, was biased towards the rear.

Consequences were especially severe for Marc Marquez, who characteristically had decided on a high-risk approach. He crashed three times on Friday and Saturday, including twice within seven minutes in Q1, which scuppered his chances of moving into Q2, leaving him 15th on the grid. But he wouldn't get there.

In Sunday morning's warm-up, he suffered a massive high-side at Turn Seven – taken in fourth gear at around 125mph. A blow to his head in a sickening landing left him dizzy and put him out of the race. Things would get worse. On the flight home, he noticed the return of the troublesome double vision, and during a worrying fortnight that followed, he would miss the next race as well.

Pol Espargaro was especially critical of the tyres, likewise

team manager Alberto Puig, perplexed by the decision, since all MotoGP bikes had been designed to extract the best from Michelin's current rear tyre profile, first introduced in 2020. "With four-year-old tyres, this bike isn't made for it," said Puig, prompting a waspish response from Michelin's Piero Taramasso, who expressed surprise that "only he" did not understand the tyre switch, and only Honda was unable to adapt. Ironically, the wet race rendered irrelevant all difficulties, but instead Espargaro suffered a lack of vision in the spray, after starting mid-pack in 15th.

This was not the only squabble of the weekend, with post-race tension between Quartararo and Miller, after the pair had made contact when contesting second place at the start of lap two. "He proceeded to ride his motorcycle into my leg," said Miller. "The Yamaha turns well, but that doesn't mean you open gas and aim for my front tyre." Quartararo was unfazed: "I don't care. He is the one in the past that also had some aggressive moves. I think my move was really not aggressive."

The Frenchman's confidence had been boosted after floundering in Qatar, usually a good Yamaha track. He claimed a first pole position since the previous June before fighting back to an impressive second in the wet on Sunday. "There are two things," he said, "… not so much of a straight, and the grip is much higher. When we have rear grip, we can be super-fast, but when we don't, there is a big drop. There is not something in the middle. It's really good or really bad."

On race eve, Bagnaia backtracked on his emotional post-race outburst in Qatar, where he had slammed Ducati for concentrating on development rather than race set-up. "The message that I passed on was that I didn't want to do it again. But … it's clear in a factory team you have to do it like this. Maybe because I was angry about a lot of questions, I said things not correct."

The levelling-up caused by the wet track produced two heroes, one of them most unexpected. As good as winner Miguel Oliveira's ride had been, for many, Darryn Binder had been the standout performer. The rookie had his first taste of fully wet conditions aboard a MotoGP machine on the sighting lap, but fought his way through the field from 22nd to sit ahead of brother Brad in eighth with two laps to go, slipping to a still fine tenth at the flag. "When it started raining before the race, I thought I may as well attack. From the out-lap to the grid, I was really impressed with the grip the wet tyres had. Every lap, I couldn't believe the feeling they gave. Before I knew it, I was catching riders in front of me – and my brother!"

MOTOGP RACE – 20 laps (shortened)

Quartararo was two-tenths clear of Martin for a fine pole, with Zarco completing the front row. Brad Binder led the second from Bastianini and Bagnaia, through from Q1.

Concerns about tyre life and track integrity remained and were only slightly alleviated by the decision to cut the race from 27 to 20 laps. Then, in the closing stages of the preceding Moto2 race, spots of rain fell, soon becoming a mighty deluge.

Bemused teams, riders and some 70,000 spectators (fewer than expected) waited for more than an hour as the drenching rain fell, the race scheduled for 15:00 finally getting going at 16:15 when it eased sufficiently. A short spell on day two of the Sepang test aside, the sighting lap was the first chance for the MotoGP field to acclimatise to their 2022 bikes in the wet.

There was plenty to admire in the way Oliveira and Miller gained two and six places respectively on the first lap, to sit behind Quartararo. Martin went the other way after bogging down off the line, likewise Bagnaia, who was 12th at the end of lap one.

For all the complaints over the weekend, the wet grip was noteworthy. Mir was left incredulous after finding the limits early on: "I was touching the elbows on ground in every corner. And I said, 'Is this really wet?' Unbelievable!"

Yet the exit of the final turn was an exception. Quartararo soon found this at the close of lap one, when he became crossed up, allowing Oliveira to breeze by. Miller followed suit at the first turn before snatching the lead at Turn Four. Rins, Martin, Zarco, Morbidelli (up from 12th on the grid) and Mir (from 18th) were just behind.

Those in the pack were disadvantaged by terrible visibility – spray in the air and rain on visors. That's what Miller and Oliveira had in hand as they moved clear of the rest.

Quartararo continued to have issues on the exit of T17, with Rins and Zarco breezing by at the start of lap four. By then, the leading duo was 2.4 seconds clear.

Meanwhile, a number of title favourites were experiencing a day to forget. Bagnaia ran off track on lap six after losing the front at Turn One, slowly falling down the order thereafter. Martin crashed out when braking upright for the same corner two laps later. Oliveira's Red Bull KTM team-mate, Brad Binder, was mired in the pack after his ride-height device malfunctioned off the start. "I did the whole race with the ride-height device completely down," he said.

Up front, it soon became clear that Miller was struggling. As Oliveira built up a handy margin, Rins, Zarco and Quartararo were all faster than the Australian the tenth time around. By lap 15, Zarco was not only third, but also pushing

Above: **The scenic seaside location brought searing heat and drenching rain. Quartararo was able to make the most of it.**
Photo: Monster Energy Yamaha

Top right: **Somkiat Chantra claimed a breakthrough Moto2 win for Honda Team Asia, the first Thai rider to do so.**
Photo: Gold & Goose

Above right: **Johann Zarco, chased by Rins, made a podium return.**
Photo: Pramac Racing

Above far right: **Rookies Diogo Moreira and Mario Aji flank Carlos Tatay, an unexpected front-row trio for Moto3.**

Right: **Moto3 unleashed, as run-away winner Foggia (7) disputes the first corner with Garcia (11).**
Photos: Gold & Goose

Miller for second, outbraking his fellow Ducati rider at Turn Ten, only to run wide and lose the place. But now Quartararo was the coming man, rallying after his earlier wobbles and passing Zarco brilliantly at Turn 16, and again on the exit of the first turn on the following lap.

The Frenchman still wasn't satisfied. A beautiful switch back on Miller at Turn 12 was good enough for second, and off he tore in search of Oliveira. The reigning champion was a full 1.1 seconds quicker than the leader the next time around as he posted the fastest lap of the race. But the KTM rider responded to win by 2.2 seconds. "If the race had seven laps more, I don't know if I'd have won," he admitted.

Zarco was third for a first podium since the previous June, Miller a couple of seconds adrift. Likewise Rins and Mir, readily admitting that the rain had saved them after dry set-up problems; Morbidelli came home a lonely seventh, 16 seconds behind.

The elder Binder won a brilliant eight-rider battle for eighth, heading Aleix Espargaro, his inspired brother, Darryn, Bastianini, Pol Espargaro, Alex Marquez, Marini and Bagnaia, all eight over the line inside 3.5 seconds. Vinales was less than two seconds down. Dovizioso pitted, after battling a Yamaha with a blank dashboard and a loose left handlebar grip – problems ranging from the esoteric to the mundane.

The unexpected early title leader-board remained surprising, with Bastianini narrowly ahead of Binder, Quartararo and Oliveira, all covered by five points; while Oliveira's win took KTM to the top of the constructors' table for the first time.

MOTO2 RACE – 16 laps (shortened)

With the race scheduled for 13:20, concerns grew about the track, the tarmac breaking up around Turns Two, Three and 17. Relief came when Race Direction confirmed a cut from 25 to 16 laps, a (slightly notional) two-thirds distance.

That meant a slight change in tactics, but it could not have predicted the rabbit-from-a-hat result. Thai rider Somkiat Chantra, who had missed the opening round with hand injuries sustained in a practice crash, posted the performance of a seasoned contender, rather than the crash-happy, erratic rider we had seen over his three previous years in the class.

Starting from fourth, after making his way through from Q1, he passed pole-sitter Jake Dixon and Sam Lowes at Turn One, and never looked back. It was no walk in the park, as rain began to pepper the track on lap four, by which time, Chantra's lead exceeded 1.5s. Any fears that he might crack under pressure were shattered emphatically when he posted fastest lap on the 12th. Coming home 3.2 seconds clear, he became the first Thai GP winner in history.

Dixon's career-first pole reflected his pleasure at gelling with his new Aspar team and, he said, showed the potential he'd had all along. Fernandez was alongside, then Lowes, making it a double British affair.

Bendsneyder (another Q1 escapee) and Arenas were alongside Chantra on row two; Qatar winner Vietti headed Arbolino and Corsi (also ex-Q1) on the third. Acosta was tenth and Aldeguer 12th, sandwiching Beaubier, but Acosta faced a long-lap penalty after crashing under a yellow flag during FP2.

The battle for second was led for four laps by Lowes, from Dixon, with Canet and Vietti soon joining in, ahead of the fading Corsi's MV Agusta.

Dixon passed Lowes on lap five at Turn Seven. Three turns later, he tucked the front, ruining what had been a fine weekend until then. Convinced that rain was at play and already struggling for rear grip, Lowes was spooked, which gave Vietti and Canet a crucial gap that they carried to the flag, the Italian and Spaniard finishing just over a second apart, to complete a multi-national podium.

Corsi crashed on the same lap, while four seconds behind Lowes, Fernandez was engaged with Ogura, Aldeguer and Arbolino. The last named had dropped away by a couple of seconds at the end, but the first three were over the line inside half a second.

Acosta had dropped from seventh to 16th while taking his long-lap the fourth time around, but immediately he started moving forward. Two laps from the end, he caught and passed Arenas to finish ninth. Roberts, Beaubier, Navarro, rookie Alcoba and Bendsneyder followed Arenas over the line, all within just over two seconds, to tie up the points.

Fellow ex-Moto3 rookies Rodrigo and Antonelli, both seasoned campaigners, were still somewhat at sea, finishing

well out of touch, 22nd and 25th, while promising teenage beginner Zonta van den Goorbergh, son of former Dutch ace Jurgen, was more impressive in 23rd.

MOTO3 RACE – 23 laps

The first and, most unusually, longest race of the day failed to yield the expected close fight for victory, with Foggia and the turquoise Leopard Honda utterly dominant. At times, he was seven-tenths faster than the rest per lap. By the 14th, he was more than five seconds clear and could cruise to the end, to win by 2.6 seconds.

Tatay was on pole, with two rookies alongside: Brazilian Diogo Moreira and local hero Mario Aji. Foggia was at the far end of row two, alongside Migno; fellow title favourites Garcia, Guevara and Oncu on the third.

Foggia had broken free of battling Aspar GasGas teammates Guevara and Garcia by lap three, leaving a growing fight for second. The Aspar infighting bunched a host of riders together, including Migno, Tatay, Sasaki, Artigas and Masia.

Amid the early exchanges, Tatay was handed a long-lap penalty for taking a short cut at Turn Nine. Fighting back, he carved through the pack to fourth with a lap to go. Guevara had just broken clear in second, and Tatay took third from Garcia on the final lap as Sasaki T-boned Migno at Turn Ten, both crashing out. Oncu was narrowly fifth from Artigas, Bartolini, Holgado and Suzuki.

Australian rookie Kelso was metres away from a top-ten when he collided with Nepa, taking both down.

Briton Scott Ogden was 13th, one place ahead of fast qualifier Aji, the first points for each of the rookies.

FIM WORLD CHAMPIONSHIP: ROUND 2

PERTAMINA GRAND PRIX OF INDONESIA

18–20 MARCH, 2022

PERTAMINA MANDALIKA CIRCUIT

Circuit: 4.313km / 2.680 miles
20 laps
Width: 15m

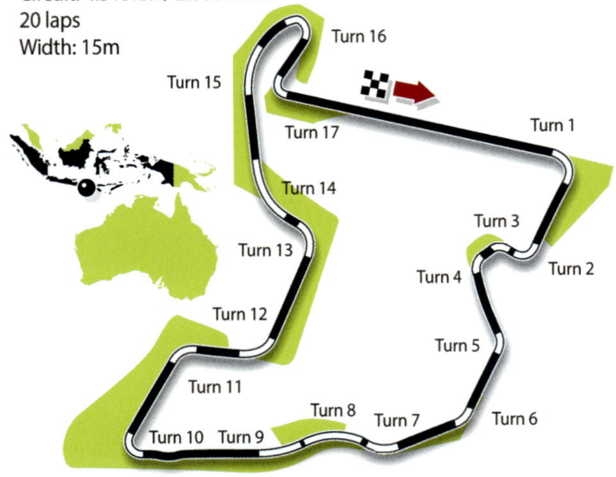

MotoGP

RACE DISTANCE: 20 laps, 53.450 miles/86.020km · RACE WEATHER: Wet (air 25°, humidity 98%, track 28°)

Pos.	Rider	Nat.	No.	Entrant	Machine	Tyres	Race tyre choice	Laps	Time & speed
1	**Miguel Oliveira**	POR	88	Red Bull KTM Factory Racing	KTM RC16	M	F: M Wet/R: M Wet	20	33m 27.223s 95.8mph/154.2km/h
2	**Fabio Quartararo**	FRA	20	Monster Energy Yamaha MotoGP	Yamaha YZR-M1	M	F: M Wet/R: M Wet	20	33m 29.428s
3	**Johann Zarco**	FRA	5	Pramac Racing	Ducati Desmosedici	M	F: M Wet/R: M Wet	20	33m 30.381s
4	**Jack Miller**	AUS	43	Ducati Lenovo Team	Ducati Desmosedici	M	F: M Wet/R: M Wet	20	33m 32.886s
5	**Alex Rins**	SPA	42	Team SUZUKI ECSTAR	Suzuki GSX-RR	M	F: M Wet/R: M Wet	20	33m 34.267s
6	**Joan Mir**	SPA	36	Team SUZUKI ECSTAR	Suzuki GSX-RR	M	F: M Wet/R: M Wet	20	33m 35.055s
7	**Franco Morbidelli**	ITA	21	Monster Energy Yamaha MotoGP	Yamaha YZR-M1	M	F: M Wet/R: M Wet	20	33m 48.338s
8	**Brad Binder**	RSA	33	Red Bull KTM Factory Racing	KTM RC16	M	F: M Wet/R: M Wet	20	33m 59.636s
9	**Aleix Espargaro**	SPA	41	Aprilia Racing	Aprilia RS-GP	M	F: M Wet/R: M Wet	20	33m 59.809s
10	**Darryn Binder**	RSA	40	WithU Yamaha RNF MotoGP Team	Yamaha YZR-M1	M	F: M Wet/R: M Wet	20	34m 00.124s
11	**Enea Bastianini**	ITA	23	Gresini Racing MotoGP	Ducati Desmosedici	M	F: M Wet/R: M Wet	20	34m 00.339s
12	**Pol Espargaro**	SPA	44	Repsol Honda Team	Honda RC213V	M	F: M Wet/R: M Wet	20	34m 00.822s
13	**Alex Marquez**	SPA	73	LCR Honda CASTROL	Honda RC213V	M	F: M Wet/R: M Wet	20	34m 00.958s
14	**Luca Marini**	ITA	10	Mooney VR46 Racing Team	Ducati Desmosedici	M	F: M Wet/R: M Wet	20	34m 02.214s
15	**Francesco Bagnaia**	ITA	63	Ducati Lenovo Team	Ducati Desmosedici	M	F: M Wet/R: M Wet	20	34m 02.986s
16	Maverick Vinales	SPA	12	Aprilia Racing	Aprilia RS-GP	M	F: M Wet/R: M Wet	20	34m 04.620s
17	Raul Fernandez	SPA	25	Tech3 KTM Factory Racing	KTM RC16	M	F: M Wet/R: M Wet	20	34m 09.198s
18	Fabio Di Giannantonio	ITA	49	Gresini Racing MotoGP	Ducati Desmosedici	M	F: M Wet/R: M Wet	20	34m 15.138s
19	Takaaki Nakagami	JPN	30	LCR Honda IDEMITSU	Honda RC213V	M	F: M Wet/R: M Wet	20	34m 16.694s
20	Marco Bezzecchi	ITA	72	Mooney VR46 Racing Team	Ducati Desmosedici	M	F: M Wet/R: M Wet	20	34m 16.696s
21	Remy Gardner	AUS	87	Tech3 KTM Factory Racing	KTM RC16	M	F: M Wet/R: M Wet	20	34m 23.187s
	Jorge Martin	SPA	89	Pramac Racing	Ducati Desmosedici	M	F: M Wet/R: M Wet	7	DNF-crash
	Andrea Dovizioso	ITA	4	WithU Yamaha RNF MotoGP Team	Yamaha YZR-M1	M	F: M Wet/R: M Wet	6	DNF-technical
	Marc Marquez	SPA	93	Repsol Honda Team	Honda RC213V	M		-	DNS-Injured

Fastest lap: Fabio Quartararo, on lap 17, 1m 38.749s, 97.4mph/156.7km/h.
Lap record: New circuit.
Event maximum speed: Marco Bezzecchi, 196.2mph/315.7km/h (qualifying).

Qualifying

Weather: Dry
Air Temp: 30° **Humidity:** 67%
Track Temp: 42°

1	Quartararo	1m 31.067s
2	Martin	1m 31.280s
3	Zarco	1m 31.378s
4	B. Binder	1m 31.433s
5	Bastianini	1m 31.504s
6	Bagnaia	1m 31.507s
7	Oliveira	1m 31.566s
8	Rins	1m 31.582s
9	Miller	1m 31.714s
10	A. Espargaro	1m 31.723s
11	Di Giannantonio	1m 31.829s
12	Morbidelli	1m 32.336s
	Q1	
13	Marini	1m 31.666s
14	Bezzecchi	1m 31.695s
15	M. Marquez	1m 31.830s
16	P. Espargaro	1m 31.831s
17	Dovizioso	1m 31.870s
18	Mir	1m 31.875s
19	A. Marquez	1m 31.987s
20	Vinales	1m 32.006s
21	Fernandez	1m 32.122s
22	Gardner	1m 32.140s
23	D. Binder	1m 32.299s
24	Nakagami	1m 32.330s

Fastest race laps

1	Quartararo	1m 38.749s
2	Zarco	1m 38.843s
3	Mir	1m 39.020s
4	Oliveira	1m 39.205s
5	Miller	1m 39.356s
6	Rins	1m 39.411s
7	Vinales	1m 39.472s
8	Bastianini	1m 39.538s
9	Morbidelli	1m 39.798s
10	B. Binder	1m 40.146s
11	D. Binder	1m 40.164s
12	A. Espargaro	1m 40.171s
13	Fernandez	1m 40.199s
14	Gardner	1m 40.245s
15	Bagnaia	1m 40.370s
16	A. Marquez	1m 40.474s
17	P. Espargaro	1m 40.485s
18	Marini	1m 40.753s
19	Nakagami	1m 41.084s
20	Martin	1m 41.087s
21	Di Giannantonio	1m 41.127s
22	Bezzecchi	1m 41.240s
23	Dovizioso	1m 42.177s

Championship Points

1	Bastianini	30
2	B. Binder	28
3	Quartararo	27
4	Oliveira	25
5	Zarco	24
6	P. Espargaro	20
7	A. Espargaro	20
8	Rins	20
9	Mir	20
10	Morbidelli	14
11	Miller	13
12	M. Marquez	11
13	D. Binder	6
14	Nakagami	6
15	Marini	5
16	Vinales	4
17	A. Marquez	3
18	Dovizioso	2
19	Gardner	1
20	Bagnaia	1

Constructor Points

1	KTM	45
2	Ducati	41
3	Yamaha	27
4	Suzuki	21
5	Honda	20
6	Aprilia	20

	Grid order	1	2	3	4	5	6	7	8	9	10	11	12	13	14	15	16	17	18	19	20	
20	QUARTARARO	88	43	43	43	88	88	88	88	88	88	88	88	88	88	88	88	88	88	88	88	1
89	MARTIN	20	88	88	88	43	43	43	43	43	43	43	43	43	43	43	20	20	20	20	20	2
5	ZARCO	43	20	20	42	42	42	42	42	42	42	5	5	5	5	20	43	5	5	5	5	3
33	B.BINDER	42	42	42	5	5	5	5	5	5	5	42	42	20	20	5	5	43	43	43	43	4
23	BASTIANINI	5	5	5	20	20	20	20	20	20	20	20	20	42	42	42	42	42	42	42	42	5
63	BAGNAIA	21	36	36	36	36	36	36	36	36	36	36	36	36	36	36	36	36	36	36	36	6
88	OLIVEIRA	89	21	21	21	21	89	89	21	21	21	21	21	21	21	21	21	21	21	21	21	7
42	RINS	36	89	89	89	89	21	21	10	10	10	10	10	10	10	10	40	40	40	33	33	8
43	MILLER	63	63	63	63	63	10	10	33	33	33	33	33	33	40	40	41	41	23	41	41	9
41	A. ESPARGARO	44	44	44	44	44	33	33	44	63	63	63	63	40	33	33	33	44	41	40	40	10
49	DI GIANNANTONIO	33	4	4	10	10	44	44	63	41	41	41	41	63	41	41	10	23	33	23	23	11
10	MARINI	4	33	10	33	33	63	63	41	44	44	40	40	41	63	44	44	33	44	44	44	12
72	BEZZECCHI	10	10	33	4	4	4	41	73	40	40	44	44	44	44	73	73	73	73	73	73	13
21	MORBIDELLI	23	73	73	41	41	41	73	40	73	73	73	73	73	73	63	23	10	10	10	10	14
44	P. ESPARGARO	73	41	41	73	73	73	40	72	23	23	23	23	23	23	23	63	63	63	63	63	15
4	DOVIZIOSO	49	23	72	72	40	40	72	23	72	25	25	25	25	25	25	25	25	25	12	12	
36	MIR	41	49	23	40	72	72	49	25	25	72	72	72	12	12	12	12	12	12	25	25	
73	A. MARQUEZ	25	72	40	49	49	49	23	49	49	49	49	12	72	72	72	72	72	72	49	49	
12	VINALES	30	25	49	25	25	25	25	12	30	30	12	49	49	49	49	49	49	49	72	30	
25	FERNANDEZ	72	40	25	23	23	23	87	87	12	12	30	30	30	30	30	30	30	30	30	72	
87	GARDNER	87	30	30	87	87	87	12	30	87	87	87	87	87	87	87	87	87	87	87	87	
40	D.BINDER	40	87	87	12	12	12	30														
30	NAKAGAMI	12	12	12	30	30	30															

Moto2

RACE DISTANCE: 16 laps, 42.760 miles/68.816km · RACE WEATHER: Dry (air 30°, humidity 72%, track 46°)

Pos.	Rider	Nat.	No.	Entrant	Machine	Laps	Time & Speed
1	**Somkiat Chantra**	THA	35	IDEMITSU Honda Team Asia	Kalex	16	25m 40.876
							99.9mph/160.7km/h
2	**Celestino Vietti**	ITA	13	Mooney VR46 Racing Team	Kalex	16	25m 44.106
3	**Aron Canet**	SPA	40	Flexbox HP40	Kalex	16	25m 45.242s
4	**Sam Lowes**	GBR	22	Elf Marc VDS Racing Team	Kalex	16	25m 48.794s
5	**Augusto Fernandez**	SPA	37	Red Bull KTM Ajo	Kalex	16	25m 53.104s
6	**Ai Ogura**	JPN	79	IDEMITSU Honda Team Asia	Kalex	16	25m 53.260s
7	**Fermin Aldeguer**	SPA	54	MB Conveyors Speed Up	Boscoscuro	16	25m 53.572s
8	**Tony Arbolino**	ITA	14	Elf Marc VDS Racing Team	Kalex	16	25m 55.423s
9	**Pedro Acosta**	SPA	51	Red Bull KTM Ajo	Kalex	16	25m 58.662s
10	**Albert Arenas**	SPA	75	Inde GASGAS Aspar Team	Kalex	16	25m 59.203s
11	**Joe Roberts**	USA	16	Italtrans Racing Team	Kalex	16	25m 59.385s
12	**Cameron Beaubier**	USA	6	American Racing	Kalex	16	25m 59.442s
13	**Jorge Navarro**	SPA	9	Flexbox HP40	Kalex	16	26m 00.587s
14	**Jeremy Alcoba**	SPA	52	Liqui Moly Intact GP	Kalex	16	26m 00.836s
15	**Bo Bendsneyder**	NED	64	Pertamina Mandalika SAG Team	Kalex	16	26m 01.427s
16	Marcel Schrotter	GER	23	Liqui Moly Intact GP	Kalex	16	26m 03.923s
17	Marcos Ramirez	SPA	42	MV Agusta Forward Racing	MV Agusta	16	26m 04.094s
18	Manuel Gonzalez	SPA	18	Yamaha VR46 Master Camp Team	Kalex	16	26m 05.055s
19	Romano Fenati	ITA	5	MB Conveyors Speed Up	Boscoscuro	16	26m 06.009s
20	Lorenzo Dalla Porta	ITA	19	Italtrans Racing Team	Kalex	16	26m 07.830s
21	Filip Salac	CZE	12	Gresini Racing Moto2	Kalex	16	26m 08.554s
22	Gabriel Rodrigo	ARG	2	Pertamina Mandalika SAG Team	Kalex	16	26m 10.424s
23	Zonta van den Goorbergh	NED	84	RW Racing GP	Kalex	16	26m 12.649s
24	Alessandro Zaccone	ITA	61	Gresini Racing Moto2	Kalex	16	26m 13.312s
25	Niccolo Antonelli	ITA	28	Mooney VR46 Racing Team	Kalex	16	26m 14.850s
	Sean Dylan Kelly	USA	4	American Racing	Kalex	13	DNF-technical
	Jake Dixon	GBR	96	Inde GASGAS Aspar Team	Kalex	12	DNF-crash
	Keminth Kubo	THA	81	Yamaha VR46 Master Camp Team	Kalex	7	DNF-crash
	Simone Corsi	ITA	24	MV Agusta Forward Racing	MV Agusta	4	DNF-crash

Fastest lap: Somkiat Chantra, on lap 12, 1m 35.591s, 100.6mph/161.9km/h.

Lap record: New circuit.

Event maximum speed: Tony Arbolino, 161.7mph/260.2km/h (qualifying).

Qualifying

Weather: Dry

Air: 32° **Humidity:** 66%

Track: 44°

1	Dixon	1m 35.799s
2	Fernandez	1m 35.901s
3	Lowes	1m 35.953s
4	Chantra	1m 36.260s
5	Bendsneyder	1m 36.337s
6	Arenas	1m 36.581s
7	Vietti	1m 36.588s
8	Arbolino	1m 36.657s
9	Corsi	1m 36.665s
10	Acosta	1m 36.751s
11	Beaubier	1m 36.900s
12	Aldeguer	1m 37.006s
13	Canet	1m 37.028s
14	Ramirez	1m 37.034s
15	Alcoba	1m 37.072s
16	Fenati	1m 37.312s
	Navarro	No Time
	Gonzalez	No Time
	Q1	
19	Alcoba	1m 36.870s
20	Corsi	1m 36.882s
21	Roberts	1m 36.905s
22	Baltus	1m 36.908s
23	Ogura	1m 36.913s
24	Schrotter	1m 37.033s
25	Salac	1m 37.218s
26	Rodrigo	1m 37.436s
27	V D Goorbergh	1m 37.582s
28	Kubo	1m 37.625s
29	Dalla Porta	1m 37.843s
30	Antonelli	1m 38.066s
31	Zaccone	1m 38.609s
	Kelly	No Time

Fastest race laps

1	Chantra	1m 35.591s
2	Vietti	1m 35.808s
3	Canet	1m 35.908s
4	Ogura	1m 35.922s
5	Fernandez	1m 35.958s
6	Lowes	1m 36.111s
7	Aldeguer	1m 36.193s
8	Dixon	1m 36.217s
9	Arbolino	1m 36.320s
10	Corsi	1m 36.371s
11	Navarro	1m 36.514s
12	Roberts	1m 36.519s
13	Acosta	1m 36.533s
14	Bendsneyder	1m 36.551s
15	Beaubier	1m 36.583s
16	Arenas	1m 36.673s
17	Schrotter	1m 36.690s
18	Alcoba	1m 36.690s
19	Ramirez	1m 36.813s
20	Fenati	1m 36.953s
21	Gonzalez	1m 36.982s
22	Salac	1m 37.137s
23	Dalla Porta	1m 37.142s
24	Antonelli	1m 37.239s
25	Rodrigo	1m 37.318s
26	V D Goorbergh	1m 37.337s
27	Zaccone	1m 37.459s
28	Kubo	1m 37.680s
29	Kelly	1m 38.259s

Championship Points

1	Vietti	45
2	Canet	36
3	Lowes	29
4	Chantra	25
5	Fernandez	24
6	Ogura	20
7	Arbolino	19
8	Roberts	13
9	Navarro	12
10	Acosta	11
11	Beaubier	11
12	Aldeguer	9
13	Arenas	9
14	Schrotter	6
15	Dixon	5
16	Alcoba	4
17	Bendsneyder	1
18	Fenati	1

Constructor Points

1	Kalex	50
2	Boscoscuro	10

Moto3

RACE DISTANCE: RACE DISTANCE: 23 laps, 61.468 miles/98.923km · RACE WEATHER: Dry (air 31°, humidity 67%, track 50°)

Pos.	Rider	Nat.	No.	Entrant	Machine	Laps	Time & Speed
1	**Dennis Foggia**	ITA	7	Leopard Racing	Honda	23	38m 51.668s
							94.9mph/152.7km/h
2	**Izan Guevara**	SPA	28	Gaviota GASGAS Aspar Team	GASGAS	23	38m 54.280s
3	**Carlos Tatay**	SPA	99	CFMOTO Racing PruestelGP	CFMOTO	23	38m 55.307s
4	**Sergio Garcia**	SPA	11	Gaviota GASGAS Aspar Team	GASGAS	23	38m 55.427s
5	**Deniz Oncu**	TUR	53	Red Bull KTM Tech3	KTM	23	38m 55.538s
6	**Xavier Artigas**	SPA	43	CFMOTO Racing PruestelGP	CFMOTO	23	38m 56.630s
7	**Jaume Masia**	SPA	5	Red Bull KTM Ajo	KTM	23	38m 56.957s
8	**Elia Bartolini**	ITA	23	QJMotor Avintia Racing Team	KTM	23	38m 57.073s
9	**Daniel Holgado**	SPA	96	Red Bull KTM Ajo	KTM	23	38m 57.201s
10	**Tatsuki Suzuki**	JPN	24	Leopard Racing	Honda	23	38m 57.355s
11	**Ryusei Yamanaka**	JPN	6	MT Helmets - MSI	KTM	23	39m 07.954s
12	**Kaito Toba**	JPN	27	CIP Green Power	KTM	23	39m 08.589s
13	**Scott Ogden**	GBR	19	VisionTrack Racing Team	Honda	23	39m 08.925s
14	**Mario Aji**	INA	64	Honda Team Asia	Honda	23	39m 16.294s
15	**Matteo Bertelle**	ITA	18	QJMotor Avintia Racing Team	KTM	23	39m 16.477s
16	Lorenzo Fellon	FRA	20	SIC58 Squadra Corse	Honda	23	39m 23.190s
17	Riccardo Rossi	ITA	54	SIC58 Squadra Corse	Honda	23	39m 23.296s
18	Joel Kelso	AUS	66	CIP Green Power	KTM	23	39m 23.872s
19	Ana Carrasco	SPA	22	BOE SKX	KTM	23	39m 32.870s
20	Joshua Whatley	GBR	70	VisionTrack Racing Team	Honda	23	39m 39.681s
21	Gerard Riu Male	SPA	87	BOE SKX	KTM	23	39m 39.758s
	Ayumu Sasaki	JPN	71	Sterilgarda Husqvarna Max	Husqvarna	22	DNF-crash
	Andrea Migno	ITA	16	Rivacold Snipers Team	Honda	22	DNF-crash
	Stefano Nepa	ITA	82	Angeluss MTA Team	KTM	22	DNF-crash
	Alberto Surra	ITA	67	Rivacold Snipers Team	Honda	17	DNF-crash
	Adrian Fernandez	SPA	31	Red Bull KTM Tech3	KTM	10	DNF-technical
	Diogo Moreira	BRA	10	MT Helmets - MSI	KTM	8	DNF-technical
	Ivan Ortola	SPA	48	Angeluss MTA Team	KTM	7	DNF-crash

Fastest lap: Jaume Masia, on lap 4, 1m 40.197s, 96.0mph/154.5km/h.

Lap record: New circuit.

Event maximum speed: Diogo Moreira, 134.5mph/216.4km/h (free practice).

Qualifying:

Weather: Dry

Air: 30° **Humidity:** 71%

Track: 39°

1	Tatay	1m 41.232s
2	Moreira	1m 41.315s
3	Aji	1m 41.567s
4	Artigas	1m 41.585s
5	Migno	1m 41.594s
6	Foggia	1m 41.674s
7	Garcia	1m 41.811s
8	Guevara	1m 41.830s
9	Oncu	1m 42.203s
10	Sasaki	1m 42.268s
11	Masia	1m 42.391s
12	Surra	1m 42.398s
13	Bartolini	1m 42.838s
14	Ortola	1m 42.878s
15	Rossi	1m 43.129s
16	Bertelle	1m 43.396s
17	Fernandez	1m 43.760s
	Ogden	No Time
	Q1	
19	Artigas	1m 42.614s
20	Surra	1m 42.637s
21	Holgado	1m 42.973s
22	Suzuki	1m 43.008s
23	Nepa	1m 43.079s
24	Kelso	1m 43.163s
25	Fellon	1m 43.192s
26	Carrasco	1m 43.776s
27	Yamanaka	1m 43.831s
28	Riu Male	1m 44.390s
29	Whatley	1m 44.478s
30	Toba	1m 44.658s

Fastest race laps

1	Masia	1m 40.197s
2	Foggia	1m 40.275s
3	Garcia	1m 40.508s
4	Kelso	1m 40.518s
5	Oncu	1m 40.561s
6	Toba	1m 40.618s
7	Artigas	1m 40.641s
8	Tatay	1m 40.648s
9	Bartolini	1m 40.661s
10	Guevara	1m 40.697s
11	Nepa	1m 40.733s
12	Fernandez	1m 40.755s
13	Suzuki	1m 40.813s
14	Holgado	1m 40.823s
15	Sasaki	1m 40.849s
16	Migno	1m 40.926s
17	Aji	1m 41.132s
18	Yamanaka	1m 41.183s
19	Bertelle	1m 41.256s
20	Ogden	1m 41.307s
21	Fellon	1m 41.664s
22	Moreira	1m 41.698s
23	Rossi	1m 41.833s
24	Ortola	1m 41.929s
25	Surra	1m 42.007s
26	Whatley	1m 42.349s
27	Carrasco	1m 42.386s
28	Riu Male	1m 42.644s

Championship Points

1	Foggia	34
2	Garcia	33
3	Guevara	28
4	Migno	25
5	Öncü	24
6	Toba	20
7	Tatay	16
8	Artigas	16
9	Yamanaka	12
10	McPhee	11
11	Moreira	10
12	Masia	9
13	Bartolini	8
14	Holgado	7
15	Suzuki	6
16	Ortola	5
17	Rossi	4
18	Nepa	3
19	Ogden	3
20	Aji	2
21	Fernandez	2
22	Bertelle	1

Constructor Points

1	Honda	50
2	GASGAS	40
3	KTM	27
4	CFMOTO	22
5	Husqvarna	11

FIM WORLD CHAMPIONSHIP · ROUND 3

ARGENTINE GRAND PRIX

TERMAS DE RIO HONDO

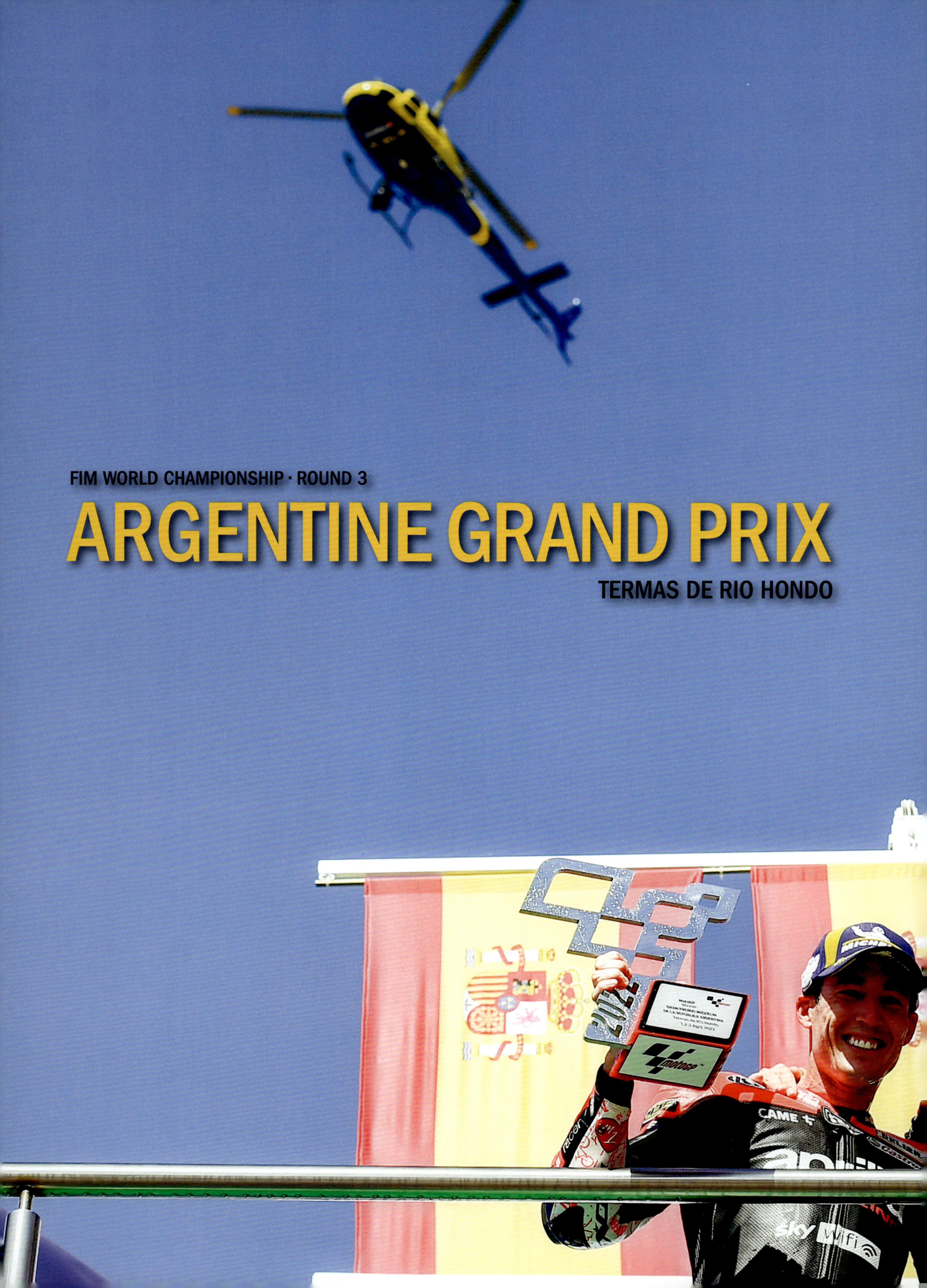

Main: Espargaro and Rivola celebrate Aprilia's first ever premier-class win.

Inset: "Hi, honey. Just won my first grand prix." Aleix calls home from *parc fermé*.

Photos: Gold & Goose

Above: **Twiddling thumbs. Air-freight problems forced Carmelo Ezpeleta to improvise a new schedule to save the race.**
Photo: Gold & Goose

Right: **Pecco Bagnaia made good points at last, but his patience was wearing thin.**
Photo: Ducati Corse

Below right: **Aprilia's Antonio Jimenez appreciated his rider's mature performance.**

Far right: **No bikes, no tools, no sweat. A KTM mechanic hunts for the appropriate emoji.**
Photos: Gold & Goose

ALEIX ESPARGARO'S 200th premier-class grand prix was a race to remember. So too for his Aprilia team. Already having shaken loose the mantle of poor relation with an improved bike now in its third year of development, the Italian marque claimed a first four-stroke pole position and fastest race lap, the Spanish rider a first victory. Achieved, it was noted, with a calm assurance nobody had expected from the often excitable 32-year-old rider.

His crew chief, Antonio Jimenez, was as surprised as anyone. "We showed everyone Aprilia is there," he said. "Normally, Aleix is not so calm. But on Saturday night, I saw a guy that was very convinced about his possibilities. He was the first one to be quiet and believe in himself. It's not easy when you've not been there before and you know you have this chance. But he managed it well. He waited for his moment."

The last time an Aprilia had started on pole had been in October, 2000, with Jeremy McWilliams and the undersized 400cc 'super-250' twin (a feat the Ulsterman repeated in 2002 at the same Phillip Island venue on the three-cylinder Proton, the last ever pole for a two-stroke). It made Espargaro the first rider in the four-stroke MotoGP era to claim pole positions with three different manufacturers – previously on Yamaha and Suzuki.

It was signal proof of the success of Dorna's levelling-up policy, accomplished through control tyres and electronics, and regulations restricting engine design and numbers, with a loophole of concessions in development, testing and engine numbers for less successful teams. Aprilia was the last such, and this was a first step towards losing this slightly inglorious distinction.

It was also the fifth successive win for a European marque, with Ducati twice in the previous season and once this, followed by KTM; and with Martin and Rins also on the podium for a third straight trio of new faces – a first since 1952 and only the third time it had occurred.

Once again, it almost didn't happen, after an unfortunate combination of freight delays in (of all places) Nairobi. It had been a fortnight since the Indonesian round, supposedly plenty of time, but both chartered aircraft suffered technical issues in Kenya. As a result, all of Friday's action was cancelled. The worst off MotoGP teams were Gresini Ducati and VR46 Ducati, with neither bikes nor equipment. Factory rider Oliveira was also short of one of his pair of KTMs, and Tech3 rider Fernandez was missing two.

Eventually, the last of the freight arrived during Friday night. Supplies of midnight oil were severely depleted, and free practice and qualifying were crammed into a busy Saturday. Instead of the usual three free practice sessions, all classes were allocated just two, albeit expanded from 40 to 50 minutes for the smaller classes, and from 45 to an hour for MotoGP, which also lost the usual FP4, effectively a non-timed 30 minutes used to concentrate on race set-up rather than single-lap times. Thereafter, the usual Q1/Q2 sessions went ahead for all three classes, in a nine-and-a-half-hour day of non-stop track action, instead of the usual Saturday of just short of seven hours, with an hour for lunch. A further extension doubled the length of the race-morning warm-up sessions, to 20 minutes for Motos 2 and 3, and 40 for MotoGP.

Qualifying produced renewed hostility between Miller and Quartararo, after the former was touring close to the line as the Frenchman approached the very fast Turn Seven. He had to abort his lap, and since he had already got the best

out of his soft rear tyre, he felt that it had compromised his qualifying, putting him on the far end of row two and arguably contributing to a disappointing eighth place. Race Direction agreed and penalised Miller three grid positions, from 11th to 14th.

Saturday was notable also for Bagnaia's near meltdown in FP2 and Q1. Looking nervous over the track's bumps and repeatedly throwing his hands into the air, the Italian, better known for a calm approach, cut a desperately frustrated figure. His annoyance at riders seeking a tow blew up at the close of FP2, when he pulled to the right of the start/finish straight and braked in a straight line to a crawl. Luckily, no one was directly behind, and he escaped sanction.

The news broke before the race that front ride-height devices that could be operated mid-race would be banned after the current season. Unsurprisingly, that triggered frustration at Ducati. While others had such a system to use off the start line, which escaped the ban, only Ducati's latest GP22 models had a mid-race system.

"Obviously, we're disappointed," said sporting director Paolo Ciabatti. "We've been trying our best to keep something within the regulations that can be used. We spent time and money to develop it last year while our competitors spent their time trying to develop something else. We think it's very unfair. It's a story that's repeating itself, from the winglets to the rear tyre deflector.

"In this case, I heard motivations we don't agree with. The cost – we know that's fully compatible with our budget. Some manufacturers spend high amounts on their riders. It's up to them. But I don't think they should criticise when we spend money on development. We heard about safety, but we don't see this as a fact."

Explaining why KTM voted for the ban, project manager Sebastian Risse said, "On the one hand, as an engineer, you like technology. On the other, you have the sporting part of racing. There is a certain philosophy of the rules, to not over-engineer things and go toward a kind of active suspension. It's a shame for a manufacturer to invest in a technology that is not really state of the art. There is a reason why there is no active suspension allowed. So why work around that with technology that is older than that. It's a big challenge for engineers, but is this really the right thing to do? The bikes are getting faster. It starts with aerodynamics. With ride-height devices, you alter the pitch of the bike. It's already a problem to have enough run-off space for a lot of tracks for these very fast bikes."

MOTOGP RACE – 25 laps

An all-Italian front row had the Aprilia ahead of a pair of Ducatis, although not the factory bikes. Espargaro had Martin and Marini alongside, with brother Pol's Honda directly behind, then Vinales in his best-so-far on the Aprilia, from Quartararo.

Martin made the early running, getting the jump into Turn One, and confidently asserted himself as Espargaro fought past brother Pol to sit second. Behind, Marini led a gaggle that included third-row-starter Rins, Vinales, the fast-away, but erratic Nakagami and Mir.

The front two were soon ahead of the fight for third, where Pol Espargaro had quickly bettered Marini on lap two. The Suzuki team-mates weren't so fortunate. Had it not taken them so long to get by the Ducati (Rins was past on lap four, Mir on lap six, after disposing of Vinales and Nakagami), they might have been able to attack at the end.

At least they weren't totally adrift. Quartararo was sliding backwards, battling a chronic lack of rear grip in the heightened afternoon temperatures. By lap two, he had been shuffled back to 13th. Binder, Bastianini, Bagnaia and soon-to-crash Zarco had all barged through. It was even worse for his fellow factory Yamaha riders. Having accidentally jammed his front ride-height starting device, Dovizioso pitted after a lap, rejoining to finish three laps down. Morbidelli retired out of 16th on lap seven with a puncture.

Up front, Martin and Espargaro traded fastest laps, the Aprilia rider apparently content to follow. Until Rins moved by Pol on the exit of Turn Seven the seventh time around and started working on the 2.5-second gap. Aleix's failure so far to have notched up a GP win – often being excitable in previous positions of promise – seemed likely to continue

Above: With the Suzukis closing, it was time for Espargaro to take control over long-time leader Martin.
Photo: Gold & Goose

Top right: Alex Rins returned to the podium, his first in nine races.
Photo: Suzuki ECSTAR

Top far right: Pramac's Jorge Martin led the most laps and finished less than a second behind the Aprilia.

Above centre right: Sergio Garcia's first win of the year meant the lead in the championship.

Above centre far right: Vietti survived a clash with young tyro Aldeguer for a second Moto2 win.

Above right: Garcia closes a devastating last lap to deny Foggia, Sasaki a close spectator.

Right: Rookie Holgado leads Suzuki, Rossi, Foggia, Kelso and Tatay.
Photos: Gold & Goose

when he made two mistakes while braking on lap ten. Martin gained an advantage of one second.

A fastest lap next time around cut the gap to three-tenths. But as Rins began shaving tenths off his deficit, already shrunk from some 2.5 seconds to less than two, Espargaro knew he had to get by.

The more agile Aprilia's turning prowess through Turns Three and Four allowed him to line up Martin on the back straight and draft by. Twice, on laps 18 and 20, he tried to outbrake the Ducati at the ensuing Turn Five. Twice he ran wide, allowing Martin back through. But with Rins now just 1.2 seconds behind, Espargaro made the move stick on lap 21, perfectly making the apex.

Martin continued to hover, just a tenth behind, and both he and the leader were sweating as a second Suzuki closed in. After Pol Espargaro crashed out of fourth on lap 15, Mir had a clear run and could focus on reeling in his team-mate. He was comfortably the fastest man on track over the final five laps.

Only on the penultimate lap did Espargaro gap his pursuer decisively, with no signs of nerves as he claimed a famous win, eight-tenths clear at the chequered flag. "I'm extremely happy," he said, after becoming the second rider in the four-stroke era to win his first premier-class race over the age of 30. "In the pre-season, I felt that I had the best machine ever in my career. Today hasn't been a wet race or a lucky race or whatever. I think yesterday we proved that we were the fastest on the qualifying and also today in the race."

Martin was content with second, his first finish after a bruising opening to the season. Likewise, Rins and Mir took positives from strong displays, as they finished just 1.3 and 1.8 seconds off the win respectively. "Maybe if I started more in front, I could fight with them," said Rins. His team-mate felt that his late-race speed had had echoes of the victorious 2020. "I got back the feeling," he said. "To be strong on the last laps was something we've been missing."

Bagnaia rode a smart race to come home fifth after a disastrous Saturday, just ahead of Binder, who mugged Vinales for sixth on the final lap. Quartararo was a frustrated eighth, bemoaning a lack of rear grip as well as the usual shortage of speed. Rookie Bezzecchi was an inspired ninth, ahead of the more experienced Bastianini and Marini, who had slipped to 11th, with Nakagami, Oliveira and Miller in close attendance. The Australian complained that a lack of confidence and front-end feel had prevented him from making a single overtake. Alex Marquez took the last point some way behind.

MOTO2 RACE – 23 laps

Dazzling new boy Aldeguer, due to turn 17 two days after the race, made history on Saturday as the youngest pole-qualifier in the history of the intermediate class. He had dominated the extended race-morning warm-up session as well, and looked on target to become the class's youngest winner to boot.

Second qualifier Fernandez was less than two-tenths down, with Arbolino alongside on the front row. Arenas led the second from Dixon and Vietti; the Honda Team Asia pair of Chantra and Ogura headed the third.

The Spanish teenager duly broke free to lead early on, Vietti in hot pursuit. Fernandez had ruled himself out from the get-go after fluffing his start, then crashing out at the first turn.

The front two soon began to pull clear, Vietti taking over on lap four, but Aldeguer stuck right with him. His run would last not quite seven laps, however. They collided at Turn 13, the last tight right hairpin, and he came off worse. Vietti had run wide on the entrance and cut back on the racing line as Aldeguer moved inside to take advantage. The Italian survived; the Spaniard spun around at speed and fell.

At that point, Chantra had been in third since lap three, when he and Canet had got ahead of Arbolino, who now was coming under pressure from Ogura. The Thai rider, fresh from his maiden Indonesian win, began to press Vietti, and was even ahead of him over the line once, on lap 11.

In reality, the Italian was controlling events, and he extended his narrow advantage through the closing laps to 1.5 seconds to claim a second win in three. Chantra was a superb second.

Canet and Ogura tussled for third all race long, only for the Japanese rider to execute a beautiful block pass at Turn 13 on the final lap for third, capping Honda Team Asia's best day to date with a first double podium.

Dixon had lost a couple of places in a muddled first lap, but came back to fifth, less than a second off the podium.

He had finally got the better of Arbolino; while Acosta won a duel with Arenas.

Bendsneyder had dropped behind both riders in the closing laps, while Lowes had closed to within half a second by the flag to complete the top ten.

A couple of seconds behind, Beaubier was comfortably clear of Schrotter, with Roberts, Gonzalez and Ramirez trailing in for the last points.

Navarro had been fighting at the rear of the top ten when he crashed out on the 21st lap, one of the last of a long crash list that included Kelly and Antonelli on lap one, then van den Goorbergh, Salac, Rodrigo and, at the end, also Dalla Porta.

MOTO3 RACE – 21 laps

Sergio Garcia's first 2022 win followed a frenetic last-lap fight with both Leopard Hondas, heading a group of seven over the line in just seven-tenths. The Spaniard had fought back from third with five corners remaining – a rapid-fire move on Suzuki at Turn Nine and then a beautifully precise pass on Foggia at the final right.

Garcia and fellow front-row starter Guevara raced into an early lead, the GasGas team-mates eking out 1.5 seconds by lap three. But by quarter-distance, Masia, Migno and close-to-home Brazilian beginner Moreira had joined them.

Foggia, qualified 11th, had made a slow start, but by lap nine he was leading the second group and took little time in chasing down the leaders, taking Suzuki with him.

Leader Guevara slowed suddenly on lap ten to dismayed retirement. Then Migno tagged third-placed Masia on the exit of Turn 13 five laps later, taking out both men.

Thereafter, Foggia seemed to have it won, taking the lead with a lap to go. Suzuki's block pass for second at Turn Five appeared to end Garcia's chances, but his inspired late salvage saved the day.

Sasaki recovered from a long-lap penalty to nab third at the last corner from Suzuki, who then was demoted to fifth for exceeding track limits on the last lap. Rossi gained fourth as a result, with rookies Moreira and Holgado hanging on at the back of the gang.

Just over a second away, Tatay led Toba and Kelso, the Australian rookie's first top-ten finish.

FIM WORLD CHAMPIONSHIP: ROUND 3

GRAN PREMIO MICHELIN DE LA REPÚBLICA ARGENTINA

1-3 APRIL, 2022

AUTÓDROMO TERMAS DE RÍO HONDO

25 laps
Length: 4.806km / 2.986 miles
Width: 16m

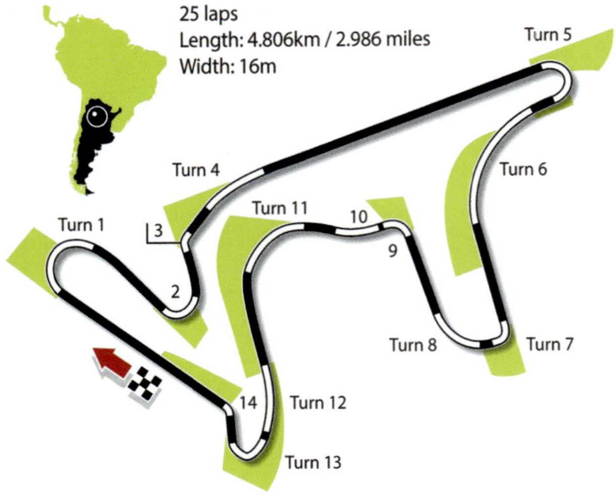

MotoGP RACE DISTANCE: 25 laps, 74.658 miles/120.150km · RACE WEATHER: Dry (air 26°, humidity 49%, track 44°)

Pos.	Rider	Nat.	No.	Entrant	Machine	Tyres	Race tyre choice	Laps	Time & speed
1	**Aleix Espargaro**	SPA	41	Aprilia Racing	Aprilia RS-GP	M	F: Hard/R: Soft	25	41m 36.198s 173.2km/h 107.6mph
2	**Jorge Martin**	SPA	89	Pramac Racing	Ducati Desmosedici	M	F: Hard/R: Soft	25	41m 37.005s
3	**Alex Rins**	SPA	42	Team SUZUKI ECSTAR	Suzuki GSX-RR	M	F: Hard/R: Soft	25	41m 37.528s
4	**Joan Mir**	SPA	36	Team SUZUKI ECSTAR	Suzuki GSX-RR	M	F: Hard/R: Soft	25	41m 38.029s
5	**Francesco Bagnaia**	ITA	63	Ducati Lenovo Team	Ducati Desmosedici	M	F: Hard/R: Soft	25	41m 42.038s
6	**Brad Binder**	RSA	33	Red Bull KTM Factory Racing	KTM RC16	M	F: Hard/R: Soft	25	41m 42.390s
7	**Maverick Vinales**	SPA	12	Aprilia Racing	Aprilia RS-GP	M	F: Hard/R: Soft	25	41m 42.738s
8	**Fabio Quartararo**	FRA	20	Monster Energy Yamaha MotoGP	Yamaha YZR-M1	M	F: Hard/R: Soft	25	41m 46.413s
9	**Marco Bezzecchi**	ITA	72	Mooney VR46 Racing Team	Ducati Desmosedici	M	F: Hard/R: Soft	25	41m 48.820s
10	**Enea Bastianini**	ITA	23	Gresini Racing MotoGP	Ducati Desmosedici	M	F: Hard/R: Soft	25	41m 49.185s
11	**Luca Marini**	ITA	10	Mooney VR46 Racing Team	Ducati Desmosedici	M	F: Hard/R: Soft	25	41m 50.160s
12	**Takaaki Nakagami**	JPN	30	LCR Honda IDEMITSU	Honda RC213V	M	F: Hard/R: Soft	25	41m 50.200s
13	**Miguel Oliveira**	POR	88	Red Bull KTM Factory Racing	KTM RC16	M	F: Hard/R: Soft	25	41m 50.654s
14	**Jack Miller**	AUS	43	Ducati Lenovo Team	Ducati Desmosedici	M	F: Hard/R: Soft	25	41m 51.096s
15	**Alex Marquez**	SPA	73	LCR Honda CASTROL	Honda RC213V	M	F: Hard/R: Soft	25	41m 59.670s
16	Raul Fernandez	SPA	25	Tech3 KTM Factory Racing	KTM RC16	M	F: Hard/R: Soft	25	42m 02.060s
17	Remy Gardner	AUS	87	Tech3 KTM Factory Racing	KTM RC16	M	F: Hard/R: Soft	25	42m 04.909s
18	Darryn Binder	RSA	40	WithU Yamaha RNF MotoGP Team	Yamaha YZR-M1	M	F: Hard/R: Soft	25	42m 04.982s
19	Stefan Bradl	GER	6	Repsol Honda Team	Honda RC213V	M	F: Hard/R: Soft	25	42m 08.141s
20	Andrea Dovizioso	ITA	4	WithU Yamaha RNF MotoGP Team	Yamaha YZR-M1	M	F: Hard/R: Soft	22	42m 57.640s
	Fabio Di Giannantonio	ITA	49	Gresini Racing MotoGP	Ducati Desmosedici	M	F: Hard/R: Soft	22	DNF-crash
	Pol Espargaro	SPA	44	Repsol Honda Team	Honda RC213V	M	F: Hard/R: Soft	14	DNF-crash
	Franco Morbidelli	ITA	21	Monster Energy Yamaha MotoGP	Yamaha YZR-M1	M	F: Hard/R: Soft	7	DNF-technical
	Johann Zarco	FRA	5	Pramac Racing	Ducati Desmosedici	M	F: Hard/R: Soft	5	DNF-crash

Fastest lap: Aleix Espargaro, on lap 11, 1m 39.375s, 108.2mph/174.1km/h.
Lap record: Valentino Rossi, 1m 39.019s, 108.6mph/174.7km/h (2015).
Event maximum speed: Francesco Bagnaia, 214.7mph/345.5km/h (race).

Qualifying

Weather: Dry
Air Temp: 26° **Humidity:** 26%
Track Temp: 38°

1	A. Espargaro	1m 37.688s
2	Martin	1m 37.839s
3	Marini	1m 38.119s
4	P. Espargaro	1m 38.165s
5	Vinales	1m 38.196s
6	Quartararo	1m 38.281s
7	Rins	1m 38.455s
8	Mir	1m 38.516s
9	Zarco	1m 38.537s
10	Nakagami	1m 38.576s
11	Miller	1m 38.584s
12	B. Binder	1m 38.932s
	Q1	
13	Bastianini	1m 38.566s
14	Bagnaia	1m 38.610s
15	Morbidelli	1m 38.805s
16	Oliveira	1m 38.871s
17	Bezzecchi	1m 38.877s
18	Dovizioso	1m 38.938s
19	A. Marquez	1m 39.095s
20	Di Giannantonio	1m 39.126s
21	Fernandez	1m 39.153s
22	Gardner	1m 39.159s
23	D. Binder	1m 39.380s
24	Bradl	1m 39.487s

Fastest race laps

1	A. Espargaro	1m 39.375s
2	Mir	1m 39.443s
3	Bagnaia	1m 39.451s
4	Rins	1m 39.453s
5	B. Binder	1m 39.505s
6	P. Espargaro	1m 39.514s
7	Martin	1m 39.522s
8	Vinales	1m 39.574s
9	Bezzecchi	1m 39.600s
10	Quartararo	1m 39.611s
11	Bastianini	1m 39.749s
12	Nakagami	1m 39.773s
13	Marini	1m 39.825s
14	Oliveira	1m 39.852s
15	Miller	1m 39.905s
16	Dovizioso	1m 39.908s
17	Zarco	1m 40.032s
18	Morbidelli	1m 40.043s
19	Fernandez	1m 40.116s
20	A. Marquez	1m 40.118s
21	Gardner	1m 40.127s
22	D. Binder	1m 40.209s
23	Di Giannantonio	1m 40.289s
24	Bradl	1m 40.452s

Championship Points

1	A. Espargaro	45
2	B. Binder	38
3	Bastianini	36
4	Rins	36
5	Quartararo	35
6	Mir	33
7	Oliveira	28
8	Zarco	24
9	Martin	20
10	P. Espargaro	20
11	Miller	15
12	Morbidelli	14
13	Vinales	13
14	Bagnaia	12
15	M. Marquez	11
16	Nakagami	10
17	Marini	10
18	Bezzecchi	7
19	D. Binder	6
20	A. Marquez	4
21	Dovizioso	2
22	Gardner	1

Constructor Points

1	Ducati	61
2	KTM	55
3	Aprilia	45
4	Suzuki	37
5	Yamaha	35
6	Honda	24

Grid order	1	2	3	4	5	6	7	8	9	10	11	12	13	14	15	16	17	18	19	20	21	22	23	24	25	·
41 A. ESPARGARO	89	89	89	89	89	89	89	89	89	89	89	89	89	89	89	89	89	89	89	89	41	41	41	41	41	1
89 MARTIN	41	41	41	41	41	41	41	41	41	41	41	41	41	41	41	41	41	41	41	41	89	89	89	89	89	2
10 MARINI	10	44	44	44	44	44	42	42	42	42	42	42	42	42	42	42	42	42	42	42	42	42	42	42	42	3
44 P. ESPARGARO	44	10	10	42	42	42	44	44	44	44	44	44	44	44	36	36	36	36	36	36	36	36	36	36	36	4
12 VINALES	42	42	42	10	10	36	36	36	36	36	36	36	36	36	12	12	12	12	12	12	12	12	12	63	63	5
20 QUARTARARO	30	36	36	36	36	10	10	10	10	12	12	12	12	12	63	63	63	63	63	63	63	63	63	12	33	6
42 RINS	36	12	12	12	12	12	12	12	12	10	10	10	63	63	33	33	33	33	33	33	33	33	33	33	12	7
36 MIR	12	33	33	33	33	33	63	63	63	63	63	63	33	33	10	10	10	20	20	20	20	20	20	20	20	8
5 ZARCO	20	30	63	63	63	63	33	33	33	33	33	33	10	10	23	20	20	10	10	72	72	72	72	72	72	9
30 NAKAGAMI	33	23	30	23	23	23	23	23	23	23	23	23	23	23	20	30	30	30	72	10	23	23	23	23	23	10
33 B.BINDER	23	63	23	30	30	30	30	30	20	20	20	20	20	20	30	72	72	72	30	23	10	10	10	10	10	11
23 BASTIANINI	63	5	5	20	5	20	20	20	30	30	30	30	30	30	88	88	23	23	23	30	30	30	30	30	30	12
63 BAGNAIA	5	20	20	5	20	88	88	88	88	88	88	88	88	88	72	23	88	88	88	88	88	88	88	88	88	13
43 MILLER	88	88	88	88	88	43	43	43	43	43	43	43	72	72	43	43	43	43	43	43	43	43	43	43	43	14
21 MORBIDELLI	25	43	43	43	43	72	72	72	72	72	72	72	43	43	73	73	73	73	73	73	73	73	73	73	73	15
88 OLIVEIRA	43	87	87	25	25	21	25	87	73	73	73	73	73	73	40	25	25	25	25	25	25	25	25	25	25	
72 BEZZECCHI	87	25	25	87	87	87	87	25	40	40	40	40	40	40	25	40	40	40	40	40	40	87	87	87	87	
4 DOVIZIOSO	21	21	40	40	72	25	40	40	25	25	25	25	25	25	87	87	87	87	87	87	87	40	40	40	40	
73 A. MARQUEZ	73	72	21	72	21	40	73	73	87	87	87	87	87	87	49	49	49	49	49	49	49	49	6	6	6	
49 DI GIANNANTONIO	72	40	72	21	73	73	49	49	49	49	49	49	49	49	6	6	6	6	6	6	6	6				
25 FERNANDEZ	49	73	73	73	40	49	6	6	6	6	6	6	6	6	*4*	*4*	*4*	*4*	*4*	*4*	*4*	*4*				
87 GARDNER	40	49	49	49	49	6	21	*4*	*4*	*4*	*4*	*4*	*4*	*4*												
40 D.BINDER	6	6	6	6	6	*4*	*4*																			
6 BRADL	4	*4*	*4*	*4*	*4*																					

4 Pit stop *4 lapped rider*

Moto2

RACE DISTANCE: 23 laps, 68.685 miles/110.538km · RACE WEATHER: Dry (air 24°, humidity 54%, track 42°)

Pos.	Rider	Nat.	No.	Entrant	Machine	Laps	Time & Speed
1	**Celestino Vietti**	ITA	13	Mooney VR46 Racing Team	Kalex	23	39m 44.098s
							103.7mph/166.9km/h
2	**Somkiat Chantra**	THA	35	IDEMITSU Honda Team Asia	Kalex	23	39m 45.636s
3	**Ai Ogura**	JPN	79	IDEMITSU Honda Team Asia	Kalex	23	39m 49.801s
4	**Aron Canet**	SPA	40	Flexbox HP40	Kalex	23	39m 49.978s
5	**Jake Dixon**	GBR	96	Autosolar GASGAS Aspar Team	Kalex	23	39m 50.682s
6	**Tony Arbolino**	ITA	14	Elf Marc VDS Racing Team	Kalex	23	39m 51.636s
7	**Pedro Acosta**	SPA	51	Red Bull KTM Ajo	Kalex	23	39m 56.275s
8	**Albert Arenas**	SPA	75	Autosolar GASGAS Aspar Team	Kalex	23	39m 56.516s
9	**Bo Bendsneyder**	NED	64	Pertamina Mandalika SAG Team	Kalex	23	39m 57.754s
10	**Sam Lowes**	GBR	22	Elf Marc VDS Racing Team	Kalex	23	39m 58.352s
11	**Cameron Beaubier**	USA	6	American Racing	Kalex	23	40m 04.175s
12	**Marcel Schrotter**	GER	23	Liqui Moly Intact GP	Kalex	23	40m 09.834s
13	**Joe Roberts**	USA	16	Italtrans Racing Team	Kalex	23	40m 12.415s
14	**Manuel Gonzalez**	SPA	18	Yamaha VR46 Master Camp Team	Kalex	23	40m 13.882s
15	**Marcos Ramirez**	SPA	42	MV Agusta Forward Racing	MV Agusta	23	40m 14.368s
16	Jeremy Alcoba	SPA	52	Liqui Moly Intact GP	Kalex	23	40m 21.982s
17	Simone Corsi	ITA	24	MV Agusta Forward Racing	MV Agusta	23	40m 22.054s
18	Romano Fenati	ITA	5	MB Conveyors Speed Up	Boscoscuro	23	40m 22.423s
19	Keminth Kubo	THA	81	Yamaha VR46 Master Camp Team	Kalex	23	40m 48.956s
	Jorge Navarro	SPA	9	Flexbox HP40	Kalex	20	DNF-crash
	Lorenzo Dalla Porta	ITA	19	Italtrans Racing Team	Kalex	20	DNF-crash
	Gabriel Rodrigo	ARG	2	Pertamina Mandalika SAG Team	Kalex	19	DNF-crash
	Filip Salac	CZE	12	Gresini Racing Moto2	Kalex	11	DNF-crash
	Alessandro Zaccone	ITA	61	Gresini Racing Moto2	Kalex	7	DNF-technical
	Fermin Aldeguer	SPA	54	MB Conveyors Speed Up	Boscoscuro	6	DNF-crash
	Zonta van den Goorbergh	NED	84	RW Racing GP	Kalex	1	DNF-crash
	Augusto Fernandez	SPA	37	Red Bull KTM Ajo	Kalex	0	DNF-crash
	Niccolo Antonelli	ITA	28	Mooney VR46 Racing Team	Kalex	0	DNF-crash
	Sean Dylan Kelly	USA	4	American Racing	Kalex	0	DNF-crash

Fastest lap: Celestino Vietti, on lap 3, 1m 42.829s, 104.5mph/168.2km/h.

Lap record: Jonas Folger, 1m 43.001s, 104.3mph/167.9km/h (2015).

Event maximum speed: Pedro Acosta, 182.4mph/293.6km/h (race).

Qualifying

Weather: Dry

Air: 26° **Humidity:** 29%

Track: 43°

1	Aldeguer	1m 43.306s
2	Fernandez	1m 43.456s
3	Arbolino	1m 43.513s
4	Arenas	1m 43.615s
5	Dixon	1m 43.622s
6	Vietti	1m 43.645s
7	Chantra	1m 43.671s
8	Ogura	1m 43.710s
9	Bendsneyder	1m 43.727s
10	Gonzalez	1m 43.761s
11	Lowes	1m 43.787s
12	Canet	1m 43.810s
13	Navarro	1m 43.839s
14	V D Goorbergh	1m 44.068s
15	Roberts	1m 44.189s
16	Beaubier	1m 44.189s
17	Acosta	1m 44.205s
18	Schrotter	1m 44.554s
	Q1	
19	Dalla Porta	1m 44.244s
20	Rodrigo	1m 44.390s
21	Corsi	1m 44.431s
22	Ramirez	1m 44.445s
23	Salac	1m 44.501s
24	Antonelli	1m 44.521s
25	Alcoba	1m 44.652s
26	Fenati	1m 44.671s
27	Kelly	1m 44.798s
28	Zaccone	1m 44.798s
29	Kubo	1m 44.876s

Fastest race laps

1	Vietti	1m 42.829s
2	Canet	1m 43.117s
3	Aldeguer	1m 43.216s
4	Chantra	1m 43.226s
5	Ogura	1m 43.312s
6	Dixon	1m 43.407s
7	Arbolino	1m 43.455s
8	Navarro	1m 43.558s
9	Arenas	1m 43.656s
10	Acosta	1m 43.662s
11	Bendsneyder	1m 43.679s
12	Lowes	1m 43.731s
13	Beaubier	1m 43.861s
14	Roberts	1m 44.183s
15	Schrotter	1m 44.210s
16	Ramirez	1m 44.214s
17	Dalla Porta	1m 44.215s
18	Gonzalez	1m 44.423s
19	Fenati	1m 44.593s
20	Corsi	1m 44.614s
21	Alcoba	1m 44.663s
22	Salac	1m 44.689s
23	Rodrigo	1m 44.701s
24	Kubo	1m 45.367s
25	Zaccone	1m 46.006s

Championship Points

	Rider	Points
1	Vietti	70
2	Canet	49
3	Chantra	45
4	Ogura	36
5	Lowes	35
6	Arbolino	29
7	Fernandez	24
8	Acosta	20
9	Arenas	17
10	Dixon	16
11	Roberts	16
12	Beaubier	16
13	Navarro	12
14	Schrotter	10
15	Aldeguer	9
16	Bendsneyder	8
17	Alcoba	4
18	Gonzalez	2
19	Ramirez	1
20	Fenati	1

Constructor Points

	Constructor	Points
1	Kalex	75
2	Boscoscuro	10
3	MV Agusta	1

Moto3

RACE DISTANCE: 21 laps, 62.713 miles/100.926km · RACE WEATHER: Dry (air 22°, humidity 58%, track 35°)

Pos.	Rider	Nat.	No.	Entrant	Machine	Laps	Time & Speed
1	**Sergio Garcia**	SPA	11	Solunion GASGAS Aspar Team	GASGAS	21	38m 23.433s
							98.0mph/157.7km/h
2	**Dennis Foggia**	ITA	7	Leopard Racing	Honda	21	38m 23.579s
3	**Ayumu Sasaki**	JPN	71	Sterilgarda Husqvarna Max	Husqvarna	21	38m 23.808s
4	**Riccardo Rossi**	ITA	54	SIC58 Squadra Corse	Honda	21	38m 23.940s
5	**Tatsuki Suzuki**	JPN	24	Leopard Racing	Honda	21	38m 23.917s
6	**Diogo Moreira**	BRA	10	MT Helmets - MSI	KTM	21	38m 24.020s
7	**Daniel Holgado**	SPA	96	Red Bull KTM Ajo	KTM	21	38m 24.148s
8	**Carlos Tatay**	SPA	99	CFMOTO Racing PruestelGP	CFMOTO	21	38m 25.465s
9	**Kaito Toba**	JPN	27	CIP Green Power	KTM	21	38m 26.531s
10	**Joel Kelso**	AUS	66	CIP Green Power	KTM	21	38m 26.830s
11	**Elia Bartolini**	ITA	23	QJMotor Avintia Racing Team	KTM	21	38m 31.082s
12	**Ryusei Yamanaka**	JPN	6	MT Helmets - MSI	KTM	21	38m 32.326s
13	**Adrian Fernandez**	SPA	31	Red Bull KTM Tech3	KTM	21	38m 32.465s
14	**Deniz Oncu**	TUR	53	Red Bull KTM Tech3	KTM	21	38m 32.635s
15	**Ivan Ortola**	SPA	48	Angeluss MTA Team	KTM	21	38m 32.882s
16	Stefano Nepa	ITA	82	Angeluss MTA Team	KTM	21	38m 46.178s
17	Taiyo Furusato	JPN	72	Honda Team Asia	Honda	21	38m 46.856s
18	Matteo Bertelle	ITA	18	QJMotor Avintia Racing Team	KTM	21	38m 47.100s
19	Lorenzo Fellon	FRA	20	SIC58 Squadra Corse	Honda	21	38m 47.243s
20	Alberto Surra	ITA	67	Rivacold Snipers Team	Honda	21	38m 47.474s
21	Mario Aji	INA	64	Honda Team Asia	Honda	21	38m 48.313s
22	Gerard Riu Male	SPA	87	BOE SKX	KTM	21	39m 00.849s
23	Joshua Whatley	GBR	70	VisionTrack Racing Team	Honda	21	39m 25.564s
	Jaume Masia	SPA	5	Red Bull KTM Ajo	KTM	16	DNF-crash
	Andrea Migno	ITA	16	Rivacold Snipers Team	Honda	14	DNF-crash
	Scott Ogden	GBR	19	VisionTrack Racing Team	Honda	13	DNF-technical
	Izan Guevara	SPA	28	Solunion GASGAS Aspar Team	GASGAS	9	DNF-technical
	Xavier Artigas	SPA	43	CFMOTO Racing PruestelGP	CFMOTO	5	DNF-technical
	Ana Carrasco	SPA	22	BOE SKX	KTM	4	DNF-crash

Fastest lap: Andrea Migno, on lap 5, 1m 48.834s, 98.7mph/158.9km/h.

Lap record: Miguel Oliveira, 1m 48.977s, 98.6mph/158.7km/h (2015).

Event maximum speed: Andrea Migno, 151.2mph/243.3km/h (race).

Qualifying:

Weather: Dry

Air: 25° **Humidity:** 35%

Track: 43°

1	Garcia	1m 48.429s
2	Sasaki	1m 48.600s
3	Guevara	1m 48.624s
4	Rossi	1m 48.726s
5	Kelso	1m 48.735s
6	Holgado	1m 48.865s
7	Artigas	1m 48.943s
8	Migno	1m 48.953s
9	Suzuki	1m 49.050s
10	Moreira	1m 49.061s
11	Foggia	1m 49.128s
12	Masia	1m 49.186s
13	Toba	1m 49.376s
14	Yamanaka	1m 49.400s
15	Ortola	1m 49.435s
16	Oncu	1m 49.531s
17	Nepa	1m 49.541s
18	Tatay	1m 49.724s
	Q1	
19	Ogden	1m 50.094s
20	Aji	1m 50.104s
21	Bartolini	1m 50.138s
22	Furusato	1m 50.209s
23	Fernandez	1m 50.229s
24	Bertelle	1m 50.423s
25	Surra	1m 50.544s
26	Fellon	1m 50.740s
27	Carrasco	1m 51.031s
28	Riu Male	1m 51.128s
29	Whatley	1m 53.108s

Fastest race laps

1	Migno	1m 48.834s
2	Masia	1m 48.836s
3	Sasaki	1m 48.984s
4	Kelso	1m 48.993s
5	Moreira	1m 49.002s
6	Rossi	1m 49.090s
7	Foggia	1m 49.125s
8	Tatay	1m 49.126s
9	Holgado	1m 49.132s
10	Suzuki	1m 49.134s
11	Oncu	1m 49.144s
12	Garcia	1m 49.150s
13	Guevara	1m 49.237s
14	Toba	1m 49.256s
15	Bartolini	1m 49.294s
16	Fernandez	1m 49.300s
17	Ortola	1m 49.361s
18	Ogden	1m 49.365s
19	Yamanaka	1m 49.419s
20	Artigas	1m 49.476s
21	Nepa	1m 49.745s
22	Bertelle	1m 49.844s
23	Surra	1m 49.855s
24	Furusato	1m 50.035s
25	Fellon	1m 50.112s
26	Aji	1m 50.154s
27	Whatley	1m 50.725s
28	Carrasco	1m 50.833s
29	Riu Male	1m 50.849s

Championship Points

	Rider	Points
1	Garcia	58
2	Foggia	54
3	Guevara	28
4	Toba	27
5	Oncu	26
6	Migno	25
7	Tatay	24
8	Moreira	20
9	Rossi	17
10	Suzuki	17
11	Sasaki	16
12	Artigas	16
13	Holgado	16
14	Yamanaka	16
15	Bartolini	13
16	McPhee	11
17	Masia	9
18	Kelso	7
19	Ortola	6
20	Fernandez	5
21	Nepa	3
22	Ogden	3
23	Aji	2
24	Bertelle	1

Constructor Points

	Constructor	Points
1	Honda	70
2	GASGAS	65
3	KTM	37
4	CFMOTO	30
5	Husqvarna	27

FIM WORLD CHAMPIONSHIP · ROUND 4

GRAND PRIX OF THE AMERICAS

CIRCUIT OF THE AMERICAS

23
alpinestars

THE return of Marc Marquez to Austin was always going to be significant. In eight previous visits, the only time he hadn't won had been in 2019, when a traction-control glitch had tipped him off when miles in the lead. He had always been on pole until 2021, when Bagnaia and Quartararo had pipped him. But he won anyway, by 4.6 seconds. In the parlance of the self-styled live-music capital of the world, Marc 'owned' CoTA.

In 2022, both he and his bike were a little below par: the Honda was still short of settings that would let him ride it to his maximum, the rider a little tentative after three weeks away, haunted by diplopia. At first, he'd even feared he might not recover: "It made me feel scared." Those feelings were mitigated after rapid improvement; the knock to his confidence took a bit longer.

In fact, he said, he'd been fit to race in Argentina, but because of the issues involved in adapting to the 2022 bike, "I didn't feel motivated to take that risk." Now, "compared to Qatar, my physical condition … I feel a bit better, but it's true that with confidence, I feel much worse. This is something that is obvious about a weekend after another injury. The championship is important, it's there, but it's not the main target now." He was not telling the whole story.

Another rare electronic glitch would rekindle the fire.

He had qualified ninth. Then, as the lights went out, at first it appeared as though he had fluffed the start. Those ahead disappeared up the hill, those behind swerved around the Honda until only the safety car was left behind as he moved away at a relative crawl.

The details remained a mystery, but Marquez was exonerated for whatever it was that had prevented the bike from producing full power: "At first, I thought, 'Did I put the pit limiter on?' But no. The alarm [a warning light] was on for all the race, but luckily in the first corner, when the holeshot [device] disengaged, the bike worked, more or less. Not perfect. There was something still wrong, but it worked in a good way."

Later, the details leaked out. Marc's bike had a new swingarm, and when a mechanic was removing the tyre warmer on the grid, he accidentally struck a sensor in an unfamiliar location. This confused the electronics to spoil his start and produce problems that lingered through the race.

Despite this, he became the star of the race as he mounted a stirring comeback from last to sixth, passing and sometimes repassing 18 riders on the way: "It was a sprint race for me. I said to myself, 'I will give everything.' I knew riding at 100 per cent, I might not finish in a good way, and with five or six laps left, my body said, 'That's it,' and I just tried to finish." It was his worst ever finish at Austin, but a turning point in his confidence.

At 3.4 miles, only second in length to 3.6-mile Silverstone, and with two more corners (20: 11 left, 9 right), CoTA had undergone a major resurfacing in less than six months since the previous visit, addressing the problems of bumps that in 2021 had prompted some riders to threaten never to return. New asphalt had been laid from Turns Two to Ten, and from Turn 12 to the entry of 16. While still not perfect, it won praise, albeit lukewarm in some cases. "From last year, for me, 80 per cent of the bumps, or even more, are better," said Quartararo. "Just Turn Ten, if you are not on the line, it is tricky." Joan Mir added. "When we come to America, there are always really bumpy tracks, and we have to live with that. Probably I don't complain because I know how bad it was last year! So I'm saying, 'Okay, it's more or less fine, but it's bumpy.'"

With most riders' contracts running out at the end of the season, the who-goes-where speculation had already begun. Most particularly, Quartararo's plans for 2023 were a hot topic, with reports linking him to a switch, probably to Honda. Nonplused by the M1's lack of development and a patchy start to 2022, he remained tight-lipped, insisting, "My priority is

to fight for the championship ... but at the end, we also have to look at my future, during this month or next month." His manager, Eric Mahe, revealed that there had been in talks with other factories. "We are checking all parameters," he said.

Similar questions had been prompted by the sudden elevated status of Aleix Espargaro. He had helped Aprilia turn the RS-GP into a race-winning bike, and he had arrived leading the championship. But it was not all celebration, with the rider and Italian factory disputing the finances. He too was being linked with a move elsewhere. "I feel super-strong, super-fast," he said. "I want to stay ... but the first talks they have with my manager were really disappointing. I feel very sad because we are completely far apart."

Just two races later, however, with Suzuki announcing that they would quit, the landscape would change, with more strong riders going for fewer strong seats.

In 2021, at this circuit, the nightmare of Moto3 mayhem had been realised in the race – a top-speed collision had tipped off Alcoba, Acosta and Migno, miraculously without injury, and earned the culprit, Deniz Oncu, a two-race suspension. So far in the new season, Moto3 misbehaviour seemed to be under some sort of control, with the threat of ever-increasing punishment: only one rider, Elia Bartolini, was sanctioned for dawdling in practice and qualifying (back-of-the-grid start and a long-lap), while Moto2's Jorge Navarro earned a long-lap for crashing under a yellow flag.

But incidents in MotoGP qualifying again prompted questions as to why the bigger classes are not scrutinised in the same way. Aleix Espargaro had crashed out in frustration after Alex Marquez and Franco Morbidelli attempted to follow him throughout Q1. Later, he lamented, "It was embarrassing." And Suzuki's Alex Rins found his qualifying efforts frustrated by riders touring on the edge of the track. "It's unacceptable," he said. "We are the big boys and we need to give an example to the others. I was in Q1, pushing, pushing, pushing – then four or five riders in front stopped. It makes no sense. It's so dangerous." Rins, who had denied Rossi a final win at this circuit in 2019, after Marquez had crashed out, made it out of Q1, by two-tenths ahead of Aleix.

MOTOGP RACE – 20 laps

Martin claimed his second 2022 pole with a new record, through from Q1 and heading a first ever Ducati lockout of the top five. Miller and Bagnaia were next, then Zarco and Bastianini. Quartararo was sixth; the Suzukis of Rins and Mir led row three from Marc Marquez.

With the leading Repsol Honda left trailing, Ducati – and namely Miller – took advantage of their Saturday superiority. A brief disruption from Martin aside, the Australian ended the first lap up front, with Bagnaia third and Bastianini fourth. Initially, Quartararo was the only man to get among the red bikes, picking off Zarco at Turn One. The Suzukis hovered menacingly in seventh and eighth, ahead of the Espargaro brothers, with Aleix leading Pol.

Miller led confidently. Zarco appeared to be the principal early threat, posting fastest time on lap three as he took fifth from Quartararo. Two laps on, he was under Bagnaia for fourth. Then it was the Italian's turn as he reclaimed the position with another fastest lap, the eighth. All the while, Bastianini was a solid third, keeping his tyres cool behind Miller and Martin.

Behind, Quartararo was going in the opposite direction. First Rins got by on lap three at Turn 11, before Mir also on lap six with a neat move into Turn One. With Morbidelli and Dovizioso contesting a distant 16th, this had all the hallmarks of being another embarrassing day for Yamaha. But the reigning champion's head never dropped as he clung on to the Suzukis.

Back in the pack, Marc Marquez was getting stuck in. There were two-in-one moves on brother Alex and Marco Bezzecchi on the first lap, then Brad Binder and Vinales

Left: **Marquez takes the applause from his Honda crew after an epic ride.**

Photo: Whit Bazemore

Below: **On the hunt. An electronics glitch left the multiple winner trailing and set for a stirring ride from last to sixth.**

Opening spread: **After biding his time, Bastianini took an impressive second win in four races.**

Photos: Gold & Goose

Above: **Rins, here briefly ahead of winner Bastianini, would seize second from Miller on the final lap.**
Photo: Suzuki ECSTAR.

Top right: **A maiden Moto2 pole came at home for American Racing's Cameron Beaubier.**

Above right: **And a maiden Moto2 win for Tony Arbolino, shadowed early on by Jake Dixon.**

Centre right: **A happy Gigi Dall'Igna gives Miller a hug after his return to the podium.**

Centre far right: **Ai Ogura enjoyed second place and a boost to his title chances.**

Below right: **Red Bull KTM's Jaume Masia takes a rest in *parc fermé* after winning a thrilling Moto3 race.**

Below far right: **Rookie Scott Ogden impressed once more with 12th, only ten seconds adrift in his first visit to the track.**
Photos: Gold & Goose

on lap five as he scrambled forward, finding passing places where others hadn't imagined them. Not even a huge moment over the bumps on the descent from Turn Ten slowed his pace as he advanced towards the top six.

Yet as he hovered five seconds off the leader, Marquez was of no concern to the front battle. Rins was, however, as he took advantage of his superior speed through the track's serpentine first sector to launch repeated late-braking attacks into Turn 11. First, he passed Bagnaia on lap six, then Zarco on lap nine after attacks at Turns 11 and 12.

Next time around, he launched another attack at the downhill hairpin at 11, this time on Bastianini, who used his Ducati power to get back ahead on the straight and was spurred into action: "I knew it was time to push."

Ahead, his first target became clearer as Martin began to falter at half-distance, losing time on to the track's two straights as his rear tyre faded. Miller soon had seven-tenths in hand as Bastianini and Rins made short work of the Pramac man, second and third on lap 12.

As well as Miller had performed, the writing was on the wall. On lap 14, Bastianini posted a new fastest lap, gapping Rins in the process. A lap later, he had wiped out the Australian's lead.

The race-winning overtake on the back straight on lap 16 was a formality, thanks again to his late-race speed. He had gained two seconds by the flag and retaken the championship lead.

The chances of a Ducati one-two were dashed at the end as Rins doggedly chased down Miller. A Turn 11 pass didn't stick, but a clinical move at the second-last corner of the race gave him second, his best since the British GP in 2021.

At a least favourite track, Mir shadowed his team-mate for fourth. As Martin dropped down the order, Bagnaia held on to fifth. But only just. Marc Marquez reached sixth on lap 17, three on from yet another two-in-one on Quartararo and Zarco. By then, his tyres were finished. Unable to attack Bagnaia, he had to defend. Twice in the final two laps, Quartararo had attacked at Turn Seven, but had failed to hold the place.

Martin, eighth, was distraught; Zarco's early promise also fizzled out. After three-quarter-distance, he fell back into the clutches of a three-way skirmish, then led by Brad Binder from Aleix Espargaro and a closing Vinales. Zarco narrowly held ninth, with the reshuffled Vinales, Espargaro and Binder following, all four over the line within the same second.

Pol and close companion Nakagami were next. Then another trio disputed the final point, with Morbidelli in charge over the last three laps, Dovizioso and Marini right behind.

Fernandez was 19th behind Oliveira; Bezzecchi crashed. The other three rookies – Gardner, Di Giannantonio and Binder – were locked together. Alex Marquez also crashed.

MOTO2 RACE – 18 laps

Hopes of a first American intermediate-class victory since John Kocinski's 250 win in Australia in 1990, and a repeat of home-hero wins by Kocinski and Jimmy Filice at Laguna Seca were boosted when Beaubier took his Kalex to a career-first pole. The five-times AMA Superbike champion had track knowledge as well as fan support on his side, and a growing familiarity in his second year on the American Racing Kalex.

Vietti and Canet were alongside; Arbolino, Arenas and Dixon behind. Second American Roberts, who lacked the AMA experience, was 16th; compatriot rookie Kelly, 28th.

Unusually, Moto2 was run first on Sunday, and the championship battle was blown wide open when the top three all crashed out in a dramatic first third of the race. An afternoon of attrition resulted in the 29 starters being whittled down to just 17 at the finish.

Vietti and Beaubier had led through the first corner, but the American had been shuffled down to fourth by the end of the lap. By then, mayhem at the end of the main straight had been triggered when Chantra missed his braking. The subsequent multiple pile-up took out four other riders: Lowes, the unfortunate Aldeguer, van den Goorbergh and Rodrigo. Chantra was hit with a long-lap penalty for the following race.

The next to go was Vietti, who had lost the lead to Canet on lap three, then crashed out of second on the fifth. That gave Canet a lead of 1.3 seconds, but the Spaniard suffered a similar fate on lap eight, losing the rear on the bump through Turn Seven and shaking his head in frustration.

Now, the gift went to Arbolino, who had just over half a

second on Dixon, who, in turn, was being pursued a second or so behind by a dogged Ogura. The rest, led by Schrotter, were already more than five seconds in arrears.

Arbolino stretched his advantage steadily, taking a maiden victory in the class by better than three seconds.

Behind him, Ogura was well placed to move decisively past Dixon when the English rider hit a neutral at the end of the long main straight on lap 12.

Other crashes had thinned the field – Corsi on the MV Agusta, after a poor start, on lap three, and shortly afterwards, Acosta, while running a promising fifth. Antonelli was one of two retirements.

Heartbreakingly, the last to go was Beaubier, on the final lap, having taken fourth from Schrotter four laps before, and while trying to fend off the German's retaliatory attacks. The latter inherited the position ahead of Navarro, who had recovered after serving his long-lap penalty. A second away, Alcoba took sixth off Bendsneyder on the last lap, with Roberts just out of touch.

A lone and off-form Fernandez was ninth, Baltus tenth, the rest trailing in.

Vietti's points lead shrank, with Ogura and Arbolino overtaking Canet to close threateningly.

MOTO3 RACE – 17 laps

Free practice had suggested that pole-qualifier Migno and second-fastest Foggia would be set to break clear, but a strong headwind on the back straight changed the picture. Slipstreaming became critical, and it bunched together a lead group of seven riders throughout a thrilling contest.

Brilliant rookie Moreira traded blows with Oncu in the early laps while the slow-starting Foggia and Migno came to life. Masia, Sasaki and front-row-starter Artigas made up the lead group after Guevara served a double long-lap for jumping the start, and team-mate Garcia was punted off at Turn 16 by the wayward Holgado.

With Masia and Migno ahead on the penultimate lap, a thrilling double move by Oncu had Foggia and Sasaki scampering to recover lost ground. Masia made the decisive move on the final lap, outbraking Migno at Turn 12. The Italian attempted a response two turns from the flag, only to run wide, allowing Masia and Foggia through for a last-gasp first and second. With Garcia out, this was enough for Foggia to regain the points lead.

Sasaki came home fourth, ahead of Oncu and Artigas, the top six covered by 1.5 seconds after Moreira high-sided out of the action on the final lap. Guevara recovered to seventh.

The next group was led by Tatay from Rossi and Suzuki to complete the top ten. Close behind, another gang of three was led over the line by Ortola, while fellow rookie Ogden snitched 12th from Nepa on the final lap.

Toba crashed out, and rookie Holgado also, twice – the second time terminally.

FIM WORLD CHAMPIONSHIP: ROUND 4

RED BULL GRAND PRIX OF THE AMERICAS

8–10 APRIL, 2022

CIRCUIT OF THE AMERICAS

Circuit: 5.513km / 3.426 miles
20 laps
Width: 15m

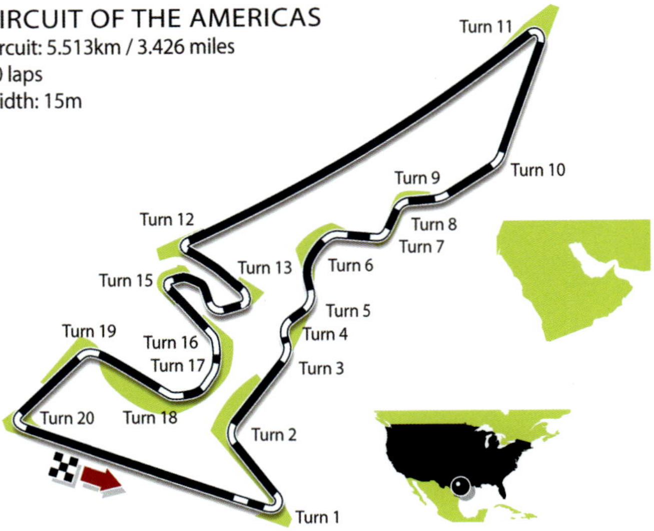

MotoGP

RACE DISTANCE: 20 laps, 68.512 miles/110.260km · RACE WEATHER: Dry (air 26°, humidity 57%, track 37°)

Pos.	Rider	Nat.	No.	Entrant	Machine	Tyres	Race tyre choice	Laps	Time & speed
1	**Enea Bastianini**	ITA	23	Gresini Racing MotoGP	Ducati Desmosedici	M	F: Hard/R: Soft	20	41m 23.111s 99.3mph/159.8km/h
2	**Alex Rins**	SPA	42	Team SUZUKI ECSTAR	Suzuki GSX-RR	M	F: Hard/R: Soft	20	41m 25.169s
3	**Jack Miller**	AUS	43	Ducati Lenovo Team	Ducati Desmosedici	M	F: Hard/R: Soft	20	41m 25.423s
4	**Joan Mir**	SPA	36	Team SUZUKI ECSTAR	Suzuki GSX-RR	M	F: Hard/R: Soft	20	41m 27.086s
5	**Francesco Bagnaia**	ITA	63	Ducati Lenovo Team	Ducati Desmosedici	M	F: Hard/R: Soft	20	41m 29.156s
6	**Marc Marquez**	SPA	93	Repsol Honda Team	Honda RC213V	M	F: Hard/R: Soft	20	41m 29.728s
7	**Fabio Quartararo**	FRA	20	Monster Energy Yamaha MotoGP	Yamaha YZR-M1	M	F: Hard/R: Soft	20	41m 29.871s
8	**Jorge Martin**	SPA	89	Pramac Racing	Ducati Desmosedici	M	F: Hard/R: Soft	20	41m 31.552s
9	**Johann Zarco**	FRA	5	Pramac Racing	Ducati Desmosedici	M	F: Hard/R: Soft	20	41m 35.486s
10	**Maverick Vinales**	SPA	12	Aprilia Racing	Aprilia RS-GP	M	F: Hard/R: Soft	20	41m 35.753s
11	**Aleix Espargaro**	SPA	41	Aprilia Racing	Aprilia RS-GP	M	F: Hard/R: Soft	20	41m 36.058s
12	**Brad Binder**	RSA	33	Red Bull KTM Factory Racing	KTM RC16	M	F: Hard/R: Soft	20	41m 36.487s
13	**Pol Espargaro**	SPA	44	Repsol Honda Team	Honda RC213V	M	F: Hard/R: Soft	20	41m 41.072s
14	**Takaaki Nakagami**	JPN	30	LCR Honda IDEMITSU	Honda RC213V	M	F: Hard/R: Soft	20	41m 41.881s
15	**Andrea Dovizioso**	ITA	4	WithU Yamaha RNF MotoGP Team	Yamaha YZR-M1	M	F: Hard/R: Soft	20	41m 52.430s
16	Franco Morbidelli	ITA	21	Monster Energy Yamaha MotoGP	Yamaha YZR-M1	M	F: Hard/R: Soft	20	41m 52.240s
17	Luca Marini	ITA	10	Mooney VR46 Racing Team	Ducati Desmosedici	M	F: Hard/R: Soft	20	41m 52.741s
18	Miguel Oliveira	POR	88	Red Bull KTM Factory Racing	KTM RC16	M	F: Hard/R: Medium	20	41m 55.113s
19	Raul Fernandez	SPA	25	Tech3 KTM Factory Racing	KTM RC16	M	F: Hard/R: Medium	20	42m 00.173s
20	Remy Gardner	AUS	87	Tech3 KTM Factory Racing	KTM RC16	M	F: Hard/R: Soft	20	42m 05.553s
21	Fabio Di Giannantonio	ITA	49	Gresini Racing MotoGP	Ducati Desmosedici	M	F: Hard/R: Soft	20	42m 05.998s
22	Darryn Binder	RSA	40	WithU Yamaha RNF MotoGP Team	Yamaha YZR-M1	M	F: Hard/R: Soft	20	43m 05.282s
	Alex Marquez	SPA	73	LCR Honda CASTROL	Honda RC213V	M	F: Hard/R: Soft	5	DNF-crash
	Marco Bezzecchi	ITA	72	Mooney VR46 Racing Team	Ducati Desmosedici	M	F: Hard/R: Soft	2	DNF-crash

Fastest lap: Enea Bastianini, on lap 14, 2m 3.521s, 99.8mph/160.6km/h.
Lap record: Marc Marquez, 2m 3.575s, 99.8mph/160.6km/h (2014).
Event maximum speed: Enea Bastianini, 217.9mph/350.6km/h (free practice).

Qualifying

Weather: Dry
Air Temp: 28° **Humidity:** 24%
Track Temp: 49°

1	Martin	2m 02.039s
2	Miller	2m 02.042s
3	Bagnaia	2m 02.167s
4	Zarco	2m 02.570s
5	Bastianini	2m 02.578s
6	Quartararo	2m 02.634s
7	Rins	2m 02.694s
8	Mir	2m 02.947s
9	M. Marquez	2m 03.038s
10	Nakagami	2m 03.054s
11	Marini	2m 03.059s
12	P. Espargaro	2m 03.096s
Q1		
13	A. Espargaro	2m 02.922s
14	Vinales	2m 03.121s
15	Dovizioso	2m 03.133s
16	Bezzecchi	2m 03.328s
17	B. Binder	2m 03.467s
18	Di Giannantonio	2m 03.576s
19	Morbidelli	2m 03.579s
20	Oliveira	2m 03.983s
21	Fernandez	2m 04.140s
22	Gardner	2m 04.185s
23	A. Marquez	2m 04.229s
24	D. Binder	2m 04.646s

Fastest race laps

1	Bastianini	2m 03.521s
2	M. Marquez	2m 03.553s
3	Vinales	2m 03.570s
4	Miller	2m 03.674s
5	Mir	2m 03.799s
6	Bagnaia	2m 03.870s
7	Zarco	2m 03.895s
8	Rins	2m 03.932s
9	Quartararo	2m 04.037s
10	Martin	2m 04.103s
11	B. Binder	2m 04.305s
12	A. Espargaro	2m 04.306s
13	P. Espargaro	2m 04.508s
14	A. Marquez	2m 04.558s
15	Nakagami	2m 04.559s
16	Fernandez	2m 04.621s
17	Marini	2m 04.694s
18	Morbidelli	2m 04.723s
19	Oliveira	2m 04.747s
20	D. Binder	2m 04.777s
21	Dovizioso	2m 04.802s
22	Di Giannantonio	2m 05.150s
23	Gardner	2m 05.218s
24	Bezzecchi	2m 39.542s

Championship Points

1	Bastianini	61
2	Rins	56
3	A. Espargaro	50
4	Mir	46
5	Quartararo	44
6	B. Binder	42
7	Miller	31
8	Zarco	31
9	Oliveira	28
10	Martin	28
11	P. Espargaro	23
12	Bagnaia	23
13	M. Marquez	21
14	Vinales	19
15	Morbidelli	14
16	Nakagami	12
17	Marini	10
18	Bezzecchi	7
19	D. Binder	6
20	A. Marquez	4
21	Dovizioso	3
22	Gardner	1

Constructor Points

1	Ducati	86
2	KTM	59
3	Suzuki	57
4	Aprilia	51
5	Yamaha	44
6	Honda	34

Lap chart

	Grid order	1	2	3	4	5	6	7	8	9	10	11	12	13	14	15	16	17	18	19	20	
89	MARTIN	43	43	43	43	43	43	43	43	43	43	43	43	43	43	43	23	23	23	23	23	1
43	MILLER	89	89	89	89	89	89	89	89	89	89	89	23	23	23	23	43	43	43	43	42	2
63	BAGNAIA	23	23	23	23	23	23	23	23	23	23	23	42	42	42	42	42	42	42	42	43	3
5	ZARCO	63	63	63	63	5	5	5	5	42	42	42	89	89	36	36	36	36	36	36	36	4
23	BASTIANINI	20	20	5	5	63	42	42	42	5	5	5	63	36	63	63	63	63	63	63	63	5
20	QUARTARARO	5	5	20	20	42	63	63	63	63	63	63	36	63	89	89	89	93	93	93	93	6
42	RINS	36	42	42	42	20	36	36	36	36	36	36	5	5	93	93	93	20	20	20	20	7
36	MIR	42	36	36	36	36	20	20	20	20	20	20	20	20	20	20	20	89	89	89	89	8
93	M. MARQUEZ	41	41	41	41	41	41	41	41	41	93	93	93	93	5	5	5	5	5	5	5	9
30	NAKAGAMI	44	44	44	44	44	44	93	93	93	41	41	41	41	41	33	33	33	41	41	12	10
10	MARINI	30	30	30	30	30	93	44	33	33	33	33	33	33	33	41	12	12	33	12	41	11
44	P. ESPARGARO	33	33	33	33	93	33	33	44	44	44	12	12	12	12	12	41	41	12	33	33	12
41	A. ESPARGARO	12	12	12	12	33	12	12	12	12	12	44	44	44	44	44	44	44	44	44	44	13
12	VINALES	10	10	93	93	12	30	30	30	30	30	30	30	30	30	30	30	30	30	30	30	14
4	DOVIZIOSO	88	88	88	88	88	88	88	88	88	88	88	88	88	88	10	10	10	21	21	21	15
72	BEZZECCHI	4	93	4	4	73	4	4	4	10	10	10	10	10	10	4	4	4	10	4	4	
33	B.BINDER	21	4	73	73	4	10	10	10	4	4	4	4	4	4	88	88	21	4	10	10	
49	DI GIANNANTONIO	93	21	21	21	10	25	25	25	25	25	25	25	21	21	21	21	88	88	88	88	
21	MORBIDELLI	73	73	10	10	87	87	21	21	21	21	21	21	25	25	25	25	25	25	25	25	
88	OLIVEIRA	72	87	87	87	25	21	87	87	87	40	40	87	87	87	87	87	87	87	87	87	
25	FERNANDEZ	40	25	25	25	21	49	40	40	40	87	87	40	40	40	40	40	49	49	49	49	
87	GARDNER	87	49	49	49	49	40	49	49	49	49	49	49	49	49	49	49	40	40	40	40	
73	A. MARQUEZ	49	40	40	40	40																
40	D.BINDER	25	72																			

40 Pit stop

Moto2

RACE DISTANCE: 18 laps, 61.661 miles/99.234km · RACE WEATHER: Dry (air 24°, humidity 64%, track 35°)

Pos.	Rider	Nat.	No.	Entrant	Machine	Laps	Time & Speed
1	**Tony Arbolino**	ITA	14	Elf Marc VDS Racing Team	Kalex	18	39m 06.552s
							94.6 mph/152.2km/h
2	**Ai Ogura**	JPN	79	IDEMITSU Honda Team Asia	Kalex	18	39m 09.991s
3	**Jake Dixon**	GBR	96	Shimoko GASGAS Aspar Team	Kalex	18	39m 11.339s
4	**Marcel Schrotter**	GER	23	Liqui Moly Intact GP	Kalex	18	39m 21.081s
5	**Jorge Navarro**	SPA	9	Flexbox HP40	Kalex	18	39m 22.899s
6	**Jeremy Alcoba**	SPA	52	Liqui Moly Intact GP	Kalex	18	39m 23.940s
7	**Bo Bendsneyder**	NED	64	Pertamina Mandalika SAG Team	Kalex	18	39m 24.183s
8	**Joe Roberts**	USA	16	Italtrans Racing Team	Kalex	18	39m 26.336s
9	**Augusto Fernandez**	SPA	37	Red Bull KTM Ajo	Kalex	18	39m 31.147s
10	**Barry Baltus**	BEL	7	RW Racing GP	Kalex	18	39m 36.843s
11	**Albert Arenas**	SPA	75	Shimoko GASGAS Aspar Team	Kalex	18	39m 40.027s
12	**Marcos Ramirez**	SPA	42	MV Agusta Forward Racing	MV Agusta	18	39m 41.337s
13	**Manuel Gonzalez**	SPA	18	Yamaha VR46 Master Camp Team	Kalex	18	39m 41.540s
14	**Filip Salac**	CZE	12	Gresini Racing Moto2	Kalex	18	39m 44.338s
15	**Romano Fenati**	ITA	5	MB Conveyors Speed Up	Boscoscuro	18	39m 44.960s
16	Lorenzo Dalla Porta	ITA	19	Italtrans Racing Team	Kalex	18	40m 26.551s
17	Sean Dylan Kelly	USA	4	American Racing	Kalex	18	40m 30.989s
	Cameron Beaubier	USA	6	American Racing	Kalex	17	DNF-crash
	Niccolo Antonelli	ITA	28	Mooney VR46 Racing Team	Kalex	12	DNF-physical
	Aron Canet	SPA	40	Flexbox HP40	Kalex	7	DNF-crash
	Celestino Vietti	ITA	13	Mooney VR46 Racing Team	Kalex	4	DNF-crash
	Pedro Acosta	SPA	51	Red Bull KTM Ajo	Kalex	3	DNF-crash
	Alessandro Zaccone	ITA	61	Gresini Racing Moto2	Kalex	3	DNF-crash
	Simone Corsi	ITA	24	MV Agusta Forward Racing	MV Agusta	2	DNF-crash
	Fermin Aldeguer	SPA	54	MB Conveyors Speed Up	Boscoscuro	0	DNF-crash
	Sam Lowes	GBR	22	Elf Marc VDS Racing Team	Kalex	0	DNF-crash
	Somkiat Chantra	THA	35	IDEMITSU Honda Team Asia	Kalex	0	DNF-crash
	Zonta van den Goorbergh	NED	84	RW Racing GP	Kalex	0	DNF-crash
	Gabriel Rodrigo	ARG	2	Pertamina Mandalika SAG Team	Kalex	0	DNF-crash

Fastest lap: Aron Canet, on lap 2, 2m 9.312s, 95.3mph/153.4km/h.

Lap record: Raul Fernandez, 2m 9.794s, 95.0mph/152.9km/h (2021).

Event maximum speed: Pedro Acosta, 180.4mph/290.3km/h (warm-up).

Qualifying

Weather: Dry

Air: 26° **Humidity:** 27%

Track: 45°

1	Beaubier	2m 08.751s
2	Vietti	2m 09.091s
3	Canet	2m 09.283s
4	Arbolino	2m 09.329s
5	Arenas	2m 09.358s
6	Dixon	2m 09.434s
7	Navarro	2m 09.462s
8	Aldeguer	2m 09.614s
9	Lowes	2m 09.900s
10	Acosta	2m 09.925s
11	Ogura	2m 10.003s
12	Bendsneyder	2m 10.020s
13	Schrotter	2m 10.069s
14	Ramirez	2m 10.127s
15	Alcoba	2m 10.152s
16	Roberts	2m 10.325s
17	Chantra	2m 10.707s
18	Fernandez	No Time
	Q1	
19	Salac	2m 10.209s
20	Baltus	2m 10.471s
21	Fenati	2m 10.599s
22	V D Goorbergh	2m 10.619s
23	Gonzalez	2m 11.078s
24	Rodrigo	2m 11.113s
25	Dalla Porta	2m 11.288s
26	Zaccone	2m 11.486s
27	Antonelli	2m 13.291s
28	Kelly	2m 13.562s
29	Corsi	2m 17.038s

Fastest race laps

1	Canet	2m 09.312s
2	Ogura	2m 09.582s
3	Vietti	2m 09.620s
4	Dixon	2m 09.634s
5	Arbolino	2m 09.651s
6	Acosta	2m 09.751s
7	Beaubier	2m 10.001s
8	Schrotter	2m 10.006s
9	Navarro	2m 10.270s
10	Roberts	2m 10.517s
11	Bendsneyder	2m 10.544s
12	Salac	2m 10.590s
13	Alcoba	2m 10.616s
14	Fernandez	2m 10.648s
15	Arenas	2m 11.005s
16	Fenati	2m 11.081s
17	Baltus	2m 11.176s
18	Gonzalez	2m 11.279s
19	Ramirez	2m 11.283s
20	Corsi	2m 11.690s
21	Dalla Porta	2m 12.386s
22	Antonelli	2m 12.890s
23	Zaccone	2m 12.901s
24	Kelly	2m 13.808s

Championship Points

1	Vietti	70
2	Ogura	56
3	Arbolino	54
4	Canet	49
5	Chantra	45
6	Lowes	35
7	Dixon	32
8	Fernandez	31
9	Roberts	24
10	Schrotter	23
11	Navarro	23
12	Arenas	22
13	Acosta	20
14	Bendsneyder	17
15	Beaubier	16
16	Alcoba	14
17	Aldeguer	9
18	Baltus	6
19	Ramirez	5
20	Gonzalez	5
21	Salac	2
22	Fenati	2

Constructor Points

1	Kalex	100
2	Boscoscuro	11
3	MV Agusta	5

Moto3

RACE DISTANCE: 17 laps, 58.236 miles/93.721km · RACE WEATHER: Dry (air 27°, humidity 53%, track 40°)

Pos.	Rider	Nat.	No.	Entrant	Machine	Laps	Time & Speed
1	**Jaume Masia**	SPA	5	Red Bull KTM Ajo	KTM	17	38m 58.286s
							89.6 mph/144.2km/h
2	**Dennis Foggia**	ITA	7	Leopard Racing	Honda	17	38m 58.458s
3	**Andrea Migno**	ITA	16	Rivacold Snipers Team	Honda	17	38m 58.680s
4	**Ayumu Sasaki**	JPN	71	Sterilgarda Husqvarna Max	Husqvarna	17	38m 58.776s
5	**Deniz Oncu**	TUR	53	Red Bull KTM Tech3	KTM	17	38m 59.399s
6	**Xavier Artigas**	SPA	43	CFMOTO Racing PruestelGP	CFMOTO	17	38m 59.862s
7	**Izan Guevara**	SPA	28	Gaviota GASGAS Aspar Team	GASGAS	17	39m 01.173s
8	**Carlos Tatay**	SPA	99	CFMOTO Racing PruestelGP	CFMOTO	17	39m 06.494s
9	**Riccardo Rossi**	ITA	54	SIC58 Squadra Corse	Honda	17	39m 06.656s
10	**Tatsuki Suzuki**	JPN	24	Leopard Racing	Honda	17	39m 06.764s
11	**Ivan Ortola**	SPA	48	Angeluss MTA Team	KTM	17	39m 08.370s
12	**Scott Ogden**	GBR	19	VisionTrack Racing Team	Honda	17	39m 08.558s
13	**Stefano Nepa**	ITA	82	Angeluss MTA Team	KTM	17	39m 08.710s
14	**Adrian Fernandez**	SPA	31	Red Bull KTM Tech3	KTM	17	39m 16.253s
15	**Lorenzo Fellon**	FRA	20	SIC58 Squadra Corse	Honda	17	39m 16.374s
16	Taiyo Furusato	JPN	72	Honda Team Asia	Honda	17	39m 18.849s
17	Ryusei Yamanaka	JPN	6	MT Helmets - MSI	KTM	17	39m 19.719s
18	Joel Kelso	AUS	66	CIP Green Power	KTM	17	39m 20.245s
19	Elia Bartolini	ITA	23	QJMotor Avintia Racing Team	KTM	17	39m 27.385s
20	Gerard Riu Male	SPA	87	BOE SKX	KTM	17	39m 32.622s
21	Mario Aji	INA	64	Honda Team Asia	Honda	17	39m 32.581s
22	David Salvador	SPA	38	Sterilgarda Husqvarna Max	Husqvarna	17	39m 37.682s
23	Ana Carrasco	SPA	22	BOE SKX	KTM	17	39m 59.195s
	Daniel Holgado	SPA	96	Red Bull KTM Ajo	KTM	16	DNF-crash
	Kaito Toba	JPN	27	CIP Green Power	KTM	16	DNF-crash
	Diogo Moreira	BRA	10	MT Helmets - MSI	KTM	15	DNF-crash
	Matteo Bertelle	ITA	18	QJMotor Avintia Racing Team	KTM	15	DNF-crash
	Sergio Garcia	SPA	11	Gaviota GASGAS Aspar Team	GASGAS	12	DNF-crash
	Joshua Whatley	GBR	70	VisionTrack Racing Team	Honda	5	DNF-physical

Fastest lap: Jaume Masia, on lap 7, 2m 16.179s, 90.5mph/145.7km/h.

Lap record: Aron Canet, 2m 15.583s, 90.9mph/146.3km/h (2017).

Event maximum speed: Jaume Masia, 150.1mph/241.6km/h (race).

Qualifying:

Weather: Dry

Air: 29° **Humidity:** 20%

Track: 48°

1	Migno	2m 15.814s
2	Foggia	2m 15.881s
3	Artigas	2m 16.066s
4	Oncu	2m 16.330s
5	Masia	2m 16.409s
6	Moreira	2m 16.416s
7	Holgado	2m 16.551s
8	Toba	2m 16.582s
9	Sasaki	2m 16.604s
10	Guevara	2m 16.609s
11	Nepa	2m 16.727s
12	Ogden	2m 16.856s
13	Bartolini	2m 16.907s
14	Tatay	2m 16.946s
15	Garcia	2m 17.114s
16	Suzuki	2m 17.515s
17	Rossi	2m 17.651s
18	Kelso	2m 17.771s
	Q1	
19	Fernandez	2m 17.659s
20	Bertelle	2m 17.672s
21	Yamanaka	2m 17.877s
22	Ortola	2m 18.005s
23	Riu Male	2m 18.345s
24	Salvador	2m 18.407s
25	Furusato	2m 18.481s
26	Carrasco	2m 19.699s
27	Whatley	2m 19.935s
	Fellon	No Time
	Aji	No Time

Fastest race laps

1	Masia	2m 16.179s
2	Sasaki	2m 16.608s
3	Guevara	2m 16.672s
4	Artigas	2m 16.739s
5	Moreira	2m 16.744s
6	Foggia	2m 16.783s
7	Migno	2m 16.809s
8	Suzuki	2m 16.859s
9	Rossi	2m 16.863s
10	Garcia	2m 16.873s
11	Ortola	2m 16.889s
12	Nepa	2m 17.034s
13	Oncu	2m 17.058s
14	Holgado	2m 17.127s
15	Tatay	2m 17.235s
16	Ogden	2m 17.394s
17	Fellon	2m 17.433s
18	Fernandez	2m 17.501s
19	Bartolini	2m 17.506s
20	Kelso	2m 17.597s
21	Toba	2m 17.614s
22	Bertelle	2m 17.630s
23	Furusato	2m 17.739s
24	Yamanaka	2m 18.082s
25	Salvador	2m 18.546s
26	Aji	2m 18.908s
27	Riu Male	2m 18.944s
28	Carrasco	2m 20.437s
29	Whatley	2m 21.246s

Championship Points

1	Foggia	74
2	Garcia	58
3	Migno	41
4	Guevara	37
5	Oncu	37
6	Masia	34
7	Tatay	32
8	Sasaki	29
9	Toba	27
10	Artigas	26
11	Rossi	24
12	Suzuki	23
13	Moreira	20
14	Holgado	16
15	Yamanaka	16
16	Bartolini	13
17	McPhee	11
18	Ortola	11
19	Kelso	7
20	Ogden	7
21	Fernandez	7
22	Nepa	6
23	Aji	2
24	Fellon	1
25	Bertelle	1

Constructor Points

1	Honda	90
2	GASGAS	74
3	KTM	62
4	Husqvarna	40
5	CFMOTO	40

FIM WORLD CHAMPIONSHIP · ROUND 5

PORTUGUESE GRAND PRIX

ALGARVE INTERNATIONAL CIRCUIT

12
CUSTOM
73
Lenovo
SUZUKI
36

Above: **Moto2 carnage, after a sudden local downpour played havoc with the leading group.**

Inset, above: **Tony Arbolino was one of 13 riders unable to restart.**
Photos: Gold & Goose

Top right: **Quartararo took a dominant win, his first in ten races.**
Photo: Monster Energy Yamaha

Above right: **Downbeat Dovi – 11th was his best yet in a dismal return to Yamaha.**

Right: **Hand on heart, maiden Moto2 winner Joe Roberts smiles to the strains of his national anthem – the first time it had been played for a podium since 2011.**

Opening spread: **A thundering spectacle – but the dry weather held for MotoGP as Mir's Suzuki led the run to Turn One.**
Photos: Gold & Goose

SELDOM has vulnerability to unexpected weather been as clearly defined as in Portimao. The return to the Algarve not only failed to deliver the balmy conditions everyone had expected, but failed in a way that proved costly for many. A total of 106 falls put the event fourth overall since 2015 (behind Valencia, 2018 – 155; Misano, 2017 – 140; and Le Mans, 2021 – 118).

Two notable victims were Bagnaia and Bastianini. Both crashed in qualifying. Bagnaia in particular was lucky to get away without a fracture that would have further dented his already battered title hopes. Rookie Raul Fernandez was out of the race after injuring his right hand in Q1.

But it was in Moto2 that the effect was at its most apparent, but somehow – miraculously – also forgiving. After two days of practice when wind, cold and rain had been seriously disruptive, a hitherto dry race day turned nasty for what was, unusually, the last race of the day. A sudden and very localised squall caused a horrifying incident from which 11 fallers emerged with a great deal of property damage, but miraculously no serious injuries.

Both the Moto3 and MotoGP races had been run in dry conditions. Dark clouds were looming by the time Moto2 started at 14:32, but the race ran for eight laps with only sparse drops falling, although rain flags had been shown since lap three.

It was just spitting – until the pack, still close, arrived at a drenched second corner.

All at once, the front three riders and six more from the top 11 fell. Erstwhile leader Aron Canet likened the aftermath to a Second World War battlefield, with riders alternately leaping for safety or lying where they had fallen, bikes scattered about. One of them (van den Goorbergh's) was snapped in half, while Corsi's MV Agusta was on fire.

Canet was the worst hurt, having suffered a broken finger and a fracture to his right wrist – the end of the radius bone, to be precise, which he had pinned immediately by surgeons to be fit to race the following week. Lowes was another victim, escaping fracture, but badly beaten after being struck by another bike. Ogura got away with it after getting to his feet and jumping over a sliding machine.

Canet, Ogura, US GP winner Arbolino and Chantra, lying second to fifth in the championship after the previous round, were disadvantaged in an entirely different way, when once again Race Direction chose the letter of the law rather than a willingness to respond to unusual circumstances. By regulation, to be eligible to restart, riders must enter the pits on their bikes within five minutes of the red flag. Only 17 of the original 30 starters made it. This championship quartet were among those who missed the cut, although Ogura and Chantra's mechanics worked feverishly to repair their bikes anyway, hoping for a change of heart that never came.

Instead, officials incurred further questions and displeasure when it was announced that the restart – a rapid-fire seven-lap sprint a full 42 minutes after the first start – would carry full points. Rules being rules and all that.

This heavily favoured Vietti, who had arrived with his early points lead cut to 14. He'd been 11th when the incident took place. Now, a relative stroll to second, while his nearest rivals no-scored, stretched his advantage to an impressive and potentially crucial 34 points.

Beaubier, lying a strong second when they all fell and also unable to restart, was another big loser. The switch in luck

went to compatriot Roberts, who took a dominant first win in the restart – the first US rider to win in any class since MotoGP Dutch TT winner Ben Spies in 2011.

The number of crashes highlighted an unusual complaint, after a puzzling sight in FP2 when Bagnaia had returned to the paddock after his first fall of the weekend carrying a handful of gravel. It was not a memento, but to underline concerns regarding the size and shape of the stones. "There are three tracks in the championship where the gravel is like this: Jerez, Mandalika and here. We were complaining already last year when Martin crashed. At this track, when you arrive to the gravel, you start to tumble a lot. This means you can get hurt by the gravel," he said.

The next day, he hadn't even reached the gravel when he did get hurt. One of the first to essay slicks on a drying track in Q1, he slammed down hard on his right shoulder. Taken to hospital, he was relieved to discover that nothing was broken. He raced – from the back of the grid – heavily strapped and in pain. A spirited run through to eighth was an impressive indication that he had overcome the teething problems with his new Ducati.

Bastianini and Gardner also fell on slicks.

MotoGP's biggest incident came when Miller wiped out Mir as they battled for third, having lost the front while trying to outbrake and repass the Suzuki. The pair had history, and Mir's sarcastic applause seemed set to trigger a fresh exchange. Instead, each gave a measured response, Miller apologetic and Mir saying that it wasn't "on purpose. I've made this mistake a couple of times."

Race controversy was reserved for Aleix Espargaro's early exchange while contesting fifth with Alex Marquez. Said Espargaro, "Like Mandalika, he rode over the limit and hit me three times. I don't understand this, because he didn't have the speed. We just lost time." Marquez explained, "He was overtaking, but all the time a little bit wide, so if the space is there, I tried to come again inside him."

After his troubled start to 2022, the younger Marquez came within one lap of placing top Honda, losing sixth to Marc by two-hundredths, nowhere near the front. By now, Honda's pre-season optimism had become a distant memory. It was hard to recall a more subdued performance by Marc, who was still struggling to find a comfortable setting. He revealed that he thought Honda had lost a part of its DNA in attempting to compensate for the previous bike's lack of rear grip. He could no longer push the front tyre, which negated one of his greatest strengths: "It's not only me, not only the bike. It's everything. Obviously, I'm not in my sweet moment and I need help from the bike. My target is not to be the first Honda. My target is to fight for the top positions."

MOTOGP RACE – 25 laps

Quartararo's first win since the previous August was a relief after the start to his title defence had been far from straightforward. He showed that when he started well and had minimum traffic ahead, he was still capable of dominating.

After pressure-cooker qualifying, the track only just fit for slicks by the end of Saturday, Quartararo was in the middle of the second row, between the Ducatis of Miller and Bezzecchi. Zarco was on pole, ahead of Mir and Aleix Espargaro. Marc Marquez was ninth, two places down on his brother and one ahead of factory team-mate Pol Espargaro. Home hero and former winner Oliveira was two seconds off pole in 11th, top KTM.

Bastianini and Bagnaia started from 18th and 25th, while Rins's muddled qualifying strategy left him 23rd, on the eighth row, and poised for a heroic first few laps.

Their early absence eased Quartararo's task, but he had to chase Mir in the first two laps. Behind them, Miller led Alex Marquez, Zarco, Aleix Espargaro, Oliveira, Pol Espargaro and Martin. And then Rins, thanks to a mesmeric first lap, during which he had claimed 13 places, the last from a strangely subdued Marc Marquez at Turn 13.

Yet it's possible that not even Rins could have lived with Quartararo. The Frenchman had shadowed Mir for three laps as they stretched more than a second clear, then breezed past on the run to Turn One. After that, with the Yamaha's speed through the twists and undulations, he made it look easy: "If I had pressure from someone behind, for sure I could manage to do 1m 39s all race."

But Mir had run into trouble: "On the second lap, I started having lots of movement; the front was really on the limit." Holding second became an ordeal. Zarco was the first threat. Having barged Alex Marquez wide at Turn 14 on the first lap, he pounced on Miller for third with a neat move at the same turn on lap two. By lap ten, he was with Mir, Miller not far away. Then, after a few bruising moments with Alex Marquez in the early laps, Aleix Espargaro once again put his Aprilia in the fight.

Likewise Rins, his progress hardly slowed. Lap eight was particularly impressive, as he passed Marquez junior, Oliveira and Espargaro senior in a breathless 60-second blitz. Then he settled behind the Aprilia as they set about reeling in the fight for second.

Subsequently, Miller made their job easier. Zarco launched a Turn One lunge on Mir on lap 16, only to run wide, but he made it work the next time around. The Australian was eager to do the same. As Miller attempted to replicate Zarco's move on the Suzuki, he tucked the front. "I went deep, Joan went deep. Joan released, I released, and I was just on the shit part of the track trying to stop the bike," he explained. They joined Martin (Turn 14, lap five) and Bastianini (Turn Eight, lap ten) on the crash list.

Above: **Outpaced by Mir and Quartararo, pole-starter Zarco fought to hold third ahead of Miller, Alex Marquez, Aleix Espargaro and Oliveira.**

Top right: **Moto3 winner Sergio Garcia leads Masia, Sasaki, Oncu and Guevara.**

Above right: **It was only for sixth, but the Marquez brothers battled to finish top Honda. In the end, it went to Marc.**

Right: **With Roberts long gone, lucky Vietti leads a depleted Moto2 field. In pursuit, Navarro (9), Schrotter (23), Gonzalez (18), Aldeguer (54), Alcoba (52) and Bendsneyder (64).**

Photos: Gold & Goose

By now, Zarco was almost a second clear, but Espargaro closed steadily to start the penultimate lap just a tenth behind. Zarco rallied, however, to claim second by six-tenths, while Aleix blamed time lost battling Alex Marquez for not finishing even higher up his second podium in three races.

After seeing his team-mate go down, Rins had nothing left and gladly settled for fourth. "When I tried to overtake Aleix, my front tyre was destroyed," he said. "I preferred to take good points." Oliveira was a lonely fifth, while a little way back, Marc Marquez finally overcame a spirited ride by brother Alex to nab sixth at the death. The senior sibling had overtaken at Turn 13 on the penultimate lap, only for Alex to accelerate past on the home straight. Marc sealed the deal next time around at the same spot, leaving Alex no time to respond. Late excitement aside, this was a troubling outing for Honda, 16 seconds off the winner.

Heavily strapped, but shrugging off the pain, Bagnaia produced a spirited rise to eighth, picking off Pol Espargaro on the final lap in one of the rides of the day; while Vinales overcame his trademark poor start for tenth.

Dovizioso was next-best Yamaha, having narrowly fended off Marini, with Morbidelli having lost touch behind. Gardner and Bezzecchi were widely spaced for the last points, with Nakagami missing out after slipping off and remounting. Brad Binder and Aprilia wild-card Savadori also crashed out; Di Giannantonio retired.

MOTO2 RACE – 7 laps (restarted)

Fate had it in for Moto2, when the weather that had seemed to relent on race day came back in the worst possible way: not quite raining, not quite dry.

Qualifying had been dry enough for slicks, although the times were still a couple of seconds off. Canet claimed his first pole of the year, ahead of Beaubier and Dixon; Arbolino had come through from Q1 to head the second row from Fernandez and Lowes. Honda Team Asia's pair, Ogura and Chantra, led the third from Roberts.

The first race, scheduled for 23 laps, started on a dry track, but rain flags appeared on lap three, making the victory fight between Canet, Beaubier and Ogura all the more nerve-racking.

The American led away, but Canet assumed the lead on lap two. Over the next two laps, Arbolino, Ogura and Fernandez took over from fast-starting Chantra as he pulled in to take a long-lap penalty, a hangover from the previous race. Dixon, a little way back, also finished lap four ahead of the Thai rider, although they swapped again on lap five.

Now, Canet and Beaubier pulled a small gap, but Ogura had the advantage of following in the increasingly tricky conditions and had closed right up by lap seven.

On the ninth, disaster. The leading trio went down at the fast Turn Two, followed in short order by eight others: Arbolino, Lowes, Fernandez, Acosta, Chantra, Corsi, Arenas and van den Goorbergh. None was able to ride back to the pit lane within the five-minute window.

The restart, a scant seven laps and almost 30 minutes after the red flag, took the survivors' grid positions from the lap-eight finishing order. Dixon, who had been running seventh and had managed to avoid the carnage, was on pole.

He led away and for the first six corners, but lost the front into the seventh. That left Roberts, already two seconds clear at the end of the first lap, to cruise home to a maiden win.

Aldeguer led the early pursuit, but Schrotter took over on lap two, with Navarro on his heels; Vietti was next past into fourth by lap three.

There was a lively scrap for second, with Navarro heading the pack for two laps before Vietti took over. He was still ahead at the end, by two-tenths from Navarro, and more than lucky to take 20 points while his main title rivals could only watch in frustration from the pits (or from the medical centre in Canet's case).

They were all still close, second to eighth past the flag in less than two seconds, with Schrotter fourth, then rookies Gonzales, Alcoba and Aldeguer. The last named was docked a position for exceeding track limits on the last lap. Baltus was next; a second adrift, Rodrigo completed the top ten.

Antonelli joined Dixon on the crash list, and with only 15 finishers, there were points for all, even Zaccone, who was one lap behind.

MOTO3 RACE – 21 laps

Moto3 had no dry time on Friday and Saturday, with Oncu coming through from Q1 to take pole ahead of rookie Aji and Fellon; Garcia was sixth. British rookies Ogden and Whatley, benefiting from the wet surface, were eighth and 18th respectively, the latter through from Q1. Foggia was down in 12th on the grid.

With only morning warm-up available to seek dry settings, the race was fraught.

Oncu led away from Aji, but Garcia was rapidly up to second and had taken the lead by the time they crossed the line for the first time.

Team-mate Guevara and Oncu disputed the pursuit, but nobody could live with Garcia early on, fully 1.6 seconds clear by lap five. But the rest started to reel him in, and Guevara led over the line for the first of several times on lap ten.

Also engaged in the front pack were Sasaki, Oncu and Masia, up from 15th on the grid. Each would enjoy brief spells heading the quintet.

But Garcia held his nerve in a tight last-lap fight for his second win of the year, by 0.069 of a second, from Masia. Sasaki, Oncu and Guevara were not much further behind; sixth-placed Tatay almost four seconds away. Migno was seventh, an off-form Foggia another two seconds down in eighth, with Australian Kelso beating fellow rookie Moreira for ninth. Ogden was at the back of that group for 13th.

FIM WORLD CHAMPIONSHIP: ROUND 5

GRANDE PREMIO TISSOT DE PORTUGAL

22–24 APRIL, 2022

CIRCUIT ALGARVE, PORTIMÃO

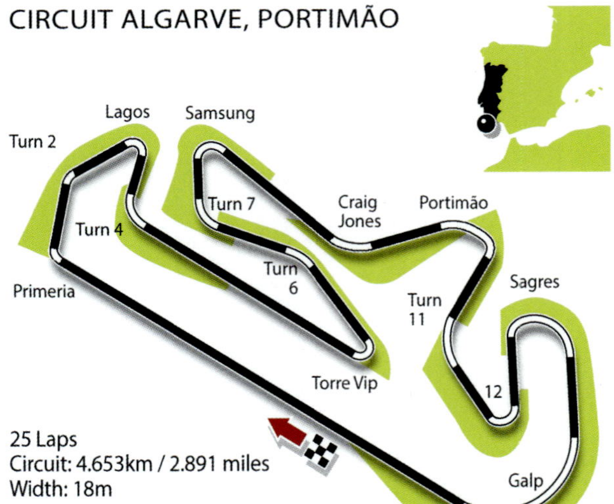

25 Laps
Circuit: 4.653km / 2.891 miles
Width: 18m

MotoGP

RACE DISTANCE: 25 laps, 71.333 miles/114.800km · RACE WEATHER: Dry (air 18°, humidity 70%, track 26°)

Pos.	Rider	Nat.	No.	Entrant	Machine	Tyres	Race tyre choice	Laps	Time & speed
1	**Fabio Quartararo**	FRA	20	Monster Energy Yamaha MotoGP	Yamaha YZR-M1	M	F: Medium/R: Medium	25	41m 39.611s 102.7mph/165.3km/h
2	**Johann Zarco**	FRA	5	Pramac Racing	Ducati Desmosedici	M	F: Medium/R: Medium	25	41m 45.020s
3	**Aleix Espargaro**	SPA	41	Aprilia Racing	Aprilia RS-GP	M	F: Medium/R: Medium	25	41m 45.679s
4	**Alex Rins**	SPA	42	Team SUZUKI ECSTAR	Suzuki GSX-RR	M	F: Medium/R: Medium	25	41m 49.244s
5	**Miguel Oliveira**	POR	88	Red Bull KTM Factory Racing	KTM RC16	M	F: Medium/R: Medium	25	41m 53.184s
6	**Marc Marquez**	SPA	93	Repsol Honda Team	Honda RC213V	M	F: Medium/R: Medium	25	41m 55.774s
7	**Alex Marquez**	SPA	73	LCR Honda CASTROL	Honda RC213V	M	F: Medium/R: Hard	25	41m 55.794s
8	**Francesco Bagnaia**	ITA	63	Ducati Lenovo Team	Ducati Desmosedici	M	F: Medium/R: Medium	25	41m 56.122s
9	**Pol Espargaro**	SPA	44	Repsol Honda Team	Honda RC213V	M	F: Medium/R: Hard	25	41m 56.380s
10	**Maverick Vinales**	SPA	12	Aprilia Racing	Aprilia RS-GP	M	F: Medium/R: Medium	25	41m 57.674s
11	**Andrea Dovizioso**	ITA	4	WithU Yamaha RNF MotoGP Team	Yamaha YZR-M1	M	F: Medium/R: Medium	25	42m 08.640s
12	**Luca Marini**	ITA	10	Mooney VR46 Racing Team	Ducati Desmosedici	M	F: Medium/R: Medium	25	42m 08.860s
13	**Franco Morbidelli**	ITA	21	Monster Energy Yamaha MotoGP	Yamaha YZR-M1	M	F: Medium/R: Medium	25	42m 12.965s
14	**Remy Gardner**	AUS	87	Tech3 KTM Factory Racing	KTM RC16	M	F: Medium/R: Medium	25	42m 19.816s
15	**Marco Bezzecchi**	ITA	72	Mooney VR46 Racing Team	Ducati Desmosedici	M	F: Medium/R: Medium	25	42m 25.663s
16	Takaaki Nakagami	JPN	30	LCR Honda IDEMITSU	Honda RC213V	M	F: Medium/R: Medium	25	42m 29.180s
17	Darryn Binder	RSA	40	WithU Yamaha RNF MotoGP Team	Yamaha YZR-M1	M	F: Medium/R: Medium	25	42m 29.914s
	Lorenzo Savadori	ITA	32	Aprilia Racing	Aprilia RS-GP	M	F: Medium/R: Medium	24	DNF-crash
	Fabio Di Giannantonio	ITA	49	Gresini Racing MotoGP	Ducati Desmosedici	M	F: Medium/R: Medium	21	DNF-crash
	Joan Mir	SPA	36	Team SUZUKI ECSTAR	Suzuki GSX-RR	M	F: Medium/R: Medium	18	DNF-crash
	Jack Miller	AUS	43	Ducati Lenovo Team	Ducati Desmosedici	M	F: Medium/R: Medium	18	DNF-crash
	Brad Binder	RSA	33	Red Bull KTM Factory Racing	KTM RC16	M	F: Medium/R: Medium	17	DNF-crash
	Enea Bastianini	ITA	23	Gresini Racing MotoGP	Ducati Desmosedici	M	F: Medium/R: Medium	9	DNF-crash
	Jorge Martin	SPA	89	Pramac Racing	Ducati Desmosedici	M	F: Medium/R: Medium	4	DNF-crash
	Raul Fernandez	SPA	25	Tech3 KTM Factory Racing	KTM RC16	M	-	-	DNS-injured

Fastest lap: Enea Bastianini, on lap 14, 2m 3.521s, 99.8mph/160.6km/h.

Lap record: Marc Marquez, 2m 3.575s, 99.8mph/160.6km/h (2014).

Event maximum speed: Enea Bastianini, 217.9mph/350.6km/h (free practice).

Qualifying

Weather: Dry

Air Temp: 16° **Humidity:** 69%

Track Temp: 24°

1	Zarco	1m 42.003s
2	Mir	1m 42.198s
3	A. Espargaro	1m 42.235s
4	Miller	1m 42.503s
5	Quartararo	1m 42.716s
6	Bezzecchi	1m 42.716s
7	A. Marquez	1m 42.903s
8	Marini	1m 43.179s
9	M. Marquez	1m 43.575s
10	P. Espargaro	1m 43.832s
11	Oliveira	1m 44.066s
12	B. Binder	1m 44.710s
	Q1	
13	Martin	1m 47.936s
14	Vinales	1m 49.332s
15	Di Giannantonio	1m 49.639s
16	Dovizioso	1m 49.695s
17	Nakagami	1m 49.889s
18	Bastianini	1m 50.618s
19	Morbidelli	1m 50.702s
20	Gardner	1m 50.953s
21	Savadori	1m 51.308s
22	D. Binder	1m 51.639s
23	Rins	1m 52.300s
24	Fernandez	1m 53.603s
25	Bagnaia	No Time

Fastest race laps

1	Quartararo	1m 39.435s
2	A. Espargaro	1m 39.523s
3	Rins	1m 39.538s
4	Bagnaia	1m 39.588s
5	Zarco	1m 39.636s
6	Miller	1m 39.671s
7	Nakagami	1m 39.741s
8	Mir	1m 39.786s
9	Vinales	1m 39.797s
10	B. Binder	1m 39.835s
11	Oliveira	1m 39.866s
12	M. Marquez	1m 39.919s
13	A. Marquez	1m 40.011s
14	P. Espargaro	1m 40.020s
15	Dovizioso	1m 40.284s
16	Marini	1m 40.287s
17	Bastianini	1m 40.307s
18	Martin	1m 40.312s
19	Gardner	1m 40.494s
20	Morbidelli	1m 40.665s
21	D. Binder	1m 41.209s
22	Bezzecchi	1m 41.310s
23	Di Giannantonio	1m 41.319s
24	Savadori	1m 41.753s

Championship Points

1	Quartararo	69
2	Rins	69
3	A. Espargaro	66
4	Bastianini	61
5	Zarco	51
6	Mir	46
7	B. Binder	42
8	Oliveira	39
9	Miller	31
10	Bagnaia	31
11	M. Marquez	31
12	P. Espargaro	30
13	Martin	28
14	Vinales	25
15	Morbidelli	17
16	Marini	14
17	A. Marquez	13
18	Nakagami	12
19	Bezzecchi	8
20	Dovizioso	8
21	D. Binder	6
22	Gardner	3

Constructor Points

1	Ducati	106
2	KTM	70
3	Suzuki	70
4	Yamaha	69
5	Aprilia	67
6	Honda	44

Grid order	1	2	3	4	5	6	7	8	9	10	11	12	13	14	15	16	17	18	19	20	21	22	23	24	25	
5 ZARCO	36	36	36	20	20	20	20	20	20	20	20	20	20	20	20	20	20	20	20	20	20	20	20	20	20	1
36 MIR	20	20	20	36	36	36	36	36	36	36	36	36	36	36	36	36	5	5	5	5	5	5	5	5	5	2
41 A. ESPARGARO	43	5	5	5	5	5	5	5	5	5	5	5	5	5	5	5	36	36	41	41	41	41	41	41	41	3
43 MILLER	5	43	43	43	43	43	43	43	43	43	43	43	43	43	43	43	43	43	42	42	42	42	42	42	42	4
20 QUARTARARO	73	73	73	73	73	73	73	41	41	41	41	41	41	41	41	41	41	41	88	88	88	88	88	88	88	5
72 BEZZECCHI	88	41	41	41	41	41	41	42	42	42	42	42	42	42	42	42	42	42	73	73	73	73	73	73	93	6
73 A. MARQUEZ	41	88	88	88	88	88	88	73	88	88	88	88	88	88	88	88	88	88	93	93	93	93	93	93	73	7
10 MARINI	44	44	44	42	42	42	42	88	73	73	73	73	73	73	73	73	73	73	44	44	44	44	44	44	63	8
93 M. MARQUEZ	89	42	42	44	44	93	93	93	93	93	93	93	93	93	93	93	93	93	63	63	63	63	63	63	44	9
44 P. ESPARGARO	42	93	93	93	93	44	44	44	44	44	44	44	44	44	44	44	44	44	12	12	12	12	12	12	12	10
88 OLIVEIRA	93	89	89	89	23	23	23	23	23	33	33	33	33	33	33	33	33	63	21	21	4	4	4	4	4	11
33 B.BINDER	30	23	23	23	33	33	33	33	33	30	63	63	63	63	63	63	63	12	4	4	21	10	10	10	10	12
89 MARTIN	23	33	33	33	30	30	30	30	30	12	12	12	12	12	12	12	12	21	10	10	10	21	21	21	21	13
12 VINALES	33	30	30	30	12	12	12	12	12	63	10	10	10	10	10	10	10	10	87	87	87	87	87	87	87	14
49 DI GIANNANTONIO	72	72	10	12	4	10	10	63	63	10	21	21	21	21	21	21	21	4	72	72	72	72	72	72	72	15
4 DOVIZIOSO	10	10	72	10	10	21	63	10	10	21	4	4	4	4	4	4	4	87	49	49	49	40	40	40	30	
30 NAKAGAMI	12	4	12	4	21	63	21	21	21	4	87	87	87	87	87	87	87	72	40	40	40	30	30	30	40	
23 BASTIANINI	4	12	4	21	63	4	72	4	4	87	72	72	72	72	72	72	72	49	32	30	30	32	32	32		
21 MORBIDELLI	49	21	21	72	72	72	4	72	87	72	49	49	49	49	49	49	49	40	30	32	32					
87 GARDNER	21	49	49	63	49	87	87	87	72	49	40	40	40	40	40	40	40	32								
32 SAVADORI	63	63	63	49	87	49	49	49	49	40	32	32	32	32	32	32	32	30								
40 D.BINDER	87	87	87	87	40	40	40	40	40	32	30	30	30	30	30	30	30									
42 RINS	40	40	40	40	32	32	32	32	32																	
63 BAGNAIA	32	32	32	32																						

Moto2

RACE DISTANCE (Part 2): 7 laps, 19.973 miles/32.144km · RACE WEATHER: Dry (air 16°, humidity 80%, track 19°)

Pos.	Rider	Nat.	No.	Entrant	Machine	Laps	Time & Speed
1	**Joe Roberts**	USA	16	Italtrans Racing Team	Kalex	7	12m 09.757s
							98.5 mph/158.5 km/h
2	**Celestino Vietti**	ITA	13	Mooney VR46 Racing Team	Kalex	7	12m 12.575s
3	**Jorge Navarro**	SPA	9	Flexbox HP40	Kalex	7	12m 12.748s
4	**Marcel Schrotter**	GER	23	Liqui Moly Intact GP	Kalex	7	12m 12.861s
5	**Manuel Gonzalez**	SPA	18	Yamaha VR46 Master Camp Team	Kalex	7	12m 12.956s
6	**Jeremy Alcoba**	SPA	52	Liqui Moly Intact GP	Kalex	7	12m 13.578s
7	**Fermin Aldeguer**	SPA	54	Lightech Speed Up	Boscoscuro	7	12m 13.541s
8	**Bo Bendsneyder**	NED	64	Pertamina Mandalika SAG Team	Kalex	7	12m 14.405s
9	**Barry Baltus**	BEL	7	RW Racing GP	Kalex	7	12m 17.860s
10	**Gabriel Rodrigo**	ARG	2	Pertamina Mandalika SAG Team	Kalex	7	12m 18.637s
11	**Romano Fenati**	ITA	5	Lightech Speed Up	Boscoscuro	7	12m 19.268s
12	**Keminth Kubo**	THA	81	Yamaha VR46 Master Camp Team	Kalex	7	12m 32.298s
13	**Sean Dylan Kelly**	USA	4	American Racing	Kalex	7	12m 34.426s
14	**Filip Salac**	CZE	12	Gresini Racing Moto2	Kalex	7	14m 02.802s
15	**Alessandro Zaccone**	ITA	61	Gresini Racing Moto2	Kalex	6	12m 30.366s
	Niccolo Antonelli	ITA	28	Mooney VR46 Racing Team	Kalex	3	DNF-crash
	Jake Dixon	GBR	96	Autosolar GASGAS Aspar Team	Kalex	0	DNF-crash
	Lorenzo Dalla Porta	ITA	19	Italtrans Racing Team	Kalex	-	DNS Part 2
	Aron Canet	SPA	40	Flexbox HP40	Kalex	-	DNS Part 2
	Cameron Beaubier	USA	6	American Racing	Kalex	-	DNS Part 2
	Tony Arbolino	ITA	14	Elf Marc VDS Racing Team	Kalex	-	DNS Part 2
	Augusto Fernandez	SPA	37	Red Bull KTM Ajo	Kalex	-	DNS Part 2
	Sam Lowes	GBR	22	Elf Marc VDS Racing Team	Kalex	-	DNS Part 2
	Ai Ogura	JPN	79	IDEMITSU Honda Team Asia	Kalex	-	DNS Part 2
	Somkiat Chantra	THA	35	IDEMITSU Honda Team Asia	Kalex	-	DNS Part 2
	Albert Arenas	SPA	75	Autosolar GASGAS Aspar Team	Kalex	-	DNS Part 2
	Marcos Ramirez	SPA	42	MV Agusta Forward Racing	Agusta	-	DNS Part 2
	Zonta van den Goorbergh	NED	84	RW Racing GP	Kalex	-	DNS Part 2
	Pedro Acosta	SPA	51	Red Bull KTM Ajo	Kalex	-	DNS Part 2
	Simone Corsi	ITA	24	MV Agusta Forward Racing	Agusta	-	DNS Part 2

Fastest lap: Joe Roberts, on lap 3, 1m 43.410s, 99.3mph/159.8km/h.

Lap record: Remy Gardner, 1m 42.504s, 100.2mph/161.2km/h (2020).

Event maximum speed: Manuel Gonzalez, 183.3mph/295.0km/h (race part 1).

Qualifying

Weather: Dry

Air: 16° **Humidity:** 64%

Track: 23°

	Rider	Time
1	Canet	1m 44.151s
2	Beaubier	1m 44.479s
3	Dixon	1m 44.501s
4	Arbolino	1m 44.560s
5	Fernandez	1m 44.788s
6	Lowes	1m 44.827s
7	Ogura	1m 44.898s
8	Chantra	1m 44.911s
9	Roberts	1m 44.915s
10	Arenas	1m 44.999s
11	Navarro	1m 45.016s
12	Schrotter	1m 45.018s
13	Vietti	1m 45.076s
14	Ramirez	1m 45.251s
15	Aldeguer	1m 45.304s
16	V D Goorbergh	1m 45.354s
17	Dalla Porta	1m 46.859s
18	Kubo	No Time
	Q1	
19	Salac	1m 46.086s
20	Acosta	1m 46.160s
21	Gonzalez	1m 46.600s
22	Bendsneyder	1m 46.712s
23	Baltus	1m 46.787s
24	Fenati	1m 46.787s
25	Rodrigo	1m 47.213s
26	Alcoba	1m 47.274s
27	Corsi	1m 47.676s
28	Zaccone	1m 47.762s
29	Kelly	1m 48.021s
30	Antonelli	1m 48.305s

Fastest race laps

	Rider	Time
1	Roberts	1m 43.410s
2	Alcoba	1m 43.676s
3	Schrotter	1m 43.782s
4	Bendsneyder	1m 43.787s
5	Vietti	1m 43.789s
6	Aldeguer	1m 43.807s
7	Gonzalez	1m 43.818s
8	Navarro	1m 43.848s
9	Baltus	1m 44.290s
10	Fenati	1m 44.460s
11	Rodrigo	1m 44.465s
12	Antonelli	1m 45.743s
13	Kubo	1m 46.326s
14	Kelly	1m 46.953s
15	Salac	1m 59.763s
16	Zaccone	2m 03.109s

Championship Points

	Rider	Points
1	Vietti	90
2	Ogura	56
3	Arbolino	54
4	Roberts	49
5	Canet	49
6	Chantra	45
7	Navarro	39
8	Schrotter	36
9	Lowes	35
10	Dixon	32
11	Fernandez	31
12	Bendsneyder	25
13	Alcoba	24
14	Arenas	22
15	Acosta	20
16	Aldeguer	18
17	Gonzalez	16
18	Beaubier	16
19	Baltus	13
20	Fenati	7
21	Rodrigo	6
22	Ramirez	5
23	Kubo	4
24	Salac	4
25	Kelly	3
26	Zaccone	1

Constructor Points

	Constructor	Points
1	Kalex	125
2	Boscoscuro	20
3	MV Agusta	5

Moto3

RACE DISTANCE: 21 laps, 59.920 miles/96.432km · RACE WEATHER: Dry (air 18°, humidity 65%, track 28°)

Pos.	Rider	Nat.	No.	Entrant	Machine	Laps	Time & Speed
1	**Sergio Garcia**	SPA	11	Valresa GASGAS Aspar Team	GASGAS	21	38m 17.725s
							93.8 mph/151.0 km/h
2	**Jaume Masia**	SPA	5	Red Bull KTM Ajo	KTM	21	38m 17.794s
3	**Ayumu Sasaki**	JPN	71	Sterilgarda Husqvarna Max	Husqvarna	21	38m 17.835s
4	**Deniz Oncu**	TUR	53	Red Bull KTM Tech3	KTM	21	38m 17.935s
5	**Izan Guevara**	SPA	28	Valresa GASGAS Aspar Team	GASGAS	21	38m 18.098s
6	**Carlos Tatay**	SPA	99	CFMOTO Racing PruestelGP	CFMOTO	21	38m 21.819s
7	**Andrea Migno**	ITA	16	Rivacold Snipers Team	Honda	21	38m 22.454s
8	**Dennis Foggia**	ITA	7	Leopard Racing	Honda	21	38m 24.895s
9	**Joel Kelso**	AUS	66	CIP Green Power	KTM	21	38m 24.966s
10	**Diogo Moreira**	BRA	10	MT Helmets - MSI	KTM	21	38m 24.890s
11	**Riccardo Rossi**	ITA	54	SIC58 Squadra Corse	Honda	21	38m 25.001s
12	**Tatsuki Suzuki**	JPN	24	Leopard Racing	Honda	21	38m 25.059s
13	**Scott Ogden**	GBR	19	VisionTrack Racing Team	Honda	21	38m 25.167s
14	**Lorenzo Fellon**	FRA	20	SIC58 Squadra Corse	Honda	21	38m 36.714s
15	**Stefano Nepa**	ITA	82	Angeluss MTA Team	KTM	21	38m 40.162s
16	Mario Aji	INA	64	Honda Team Asia	Honda	21	38m 40.352s
17	Kaito Toba	JPN	27	CIP Green Power	KTM	21	38m 43.136s
18	Matteo Bertelle	ITA	18	QJMotor Avintia Racing Team	KTM	21	38m 43.920s
19	Elia Bartolini	ITA	23	QJMotor Avintia Racing Team	KTM	21	38m 43.938s
20	Xavier Artigas	SPA	43	CFMOTO Racing PruestelGP	CFMOTO	21	38m 44.305s
21	Ryusei Yamanaka	JPN	6	MT Helmets - MSI	KTM	21	38m 44.942s
22	David Salvador	SPA	38	Sterilgarda Husqvarna Max	Husqvarna	21	38m 48.127s
23	Gerard Riu Male	SPA	87	BOE SKX	KTM	21	39m 00.651s
24	Syarifuddin Azman	MAL	63	Rivacold Snipers Team	Honda	21	39m 00.714s
25	Taiyo Furusato	JPN	72	Honda Team Asia	Honda	21	39m 08.257s
26	Joshua Whatley	GBR	70	VisionTrack Racing Team	Honda	21	39m 08.627s
27	David Alonso	COL	80	GASGAS Aspar Team	GASGAS	21	39m 08.924s
28	Ana Carrasco	SPA	22	BOE SKX	KTM	21	39m 11.730s
	Daniel Holgado	SPA	96	Red Bull KTM Ajo	KTM	17	DNF-crash
	Ivan Ortola	SPA	48	Angeluss MTA Team	KTM	7	DNF-crash

Fastest lap: Jaume Masia, on lap 9, 1m 48.201s, 94.9mph/152.7km/h.

Lap record: Gabriel Rodrigo, 1m 47.610s, 95.4mph/153.6km/h (2021).

Event maximum speed: Ayumu Sasaki, 156.4mph/251.7km/h (race).

Qualifying:

Weather: Wet

Air: 15° **Humidity:** 85%

Track: 21°

	Rider	Time
1	Oncu	2m 03.955s
2	Aji	2m 03.972s
3	Fellon	2m 04.447s
4	Tatay	2m 04.501s
5	Suzuki	2m 04.563s
6	Garcia	2m 05.005s
7	Rossi	2m 05.137s
8	Ogden	2m 05.202s
9	Guevara	2m 05.311s
10	Sasaki	2m 05.395s
11	Migno	2m 05.608s
12	Foggia	2m 05.772s
13	Holgado	2m 05.967s
14	Moreira	2m 06.270s
15	Masia	2m 06.532s
16	Yamanaka	2m 07.020s
17	Nepa	2m 07.238s
18	Whatley	2m 08.626s
	Q1	
19	Artigas	2m 08.477s
20	Azman	2m 08.977s
21	Salvador	2m 09.228s
22	Kelso	2m 09.502s
23	Ortola	2m 09.654s
24	Toba	2m 10.039s
25	Bartolini	2m 10.365s
26	Bertelle	2m 10.514s
27	Riu Male	2m 11.241s
28	Carrasco	2m 12.481s
29	Alonso	2m 13.508s
30	Furusato	No Time

Fastest race laps

	Rider	Time
1	Masia	1m 48.201s
2	Oncu	1m 48.543s
3	Sasaki	1m 48.558s
4	Guevara	1m 48.611s
5	Kelso	1m 48.816s
6	Migno	1m 48.848s
7	Garcia	1m 48.850s
8	Holgado	1m 48.900s
9	Moreira	1m 48.967s
10	Tatay	1m 48.981s
11	Suzuki	1m 48.993s
12	Rossi	1m 49.071s
13	Foggia	1m 49.083s
14	Aji	1m 49.141s
15	Fellon	1m 49.165s
16	Ogden	1m 49.244s
17	Ortolá	1m 49.384s
18	Nepa	1m 49.418s
19	Toba	1m 49.476s
20	Yamanaka	1m 49.514s
21	Artigas	1m 49.555s
22	Salvador	1m 49.700s
23	Bartolini	1m 49.878s
24	Bertelle	1m 49.926s
25	Alonso	1m 50.540s
26	Riu Male	1m 50.545s
27	Azman	1m 50.596s
28	Whatley	1m 50.746s
29	Furusato	1m 50.929s
30	Carrasco	1m 50.931s

Championship Points

	Rider	Points
1	Garcia	83
2	Foggia	82
3	Masia	54
4	Migno	50
5	Oncu	50
6	Guevara	48
7	Sasaki	45
8	Tatay	42
9	Rossi	29
10	Toba	27
11	Suzuki	27
12	Artigas	26
13	Moreira	26
14	Holgado	16
15	Yamanaka	16
16	Kelso	14
17	Bartolini	13
18	McPhee	11
19	Ortolá	11
20	Ogden	10
21	Nepa	7
22	Fernandez	7
23	Fellon	3
24	Aji	2

Constructor Points

	Constructor	Points
1	GASGAS	99
2	Honda	99
3	KTM	82
4	Husqvarna	56
5	CFMOTO	50

FIM WORLD CHAMPIONSHIP · ROUND 6

SPANISH GRAND PRIX

JEREZ-ANGEL NIETO CIRCUIT

Main: Open gates, and a crowd of more than 50,000 watched Bagnaia and Quartararo duel in the sun.

Inset, left: Pecco was smiling at last.
Photos: Gold & Goose

Inset, far left: Bagnaia's Ducati kept Quartararo's Yamaha at bay in a race-long battle.
Photo: Ducati Corse

Above: Marquez's trademark super-save gave Espargaro the chance to pass both him and Miller.

Top right: Jorge Lorenzo was on hand for induction to the MotoGP Hall of Fame.
Photos: Gold & Goose

Above right: Suzuki's Alex Rins would be left to ponder his future.

Right: Likewise, Joan Mir was lost after Suzuki's post-race bombshell.
Photos: Suzuki ECSTAR

OVERTAKING was in the news at Jerez. Or the lack of it. It had become very hard in modern MotoGP, apparently. Thanks to the similarity in performance of bikes with same-size, four-cylinder engines, the same electronics, tyres, brakes and (but for KTM) suspension; thanks to new aerodynamics spilling dirty air on to following machines; thanks to those following bikes suffering overheating front tyres; thanks to the downforce further stressing the tyres; thanks to a high level of well-developed talent. For all sorts of reason, passing had become fraught.

For example, said Jack Miller, both he and Mir had fallen in Portugal because neither could find a clean way past.

Many other riders agreed, but not all.

Among them was Bagnaia, who pointed to his Portuguese run from 24th to eighth, and Rins's from 23rd to fourth, and in Argentina, from 13th to fifth. "It depends," he said. "If you are fast, you can have a good overtake."

A processional Jerez race undermined his theory – though his first win of the season made up for any resultant dismay. Pecco, still in pain from Portimao, had seized a narrow pole ahead of race favourite Quartararo, then took the lead into Turn One. It remained narrow, but commanding. There was no way past.

So down the field, with minimal changes from first lap to last. The exception was Marc Marquez, forced to follow other riders to scrape on to the second row. He'd got away fourth, sandwiched between Miller and Aleix Espargaro, but it took him until lap 21 to force past the Australian. At the end of that lap, he ran too hot into the final hairpin.

There followed about the only excitement of the afternoon. Front and rear slid, the bike at almost 70 degrees. Then, for the first time in almost two years, knee and elbow digging in, the old Marc was back. Though rather winsomely he credited "the Spanish crowd" for picking him up.

The confusion let Espargaro and Miller back through, but on the final lap, Marc managed to regain fourth, his best of the year so far.

While his antics gladdened the heart, the Honda continued to cause concern: "In big circuits, [it] is working really well, like pre-season in Malaysia and in Qatar. But at a small circuit, where you need to turn in a short time, that's where we struggle a lot." The new machine, designed for Michelin's grippy rear, forced wider, sweeping lines. Marc's most ferocious weapon – front-end stability under heavy braking, then quick turning – had been blunted.

At Yamaha, a revelation from team boss Lin Jarvis explained the company's growing confidence in retaining Quartararo, in spite of his complaints about speed and horsepower. In fact, they had developed a new engine, only to run into reliability problems, which had forced them to shelve it. The factory had apologised to the rider; contract renewal talks were "progressing well". Fabio would neither confirm nor deny, saying with a cheeky grin, "I have not signed anything."

Jorge Lorenzo was inducted into the MotoGP Hall of Fame, the 34th official Legend. With three MotoGP and two 250 titles, perhaps most impressively, he had defeated fellow greats Stoner, Marquez, Rossi and Pedrosa in epic title fights. It had started at Jerez in 2002. "I arrived here 20 years ago to make my debut and I was still 14 on Friday," said Lorenzo. "I went to watch at a few corners with a scooter and I saw the likes of Cecchinello, Pedrosa, Poggiali all so aggressive and so fast that I wondered if some day I could arrive at that level." The next day, he was old enough to give it a try.

Aprilia's third podium of the year and fourth in 24 months meant the loss of concession-team status – a sacrifice more sweet than bitter, after seven years of trying. It meant an immediate end to unlimited testing. Other privileges – including two extra engines, free engine development and extra wild-card entries – would remain until the end of the season.

The cost of the loss varies. KTM lost concessions in 2020, and since then results remained patchy, in spite of two more wins in the following season. In 2022, after a promising start, they were back in the doldrums in warmer conditions, both factory riders complaining that the bike's preference for very hard braking was limiting, and that at Jerez, the hardest Michelin was not hard enough – a familiar comment.

Suzuki had finally lost their concessions in 2018, and hardly looked back, taking riders' and teams' titles with Mir in

2020. A downbeat 2021 had now been followed by a storming return to form. With the GSX-RR, already thought to be the best handling and most tyre friendly, they had achieved something that Yamaha, with its similar inline engine, had failed to do: deliver a power boost to put it right up among the best in the top-speed charts.

Thus bombshell news at the season's first post-race tests on Monday came as even more of a shock. Suzuki were to pull out of MotoGP at the end of the season.

This was not an official announcement, but it had leaked out after team members had been informed privately. A fortnight later, there was an official, somewhat vague, statement from the factory. Dorna, however, had been quick to respond to "a rumour", pointing out that there would be a financial cost for breaking the five-year contract (signed in April, 2021 and valid until 2026), and that there would be no difficulty in filling the gap.

With the paddock left to speculate, the blame was attributed to economic reasons, brought about by the Covid-19 pandemic and Russian invasion of Ukraine, plus the possibility of pending costs of an intensifying 'dieselgate' investigation into the car side of the company, which uses engines from an outside supplier.

The decision came out of the blue to shocked riders and team management. In the preceding weeks, newly appointed manager Livio Suppo had repeatedly stated that the factory was keen to re-sign both current riders. Now, the future of Mir and Rins, and the rest of the team, had been cast to the wind.

With the need to maximise results even more acute than ever, and with a serious knock-on effect to the whole rider market, the paddock was left to consider the fall-out over the coming weeks.

MOTOGP RACE – 25 laps

On Friday, it had looked like it was Fabio's game. Bagnaia had other ideas, however, and in Q2, he displaced the defending champion from pole by a massive margin. Espargaro's Aprilia was alongside; Miller led row two from Marc Marquez and Zarco.

The race marked a return to normality, and not just with the presence of 56,000 boisterous Spanish fans. After five 'anyone-can-win' races, the big beasts were back, and 2021's top two riders finally faced off in a contest that was likely to be repeated in forthcoming races.

On a hot, greasy track, Bagnaia and Quartararo delivered a masterclass, cementing their reputations as the leading names. This was as much a battle of wits, as the latter's repeated attempts to push the former into a mistake failed to pay off. His lead over, the reigning champion never exceeded eight-tenths; Bagnaia, though, didn't blink.

It was an exhibition of brilliance, high on tension to the wire, but also a drab follow-my-leader affair, with just four overtakes in the top six from lap two to the end. The issue was complicated because Andalusian heat and the all-action track always push front tyres to the limit. Furthermore, as Mir explained, "The wings and ride-height devices put more load on the front." The question of rising tyre pressures and how to avoid them would trigger controversy in the following week, with Bagnaia's team accused of bending minimum-pressure rules.

Thus the start was critical. Bagnaia got the jump, Quartararo shadowing him away, with Miller third ahead of Nakagami and Marquez sneaking under Espargaro's Aprilia on the exit of Turn One. Mir took seventh from Bezzecchi at Turn Six, while team-mate Rins was unable to repeat his Portimao

Above: **Miller and Espargaro battle over third. The Spaniard won out.**

Top right: **Tech3 KTM's Raul Fernandez was sidelined for his home race, thanks to injury in Portugal. His troubled rookie season continued.**

Top far right: **Aldeguer remonstrates with Dixon after they tangled. The Spaniard remounted, only to retire four laps later.**

Above right: **Ogura leads the courageous Canet and Arbolino in Moto2.**

Centre and far right: **Prizes and plaudits for Canet and Guevara.**

Below right: **Inches in it – Masia (5), Garcia (11) and Guevara (28) play Moto3 tag.**

Photos: Gold & Goose

heroics, dropping from 13th before running off-track on lap nine and rejoining way out of contention.

There was more action at the last hairpin: Marquez pounced on Nakagami, Espargaro following through. And Mir was past the Japanese rider on the following lap, his late-braking move coming at Turn Six.

Quartararo didn't have the speed through Turn 12, the last of Jerez's fast rights, to line up the Ducati at the final turn. "I knew if I couldn't overtake him the first three laps, it was going to be difficult for our front tyre," he said. He dropped back slightly, hoping to give the tyre a chance to cool down for a final assault.

The chasing Miller couldn't match their pace as they edged clear. Attention instead turned to holding third. Marquez finally attacked at the unlikeliest of places on lap 21: Turn Five. As Miller reacted, Marquez cemented the spot with some fine braking into the far hairpin. But it didn't last, as a massive front-end slide at the final turn allowed his two pursuers through, with a two-in-one for Espargaro. From there, the Aprilia broke clear.

It was still all to play for going into the final lap. Quartararo had reduced Bagnaia's lead and pushed to within two-tenths with just one sector remaining. Any move would have been too risky, however. Bagnaia won by just under three-tenths. "The gap was five-tenths, four-tenths, five-tenths all race. In this situation, I didn't have time to think about my shoulder," he said.

Quartararo was content with increasing his championship lead, but Espargaro thought that he could have run with the leaders and was frustrated about his ultimately comfortable third, a massive ten seconds behind (the same gap that covered from third to 11th). Stuck behind Miller and Marquez, "I had a lot more pace, but they braked very late, stopping in the middle of the corner."

Marquez nabbed fourth from Miller on the final lap with a fine Turn Eight move; Mir was a frustrated sixth, unable to keep his front tyre pressure under control, but ahead of Nakagami and Bastianini, who finally managed to take eighth off Bezzecchi on the last lap. Brad Binder was the best of the KTMs in a distant tenth.

Then Pol Espargaro, Oliveira and Alex Marquez, unable to do anything about one another, followed by Vinales, who had made progress after qualifying 12th, but finished the first lap 22nd after trouble with his launch. His last victims had been Morbidelli and Marini, the former taking the final point.

With the injured Fernandez still out, Di Giannantonio was top rookie, chasing veteran Dovizioso home in 18th; Gardner had lost a wing in a first-lap shoving match and trailed in 20th; Darryn Binder crashed out of a place in the points.

Martin and Honda wild-card Stefan Bradl had fallen on the first lap. Both had rejoined, only for Bradl to crash out again. Zarco also crashed after a frustrating time failing to get past Bastianini for eighth.

MOTO2 RACE – 23 laps

After the debacle of Portimao, riders were anxious to get going for a race that could restore some natural justice, and five of the most notable victims took the top spots in qualifying. With the top 14 inside one second, Ogura claimed pole by a hundredth from Arbolino, with Lowes completing the front row. Canet led the second from Aldeguer. Alongside, the previous Sunday's major beneficiary, Vietti.

Canet's was a brave effort less than a week after surgeons had pinned his broken left wrist with two screws.

Ogura followed pole with a lights-to-flag victory. Each was a career first, never achieved in three years in Moto3. It was a timely accomplishment for the Honda-favoured rider, considering Nakagami's struggles in MotoGP, reinforcing his prospects of promotion.

On a normal weekend, this would have been the main story of the race, but the ride of the day belonged to Canet. Through practice, it was obvious that he had been in pain. To see him take off in second and hold his place in a strong leading quintet was deeply impressive.

The group was soon reduced to four and then three, with

Lowes crashing out on lap seven and Chantra following suit a lap later.

By mid-race, Canet was clearly tiring. A mistake at Turn Six on lap 17 gave Ogura breathing space for the first time, his lead increasing from two- to seven-tenths.

Arbolino was suffering issues of his own, as arm-pump in his right arm slowed him late on. That left Ogura to coast home, 2.5 seconds ahead of the heroic Canet. Arbolino was another second behind.

Fernandez, who had qualified ninth and finished the first lap eighth, profited from crashes ahead of him, as well as a good run past Vietti for fourth. Behind him, Schrotter also got the better of a fading Vietti with six laps to go.

The points leader was followed by the duelling pair of Bendsneyder and Roberts, the Dutchman getting back ahead of the American around half-distance and holding him narrowly at bay to the flag.

Arenas and Navarro trailed in to complete the top ten.

Once again, Aldeguer was unlucky, taking fifth off Vietti on lap eight only to slip off next time around after colliding with Dixon. He remounted, but pitted at the end of lap 13. Many others fell victim to slippery conditions. Acosta had already gone, out of the top ten on the second lap; Dixon lasted until the ninth, lying eighth thanks to the crashes ahead after qualifying 11th.

Beaubier suffered a dire weekend: qualified 25th and retiring from the race.

Ogura's win to Vietti's downbeat sixth cut the Italian's championship lead to a more manageable 19 points.

MOTO3 RACE – 22 laps

KTMs, under various names, held the high ground at a track that favoured their point-and-squirt style. GasGas pair Guevara and Garcia led the front row from Masia's KTM, and while Foggia managed to slot his Honda into fourth, it would prove a false dawn at one of his worst tracks. The next best NSF250RW was that of impressive rookie Ogden, 11th, then Migno, 13th.

The race proved the point, with the Austrian bikes taking the first 11 places. Ogden, in 12th, was top Honda again; Migno was 14th, while Foggia had faded throughout to a distant 18th, a slump his Leopard team found inexplicable.

Guevara emerged victorious from a hectic six-strong lead pack, past the flag in less than a second, with a brilliant last-corner attack. He had entered Turn 13 behind Oncu and Garcia, but braked very late and ran around the outside of both.

Masia and Moreira had been with the front group at the start, Oncu and Artigas joining before half-distance. Swapping back and forth slowed the pace, so that as well as Rossi and Holgado, Sasaki also joined them, in spite of serving a long-lap penalty after a back-of-the-grid start for careless riding in qualifying.

His own long-lap (exceeding track limits) blunted Moreira's charge, and Holgado faded, leaving six to flash over the line: Guevara, Garcia, Masia, Oncu, Artigas, Sasaki. Phew!

Toba and Yamanaka scrapped to the end, Holgado and Moreira likewise to complete the top ten.

Australian Kelso retired hurt after a freak morning warm-up incident, hit by Ortola's riderless bike, after the Spaniard and Rossi had collided on the back straight. Rossi earned a long-lap penalty for causing the crash.

FIM WORLD CHAMPIONSHIP: ROUND 6

GUEVRA GRAN PREMIO RED BULL DE ESPAÑA

29 APRIL–1 MAY, 2022

CIRCUITO DE JEREZ

25 laps
Length: 4.423 km. / 2.748 miles
Width: 11m

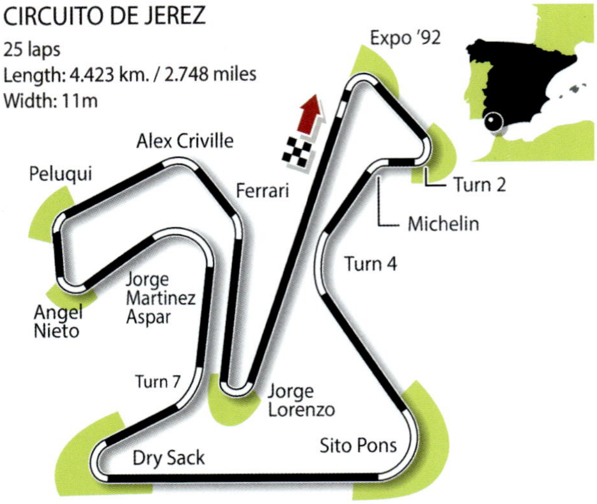

MotoGP

RACE DISTANCE: 25 laps, 68.708 miles/110.575km · RACE WEATHER: Dry (air 27°, humidity 35%, track 44°)

Pos.	Rider	Nat.	No.	Entrant	Machine	Tyres	Race tyre choice	Laps	Time & speed
1	**Francesco Bagnaia**	ITA	63	Ducati Lenovo Team	Ducati Desmosedici	M	F: Hard/R: Medium	25	41m 00.554s 100.5mph/161.7km/h
2	**Fabio Quartararo**	FRA	20	Monster Energy Yamaha MotoGP	Yamaha YZR-M1	M	F: Hard/R: Medium	25	41m 00.839s
3	**Aleix Espargaro**	SPA	41	Aprilia Racing	Aprilia RS-GP	M	F: Hard/R: Medium	25	41m 11.531s
4	**Marc Marquez**	SPA	93	Repsol Honda Team	Honda RC213V	M	F: Hard/R: Medium	25	41m 13.230s
5	**Jack Miller**	AUS	43	Ducati Lenovo Team	Ducati Desmosedici	M	F: Hard/R: Medium	25	41m 13.511s
6	**Joan Mir**	SPA	36	Team SUZUKI ECSTAR	Suzuki GSX-RR	M	F: Hard/R: Medium	25	41m 14.488s
7	**Takaaki Nakagami**	JPN	30	LCR Honda IDEMITSU	Honda RC213V	M	F: Hard/R: Medium	25	41m 15.483s
8	**Enea Bastianini**	ITA	23	Gresini Racing MotoGP	Ducati Desmosedici	M	F: Hard/R: Medium	25	41m 18.990s
9	**Marco Bezzecchi**	ITA	72	Mooney VR46 Racing Team	Ducati Desmosedici	M	F: Hard/R: Medium	25	41m 19.384s
10	**Brad Binder**	RSA	33	Red Bull KTM Factory Racing	KTM RC16	M	F: Hard/R: Medium	25	41m 20.610s
11	**Pol Espargaro**	SPA	44	Repsol Honda Team	Honda RC213V	M	F: Hard/R: Medium	25	41m 21.410s
12	**Miguel Oliveira**	POR	88	Red Bull KTM Factory Racing	KTM RC16	M	F: Hard/R: Medium	25	41m 23.685s
13	**Alex Marquez**	SPA	73	LCR Honda CASTROL	Honda RC213V	M	F: Hard/R: Medium	25	41m 25.860s
14	**Maverick Vinales**	SPA	12	Aprilia Racing	Aprilia RS-GP	M	F: Hard/R: Medium	25	41m 27.912s
15	**Franco Morbidelli**	ITA	21	Monster Energy Yamaha MotoGP	Yamaha YZR-M1	M	F: Hard/R: Medium	25	41m 28.073s
16	Luca Marini	ITA	10	Mooney VR46 Racing Team	Ducati Desmosedici	M	F: Hard/R: Medium	25	41m 29.832s
17	Andrea Dovizioso	ITA	4	WithU Yamaha RNF MotoGP Team	Yamaha YZR-M1	M	F: Hard/R: Medium	25	41m 35.758s
18	Fabio Di Giannantonio	ITA	49	Gresini Racing MotoGP	Ducati Desmosedici	M	F: Hard/R: Medium	25	41m 35.915s
19	Alex Rins	SPA	42	Team SUZUKI ECSTAR	Suzuki GSX-RR	M	F: Hard/R: Medium	25	41m 39.476s
20	Remy Gardner	AUS	87	Tech3 KTM Factory Racing	KTM RC16	M	F: Hard/R: Medium	25	41m 43.932s
21	Lorenzo Savadori	ITA	32	Aprilia Racing	Aprilia RS-GP	M	F: Hard/R: Medium	25	41m 44.853s
22	Jorge Martin	SPA	89	Pramac Racing	Ducati Desmosedici	M	F: Hard/R: Medium	25	42m 08.235s
	Stefan Bradl	GER	6	Team HRC	Honda RC213V	M	F: Hard/R: Medium	10	DNF-crash
	Johann Zarco	FRA	5	Pramac Racing	Ducati Desmosedici	M	F: Hard/R: Medium	9	DNF-crash
	Darryn Binder	RSA	40	WithU Yamaha RNF MotoGP Team	Yamaha YZR-M1	M	F: Hard/R: Medium	5	DNF-crash

Fastest lap: Francesco Bagnaia, on lap 5, 1m 37.669s, 101.3mph/163.0km/h.

Lap record: Fabio Quartararo, 1m 37.770s, 101.2mph/162.8km/h (2021).

Event maximum speed: Johann Zarco, 186.4mph/300.0km/h (qualifying).

Qualifying

Weather: Dry
Air Temp: 24° **Humidity:** 43%
Track Temp: 43°

Pos.	Rider	Time
1	Bagnaia	1m 36.170s
2	Quartararo	1m 36.623s
3	A. Espargaro	1m 36.933s
4	Miller	1m 37.049s
5	M. Marquez	1m 37.145s
6	Zarco	1m 37.220s
7	Nakagami	1m 37.254s
8	Bezzecchi	1m 37.285s
9	Mir	1m 37.330s
10	Martin	1m 37.526s
11	Bastianini	1m 37.618s
12	Vinales	1m 37.675s
	Q1	
13	P. Espargaro	1m 37.138s
14	Rins	1m 37.401s
15	B. Binder	1m 37.544s
16	Morbidelli	1m 37.668s
17	Di Giannantonio	1m 37.882s
18	Gardner	1m 37.889s
19	Marini	1m 37.910s
20	Bradl	1m 37.937s
21	Oliveira	1m 37.958s
22	A. Marquez	1m 38.014s
23	Dovizioso	1m 38.064s
24	Savadori	1m 38.244s
25	D. Binder	1m 38.405s

Fastest race laps

Pos.	Rider	Time
1	Bagnaia	1m 37.669s
2	Quartararo	1m 37.678s
3	M. Marquez	1m 38.059s
4	Miller	1m 38.140s
5	A. Espargaro	1m 38.184s
6	Mir	1m 38.222s
7	Zarco	1m 38.429s
8	Nakagami	1m 38.472s
9	P. Espargaro	1m 38.545s
10	B. Binder	1m 38.550s
11	Bezzecchi	1m 38.553s
12	Rins	1m 38.556s
13	Bastianini	1m 38.567s
14	Oliveira	1m 38.609s
15	Morbidelli	1m 38.643s
16	Vinales	1m 38.678s
17	Martin	1m 38.740s
18	A. Marquez	1m 38.851s
19	Bradl	1m 38.926s
20	D. Binder	1m 38.948s
21	Dovizioso	1m 38.983s
22	Marini	1m 39.029s
23	Gardner	1m 39.068s
24	Di Giannantonio	1m 39.142s
25	Savadori	1m 39.409s

Championship Points

Pos.	Rider	Points
1	Quartararo	89
2	A. Espargaro	82
3	Bastianini	69
4	Rins	69
5	Bagnaia	56
6	Mir	56
7	Zarco	51
8	B. Binder	48
9	M. Marquez	44
10	Oliveira	43
11	Miller	42
12	P. Espargaro	35
13	Martin	28
14	Vinales	27
15	Nakagami	21
16	Morbidelli	18
17	A. Marquez	16
18	Bezzecchi	15
19	Marini	14
20	Dovizioso	8
21	D. Binder	6
22	Gardner	3

Constructor Points

Pos.	Constructor	Points
1	Ducati	131
2	Yamaha	89
3	Aprilia	83
4	Suzuki	80
5	KTM	76
6	Honda	57

Grid order	1	2	3	4	5	6	7	8	9	10	11	12	13	14	15	16	17	18	19	20	21	22	23	24	25	
63 BAGNAIA	63	63	63	63	63	63	63	63	63	63	63	63	63	63	63	63	63	63	63	63	63	63	63	63	63	1
20 QUARTARARO	20	20	20	20	20	20	20	20	20	20	20	20	20	20	20	20	20	20	20	20	20	20	20	20	20	2
41 A. ESPARGARO	43	43	43	43	43	43	43	43	43	43	43	43	43	43	43	43	43	43	43	43	41	41	41	41	41	3
43 MILLER	93	93	93	93	93	93	93	93	93	93	93	93	93	93	93	93	93	93	93	93	93	43	43	43	93	4
93 M. MARQUEZ	41	41	41	41	41	41	41	41	41	41	41	41	41	41	41	41	41	41	41	41	43	93	93	93	43	5
5 ZARCO	30	36	36	36	36	36	36	36	36	36	36	36	36	36	36	36	36	36	36	36	36	36	36	36	36	6
30 NAKAGAMI	36	30	30	30	30	30	30	30	30	30	30	30	30	30	30	30	30	30	30	30	30	30	30	30	30	7
72 BEZZECCHI	72	72	72	72	72	72	72	72	72	72	72	72	72	72	72	72	72	72	72	72	72	72	72	72	23	8
36 MIR	5	5	5	5	5	5	5	5	5	33	33	23	23	23	23	23	23	23	23	23	23	23	23	23	72	9
89 MARTIN	33	33	33	33	33	33	33	33	33	23	23	33	33	33	33	33	33	33	33	33	33	33	33	33	33	10
23 BASTIANINI	23	23	23	23	23	23	23	23	23	44	44	44	44	44	44	44	44	44	44	44	44	44	44	44	44	11
12 VINALES	44	42	44	44	44	44	44	44	44	88	88	88	88	88	88	88	88	88	88	88	88	88	88	88	88	12
44 P. ESPARGARO	42	44	88	88	88	88	88	88	88	73	73	73	73	73	73	73	73	73	73	73	73	73	73	73	73	13
42 RINS	88	88	42	42	73	42	42	42	73	10	10	10	10	10	10	10	10	10	10	10	12	12	12	12	12	14
33 B.BINDER	21	73	73	73	42	73	73	73	10	12	12	12	12	12	12	12	12	12	12	12	10	10	21	21	21	15
21 MORBIDELLI	73	21	21	21	21	21	10	10	12	21	21	21	21	21	21	21	21	21	21	21	21	21	10	10	10	
49 DI GIANNANTONIO	10	10	10	10	40	10	21	12	21	4	4	4	4	4	4	4	4	4	4	4	4	4	4	4	4	
87 GARDNER	40	40	40	40	10	12	12	21	4	49	49	49	49	49	49	49	49	49	49	49	49	49	49	49	49	
10 MARINI	87	87	87	87	12	87	4	4	49	87	87	87	87	87	87	87	87	87	87	42	42	42	42	42	42	
6 BRADL	49	12	12	12	87	4	87	49	87	32	32	32	32	32	32	32	32	42	42	87	87	87	87	87	87	
88 OLIVEIRA	4	49	4	4	4	49	49	87	32	42	42	42	42	42	42	42	42	32	32	32	32	32	32	32	32	
73 A. MARQUEZ	12	4	49	49	49	32	32	32	42	6	89	89	89	89	89	89	89	89	89	89	89	89	89	89	89	
4 DOVIZIOSO	32	32	32	32	32	6	6	6	6	89																
32 SAVADORI	6	6	6	6	6	89	89	89	89																	
40 D.BINDER	89	89	89	89	89																					

40 Pit stop

Moto2

RACE DISTANCE: 23 laps, 63.211 miles/101.729km · RACE WEATHER: Dry (air 26°, humidity 32%, track 39°)

Pos.	Rider	Nat.	No.	Entrant	Machine	Laps	Time & Speed
1	**Ai Ogura**	JPN	79	IDEMITSU Honda Team Asia	Kalex	23	39m 16.357s
							96.6mph/155.4km/h
2	**Aron Canet**	SPA	40	Flexbox HP40	Kalex	23	39m 18.866s
3	**Tony Arbolino**	ITA	14	Elf Marc VDS Racing Team	Kalex	23	39m 20.026s
4	**Augusto Fernandez**	SPA	37	Red Bull KTM Ajo	Kalex	23	39m 21.715s
5	**Marcel Schrotter**	GER	23	Liqui Moly Intact GP	Kalex	23	39m 25.602s
6	**Celestino Vietti**	ITA	13	Mooney VR46 Racing Team	Kalex	23	39m 28.479s
7	**Bo Bendsneyder**	NED	64	Pertamina Mandalika SAG Team	Kalex	23	39m 30.275s
8	**Joe Roberts**	USA	16	Italtrans Racing Team	Kalex	23	39m 30.421s
9	**Albert Arenas**	SPA	75	Autosolar GASGAS Aspar Team	Kalex	23	39m 35.337s
10	**Jorge Navarro**	SPA	9	Flexbox HP40	Kalex	23	39m 44.124s
11	**Alessandro Zaccone**	ITA	61	Gresini Racing Moto2	Kalex	23	39m 47.893s
12	**Jeremy Alcoba**	SPA	52	Liqui Moly Intact GP	Kalex	23	39m 49.665s
13	**Stefano Manzi**	ITA	62	Yamaha VR46 Master Camp Team	Kalex	23	39m 49.992s
14	**Barry Baltus**	BEL	7	RW Racing GP	Kalex	23	39m 50.108s
15	**Lorenzo Dalla Porta**	ITA	19	Italtrans Racing Team	Kalex	23	39m 50.193s
16	Manuel Gonzalez	SPA	18	Yamaha VR46 Master Camp Team	Kalex	23	39m 50.397s
17	Gabriel Rodrigo	ARG	2	Pertamina Mandalika SAG Team	Kalex	23	39m 53.649s
18	Simone Corsi	ITA	24	MV Agusta Forward Racing	MV Agusta	23	39m 57.485s
19	Zonta van den Goorbergh	NED	84	RW Racing GP	Kalex	23	39m 57.664s
20	Pedro Acosta	SPA	51	Red Bull KTM Ajo	Kalex	23	40m 02.798s
21	Filip Salac	CZE	12	Gresini Racing Moto2	Kalex	23	40m 09.430s
22	Sean Dylan Kelly	USA	4	American Racing	Kalex	23	40m 12.514s
23	Niccolo Antonelli	ITA	28	Mooney VR46 Racing Team	Kalex	23	40m 12.878s
	Fermin Aldeguer	SPA	54	Lightech Speed Up	Boscoscuro	13	DNF-crash
	Marcos Ramirez	SPA	42	MV Agusta Forward Racing	MV Agusta	9	DNF-crash
	Jake Dixon	GBR	96	Autosolar GASGAS Aspar Team	Kalex	8	DNF-crash
	Somkiat Chantra	THA	35	IDEMITSU Honda Team Asia	Kalex	7	DNF-crash
	Cameron Beaubier	USA	6	American Racing	Kalex	7	DNF-technical
	Sam Lowes	GBR	22	Elf Marc VDS Racing Team	Kalex	6	DNF-crash
	Romano Fenati	ITA	5	Lightech Speed Up	Boscoscuro	4	DNF-crash

Fastest lap: Sam Lowes, on lap 3, 1m 41.757s, 97.2mph/156.4km/h.

Lap record: Sam Lowes, 1m 41.313s, 97.6mph/157.1km/h (2021).

Event maximum speed: Lorenzo Dalla Porta, 159.4mph/256.5km/h (free practice).

Qualifying

Weather: Dry

Air: 26° **Humidity:** 39%

Track: 42°

Pos.	Rider	Time
1	Ogura	1m 41.289s
2	Arbolino	1m 41.299s
3	Lowes	1m 41.321s
4	Canet	1m 41.369s
5	Aldeguer	1m 41.620s
6	Vietti	1m 41.741s
7	Chantra	1m 41.753s
8	Bendsneyder	1m 41.815s
9	Fernandez	1m 41.901s
10	Acosta	1m 41.914s
11	Dixon	1m 41.966s
12	Arenas	1m 42.072s
13	Navarro	1m 42.097s
14	Roberts	1m 42.100s
15	Rodrigo	1m 42.367s
16	Dalla Porta	1m 42.381s
17	Baltus	1m 42.631s
18	Schrotter	1m 42.818s
	Q1	
19	Ramirez	1m 41.907s
20	Gonzalez	1m 41.950s
21	Zaccone	1m 42.051s
22	Salac	1m 42.063s
23	Alcoba	1m 42.090s
24	V D Goorbergh	1m 42.287s
25	Beaubier	1m 42.295s
26	Manzi	1m 42.634s
27	Fenati	1m 42.694s
28	Corsi	1m 42.828s
29	Kelly	1m 43.211s
30	Antonelli	1m 43.229s

Fastest race laps

Pos.	Rider	Time
1	Lowes	1m 41.757s
2	Canet	1m 41.810s
3	Arbolino	1m 41.885s
4	Ogura	1m 41.920s
5	Fernandez	1m 41.925s
6	Acosta	1m 41.983s
7	Aldeguer	1m 41.992s
8	Schrotter	1m 41.999s
9	Vietti	1m 42.016s
10	Chantra	1m 42.017s
11	Dixon	1m 42.235s
12	Navarro	1m 42.418s
13	Roberts	1m 42.422s
14	Arenas	1m 42.441s
15	Bendsneyder	1m 42.509s
16	Baltus	1m 42.593s
17	Beaubier	1m 42.771s
18	Rodrigo	1m 42.775s
19	Gonzalez	1m 42.824s
20	Zaccone	1m 42.883s
21	Alcoba	1m 42.946s
22	Manzi	1m 42.958s
23	Dalla Porta	1m 42.974s
24	Ramirez	1m 42.994s
25	Fenati	1m 43.426s
26	Corsi	1m 43.593s
27	Salac	1m 43.595s
28	V D Goorbergh	1m 43.604s
29	Antonelli	1m 43.969s
30	Kelly	1m 44.073s

Championship Points

Pos.	Rider	Points
1	Vietti	100
2	Ogura	81
3	Arbolino	70
4	Canet	69
5	Roberts	57
6	Schrotter	47
7	Chantra	45
8	Navarro	45
9	Fernandez	44
10	Lowes	35
11	Bendsneyder	34
12	Dixon	32
13	Arenas	29
14	Alcoba	28
15	Acosta	20
16	Aldeguer	18
17	Gonzalez	16
18	Beaubier	16
19	Baltus	15
20	Fenati	7
21	Rodrigo	6
22	Zaccone	6
23	Ramirez	5
24	Kubo	4
25	Salac	4
26	Kelly	3
27	Manzi	3
28	Dalla Porta	1

Constructor Points

Pos.	Constructor	Points
1	Kalex	150
2	Boscoscuro	20
3	MV Agusta	5

Moto3

RACE DISTANCE: 22 laps, 60.463 miles/97.306km · RACE WEATHER: Dry (air 26°, humidity 32%, track 35°)

Pos.	Rider	Nat.	No.	Entrant	Machine	Laps	Time & Speed
1	**Izan Guevara**	SPA	28	Gaviota GASGAS Aspar Team	GASGAS	22	39m 19.873s
							92.2mph/148.4km/h
2	**Sergio Garcia**	SPA	11	Gaviota GASGAS Aspar Team	GASGAS	22	39m 19.934s
3	**Jaume Masia**	SPA	5	Red Bull KTM Ajo	KTM	22	39m 20.081s
4	**Deniz Oncu**	TUR	53	Red Bull KTM Tech3	KTM	22	39m 20.192s
5	**Xavier Artigas**	SPA	43	CFMOTO Racing PruestelGP	CFMOTO	22	39m 20.290s
6	**Ayumu Sasaki**	JPN	71	Sterilgarda Husqvarna Max	Husqvarna	22	39m 20.720s
7	**Kaito Toba**	JPN	27	CIP Green Power	KTM	22	39m 23.660s
8	**Ryusei Yamanaka**	JPN	6	MT Helmets - MSI	KTM	22	39m 23.855s
9	**Daniel Holgado**	SPA	96	Red Bull KTM Ajo	KTM	22	39m 25.684s
10	**Diogo Moreira**	BRA	10	MT Helmets - MSI	KTM	22	39m 25.961s
11	**Matteo Bertelle**	ITA	18	QJMotor Avintia Racing Team	KTM	22	39m 30.942s
12	**Scott Ogden**	GBR	19	VisionTrack Racing Team	Honda	22	39m 31.015s
13	**Ivan Ortola**	SPA	48	Angeluss MTA Team	KTM	22	39m 35.419s
14	**Andrea Migno**	ITA	16	Rivacold Snipers Team	Honda	22	39m 35.535s
15	**Stefano Nepa**	ITA	82	Angeluss MTA Team	KTM	22	39m 35.560s
16	Elia Bartolini	ITA	23	QJMotor Avintia Racing Team	KTM	22	39m 35.601s
17	Mario Aji	INA	64	Honda Team Asia	Honda	22	39m 36.455s
18	Dennis Foggia	ITA	7	Leopard Racing	Honda	22	39m 37.402s
19	David Salvador	SPA	38	Sterilgarda Husqvarna Max	Husqvarna	22	39m 43.211s
20	Gerard Riu Male	SPA	87	BOE SKX	KTM	22	39m 45.281s
21	Taiyo Furusato	JPN	72	Honda Team Asia	Honda	22	39m 45.442s
22	Syarifuddin Azman	MAL	63	Rivacold Snipers Team	Honda	22	40m 04.039s
23	Ana Carrasco	SPA	22	BOE SKX	KTM	22	40m 04.210s
	Riccardo Rossi	ITA	54	SIC58 Squadra Corse	Honda	14	DNF-crash
	Tatsuki Suzuki	JPN	24	Leopard Racing	Honda	6	DNF-crash
	Adrian Fernandez	SPA	31	Red Bull KTM Tech3	KTM	5	DNF-injured
	Carlos Tatay	SPA	99	CFMOTO Racing PruestelGP	CFMOTO	3	DNF-crash
	Joel Kelso	AUS	66	CIP Green Power	KTM	3	DNF-injured

Fastest lap: Izan Guevara, on lap 2, 1m 46.084s, 93.2mph/150.0km/h.

Lap record: Jaume Masia, 1m 46.060s, 93.3mph/150.1km/h (2020).

Event maximum speed: Izan Guevara, 137.2mph/220.8km/h (race).

Qualifying:

Weather: Wet

Air: 22° **Humidity:** 49%

Track: 41°

Pos.	Rider	Time
1	Guevara	1m 45.880s
2	Garcia	1m 46.004s
3	Masia	1m 46.051s
4	Foggia	1m 46.170s
5	Oncu	1m 46.214s
6	Artigas	1m 46.225s
7	Sasaki	1m 46.312s
8	Rossi	1m 46.315s
9	Moreira	1m 46.384s
10	Tatay	1m 46.395s
11	Ogden	1m 46.454s
12	Yamanaka	1m 46.483s
13	Migno	1m 46.815s
14	Kelso	1m 46.918s
15	Ortola	1m 47.165s
16	Salvador	1m 47.242s
17	Bertelle	1m 48.204s
18	Toba	No Time
	Q1	
19	Holgado	1m 47.486s
20	Suzuki	1m 47.489s
21	Fernandez	1m 47.502s
22	Riu Male	1m 47.625s
23	Bartolini	1m 47.778s
24	Furusato	1m 47.819s
25	Azman	1m 48.075s
26	Nepa	1m 48.303s
27	Aji	1m 48.341s
28	Carrasco	1m 49.241s

Fastest race laps

Pos.	Rider	Time
1	Guevara	1m 46.084s
2	Masia	1m 46.105s
3	Oncu	1m 46.128s
4	Garcia	1m 46.178s
5	Sasaki	1m 46.179s
6	Artigas	1m 46.281s
7	Rossi	1m 46.484s
8	Holgado	1m 46.532s
9	Yamanaka	1m 46.553s
10	Tatay	1m 46.579s
11	Toba	1m 46.655s
12	Moreira	1m 46.704s
13	Ogden	1m 46.714s
14	Suzuki	1m 46.720s
15	Bertelle	1m 46.728s
16	Migno	1m 46.749s
17	Ortola	1m 46.844s
18	Salvador	1m 46.873s
19	Foggia	1m 46.979s
20	Nepa	1m 46.982s
21	Bartolini	1m 47.046s
22	Fernandez	1m 47.161s
23	Aji	1m 47.204s
24	Furusato	1m 47.383s
25	Riu Male	1m 47.694s
26	Carrasco	1m 47.989s
27	Azman	1m 48.198s
28	Kelso	1m 48.846s

Championship Points

Pos.	Rider	Points
1	Garcia	103
2	Foggia	82
3	Guevara	73
4	Masia	70
5	Oncu	63
6	Sasaki	55
7	Migno	52
8	Tatay	42
9	Artigas	37
10	Toba	36
11	Moreira	32
12	Rossi	29
13	Suzuki	27
14	Yamanaka	24
15	Holgado	23
16	Kelso	14
17	Ortola	14
18	Ogden	14
19	Bartolini	13
20	McPhee	11
21	Nepa	8
22	Fernandez	7
23	Bertelle	6
24	Fellon	3
25	Aji	2

Constructor Points

Pos.	Constructor	Points
1	GASGAS	124
2	Honda	103
3	KTM	98
4	Husqvarna	66
5	CFMOTO	61

SHARK
GRAND PRIX de
FRANCE
LE MANS
MICHELIN
PAYS DE LA LOIRE
Sarthe

FIM WORLD CHAMPIONSHIP · ROUND 7

FRENCH GRAND PRIX

LE MANS CIRCUIT

Inset, above: Covid restrictions had ended, and huge crowds descended on the Sarthe circuit.
Photo: Gold & Goose

Main: Fine weather for once at Le Mans as the MotoGP field streams away from the start.
Photo: Suzuki ECSTAR

Above: **Bastianini outpaced Miller on his way forward for a third win of the year.**

Above right: **Quartararo couldn't satisfy the local fans' hopes for a French victory.**

Right: **Zarco and Marquez were never in the hunt.**

Below right: **Alex Rins was an early casualty after a spectacular high-speed run across the gravel.**

Photos: Gold & Goose

THE combination of post-pandemic open gates and a French world champion brought the fans flocking to Le Mans – a race-day crowd of more than 110,000 being the largest for almost two decades. Records were broken on track, too, in a weekend of unusually benign weather, although a brief blip during Sunday's opening Moto3 race caused red flags and mayhem.

Sadly, fortune did not complete the full circle. Quartararo's prowess had engendered hopes of a first ever French premier-class win at the famous venue, indeed the first at any home track since Pierre Monneret had beaten fellow Gilera rider Alfredo Milani by 16 seconds at Reims in 1954. Circumstances, and the speed and braking prowess of the Ducatis quashed them.

For a third time in seven races, however, it was the 'wrong' Ducati. Sophomore Bastianini wore down Miller and then pushed Bagnaia into a second race crash. Once again, his win displayed maturity and racecraft above his status as a second-string satellite rider.

It was another rock in the already turbulent waters of the silly season. With only four riders under contract for 2023 (Bagnaia, Brad Binder, Marc Marquez and Morbidelli), rider managers were at full tilt, and rumours seething. Now Bastianini was tipped to gazump Martin's expected promotion to replace Miller on the second factory Ducati. The unexpected availability of both Suzuki riders, Mir and Rins, was another key factor. With more talented riders than top-level seats, it had become a buyers' market for the factories; conversely, riders were starting to complain of reduced payments. Ducati were playing musical chairs with their eight-strong talent pool, while Aleix Espargaro's renewal talks with Aprilia were in a state of stalemate over payment.

Suzuki's withdrawal was finally confirmed officially on Saturday. A terse 98-word factory statement acknowledged negotiations with Dorna to cancel their contract, citing "the current economic situation and the need to concentrate ... effort on the big changes that the automotive world is facing." A predicted penalty payment to Dorna in the region of 20 million euros was small beer compared with the US $1.4-billion investment planned for Suzuki's electric-vehicle plant in India.

Harder to put a price on was the PR disaster, exacerbated by stories emerging from unexpectedly displaced riders and team staff. Team officials were tight-lipped, but Rins spoke for many. He said that he'd been "fully crying" when informed on the evening of the tests: "I gave everything to this team, since 2017 trying to have a competitive, winning bike." None of the higher factory bosses had spoken to the riders nor the majority of team members to explain their reasoning. "It's a little bit strange," said Rins. "The Suzuki president – Toshihiro-San – he is super-friendly with me. He sent me a video saying, 'Congratulations,' when my baby was born. But I didn't receive anything."

Of the two riders, 2020 World Champion Mir appeared more likely to land on his feet, already strongly tipped to replace Pol Espargaro at Repsol Honda for 2023. His manager, Paco Sanchez, said, "I read that we have signed with Yamaha or with Honda, but these are false. Are we close to sign with one of them? Yes, we could be."

Meanwhile, Dorna confirmed strong interest from both factories and independent teams ready to take Suzuki's two grid slots. Moto3's Leopard Racing and the Moto2 American Racing Team were interested, but Dorna CEO Carmelo Ezpeleta intimated that he would be perfectly fine with the grid shrinking from 24 bikes to 22. "For us, a championship with five manufacturers and six private teams is exactly the same as we had last year, and it's okay for us," he said. "Depending on how the proposals look, we will decide if we want to replace Suzuki or we will continue with the situation as it is without Suzuki."

There was shrinkage elsewhere, as Yamaha Racing MD Lin Jarvis revealed that they might field only two machines in 2023, with the satellite RNF squad soon to confirm a switch to Aprilia. Jarvis explained that they had a year-by-year contract with the satellite outfit. "We'd ideally like to extend the contract with RNF for another year," he said. The poor performance of the bikes was a big negative, however.

Meanwhile, another hangover from Jerez was a fresh controversy, following the revelation that Pecco Bagnaia's front tyre pressure had been below the legal amount for the entirety of the race. Should he have been disqualified? The answer was submerged in a soup of reticence and uncertainty, as it became clear that the regulation for a minimum front tyre pressure of 27.5psi (1.9 bar) was, by a gentleman's agreement between Dorna and the MSMA, not enforceable; and Bagnaia angrily pointed out that as many as 18 riders had been below the minimum pressure for more than half-race distance at least once in the current season.

Michelin blamed the use of different pressure sensors, while Dorna tech director Danny Aldridge was "evaluating a new … monitoring protocol" for 2023, using a standardised 'control' sensor. But there was another aspect to the affair: teams start their riders with tyres below minimum pressure to take account of temperature and thence pressure increases during the race, especially if the airflow is masked when following closely behind another bike. Bagnaia had nobody in front of him all race, so that didn't happen. On the other hand, Quartararo in particular had had races spoiled on the Yamaha, with its reliance on high corner speed, when the front tyre pressure had increased and the optimal profile been lost.

There was yet another aspect, after a second successive processional race. At one point, seven machines were at the front, but only the Ducatis of Bagnaia and Bastianini could overtake. The spectacle was similar to the previous race at Jerez: bikes circulating together at close to identical speed, albeit several metres apart, from one lap to the next – further evidence that Michelin's front tyre couldn't deal with the extra pressures of braking brought on by aerodynamics and ride-height devices. Luca Marini summed up a common theme: "With the tyres now, it's really, really difficult to overtake because the front pressure goes up and the temperature goes up. Then everyone is braking very late. You just stay behind the rider in front and wait for him to make a mistake. Michelin improved the rear tyre a lot compared to 2019. Now they need to focus on the front."

MOTOGP RACE – 27 laps

Bagnaia's second pole in a row came by less than a tenth from team-mate Miller, the Ducatis joined on the front row by Aleix Espargaro, his Aprilia's third in succession. Quartararo led row two, again by far the fastest Yamaha, with Morbidelli, Dovizioso and Darryn Binder 19th, 20th and 23rd, almost a full second slower.

Bastianini and Zarco completed row two; Mir – through with Martin from Q1 – led the third. Again, the KTMs were all at sea on a twisty track, Brad Binder and Oliveira 17th and 18th; rookies Gardner and Fernandez, the latter becoming increasingly disillusioned, at the back.

Miller and Rins were the only top riders to choose Michelin's soft front, and the Australian led a dream getaway for Ducati from Bastianini and Bagnaia. The Suzukis of Rins and Mir followed, while Quartararo was squeezed at the Dunlop chicane, dropping to eighth behind Nakagami and Aleix Espargaro, although ahead of Marc Marquez, who had started tenth.

The early action was lively. First, Bastianini made his sole mistake at Garage Vert, running wide to let Bagnaia and Rins past. Espargaro dived under Nakagami for sixth at Turn Nine; two corners later, Quartararo also pushed past the Japanese rider, only for Nakagami to fight back at Turn 13, pushing both wide and creating an opening for Marquez to dive under the pair.

There was more drama on the next two laps. First, Quartararo's retaliation on Nakagami, shunting the Honda rider off wide at the first part of the Dunlop chicane. As he rejoined, the field bunched up behind him into La Chapelle at the bottom of the hill. In the melee, Brad Binder lost his left winglet in a shunt with Zarco.

Next time around, Rins was dragged down the front straight in Bagnaia's slipstream, too fast into the daunting Turn One/Two set. He lifted, but ran across the gravel at unabated speed, rejoining the track at 120mph and at right angles at the second part of the chicane. By some miracle, he didn't hit Miller, but crossing the kerb had sent him airborne, and he landed with his wheels out of line and crashed, rejoining at the back, only to retire shortly afterwards.

One lap later, the fourth, Miller ran wide on the exit of Museum and Bagnaia moved under him. From this point, with Bastianini, Mir and Espargaro behind, and Quartararo now past Marquez for sixth, the race settled down.

Marquez gradually dropped back, while the top six were

Above: **Bagnaia's plan for patience came crashing down after Bastianini had stolen the lead.**

Above right: **Augusto Fernandez took a long delayed Moto2 win after team-mate Acosta crashed out.**

Above far right: **Jack Miller entertained with his famous stoppie to celebrate his return to the podium.**

Right: **Still hampered by injury, Canet took second, while Chantra (35) would deny Beaubier (6) a first Moto2 podium.**

Below right: **Jaume Masia (5) emerged victorious in the restarted Moto3 race, ahead of Sasaki (71). Foggia, partly hidden, fell victim to Guevara (28).**

Photos: Gold & Goose

never more than three seconds apart. A few critical moves would decide the race.

On lap 11, Bagnaia was inching clear of Miller, while Bastianini upped his pace to pass the Australian at Garage Vert. Three laps later, Mir misjudged his braking for Turn 13 and crashed out, blaming "less air and some turbulence" when behind a Ducati, compounding a wretched fortnight for the Suzuki team.

Now Bastianini was pressing Bagnaia, just over half a second ahead. On lap 20, they crossed the line almost together – 90 seconds later, Bagnaia's world came crashing down.

Bastianini had expertly taken the lead into the chicane. Bagnaia fought back on the exit of La Chapelle, only to fluff his braking into Garage Vert, losing nine-tenths after running wide. Time to regroup: "I was thinking, 'No pressure. I will retake him – not soon, but with consistency.' But I arrived at the second-last corner, I entered a bit slower. And crashed."

Bastianini could cruise home almost three seconds clear of Miller, a title candidate once more. He had learned while following Bagnaia, he said: "All weekend, he was faster than me in two points. I changed some of my lines and closed the gap." Miller observed that Bastianini had been "good on the tyres ... he rode a perfect race."

Espargaro clung on to third, narrowly fending off Quartararo's late attempts at a home podium by a tenth.

Zarco, never in the hunt up front, secured fifth. Honda's woes continued, with Nakagami following Marquez for a distant sixth and seventh.

Reliably heroic, in spite of his missing winglet, Brad Binder collected eighth ahead of Marini and Vinales. Once again, the latter had recovered from a shocking getaway, finishing lap one last. Oliveira had been tussling with Binder until he crashed with three laps to go.

Pol Espargaro was close in 11th after running wide, and dropping behind Marini and Vinales; Bezzecchi was close behind. Di Giannantonio, Alex Marquez (after a long-lap penalty) and Morbidelli wrapped up the points; Dovizioso and a distant Darryn Binder tailed in.

Martin fell from an undistinguished 11th soon after half-distance. Both satellite KTM riders Gardner and Fernandez also crashed out.

MOTO2 RACE – 25 laps

Moto3 champion Pedro Acosta's middle-class debut had disappointed many observers, who had expected his dominance in the smallest class to transfer seamlessly, especially after he had been fastest at the pre-season Portimao tests. He came close in France, only to fall while working on a commanding lead.

His first pole – indeed his first front row – was by better than a tenth from Dixon and Fernandez. Lowes was fourth, but unfit after a heavy crash in qualifying – he'd been fastest at the time. That put Arenas at the head of row two from Lopez and Canet, his right wrist still far from full strength. Lopez had been drafted into the Boscoscuro team to replace Fenati, sacked after a disappointing start to the season; it was the Spanish Moto3 veteran's fifth Moto2 race.

Ogura led the third row, still just half a second off pole in a tight set of times.

The race was eventful, but not for eventual winner Fernandez. He took off in second and seemed destined to stay there, pulling rapidly clear of the pursuit, but seeming able only to follow team-mate Acosta.

By lap ten, Acosta was trying to break clear, crossing the line eight-tenths ahead. But his sprint didn't last even half a lap more. The front tucked under at La Chapelle, handing Fernandez a comfortable first win since the San Marino GP in September, 2019.

Arenas had led the pursuit on the first lap, from Lopez, Ramirez, Canet and Dixon. On the second, Arbolino and Aldeguer fell together from the middle of the pack; two laps later, Dixon also fell, after losing a place to a charging Beaubier, up from the sixth row.

By now, Lopez was heading a lively battle for third, from Canet, Arenas, Beaubier and Chantra, eighth on lap one.

On lap six, Arenas and Lopez collided and fell on the exit from Museum. That left Canet, Chantra and Beaubier to contest the remaining podium places. It was going Chantra's way, as he had moved to second by lap 15. But a mistake when braking at Garage Vert four laps later allowed his two pursuers through. Canet held on to second, with Chantra depriving Beaubier of a maiden podium with a move two laps from the flag.

Ogura had finished lap one 12th, but gained positions in the later stages for a potentially valuable fifth. His last victim had been Schrotter, who led Roberts, Vietti, Navarro and substitute rider Manzi, with rookie Gonzalez only half a second behind. Vietti had qualified 18th and finished lap one 21st, but he picked his way steadily forward, overtaking Navarro on the final lap; his points lead over Ogura and Canet shrank to 16 and 19 respectively.

Dalla Porta, a tussling Alcoba and Bendsneyder, and a distant Salac took the remaining points.

Just 19 of 29 starters finished, the crash list swelled by Antonelli on lap one, plus Rodrigo, Ramirez and Baltus.

MOTO3 RACE – 14 laps (shortened)

Foggia claimed a career-first pole position, ahead of Honda team-mate Suzuki and Masia, but the race was thrown into chaos by the briefest of rain showers on the opening lap. GasGas team-mates Garcia and Guevara, plus Migno, Sasaki, Toba and rookie Ortola all fell in a heap in the final corner, followed by Holgado and Bartolini a little further around. Red flag.

Twenty-five minutes on, the track was dry enough for slicks, but with wet patches remaining. The 14-lap rerun was a corker.

Few were willing to push initially in the patchy conditions, and a massive lead group quickly formed. This was soon whittled down to five.

Foggia did much of the leading, Masia, Suzuki and Sasaki never far away. Guevara, meanwhile, recovered from a tepid start to launch a late attack, while an uncharacteristic mistake on the penultimate lap resulted in Garcia becoming mired in a fight behind.

Twice Masia had to scrap on the final lap. A beautiful pass on Foggia at Turn Three gave him the lead, only for Sasaki – also past the Italian at Museum – to audaciously snatch it on the switchback into Turn 12. But Masia was finally showing signs that his fighting instincts could match his talent. A clinical move on Sasaki at Turn 13 was enough for his second victory of the year.

Guevara nabbed third from a bemused Foggia; Suzuki was fifth, the top five covered by just 0.529 of a second, with Tatay leading Garcia home in sixth.

FIM WORLD CHAMPIONSHIP: ROUND 7

SHARK GRAND PRIX DE FRANCE

13–15 MAY, 2022

LE MANS – BUGATTI

28 laps
Length: 4.185 km / 2.600 miles
Width: 13m

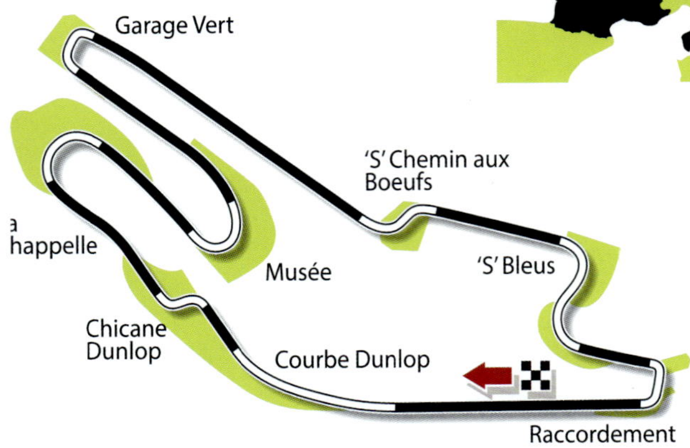

MotoGP

RACE DISTANCE: 27 laps, 70.212 miles/112.995km · RACE WEATHER: Dry (air 28°, humidity 41%, track 36°)

Pos.	Rider	Nat.	No.	Entrant	Machine	Tyres	Race tyre choice	Laps	Time & speed
1	**Enea Bastianini**	ITA	23	Gresini Racing MotoGP	Ducati Desmosedici	M	F: Medium/R: Soft	27	41m 34.613s 101.3mph/163.0km/h
2	**Jack Miller**	AUS	43	Ducati Lenovo Team	Ducati Desmosedici	M	F: Soft/R: Soft	27	41m 37.331s
3	**Aleix Espargaro**	SPA	41	Aprilia Racing	Aprilia RS-GP	M	F: Medium/R: Soft	27	41m 38.795s
4	**Fabio Quartararo**	FRA	20	Monster Energy Yamaha MotoGP	Yamaha YZR-M1	M	F: Medium/R: Soft	27	41m 38.901s
5	**Johann Zarco**	FRA	5	Pramac Racing	Ducati Desmosedici	M	F: Soft/R: Soft	27	41m 45.752s
6	**Marc Marquez**	SPA	93	Repsol Honda Team	Honda RC213V	M	F: Medium/R: Soft	27	41m 49.768s
7	**Takaaki Nakagami**	JPN	30	LCR Honda IDEMITSU	Honda RC213V	M	F: Medium/R: Soft	27	41m 51.293s
8	**Brad Binder**	RSA	33	Red Bull KTM Factory Racing	KTM RC16	M	F: Hard/R: Soft	27	41m 53.072s
9	**Luca Marini**	ITA	10	Mooney VR46 Racing Team	Ducati Desmosedici	M	F: Soft/R: Soft	27	41m 55.154s
10	**Maverick Vinales**	SPA	12	Aprilia Racing	Aprilia RS-GP	M	F: Medium/R: Soft	27	41m 56.099s
11	**Pol Espargaro**	SPA	44	Repsol Honda Team	Honda RC213V	M	F: Medium/R: Soft	27	41m 57.320s
12	**Marco Bezzecchi**	ITA	72	Mooney VR46 Racing Team	Ducati Desmosedici	M	F: Medium/R: Soft	27	41m 58.021s
13	**Fabio Di Giannantonio**	ITA	49	Gresini Racing MotoGP	Ducati Desmosedici	M	F: Medium/R: Soft	27	42m 01.045s
14	**Alex Marquez**	SPA	73	LCR Honda CASTROL	Honda RC213V	M	F: Medium/R: Soft	27	42m 03.323s
15	**Franco Morbidelli**	ITA	21	Monster Energy Yamaha MotoGP	Yamaha YZR-M1	M	F: Medium/R: Soft	27	42m 04.046s
16	Andrea Dovizioso	ITA	4	WithU Yamaha RNF MotoGP Team	Yamaha YZR-M1	M	F: Medium/R: Soft	27	42m 12.762s
17	Darryn Binder	RSA	40	WithU Yamaha RNF MotoGP Team	Yamaha YZR-M1	M	F: Medium/R: Soft	27	42m 34.361s
	Miguel Oliveira	POR	88	Red Bull KTM Factory Racing	KTM RC16	M	F: Hard/R: Soft	24	DNF-crash
	Francesco Bagnaia	ITA	63	Ducati Lenovo Team	Ducati Desmosedici	M	F: Medium/R: Soft	20	DNF-crash
	Jorge Martin	SPA	89	Pramac Racing	Ducati Desmosedici	M	F: Medium/R: Soft	16	DNF-crash
	Joan Mir	SPA	36	Team SUZUKI ECSTAR	Suzuki GSX-RR	M	F: Medium/R: Soft	13	DNF-crash
	Raul Fernandez	SPA	25	Tech3 KTM Factory Racing	KTM RC16	M	F: Medium/R: Soft	6	DNF-crash
	Alex Rins	SPA	42	Team SUZUKI ECSTAR	Suzuki GSX-RR	M	F: Soft/R: Soft	5	DNF-crash
	Remy Gardner	AUS	87	Tech3 KTM Factory Racing	KTM RC16	M	F: Hard/R: Soft	3	DNF-crash

Fastest lap: Francesco Bagnaia, on lap 4, 1m 31.778s, 102.0mph/164.1km/h.
Lap record: Maverick Vinales, 1m 32.309s, 101.4mph/163.2km/h (2017).
Event maximum speed: Alex Marquez, 201.1mph/323.7km/h (race).

Qualifying

Weather: Dry
Air Temp: 27° **Humidity:** 35%
Track Temp: 35°

1	Bagnaia	1m 30.450s
2	Miller	1m 30.519s
3	A. Espargaro	1m 30.609s
4	Quartararo	1m 30.688s
5	Bastianini	1m 30.711s
6	Zarco	1m 30.863s
7	Mir	1m 30.943s
8	Rins	1m 30.977s
9	Martin	1m 31.068s
10	M. Marquez	1m 31.148s
11	P. Espargaro	1m 31.526s
12	Nakagami	1m 31.595s
	Q1	
13	Bezzecchi	1m 30.940s
14	Vinales	1m 31.271s
15	Marini	1m 31.363s
16	Di Giannantonio	1m 31.487s
17	Oliveira	1m 31.547s
18	B. Binder	1m 31.610s
19	Morbidelli	1m 31.617s
20	Dovizioso	1m 31.618s
21	A. Marquez	1m 31.763s
22	Gardner	1m 31.820s
23	D. Binder	1m 32.596s
24	Fernandez	1m 32.767s

Fastest race laps

1	Bagnaia	1m 31.778s
2	Bastianini	1m 31.885s
3	A. Espargaro	1m 31.946s
4	Quartararo	1m 31.947s
5	Mir	1m 32.000s
6	Rins	1m 32.052s
7	Bezzecchi	1m 32.076s
8	Zarco	1m 32.145s
9	Miller	1m 32.163s
10	Martin	1m 32.294s
11	M. Marquez	1m 32.349s
12	Nakagami	1m 32.394s
13	Vinales	1m 32.397s
14	B. Binder	1m 32.404s
15	Marini	1m 32.409s
16	P. Espargaro	1m 32.461s
17	Oliveira	1m 32.484s
18	Di Giannantonio	1m 32.636s
19	A. Marquez	1m 32.729s
20	Morbidelli	1m 32.760s
21	Dovizioso	1m 32.870s
22	Gardner	1m 33.272s
23	Fernandez	1m 33.445s
24	D. Binder	1m 33.528s

Championship Points

1	Quartararo	102
2	A. Espargaro	98
3	Bastianini	94
4	Rins	69
5	Miller	62
6	Zarco	62
7	Bagnaia	56
8	B. Binder	56
9	Mir	56
10	M. Marquez	54
11	Oliveira	43
12	P. Espargaro	40
13	Vinales	33
14	Nakagami	30
15	Martin	28
16	Marini	21
17	Morbidelli	19
18	Bezzecchi	19
19	A. Marquez	18
20	Dovizioso	8
21	D. Binder	6
22	Di Giannantonio	3
23	Gardner	3

Constructor Points

1	Ducati	156
2	Yamaha	102
3	Aprilia	99
4	KTM	84
5	Suzuki	80
6	Honda	67

Grid order	1	2	3	4	5	6	7	8	9	10	11	12	13	14	15	16	17	18	19	20	21	22	23	24	25	26	27	
63 BAGNAIA	43	43	43	63	63	63	63	63	63	63	63	63	63	63	63	63	63	63	63	63	23	23	23	23	23	23	23	1
43 MILLER	63	63	63	43	43	43	43	43	43	43	43	23	23	23	23	23	23	23	23	23	43	43	43	43	43	43	43	2
41 A. ESPARGARO	42	42	23	23	23	23	23	23	23	23	23	43	43	43	43	43	43	43	43	43	41	41	41	41	41	41	41	3
20 QUARTARARO	23	23	36	36	36	36	36	36	36	36	36	36	36	41	41	41	41	41	41	41	20	20	20	20	20	20	20	4
23 BASTIANINI	36	36	41	41	41	41	41	41	41	41	41	41	41	20	20	20	20	20	20	20	5	5	5	5	5	5	5	5
36 MIR	41	41	20	20	20	20	20	20	20	20	20	20	20	93	93	93	5	5	5	5	93	93	93	93	93	93	93	6
42 RINS	93	93	93	93	93	93	93	93	93	93	93	93	93	5	5	5	93	93	93	93	30	30	30	30	30	30	30	7
89 MARTIN	20	20	30	30	30	30	30	30	5	5	5	5	5	30	30	30	30	30	30	30	33	33	33	33	33	33	33	8
5 ZARCO	30	30	5	5	5	5	5	5	30	30	30	30	30	88	88	88	88	33	33	33	88	88	88	88	10	10	10	9
93 M. MARQUEZ	5	5	33	33	33	33	33	89	89	89	89	89	88	33	33	33	33	88	88	88	44	44	44	44	12	12	12	10
44 P. ESPARGARO	89	33	44	89	89	89	89	33	33	33	33	33	33	89	89	89	44	44	44	44	10	10	10	10	44	44	44	11
30 NAKAGAMI	33	44	89	44	44	44	44	44	88	88	88	88	89	44	44	44	10	10	10	10	12	12	12	12	72	72	72	12
72 BEZZECCHI	44	88	88	88	88	88	88	88	44	44	44	44	44	10	10	10	12	12	12	12	49	49	49	49	49	49	49	13
12 VINALES	73	89	73	73	73	73	73	10	10	10	10	10	10	12	12	12	49	49	49	49	72	72	72	72	73	73	73	14
10 MARINI	88	73	10	10	10	10	10	73	49	49	49	49	12	49	49	49	72	72	72	72	73	73	73	73	21	21	21	15
49 DI GIANNANTONIO	10	10	87	49	49	49	49	49	73	73	73	12	49	72	72	72	73	73	73	73	21	21	21	21	4	4	4	
88 OLIVEIRA	72	72	49	21	21	12	12	12	12	12	12	21	72	21	73	73	21	21	21	21	4	4	4	4	40	40	40	
33 B.BINDER	21	87	72	12	12	21	21	21	21	21	21	72	21	73	21	21	4	4	4	4	40	40	40	40				
21 MORBIDELLI	49	49	21	4	4	4	72	4	4	72	72	73	73	4	4	4	40	40	40	40								
4 DOVIZIOSO	87	21	4	72	72	72	4	72	72	4	4	4	4	40	40	40												
73 A. MARQUEZ	40	4	12	25	25	25	40	40	40	40	40	40	40															
87 GARDNER	4	12	25	40	40	40																						
40 D.BINDER	25	25	40	42	42																							
25 FERNANDEZ	12	40	42																									

42 Pit stop

Moto2

RACE DISTANCE: 25 laps, 65.011 miles/104.625km · RACE WEATHER: Dry (air 27°, humidity 47%, track 32°)

Pos.	Rider	Nat.	No.	Entrant	Machine	Laps	Time & Speed
1	**Augusto Fernandez**	SPA	37	Red Bull KTM Ajo	Kalex	25	40m 31.726s
							96.2mph/154.8km/h
2	**Aron Canet**	SPA	40	Flexbox HP40	Kalex	25	40m 35.472s
3	**Somkiat Chantra**	THA	35	IDEMITSU Honda Team Asia	Kalex	25	40m 36.354s
4	**Cameron Beaubier**	USA	6	American Racing	Kalex	25	40m 36.471s
5	**Ai Ogura**	JPN	79	IDEMITSU Honda Team Asia	Kalex	25	40m 47.102s
6	**Marcel Schrotter**	GER	23	Liqui Moly Intact GP	Kalex	25	40m 49.273s
7	**Joe Roberts**	USA	16	Italtrans Racing Team	Kalex	25	40m 50.761s
8	**Celestino Vietti**	ITA	13	Mooney VR46 Racing Team	Kalex	25	40m 51.580s
9	**Jorge Navarro**	SPA	9	Flexbox HP40	Kalex	25	40m 52.492s
10	**Stefano Manzi**	ITA	62	Yamaha VR46 Master Camp Team	Kalex	25	40m 52.605s
11	**Manuel Gonzalez**	SPA	18	Yamaha VR46 Master Camp Team	Kalex	25	40m 53.107s
12	**Lorenzo Dalla Porta**	ITA	19	Italtrans Racing Team	Kalex	25	40m 55.618s
13	**Jeremy Alcoba**	SPA	52	Liqui Moly Intact GP	Kalex	25	40m 58.607s
14	**Bo Bendsneyder**	NED	64	Pertamina Mandalika SAG Team	Kalex	25	40m 58.678s
15	**Filip Salac**	CZE	12	Gresini Racing Moto2	Kalex	25	41m 03.789s
16	Simone Corsi	ITA	24	MV Agusta Forward Racing	MV Agusta	25	41m 08.438s
17	Zonta van den Goorbergh	NED	84	RW Racing GP	Kalex	25	41m 22.548s
18	Alessandro Zaccone	ITA	61	Gresini Racing Moto2	Kalex	25	41m 31.417s
19	Albert Arenas	SPA	75	Inde GASGAS Aspar Team	Kalex	24	41m 10.731s
20	Sean Dylan Kelly	USA	4	American Racing	Kalex	23	40m 45.451s
21	Jake Dixon	GBR	96	Inde GASGAS Aspar Team	Kalex	23	41m 15.782s
	Barry Baltus	BEL	7	RW Racing GP	Kalex	19	DNF-crash
	Marcos Ramirez	SPA	42	MV Agusta Forward Racing	MV Agusta	12	DNF-crash
	Pedro Acosta	SPA	51	Red Bull KTM Ajo	Kalex	10	DNF-crash
	Gabriel Rodrigo	ARG	2	Pertamina Mandalika SAG Team	Kalex	9	DNF-crash
	Alonso Lopez	SPA	21	MB Conveyors Speed Up	Boscoscuro	6	DNF-crash
	Fermin Aldeguer	SPA	54	MB Conveyors Speed Up	Boscoscuro	1	DNF-crash
	Tony Arbolino	ITA	14	Elf Marc VDS Racing Team	Kalex	1	DNF-crash
	Niccolo Antonelli	ITA	28	Mooney VR46 Racing Team	Kalex	0	DNF-crash
	Sam Lowes	GBR	22	ELF Marc VDS Racing Team	Kalex	-	DNS-injured

Fastest lap: Augusto Fernandez, on lap 5, 1m 36.276s, 97.2mph/156.4km/h.

Lap record: Jorge Navarro, 1m 36.764s, 96.7mph/155.6km/h (2019).

Event maximum speed: Tony Arbolino, 168.3mph/270.9km/h (free practice).

Qualifying

Weather: Dry

Air: 27° **Humidity:** 34%

Track: 36°

1	Acosta	1m 35.803s
2	Dixon	1m 35.921s
3	Fernandez	1m 35.963s
4	Lowes	1m 36.071s
5	Arenas	1m 36.088s
6	Lopez	1m 36.269s
7	Canet	1m 36.303s
8	Ogura	1m 36.309s
9	Bendsneyder	1m 36.341s
10	Arbolino	1m 36.351s
11	Chantra	1m 36.461s
12	Navarro	1m 36.472s
13	Schrotter	1m 36.502s
14	Ramirez	1m 36.743s
15	Dalla Porta	1m 36.962s
16	Manzi	1m 36.979s
17	Beaubier	1m 37.037s
18	Aldeguer	1m 37.098s
	Q1	
19	Vietti	1m 36.310s
20	Rodrigo	1m 36.434s
21	Corsi	1m 36.478s
22	Baltus	1m 36.528s
23	Salac	1m 36.599s
24	Gonzalez	1m 36.623s
25	Roberts	1m 36.766s
26	V D Goorbergh	1m 37.031s
27	Alcoba	1m 37.105s
28	Antonelli	1m 37.422s
29	Zaccone	1m 37.778s
30	Kelly	1m 38.454s

Fastest race laps

1	Fernandez	1m 36.276s
2	Acosta	1m 36.318s
3	Beaubier	1m 36.632s
4	Chantra	1m 36.646s
5	Canet	1m 36.787s
6	Vietti	1m 36.989s
7	Dixon	1m 37.013s
8	Lopez	1m 37.035s
9	Ramirez	1m 37.201s
10	Schrotter	1m 37.220s
11	Ogura	1m 37.250s
12	Navarro	1m 37.284s
13	Arenas	1m 37.312s
14	Manzi	1m 37.321s
15	Corsi	1m 37.328s
16	Salac	1m 37.373s
17	Baltus	1m 37.390s
18	Roberts	1m 37.450s
19	Gonzalez	1m 37.470s
20	Dalla Porta	1m 37.478s
21	Rodrigo	1m 37.494s
22	Bendsneyder	1m 37.513s
23	Alcoba	1m 37.568s
24	V D Goorbergh	1m 38.226s
25	Zaccone	1m 38.344s
26	Kelly	1m 39.428s

Championship Points

1	Vietti	108
2	Ogura	92
3	Canet	89
4	Arbolino	70
5	Fernandez	69
6	Roberts	66
7	Chantra	61
8	Schrotter	57
9	Navarro	52
10	Bendsneyder	36
11	Lowes	35
12	Dixon	32
13	Alcoba	31
14	Beaubier	29
15	Arenas	29
16	Gonzalez	21
17	Acosta	20
18	Aldeguer	18
19	Baltus	15
20	Manzi	9
21	Fenati	7
22	Rodrigo	6
23	Zaccone	6
24	Dalla Porta	5
25	Ramirez	5
26	Salac	5
27	Kubo	4
28	Kelly	3

Constructor Points

1	Kalex	175
2	Boscoscuro	20
3	MV Agusta	5

Moto3

RACE DISTANCE (Part 2): 14 laps, 36.406 miles/58.590km · RACE WEATHER: Dry (air 21°, humidity 66%, track 23°)

Pos.	Rider	Nat.	No.	Entrant	Machine	Laps	Time & Speed
1	**Jaume Masia**	SPA	5	Red Bull KTM Ajo	KTM	14	24m 04.119s
							90.7mph/146.0km/h
2	**Ayumu Sasaki**	JPN	71	Sterilgarda Husqvarna Max	Husqvarna	14	24m 04.269s
3	**Izan Guevara**	SPA	28	Gaviota GASGAS Aspar Team	GASGAS	14	24m 04.339s
4	**Dennis Foggia**	ITA	7	Leopard Racing	Honda	14	24m 04.441s
5	**Tatsuki Suzuki**	JPN	24	Leopard Racing	Honda	14	24m 04.648s
6	**Carlos Tatay**	SPA	99	CFMOTO Racing PruestelGP	CFMOTO	14	24m 05.713s
7	**Sergio Garcia**	SPA	11	Gaviota GASGAS Aspar Team	GASGAS	14	24m 06.126s
8	**Ryusei Yamanaka**	JPN	6	MT Helmets - MSI	KTM	14	24m 06.394s
9	**Deniz Oncu**	TUR	53	Red Bull KTM Tech3	KTM	14	24m 06.621s
10	**Andrea Migno**	ITA	16	Rivacold Snipers Team	Honda	14	24m 07.036s
11	**Daniel Holgado**	SPA	96	Red Bull KTM Ajo	KTM	14	24m 07.144s
12	**John McPhee**	GBR	17	Sterilgarda Husqvarna Max	Husqvarna	14	24m 07.312s
13	**Riccardo Rossi**	ITA	54	SIC58 Squadra Corse	Honda	14	24m 07.449s
14	**Diogo Moreira**	BRA	10	MT Helmets - MSI	KTM	14	24m 12.112s
15	**Kaito Toba**	JPN	27	CIP Green Power	KTM	14	24m 14.010s
16	Elia Bartolini	ITA	23	QJMotor Avintia Racing Team	KTM	14	24m 14.253s
17	Stefano Nepa	ITA	82	Angeluss MTA Team	KTM	14	24m 14.563s
18	Ivan Ortola	SPA	48	Angeluss MTA Team	KTM	14	24m 14.649s
19	Matteo Bertelle	ITA	18	QJMotor Avintia Racing Team	KTM	14	24m 14.931s
20	Adrian Fernandez	SPA	31	Red Bull KTM Tech3	KTM	14	24m 16.501s
21	Jose Rueda	SPA	98	Rivacold Snipers Team	Honda	14	24m 16.554s
22	Mario Aji	INA	64	Honda Team Asia	Honda	14	24m 16.671s
23	Lorenzo Fellon	FRA	20	SIC58 Squadra Corse	Honda	14	24m 16.816s
24	Gerard Riu Male	SPA	87	BOE SKX	KTM	14	24m 21.135s
25	Taiyo Furusato	JPN	72	Honda Team Asia	Honda	14	24m 31.080s
26	Joshua Whatley	GBR	70	VisionTrack Racing Team	Honda	14	24m 31.397s
27	Ana Carrasco	SPA	22	BOE SKX	KTM	14	24m 36.319s
	Xavier Artigas	SPA	43	CFMOTO Racing PruestelGP	CFMOTO	11	DNF-crash
	Scott Ogden	GBR	19	VisionTrack Racing Team	Honda	3	DNF-crash

Fastest lap: Izan Guevara, on lap 12, 1m 42.081s, 91.7mph/147.5km/h.

Lap record: Celestino Vietti, 1m 41.690s, 92.0mph/148.1km/h (2020).

Event maximum speed: Dennis Foggia, 141.4mph/227.6km/h (free practice).

Qualifying:

Weather: Dry

Air: 24° **Humidity:** 41%

Track: 30°

1	Foggia	1m 41.621s
2	Suzuki	1m 41.772s
3	Masia	1m 41.778s
4	Moreira	1m 41.879s
5	Tatay	1m 41.961s
6	Migno	1m 41.989s
7	Garcia	1m 41.999s
8	Guevara	1m 42.024s
9	Rossi	1m 42.026s
10	Oncu	1m 42.046s
11	Kelso	1m 42.099s
12	Sasaki	1m 42.252s
13	Yamanaka	1m 42.276s
14	Holgado	1m 42.439s
15	Artigas	1m 42.479s
16	Fellon	1m 42.533s
17	McPhee	1m 42.581s
18	Bertelle	1m 42.657s
	Q1	
19	Bartolini	1m 42.712s
20	Ogden	1m 42.821s
21	Fernandez	1m 42.851s
22	Nepa	1m 42.874s
23	Toba	1m 42.919s
24	Rueda	1m 43.173s
25	Ortola	1m 43.323s
26	Furusato	1m 43.512s
27	Riu Male	1m 43.537s
28	Aji	1m 43.707s
29	Whatley	1m 44.689s
30	Carrasco	1m 44.763

Fastest race laps

1	Guevara	1m 42.081s
2	Masia	1m 42.203s
3	Foggia	1m 42.260s
4	Sasaki	1m 42.264s
5	Yamanaka	1m 42.314s
6	Suzuki	1m 42.329s
7	Holgado	1m 42.367s
8	Oncu	1m 42.379s
9	Tatay	1m 42.413s
10	McPhee	1m 42.423s
11	Migno	1m 42.426s
12	Bertelle	1m 42.431s
13	Garcia	1m 42.432s
14	Rossi	1m 42.511s
15	Artigas	1m 42.521s
16	Moreira	1m 42.800s
17	Toba	1m 42.831s
18	Fernandez	1m 42.876s
19	Bartolini	1m 42.891s
20	Nepa	1m 42.893s
21	Ortola	1m 42.925s
22	Fellon	1m 43.075s
23	Rueda	1m 43.078s
24	Aji	1m 43.083s
25	Riu Male	1m 43.321s
26	Furusato	1m 43.738s
27	Ogden	1m 43.812s
28	Whatley	1m 43.947s
29	Carrasco	1m 44.407s

Championship Points

1	Garcia	112
2	Masia	95
3	Foggia	95
4	Guevara	89
5	Sasaki	75
6	Oncu	70
7	Migno	58
8	Tatay	52
9	Suzuki	38
10	Toba	37
11	Artigas	37
12	Moreira	34
13	Rossi	32
14	Yamanaka	32
15	Holgado	28
16	McPhee	15
17	Kelso	14
18	Ortola	14
19	Ogden	14
20	Bartolini	13
21	Nepa	8
22	Fernandez	7
23	Bertelle	6
24	Fellon	3
25	Aji	2

Constructor Points

1	GASGAS	140
2	KTM	123
3	Honda	116
4	Husqvarna	86
5	CFMOTO	71

Main: Bagnaia forces the pace; Quartararo and Espargaro pursue him in vain.

Inset, above: Wrapped in the Italian *tricolore*, Pecco savours his home victory.
Photos: Ducati Corse

Inset, bottom right: No Valentino meant plenty of empty seats.
Photo: Gold & Goose

FIM WORLD CHAMPIONSHIP · ROUND 8

ITALIAN GRAND PRIX

MUGELLO CIRCUIT

Above: **A standing ovation for Rossi as his number 46 is officially retired.**

Top right: **A double front row for VR46 pair Marini and Bezzecchi.**
Photos: Gold & Goose

Above right: **Sombre faces for Marquez and Puig as they announce his departure for yet another major operation.**
Photo: Repsol Honda

Right: **A surprise rookie pole lit up Fabio Di Giannantonio's smile.**

Far right, top: **Oliveira reflects on losing his seat at KTM.**

Far right, bottom: **Double trouble. Martin was struggling with injury and a fast, but feisty Ducati.**
Photos: Gold & Goose

MUGELLO without Valentino? Unthinkable – at least for a significant number of absent fans. The turnstiles were open for the first time after the pandemic, but the numbers were way down. An official tally of 43,661 on race Sunday was 40,000 down on 2019, 55,000 fewer than in 2017. Cumulative weekend totals suffered similarly: 74,078 over three days, compared with almost 140,000 in 2019, and more than 150,000 (2018) and 164,418 (2017).

Valentino was there, however. In a rare weekend off from car racing, Rossi attended an inevitably cheesy Saturday start-line ceremony, where his number 46 was officially retired from MotoGP. Not an honour he'd sought, he had long made clear; in the same way, he disapproved of naming corners after riders. But the choice was not his, and 46 joined previously retired MotoGP numbers: Kevin Schwantz's 34 the first, followed by posthumous tributes to Daijiro Kato (74), Marco Simoncelli (58) and Nicky Hayden (69).

Another departure hit the headlines at a special Repsol Honda press conference later on Saturday. Team manager Alberto Puig and Marc Marquez announced that the rider would quit the team after the following day's race for a fourth operation on his right humerus fracture, sustained in July, 2020. With shades of Mick Doohan's repeatedly readjusted leg, the limb needed realignment.

Marquez had considered the surgery the previous winter when sidelined with diplopia, but his doctors had said no. That had changed. "The bone is ready," explained Puig. "In the past, it was soft, and not recommended." Marc had been given the go-ahead only on Saturday. Had it come a day or two earlier, he would have withdrawn from this race.

Only after a successful three-hour operation the following Tuesday, by specialist Joaquim Sanchez Sotelo at the Mayo Clinic in Rochester, Minnesota, was the scale of the adjustment revealed. The humerus had been sawn through and rotated through an astonishing 30 degrees to correct the accumulated displacement over three previous operations. On each occasion, a titanium plate had been fixed to the bone, the second of them just a week after the first, following his ill-advised and abortive return to the track days after surgery. Subsequently, the much-drilled bone had developed an infection, requiring a further eight-hour surgery, when a third plate had been attached.

By that stage, the angle of the elbow to shoulder had drifted so much that "I could not ride as I like. I don't have the rotation, so on the straight I have the arm more open than normal. Then in left corners, I'm with the elbow completely up to compensate. In all races, I had arm-pump. Then the pain in the shoulder arrive. I needed to ride really smooth. That is not my style."

His departure deepened Honda's plight. The balance of the new bike suited none of their four riders, but Marc was the best equipped at least to find ways around the problem. Pol Espargaro was trying hard, but after a promising start was struggling; Nakagami was not infrequently faster over one lap, but hard pushed over race distance; the unhappy younger Marquez wasn't far away, but in super-close MotoGP, that left him trailing. Test rider Stefan Bradl was back for a second outing, but lacked edge. In 2020, Honda had endured their first year since 1983 without a single win; 2022 was shaping up for an unwelcome repeat.

There was more hospital news from Jorge Martin, who blamed his Le Mans race crash on numbness in his right hand, a persistent problem stemming from his heavy Portimao crash early the previous season. Surgery to address nerve damage was scheduled for the short break after the following weekend's race.

Martin also repeated his complaint about the intractability of the 2022 Ducati engine, compared with the more flexible hybrid given to the factory pair of Bagnaia and Miller

after pre-season tests. It did drive him to a new top-speed record, however: 225.93mph, set in the early laps with the advantage of a double slipstream, 0.75mph faster than the previous year's record shared by Zarco's Ducati (Qatar) and Binder's KTM (Mugello). "It's nice, but it's dangerous when you are arriving at the first corner," Martin said. "It's crazy how the air is moving the bike."

For Ducati's home race, Bagnaia, Miller and Bastianini had led an armada of *Ducatisti* across the Apennines from the Bologna factory, over the Raticosa and Futa passes, the route of the fabled Mille Miglia race. The celebrations concealed a dilemma, however. It now seemed certain that Miller would not retain his factory seat. Whether Martin or the suddenly tempting Bastianini would take his place would be debated for weeks to come.

There were changes also at KTM, targeting Miller, Rins or possibly the return of Pol Espargaro for the factory team. Oliveira had been informed that he had to be prepared to step down to the satellite squad, albeit on equal machinery. "I told the management that I do not accept the Tech3 spot and I want my factory seat," he said on Sunday. "With this not being possible, I will sure take other options into consideration."

There was definite news from Aprilia. Not only had they re-signed Aleix Espargaro (money quibbles over) and Vinales for two more years, but they had also reached agreement with Razlan Razali and his RNF team for a two-rider satellite squad, with the twin aim (according to Aprilia's Massimo Rivola) of chasing results, and developing young riding and engineering talent. Rins and Raul Fernandez were likely prospects for 2023.

A post-race row blew up between Rins and Nakagami, after they had touched and the Spaniard fallen. Rins blasted the stewards for not penalising the Japanese rider: "Ask the riders ... he's one of the most dangerous on track in terms of overtakes." This was a prelude to an even bigger incident a week later.

The longest MotoGP calendar in history was reduced by one, the Finnish GP, due to be held on 10th July, was postponed for a fifth year. Delayed homologation works were blamed, as well as "risks caused by the ongoing geopolitical situation in the region." The organisers had been banking on Russian fans crossing the nearby border. Current tensions between Russia and Finland, keen to join NATO in the wake of the invasion of Ukraine, made that impossible.

MOTOGP RACE – 23 laps

On a day with some wet-weather interruptions, a surprise maiden pole for Di Giannantonio, through from Q1, where he was also fastest, less than a tenth ahead of Marc Marquez. A disconsolate Miller was third in the session, left to a fifth-row start.

Di Giannantonio led fellow rookie Bezzecchi and VR46 team-mate Marini, an all-Italian theme continued by two more Ducatis heading row two: Zarco from Bagnaia. Only then came Quartararo. Aleix Espargaro led row three from brother Pol, with Nakagami top Honda between them. Marc Marquez, short of tyres and enthusiasm, was 12th after running only four timed laps.

The new wave held their own off the start, Marini leading Di Giannantonio and Bezzecchi out of the first corner, Bezzecchi in front at the end of the lap. At the Casanova plunge off the hill, Aleix signalled his intentions with a neat move on Quartararo for fourth, with Zarco sixth and the ever-impressive Binder seventh, up nine places from the start.

Bagnaia, crowded out over the crest on the run from the start, was ninth; Bastianini 12th – and Miller down in 22nd after being pushed almost off the track in the first corner. He remained mired and struggled to pass riders who normally would be easy, thanks to a flat spot in third gear that ruined his run on to the straight.

Bagnaia wasn't for hanging around. By lap two, he was

past Binder and Zarco for sixth, then Espargaro and Di Giannantonio next time around.

Now he spied the Frenchman up ahead, third behind Marini. Lack of straight-line speed notwithstanding, Quartararo had been quickly back past Espargaro and Di Giannantonio on lap two, then had swooped past Marini for second at Savelli. He was in the thick of the Ducatis.

That spurred Bagnaia to greater heights. He drafted past Di Giannantonio at the start of lap five, setting fastest lap of the race (a new record), and drifting past Marini and Quartararo on the run past the pits.

Now only his friend and training partner Bezzecchi, leading his first premier-class race, was ahead. He settled in to follow for the next four laps. At the same time, Aleix's hopes of joining the fight for victory took a hit when he missed his braking for the first corner at the start of lap six, losing hard won places, if only briefly, to Di Giannantonio and Zarco.

Di Giannantonio's challenge waned and he slipped down the order, complaining afterwards of zero rear grip.

In the pack, there had been several early crashes. Pol Espargaro was out on lap five at the high-speed Arrabbiata Two, after dropping from ninth on the grid to 16th. Both Suzuki riders crashed on lap eight: Mir at Turn One from 16th, and Rins further around after a collision while trying to wrest 12th from Nakagami.

Up front, the race was reaching its critical phase. Starting lap nine, Bagnaia powered past Bezzecchi to lead for the first time. As he edged clear, Ducati's strength in numbers paid off. Quartararo was all over Bezzecchi's rear tyre, but it took until lap 11 to get through with an on-the-brink late braking move into Scarperia. He had to spend the next lap defending as Bezzecchi attacked again on the straight, forcing another bout of braking brinkmanship into the first turn.

Crucially, Bagnaia now had a second in hand. For the remaining laps, they traded blows. Quartararo was majestic through the sinuous second and third sectors, taking three- or four-tenths out of the Italian every time, only to lose it down the straight. He didn't give up, however. Bagnaia was 1.1 seconds clear as they started the last lap, Quartararo just half a second down into the final chicane – but not close enough to pounce. Bagnaia's second win of the season was by six-tenths.

Behind, some entertaining intra-team fighting between Bezzecchi and Marini allowed Espargaro, Zarco and Bastianini back into play. The last named crashed at Materassi on lap 14 just after passing Zarco; it was his second fall in four races.

Espargaro finally got fourth off Marini on the same lap, then pounced on Bezzecchi three laps later for a fourth successive podium, reinforcing second overall.

Zarco also passed the VR46 pair late on for fourth, Binder working his usual miracles to finish two-tenths behind Marini in seventh. Some way back, Nakagami had passed the fading Di Giannantonio and Martin, and finally Oliveira for eighth. Marquez was close behind the pair; a second down, Di Giannantonio was awarded 11th from Vinales in a video finish, the Aprilia rider again speeding up after finishing the first lap 23rd.

Martin held off Alex Marquez, while Miller was two-tenths adrift for the last point. Rookie Darryn Binder was 16th, second-best Yamaha, narrowly ahead of Morbidelli.

MOTO2 RACE – 21 laps

A pair of riders book-ended the Italian GP, at least in terms of age and experience. On one side, Mattia Pasini had returned, 19 years after his debut, for a 240th GP start, wildcarding on the private Kalex he uses to keep himself fresh. Aged 36, he threatened to qualify on the front row – but finished at the bottom end of the points.

On the other, half his age, Pedro Acosta, lining up for grand prix start number 26, his eighth in the class. He did make it to the front row, and all the way to his first win, which he felt, after leading pre-season tests and coming close at Le Mans, was definitely overdue.

He became the youngest rider in history to win in the intermediate class. At 18 years and 4 days, he took the record from Marc Marquez, who had been 83 days older when he rode to his first Moto2 win 11 years before.

Acosta succeeded in the race's critical phase where he had failed just two weeks before. At Le Mans, the Spaniard had crashed out of the lead while striving to break the challenge of team-mate Fernandez. This time, it was Canet who fell, at Bucine on lap 13, trying to keep up.

Canet had qualified on pole for a second time, Acosta and Lowes alongside. Vietti and Ogura were on the second, with the remarkable Pasini (through from Q1) sandwiched between them.

Above: A fourth successive podium – Aleix Espargaro was riding the crest of a wave.

Above right Veteran Mattia Pasini was an impressive Moto2 wild-card.

Top: Bezzecchi (72) and Marini (10) were hard pressed by Brad Binder (33) in their battle for fifth.

Right: Tatsuki Suzuki (24) overcame a long-lap penalty to snitch the final podium slot from Andre Migno (16). Guevara (hidden) and Garcia (11) beat them both.

Photos: Gold & Goose

Above: **Dash to Turn One: Di Giannantonio leads Marini, Bezzechi and Zarco (on the paint). Bagnaia and Quartararo prepare to pounce.**

Top: **Pedro Acosta leads Canet, Arbolino, Lowes and Roberts.**

Above right: **Acosta's first Moto2 win followed directly.**

Photos: Gold & Goose

Acosta led the first lap and all the others except for the third, when a persistent Canet got ahead over the line.

The youngster stayed at the head of a lively seven-rider fight, which included Roberts, Ogura, team-mates Lowes and Arbolino, and Vietti.

It was Canet who challenged most consistently, but when his compatriot put the pressure on, he fell. After that, and although Augusto Fernandez had set fastest lap early on, a second short of the record, none could live with Acosta's late speed. Not only did he cruise home to win by four seconds, but also he pulled the lead group apart, with Roberts achieving a second podium of the season.

There was drama late on lap 19 as Arbolino, suffering from arm-pump, took out Lowes at Luco, earning him a long-lap penalty. Then Vietti retired from third with a mechanical issue, leaving the final podium place to Ogura.

Fernandez had passed Arbolino after his penalty, only for the Italian to draft him to the line and take fourth by a wheel's breadth. Dixon was another two-tenths down, with Beaubier on his heels; Lopez, Schrotter and Arenas completed the top ten, with Bendsneyder and Navarro still close. Pasini had dropped back to 15th, losing a place to teenager Aldeguer on the final lap.

Ogura's podium and Vietti's no-score were redress for the Japanese rider's Portuguese misfortunes, and now they were tied on points at the top of the table.

MOTO3 RACE – 20 laps

Mugello is a classic Moto3 playground, guaranteeing ludicrously close racing, desperate tactics and an elbows-out, swerving run to the finish line. The 2022 race was no exception, with seven riders starting the final lap together, each harbouring realistic hopes of victory.

It followed a typically chaotic encounter, as Foggia began a run of somewhat random ill fortune shortly after starting an escape bid up front on the 11th lap. He blamed running over a discarded tear-off visor for an otherwise inexplicable crash going through Casanova-Savelli. Somehow, the chasing pack missed his bike as it slid across the track.

That left Aspar duo Garcia and Guevara to slug it out on the last lap, with Suzuki, Migno, Yamanaka, Rossi and impressive rookie Moreiro. Suzuki had recovered from a long-lap penalty incurred for a mid-race Turn One collision with pole-sitter Oncu, who had spent the second half of the race recovering from 20th to a single point for 15th.

Guevara led the group out of the first turn, but fourth-placed Garcia got to work, taking Migno, Suzuki and Guevara in the last three turns. However, Guevara outdragged him to the line by two-hundredths, but had touched the green at the last chicane and was docked one place. Suzuki was third, then Migno and Yamanaka, a career-best fifth. Rossi gained sixth when Moreira high-sided out on the last corner.

Ortola led the next big gang for seventh, with Bartolini, Bertelle and Fernandez completing the top ten; Munoz, Kelso and Aji were close at hand.

McPhee, in his second race back, crashed out of the top ten at half-distance; fast rookie Holgado likewise, and Scott Ogden on the first lap.

FIM WORLD CHAMPIONSHIP: ROUND 8

GRAN PREMIO D'ITALIA OAKLEY

27-29 MAY, 2022

AUTODROMO INTERNAZIONALE DEL MUGELLO

23 laps
Length: 5.245 km / 3,259 miles
Width: 14m

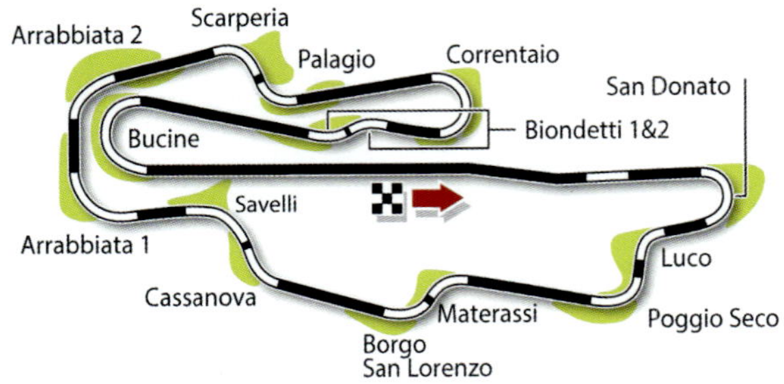

MotoGP

RACE DISTANCE: 23 laps, 74.959 miles/120.635km · RACE WEATHER: Dry (air 22°, humidity 60%, track 36°)

Pos.	Rider	Nat.	No.	Entrant	Machine	Tyres	Race tyre choice	Laps	Time & speed
1	**Francesco Bagnaia**	ITA	63	Ducati Lenovo Team	Ducati Desmosedici	M	F: Medium/R: Medium	23	41m 18.923s 108.8mph/175.1km/h
2	**Fabio Quartararo**	FRA	20	Monster Energy Yamaha MotoGP	Yamaha YZR-M1	M	F: Hard/R: Medium	23	41m 19.558s
3	**Aleix Espargaro**	SPA	41	Aprilia Racing	Aprilia RS-GP	M	F: Hard/R: Medium	23	41m 20.906s
4	**Johann Zarco**	FRA	5	Prima Pramac Racing	Ducati Desmosedici	M	F: Medium/R: Medium	23	41m 21.513s
5	**Marco Bezzecchi**	ITA	72	Mooney VR46 Racing Team	Ducati Desmosedici	M	F: Medium/R: Medium	23	41m 21.990s
6	**Luca Marini**	ITA	10	Mooney VR46 Racing Team	Ducati Desmosedici	M	F: Medium/R: Medium	23	41m 22.798s
7	**Brad Binder**	RSA	33	Red Bull KTM Factory Racing	KTM RC16	M	F: Hard/R: Medium	23	41m 22.990s
8	**Takaaki Nakagami**	JPN	30	LCR Honda IDEMITSU	Honda RC213V	M	F: Medium/R: Soft	23	41m 29.867s
9	**Miguel Oliveira**	POR	88	Red Bull KTM Factory Racing	KTM RC16	M	F: Hard/R: Medium	23	41m 30.179s
10	**Marc Marquez**	SPA	93	Repsol Honda Team	Honda RC213V	M	F: Hard/R: Medium	23	41m 30.723s
11	**Fabio Di Giannantonio**	ITA	49	Gresini Racing MotoGP	Ducati Desmosedici	M	F: Medium/R: Medium	23	41m 31.839s
12	**Maverick Vinales**	SPA	12	Aprilia Racing	Aprilia RS-GP	M	F: Hard/R: Soft	23	41m 31.840s
13	**Jorge Martin**	SPA	89	Prima Pramac Racing	Ducati Desmosedici	M	F: Medium/R: Medium	23	41m 36.163s
14	**Alex Marquez**	SPA	73	LCR Honda CASTROL	Honda RC213V	M	F: Medium/R: Soft	23	41m 36.491s
15	**Jack Miller**	AUS	43	Ducati Lenovo Team	Ducati Desmosedici	M	F: Medium/R: Medium	23	41m 36.610s
16	Darryn Binder	RSA	40	WithU Yamaha RNF MotoGP Team	Yamaha YZR-M1	M	F: Hard/R: Medium	23	41m 39.188s
17	Franco Morbidelli	ITA	21	Monster Energy Yamaha MotoGP	Yamaha YZR-M1	M	F: Hard/R: Medium	23	41m 39.219s
18	Michele Pirro	ITA	51	Aruba.it Racing	Ducati Desmosedici	M	F: Medium/R: Medium	23	41m 40.228s
19	Remy Gardner	AUS	87	Tech3 KTM Factory Racing	KTM RC16	M	F: Medium/R: Medium	23	41m 49.471s
20	Andrea Dovizioso	ITA	4	WithU Yamaha RNF MotoGP Team	Yamaha YZR-M1	M	F: Medium/R: Medium	23	41m 49.934s
21	Raul Fernandez	SPA	25	Tech3 KTM Factory Racing	KTM RC16	M	F: Hard/R: Medium	23	42m 01.646s
22	Lorenzo Savadori	ITA	32	Aprilia Racing	Aprilia RS-GP	M	F: Hard/R: Medium	22	41m 58.611s
	Enea Bastianini	ITA	23	Gresini Racing MotoGP	Ducati Desmosedici	M	F: Medium/R: Soft	13	DNF-crash
	Alex Rins	SPA	42	Team SUZUKI ECSTAR	Suzuki GSX-RR	M	F: Medium/R: Medium	7	DNF-crash
	Joan Mir	SPA	36	Team SUZUKI ECSTAR	Suzuki GSX-RR	M	F: Medium/R: Medium	7	DNF-crash
	Pol Espargaro	SPA	44	Repsol Honda Team	Honda RC213V	M	F: Medium/R: Soft	4	DNF-crash

Fastest lap: Francesco Bagnaia, on lap 5, 1m 46.588s, 110.0mph/177.1km/h.

Lap record: Johann Zarco, 1m 46.810s, 109.8mph/176.7km/h (2021).

Event maximum speed: Jorge Martin, 225.9mph/363.6km/h (race, new all-time MotoGP record).

Qualifying

Weather: Dry
Air Temp: 23° **Humidity:** 63%
Track Temp: 31°

1	Di Giannantonio	1m 46.156s
2	Bezzecchi	1m 46.244s
3	Marini	1m 46.327s
4	Zarco	1m 46.383s
5	Bagnaia	1m 46.471s
6	Quartararo	1m 46.506s
7	A. Espargaro	1m 46.507s
8	Nakagami	1m 46.561s
9	P. Espargaro	1m 46.667s
10	Bastianini	1m 46.679s
11	Martin	1m 47.223s
12	M. Marquez	1m 47.468s
	Q1	
13	Miller	1m 47.621s
14	Pirro	1m 48.209s
15	Oliveira	1m 48.231s
16	B. Binder	1m 48.255s
17	Mir	1m 48.732s
18	A. Marquez	1m 48.846s
19	Gardner	1m 48.907s
20	D. Binder	1m 49.471s
21	Rins	1m 50.266s
22	Savadori	1m 50.270s
23	Morbidelli	1m 55.369s
24	Vinales	1m 56.479s
25	Fernandez	1m 57.106s
26	Dovizioso	1m 57.671s

Fastest race laps

1	Bagnaia	1m 46.588s
2	Bezzecchi	1m 46.676s
3	Quartararo	1m 46.868s
4	Bastianini	1m 46.910s
5	Oliveira	1m 46.968s
6	Zarco	1m 46.970s
7	A. Espargaro	1m 46.971s
8	Di Giannantonio	1m 47.031s
9	Nakagami	1m 47.046s
10	Marini	1m 47.081s
11	Rins	1m 47.129s
12	M. Marquez	1m 47.133s
13	B. Binder	1m 47.225s
14	Mir	1m 47.426s
15	Vinales	1m 47.525s
16	D. Binder	1m 47.619s
17	Martin	1m 47.619s
18	Morbidelli	1m 47.626s
19	A. Marquez	1m 47.741s
20	Miller	1m 47.742s
21	Pirro	1m 47.824s
22	P. Espargaro	1m 48.048s
23	Gardner	1m 48.051s
24	Fernandez	1m 48.063s
25	Dovizioso	1m 48.272s
26	Savadori	1m 48.586s

Championship Points

1	Quartararo	122
2	A. Espargaro	114
3	Bastianini	94
4	Bagnaia	81
5	Zarco	75
6	Rins	69
7	B. Binder	65
8	Miller	63
9	M. Marquez	60
10	Mir	56
11	Oliveira	50
12	P. Espargaro	40
13	Nakagami	38
14	Vinales	37
15	Martin	31
16	Marini	31
17	Bezzecchi	30
18	A. Marquez	20
19	Morbidelli	19
20	Di Giannantonio	8
21	Dovizioso	8
22	D. Binder	6
23	Gardner	3

Constructor Points

1	Ducati	181
2	Yamaha	122
3	Aprilia	115
4	KTM	93
5	Suzuki	80
6	Honda	75

	Grid order	1	2	3	4	5	6	7	8	9	10	11	12	13	14	15	16	17	18	19	20	21	22	23	
49	DI GIANNANTONIO	72	72	72	72	72	72	72	72	63	63	63	63	63	63	63	63	63	63	63	63	63	63	63	1
72	BEZZECCHI	10	10	10	20	63	63	63	63	72	72	20	20	20	20	20	20	20	20	20	20	20	20	20	2
10	MARINI	49	20	20	10	20	20	20	20	20	20	72	10	72	72	72	72	41	41	41	41	41	41	41	3
5	ZARCO	41	49	63	63	10	10	10	10	10	10	10	72	10	41	41	41	72	72	72	72	72	72	5	4
63	BAGNAIA	20	41	49	49	49	49	41	41	41	41	41	41	41	10	10	10	5	5	5	5	5	5	72	5
20	QUARTARARO	5	63	41	41	41	41	49	49	5	5	5	5	23	5	5	5	10	10	10	10	10	10	10	6
41	A. ESPARGARO	33	5	5	5	5	5	5	23	23	23	23	23	5	33	33	33	33	33	33	33	33	33	33	7
30	NAKAGAMI	63	33	33	33	23	23	23	5	33	33	33	33	33	88	88	30	30	30	30	30	30	30	30	8
44	P. ESPARGARO	30	93	93	93	33	33	33	33	49	88	88	88	88	49	30	88	88	88	88	88	88	88	88	9
23	BASTIANINI	93	30	23	23	93	93	88	88	88	49	49	49	49	30	49	49	49	49	49	93	93	93	93	10
93	M. MARQUEZ	88	23	88	88	88	88	93	93	93	93	93	93	30	93	93	93	93	93	93	49	49	49	49	11
43	MILLER	23	88	30	30	30	30	30	30	30	30	30	30	93	12	12	12	12	12	12	12	12	12	12	12
51	PIRRO	73	73	73	42	42	42	42	89	73	73	89	89	89	73	73	89	89	89	89	89	89	89	89	13
89	MARTIN	44	42	42	73	73	73	89	73	89	89	73	73	12	89	89	73	73	73	73	73	73	73	73	14
88	OLIVEIRA	42	44	44	89	89	89	73	43	43	43	43	43	73	43	43	43	43	43	43	43	43	43	43	15
33	B.BINDER	89	89	89	44	36	36	36	51	12	12	12	12	43	51	51	51	51	51	51	51	21	21	40	
36	MIR	40	40	36	36	43	43	43	12	51	51	51	51	51	21	21	21	21	21	21	21	40	40	21	
73	A. MARQUEZ	51	36	51	43	51	51	51	21	21	21	21	21	21	40	40	40	40	40	40	40	51	51	51	
87	GARDNER	36	51	43	51	12	12	12	40	40	40	40	40	40	87	87	87	87	87	87	87	87	87	87	
40	D.BINDER	87	87	87	87	87	87	21	87	87	87	87	87	87	4	4	4	4	4	4	4	4	4	4	
42	RINS	4	43	12	12	21	21	87	25	25	25	25	4	4	25	25	25	25	25	25	25	25	25	25	
32	SAVADORI	43	12	21	40	40	40	40	4	4	4	4	25	25	*32*	*32*	*32*	*32*	*32*	*32*	*32*	*32*	*32*		
21	MORBIDELLI	12	4	40	21	25	25	25	*32*	*32*	*32*	*32*	*32*	*32*											
12	VNALES	21	21	4	25	4	4	4																	
25	FERNANDEZ	25	25	25	4	32	32	*32*																	
4	DOVIZIOSO	32	32	32	32																				

32 Pit stop · *32 Lapped rider*

Moto2

RACE DISTANCE: 21 laps, 68.441 miles/110.145km · RACE WEATHER: Dry (air 21°, humidity 64%, track 29°)

Pos.	Rider	Nat.	No.	Entrant	Machine	Laps	Time & Speed
1	**Pedro Acosta**	SPA	51	Red Bull KTM Ajo	Kalex	21	39m 35.930s
							103.6mph/166.8km/h
2	**Joe Roberts**	USA	16	Italtrans Racing Team	Kalex	21	39m 39.981s
3	**Ai Ogura**	JPN	79	IDEMITSU Honda Team Asia	Kalex	21	39m 42.679s
4	**Tony Arbolino**	ITA	14	Elf Marc VDS Racing Team	Kalex	21	39m 48.242s
5	**Augusto Fernandez**	SPA	37	Red Bull KTM Ajo	Kalex	21	39m 48.257s
6	**Jake Dixon**	GBR	96	Inde GASGAS Aspar Team	Kalex	21	39m 48.443s
7	**Cameron Beaubier**	USA	6	American Racing	Kalex	21	39m 48.779s
8	**Alonso Lopez**	SPA	21	MB Conveyors Speed Up	Boscoscuro	21	39m 49.244s
9	**Marcel Schrotter**	GER	23	Liqui Moly Intact GP	Kalex	21	39m 50.633s
10	**Albert Arenas**	SPA	75	Inde GASGAS Aspar Team	Kalex	21	39m 50.678s
11	**Bo Bendsneyder**	NED	64	Pertamina Mandalika SAG Team	Kalex	21	39m 51.071s
12	**Jorge Navarro**	SPA	9	Flexbox HP40	Kalex	21	39m 51.355s
13	**Filip Salac**	CZE	12	Gresini Racing Moto2	Kalex	21	39m 53.184s
14	**Fermin Aldeguer**	SPA	54	MB Conveyors Speed Up	Boscoscuro	21	39m 53.999s
15	**Mattia Pasini**	ITA	11	Inde GASGAS Aspar Team	Kalex	21	39m 54.680s
16	Barry Baltus	BEL	7	RW Racing GP	Kalex	21	39m 59.899s
17	Jeremy Alcoba	SPA	52	Liqui Moly Intact GP	Kalex	21	40m 03.578s
18	Niccolo Antonelli	ITA	28	Mooney VR46 Racing Team	Kalex	21	40m 05.216s
19	Alessandro Zaccone	ITA	61	Gresini Racing Moto2	Kalex	21	40m 06.151s
20	Manuel Gonzalez	SPA	18	Yamaha VR46 Master Camp Team	Kalex	21	40m 11.130s
21	Zonta van den Goorbergh	NED	84	RW Racing GP	Kalex	21	40m 11.153s
22	Keminth Kubo	THA	81	Yamaha VR46 Master Camp Team	Kalex	21	40m 25.707s
23	Sean Dylan Kelly	USA	4	American Racing	Kalex	21	40m 25.827s
	Simone Corsi	ITA	24	MV Agusta Forward Racing	MV Agusta	20	DNF-ret in pit
	Celestino Vietti	ITA	13	Mooney VR46 Racing Team	Kalex	18	DNF-technical
	Sam Lowes	GBR	22	Elf Marc VDS Racing Team	Kalex	18	DNF-crash
	Aron Canet	SPA	40	Flexbox HP40	Kalex	12	DNF-crash
	Lorenzo Dalla Porta	ITA	19	Italtrans Racing Team	Kalex	11	DNF-crash
	Marcos Ramirez	SPA	42	MV Agusta Forward Racing	MV Agusta	10	DNF-crash
	Somkiat Chantra	THA	35	IDEMITSU Honda Team Asia	Kalex	4	DNF-crash

Fastest lap: Augusto Fernandez, on lap 9, 1m 52.323s, 104.5mph/168.1km/h.

Lap record: Sam Lowes, 1m 51.208s, 105.4mph/169.7km/h (2021).

Event maximum speed: Pedro Acosta, 185.9mph/299.1km/h (free practice).

Qualifying

Weather: Dry

Air: 23° **Humidity:** 73%

Track: 30°

1	Canet	1m 51.121s
2	Acosta	1m 51.246s
3	Lowes	1m 51.279s
4	Vietti	1m 51.381s
5	Pasini	1m 51.465s
6	Ogura	1m 51.478s
7	Roberts	1m 51.552s
8	Arbolino	1m 51.566s
9	Dixon	1m 51.631s
10	Baltus	1m 51.754s
11	Dalla Porta	1m 51.760s
12	Navarro	1m 51.789s
13	Arenas	1m 51.849s
14	Fernandez	1m 51.940s
15	Aldeguer	1m 51.954s
16	Ramirez	1m 52.045s
17	Bendsneyder	1m 52.056s
18	Beaubier	1m 52.656s
	Q1	
19	Lopez	1m 52.006s
20	Schrotter	1m 52.066s
21	Alcoba	1m 52.139s
22	Zaccone	1m 52.438s
23	Salac	1m 52.451s
24	Chantra	1m 52.522s
25	Corsi	1m 52.746s
26	V D Goorbergh	1m 52.755s
27	Gonzalez	1m 53.036s
28	Antonelli	1m 53.115s
29	Rodrigo	1m 53.153s
30	Kubo	1m 53.763s
31	Kelly	1m 54.218s

Fastest race laps

1	Fernandez	1m 52.323s
2	Canet	1m 52.356s
3	Bendsneyder	1m 52.357s
4	Arbolino	1m 52.396s
5	Vietti	1m 52.400s
6	Salac	1m 52.410s
7	Acosta	1m 52.437s
8	Roberts	1m 52.453s
9	Ogura	1m 52.498s
10	Beaubier	1m 52.526s
11	Lopez	1m 52.536s
12	Pasini	1m 52.564s
13	Dixon	1m 52.566s
14	Arenas	1m 52.633s
15	Lowes	1m 52.686s
16	Chantra	1m 52.726s
17	Navarro	1m 52.751s
18	Dalla Porta	1m 52.793s
19	Schrotter	1m 52.888s
20	Aldeguer	1m 52.892s
21	Ramirez	1m 53.082s
22	Alcoba	1m 53.127s
23	Baltus	1m 53.134s
24	Zaccone	1m 53.230s
25	Corsi	1m 53.380s
26	V D Goorbergh	1m 53.445s
27	Antonelli	1m 53.456s
28	Gonzalez	1m 53.565s
29	Kubo	1m 54.212s
30	Kelly	1m 54.666s

Championship Points

1	Vietti	108
2	Ogura	108
3	Canet	89
4	Roberts	86
5	Arbolino	83
6	Fernandez	80
7	Schrotter	64
8	Chantra	61
9	Navarro	56
10	Acosta	45
11	Dixon	42
12	Bendsneyder	41
13	Beaubier	38
14	Lowes	35
15	Arenas	35
16	Alcoba	31
17	Gonzalez	21
18	Aldeguer	20
19	Baltus	15
20	Manzi	9
21	Lopez	8
22	Salac	8
23	Fenati	7
24	Rodrigo	6
25	Zaccone	6
26	Dalla Porta	5
27	Ramirez	5
28	Kubo	4
29	Kelly	3
30	Pasini	1

Constructor Points

1	Kalex	200
2	Boscoscuro	28
3	MV Agusta	5

Moto3

RACE DISTANCE: 20 laps, 65.182 miles/104.900km · RACE WEATHER: Dry (air 20°, humidity 70%, track 23°)

Pos.	Rider	Nat.	No.	Entrant	Machine	Laps	Time & Speed
1	**Sergio Garcia**	SPA	11	Valresa GASGAS Aspar Team	GASGAS	20	39m 43.214s
							98.4mph/158.4km/h
2	**Izan Guevara**	SPA	28	Valresa GASGAS Aspar Team	GASGAS	20	39m 43.193s
3	**Tatsuki Suzuki**	JPN	24	Leopard Racing	Honda	20	39m 43.226s
4	**Andrea Migno**	ITA	16	Rivacold Snipers Team	Honda	20	39m 43.351s
5	**Ryusei Yamanaka**	JPN	6	MT Helmets - MSI	KTM	20	39m 43.448s
6	**Riccardo Rossi**	ITA	54	SIC58 Squadra Corse	Honda	20	39m 44.213s
7	**Ivan Ortola**	SPA	48	Angeluss MTA Team	KTM	20	39m 48.601s
8	**Elia Bartolini**	ITA	23	QJMotor Avintia Racing Team	KTM	20	39m 48.691s
9	**Matteo Bertelle**	ITA	18	QJMotor Avintia Racing Team	KTM	20	39m 48.694s
10	**Adrian Fernandez**	SPA	31	Red Bull KTM Tech3	KTM	20	39m 48.961s
11	**David Munoz**	SPA	44	BOE Motorsports	KTM	20	39m 48.965s
12	**Joel Kelso**	AUS	66	CIP Green Power	KTM	20	39m 49.203s
13	**Mario Aji**	INA	64	Honda Team Asia	Honda	20	39m 49.323s
14	**Lorenzo Fellon**	FRA	20	SIC58 Squadra Corse	Honda	20	39m 55.857s
15	**Deniz Oncu**	TUR	53	Red Bull KTM Tech3	KTM	20	39m 59.903s
16	Kaito Toba	JPN	27	CIP Green Power	KTM	20	39m 59.952s
17	Jaume Masia	SPA	5	Red Bull KTM Ajo	KTM	20	40m 00.003s
18	Taiyo Furusato	JPN	72	Honda Team Asia	Honda	20	40m 02.663s
19	Carlos Tatay	SPA	99	CFMOTO Racing PruestelGP	CFMOTO	20	40m 15.618s
20	Xavier Artigas	SPA	43	CFMOTO Racing PruestelGP	CFMOTO	20	40m 16.635s
21	Joshua Whatley	GBR	70	VisionTrack Racing Team	Honda	20	40m 24.626s
22	Ana Carrasco	SPA	22	BOE Motorsports	KTM	20	40m 57.291s
	Diogo Moreira	BRA	10	MT Helmets - MSI	KTM	19	DNF-crash
	Dennis Foggia	ITA	7	Leopard Racing	Honda	10	DNF-crash
	John McPhee	GBR	17	Sterilgarda Husqvarna Max	Husqvarna	10	DNF-crash
	Daniel Holgado	SPA	96	Red Bull KTM Ajo	KTM	10	DNF-crash
	Stefano Nepa	ITA	82	Angeluss MTA Team	KTM	3	DNF-crash
	Scott Ogden	GBR	19	VisionTrack Racing Team	Honda	0	DNF-crash

Fastest lap: Riccardo Rossi, on lap 9, 1m 57.234s, 100.0mph/161.0km/h.

Lap record: Fabio Di Giannantonio, 1m 56.628s, 100.5mph/161.8km/h (2018).

Event maximum speed: Dennis Foggia, 153.2mph/246.5km/h (free practice).

Qualifying:

Weather: Dry

Air: 31° **Humidity:** 44%

Track: 52°

1	Oncu	1m 56.811s
2	Holgado	1m 56.908s
3	Foggia	1m 57.094s
4	Garcia	1m 57.232s
5	Guevara	1m 57.236s
6	McPhee	1m 57.299s
7	Moreira	1m 57.405s
8	Rossi	1m 57.450s
9	Yamanaka	1m 57.513s
10	Masia	1m 57.532s
11	Suzuki	1m 57.553s
12	Fellon	1m 57.702s
13	Bertelle	1m 57.794s
14	Ogden	1m 57.958s
15	Munoz	1m 58.089s
16	Migno	1m 58.188s
17	Tatay	1m 58.189s
18	Nepa	1m 58.466s
	Q1	
19	Fernandez	1m 58.645s
20	Kelso	1m 58.804s
21	Ortola	1m 58.832s
22	Furusato	1m 59.009s
23	Aji	1m 59.018s
24	Bartolini	1m 59.021s
25	Toba	1m 59.133s
26	Artigas	1m 59.185s
27	Whatley	1m 59.430s
28	Carrasco	2m 00.488s
	Surra	No Time

Fastest race laps

1	Rossi	1m 57.234s
2	Garcia	1m 57.282s
3	Suzuki	1m 57.397s
4	Oncu	1m 57.410s
5	Yamanaka	1m 57.538s
6	Guevara	1m 57.547s
7	Masia	1m 57.563s
8	Ortola	1m 57.563s
9	Fellon	1m 57.581s
10	Munoz	1m 57.583s
11	Tatay	1m 57.624s
12	Foggia	1m 57.645s
13	Bartolini	1m 57.699s
14	Holgado	1m 57.725s
15	Moreira	1m 57.726s
16	McPhee	1m 57.752s
17	Bertelle	1m 57.830s
18	Migno	1m 57.834s
19	Kelso	1m 57.837s
20	Fernandez	1m 57.859s
21	Aji	1m 57.878s
22	Nepa	1m 58.065s
23	Toba	1m 58.733s
24	Artigas	1m 59.025s
25	Furusato	1m 59.237s
26	Whatley	1m 59.528s
27	Carrasco	2m 01.686s

Championship Points

1	Garcia	137
2	Guevara	109
3	Masia	95
4	Foggia	95
5	Sasaki	75
6	Migno	71
7	Oncu	71
8	Suzuki	54
9	Tatay	52
10	Yamanaka	43
11	Rossi	42
12	Toba	37
13	Artigas	37
14	Moreira	34
15	Holgado	28
16	Ortola	23
17	Bartolini	21
18	Kelso	18
19	McPhee	15
20	Ogden	14
21	Bertelle	13
22	Fernandez	13
23	Nepa	8
24	Munoz	5
25	Aji	5
26	Fellon	5

Constructor Points

1	GASGAS	165
2	KTM	134
3	Honda	132
4	Husqvarna	86
5	CFMOTO	71

FIM WORLD CHAMPIONSHIP · ROUND 9

CATALAN GRAND PRIX

BARCELONA-CATALUNYA CIRCUIT

YAMAHA
AKRAPOVIC
NGK
SPARK PLUGS
Beta
TANIDA
2D
YAMAHA
AKRAPOVIC

Above: **Aleix Espargaro manfully resisted the Pramac challenge of Martin and Zarco to claim second. Or so he thought…**
Photos: Gold & Goose

Right: **The Aprilia rider waves to a baffled crowd following his premature finish.**

Centre right: **Head in hands, Aleix was distraught.**
Photos: Courtesy of MotoGP

Far right: **Alex Rins sustained a fractured wrist in the first-corner melee.**
Photo: Suzuki ECSTAR

Below right: **Rins is sent flying, Bagnaia is about to follow suit, while culprit Nakagami is already prone on the track.**
Photos: Gold & Goose

Opening spread: **Me and my M1 – Quartararo was exemplary at a track where he expected to pay the price of poor top speed.**
Photo: Monster Energy Yamaha

ALEIX ESPARGARO, hanging his head in the Aprilia pit, was inconsolable. "My fault," he sobbed. A simple rookie's error had robbed him of second place, cost him nine priceless points and jeopardised the Italian squad's lead in the teams' championship. It also ended a run of four consecutive podiums and spoiled his family celebrations at the track closest to his home.

He could explain if not excuse the lapse. Normally, he would use his own pit board to count down the laps, but his pit was very close to the last corner. "Some laps, I had no time to watch the laps and the gap with Martin. But then I saw the tower, and I saw L1, so I did one lap and then I didn't remember that here in Barcelona, last lap is 0, not 1. And I closed the gas on the straight."

As he waved to the crowd in celebration and took a leisurely line into the first corners, not only Martin, but also Zarco, Mir and Marini flashed past at full racing speed. Hastily rebooting, he managed to repass Marini for fifth, before slumping over the tank in despair.

But he is in good company. Not only did 2009 champion Julian Simon lose that year's 125 race to Iannone in precisely the same way, but even racing royalty Mick Doohan and Wayne Rainey had fallen into the same last-lap trap.

Rainey ceded victory at Suzuki to Kevin Schwantz in 1989; 2000 World Champion Kenny Roberts gave the race to Toni Elias and Valentino Rossi at Estoril in 2006. And in Moto3, Alex Rins stood upright, fists pumping, over the line at Brno in 2014 – and dropped to ninth. Doohan did it differently in Germany in 2006. About to mount his last-lap attack on Luca Cadalora, he saw the chequered flag instead. Perhaps this roll call could help Espargaro forget.

His was not the only gaffe in the punishing heat. Or was the stewards' decision not to punish Takaaki Nakagami's costly first-corner blunder a well-reasoned response? Certainly, the riders and teams, by and large, thought the complete opposite, and the controversy would continue in races to come.

At first, the anger was turned on the rider, already smarting at condemnation for his collision with Rins at the previous race – although when Rins had asked riders at Friday's Safety Commission meeting whether the Japanese rider should have been sanctioned, the majority had said no.

Now, selected over Repsol's Espargaro to use Marquez's upgraded chassis, he had qualified 12th, but he got a flying start and was lying around fourth in the braking zone. Too fast and too late, he lost the front and fell. While his bike skittled the adjacent Rins's Suzuki, the rider head-butted the back of Bagnaia's Ducati, who also crashed. Perhaps mercifully the consequences were light considering that all the other riders escaped involvement, but they were severe enough for Bagnaia, who had qualified second and was hoping to continue his comeback after the Mugello win; and for Rins, who fractured his left wrist. Nakagami didn't break anything, but was concussed and badly knocked about.

This certainly looked like a punishable error to most. Compatriot Quartararo reflected the general anger: "In the first laps, we all need to be conscious that we are racing big bikes, that the weight is minimum 160 kilos. If you get hit by a bike like this, you can pass away … this is the most dangerous place for us." As Zarco – a close observer – had it: "Today, he totally lost all this credit that we gave to him during the Safety Commission. That's a pity for him. Now I don't know what they're going to say."

That turned out to be nothing. Silence. Which directed the incredulity and anger once again at the stewards and panel chairman Freddie Spencer, who by now was fully aware that this position was never going to win him any popularity contests. Bagnaia opined, "I am not angry, I'm just disappointed. Nakagami was trying to overtake ten riders in the first braking. If I was not there, he was surely in the gravel, and his race was already finished."

Rins went further, suggesting that the FIM stewards were not fit for purpose: "I already said to Freddie in Mugello that in my opinion they need to penalise Nakagami with the same penalty as Deniz Oncu last year [the Turkish rider had been banned for two races for dangerous riding]. But it's crazy. I mean for sure, and today they demonstrated on TV that the stewards are not at the level of MotoGP."

News from America confirmed a completely uneventful three-hour surgery to Marc Marquez's arm, with a predicted four- to six-month recovery time, so rumours that he was targeting a late-2022 return were not completely implausible. Meanwhile, Bradl continued as his substitute, while Pol Espargaro's status in the factory team remained open to

interpretation, with Nakagami given the latest chassis and swing-arm instead of him.

No wonder his name was among those at the top of the ever-active rumour mill. It was now confirmed that Jack Miller would be joining Binder in KTM's factory team, but Espargaro was also of interest to the Austrians, with hints of a return to orange, although this time with the satellite team.

There was no rumour at Yamaha, where it was confirmed that Quartararo had agreed terms for another two years after months of negotiation and fulsome promises. "Not an easy decision," he admitted, but he had been convinced to stay because he believed in Yamaha's capacity to solve problems: "They know where they need to improve. And they know clearly it's the power."

Searing heat with track temperatures at times up to 58 degrees led to plenty of talk about deterioration in the track, last resurfaced in 2018. Grip was at a premium, and race tyre management crucial. Aleix Espargaro said that it was "just like Brno, and now we don't have Brno, so it is the lowest grip on the current calendar."

That made Michelin's latest news less than comforting – that from 2023, riders would have just two rear tyre compounds, as opposed to three, over the same allocation of seven softer and five harder.

MOTOGP RACE – 24 laps

In spite of the heat, Aleix Espargaro managed a new outright fastest lap en route to his second pole of the season, having led free practice as well. Bagnaia and Quartararo lined up alongside; Zarco led the fast-again Di Giannantonio and Martin on row two. Vinales, on the second Aprilia, through from Q1, was in the middle of row three, sandwiched by Rins and Marini.

In continuing heat, Bagnaia had predicted a race of survival. Thanks to Nakagami's indiscretion, he wouldn't survive long, with Rins and the Japanese rider also down and out at the first corner.

It was the start of a perfect afternoon for Quartararo, already ahead of Aleix Espargaro and Martin – a position that would never be challenged.

In their wake, Zarco had been slowed by the Turn One chaos, with Pol Espargaro, Mir, Marini, fast-away Vinales, Di Giannantonio, Bastianini, and the KTMs of Binder and Oliveira never in touch with the leaders.

Anxious to avoid increasing front tyre pressure if trapped behind an Aprilia or Ducati, bikes that were faster in a straight line, Quartararo set about building a commanding lead as early as possible. His advantage stood at four-tenths after lap one, then seven-tenths on lap two. It was difficult to see anyone other than the Frenchman winning when Martin, full of confidence on the brakes after reverting to a front fork setting from the start of the year, passed Espargaro on lap three. Now Yamaha's leading man had better than a full second in hand.

Zarco made it a three-way fight for second place, latching on to the Aprilia's rear, while the fight for fifth settled down after early confusion. Mir edged clear of Marini, while Bastianini grew impatient when scrapping with Vinales, crashing out of seventh. In a nightmare eighth lap for the Gresini

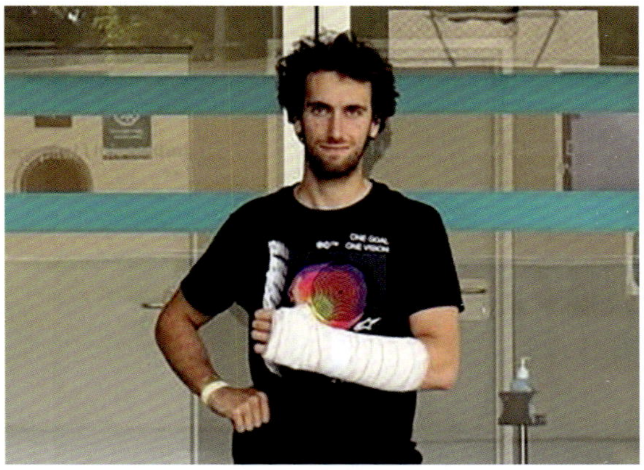

team, Di Giannantonio followed suit, a gust of wind having caught him out at the penultimate turn.

Crashes weren't the only means of coming apart. Tyre issues took their toll, with Pol Espargaro dropping at an alarming rate, and Miller not once competitive. The Australian was furious after spinning to a limp 14th: "I had nothing on the right side of the tyre, start to finish, and at the end, I was spinning in a straight line, doing times I know I can do with the Panigale [street bike] with tyres off the shelf. Last year, I was on the podium, today I'm 30 seconds away."

There were no such rubber problems up front. Quartararo's Sunday-stroll mien belied devastating pace and consistency, able to run 1m 40s until lap 14. With his pursuers lapping in the 1m 41s, he built up a commanding cushion to come home 6.4 seconds clear at the flag.

Second was where the fun was. On Friday, the superiority of Espargaro and Aprilia's RS-GP in low-grip conditions had been clear, and his pole time reinforced the notion of him being pre-race favourite. Thus his frustration at being stuck behind Martin for long spells was understandable. Espargaro retook second place with a neat Turn One move on the tenth lap, only to lose out at the same place six laps later. He appeared to have made the decisive move back at Turn One once more on lap 21, and Martin had finally given up hope, only for Aleix's first serious error of judgement of the year to hand back second place, and Zarco a surprise third.

Mir's fourth brought a run of rotten results to an end, with Espargaro retaking the fifth he had lost briefly to Marini at Turn Five on that painful final lap. Vinales was close after a gamble with a soft rear Michelin that didn't bring the benefits he had anticipated. Binder was a solid eighth, ahead of Oliveira. Alex Marquez rescued tenth from 25th on the grid on an otherwise disastrous day for Honda – Bradl had crashed out on the first lap after qualifying 21st.

Remy Gardner was just a second adrift in a best-yet 11th, after taking Darryn Binder in the rookie battle, the pair outfoxing the mystifyingly slow Morbidelli on the final lap. Miller and Fernandez wrapped up the points; wild-card Pirro and the badly faded Pol Espargaro trailed in.

Bezzecchi had also crashed out early on, in a race with only 17 finishers.

Quartararo's second win, on a track where his top-speed disadvantage and the blazing conditions might have been expected to cost him more, also marked a significant moment, thanks to his rival's error, in stretching his championship lead to more than 20 points. Do weekends come any sweeter?

MOTO2 RACE – 22 laps

Celestino Vietti's second pole of the year was a promising return to form after three difficult races, and the omens would prove reliable as his championship campaign regained momentum, while main challenger Ogura's faltered. At the same time, both Canet and new challenger Fernandez were coming into the picture more strongly.

Vietti had to go through Q1, where he was second fastest to Lopez. Arbolino and Navarro also came through. The Italian topped Q2 from Canet, with Roberts (fast also in free practice) completing row one; Dixon led the second from Arenas and Lowes. Ogura was down on row four, more than half a second off the pace.

It was a race of more than one dimension. The first lasted until just short of half-distance for Roberts, who led through the first corner and immediately embarked on an escape attempt, defying any need for caution or tyre management in the heat.

By the end of lap ten, he was better than 2.4 seconds clear. It all came to an end at Turn Five, the notorious left-hand hairpin after a long set of rights, and with it a run of points scored at every race of the season so far.

That handed the lead to Dixon, temporarily ahead of long-time pursuer Canet, while behind Vietti was engaged to and fro in a lively fight with Arenas, Fernandez and Schrotter.

Canet took over up front on lap 14, with Vietti soon getting clear of the scrap to set about him. From there to the end, they traded blows, the lead changing hands between them four times in the final eight laps.

As they started the last, it appeared that Canet had done

Above: **High-speed scrum on the opening lap, with the Ducatis of Di Giannantonio, Miller and Bastianini up front.**

Below: **Martin and Zarco celebrate their Pramac double podium.**

Below right: **Vietti (13) and Canet traded blows in Moto2. The Italian narrowly prevailed.**

Right: **In Moto3, precocious rookie Munoz leads Garcia and Suzuki, with Oncu and Masia in pursuit.**

Photos: Gold & Goose

Left: Aleix Espargaro celebrates pole with daughter Mia. He dedicated his race to the cardiac team who had been treating her.

Below left: Joe Roberts ran away in Moto2, only to crash out, his first no-score of the season.

Below: Teenager David Munoz snatched second in only his second grand prix.

Photos: Gold & Goose

enough, with a neat move into the first corner. But Vietti's response, at the exit from Turn Ten, was enough to hold off the Spaniard by 0.081 of a second for a third win of the year.

Another last-lap attack resulted in Fernandez nabbing third from Dixon with just three turns remaining, the leading quartet covered by six-tenths.

With three laps to go, Arenas suffered a mechanical problem and retired frustrated. By then, Schrotter had got the better of him for fifth, while five seconds away, Acosta was sixth, promoted not only by the departure of Arenas, but also a lap-20 crash for Sam Lowes.

Acosta kept Ogura narrowly behind to the line; less than a second adrift came Lopez on the top Boscoscuro. Gonzalez was a lone ninth; Arbolino tenth after a long-lap penalty for exceeding track limits.

Cameron Beaubier had qualified way down in 23rd and was an early faller, still nowhere near the points. Toledo and Salac also crashed out.

MOTO3 RACE – 21 laps

Spain's talent conveyor belt had already produced 17-year-old Izan Guevara to flirt with title success in 2022, but he was a relative veteran compared with rookie David Munoz, who had turned 16 just in time to make his GP debut in Italy the previous weekend, and who finished runner-up at his second attempt, upsetting a number of more experienced riders in the final laps.

It was typically frantic: five laps in, just 3.8 seconds covered the top 25. Then pole-sitter Foggia found another random way to suffer. He'd led the early laps and was in the front pack when his chain jumped its sprocket after he ran over the corrugations of the kerb.

A Turn Ten collision between Salvador, Holgado and Yamanaka on lap nine splintered the lead group temporarily. It was soon back together, however, at least until Guevara started gapping them on lap 15. The Majorcan was seven-tenths faster than second-placed Oncu two laps later, and that was enough for the decisive break.

Garcia, Munoz and Suzuki benefited as Oncu ran wide, but could do little as Guevara eased clear to win his second race of the year by almost two seconds.

Behind, Munoz jumped from fourth to second on the final lap, passing Garcia on the entry to Turn Five, then barging past Suzuki on the exit. Suzuki then nabbed third from Garcia on the final turn, after the Spaniard had mistakenly assumed one lap remained. Oncu was fifth ahead of Tatay, McPhee and Masia.

Rossi crossed the line ninth, but was dropped to 11th behind Fernandez and Artigas with a three-second penalty for failing to take a long-lap. Fellon suffered the same sanction.

FIM WORLD CHAMPIONSHIP: ROUND 9

GRAN PREMI MONSTER ENERGY DE CATALUNYA

3–5 JUNE, 2022

CIRCUIT DE CATALUNYA

25 laps
Length: 4.657km/2.894 miles
Width: 12m

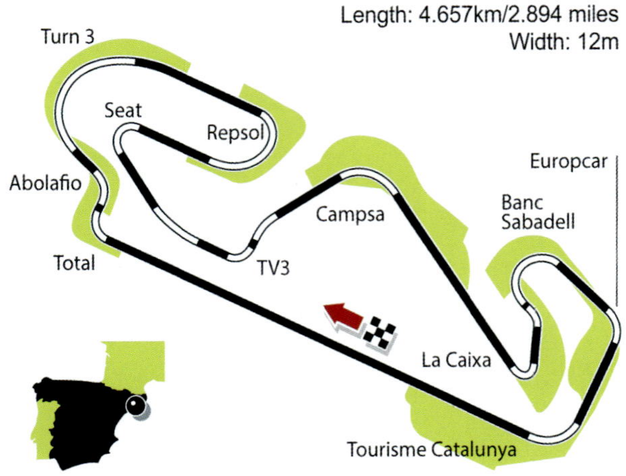

MotoGP

RACE DISTANCE: 24 laps, 69.449 miles/111.768km · RACE WEATHER: Dry (air 30°, humidity 47%, track 55°)

Pos.	Rider	Nat.	No.	Entrant	Machine	Tyres	Race tyre choice	Laps	Time & speed
1	**Fabio Quartararo**	FRA	20	Monster Energy Yamaha MotoGP	Yamaha YZR-M1	M	F: Medium/R: Medium	24	40m 29.360s 102.9mph/165.6km/h
2	**Jorge Martin**	SPA	89	Prima Pramac Racing	Ducati Desmosedici	M	F: Medium/R: Medium	24	40m 35.833s
3	**Johann Zarco**	FRA	5	Prima Pramac Racing	Ducati Desmosedici	M	F: Medium/R: Hard	24	40m 37.745s
4	**Joan Mir**	SPA	36	Team SUZUKI ECSTAR	Suzuki GSX-RR	M	F: Medium/R: Medium	24	40m 40.841s
5	**Aleix Espargaro**	SPA	41	Aprilia Racing	Aprilia RS-GP	M	F: Medium/R: Medium	24	40m 43.755s
6	**Luca Marini**	ITA	10	Mooney VR46 Racing Team	Ducati Desmosedici	M	F: Medium/R: Medium	24	40m 44.790s
7	**Maverick Vinales**	SPA	12	Aprilia Racing	Aprilia RS-GP	M	F: Medium/R: Soft	24	40m 45.335s
8	**Brad Binder**	RSA	33	Red Bull KTM Factory Racing	KTM RC16	M	F: Hard/R: Medium	24	40m 50.796s
9	**Miguel Oliveira**	POR	88	Red Bull KTM Factory Racing	KTM RC16	M	F: Hard/R: Medium	24	40m 56.160s
10	**Alex Marquez**	SPA	73	LCR Honda CASTROL	Honda RC213V	M	F: Medium/R: Soft	24	40m 59.820s
11	**Remy Gardner**	AUS	87	Tech3 KTM Factory Racing	KTM RC16	M	F: Hard/R: Medium	24	41m 01.803s
12	**Darryn Binder**	RSA	40	WithU Yamaha RNF MotoGP Team	Yamaha YZR-M1	M	F: Medium/R: Medium	24	41m 02.241s
13	**Franco Morbidelli**	ITA	21	Monster Energy Yamaha MotoGP	Yamaha YZR-M1	M	F: Medium/R: Hard	24	41m 02.528s
14	**Jack Miller**	AUS	43	Ducati Lenovo Team	Ducati Desmosedici	M	F: Medium/R: Hard	24	41m 04.053s
15	**Raul Fernandez**	SPA	25	Tech3 KTM Factory Racing	KTM RC16	M	F: Hard/R: Medium	24	41m 07.204s
16	Michele Pirro	ITA	51	Aruba.it Racing	Ducati Desmosedici	M	F: Medium/R: Medium	24	41m 13.893s
17	Pol Espargaro	SPA	44	Repsol Honda Team	Honda RC213V	M	F: Medium/R: Hard	24	41m 15.559s
	Andrea Dovizioso	ITA	4	WithU Yamaha RNF MotoGP Team	Yamaha YZR-M1	M	F: Medium/R: Medium	17	DNF-crash
	Fabio Di Giannantonio	ITA	49	Gresini Racing MotoGP	Ducati Desmosedici	M	F: Medium/R: Medium	8	DNF-crash
	Enea Bastianini	ITA	23	Gresini Racing MotoGP	Ducati Desmosedici	M	F: Medium/R: Medium	7	DNF-crash
	Marco Bezzecchi	ITA	72	Mooney VR46 Racing Team	Ducati Desmosedici	M	F: Medium/R: Hard	5	DNF-crash
	Francesco Bagnaia	ITA	63	Ducati Lenovo Team	Ducati Desmosedici	M	F: Medium/R: Medium	1	DNF-crash
	Alex Rins	SPA	42	Team SUZUKI ECSTAR	Suzuki GSX-RR	M	F: Medium/R: Medium	0	DNF-crash
	Takaaki Nakagami	JPN	30	LCR Honda IDEMITSU	Honda RC213V	M	F: Medium/R: Medium	0	DNF-crash
	Stefan Bradl	GER	6	Repsol Honda Team	Honda RC213V	M	F: Medium/R: Hard	0	DNF-crash

Fastest lap: Fabio Quartararo, on lap 3, 1m 40.186s, 104.0mph/167.3km/h.

Lap record: Johann Zarco, 1m 39.939s, 104.2mph/167.7km/h (2021).

Event maximum speed: Enea Bastianini, 219.3mph/352.9km/h (free practice).

Qualifying

Weather: Dry
Air Temp: 33° **Humidity:** 26%
Track Temp: 58°

	Rider	Time
1	A. Espargaro	1m 38.742s
2	Bagnaia	1m 38.773s
3	Quartararo	1m 38.959s
4	Zarco	1m 39.027s
5	Di Giannantonio	1m 39.099s
6	Martin	1m 39.142s
7	Rins	1m 39.145s
8	Vinales	1m 39.397s
9	Marini	1m 39.451s
10	P. Espargaro	1m 39.477s
11	Miller	1m 39.523s
12	Nakagami	1m 39.611s
	Q1	
13	Bezzecchi	1m 39.240s
14	Bastianini	1m 39.246s
15	B. Binder	1m 39.249s
16	Oliveira	1m 39.420s
17	Mir	1m 39.664s
18	Morbidelli	1m 39.884s
19	Dovizioso	1m 40.071s
20	Gardner	1m 40.113s
21	Bradl	1m 40.298s
22	Pirro	1m 40.351s
23	D. Binder	1m 40.373s
24	Fernandez	1m 40.587s

Fastest race laps

	Rider	Time
1	Quartararo	1m 40.186s
2	Martin	1m 40.484s
3	A. Espargaro	1m 40.611s
4	Zarco	1m 40.639s
5	Mir	1m 40.762s
6	Bastianini	1m 40.896s
7	Marini	1m 40.930s
8	Vinales	1m 40.948s
9	Di Giannantonio	1m 41.090s
10	Oliveira	1m 41.144s
11	Morbidelli	1m 41.194s
12	B. Binder	1m 41.195s
13	D. Binder	1m 41.271s
14	Bezzecchi	1m 41.307s
15	A. Marquez	1m 41.413s
16	Gardner	1m 41.504s
17	Miller	1m 41.512s
18	Fernandez	1m 41.560s
19	Dovizioso	1m 41.588s
20	P. Espargaro	1m 41.642s
21	Pirro	1m 42.131s

Championship Points

	Rider	Points
1	Quartararo	147
2	A. Espargaro	125
3	Bastianini	94
4	Zarco	91
5	Bagnaia	81
6	B. Binder	73
7	Rins	69
8	Mir	69
9	Miller	65
10	M. Marquez	60
11	Oliveira	57
12	Martin	51
13	Vinales	46
14	Marini	41
15	P. Espargaro	40
16	Nakagami	38
17	Bezzecchi	30
18	A. Marquez	26
19	Morbidelli	22
20	D. Binder	10
21	Di Giannantonio	8
22	Dovizioso	8
23	Gardner	8
24	Fernandez	1

Constructor Points

	Constructor	Points
1	Ducati	201
2	Yamaha	147
3	Aprilia	126
4	KTM	101
5	Suzuki	93
6	Honda	81

Grid order	1	2	3	4	5	6	7	8	9	10	11	12	13	14	15	16	17	18	19	20	21	22	23	24	•
41 A. ESPARGARO	20	20	20	20	20	20	20	20	20	20	20	20	20	20	20	20	20	20	20	20	20	20	20	20	1
63 BAGNAIA	41	41	89	89	89	89	89	89	89	41	41	41	41	41	41	89	89	89	89	89	41	41	41	89	2
20 QUARTARARO	89	89	41	41	41	41	41	41	41	89	89	89	89	89	89	41	41	41	41	41	89	89	89	5	3
5 ZARCO	5	5	5	5	5	5	5	5	5	5	5	5	5	5	5	5	5	5	5	5	5	5	5	36	4
49 DI GIANNANTONIO	44	44	36	10	36	36	36	36	36	36	36	36	36	36	36	36	36	36	36	36	36	36	36	41	5
89 MARTIN	10	36	10	36	10	10	10	10	10	10	10	10	10	10	10	10	10	10	10	10	10	10	10	10	6
42 RINS	36	10	44	44	23	23	23	12	12	12	12	12	12	12	12	12	12	12	12	12	12	12	12	12	7
12 VINALES	12	12	12	12	12	12	12	33	33	33	33	33	33	33	33	33	33	33	33	33	33	33	33	33	8
10 MARINI	49	49	49	23	44	33	33	88	88	88	88	88	88	88	88	88	88	88	88	88	88	88	88	88	9
44 P. ESPARGARO	23	23	23	33	33	88	88	40	40	73	73	73	73	73	73	73	73	73	73	73	73	73	73	73	10
43 MILLER	33	33	33	88	88	44	49	44	44	40	40	40	43	43	43	43	43	43	43	43	43	40	40	87	11
30 NAKAGAMI	88	88	88	49	49	49	40	73	73	44	44	43	40	40	40	40	40	40	40	40	40	87	21	40	12
72 BEZZECCHI	43	40	40	72	40	40	44	87	87	43	43	44	87	21	87	87	87	87	87	87	87	21	87	21	13
23 BASTIANINI	40	43	72	40	87	73	73	43	43	87	87	87	21	87	21	21	21	21	21	21	21	43	43	43	14
33 B.BINDER	72	72	43	87	73	87	87	4	4	4	4	4	44	44	44	4	25	25	25	25	25	25	25	25	15
88 OLIVEIRA	87	87	87	73	43	43	43	21	21	21	21	21	4	4	4	44	44	44	44	44	44	44	44	51	
36 MIR	73	73	73	43	25	25	25	25	25	25	25	25	25	25	25	25	51	51	51	51	51	51	51	44	
21 MORBIDELLI	25	25	25	25	4	4	4	51	51	51	51	51	51	51	51	51	4								
4 DOVIZIOSO	4	4	4	4	21	21	21	49																	
87 GARDNER	51	51	21	21	51	51	51																		
6 BRADL	21	21	51	51	72																				
51 PIRRO	*63*																								
40 D.BINDER																									
25 FERNANDEZ																									
73 A. MARQUEZ																									

72 Pit stop *63 Lapped rider*

Moto2

RACE DISTANCE: 22 laps, 63.662 miles/102.454km · RACE WEATHER: Dry (air 28°, humidity 51%, track 50°)

Pos.	Rider	Nat.	No.	Entrant	Machine	Laps	Time & Speed
1	**Celestino Vietti**	ITA	13	Mooney VR46 Racing Team	Kalex	22	38m 42.958s
							98.6/mph/158.7 km/h
2	**Aron Canet**	SPA	40	Flexbox HP40	Kalex	22	38m 43.039s
3	**Augusto Fernandez**	SPA	37	Red Bull KTM Ajo	Kalex	22	38m 43.480s
4	**Jake Dixon**	GBR	96	Inde GASGAS Aspar Team	Kalex	22	38m 43.604s
5	**Marcel Schrotter**	GER	23	Liqui Moly Intact GP	Kalex	22	38m 44.428s
6	**Pedro Acosta**	SPA	51	Red Bull KTM Ajo	Kalex	22	38m 49.256s
7	**Ai Ogura**	JPN	79	IDEMITSU Honda Team Asia	Kalex	22	38m 49.278s
8	**Alonso Lopez**	SPA	21	Lightech Speed Up	Boscoscuro	22	38m 50.187s
9	**Manuel Gonzalez**	SPA	18	Yamaha VR46 Master Camp Team	Kalex	22	38m 53.704s
10	**Tony Arbolino**	ITA	14	Elf Marc VDS Racing Team	Kalex	22	38m 55.014s
11	**Lorenzo Dalla Porta**	ITA	19	Italtrans Racing Team	Kalex	22	38m 55.572s
12	**Somkiat Chantra**	THA	35	IDEMITSU Honda Team Asia	Kalex	22	38m 56.164s
13	**Bo Bendsneyder**	NED	64	Pertamina Mandalika SAG Team	Kalex	22	39m 01.293s
14	**Jorge Navarro**	SPA	9	Flexbox HP40	Kalex	22	39m 01.453s
15	**Fermin Aldeguer**	SPA	54	Lightech Speed Up	Boscoscuro	22	39m 02.852s
16	Stefano Manzi	ITA	62	Yamaha VR46 Master Camp Team	Kalex	22	39m 04.679s
17	Barry Baltus	BEL	7	RW Racing GP	Kalex	22	39m 05.227s
18	Jeremy Alcoba	SPA	52	Liqui Moly Intact GP	Kalex	22	39m 05.471s
19	Niccolo Antonelli	ITA	28	Mooney VR46 Racing Team	Kalex	22	39m 19.827s
20	Zonta van den Goorbergh	NED	84	RW Racing GP	Kalex	22	39m 19.978s
21	Sean Dylan Kelly	USA	4	American Racing	Kalex	22	39m 21.378s
22	Simone Corsi	ITA	24	MV Agusta Forward Racing	MV Agusta	22	39m 28.570s
23	Piotr Biesiekirski	POL	74	Pertamina Mandalika SAG EUVIC	Kalex	22	39m 30.284s
24	Marcos Ramirez	SPA	42	MV Agusta Forward Racing	MV Agusta	22	39m 37.556s
	Albert Arenas	SPA	75	Inde GASGAS Aspar Team	Kalex	19	DNF-technical
	Sam Lowes	GBR	22	Elf Marc VDS Racing Team	Kalex	19	DNF-crash
	Alessandro Zaccone	ITA	61	Gresini Racing Moto2	Kalex	14	DNF-ret in pit
	Joe Roberts	USA	16	Italtrans Racing Team	Kalex	10	DNF-crash
	Cameron Beaubier	USA	6	American Racing	Kalex	4	DNF-crash
	Filip Salac	CZE	12	Gresini Racing Moto2	Kalex	3	DNF-crash
	Alex Toledo	SPA	55	Pertamina Mandalika SAG Team	Kalex	2	DNF-crash

Fastest lap: Aron Canet, on lap 2, 1m 44.550s, 99.6mph/160.3km/h.

Lap record: Raul Fernandez, 1m 43.757s, 100.4mph/161.5km/h (2021).

Event maximum speed: Somkiat Chantra, 184.9mph/297.5km/h (race).

Qualifying

Weather: Dry

Air: 29° **Humidity:** 51%

Track: 51°

1	Vietti	1m 43.823s
2	Canet	1m 43.831s
3	Roberts	1m 44.002s
4	Dixon	1m 44.045s
5	Arenas	1m 44.049s
6	Lowes	1m 44.190s
7	Bendsneyder	1m 44.407s
8	Fernandez	1m 44.430s
9	Schrotter	1m 44.477s
10	Ogura	1m 44.491s
11	Lopez	1m 44.579s
12	Acosta	1m 44.691s
13	Salac	1m 44.702s
14	Gonzalez	1m 44.712s
15	Dalla Porta	1m 44.748s
16	Navarro	1m 44.778s
17	Baltus	1m 44.833s
18	Arbolino	1m 44.878s
	Q1	
19	Chantra	1m 44.911s
20	Aldeguer	1m 44.974s
21	Toledo	1m 45.217s
22	Manzi	1m 45.226s
23	Beaubier	1m 45.269s
24	V D Goorbergh	1m 45.368s
25	Antonelli	1m 45.687s
26	Alcoba	1m 45.812s
27	Corsi	1m 45.831s
28	Zaccone	1m 45.861s
29	Kelly	1m 46.326s
30	Ramirez	1m 46.491s
31	Biesiekirski	1m 46.718s

Fastest race laps

1	Canet	1m 44.550s
2	Roberts	1m 44.592s
3	Dixon	1m 44.623s
4	Schrotter	1m 44.715s
5	Ogura	1m 44.745s
6	Arenas	1m 44.803s
7	Fernandez	1m 44.806s
8	Lowes	1m 44.895s
9	Lopez	1m 44.920s
10	Acosta	1m 44.929s
11	Vietti	1m 44.935s
12	Arbolino	1m 45.096s
13	Gonzalez	1m 45.101s
14	Salac	1m 45.143s
15	Dalla Porta	1m 45.284s
16	Chantra	1m 45.465s
17	Beaubier	1m 45.544s
18	Baltus	1m 45.578s
19	Bendsneyder	1m 45.609s
20	Navarro	1m 45.667s
21	Manzi	1m 45.676s
22	Aldeguer	1m 45.727s
23	Alcoba	1m 45.951s
24	V D Goorbergh	1m 46.346s
25	Kelly	1m 46.362s
26	Toledo	1m 46.368s
27	Antonelli	1m 46.448s
28	Corsi	1m 46.678s
29	Biesiekirski	1m 46.685s
30	Zaccone	1m 46.702s
31	Ramirez	1m 46.714s

Championship Points

1	Vietti	133
2	Ogura	117
3	Canet	109
4	Fernandez	96
5	Arbolino	89
6	Roberts	86
7	Schrotter	75
8	Chantra	65
9	Navarro	58
10	Acosta	55
11	Dixon	55
12	Bendsneyder	44
13	Beaubier	38
14	Lowes	35
15	Arenas	35
16	Alcoba	31
17	Gonzalez	28
18	Aldeguer	21
19	Lopez	16
20	Baltus	15
21	Dalla Porta	10
22	Manzi	9
23	Salac	8
24	Fenati	7
25	Rodrigo	6
26	Zaccone	6
27	Ramirez	5
28	Kubo	4
29	Kelly	3
30	Pasini	1

Constructor Points

1	Kalex	225
2	Boscoscuro	36
3	MV Agusta	5

Moto3

RACE DISTANCE: 21 laps, 60.768 miles/97.797km · RACE WEATHER: Dry (air 27°, humidity 54%, track 42°)

Pos.	Rider	Nat.	No.	Entrant	Machine	Laps	Time & Speed
1	**Izan Guevara**	SPA	28	Valresa GASGAS Aspar Team	GASGAS	21	38m 22.351s
							95.0 mph/152.9 km/h
2	**David Munoz**	SPA	44	BOE Motorsports	KTM	21	38m 24.326s
3	**Tatsuki Suzuki**	JPN	24	Leopard Racing	Honda	21	38m 24.336s
4	**Sergio Garcia**	SPA	11	Valresa GASGAS Aspar Team	GASGAS	21	38m 24.387s
5	**Deniz Oncu**	TUR	53	Red Bull KTM Tech3	KTM	21	38m 25.103s
6	**Carlos Tatay**	SPA	99	CFMOTO Racing PruestelGP	CFMOTO	21	38m 25.485s
7	**John McPhee**	GBR	17	Sterilgarda Husqvarna Max	Husqvarna	21	38m 25.692s
8	**Jaume Masia**	SPA	5	Red Bull KTM Ajo	KTM	21	38m 25.984s
9	**Adrian Fernandez**	SPA	31	Red Bull KTM Tech3	KTM	21	38m 27.636s
10	**Xavier Artigas**	SPA	43	CFMOTO Racing PruestelGP	CFMOTO	21	38m 27.906s
11	**Riccardo Rossi**	ITA	54	SIC58 Squadra Corse	Honda	21	38m 29.977s
12	**Joel Kelso**	AUS	66	CIP Green Power	KTM	21	38m 31.566s
13	**Matteo Bertelle**	ITA	18	QJMotor Avintia Racing Team	KTM	21	38m 33.676s
14	**Scott Ogden**	GBR	19	VisionTrack Racing Team	Honda	21	38m 33.730s
15	**Kaito Toba**	JPN	27	CIP Green Power	KTM	21	38m 46.995s
16	Stefano Nepa	ITA	82	Angeluss MTA Team	KTM	21	38m 47.358s
17	Elia Bartolini	ITA	23	QJMotor Avintia Racing Team	KTM	21	38m 47.387s
18	Ivan Ortola	SPA	48	Angeluss MTA Team	KTM	21	38m 47.516s
19	Syarifuddin Azman	MAL	63	VisionTrack Racing Team	Honda	21	38m 47.561s
20	Lorenzo Fellon	FRA	20	SIC58 Squadra Corse	Honda	21	38m 47.590s
21	Ryusei Yamanaka	JPN	6	MT Helmets - MSI	KTM	21	39m 02.738s
22	Ana Carrasco	SPA	22	BOE Motorsports	KTM	21	39m 20.399s
	Marcos Uriarte	SPA	89	Rivacold Snipers Team	Honda	15	DNF-crash
	Andrea Migno	ITA	16	Rivacold Snipers Team	Honda	14	DNF-ret in pit
	Joshua Whatley	GBR	70	VisionTrack Racing Team	Honda	12	DNF-ret in pit
	Taiyo Furusato	JPN	72	Honda Team Asia	Honda	9	DNF-crash
	David Salvador	SPA	38	Sterilgarda Husqvarna Max	Husqvarna	8	DNF-crash
	Daniel Holgado	SPA	96	Red Bull KTM Ajo	KTM	8	DNF-crash
	Mario Aji	INA	64	Honda Team Asia	Honda	8	DNF-crash
	Dennis Foggia	ITA	7	Leopard Racing	Honda	6	DNF-technical

Fastest lap: Jaume Masia, on lap 2, 1m 48.380s, 96.1mph/154.6km/h.

Lap record: Darryn Binder, 1m 48.209s, 96.3mph/154.9km/h (2021).

Event maximum speed: Jaume Masia, 155.3mph/250.0km/h (race).

Qualifying:

Weather: Dry

Air: 31° **Humidity:** 43%

Track: 53°

1	Foggia	1m 48.290s
2	Oncu	1m 48.428s
3	Guevara	1m 48.537s
4	Fellon	1m 48.574s
5	Yamanaka	1m 48.693s
6	Rossi	1m 48.726s
7	Garcia	1m 48.729s
8	Toba	1m 48.744s
9	Kelso	1m 48.806s
10	Suzuki	1m 48.858s
11	McPhee	1m 48.925s
12	Bertelle	1m 48.965s
13	Ogden	1m 49.258s
14	Masia	1m 49.288s
15	Migno	1m 49.314s
16	Salvador	1m 49.394s
17	Holgado	1m 49.407s
18	Tatay	1m 49.832s
	Q1	
19	Aji	1m 49.873s
20	Munoz	1m 49.957s
21	Artigas	1m 49.971s
22	Furusato	1m 49.986s
23	Bartolini	1m 50.137s
24	Fernandez	1m 50.230s
25	Nepa	1m 50.277s
26	Azman	1m 50.448s
27	Uriarte	1m 50.823s
28	Ortola	1m 51.642s
29	Carrasco	1m 51.812s
	Whatley	No Time

Fastest race laps

1	Masia	1m 48.380s
2	Suzuki	1m 48.540s
3	Salvador	1m 48.563s
4	McPhee	1m 48.612s
5	Munoz	1m 48.628s
6	Holgado	1m 48.715s
7	Artigas	1m 48.737s
8	Bertelle	1m 48.787s
9	Tatay	1m 48.825s
10	Toba	1m 48.868s
11	Rossi	1m 48.874s
12	Guevara	1m 48.900s
13	Oncu	1m 48.930s
14	Fernandez	1m 48.945s
15	Garcia	1m 48.957s
16	Yamanaka	1m 48.972s
17	Migno	1m 49.042s
18	Fellon	1m 49.079s
19	Nepa	1m 49.137s
20	Azman	1m 49.142s
21	Ogden	1m 49.149s
22	Aji	1m 49.175s
23	Foggia	1m 49.236s
24	Kelso	1m 49.270s
25	Ortola	1m 49.568s
26	Furusato	1m 49.772s
27	Bartolini	1m 49.827s
28	Uriarte	1m 50.583s
29	Carrasco	1m 50.847s
30	Whatley	1m 51.468s

Championship Points

1	Garcia	150
2	Guevara	134
3	Masia	103
4	Foggia	95
5	Oncu	82
6	Sasaki	75
7	Migno	71
8	Suzuki	70
9	Tatay	62
10	Rossi	47
11	Artigas	43
12	Yamanaka	43
13	Toba	38
14	Moreira	34
15	Holgado	28
16	Munoz	25
17	McPhee	24
18	Ortola	23
19	Kelso	22
20	Bartolini	21
21	Fernandez	20
22	Bertelle	16
23	Ogden	16
24	Nepa	8
25	Aji	5
26	Fellon	5

Constructor Points

1	GASGAS	190
2	KTM	154
3	Honda	148
4	Husqvarna	95
5	CFMOTO	81

FIM WORLD CHAMPIONSHIP · ROUND 10

GERMAN GRAND PRIX

SACHSENRING CIRCUIT

Main: Quartararo gave a master-class for a second successive win.
Photo: Monster Energy Yamaha

Insets, top to bottom: Going, going, gone. Bagnaia was the picture of dejection as he did the notorious walk of shame.
Photos: Gold & Goose & Ducati Corse

Above: **On the move. Miller leads a blur of colour provided by Vinales, Di Giannantonio, Marini and Martin.**
Photo: Ducati Corse

Top right: **A frustrated Bradl found his Repsol Honda's performance "unacceptable".**
Photo: Repsol Honda

Top far right: **Maverick Vinales had his best race of the year curtailed by a ride-height device malfunction.**

Centre row, from left: **Team principals Razlan Razali, Aki Ajo and Paolo Ciabatti held all the cards in the 2023 riders' contract negotiations.**

Right: **Another second moved Zarco into third spot in the championship.**
Photos: Gold & Goose

IF ever such a concept can be considered, then Honda could be said to have owned the Sachsenring. Not just through its most successful rider ever, although Marc Marquez's victory record there is unrivalled, stretching back to 2010 in 125s and 2011/12 in Moto2, before he took over the premier class in 2013. For three years straight before that, Dani Pedrosa had won at the Sachsenring, as well as for a first time in 2007. Even in the nine preceding years at the little track outside Chemnitz, Honda had won five times with both two-strokes and four-strokes, ridden by Doohan, Barros, Rossi, Gibernau and Biaggi.

How poignant that the 2022 event, the first in a decade sans Marc, should create a different historic landmark – the first time since 1982 without a single Honda in the points. Nakagami crashed out of tenth; Pol Espargaro pulled in with breathing difficulties resulting from rib injuries in a heavy FP1 fall, Alex Marquez retired with a failed ride-height device, and Bradl trailed in a disconsolate 16th and last, stricken with such severe overheating that he'd had to slow down to avoid the slipstream of rivals, a situation he bluntly described as unacceptable.

Small comfort that at the next round at Assen, Yamaha would suffer the same pointless fate, since in Germany Quartararo had won in a style reminiscent of Marquez's majestic domination.

But there was a crumb or two perhaps of positive news from Marc, after his latest checkup in Madrid. "I have no pain; this is very important," he said. "It allows me to rest and follow the doctors' rules: a healthy diet, drink a lot and try to hang out with our dogs because it is important that the body is not inactive." Team manager Alberto Puig expressed hope that he would be able to ride before the end of the year: "I don't know when, but it will be very important for Marc to test the new bike at the end of the season."

In another weekend of blazing heat, there were hangovers from Catalunya. Alex Rins rode competitively on Friday, but withdrew on Saturday after waking in considerable pain as a result of his efforts. He was hoping that his left wrist fracture would be more race-ready for Assen in a week's time. But he was more philosophical about the Montmelo crash, softening some of his heat-of-the-moment criticism of the Stewards' Panel: "Saying that Freddie [Spencer] is too old … they were not the correct words." He did request that the stewards should attend the Friday Safety Commission meetings, to interact directly with the riders.

For his part, Nakagami was apologetic, but he excused himself for having been caught unawares by the suction effect of Bagnaia's Ducati slipstream, a factor exacerbated by its aero bodywork: "The braking point was under control, but I had a big slipstream behind Pecco." The same had happened to Rins behind Bagnaia at Le Mans, causing him to run off at Turn One and crash.

Another contemporary development was back in the spotlight, after both Vinales and Alex Marquez retired with ride-height device malfunctions. The system was due to be outlawed from 2023, but Aleix Espargaro was one who didn't want to wait until then: "I would ban it tomorrow, even if my one works very well and I like it. The bike accelerates better, but if everybody removed them, the bikes would accelerate at the same level for everyone. I think we'd have more overtakes because we will make more wheelie and more mistakes in acceleration."

Vinales's best Aprilia race so far was abruptly curtailed: "I was one-tenth from Aleix, going to attack, and then I start to feel the bike a little bit more down and starting to chatter. Then all of a sudden, boom, down! I felt my foot on the ground. I thought I had a flat tyre, because I nearly highsided." Showing a change in mentality, he pitted without any sign of temperament.

As usual, tyres were under fire, with Pol Espargaro blaming his FP1 crash on an unpredictable tyre that had already been through one heating cycle, without having been used. Michelin explained that such tyres were "those allocated to a rider during the weekend, and which were heated by the team in anticipation of using them, but subsequently not used. These tyres were then returned to Michelin and are reallocated to that same rider at a later date.

"It is not responsible or sustainable to scrap new/unused tyres. The teams only receive the preheated tyres that they heated themselves," said a representative. "Therefore, those riders/teams that manage their allocation well, and do not heat too many tyres, will receive fewer preheated tyres at fu-

ture races. As the teams are responsible for managing their own tyre allocation, they know exactly how long the tyres have been heated for, and to what temperature."

Jack Miller was now free to speak about his new deal with KTM. He cited as indispensible his good relations with Aki Ajo, his personal manager and a key figure for the Austrian factory, and team manager Francesco Guidotti, formerly his crew chief at Pramac Ducati. Likewise, the lure of a two-year contract as a reason. In five years at Ducati, he had only ever had one-year deals.

Again, Ducati extended their deadline for deciding on his replacement in the factory team for 2023, still between Martin and Bastianini, scotching rumours that Joan Mir was a candidate. Sporting director Paolo Ciabatti also confirmed that the factory was close to confirming an extension for Johann Zarco at Pramac for 2023.

Other rumours swirled around the new RNF Aprilia team, with up to six names in the ring. They included Oliveira, whose expected move to Gresini hit a snag over his personal sponsor, Hyundai (Ducati is owned by Audi). Rins, Fernandez, Gardner, Binder and Vietti were also mentioned as possible signings to Aprilia's new satellite team. "There are so many riders in the market right now, we can afford to wait," said team owner Razlan Razali, who added that he saw little point in looking outside MotoGP. But ruling out Vietti came as a surprise to exasperated Aprilia CEO Massimo Rivola: "Did Razlan say that? Then I need to speak to him!"

Aron Canet was struggling with an uncomfortable and unusual problem. He had suffered facial injuries in a road accident during the break after the previous race and was stricken with persistent nose-bleeds whenever he rode – hardly stemmed by wads of cotton wool, and severely hampering his progress.

MOTOGP RACE – 30 laps

Once again, Di Giannantonio led Q1, Bezzecchi coming through with him, and the battered Pol Espargaro out by four-thousandths; but it was Bagnaia's factory Ducati on a third pole of the season, with Quartararo and Zarco alongside. Aleix Espargaro led row two from Di Giannantonio and Jack

Above: **Luca Marini leads Brad Binder in their lively scrap. The Italian would escape for fifth.**

Top right: **Izan Guevara hit the front running to break the Moto3 field.**
Photos: Gold & Goose

Above right and far right: **Jack Miller enjoyed his podium after overcoming a long-lap penalty.**
Photos: Ducati Corse

Centre right: **Moto3 muddle at Turn One. Riccardo Rossi crashes out, forcing McPhee and Tatay off track and into the gravel.**

Right: **Moto2 winner Augusto Fernandez heads Lowes (22), Schrotter (23), Acosta (51) and Arenas (75).**
Photos: Gold & Goose

Miller, but the Australian faced a long-lap penalty after falling at the bottom of the hill where yellow flags were still being shown for Aleix Espargaro's earlier tumble.

A sell-out crowd of more than 95,000, baking in stifling 35-degree heat, watched Quartararo make it look easy. At first, it had appeared to be a two-rider slog, Bagnaia slotted behind the Yamaha, with intentions of playing the long game over 30 laps. He had the hard rear tyre; Quartararo (along with only Pol Espargaro and Vinales) had risked the soft.

But in a sight all too common in 2022, Bagnaia's challenge wilted just four laps in. A slow crash at the first corner not only ended the victory contest, but also might well have condemned Ducati to another year in which the riders' title remained elusive.

Especially given Quartararo's form. Shrugging off a head cold, he had it all wrapped up with barely a third of the distance gone, finishing just under five seconds clear of new top Ducati rider Zarco for a second French one-two of the year. He had now led every one of the last 54 laps of racing.

He overhauled pole-sitter Bagnaia on the run to Turn One, but the Ducati swarmed all over him in the early exchanges. Behind, Aleix Espargaro took third from Zarco at Turn One, with Di Giannantonio heading Miller in fifth. For once, Vinales was in the mood early on, nabbing seventh from Marini at the final turn.

Lap two was busy. First Bagnaia lunged under Quartararo at Turn One, but the reigning champion held a tight line to regain the lead into Turn Two. Then Miller took fifth from Di Giannantonio at Turn Eight, while Zarco produced the move of the race at the downhill Turn 11, running inside Espargaro's Aprilia at the apex. And Vinales gained another place at the final turn, this time from Di Giannantonio.

Next time around, Quartararo's fastest lap gained him better than half a second, but Bagnaia was banking on his hard tyre playing in his favour: "I was planning to close the gap later on." Instead, he crashed out on the next lap. He was unable to explain why, and it was scant consolation that Mir also fell there immediately behind him, from 13th.

Zarco was clear in second, with Espargaro convinced he had a duff front tyre. "I went into the grid with a used tyre, the bike was okay. As soon as I put in the new one, I arrived at T1 and the bike started to vibrate," he explained. From there, it was damage limitation, defending first from team-mate Vinales, before Miller joined after his long-lap had dropped him from fourth to seventh. He quickly recovered, passing first Martin, then Di Giannantonio. Then he gained another place as Vinales slowed before retiring, his rear ride height collapsed.

Now Miller began pressing. First, he showed his hand at Turn One on lap 23, only to run wide. The Aprilia did the same five laps later, leaving the Australian clear in third, three seconds behind Zarco.

An entertaining four-way scrap for fifth had Di Giannantonio, Martin, Marini and Brad Binder swapping through the middle third of the race. Marini prevailed, with classy moves on Di Giannantonio, then Martin on laps 21 and 23. After that, he was the fastest rider on track, and even threatened to reel in Miller and Espargaro, less than two seconds ahead.

Martin was sixth, relieved to notch up a third straight finish. Binder worked more miracles for KTM, qualifying 15th, but holding Di Giannantonio at bay for seventh – the Italian's first top-ten,

Oliveira was nowhere near; then Bastianini a subdued tenth, suffering the absence of his crew chief through Covid. The next three – Bezzecchi, Fernandez, Morbidelli – were spaced out, then veteran Dovizioso narrowly held off rookie Gardner for the final points, Bradl another 20 seconds away.

Darryn Binder fell early on at the last corner, remounting to retire; Marquez had dropped to last with ride-height adjustment failure, retiring after six laps; Nakagami crashed out of the top ten at the fast Turn Eight on the seventh; Pol Espargaro battled on for 22 laps before succumbing to pain and breathing problems.

MOTO2 RACE – 28 laps

Lowes claimed a first pole of the year alongside Arenas, in his career first front row. Fernandez was third; Dixon led the second row from Schrotter and Canet. Vietti had to come through from Q1 and was eighth. It goes without saying at this track that the times were close, the top 16 all inside one second.

The race results would be similarly mixed up. Fernandez's dominant victory, his second of the year, reinforced his mid-

season arrival as a serious title contender after a few false starts; while Vietti's lead shrank once again after he crashed out of 11th. Likewise, Ogura (eighth) and the struggling Canet (ninth) faced disappointment.

Lowes got the jump to lead the opening five laps, with home hero Schrotter, Arenas and Fernandez close behind. Yet once Fernandez made a neat move on the Englishman on the sixth lap, there was no turning back.

At the same time, Acosta added spice to the fight as he joined in from 11th on the grid. He rapidly picked off Arenas, and on lap eight also Schrotter. Now, with Lowes losing touch with the leader, the rookie started to close.

On lap 15, Lowes hit a neutral, giving Acosta the chance to get ahead for the first time.

He was not the only newbie enjoying the tight bends. Aldeguer, qualified 13th, had been making his way forward in the top ten for the first half of the race, following Canet, who had been slow away to finish lap one tenth. Aldeguer had taken a few more laps to pass Arbolino and Roberts, but just after half-distance, he was on Canet's back wheel again, and on lap 16 ahead of him and setting about Arenas.

Schrotter took third from Lowes at Turn One on the penultimate lap, only for the Brit to respond 11 corners on. Then Lowes lined up Acosta on the run to the race's final turn, but shut the throttle when they made contact, and the Spaniard retained second. Schrotter and Aldeguer were right behind, and the latter hung on to fifth in spite of a post-race three-second penalty for exceeding track limits.

Arenas was sixth; then a gang of four, with Lopez just clear of Ogura, Canet and Arbolino, the trio over the line inside two-tenths of a second.

Dixon was eventually 11th, having regained the place on the final lap from Gonzalez after a protracted scrap. Americans Roberts and Beaubier were out of touch behind, with Chantra taking the final point.

Vietti had dropped to 13th and was battling with Dixon when he crashed out; Navarro, Antonelli and Kubo also fell. Vietti still led overall in spite of failing to score, but by only eight points from Ogura, with Fernandez now closing impressively, another four points away.

MOTO3 RACE – 27 laps

In the past, Moto3 races at the Sachsenring had followed the usual pattern, with big groups disputing the lead. This time, Guevara changed the rules with a start-to-finish runaway win by almost five seconds.

He led away from pole, and controlled the early exchanges from the front of an eight-rider group that included teammates Foggia and Suzuki, his own stablemate Garcia and Sasaki. It had been led for a couple of laps by exciteable rookie Holgado.

But from lap six, the outcome was all but decided. By then, Guevara had edged a half-second clear of Foggia and the rest. The margin stretched steadily, with Guevara coming home 4.8 seconds clear, annihilating the previous race record by 11.9 seconds.

His speed stretched the pursuit. Foggia, Garcia and Sasaki circulated together until the end, with Foggia faultless until the flag. Not even a late dive at the final corner by Garcia could catch him out – the Italian regained the advantage on the cutback to secure second, and a first podium since Austin. Garcia was third, with Sasaki a second back in fourth, a heroic return after his horrendous fall at Mugello. Suzuki was a lonely fifth, three seconds back, while Holgado faded to sixth, just ahead of Deniz Oncu, who had recovered well from a double long-lap penalty for jumping the start from 24th on the grid.

Fernandez was close; Munoz and Ortola led Migno and Masia some seven seconds adrift. Rookies Ogden and Kelso were among five fallers, both in the top ten at the time.

At the halfway point, Guevara had closed to within seven points of Garcia; with Foggia 51 points behind the leader.

FIM WORLD CHAMPIONSHIP: ROUND 10

LIQUI MOLY MOTORRAD GRAND PRIX DEUTSCHLAND

17–19 JUNE, 2022

SACHSENRING GP CIRCUIT

30 laps
Length: 3.700 km / 2.280 miles
Width: 12m

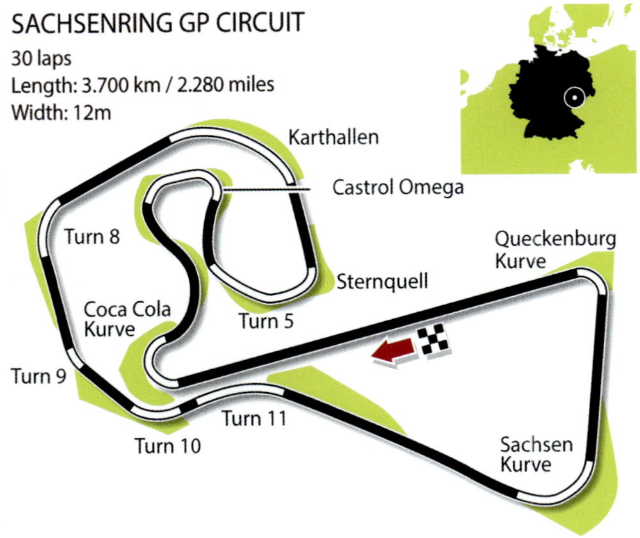

MotoGP

RACE DISTANCE: 30 laps, 68.432 miles/110.130km · RACE WEATHER: Dry (air 35°, humidity 22%, track 51°)

Pos.	Rider	Nat.	No.	Entrant	Machine	Tyres	Race tyre choice	Laps	Time & speed
1	**Fabio Quartararo**	FRA	20	Monster Energy Yamaha MotoGP	Yamaha YZR-M1	M	F: Hard/R: Medium	30	41m 12.816s 99.6mph/160.3km/h
2	**Johann Zarco**	FRA	5	Prima Pramac Racing	Ducati Desmosedici	M	F: Hard/R: Hard	30	41m 17.755s
3	**Jack Miller**	AUS	43	Ducati Lenovo Team	Ducati Desmosedici	M	F: Hard/R: Hard	30	41m 21.188s
4	**Aleix Espargaro**	SPA	41	Aprilia Racing	Aprilia RS-GP	M	F: Hard/R: Hard	30	41m 21.929s
5	**Luca Marini**	ITA	10	Mooney VR46 Racing Team	Ducati Desmosedici	M	F: Hard/R: Hard	30	41m 24.495s
6	**Jorge Martin**	SPA	89	Prima Pramac Racing	Ducati Desmosedici	M	F: Hard/R: Hard	30	41m 25.980s
7	**Brad Binder**	RSA	33	Red Bull KTM Factory Racing	KTM RC16	M	F: Hard/R: Hard	30	41m 28.221s
8	**Fabio Di Giannantonio**	ITA	49	Gresini Racing MotoGP	Ducati Desmosedici	M	F: Hard/R: Hard	30	41m 28.667s
9	**Miguel Oliveira**	POR	88	Red Bull KTM Factory Racing	KTM RC16	M	F: Hard/R: Hard	30	41m 32.556s
10	**Enea Bastianini**	ITA	23	Gresini Racing MotoGP	Ducati Desmosedici	M	F: Medium/R: Hard	30	41m 34.427s
11	**Marco Bezzecchi**	ITA	72	Mooney VR46 Racing Team	Ducati Desmosedici	M	F: Hard/R: Hard	30	41m 35.991s
12	**Raul Fernandez**	SPA	25	Tech3 KTM Factory Racing	KTM RC16	M	F: Hard/R: Hard	30	41m 39.364s
13	**Franco Morbidelli**	ITA	21	Monster Energy Yamaha MotoGP	Yamaha YZR-M1	M	F: Hard/R: Hard	30	41m 41.830s
14	**Andrea Dovizioso**	ITA	4	WithU Yamaha RNF MotoGP Team	Yamaha YZR-M1	M	F: Hard/R: Hard	30	41m 43.496s
15	**Remy Gardner**	AUS	87	Tech3 KTM Factory Racing	KTM RC16	M	F: Hard/R: Hard	30	41m 43.628s
16	Stefan Bradl	GER	6	Repsol Honda Team	Honda RC213V	M	F: Hard/R: Hard	30	42m 04.856s
	Pol Espargaro	SPA	44	Repsol Honda Team	Honda RC213V	M	F: Hard/R: Medium	22	DNF-physical
	Maverick Vinales	SPA	12	Aprilia Racing	Aprilia RS-GP	M	F: Hard/R: Medium	19	DNF-technical
	Takaaki Nakagami	JPN	30	LCR Honda IDEMITSU	Honda RC213V	M	F: Hard/R: Hard	6	DNF-crash
	Alex Marquez	SPA	73	LCR Honda CASTROL	Honda RC213V	M	F: Hard/R: Hard	6	DNF-technical
	Darryn Binder	RSA	40	WithU Yamaha RNF MotoGP Team	Yamaha YZR-M1	M	F: Hard/R: Hard	5	DNF-crash
	Francesco Bagnaia	ITA	63	Ducati Lenovo Team	Ducati Desmosedici	M	F: Hard/R: Hard	3	DNF-crash
	Joan Mir	SPA	36	Team SUZUKI ECSTAR	Suzuki GSX-RR	M	F: Hard/R: Hard	3	DNF-crash

Fastest lap: Fabio Quartararo, on lap 3, 1m 21.584s, 100.6mph/161.9km/h.

Lap record: Marc Marquez, 1m 21.228s, 101.0mph/162.6km/h (2019).

Event maximum speed: Jorge Martin, 189.0mph/304.2km/h (free practice).

Qualifying

Weather: Dry
Air Temp: 33° **Humidity:** 24%
Track Temp: 50°

1	Bagnaia	1m 19.931s
2	Quartararo	1m 20.007s
3	Zarco	1m 20.030s
4	A. Espargaro	1m 20.120s
5	Di Giannantonio	1m 20.128s
6	Miller	1m 20.150s
7	Marini	1m 20.168s
8	Martin	1m 20.219s
9	Vinales	1m 20.468s
10	Nakagami	1m 20.562s
11	Bezzecchi	1m 20.593s
12	Mir	1m 20.732s
	Q1	
13	P. Espargaro	1m 20.604s
14	Oliveira	1m 20.656s
15	B. Binder	1m 20.757s
16	A. Marquez	1m 20.888s
17	Bastianini	1m 20.905s
18	Bradl	1m 20.908s
19	Dovizioso	1m 20.965s
20	Morbidelli	1m 21.020s
21	Gardner	1m 21.089s
22	Fernandez	1m 21.322s
23	D. Binder	1m 21.322s

Fastest race laps

1	Quartararo	1m 21.584s
2	Zarco	1m 21.718s
3	Vinales	1m 21.770s
4	Miller	1m 21.865s
5	A. Espargaro	1m 21.938s
6	Bagnaia	1m 21.949s
7	B. Binder	1m 21.996s
8	Martin	1m 22.004s
9	Di Giannantonio	1m 22.005s
10	Marini	1m 22.039s
11	Oliveira	1m 22.183s
12	Nakagami	1m 22.335s
13	Bastianini	1m 22.363s
14	Fernandez	1m 22.376s
15	P. Espargaro	1m 22.380s
16	Morbidelli	1m 22.394s
17	Bezzecchi	1m 22.469s
18	Gardner	1m 22.469s
19	Dovizioso	1m 22.518s
20	Mir	1m 22.652s
21	Bradl	1m 23.190s
22	D. Binder	1m 23.230s
23	A. Marquez	1m 23.458s

Championship Points

1	Quartararo	172
2	A. Espargaro	138
3	Zarco	111
4	Bastianini	100
5	B. Binder	82
6	Bagnaia	81
7	Miller	81
8	Rins	69
9	Mir	69
10	Oliveira	64
11	Martin	61
12	M. Marquez	60
13	Marini	52
14	Vinales	46
15	P. Espargaro	40
16	Nakagami	38
17	Bezzecchi	35
18	A. Marquez	26
19	Morbidelli	25
20	Di Giannantonio	16
21	D. Binder	10
22	Dovizioso	10
23	Gardner	9
24	Fernandez	5

Constructor Points

1	Ducati	221
2	Yamaha	172
3	Aprilia	139
4	KTM	110
5	Suzuki	93
6	Honda	81

Grid Order	1	2	3	4	5	6	7	8	9	10	11	12	13	14	15	16	17	18	19	20	21	22	23	24	25	26	27	28	29	30	
63 BAGNAIA	20	20	20	20	20	20	20	20	20	20	20	20	20	20	20	20	20	20	20	20	20	20	20	20	20	20	20	20	20	20	1
20 QUARTARARO	63	63	63	5	5	5	5	5	5	5	5	5	5	5	5	5	5	5	5	5	5	5	5	5	5	5	5	5	5	5	2
5 ZARCO	41	5	5	41	41	41	41	41	41	41	41	41	41	41	41	41	41	41	41	41	41	41	41	41	41	41	41	43	43	43	3
41 A. ESPARGARO	5	41	41	43	12	12	12	12	12	12	12	12	12	12	12	12	12	43	43	43	43	43	43	43	43	43	43	41	41	41	4
49 DI GIANNANTONIO	49	43	43	12	49	49	49	49	49	49	49	43	43	43	43	43	43	12	49	49	89	89	10	10	10	10	10	10	10	10	5
43 MILLER	43	12	12	49	89	89	43	43	43	43	43	49	49	49	49	49	49	49	89	89	10	10	89	89	89	89	89	89	89	89	6
10 MARINI	12	49	49	89	43	43	89	89	89	89	89	89	89	89	89	89	89	89	10	10	49	33	33	33	33	33	33	33	33	33	7
89 MARTIN	10	10	89	33	33	33	33	33	33	33	33	10	10	10	10	10	10	10	33	33	33	49	49	49	49	49	49	49	49	49	8
12 VINALES	30	89	10	10	10	10	10	10	10	10	10	33	33	33	33	33	33	33	88	88	88	88	88	88	88	88	88	88	88	88	9
30 NAKAGAMI	89	30	33	30	30	30	44	44	88	88	88	88	88	88	88	88	88	88	12	23	23	23	23	23	23	23	23	23	23	23	10
72 BEZZECCHI	33	33	30	44	44	44	88	88	44	44	44	44	44	44	44	44	44	23	23	72	72	72	72	72	72	72	72	72	72	72	11
36 MIR	36	44	44	88	88	88	72	72	72	72	72	72	72	72	72	23	23	44	72	21	21	21	21	25	25	25	25	25	25	25	12
44 P. ESPARGARO	44	36	36	72	72	72	23	23	23	23	23	23	23	23	23	72	72	72	44	44	44	25	25	21	21	21	21	21	21	21	13
88 OLIVEIRA	88	88	88	4	23	23	4	4	4	4	4	4	4	21	21	21	21	21	21	25	25	87	87	87	87	87	4	4	4	4	14
33 B.BINDER	73	72	72	23	4	4	21	21	21	21	21	21	21	4	4	4	25	25	25	4	87	4	4	4	4	4	87	87	87	87	15
73 A. MARQUEZ	72	73	4	21	21	21	87	87	87	25	25	25	25	25	25	25	4	4	4	87	4	44	6	6	6	6	6	6	6	6	
23 BASTIANINI	21	4	23	87	87	87	25	25	25	87	87	87	87	87	87	87	87	87	87	6	6	6									
6 BRADL	4	21	73	73	25	25	6	6	6	6	6	6	6	6	6	6	6	6	6												
4 DOVIZIOSO	6	23	21	25	6	6																									
21 MORBIDELLI	25	6	40	6	73	73																									
87 GARDNER	23	40	6	40	40																										
25 FERNANDEZ	40	25	25																												
40 D.BINDER	87	87	87																												

40 Pit stop

Moto2

RACE DISTANCE: 28 laps, 63.870 miles/102.788km · RACE WEATHER: Dry (air 35°, humidity 22%, track 51°)

Pos.	Rider	Nat.	No.	Entrant	Machine	Laps	Time & Speed
1	**Augusto Fernandez**	SPA	37	Red Bull KTM Ajo	Kalex	28	39m 44.019s
							96.4mph/155.2km/h
2	**Pedro Acosta**	SPA	51	Red Bull KTM Ajo	Kalex	28	39m 51.723s
3	**Sam Lowes**	GBR	22	Elf Marc VDS Racing Team	Kalex	28	39m 51.863s
4	**Marcel Schrotter**	GER	23	Liqui Moly Intact GP	Kalex	28	39m 51.978s
5	**Fermin Aldeguer**	SPA	54	MB Conveyors Speed Up	Boscoscuro	28	39m 55.188s
6	**Albert Arenas**	SPA	75	GASGAS Aspar Team	Kalex	28	39m 55.654s
7	**Alonso Lopez**	SPA	21	MB Conveyors Speed Up	Boscoscuro	28	39m 56.824s
8	**Ai Ogura**	JPN	79	IDEMITSU Honda Team Asia	Kalex	28	39m 57.658s
9	**Aron Canet**	SPA	40	Flexbox HP40	Kalex	28	39m 57.783s
10	**Tony Arbolino**	ITA	14	Elf Marc VDS Racing Team	Kalex	28	39m 57.819s
11	**Jake Dixon**	GBR	96	GASGAS Aspar Team	Kalex	28	40m 02.572s
12	**Manuel Gonzalez**	SPA	18	Yamaha VR46 Master Camp Team	Kalex	28	40m 02.680s
13	**Joe Roberts**	USA	16	Italtrans Racing Team	Kalex	28	40m 05.808s
14	**Cameron Beaubier**	USA	6	American Racing	Kalex	28	40m 07.146s
15	**Somkiat Chantra**	THA	35	IDEMITSU Honda Team Asia	Kalex	28	40m 10.439s
16	Bo Bendsneyder	NED	64	Pertamina Mandalika SAG Team	Kalex	28	40m 12.625s
17	Sean Dylan Kelly	USA	4	American Racing	Kalex	28	40m 23.236s
18	Zonta van den Goorbergh	NED	84	RW Racing GP	Kalex	28	40m 30.448s
19	Alessandro Zaccone	ITA	61	Gresini Racing Moto2	Kalex	28	40m 30.804s
20	Jeremy Alcoba	SPA	52	Liqui Moly Intact GP	Kalex	28	40m 31.321s
21	Alex Toledo	SPA	55	Pertamina Mandalika SAG Team	Kalex	28	40m 40.085s
	Celestino Vietti	ITA	13	Mooney VR46 Racing Team	Kalex	21	DNF-crash
	Keminth Kubo	THA	81	Yamaha VR46 Master Camp Team	Kalex	20	DNF-crash
	Marcos Ramirez	SPA	42	MV Agusta Forward Racing	MV Agusta	19	DNF-ret in pit
	Filip Salac	CZE	12	Gresini Racing Moto2	Kalex	18	DNF-ret in pit
	Barry Baltus	BEL	7	RW Racing GP	Kalex	17	DNF-ret in pit
	Niccolo Antonelli	ITA	28	Mooney VR46 Racing Team	Kalex	10	DNF-crash
	Lorenzo Dalla Porta	ITA	19	Italtrans Racing Team	Kalex	10	DNF-ret in pit
	Simone Corsi	ITA	24	MV Agusta Forward Racing	MV Agusta	7	DNF-technical
	Jorge Navarro	SPA	9	Flexbox HP40	Kalex	3	DNF-crash

Fastest lap: Augusto Fernandez, on lap 4, 1m 24.331s, 97.4mph/156.7km/h.

Lap record: Remy Gardner, 1m 23.767s, 98.0mph/157.7km/h (2021).

Event maximum speed: Filip Salac, 160.1mph/257.7km/h (free practice).

Qualifying

Weather: Dry

Air: 34° **Humidity:** 24%

Track: 50°

1	Lowes	1m 23.493s
2	Arenas	1m 23.765s
3	Fernandez	1m 23.825s
4	Dixon	1m 23.897s
5	Schrotter	1m 23.913s
6	Canet	1m 23.973s
7	Arbolino	1m 24.091s
8	Vietti	1m 24.130s
9	Roberts	1m 24.134s
10	Beaubier	1m 24.222s
11	Acosta	1m 24.268s
12	Lopez	1m 24.314s
13	Aldeguer	1m 24.315s
14	Ogura	1m 24.318s
15	Dalla Porta	1m 24.334s
16	Salac	1m 24.344s
17	Gonzalez	1m 24.643s
18	Bendsneyder	1m 24.710s
	Q1	
19	Baltus	1m 24.189s
20	Navarro	1m 24.271s
21	Chantra	1m 24.492s
22	Ramirez	1m 24.526s
23	Kelly	1m 24.829s
24	V D Goorbergh	1m 24.938s
25	Corsi	1m 25.069s
26	Zaccone	1m 25.179s
27	Antonelli	1m 25.205s
28	Kubo	1m 25.490s
29	Toledo	1m 25.552s
30	Alcoba	1m 25.572s

Fastest race laps

1	Fernandez	1m 24.331s
2	Acosta	1m 24.501s
3	Schrotter	1m 24.534s
4	Canet	1m 24.555s
5	Arenas	1m 24.584s
6	Aldeguer	1m 24.649s
7	Lowes	1m 24.676s
8	Roberts	1m 24.689s
9	Dixon	1m 24.715s
10	Arbolino	1m 24.720s
11	Lopez	1m 24.819s
12	Ogura	1m 24.891s
13	Gonzalez	1m 24.955s
14	Dalla Porta	1m 24.992s
15	Vietti	1m 25.036s
16	Salac	1m 25.044s
17	Beaubier	1m 25.085s
18	Chantra	1m 25.103s
19	Baltus	1m 25.292s
20	Bendsneyder	1m 25.299s
21	Navarro	1m 25.589s
22	Alcoba	1m 25.748s
23	Zaccone	1m 25.774s
24	Corsi	1m 25.808s
25	Kelly	1m 25.835s
26	V D Goorbergh	1m 25.841s
27	Ramirez	1m 25.937s
28	Kubo	1m 26.021s
29	Antonelli	1m 26.045s
30	Toledo	1m 26.135s

Championship Points

1	Vietti	133
2	Ogura	125
3	Fernandez	121
4	Canet	116
5	Arbolino	95
6	Roberts	89
7	Schrotter	88
8	Acosta	75
9	Chantra	66
10	Dixon	60
11	Navarro	58
12	Lowes	51
13	Arenas	45
14	Bendsneyder	44
15	Beaubier	40
16	Aldeguer	32
17	Gonzalez	32
18	Alcoba	31
19	Lopez	25
20	Baltus	15
21	Dalla Porta	10
22	Manzi	9
23	Salac	8
24	Fenati	7
25	Rodrigo	6
26	Zaccone	6
27	Ramirez	5
28	Kubo	4
29	Kelly	3
30	Pasini	1

Constructor Points

1	Kalex	250
2	Boscoscuro	47
3	MV Agusta	5

Moto3

RACE DISTANCE: 27 laps, 61.588 miles/99.117km · RACE WEATHER: Dry (air 32°, humidity 27%, track 42°)

Pos.	Rider	Nat.	No.	Entrant	Machine	Laps	Time & Speed
1	**Izan Guevara**	SPA	28	GASGAS Aspar Team	GASGAS	27	39m 14.946
							94.1mph/151.5km/h
2	**Dennis Foggia**	ITA	7	Leopard Racing	Honda	27	39m 19.799s
3	**Sergio Garcia**	SPA	11	GASGAS Aspar Team	GASGAS	27	39m 19.910s
4	**Ayumu Sasaki**	JPN	71	Sterilgarda Husqvarna Max	Husqvarna	27	39m 20.887s
5	**Tatsuki Suzuki**	JPN	24	Leopard Racing	Honda	27	39m 24.027s
6	**Daniel Holgado**	SPA	96	Red Bull KTM Ajo	KTM	27	39m 27.772s
7	**Deniz Oncu**	TUR	53	Red Bull KTM Tech3	KTM	27	39m 28.372s
8	**Adrian Fernandez**	SPA	31	Red Bull KTM Tech3	KTM	27	39m 29.610s
9	**David Munoz**	SPA	44	BOE Motorsports	KTM	27	39m 36.001s
10	**Ivan Ortola**	SPA	48	Angeluss MTA Team	KTM	27	39m 36.218s
11	**Andrea Migno**	ITA	16	Rivacold Snipers Team	Honda	27	39m 36.398s
12	**Jaume Masia**	SPA	5	Red Bull KTM Ajo	KTM	27	39m 36.475s
13	**Xavier Artigas**	SPA	43	CFMOTO Racing PruestelGP	CFMOTO	27	39m 46.816s
14	**Elia Bartolini**	ITA	23	QJMotor Avintia Racing Team	KTM	27	39m 46.738s
15	**Stefano Nepa**	ITA	82	Angeluss MTA Team	KTM	27	39m 46.895s
16	Diogo Moreira	BRA	10	MT Helmets - MSI	KTM	27	39m 47.066s
17	Taiyo Furusato	JPN	72	Honda Team Asia	Honda	27	39m 47.174s
18	Lorenzo Fellon	FRA	20	SIC58 Squadra Corse	Honda	27	39m 47.267s
19	John McPhee	GBR	17	Sterilgarda Husqvarna Max	Husqvarna	27	40m 00.169s
20	Kaito Toba	JPN	27	CIP Green Power	KTM	27	40m 06.788s
21	Alberto Surra	ITA	67	Rivacold Snipers Team	Honda	27	40m 10.510s
22	Ana Carrasco	SPA	22	BOE Motorsports	KTM	27	40m 32.811s
23	Mario Aji	INA	64	Honda Team Asia	Honda	22	40m 02.478s
	Carlos Tatay	SPA	99	CFMOTO Racing PruestelGP	CFMOTO	17	DNF-crash
	Joshua Whatley	GBR	70	VisionTrack Racing Team	Honda	14	DNF-ret in pit
	Ryusei Yamanaka	JPN	6	MT Helmets - MSI	KTM	14	DNF-ret in pit
	Joel Kelso	AUS	66	CIP Green Power	KTM	9	DNF-crash
	Scott Ogden	GBR	19	VisionTrack Racing Team	Honda	4	DNF-crash
	Matteo Bertelle	ITA	18	QJMotor Avintia Racing Team	KTM	4	DNF-crash
	Riccardo Rossi	ITA	54	SIC58 Squadra Corse	Honda	0	DNF-crash

Fastest lap: Deniz Oncu, on lap 4, 1m 26.253s, 95.2mph/153.2km/h.

Lap record: Can Oncu, 1m 26.714s, 94.7mph/152.4km/h (2019).

Event maximum speed: Stefano Nepa, 134.7mph/216.8km/h (free practice).

Qualifying:

Weather: Dry

Air: 31° **Humidity:**25%

Track: 47°

1	Guevara	1m 25.869s
2	Foggia	1m 26.164s
3	Holgado	1m 26.189s
4	Sasaki	1m 26.299s
5	Suzuki	1m 26.325s
6	Yamanaka	1m 26.467s
7	Munoz	1m 26.617s
8	Garcia	1m 26.626s
9	Bertelle	1m 26.640s
10	Ogden	1m 26.645s
11	Kelso	1m 26.649s
12	Migno	1m 26.734s
13	McPhee	1m 26.751s
14	Fernandez	1m 26.759s
15	Rossi	1m 27.101s
16	Artigas	1m 27.256s
17	Tatay	1m 27.474s
18	Masia	No Time
	Q1	
19	Moreira	1m 27.192s
20	Furusato	1m 27.254s
21	Nepa	1m 27.418s
22	Fellon	1m 27.462s
23	Bartolini	1m 27.693s
24	Oncu	1m 28.001s
25	Surra	1m 28.019s
26	Ortola	1m 28.101s
27	Toba	1m 28.109s
28	Whatley	1m 28.114s
29	Aji	1m 28.186s
30	Carrasco	1m 29.017s

Fastest race laps

1	Oncu	1m 26.253s
2	Sasaki	1m 26.523s
3	Yamanaka	1m 26.535s
4	Holgado	1m 26.538s
5	Garcia	1m 26.608s
6	Guevara	1m 26.701s
7	Masia	1m 26.712s
8	Suzuki	1m 26.752s
9	Foggia	1m 26.800s
10	Kelso	1m 26.846s
11	Munoz	1m 26.878s
12	Ortola	1m 26.960s
13	Migno	1m 27.005s
14	Ogden	1m 27.025s
15	Bertelle	1m 27.055s
16	Fellon	1m 27.136s
17	Fernandez	1m 27.147s
18	Nepa	1m 27.266s
19	Bartolini	1m 27.272s
20	Artigas	1m 27.277s
21	Furusato	1m 27.292s
22	Moreira	1m 27.301s
23	Aji	1m 27.423s
24	Toba	1m 27.552s
25	McPhee	1m 27.803s
26	Tatay	1m 28.171s
27	Whatley	1m 28.353s
28	Surra	1m 28.427s
29	Carrasco	1m 28.756s

Championship Points

1	Garcia	166
2	Guevara	159
3	Foggia	115
4	Masia	107
5	Oncu	91
6	Sasaki	88
7	Suzuki	81
8	Migno	76
9	Tatay	62
10	Rossi	47
11	Artigas	46
12	Yamanaka	43
13	Toba	38
14	Holgado	38
15	Moreira	34
16	Munoz	32
17	Ortola	29
18	Fernandez	28
19	McPhee	24
20	Bartolini	23
21	Kelso	22
22	Bertelle	16
23	Ogden	16
24	Nepa	9
25	Aji	5
26	Fellon	5

Constructor Points

1	GASGAS	215
2	Honda	168
3	KTM	164
4	Husqvarna	108
5	CFMOTO	84

FIM WORLD CHAMPIONSHIP · ROUND 11

DUTCH TT

ASSEN CIRCUIT

SUOMY
Lenovo
Riello
VARGROUP
63
FRECCIAROSSA
Lenovo
FRECCIAROSSA
Lenovo
CARRERA
UnipolSai
Lenovo
Lenovo
MOTUL

Above: **Impact. 'Over-ambitious' Quartararo collides with Aleix Espargaro and falls.**

Top right: **Outcome. The Aprilia rider stayed on board to embark on an epic ride from 15th to fourth.**

Above right: **Consequence. Having remounted dead last, Quartararo crashed out terminally on lap 12.**

Right: **Rookie Bezzecchi claimed a first podium for Rossi's new team.**
Photos: Gold & Goose

Opening spread: **Focused and faultless, Bagnaia began a run of wins that ignited his title charge.**
Photo: Ducati Corse

THE last race before the longest-ever summer break provided welcome relief after the championship had seemed to be heading towards a predictable repeat. Fulfilling the 'Anything can happen, and usually does' mantra beloved of old-school commentators, Bagnaia and Quartararo traded roles.

While the Italian took masterly control from lights to flag, the Frenchman blundered and fell – twice. The second occasion, at the same Strubben hairpin, was terminal, leading to his first no-score of the year; the first had already triggered consequences, for the rider and for the man he nearly knocked off. That was Aleix Espargaro, punted into the gravel and only narrowly staying on board. He dropped from second to 15th, then embarked on the ride of the weekend, setting a new lap record on his way to the overtake of the season, possibly the decade. It was at the final Geert Timmer chicane, scene of much drama over the years, where he came from miles behind to swoop past both Brad Binder and Jack Miller in one go, seizing an epic fourth, a mere 1.3 seconds off the podium.

To add to Aprilia's delight, Espargaro's team-mate, Maverick Vinales, was third, by far his best finish of the season so far, and further proof – if any were needed – of the RSV's strength.

The other consequence was censure from the ever controversial stewards' panel, which imposed a long-lap penalty for (and this was a new one) being "overly ambitious". This was to be served when the circus returned to action at Silverstone in August.

Already facing serial criticism for inconsistency in punishing some riders and not others (notably Nakagami, who got away with a much more destructive example of being overly ambitious at Catalunya), panel chairman Freddie Spencer and his cohorts received a fresh blast, with both barrels.

A livid Quartararo took to Instagram, saying, "Now you can't try an overtake because they think you are too ambitious. From the beginning of the year, some riders made 'racing incident', but apparently mine was too dangerous. Congratulations to the stewards for the amazing job you are doing. Next time, I [won't] try any overtake."

Yamaha racing MD Lin Jarvis followed with a stern statement two days later: "We are disappointed to see the inequality with which penalties are applied by the FIM MotoGP Stewards panel." He questioned the whole process, saying that Yamaha "wanted to appeal the decision of the Stewards on Sunday at the Assen track, but this type of penalty is not open to discussion or appeal. We then wanted to raise the issue, as a matter of principle, with CAS [Court of Arbitration of Sport], but equally such a matter is not open to appeal." The regulations mean that the stewards' decisions are final. Another blow to the teams' and riders' shaken confidence in Spencer and his fellows.

There were other surprises for the 104,000 fans, who had returned in full strength. It had been difficult to foresee three Ducatis scrapping for the podium at a track that had been like kryptonite for the Desmosedici in years gone by; and that rookie Marco Bezzecchi would push Bagnaia hardest, in just his 11th premier-class race; likewise that Vinales would score third precisely one year on from when he had decided to prematurely end a doomed relationship with Yamaha.

Quartararo had just one no-pointer to regret; Bagnaia four, with three wins and three crashes over the previous six rounds. Having spent the days since Sachsenring attempting to understand what had gone wrong, his analysis was slightly unexpected: "Three times, I crashed this year ... the first in Quatar [where] I was pushing because I was behind. But at Le Mans and in Germany, in the same moment that I crashed, I had said, 'I will be more calm, breathe and then come back'. Maybe with our bike when you are not pushing the tyres, it's easier to crash. Maybe it's also concentration ... perhaps thinking to be more calm and to breathe is not a thing that helps me."

A few rider managers were still doing the rounds. Zarco's reward for acting as factory guinea pig – crucially placed top Ducati while the only rider to persist with the front ride-height device – was close to finalisation. He would stay with Pra-

mac with a factory bike. Alex Marquez had signed for Gresini Ducati, opening the way for Alex Rins to take his place at LCR Honda. The former hoped to revive his brief, but increasingly downbeat spell in the premier class; Rins rejected Gresini in favour of the chance of a factory bike. Oliveira was a step closer to joining the new RNF Aprilia team, Pol Espargaro the Tech3 KTM squad.

In the other direction, Yamaha's hopes that Superbike star Toprak Razgatlioglu might move to MotoGP remained on hold, after the reigning champion had completed his first R1 outing – 40 sweltering laps at Aragon before rain stopped play. The Turk had decided to stay in WorldSBK for 2023. Quartararo felt he was ready for MotoGP, although "of course, it is a totally different story ... it's a much more rigid bike, much more different to ride." The Turk's manager, Kenan Sofuoglu, was in Assen and didn't mince his words. Yamaha had been speaking about Toprak joining the B-team. "I told them we are never interested in a B-team. Only an official factory team. Without that, we are not interested."

Honda's ill fortune continued, with a week being too short for Pol Espargaro's ribs to heal after his Sachsenring spill. He rode on the first day in pain through the many fast changes of direction, but awoke on Saturday realising that he couldn't carry on: "The injury got worse. When I woke up, I struggled to walk, to breath. But it's more painful to hear the bikes on the track without me than the pain in my body."

Compatriot Aron Canet was stricken in a different way, forced to withdraw from Moto2 on Saturday after overnight hospital treatment to try to staunch the persistent nosebleed that had troubled him in Germany actually made it worse. He was quickest on Friday morning, but unable to complete a single timed lap on Saturday morning because of copious bleeding from the burst capillary.

MOTOGP RACE – 26 laps

Qualifying predicted a two-rider race as Bagnaia and Quartararo traded places and fastest laps, smashing the all-time record. The Italian ended up on top, by just over a tenth, his fourth pole of the year.

With Martin third, Bezzecchi leading row two from Aleix Espargaro and Miller, and Zarco heading row three, Ducatis crowded out five of the top seven times, all inside seven-tenths. In stark contrast, the next best Yamaha was Dovizioso's in 17th, 1.4 seconds down, with Morbidelli and Binder 20th and 24th.

Bagnaia got the jump, Espargaro second, after Quartararo ran a little wide at Turn One. Martin also got past.

Having led every lap of the previous two outings, Quartararo was keen to continue. By Turn Five, he was back to second with quick-fire moves on Martin (Turn Four) and Espargaro (Turn Five). But Espargaro promptly retaliated with a gutsy move at the very fast Ruskenhoek.

Bagnaia had eked out nine-tenths on the first lap, a contrast to the pursuit pack, which included Bezzecchi, Miller, Binder, Nakagami and (at last) also Vinales, all swarming behind Martin.

It was settling to be a three-way classic, as Espargaro and Quartararo exchanged fastest laps on the second and third. Four-tenths covered the trio as they began that fateful fifth lap. Then Quartararo suffered a rare error of judgement. Or, if Espargaro was to be believed, overconfidence: "I was very strong in that place and Fabio knew it." As the Yamaha man fired his M1 under at the Strubben hairpin, Espargaro attempted to defend: "I closed the line like him and we collided." Quartararo was down, Espargaro in the gravel, and Bagnaia now clear by a full second. "A stupid mistake," the reigning champion conceded.

Race done? Far from it. Bezzecchi had deposed Martin on lap three and now was the principle challenger in second. Binder was fourth, ahead of Vinales, Nakagami and Miller, who had served a long-lap penalty on the fourth lap for another qualifying misdemeanour.

Above: **Vinales – here leading Brad Binder, Miller and Nakagami – showed he'd bonded with the Aprilia.**

Top right: **Bezzecchi's podium, in only his 11th MotoGP race, was evidence of precocious potential.**

Above right: **What a difference a year made for Vinales.**

Above far right: **Self-styled 'Crazy Boy' Ayumu Sasaki, back from injury, claimed a first Moto3 win.**

Right: **Moto2 title battle shapes up as Augusto Fernandez holds off the challenging Ai Ogura.**

Photos: Gold & Goose

For eight laps, Bagnaia couldn't build on his advantage, partly due to fears of repeating the mistake of the previous weekend. "I was trying to manage the gap," he explained. "I didn't need to be on the limit."

Meanwhile, Espargaro had rejoined in 15th, Quartararo in 24th. The former eschewed the safe option of picking up a handful of points: "In that moment, I said, 'Your race is done. Nothing will change if you score two or three points, doesn't matter. Today is the day you have to prove you are fast.'" By the 11th lap, he had already recovered four places. The best was yet to come.

Quartararo would face further ignominy, however. He had pitted, intending to retire, but his crew, thinking that a rain shower might disrupt proceedings, sent him out again – only to high-side out of Strubben on lap 12, a traction control sensor having come loose in the previous fall.

The Yamaha crew weren't entirely wrong. A personal best lap on the 12th extended Bagnaia's lead to 1.5 seconds, and he appeared unbreakable – until a light shower of rain on lap 17. That brought Bezzecchi back into it, soon barely a second down.

But Bagnaia upped his pace once more for a third win, rekindling hopes of a championship comeback. Bezzecchi was an astounding second, commending his crew chief's insistence on running Michelin's soft rear compound – Miller was the only other top-ten man to use it.

The late drama lay elsewhere. Martin was spooked by the rain and dropped behind Vinales, Binder and Miller in short order. Miller had the best pace and dispensed with Binder at Turn One on lap 21. Soon he was all over Vinales, but his attack at the chicane on the penultimate lap resulted in him running wide and losing vital ground. From there, Vinales brought it home.

Aprilia's day was about to get better. Espargaro had been cutting through the top ten with brutal efficiency, moving by Mir and Zarco with bold moves at Hoge Heide and then the chicane on lap 16 to sit eighth. He passed Oliveira two laps later for seventh, before doing Martin at the chicane on the penultimate lap. Then, as Binder moved under Miller at the same spot on the final lap, Espargaro decided to outbrake both in a heroic move. Binder was full of admiration, Miller was resigned, after being pushed off track: "I copped a handlebar to the elbow. I wasn't expecting it. That was my fault."

Mir got eighth from Oliveira late on, with Rins tenth; Bastianini was a second behind; then Nakagami, Zarco, Di Giannantonio and Marquez spaced out to complete the points. The only change in the latter part of the race had been when Dovizioso had taken a distant 16th off Marini on the last lap.

Morbidelli's dire season continued, with a long-lap penalty, then a double long-lap for not taking the first in timely manner, and finally a crash. Darryn Binder also crashed out.

Quartararo's points lead was trimmed to 21 over Espargaro; Bagnaia closed on Zarco for third.

MOTO2 RACE – 24 laps

Canet's withdrawal had a clear impact on the race and on an increasingly tense title fight, while compatriot Augusto Fernandez showed he was the comeback man of Moto2, fighting through to a second straight victory that drew him level at the head of the points.

Dixon took a second pole of the season, heading a somewhat unexpected Arenas and his own compatriot, Lowes, on the front row. Ogura led the second from Lopez and Navarro, through from Q1. Home hopes rested on Bendsneyder, eighth behind Roberts and ahead of Fernandez; van den Goorbergh was down in 21st.

Lowes's hopes of redemption faded at the first corner, af-

ter a false neutral sent him out on to the run-off, rejoining down in 26th. He'd gained only one place when the same shifting problem triggered a seventh race crash on lap four.

Dixon took a flyer off the line, but a bold move at Stekkenwal allowed Lopez to seize a lead he would hold for the next seven laps. On the second, Ogura, in fourth, narrowly stayed on board after a near high-side at Mandeveen, and on the next lap, another slip dropped him to 15th, three places behind title leader Vietti, languishing after qualifying 11th.

In their absence, a thriller ensued. Behind Lopez, teammates Dixon and Arenas squabbled among a lead group of nine riders that also included Fernandez, Schrotter, Bendsneyder and Beaubier, who had charged through from 18th on the grid.

Schrotter hit the front on lap eight, but lasted just over three laps before crashing out at the Strubben. Arenas briefly took over at the head of the group, but Fernandez was biding his time and grabbed the initiative from his compatriot with eight laps to spare.

By then, Vietti had towed Ogura towards the lead fight, and the pair carved their way through to challenge for the podium places.

Ogura was stronger, taking fourth off Beaubier on lap 20. The American crashed out next time around, while Ogura disposed of Dixon and Arenas to take second.

Fernandez couldn't be caught, crossing the line just over half a second clear of the Japanese rider. Dixon recovered to third after Arenas crashed out on the penultimate lap, with Vietti fourth. Seven-tenths covered the lead quartet at the flag. Bendsneyder was fifth, a second back, with Lopez another four seconds away, busily holding off Arbolino for sixth.

Roberts led the next trio from Gonzalez and Salac, completing the top ten; Aldeguer was a lone 11th after a long-lap penalty for exceeding track limits; Navarro, Chantra, Alcoba and Baltus wrapped up the points. Antonelli's ghastly rookie season continued with another crash from near the back.

The title fight could hardly have been any tighter: Vietti and Fernandez just one point clear of Ogura, with the unfortunate Canet now 30 behind.

MOTO3 RACE – 22 laps

Thirty days previously, Ayumu Sasaki had suffered a broken collarbone among other injuries after being run over in a sickening crash at Mugello. At Assen, he followed a career second pole position with a brilliant maiden win.

The 21-year-old Japanese Husqvarna rider held off teammates Guevara and Garcia in a hectic eight-rider fight.

Guevara, runaway winner of the previous two races, led the majority of the race. At first, he was just clear of Sasaki, Suzuki, Masia and excitable rookie Munoz, while Foggia recovered from a long-lap penalty, served on lap ten for cutting the chicane.

Soon the pack grew bigger, as McPhee, Artigas and Garcia, from 18th on the grid and handicapped by top-speed issues, joined the lead group.

The moves came thick and fast, with Munoz on the very edge. Something had to give. First Foggia high-sided entering Turn Two after the rookie had pushed him wide in the turn before. Sasaki eventually deposed Guevara on lap 20 with a beautiful move at the Strubben.

Finally, Munoz took out Masia on the last lap, with McPhee following them both into the gravel. That left Sasaki clear to fend off late attacks from Suzuki and Guevara to win by three-tenths. Guevara got Suzuki into the chicane for second, while Garcia edged by to the line for third. Artigas was a close fifth. Ten seconds down, Holgado led Nepa, Yamanaka, Oncu, Toba, Rossi, Ortola and Fellon in a gaggle, sixth to 13th within 1.5 seconds.

Ogden was an early faller; Kelso had been in the lead group and started the final lap 13th, only for Fernandez to knock him off. The Australian suffered fractures to his right ankle and foot; the Spaniard earned a long-lap penalty.

TT ASSEN

26 laps
Length: 4.542km / 2.822 miles
Width: 14m

MotoGP

RACE DISTANCE: 26 laps, 73.379 miles/118.092km · RACE WEATHER: Dry (air 22°, humidity 59%, track 30°)

Pos.	Rider	Nat.	No.	Entrant	Machine	Tyres	Race tyre choice	Laps	Time & speed
1	**Francesco Bagnaia**	ITA	63	Ducati Lenovo Team	Ducati Desmosedici	M	F: Soft/R: Hard	26	40m 25.205s 108.9mph/175.2km/h
2	**Marco Bezzecchi**	ITA	72	Mooney VR46 Racing Team	Ducati Desmosedici	M	F: Medium/R: Soft	26	40m 25.649s
3	**Maverick Vinales**	SPA	12	Aprilia Racing	Aprilia RS-GP	M	F: Medium/R: Hard	26	40m 26.414s
4	**Aleix Espargaro**	SPA	41	Aprilia Racing	Aprilia RS-GP	M	F: Medium/R: Hard	26	40m 27.790s
5	**Brad Binder**	RSA	33	Red Bull KTM Factory Racing	KTM RC16	M	F: Medium/R: Hard	26	40m 27.926s
6	**Jack Miller**	AUS	43	Ducati Lenovo Team	Ducati Desmosedici	M	F: Soft/R: Soft	26	40m 28.250s
7	**Jorge Martin**	SPA	89	Prima Pramac Racing	Ducati Desmosedici	M	F: Medium/R: Hard	26	40m 29.545s
8	**Joan Mir**	SPA	36	Team SUZUKI ECSTAR	Suzuki GSX-RR	M	F: Medium/R: Hard	26	40m 33.390s
9	**Miguel Oliveira**	POR	88	Red Bull KTM Factory Racing	KTM RC16	M	F: Medium/R: Hard	26	40m 33.530s
10	**Alex Rins**	SPA	42	Team SUZUKI ECSTAR	Suzuki GSX-RR	M	F: Medium/R: Hard	26	40m 33.801s
11	**Enea Bastianini**	ITA	23	Gresini Racing MotoGP	Ducati Desmosedici	M	F: Soft/R: Soft	26	40m 34.988s
12	**Takaaki Nakagami**	JPN	30	LCR Honda IDEMITSU	Honda RC213V	M	F: Medium/R: Soft	26	40m 35.822s
13	**Johann Zarco**	FRA	5	Prima Pramac Racing	Ducati Desmosedici	M	F: Medium/R: Soft	26	40m 39.610s
14	**Fabio Di Giannantonio**	ITA	49	Gresini Racing MotoGP	Ducati Desmosedici	M	F: Soft/R: Soft	26	40m 42.886s
15	**Alex Marquez**	SPA	73	LCR Honda CASTROL	Honda RC213V	M	F: Medium/R: Soft	26	40m 51.071s
16	Andrea Dovizioso	ITA	4	WithU Yamaha RNF MotoGP Team	Yamaha YZR-M1	M	F: Medium/R: Hard	26	40m 54.916s
17	Luca Marini	ITA	10	Mooney VR46 Racing Team	Ducati Desmosedici	M	F: Medium/R: Hard	26	40m 55.501s
18	Stefan Bradl	GER	6	Repsol Honda Team	Honda RC213V	M	F: Medium/R: Soft	26	40m 57.430s
19	Remy Gardner	AUS	87	Tech3 KTM Factory Racing	KTM RC16	M	F: Medium/R: Hard	26	41m 00.152s
20	Lorenzo Savadori	ITA	32	Aprilia Racing	Aprilia RS-GP	M	F: Medium/R: Hard	26	41m 01.003s
	Raul Fernandez	SPA	25	Tech3 KTM Factory Racing	KTM RC16	M	F: Medium/R: Hard	18	DNF-physical
	Fabio Quartararo	FRA	20	Monster Energy Yamaha MotoGP	Yamaha YZR-M1	M	F: Medium/R: Hard	11	DNF-crash
	Darryn Binder	RSA	40	WithU Yamaha RNF MotoGP Team	Yamaha YZR-M1	M	F: Medium/R: Hard	8	DNF-crash
	Franco Morbidelli	ITA	21	Monster Energy Yamaha MotoGP	Yamaha YZR-M1	M	F: Medium/R: Hard	8	DNF-crash

Fastest lap: Aleix Espargaro, on lap 15, 1m 32.500s, 109.8mph/176.7km/h.

Lap record: Fabio Quartararo, 1m 32.869s, 109.4mph/176.0km/h (2021).

Event maximum speed: Enea Bastianini, 195.5mph/314.6km/h (free practice).

Qualifying

Weather: Dry
Air Temp: 21° **Humidity:** 73%
Track Temp: 29°

1	Bagnaia	1m 31.504s
2	Quartararo	1m 31.620s
3	Martin	1m 31.708s
4	Bezzecchi	1m 31.796s
5	A. Espargaro	1m 31.868s
6	Miller	1m 32.124s
7	Zarco	1m 32.175s
8	Oliveira	1m 32.272s
9	Rins	1m 32.307s
10	B. Binder	1m 32.367s
11	Vinales	1m 32.424s
12	Nakagami	1m 32.967s
	Q1	
13	Marini	1m 32.787s
14	Mir	1m 32.898s
15	Di Giannantonio	1m 32.912s
16	Bastianini	1m 33.005s
17	Dovizioso	1m 33.009s
18	Bradl	1m 33.029s
19	Gardner	1m 33.093s
20	Morbidelli	1m 33.096s
21	A. Marquez	1m 33.113s
22	Savadori	1m 33.467s
23	Fernandez	1m 33.652s
24	D. Binder	1m 33.998s

Fastest race laps

1	A. Espargaro	1m 32.500s
2	Quartararo	1m 32.603s
3	Bagnaia	1m 32.608s
4	Rins	1m 32.629s
5	Mir	1m 32.635s
6	Martin	1m 32.673s
7	Vinales	1m 32.688s
8	Bezzecchi	1m 32.689s
9	B. Binder	1m 32.694s
10	Miller	1m 32.769s
11	Nakagami	1m 32.862s
12	Zarco	1m 32.874s
13	Bastianini	1m 32.897s
14	Oliveira	1m 32.969s
15	Di Giannantonio	1m 33.057s
16	A. Marquez	1m 33.246s
17	Dovizioso	1m 33.582s
18	Bradl	1m 33.676s
19	D. Binder	1m 33.722s
20	Savadori	1m 33.727s
21	Gardner	1m 33.742s
22	Marini	1m 33.774s
23	Morbidelli	1m 33.999s
24	Fernandez	1m 34.068s

Championship Points

1	Quartararo	172
2	A. Espargaro	151
3	Zarco	114
4	Bagnaia	106
5	Bastianini	105
6	B. Binder	93
7	Miller	91
8	Mir	77
9	Rins	75
10	Oliveira	71
11	Martin	70
12	Vinales	62
13	M. Marquez	60
14	Bezzecchi	55
15	Marini	52
16	Nakagami	42
17	P. Espargaro	40
18	A. Marquez	27
19	Morbidelli	25
20	Di Giannantonio	18
21	D. Binder	10
22	Dovizioso	10
23	Gardner	9
24	Fernandez	5

Constructor Points

1	Ducati	246
2	Yamaha	172
3	Aprilia	155
4	KTM	121
5	Suzuki	101
6	Honda	85

Grid order	1	2	3	4	5	6	7	8	9	10	11	12	13	14	15	16	17	18	19	20	21	22	23	24	25	26	
63 BAGNAIA	63	63	63	63	63	63	63	63	63	63	63	63	63	63	63	63	63	63	63	63	63	63	63	63	63	63	1
20 QUARTARARO	41	41	41	41	72	72	72	72	72	72	72	72	72	72	72	72	72	72	72	72	72	72	72	72	72	72	2
89 MARTIN	20	20	20	20	89	89	89	89	89	89	89	89	89	89	89	89	12	12	12	12	12	12	12	12	12	12	3
72 BEZZECCHI	89	89	72	72	33	33	33	33	33	12	12	12	12	12	12	12	89	33	33	33	43	43	43	43	43	41	4
41 A. ESPARGARO	72	72	89	89	12	12	12	12	12	33	33	33	33	33	33	33	33	43	43	43	33	33	33	33	33	33	5
43 MILLER	43	43	43	33	30	30	30	43	43	43	43	43	43	43	43	43	43	89	89	89	89	89	89	89	41	43	6
5 ZARCO	33	33	33	12	43	43	43	30	30	30	30	30	30	30	30	88	88	41	41	41	41	41	41	41	89	89	7
88 OLIVEIRA	30	30	30	30	88	88	88	88	88	88	88	88	88	88	88	41	41	88	88	36	36	36	36	36	36	36	8
42 RINS	12	12	12	88	5	5	5	5	5	5	5	5	5	5	5	36	36	36	36	88	88	88	88	88	88	88	9
33 B.BINDER	88	88	88	43	49	49	49	49	36	36	36	36	36	36	36	5	42	42	42	42	42	42	42	42	42	42	10
12 VINALES	49	5	5	5	36	36	36	36	49	23	23	23	41	41	41	30	5	30	30	23	23	23	23	23	23	23	11
30 NAKAGAMI	5	49	49	49	23	23	23	23	23	49	41	41	23	42	42	42	30	23	23	30	30	30	30	30	30	30	12
10 MARINI	23	23	23	23	73	73	42	41	41	41	49	42	42	23	23	23	23	5	5	5	5	5	5	5	5	5	13
36 MIR	73	73	36	36	42	42	41	42	42	42	42	49	49	49	49	49	49	49	49	49	49	49	49	49	49	49	14
49 DI GIANNANTONIO	42	36	73	73	41	41	73	73	73	73	73	73	73	73	73	73	73	73	73	73	73	73	73	73	73	73	15
23 BASTIANINI	36	42	42	42	6	10	10	10	10	10	10	10	10	10	10	10	10	10	10	10	10	10	10	10	10	4	
4 DOVIZIOSO	6	6	6	6	10	6	6	6	6	6	6	6	6	6	6	6	6	6	6	6	6	6	4	4	4	10	
6 BRADL	10	10	10	10	40	40	40	40	4	4	87	87	87	4	4	4	4	4	4	4	4	4	6	6	6	6	
87 GARDNER	25	25	25	40	21	87	87	87	87	87	4	4	4	87	87	87	87	87	87	87	87	87	87	87	87	87	
21 MORBIDELLI	40	40	40	21	87	4	4	4	32	32	32	32	32	32	32	32	32	32	32	32	32	32	32	32	32	32	
73 A. MARQUEZ	21	21	21	87	4	25	25	32	25	25	25	25	25	25	25	25	25	25									
32 SAVADORI	32	4	87	4	25	32	32	25	20	*20*	*20*																
25 FERNANDEZ	4	87	4	25	32	21	21	20																			
40 D.BINDER	87	32	32	32	20	20	20	*21*																			

25 Pit stop *20 Lapped rider*

Moto2

RACE DISTANCE: 24 laps, 67.734 miles/109.008km · RACE WEATHER: Dry (air 21°, humidity 63%, track 30°)

Pos.	Rider	Nat.	No.	Entrant	Machine	Laps	Time & Speed
1	**Augusto Fernandez**	SPA	37	Red Bull KTM Ajo	Kalex	24	39m 07.133s 103.8mph/167.1km/h
2	**Ai Ogura**	JPN	79	IDEMITSU Honda Team Asia	Kalex	24	39m 07.793s
3	**Jake Dixon**	GBR	96	Inde GASGAS Aspar Team	Kalex	24	39m 07.858s
4	**Celestino Vietti**	ITA	13	Mooney VR46 Racing Team	Kalex	24	39m 07.891s
5	**Bo Bendsneyder**	NED	64	Pertamina Mandalika SAG Team	Kalex	24	39m 08.618s
6	**Alonso Lopez**	SPA	21	MB Conveyors Speed Up	Boscoscuro	24	39m 12.550s
7	**Tony Arbolino**	ITA	14	Elf Marc VDS Racing Team	Kalex	24	39m 12.686s
8	**Joe Roberts**	USA	16	Italtrans Racing Team	Kalex	24	39m 14.529s
9	**Manuel Gonzalez**	SPA	18	Yamaha VR46 Master Camp Team	Kalex	24	39m 14.722s
10	**Filip Salac**	CZE	12	Gresini Racing Moto2	Kalex	24	39m 14.824s
11	**Fermin Aldeguer**	SPA	54	MB Conveyors Speed Up	Boscoscuro	24	39m 16.455s
12	**Jorge Navarro**	SPA	9	Flexbox HP40	Kalex	24	39m 22.161s
13	**Somkiat Chantra**	THA	35	IDEMITSU Honda Team Asia	Kalex	24	39m 24.576s
14	**Jeremy Alcoba**	SPA	52	Liqui Moly Intact GP	Kalex	24	39m 26.321s
15	**Barry Baltus**	BEL	7	RW Racing GP	Kalex	24	39m 26.389s
16	Lorenzo Dalla Porta	ITA	19	Italtrans Racing Team	Kalex	24	39m 27.031s
17	Marcos Ramirez	SPA	42	MV Agusta Forward Racing	MV Agusta	24	39m 35.802s
18	Zonta van den Goorbergh	NED	84	RW Racing GP	Kalex	24	39m 35.920s
19	Sean Dylan Kelly	USA	4	American Racing	Kalex	24	39m 51.677s
20	Simone Corsi	ITA	24	MV Agusta Forward Racing	MV Agusta	24	39m 51.745s
21	Keminth Kubo	THA	81	Yamaha VR46 Master Camp Team	Kalex	24	39m 57.969s
22	Alex Toledo	SPA	55	Pertamina Mandalika SAG Team	Kalex	24	39m 58.142s
	Albert Arenas	SPA	75	Inde GASGAS Aspar Team	Kalex	22	DNF-crash
	Niccolo Antonelli	ITA	28	Mooney VR46 Racing Team	Kalex	22	DNF-crash
	Cameron Beaubier	USA	6	American Racing	Kalex	20	DNF-crash
	Alessandro Zaccone	ITA	61	Gresini Racing Moto2	Kalex	13	DNF-ret in pit
	Marcel Schrotter	GER	23	Liqui Moly Intact GP	Kalex	11	DNF-crash
	Sam Lowes	GBR	22	Elf Marc VDS Racing Team	Kalex	3	DNF-crash

Fastest lap: Celestino Vietti, on lap 24, 1m 36.729s, 105.0mph/169.0km/h.

Lap record: Raul Fernandez, 1m 36.690s, 105.1mph/169.1km/h (2021).

Event maximum speed: Ai Ogura, 163.2mph/262.6km/h (race).

Qualifying

Weather: Dry

Air: 21° **Humidity:** 71%

Track: 28°

Pos.	Rider	Time
1	Dixon	1m 36.736s
2	Arenas	1m 36.747s
3	Lowes	1m 36.767s
4	Ogura	1m 36.787s
5	Lopez	1m 36.842s
6	Navarro	1m 36.860s
7	Roberts	1m 36.884s
8	Bendsneyder	1m 36.919s
9	Fernandez	1m 36.967s
10	Schrotter	1m 37.028s
11	Vietti	1m 37.085s
12	Salac	1m 37.124s
13	Arbolino	1m 37.165s
14	Baltus	1m 37.283s
15	Gonzalez	1m 37.365s
16	Chantra	1m 37.444s
17	Zaccone	1m 37.452s
18	Beaubier	1m 37.532s
	Q1	
19	Dalla Porta	1m 37.342s
20	Aldeguer	1m 37.389s
21	V D Goorbergh	1m 37.742s
22	Ramirez	1m 37.759s
23	Alcoba	1m 37.761s
24	Kelly	1m 38.058s
25	Corsi	1m 38.150s
26	Toledo	1m 38.251s
27	Antonelli	1m 38.509s
28	Kubo	1m 38.861s

Fastest race laps

Pos.	Rider	Time
1	Vietti	1m 36.729s
2	Beaubier	1m 37.019s
3	Ogura	1m 37.049s
4	Dixon	1m 37.094s
5	Arenas	1m 37.125s
6	Bendsneyder	1m 37.132s
7	Arbolino	1m 37.171s
8	Schrotter	1m 37.180s
9	Fernandez	1m 37.244s
10	Salac	1m 37.288s
11	Lopez	1m 37.291s
12	Roberts	1m 37.379s
13	Gonzalez	1m 37.454s
14	Aldeguer	1m 37.457s
15	Chantra	1m 37.472s
16	Navarro	1m 37.525s
17	Baltus	1m 37.598s
18	Zaccone	1m 37.732s
19	Dalla Porta	1m 37.844s
20	Alcoba	1m 37.868s
21	Ramirez	1m 37.936s
22	V D Goorbergh	1m 38.153s
23	Lowes	1m 38.351s
24	Corsi	1m 38.644s
25	Toledo	1m 38.705s
26	Kelly	1m 38.784s
27	Antonelli	1m 38.830s
28	Kubo	1m 38.911s

Championship Points

Pos.	Rider	Points
1	Vietti	146
2	Fernandez	146
3	Ogura	145
4	Canet	116
5	Arbolino	104
6	Roberts	97
7	Schrotter	88
8	Dixon	76
9	Acosta	75
10	Chantra	69
11	Navarro	62
12	Bendsneyder	55
13	Lowes	51
14	Arenas	45
15	Beaubier	40
16	Gonzalez	39
17	Aldeguer	37
18	Lopez	35
19	Alcoba	33
20	Baltus	16
21	Salac	14
22	Dalla Porta	10
23	Manzi	9
24	Fenati	7
25	Rodrigo	6
26	Zaccone	6
27	Ramirez	5
28	Kubo	4
29	Kelly	3
30	Pasini	1

Constructor Points

Pos.	Constructor	Points
1	Kalex	275
2	Boscoscuro	57
3	MV Agusta	5

Moto3

RACE DISTANCE: 22 laps, 62.090 miles/99.924km · RACE WEATHER: Dry (air 20°, humidity 68%, track 27°)

Pos.	Rider	Nat.	No.	Entrant	Machine	Laps	Time & Speed
1	**Ayumu Sasaki**	JPN	71	Sterilgarda Husqvarna Max	Husqvarna	22	37m 28.371s 99.4mph/159.9km/h
2	**Izan Guevara**	SPA	28	GASGAS Aspar Team	GASGAS	22	37m 28.685s
3	**Sergio Garcia**	SPA	11	GASGAS Aspar Team	GASGAS	22	37m 28.763s
4	**Tatsuki Suzuki**	JPN	24	Leopard Racing	Honda	22	37m 28.770s
5	**Xavier Artigas**	SPA	43	CFMOTO Racing PruestelGP	CFMOTO	22	37m 29.032s
6	**Daniel Holgado**	SPA	96	Red Bull KTM Ajo	KTM	22	37m 39.911s
7	**Stefano Nepa**	ITA	82	Angeluss MTA Team	KTM	22	37m 39.977s
8	**Ryusei Yamanaka**	JPN	6	MT Helmets - MSI	KTM	22	37m 40.596s
9	**Deniz Oncu**	TUR	53	Red Bull KTM Tech3	KTM	22	37m 40.680s
10	**Kaito Toba**	JPN	27	CIP Green Power	KTM	22	37m 40.739s
11	**Riccardo Rossi**	ITA	54	SIC58 Squadra Corse	Honda	22	37m 40.967s
12	**Ivan Ortola**	SPA	48	Angeluss MTA Team	KTM	22	37m 41.249s
13	**Lorenzo Fellon**	FRA	20	SIC58 Squadra Corse	Honda	22	37m 41.347s
14	**Carlos Tatay**	SPA	99	CFMOTO Racing PruestelGP	CFMOTO	22	37m 46.274s
15	**Andrea Migno**	ITA	16	Rivacold Snipers Team	Honda	22	37m 49.286s
16	Diogo Moreira	BRA	10	MT Helmets - MSI	KTM	22	37m 58.977s
17	Alberto Surra	ITA	67	Rivacold Snipers Team	Honda	22	38m 05.790s
18	Mario Aji	INA	64	Honda Team Asia	Honda	22	38m 12.379s
19	Luca Lunetta	ITA	85	QJMotor Avintia Racing Team	KTM	22	38m 12.503s
20	Joshua Whatley	GBR	70	VisionTrack Racing Team	Honda	22	38m 12.506s
21	Taiyo Furusato	JPN	72	Honda Team Asia	Honda	22	38m 12.737s
22	Ana Carrasco	SPA	22	BOE Motorsports	KTM	22	38m 12.857s
	Jaume Masia	SPA	5	Red Bull KTM Ajo	KTM	21	DNF-crash
	David Munoz	SPA	44	BOE Motorsports	KTM	21	DNF-crash
	John McPhee	GBR	17	Sterilgarda Husqvarna Max	Husqvarna	21	DNF-crash
	Adrian Fernandez	SPA	31	Red Bull KTM Tech3	KTM	21	DNF-crash
	Joel Kelso	AUS	66	CIP Green Power	KTM	21	DNF-crash
	Dennis Foggia	ITA	7	Leopard Racing	Honda	17	DNF-crash
	Scott Ogden	GBR	19	VisionTrack Racing Team	Honda	5	DNF-crash
	Elia Bartolini	ITA	23	QJMotor Avintia Racing Team	KTM	4	DNF-crash

Fastest lap: John McPhee, on lap 13, 1m 41.190s, 100.4mph/161.5km/h.

Lap record: Pedro Acosta, 1m 41.618s, 100.0mph/160.9km/h (2021).

Event maximum speed: Dennis Foggia, 136.8mph/220.1km/h (race).

Qualifying:

Weather: Dry

Air: 24° **Humidity:** 57%

Track: 31°

Pos.	Rider	Time
1	Sasaki	1m 41.296s
2	Suzuki	1m 41.362s
3	Guevara	1m 41.502s
4	Munoz	1m 41.664s
5	Foggia	1m 41.765s
6	Masia	1m 41.811s
7	Fernandez	1m 41.995s
8	Fellon	1m 42.014s
9	Artigas	1m 42.032s
10	Kelso	1m 42.064s
11	McPhee	1m 42.121s
12	Holgado	1m 42.134s
13	Yamanaka	1m 42.177s
14	Nepa	1m 42.185s
15	Migno	1m 42.210s
16	Rossi	1m 42.279s
17	Oncu	1m 42.561s
18	Garcia	1m 42.687s
	Q1	
19	Moreira	1m 42.211s
20	Toba	1m 42.217s
21	Ortola	1m 42.389s
22	Bartolini	1m 42.569s
23	Tatay	1m 42.597s
24	Ogden	1m 42.609s
25	Surra	1m 43.304s
26	Furusato	1m 43.426s
27	Aji	1m 43.686s
28	Carrasco	1m 43.812s
29	Whatley	1m 43.915s
30	Lunetta	1m 44.077s

Fastest race laps

Pos.	Rider	Time
1	McPhee	1m 41.190s
2	Foggia	1m 41.202s
3	Suzuki	1m 41.283s
4	Munoz	1m 41.403s
5	Masia	1m 41.465s
6	Guevara	1m 41.493s
7	Sasaki	1m 41.497s
8	Yamanaka	1m 41.517s
9	Artigas	1m 41.549s
10	Garcia	1m 41.564s
11	Holgado	1m 41.567s
12	Oncu	1m 41.624s
13	Toba	1m 41.641s
14	Ortola	1m 41.648s
15	Rossi	1m 41.661s
16	Migno	1m 41.691s
17	Fernandez	1m 41.711s
18	Nepa	1m 41.711s
19	Kelso	1m 41.712s
20	Moreira	1m 41.776s
21	Tatay	1m 41.815s
22	Fellon	1m 41.876s
23	Bartolini	1m 42.040s
24	Surra	1m 42.060s
25	Ogden	1m 42.108s
26	Aji	1m 42.492s
27	Whatley	1m 42.966s
28	Furusato	1m 43.027s
29	Carrasco	1m 43.070s
30	Lunetta	1m 43.142s

Championship Points

Pos.	Rider	Points
1	Garcia	182
2	Guevara	179
3	Foggia	115
4	Sasaki	113
5	Masia	107
6	Oncu	98
7	Suzuki	94
8	Migno	77
9	Tatay	64
10	Artigas	57
11	Rossi	52
12	Yamanaka	51
13	Holgado	48
14	Toba	44
15	Moreira	34
16	Ortola	33
17	Munoz	32
18	Fernandez	28
19	McPhee	24
20	Bartolini	23
21	Kelso	22
22	Nepa	18
23	Bertelle	16
24	Ogden	16
25	Fellon	8
26	Aji	5

Constructor Points

Pos.	Constructor	Points
1	GASGAS	235
2	Honda	181
3	KTM	174
4	Husqvarna	133
5	CFMOTO	95

FIM WORLD CHAMPIONSHIP · ROUND 12

BRITISH GRAND PRIX

SILVERSTONE CIRCUIT

STER
ERGY

Above: **Close company mid-race as Bagnaia, Miller and Martin chase down Rins, followed by Quartararo and Vinales.**
Photo: Ducati Corse

Centre, from top: **Aleix Espargaro's weekend was painful and difficult; starting a trend – Ducati's 'stegosaurus' tail-fins; thank you and goodbye – Dovizioso announced his early departure; British Superbike rising star Rory Skinner made a creditable wild-card Moto2 debut.**

Far right: **Acrobatic Zarco took pole and the early lead – but it was short-lived.**
Photos: Gold & Goose

Opening spread: **In glorious sunshine, Zarco leads Quartararo, Vinales, Miller and the rest off the line.**
Photo: Monster Energy Yamaha

THE resumption of hostilities at a sun-soaked Silverstone, basking in a most unfamiliar heatwave, was mainly about the top three in the championship. Maverick Vinales's first front row and second successive podium on the Aprilia were an enjoyable sideshow, likewise the amusing 'stegosaurus' fins on a couple of Ducatis. The most important things happened to Quartararo, Aleix Espargaro and Bagnaia.

The last named's successive victory, first double of the year, moved him to third overall, displacing record-speed pole-qualifier Zarco, who led early on only to crash out. The nature of his win, achieved by metronomic consistency (his best lap was only 13th fastest) finally overshadowed a minor flurry in the wake of a drink-driving offence during the holiday – after dodging the issue before the race, he finally said, "I will celebrate with some drinks tonight ... then take a taxi".

More importantly, it cut the points deficit from 66 to 49, and with eight races remaining, four of which he had won the previous year, and with Quartararo's Yamaha appearing vulnerable in the heat, the Italian's prospects were looking considerably brighter.

Quartararo's problems multiplied after he served the long-lap penalty imposed after Assen. In itself, the cost of this was less than expected – 1.5 seconds or less, which should have been recoverable: he had won by more than 2.6 seconds in 2021. This minor inconvenience was thanks to the short loop's simple and friendly layout, and that Turn 14, where it was placed, was one of a series of slow corners. At Misano, a tighter and much less convenient long-lap loop covers two corners and seriously spoils the exit on to the fastest straight on the track, and can cost four or more seconds. This disparity led to yet more complaints about inconsistent penalties, joining the chorus questioning the difference between Quartararo's Dutch TT slip-up, and the much costlier and more dangerous Nakagami incident at Catalunya, which went unpunished.

But it dropped the title leader from second to fifth, and put him in the dirty air behind four Ducatis and a Suzuki. It was possible to pass the Italian bikes, as Rins proved when he forced through to lead six laps, only to drop back with a "not normal" loss of rear grip. But Quartararo simply couldn't manage it, also blaming an overheated rear tyre (rather than the usual front), and he dropped back to eighth.

He almost lost that to Espargaro on the last lap, but the failed overtake was the least of the current title runner-up's difficulties at the track where, in 2021, he had claimed Aprilia's first podium, and which obviously suited the Italian bikes. This was an agonising afternoon of courage and damage limitation. A huge high-side on Saturday had left him with painful foot injuries and barely able to walk – a heel fracture was found back in Spain on Monday. Losing only one point to Quartararo was a mercy.

Ducati's new rear winglets, two pairs at an angle on the seat back, caused plenty of talk, but had little effect on progress, according to Miller, who nonetheless used them for the race. So too did Bastianini, whose opinion was different – they helped somewhat with braking, he said. It was as much his canny racecraft and tyre preservation, however, that took him from 11th until almost half-distance to fourth at the finish. Most importantly, he had passed Martin (who had tried the stego-wings in practice, but raced without them) on the last lap. With Ducati's either/or decision deferred, this was a boost to his factory-team hopes. Ducati tail-fins, meanwhile, would soon be universal.

During the break, Andrea Dovizioso had announced that he would be quitting before the end of his contract with the RNF satellite Yamaha team, directly after the San Marino GP, his home race. The former 125 champion and twice 250, and thrice MotoGP runner-up had had enough, his hopes of getting back to speed on the Yamaha thoroughly dashed. Between his Honda debut and his Ducati glory years, Dovi had spent a year as team-mate to Cal Crutchlow in the satel-

lite Yamaha team, claiming six podiums and finishing fourth overall. In 2021, he had rejoined the now Malaysian-run satellite in place of the injured Morbidelli for the last five races, staying on for 2022 to replace the departed Rossi. But the bike proved anything but the friendly machine he had known before, particularly lacking in rear grip for acceleration, while he – now aged 36 – found himself unable "to reset the microchip in my brain". In 12 races, he had scored points only four times, and not one top-ten. Dovi, who in 343 starts so far over 22 years had never missed a race through injury, would be replaced for the last six rounds by former teammate and now Yamaha test rider Crutchlow.

Honda's grim season continued, with all four riders far from the race pace and none making it through from Q1 to Q2 – in 2021, Pol Espargaro had been on pole and finished third. Bradl was further hindered by a three-position grid penalty for riding slowly on the racing line in qualifying. Lead rider Pol spoke of a season that, after his single podium in Qatar, had gone "from paradise to hell in a couple of races", but he confirmed that at least he had signed for "another team" for the next two years. Everyone knew it was the KTM satellite squad, but he was not at liberty to confirm the name.

Moto3 champion Pedro Acosta was on hand, after missing the Dutch TT as a result of breaking his left femur while training on his motocross bike in the run-up to that race. His doctors in Spain had ruled him fit to ride, but the medical team at the track thought otherwise, and he remained *hors de combat*.

MOTOGP RACE – 20 laps

Zarco's second pole of the season was at record speed, denying Vinales a first Aprilia pole by a tenth. Miller made the front row a Ducati sandwich; Quartararo led the second from Bagnaia and the plucky Espargaro; while Bezzecchi and Bastianini – both through from Q1 – led the third from Martin.

Zarco got the jump into the first turn. Despite minimal testing over the weekend, all Ducatis opted for Michelin's hard rear in light of track temperatures exceeding 43 degrees. Crucially, Quartararo didn't follow suit.

Aggressive off the line, he tagged Vinales as he pushed his way into second, Miller and Bagnaia just behind. In a scrappy start, Bastianini was barged into Bezzecchi by Martin at Turn One, snapping off his left front wing and dropping him to 11th.

Rins followed an opposite trajectory, gaining six places to sit fifth, ahead of Vinales, an uncomfortable Aleix Espargaro and Martin. Mir and Oliveira were involved in the fun, in a gang of 11. For a handful of minutes, everyone tucked in line, following Zarco's high rhythm at the front. But soon the adventures began.

First, Rins nabbed fourth off Bagnaia at the Loop on lap three, before Martin edged past Espargaro for seventh. Then Quartararo took his much-anticipated long-lap penalty on the fourth. While he lost just a second to the leader, he fell three places to fifth, behind Bagnaia.

Then came the first big moment. Trail-braking into Vale on lap five, Zarco tucked the front, crashing out. "It's pretty hard to put all the things together," he said as his winless run stretched to 95.

Now Miller led briefly, until Rins pounced at Vale on lap six. From that point, it looked like the Suzuki man's race. He immediately gapped the factory Ducatis to the tune of almost half a second. It wouldn't last.

About now, Quartararo's challenge was blunted. Boxed in behind a group of bikes, his rear tyre gathered heat alarmingly. "When there's just one bike in front, it's okay," he said later, "but as soon as there is more than one, the rear tyre was so hot and we lost performance – just a nightmare." Fourth became fifth as Martin drafted past into Stowe, then sixth as Vinales did the same two laps later.

Now it was Bagnaia's turn to threaten. He outbraked Miller

Above: **A clinical move. With three laps remaining, Vinales takes second off Miller.**

Top right: **Midfield maelstrom as Aleix Espargaro fends off Oliveira, Bastianini and Binder.**

Above right: **Fernandez (Kalex) leans on long-time Moto2 leader Lopez's Boscoscuro before breaking the youngster's heart.**

Above centre right: **Jake Dixon pleased the home crowd with third.**

Above centre far right: **Back on top, Foggia can barely contain himself.**

Right: **Foggia keeps his Honda narrowly ahead of Masia (5), Oncu and the rest in a titanic struggle.**

Photos: Gold & Goose

cleanly at Stowe on lap seven for second, and steadily reeled in Rins as the Suzuki's rear tyre began to fade. He hit the front on lap 12 on the run to Stowe. Miller followed two laps later at Village. Just a second covered the Bagnaia/Miller/Rins/Martin/Vinales quintet.

Then Vinales came alive. The Catalan could hold tremendous speed through Farm, the scene of his team-mate's demise the previous day, allowing him to pounce a turn later at Village, with a series of brilliantly clinical moves that carried him from fifth to second in four breathless laps. First, he slid under Martin on lap 16, having tried there three laps before, only to lose the place again. On lap 17, he was by Rins, clearly struggling, and on lap 18, Miller was powerless to react as the Aprilia took second.

With Bagnaia six-tenths ahead, Vinales scented the chance of victory. He had annihilated the advantage as they exited Farm and dived into the lead at Village. But this pass lacked the earlier precision; Bagnaia's retaliation into The Loop was immediate. Then, two critical last-lap mistakes (missing the apex at both Copse and Stowe) allowed Bagnaia a fourth win of the year, Ducati's 200th podium.

Miller was always there, taking third barely a tenth behind.

Vinales wasn't the only late charger. Bastianini's ride was inspired, despite running with just one wing. Eleventh on lap nine, he scythed through the field, with rapid-fire moves on Espargaro and Mir (lap 14) putting him seventh (Mir tucked the front at Stowe soon after). Then he preyed on Quartararo (lap 16) and Rins (19), both struggling with rear tyre wear. And the best of them all was on Martin, picking his pocket for fourth at Brooklands, three turns from the chequered flag, and leaving him fuming.

Oliveira was a sterling sixth ahead of Rins, Quartararo was frustrated in eighth, while Aleix Espargaro was a heroic ninth, just clear of Bezzecchi in tenth. Only 6.6 seconds covered them, the second closest top ten in MotoGP history.

Binder was a second behind in 11th, ruing his medium/medium tyre choice in the heat. Marini, Nakagami and Pol Espargaro were close in his wake, while Morbidelli claimed the last point, comfortably clear of Dovizioso, Marquez and the rest.

MOTO2 RACE – 18 laps

The weekend could hardly have started worse for hopeful home hero Lowes, who had completed only two timed laps in Friday's FP1 when a big high-side dislocated his left shoulder. That ruled him out of this race and the next four races into the bargain, a fracture to his humerus being found the following week.

That left Dixon and wide-eyed wild-card debutant Skinner to carry the hopes of the home crowd, and the experienced Dixon obliged. He was fastest in free practice and claimed a second successive podium,

He could qualify no better than sixth, however, albeit only four-tenths adrift of rampant pole-man Fernandez. Roberts and Ogura completed the front row; Arenas and Vietti led the second.

Unusually the last race of the day, to oblige European TV schedules, this one was a thriller, just like Moto3 and MotoGP before it. Battle raged all the way to the last corner, where Fernandez finally took control of what until then had been a rather topsy-turvy championship with a third successive win, his fourth of the year, and fourth straight podium into the bargain.

Rather than his three principal title rivals, it was Boscoscuro-mounted class rookie Lopez, in his tenth Moto2 race, who provided the heartiest challenge. In an all-action start, he took early control with a neat second-lap move on first-lap leader Ogura, with Roberts, Fernandez, team-mates Arenas and Dixon, and Canet in hot pursuit. Erstwhile points leader Vietti dropped from ninth to 12th, serving a long-lap penalty for a practice-start infringement in FP2.

As Canet, Ogura and Fernandez scrapped for second, Lopez began edging clear. By lap 12, his lead exceeded one second for the first time, but at that point, Fernandez found his groove. Breaking clear of the tussle behind, he joined his compatriot up front with four laps to go.

He found a stubborn opponent, defending brilliantly, while the Boscoscuro chassis clearly worked well at this circuit. Lopez offered few chances to overtake. He started the final lap ahead, but Fernandez's brilliant late-braking move at

Brooklands was enough to break the younger rider's heart and seal a third straight win by a mere seven-hundredths of a second.

Behind, Dixon emerged from an intense scrap with Ogura and Canet to hunt down the leading pair. Posting his fastest lap on the final circuit, he closed to within six-tenths to clinch third.

Ogura regained fourth from Canet on the final lap; Vietti was a gallant sixth, having caught and passed the fading Roberts with two laps to go. The American was still comfortably clear of Navarro, Salac and Bendsneyder, all three of whom had passed Gonzalez in the closing stages.

Arbolino, Chantra, Alcoba and then, a couple of seconds down, Aldeguer wrapped up the points. Schrotter had been with the group, but crashed out on the penultimate lap. Arenas was another crash victim, chasing team-mate Dixon when he fell on lap 11.

In this way, Fernandez moved 13 points clear of Ogura, with Vietti still close and Canet not yet entirely out of it.

MOTO3 RACE – 17 laps

Brazilian rookie Moreira claimed a first pole position ahead of Guevara and Yamanaka, but a breathless Moto3 race played to experience instead, on a day that couldn't have gone any better for Foggia. He scored a crucial win, his first since March, while his two title rivals, Garcia and Guevara, were wiped out in separate incidents.

The margins were finer than ever. With five laps left, the top 15 were covered by 1.6 seconds, the first 21 by 3.3. Something had to give.

Soon they started falling from the lead fight. First, Sasaki rode into the back of Garcia at Village on lap 15; then Ortola took down Guevara at Stowe on the final lap. Somewhere amid the mayhem, main protagonist Suzuki also fell from the podium fight.

Despite his rivals' misfortune, no one could dispute Foggia's credentials here. He led most of the race and stayed calm after his first escape bid failed – he'd been half a second clear of Oncu, Masia and Sasaki on lap eight, only to start from zero four laps on.

Oncu began the final lap ahead, only for Foggia and Masia to draft by at Becketts, the Italian holding the Spaniard at bay to the end. There was still time for enthusiastic teen Munoz to crash out of third two corners from home, handing Oncu a well-deserved podium. Toba dive-bombed McPhee with two turns to go for fourth, a move that pushed the Scot wide, allowing Nepa and Moreira through to fifth and sixth.

FIM WORLD CHAMPIONSHIP: ROUND 12

MONSTER ENERGY BRITISH GRAND PRIX

5–7 AUGUST, 2022

SILVERSTONE GRAND PRIX CIRCUIT

20 laps
Length: 5.900km / 3.670 miles
Width: 15m

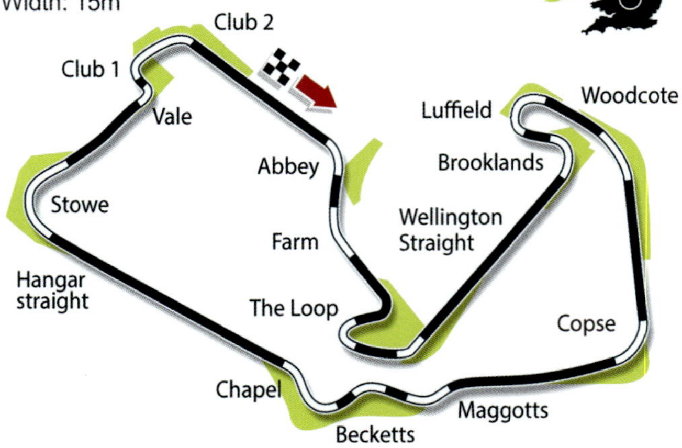

MotoGP

RACE DISTANCE: 20 laps, 73.322 miles/118.000km · RACE WEATHER: Dry (air 22°, humidity 46%, track 43°)

Pos.	Rider	Nat.	No.	Entrant	Machine	Tyres	Race tyre choice	Laps	Time & speed
1	**Francesco Bagnaia**	ITA	63	Ducati Lenovo Team	Ducati Desmosedici	M	F: Medium/R: Hard	20	40m 10.260s
									109.5mph/176.2km/h
2	**Maverick Vinales**	SPA	12	Aprilia Racing	Aprilia RS-GP	M	F: Medium/R: Hard	20	40m 10.686s
3	**Jack Miller**	AUS	43	Ducati Lenovo Team	Ducati Desmosedici	M	F: Soft/R: Hard	20	40m 10.874s
4	**Enea Bastianini**	ITA	23	Gresini Racing MotoGP	Ducati Desmosedici	M	F: Soft/R: Hard	20	40m 11.911s
5	**Jorge Martin**	SPA	89	Prima Pramac Racing	Ducati Desmosedici	M	F: Medium/R: Hard	20	40m 12.010s
6	**Miguel Oliveira**	POR	88	Red Bull KTM Factory Racing	KTM RC16	M	F: Medium/R: Hard	20	40m 12.987s
7	**Alex Rins**	SPA	42	Team SUZUKI ECSTAR	Suzuki GSX-RR	M	F: Medium/R: Hard	20	40m 13.281s
8	**Fabio Quartararo**	FRA	20	Monster Energy Yamaha MotoGP	Yamaha YZR-M1	M	F: Soft/R: Medium	20	40m 14.079s
9	**Aleix Espargaro**	SPA	41	Aprilia Racing	Aprilia RS-GP	M	F: Medium/R: Hard	20	40m 14.218s
10	**Marco Bezzecchi**	ITA	72	Mooney VR46 Racing Team	Ducati Desmosedici	M	F: Medium/R: Hard	20	40m 16.906s
11	**Brad Binder**	RSA	33	Red Bull KTM Factory Racing	KTM RC16	M	F: Medium/R: Medium	20	40m 17.990s
12	**Luca Marini**	ITA	10	Mooney VR46 Racing Team	Ducati Desmosedici	M	F: Medium/R: Hard	20	40m 23.699s
13	**Takaaki Nakagami**	JPN	30	LCR Honda IDEMITSU	Honda RC213V	M	F: Medium/R: Medium	20	40m 23.966s
14	**Pol Espargaro**	SPA	44	Repsol Honda Team	Honda RC213V	M	F: Medium/R: Medium	20	40m 24.166s
15	**Franco Morbidelli**	ITA	21	Monster Energy Yamaha MotoGP	Yamaha YZR-M1	M	F: Soft/R: Medium	20	40m 26.619s
16	Andrea Dovizioso	ITA	4	WithU Yamaha RNF MotoGP Team	Yamaha YZR-M1	M	F: Medium/R: Hard	20	40m 31.065s
17	Alex Marquez	SPA	73	LCR Honda CASTROL	Honda RC213V	M	F: Medium/R: Medium	20	40m 31.359s
18	Remy Gardner	AUS	87	Tech3 KTM Factory Racing	KTM RC16	M	F: Medium/R: Medium	20	40m 34.839s
19	Stefan Bradl	GER	6	Repsol Honda Team	Honda RC213V	M	F: Soft/R: Hard	20	40m 39.033s
20	Darryn Binder	RSA	40	WithU Yamaha RNF MotoGP Team	Yamaha YZR-M1	M	F: Medium/R: Medium	20	40m 43.913s
21	Raul Fernandez	SPA	25	Tech3 KTM Factory Racing	KTM RC16	M	F: Medium/R: Medium	20	40m 45.861s
22	Fabio Di Giannantonio	ITA	49	Gresini Racing MotoGP	Ducati Desmosedici	M	F: Soft/R: Hard	20	40m 46.720s
	Joan Mir	SPA	36	Team SUZUKI ECSTAR	Suzuki GSX-RR	M	F: Medium/R: Hard	14	DNF-crash
	Johann Zarco	FRA	5	Prima Pramac Racing	Ducati Desmosedici	M	F: Medium/R: Hard	8	DNF-crash

Fastest lap: Alex Rins, on lap 4, 1m 59.346s, 110.5mph/177.9km/h.

Lap record: Marc Marquez, 1m 59.936s, 110.0mph/177.0km/h (2019).

Event maximum speed: Enea Bastianini, 211.6mph/340.6km/h (qualifying).

Qualifying

Weather: Dry
Air Temp: 22° **Humidity:** 37%
Track Temp: 44°

1	Zarco	1m 57.767s
2	Vinales	1m 57.865s
3	Miller	1m 57.931s
4	Quartararo	1m 57.938s
5	Bagnaia	1m 57.961s
6	A. Espargaro	1m 57.966s
7	Bezzecchi	1m 58.101s
8	Bastianini	1m 58.106s
9	Martin	1m 58.174s
10	Marini	1m 58.317s
11	Rins	1m 58.318s
12	Mir	1m 58.543s
	Q1	
13	Oliveira	1m 58.853s
14	B. Binder	1m 58.932s
15	Di Giannantonio	1m 58.948s
16	Gardner	1m 59.120s
17	A. Marquez	1m 59.288s
18	Bradl	1m 59.339s
19	P. Espargaro	1m 59.367s
20	Morbidelli	1m 59.390s
21	Nakagami	1m 59.614s
22	Fernandez	1m 59.920s
23	D. Binder	1m 59.931s
24	Dovizioso	2m 00.232s

Fastest race laps

1	Rins	1m 59.346s
2	Martin	1m 59.498s
3	Zarco	1m 59.530s
4	Quartararo	1m 59.593s
5	Miller	1m 59.656s
6	Vinales	1m 59.674s
7	Bezzecchi	1m 59.744s
8	Mir	1m 59.781s
9	A. Espargaro	1m 59.857s
10	B. Binder	1m 59.867s
11	Bastianini	1m 59.878s
12	Gardner	1m 59.953s
13	Bagnaia	1m 59.956s
14	Oliveira	1m 59.956s
15	Marini	2m 00.237s
16	P. Espargaro	2m 00.335s
17	Morbidelli	2m 00.382s
18	Bradl	2m 00.434s
19	Nakagami	2m 00.436s
20	D. Binder	2m 00.582s
21	A. Marquez	2m 00.693s
22	Dovizioso	2m 00.826s
23	Fernandez	2m 01.067s
24	Di Giannantonio	2m 01.296s

Championship Points

1	Quartararo	180
2	A. Espargaro	158
3	Bagnaia	131
4	Bastianini	118
5	Zarco	114
6	Miller	107
7	B. Binder	98
8	Rins	84
9	Vinales	82
10	Oliveira	81
11	Martin	81
12	Mir	77
13	Bezzecchi	61
14	M. Marquez	60
15	Marini	56
16	Nakagami	45
17	P. Espargaro	42
18	A. Marquez	27
19	Morbidelli	26
20	Di Giannantonio	18
21	D. Binder	10
22	Dovizioso	10
23	Gardner	9
24	Fernandez	5

Constructor Points

1	Ducati	271
2	Yamaha	180
3	Aprilia	175
4	KTM	131
5	Suzuki	110
6	Honda	88

Grid order		1	2	3	4	5	6	7	8	9	10	11	12	13	14	15	16	17	18	19	20	
5	ZARCO	5	5	5	5	43	42	42	42	42	42	42	63	63	63	63	63	63	63	63	63	1
12	VINALES	20	20	20	43	42	43	63	63	63	63	63	42	42	43	43	43	43	12	12	12	2
43	MILLER	43	43	43	42	63	63	43	43	43	43	43	43	43	42	42	42	12	43	43	43	3
20	QUARTARARO	63	63	42	63	20	20	89	89	89	89	89	89	12	12	89	12	89	89	89	23	4
63	BAGNAIA	42	42	63	20	12	89	20	20	12	12	12	12	89	89	12	89	42	42	23	89	5
41	A. ESPARGARO	12	12	12	12	89	12	12	12	20	20	20	20	20	20	20	23	23	23	42	88	6
72	BEZZECCHI	41	41	89	89	41	41	41	36	36	36	36	36	36	36	23	20	20	20	88	42	7
23	BASTIANINI	36	36	41	41	36	36	36	41	41	41	41	41	41	23	41	88	88	88	20	20	8
89	MARTIN	89	89	36	36	88	88	88	88	88	88	88	88	23	41	88	41	41	41	41	41	9
10	MARINI	88	88	88	88	23	33	33	33	33	23	23	23	88	88	33	33	33	33	72	72	10
42	RINS	23	23	23	23	33	23	23	23	23	33	33	33	33	33	72	72	72	72	33	33	11
36	MIR	73	33	33	33	72	72	72	72	72	72	72	72	72	72	10	10	10	10	10	10	12
88	OLIVEIRA	33	73	87	72	87	21	21	21	21	10	10	10	10	10	21	21	21	21	30	30	13
33	B.BINDER	72	87	72	87	21	87	10	10	10	21	21	21	21	21	30	30	30	30	44	44	14
49	DI GIANNANTONIO	87	72	73	21	10	10	87	87	87	87	30	30	30	30	44	44	44	44	21	21	15
87	GARDNER	21	21	21	73	73	73	73	73	73	73	73	44	44	44	73	73	73	73	73	4	
73	A. MARQUEZ	10	10	10	10	30	30	30	30	30	30	44	73	73	73	87	87	87	87	4	73	
44	P. ESPARGARO	40	40	40	30	40	44	44	44	44	44	87	87	87	87	4	4	4	4	87	87	
21	MORBIDELLI	30	30	30	40	44	40	40	40	40	40	4	4	4	4	6	6	6	6	6	6	
30	NAKAGAMI	44	4	44	44	4	4	4	4	4	4	40	40	40	6	40	40	40	40	40	40	
6	BRADL	4	44	4	4	6	6	6	6	6	6	6	6	6	40	25	25	49	25	25	25	
25	FERNANDEZ	6	6	6	25	25	25	49	49	49	49	25	25	25	25	49	49	25	49	49	49	
40	D.BINDER	49	49	25	6	49	49	25	25	25	25	49	49	49	49							
4	DOVIZIOSO	25	25	49	49	5	5	5	5													

5 Pit stop

Moto2

RACE DISTANCE: 18 laps, 65.990 miles/106.200km · RACE WEATHER: Dry (air 23°, humidity 41%, track 46°)

Pos.	Rider	Nat.	No.	Entrant	Machine	Laps	Time & Speed
1	**Augusto Fernandez**	SPA	37	Red Bull KTM Ajo	Kalex	18	37m 38.670s
							105.1mph/169.2km/h
2	**Alonso Lopez**	SPA	21	CAG Speed Up	Boscoscuro	18	37m 38.740s
3	**Jake Dixon**	GBR	96	GASGAS Aspar Team	Kalex	18	37m 39.332s
4	**Ai Ogura**	JPN	79	IDEMITSU Honda Team Asia	Kalex	18	37m 40.411s
5	**Aron Canet**	SPA	40	Flexbox HP40	Kalex	18	37m 40.616s
6	**Celestino Vietti**	ITA	13	Mooney VR46 Racing Team	Kalex	18	37m 44.110s
7	**Joe Roberts**	USA	16	Italtrans Racing Team	Kalex	18	37m 46.198s
8	**Jorge Navarro**	SPA	9	Flexbox HP40	Kalex	18	37m 49.317s
9	**Filip Salac**	CZE	12	Gresini Racing Moto2	Kalex	18	37m 50.316s
10	**Bo Bendsneyder**	NED	64	Pertamina Mandalika SAG Team	Kalex	18	37m 50.929s
11	**Manuel Gonzalez**	SPA	18	Yamaha VR46 Master Camp Team	Kalex	18	37m 52.710s
12	**Tony Arbolino**	ITA	14	Elf Marc VDS Racing Team	Kalex	18	37m 53.472s
13	**Somkiat Chantra**	THA	35	IDEMITSU Honda Team Asia	Kalex	18	37m 54.768s
14	**Jeremy Alcoba**	SPA	52	Liqui Moly Intact GP	Kalex	18	37m 55.955s
15	**Fermin Aldeguer**	SPA	54	CAG Speed Up	Boscoscuro	18	37m 57.923s
16	Barry Baltus	BEL	7	RW Racing GP	Kalex	18	37m 58.006s
17	Lorenzo Dalla Porta	ITA	19	Italtrans Racing Team	Kalex	18	38m 06.214s
18	Alessandro Zaccone	ITA	61	Gresini Racing Moto2	Kalex	18	38m 11.663s
19	Niccolo Antonelli	ITA	28	Mooney VR46 Racing Team	Kalex	18	38m 13.666s
20	Simone Corsi	ITA	24	MV Agusta Forward Racing	MV Agusta	18	38m 18.857s
21	Rory Skinner	GBR	33	American Racing	Kalex	18	38m 19.271s
22	Sean Dylan Kelly	USA	4	American Racing	Kalex	18	38m 19.613s
23	Keminth Kubo	THA	81	Yamaha VR46 Master Camp Team	Kalex	18	38m 23.696s
24	Piotr Biesiekirski	POL	74	Pertamina Mandalika SAG Team	Kalex	18	38m 35.282s
	Marcel Schrotter	GER	23	Liqui Moly Intact GP	Kalex	16	DNF-crash
	Albert Arenas	SPA	75	GASGAS Aspar Team	Kalex	10	DNF-crash
	Marcos Ramirez	SPA	42	MV Agusta Forward Racing	MV Agusta	7	DNF-technical
	Cameron Beaubier	USA	6	American Racing	Kalex	4	DNF-crash
	Zonta van den Goorbergh	NED	84	RW Racing GP	Kalex	3	DNF-crash

Fastest lap: Augusto Fernandez, on lap 13, 2m 4.784s, 105.8mph/170.2km/h.

Lap record: Jorge Navarro, 2m 4.312s, 106.1mph/170.8km/h (2021).

Event maximum speed: Celestino Vietti, 176.1mph/283.4km/h (race).

Qualifying

Weather: Dry

Air: 22° **Humidity:** 34% **Track:** 43°

Pos.	Rider	Time
1	Fernandez	2m 04.103s
2	Roberts	2m 04.137s
3	Ogura	2m 04.280s
4	Arenas	2m 04.386s
5	Vietti	2m 04.498s
6	Dixon	2m 04.505s
7	Bendsneyder	2m 04.560s
8	Lopez	2m 04.697s
9	Schrotter	2m 04.887s
10	Canet	2m 04.891s
11	Arbolino	2m 04.899s
12	Navarro	2m 04.909s
13	Beaubier	2m 04.934s
14	Alcoba	2m 05.058s
15	Gonzalez	2m 05.090s
16	Chantra	2m 05.197s
17	Salac	2m 05.342s
18	Zaccone	2m 05.449s
	Q1	
19	Navarro	2m 04.670s
20	Gonzalez	2m 04.788s
21	Zaccone	2m 04.905s
22	Chantra	2m 05.156s
23	Dalla Porta	2m 05.175s
24	Aldeguer	2m 05.227s
25	Baltus	2m 05.485s
26	VD Goorbergh	2m 05.691s
27	Ramirez	2m 05.763s
28	Skinner	2m 05.937s
29	Corsi	2m 06.138s
30	Antonelli	2m 06.220s
31	Kubo	2m 06.441s
32	Kelly	2m 06.543s
33	Biesiekirski	2m 07.270s

Fastest race laps

Pos.	Rider	Time
1	Fernandez	2m 04.784s
2	Dixon	2m 04.799s
3	Canet	2m 04.819s
4	Lopez	2m 04.896s
5	Ogura	2m 04.963s
6	Arenas	2m 05.005s
7	Roberts	2m 05.064s
8	Vietti	2m 05.073s
9	Arbolino	2m 05.121s
10	Beaubier	2m 05.124s
11	Gonzalez	2m 05.158s
12	Navarro	2m 05.200s
13	Bendsneyder	2m 05.334s
14	Salac	2m 05.356s
15	Schrotter	2m 05.456s
16	Alcoba	2m 05.582s
17	Baltus	2m 05.673s
18	Chantra	2m 05.701s
19	Aldeguer	2m 05.746s
20	Dalla Porta	2m 05.898s
21	Zaccone	2m 06.004s
22	VD Goorbergh	2m 06.330s
23	Antonelli	2m 06.497s
24	Corsi	2m 06.882s
25	Skinner	2m 06.889s
26	Ramirez	2m 06.915s
27	Kelly	2m 06.983s
28	Kubo	2m 07.127s
29	Biesiekirski	2m 07.389s

Championship Points

Pos.	Rider	Points
1	Fernandez	171
2	Ogura	158
3	Vietti	156
4	Canet	127
5	Arbolino	108
6	Roberts	106
7	Dixon	92
8	Schrotter	88
9	Acosta	75
10	Chantra	72
11	Navarro	70
12	Bendsneyder	61
13	Lopez	55
14	Lowes	51
15	Arenas	45
16	Gonzalez	44
17	Beaubier	40
18	Aldeguer	38
19	Alcoba	35
20	Salac	21
21	Baltus	16
22	Dalla Porta	10
23	Manzi	9
24	Fenati	7
25	Rodrigo	6
26	Zaccone	6
27	Ramirez	5
28	Kubo	4
29	Kelly	3
30	Pasini	1

Constructor Points

Pos.	Constructor	Points
1	Kalex	300
2	Boscoscuro	77
3	MV Agusta	5

Moto3

17 laps, 62.324 miles/100.300km · RACE WEATHER: Dry (air 20°, humidity 52%, track 37°)

Pos.	Rider	Nat.	No.	Entrant	Machine	Laps	Time & Speed
1	**Dennis Foggia**	ITA	7	Leopard Racing	Honda	17	37m 30.120s
							99.7mph/160.4km/h
2	**Jaume Masia**	SPA	5	Red Bull KTM Ajo	KTM	17	37m 30.372s
3	**Deniz Oncu**	TUR	53	Red Bull KTM Tech3	KTM	17	37m 30.417s
4	**Kaito Toba**	JPN	27	CIP Green Power	KTM	17	37m 30.858s
5	**Stefano Nepa**	ITA	82	Angeluss MTA Team	KTM	17	37m 30.882s
6	**Diogo Moreira**	BRA	10	MT Helmets - MSI	KTM	17	37m 31.001s
7	**John McPhee**	GBR	17	Sterilgarda Husqvarna Max	Husqvarna	17	37m 31.052s
8	**Ryusei Yamanaka**	JPN	6	MT Helmets - MSI	KTM	17	37m 31.056s
9	**Andrea Migno**	ITA	16	Rivacold Snipers Team	Honda	17	37m 31.228s
10	**Carlos Tatay**	SPA	99	CFMOTO Racing PruestelGP	CFMOTO	17	37m 31.910s
11	**Xavier Artigas**	SPA	43	CFMOTO Racing PruestelGP	CFMOTO	17	37m 31.947s
12	**Scott Ogden**	GBR	19	VisionTrack Racing Team	Honda	17	37m 32.170s
13	**Lorenzo Fellon**	FRA	20	SIC58 Squadra Corse	Honda	17	37m 32.306s
14	**Riccardo Rossi**	ITA	54	SIC58 Squadra Corse	Honda	17	37m 32.503s
15	**Adrian Fernandez**	SPA	31	Red Bull KTM Tech3	KTM	17	37m 51.149s
16	Elia Bartolini	ITA	23	QJMotor Avintia Racing Team	KTM	17	37m 51.184s
17	Mario Aji	INA	64	Honda Team Asia	Honda	17	37m 51.308s
18	Taiyo Furusato	JPN	72	Honda Team Asia	Honda	17	37m 51.363s
19	Alberto Surra	ITA	67	Rivacold Snipers Team	Honda	17	37m 51.550s
20	Nicola Fabio Carraro	ITA	9	QJMotor Avintia Racing Team	KTM	17	37m 51.574s
21	Joshua Whatley	GBR	70	VisionTrack Racing Team	Honda	17	38m 00.400s
22	Marc Garcia	SPA	41	CIP Green Power	KTM	17	38m 12.273s
23	Ana Carrasco	SPA	22	BOE Motorsports	KTM	17	38m 12.285s
	Daniel Holgado	SPA	96	Red Bull KTM Ajo	KTM	17	DNF-ret in pit
	Ivan Ortola	SPA	48	Angeluss MTA Team	KTM	16	DNF-crash
	David Munoz	SPA	44	BOE Motorsports	KTM	16	DNF-crash
	Tatsuki Suzuki	JPN	24	Leopard Racing	Honda	16	DNF-crash
	Izan Guevara	SPA	28	Gaviota GASGAS Aspar Team	GASGAS	16	DNF-crash
	Sergio Garcia	SPA	11	Gaviota GASGAS Aspar Team	GASGAS	14	DNF-crash
	Ayumu Sasaki	JPN	71	Sterilgarda Husqvarna Max	Husqvarna	14	DNF-crash

Fastest lap: Deniz Oncu, on lap 11, 2m 11.011s, 100.7mph/162.1km/h.

Lap record: Izan Guevara, 2m 11.347s, 100.5mph/161.7km/h (2021).

Event maximum speed: David Munoz, 150.7mph/242.6km/h (race).

Qualifying:

Weather: Dry

Air: 20° **Humidity:** 41% **Track:** 41°

Pos.	Rider	Time
1	Moreira	2m 10.951s
2	Guevara	2m 11.019s
3	Yamanaka	2m 11.029s
4	Rossi	2m 11.059s
5	Nepa	2m 11.131s
6	Oncu	2m 11.180s
7	Foggia	2m 11.206s
8	Suzuki	2m 11.245s
9	Sasaki	2m 11.457s
10	McPhee	2m 11.560s
11	Garcia	2m 11.570s
12	Holgado	2m 11.623s
13	Migno	2m 11.628s
14	Toba	2m 11.646s
15	Artigas	2m 11.827s
16	Fellon	2m 12.155s
17	Furusato	2m 12.255s
18	Ortola	2m 12.699s
	Q1	
19	Munoz	2m 11.732s
20	Fernandez	2m 11.750s
21	Masia	2m 11.787s
22	Tatay	2m 11.827s
23	Bartolini	2m 12.061s
24	Ogden	2m 12.289s
25	Carraro	2m 12.340s
26	Whatley	2m 12.631s
27	Surra	2m 12.651s
28	Aji	2m 13.818s
29	Carrasco	2m 14.092s
30	Garcia	2m 14.602s

Fastest race laps

Pos.	Rider	Time
1	Oncu	2m 11.011s
2	Masia	2m 11.094s
3	McPhee	2m 11.178s
4	Sasaki	2m 11.179s
5	Garcia	2m 11.183s
6	Suzuki	2m 11.327s
7	Moreira	2m 11.361s
8	Nepa	2m 11.397s
9	Munoz	2m 11.417s
10	Guevara	2m 11.422s
11	Yamanaka	2m 11.463s
12	Ortola	2m 11.496s
13	Artigas	2m 11.502s
14	Holgado	2m 11.534s
15	Rossi	2m 11.557s
16	Toba	2m 11.576s
17	Ogden	2m 11.586s
18	Fellon	2m 11.588s
19	Migno	2m 11.594s
20	Foggia	2m 11.599s
21	Tatay	2m 11.688s
22	Fernandez	2m 11.973s
23	Bartolini	2m 12.295s
24	Aji	2m 12.430s
25	Furusato	2m 12.570s
26	Surra	2m 12.628s
27	Carraro	2m 12.703s
28	Whatley	2m 12.961s
29	Carrasco	2m 13.567s
30	Garcia	2m 13.601s

Championship Points

Pos.	Rider	Points
1	Garcia	182
2	Guevara	179
3	Foggia	140
4	Masia	127
5	Oncu	114
6	Sasaki	113
7	Suzuki	94
8	Migno	84
9	Tatay	70
10	Artigas	62
11	Yamanaka	59
12	Toba	57
13	Rossi	54
14	Holgado	48
15	Moreira	44
16	McPhee	33
17	Ortola	33
18	Munoz	32
19	Nepa	29
20	Fernandez	29
21	Bartolini	23
22	Kelso	22
23	Ogden	20
24	Bertelle	16
25	Fellon	11
26	Aji	5

Constructor Points

Pos.	Constructor	Points
1	GASGAS	235
2	Honda	206
3	KTM	194
4	Husqvarna	142
5	CFMOTO	101

FIM WORLD CHAMPIONSHIP · ROUND 13

AUSTRIAN GRAND PRIX

RED BULL RING

CryptoDATA
Wispr
Download Now
#DiscoverPrivacy

Above: Ducatis take control in the sprint from the start.
Photo: Bernd Fischer

Top right: Bastianini's maiden pole was deflated by a slow puncture in the race.

Top far right: Steadily improving, Marini took a career-best fourth.

Above right: New chicane drew the teeth from a notoriously dangerous second corner.
Photos: Gold & Goose

Centre right: Stefan Bradl and Marquez crew chief Santi Hernandez talk Honda problems.

Right: Watching brief. Marc Marquez was back on the scene, but not on the bike.
Photos: Repsol Honda

Opening spread: Three in a row for Bagnaia, six out of seven for Ducati – and a towering second place for Quartararo.
Photo: Ducati Corse

SPIELBERG'S alpine foothills were alive with the sound of rumours, speculation running rife in advance of a pair of 'special' press conferences. One was to reintroduce the long-absent Marc Marquez to the paddock. Maybe to retire? The other for a portentous announcement by Dorna, IRTA and the FIM, MotoGP's holy trinity. Which could have been about almost anything.

Marquez first. Looking tanned, fit and cheerful, he was there to bond again with his team after 12 weeks of separation, and to contribute to putting Honda back on track after a dismal spell with only three wins (all by him) over 44 races and counting.

"I had the experience of 2020–2021, when I was a long time without coming to the circuits. I disconnected too much and when I came back everything was too new. So this time, I tried to keep in contact a lot with [crew chief] Santi, with Stefan Bradl, especially with my team. One reason to be here is not to see the bikes on the track. It's to speak with Honda, the engineers, to be involved about the project."

His recovery was going well, although "in the end, it's an arm with four operations. But at least now it's working in a normal way." He intended to race before the end of the year. The best way to assess his recovery and to decide his future was "on the bike". All dependent on a medical assessment in the following week, which happily cleared him to step up his rehabilitation.

Team manager Alberto Puig expressed the hope that he'd be ready for the official tests after the following race at Misano. With 2023 parts and ideas expected, Puig commented darkly that without him, the tests would be without much purpose, a stinging reflection on the lack of progress by engineers and riders with the troublesome 2022 bike.

The next shake-up came on Saturday, with news that starting in 2023, there would be a Saturday afternoon half-points, half-distance sprint race.

According to IRTA President Herve Poncharal, the move was "just the tip of the iceberg" in terms of new ideas designed to address an unacknowledged nascent downturn in interest and popularity, only partly due to the departure of world superstar Rossi.

"We are trying to offer a better show, for the fans, the promoters and television," said Dorna CEO Carmelo Ezpeleta. Some details – like how a sprint-race win would count towards a rider's GP statistics – remained to be worked out. Also neglected was involvement of the riders in the decision – or even to inform them, leading to a flurry of unrest.

Many were perturbed by the thought that missing a weekend through injury (possibly sustained off track) would potentially cost 37 points rather than 25. Quartararo led the initial complaints. "They don't ask us, and at the end, I think we all prefer to make a good race on Sunday. A sprint race is stupid," he said, although later he would soften his opinion. Miller led a muted chorus in favour: "It will throw a good element in – all or nothing. You want to risk more, not worry about tyres, fuel or even physical condition."

Losing a practice session perturbed KTM crew chief Paul Trevathan: "[Set-up] will all be based on a feeling. You won't have enough data to quantify it. The bike has to be an all-round package so when it rolls out on track, it's working."

The lack of consultation with riders revived talk of a union, and the retiring Dovizioso showed interest in heading such an organisation: "Already they start to speak with me about that, and I'm happy if the people are thinking about me, but … everything has to be clear, so I don't know."

But when the idea was put to Ezpeleta at the conference, the atmosphere became combative. "The Safety Commission *is* a rider's union. Never in any sport does the protagonist have the power that they have in MotoGP," he blustered. "This is something you take from the opinion of some of the riders … but I didn't see any rider talking to me about this. The conversation [in Friday's Safety Commission] was very good. We talked a lot." Pressed further, his temper began

to fray: "Do you think it's a necessity to create a union? If the riders need something, they will talk to me, not to you."

The simple, but exciting Red Bull Ring was slightly, though drastically altered, with a new right-left chicane between Turns One and Three, adding 31 yards in length and 6.1 seconds to the best lap. Average speed dropped from 116.9mph to 109.5 – no longer fastest lap of the year. Either of the forthcoming Thai or Australian GPs, whose pre-pandemic best speeds had both been faster than 113mph (Thailand fastest at 113.5), would take over, given dry weather.

This was a robust response to the terrifying crashes in 2020 and 2021, eliminating the scary, flat-out blind left kink, where riders started braking for the slow Turn Three while downshifting from top gear. The track lost a fine flowing corner, but was much safer. Miller was one among a few fans: "It's a nice addition ... completely blind heading in, a lot of different changes of camber as you go in, so the bike's moving around a lot. I'm burying the rear brake to get it sliding going in. It's the most aggressive change of direction I think on the calendar."

It also offered Quartararo the chance for a potential 'best overtake of the year' during one of the best rides of the year. His victim, ironically, was Miller.

A new so-called 'factory team' was announced. In fact, GasGas was just a new name for Tech3's satellite KTM team, running identical bikes modified only by changing the badges.

The KTM riders were now settled, Miller joining Brad Binder in the factory squad. The displaced Oliveira was again publicly offered a GasGas seat, at least nominally retaining factory status, but he would decline, preferring instead to switch to the newly Aprilia-equipped RNF team, joined there by Raul Fernandez, whose rookie Tech3 year had proved fraught. In his place, the returning Pol Espargaro and, it was rumoured (and would later prove true), Augusto Fernandez, currently going strong in Moto2.

That left reigning Moto2 champion Remy Gardner high and dry, and very disappointed. At this late stage, it would be hard to find a good ride even back in Moto2. He had outscored fellow rookie team-mate Fernandez, but some overly frank remarks appeared not to have endeared him to the Austrian factory. He found a 2023 ride in WorldSBK.

MOTOGP RACE – 28 laps

Bagnaia led from start to finish to become the first Ducati rider with three successive wins since Stoner in 2008, gaining important ground in the championship. But the hero of the race was Quartararo, after a bitter fight to second through a hoard of faster Ducatis at a horsepower-hungry circuit, where Desmosedicis had won six out of eight races, and Yamaha none. After a shaky start, he reeled in all but one of them, finally less than half a second away from a win nobody could have expected.

Bastianini had snitched a maiden pole ahead of Bagnaia by a mere two-thousandths, at the head of a Ducati quintet, Miller a close third. Martin led the second row, with Zarco sixth. Sandwiched between them, speed and acceleration deficits notwithstanding, Quartararo – a heroic effort. The next best Yamaha was Morbidelli's down in 16th, albeit only half a second slower.

The Aprilias were also strong, Vinales and Espargaro bracketing the third row, with Rins's Suzuki between them.

Bagnaia got the jump followed by Bastianini, Miller and Martin. Quartararo was fifth, but ran wide at the next corner and was forced to defend from fast-starting Vinales, who eventually got by at the penultimate turn. By then, the four Dukes were almost a second clear.

Mir's wretched run continued, as he high-sided out of seventh at Turn Four, suffering a right ankle fracture and ligament damage that kept him out for four more races. That left Marini, Espargaro, Zarco and Rins disputing the position.

Soon there were signs that Bastianini was not as com-

Above: On the limit. Jack Miller keeps himself clear of Jorge Martin.
Photo: Bernd Fischer

Top right: Damage limitation. Second place was something to be proud of for Quartararo.
Photo: Monster Energy Yamaha

Above right: Ai Ogura forces back past team-mate Chantra, after the Honda Team Asia pit board hadn't clarified the issue.

Centre right: "This close" for Leopard Racing's Tatsuki Suzuki. The Honda rider was just 0.064 of a second behind double-winner Sasaki's Husqvarna.

Centre far right: Rising rookie David Munoz took a second Moto3 podium.

Right: Sensational Sasaki overcame two long-lap penalties to overhaul Suzuki, Oncu and Munoz.
Photos: Gold & Goose

posed as usual. Miller demoted him to third at the start of lap four, and Martin also got by after a brief to-and-fro through Turns Six and Seven. It was personal between the two rivals for 2023's factory seat, and Bastianini got past again at the start of lap six. Then, at Turn Nine, he ran wide, and cracked his front wheel rim as he rejoined over the kerb. His tyre deflating, he narrowly avoided hitting Zarco, sending the Frenchman wide, and losing places to Vinales and Marini, before running straight on shortly afterwards.

Now Quartararo's afternoon took on a different complexion. He'd been under threat from Espargaro and Zarco, but once Bastianini had gone and Vinales also run wide, he escaped to close on Martin.

The factory Ducatis were still 1.7 seconds clear, and Miller was about to give his team-mate an inadvertent hurry-up. Both were on Michelin's soft front (Martin, Quartararo and Espargaro chose the hard), and Miller desperately needed fresh air to cool the rubber, but a failed lap-seven attack at Turn Nine spurred on Bagnaia, who gained a breathing space of six-tenths.

Martin was also picking up speed, gaining on Miller, with Quartararo soon to dispose of Espargaro and close up on the Ducatis.

The pace was intense, and on lap 17, Martin messed up his braking into the chicane, rejoining behind Quartararo. With six laps remaining, the leading quartet was covered by 2.2 seconds. The Ducatis had the advantage on the front straight and out of Turn Three; Quartararo worked his magic in the tighter sections later in the lap, gaining visibly through the fast left Turns Six and Seven.

With three laps left and his front tyre graining, Miller was on the defensive, and as he braked early for the chicane to achieve a good exit, Quartararo released his brakes, going around the outside to take the inside for the following left. "I had to try something," he said later.

Bagnaia now had a healthy 1.6-second margin, but Quartararo (who later said, "Every lap was like qualifying.") gave it everything, regaining half a second on the penultimate lap and halving the lead on the last.

Martin's hopes of gaining the podium from Miller foundered when he crashed in the attempt at the first corner of the final lap. That promoted Marini to a best-yet fourth, six seconds adrift, after a solid ride and finally fighting off Zarco.

Espargaro dropped back in sixth, unhappy with the feel of the stiffer rear tyre carcass that Michelin had brought for this track. Nonethess, he was narrowly ahead of Binder, struggling with front-end vibration in the last lap. Rins was another three-tenths behind.

Bezzecchi recovered well from 20th on the grid for ninth. Close behind, Martin had remounted for tenth, holding off Di Giannantonio and Oliveira. Next, Vinales, who also experienced rear tyre issues and had faded. Marquez was a lone 14th, and Dovizioso took the last point, a second clear of Pol Espargaro.

Gardner, Nakagami, Darryn Binder and Morbidelli all fell, Gardner remounting for last place.

MOTO2 RACE – 25 laps

This was Ai Ogura's weekend, starting with a second pole position and closing with a second race win to take over the title lead for the first time. He was nearly robbed at the last gasp, however – by his own team-mate (and flat-mate), Somkiat Chantra.

Honda's bright hope had Lopez's Boscoscuro alongside, on a grid where the top 11 were otherwise on Kalexes, with erstwhile points leader Fernandez – winner of the previous three races – in third.

Dixon led row two from Chantra and Acosta; Vietti headed the third.

Ogura led away from Fernandez, with relative beginner Lopez having taken over second by the end of the lap, and then diving into the lead for two more; while Chantra moved past Dixon into third on lap two.

The early exchanges were frenetic, with Vietti, Canet, Dixon, and team-mates Acosta and Fernandez fiercely trading blows. That allowed the Honda Team Asia pair to escape.

For a while, it seemed as though Vietti might join them. He

had finally taken control of the pursuit on lap ten, and over the next six, he closed a gap of 1.6 seconds, posting fastest lap in the process. He was poised to attack Chantra at Turn Three on lap 17, but ran a little wide and crashed.

At this point, Acosta was leading the chase brawl, some six seconds adrift. With Ogura a title contender, it was assumed that Chantra would take up station behind him and cruise to the team's first one-two finish.

Not so. The Thai rider chased down Ogura in the final laps. Despite his team signaling, 'P2 OK' for the last five laps, it looked increasingly as though he was lining up an attack. And he was.

To the surprise of all, at the penultimate corner, he dived inside Ogura to lead into the last turn. The cool-tempered Japanese rider probably raised an eyebrow as he cut back under him to lead past the flag by less than two-tenths.

Asked if he had noticed the pit signal, a smiling Chantra replied that he had only seen 'P2', not the 'OK'. Ogura playfully countered, "I said to the crew, 'Next time, bring a bigger OK.'"

Dixon stole third from Acosta at the final turn, having recovered from hitting a false neutral on lap seven. Fernandez was right behind in fifth, a second ahead of Canet; Lopez faded to seventh.

Schrotter led the next group, spaced out at the end, from Arenas, Alcoba and Navarro; then Baltus and a battling Beaubier, Roberts and Bendsneyder wrapped up the points.

Briton Rory Skinner had a second successive 21st place in his second wild-card ride, a creditable debut. At Silverstone and in this race, he had been engaged throughout with Italian veteran Simone Corsi.

Australian teenager Senna Agius – riding as replacement for Sam Lowes, who had been ruled out by his British GP injuries – was an impressive 17th, in spite of a long-lap penalty for exceeding track limits.

As well as Vietti, a nine-strong crash list included Aldeguer, Arbolino, Dalla Porta and Kelly.

Ogura took a slender lead in the points, just one ahead of Fernandez.

MOTO3 RACE – 23 laps

Rookie Daniel Holgado claimed a maiden pole on an all-KTM front row, from Sasaki and Oncu, with Foggia in the middle of row two. Guevara was eighth, points leader Garcia 11th.

It was anybody's race – except surely for Sasaki, saddled with a double long-lap penalty after knocking Garcia off at the previous race. But the Japanese 21-year-old was undeterred. He led away and was still in front when he took the first penalty on lap three, dropping to 17th. He lost four more places with the second penalty two laps later. The fight back was immediate and ruthless, with a string of four lap records in five laps.

He was in the lead group by lap nine. This comprised Guevara, Holgado, Suzuki, Oncu, Munoz, Garcia and Moreira. Sasaki was past all of them in four laps.

From there, he stretched their legs. Only Suzuki, Oncu and Munoz could match his pace, but despite his best efforts, Suzuki was 0.064 of a second behind over the line.

Munoz nicked third off Oncu two turns from the flag; Garcia narrowly led home Moreira, Guevara and Holgado. Four seconds down, McPhee led Toba and the rest – and off-colour Foggia was 12th.

Masia had been with the group, but crashed, remounting to finish outside the points. Tatay was another faller. Scott Ogden narrowly missed the points in 16th, but then was dropped to 21st with a three-second penalty for exceeding track limits.

Australian teenager Joel Kelso, back from injury, ran in the points in the early stages, but dropped to 22nd, still not fully fit.

Garcia extended his narrow lead in the title chase over Guevara to five points.

FIM WORLD CHAMPIONSHIP: ROUND 13

CryptoDATA MOTORRAD GRAND PRIX VON ÖSTERREICH

19–21 AUGUST, 2022

RED BULL RING, SPIELBERG

Circuit: 4.326km / 2.688 miles
28 laps

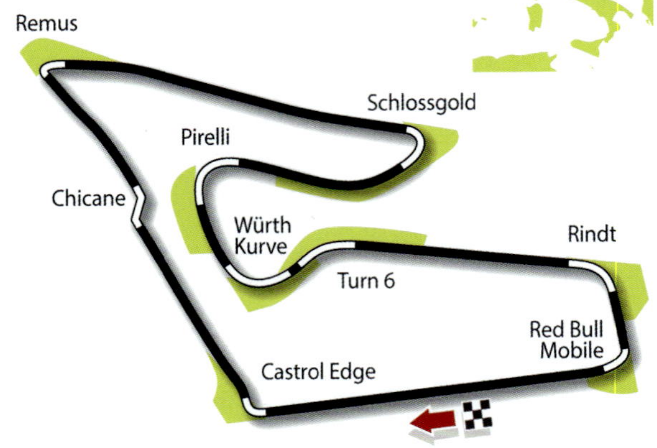

MotoGP

RACE DISTANCE: 28 laps, 75.648 miles/121.744km · RACE WEATHER: Dry (air 21°, humidity 59%, track 23°)

Pos.	Rider	Nat.	No.	Entrant	Machine	Tyres	Race tyre choice	Laps	Time & speed
1	**Francesco Bagnaia**	ITA	63	Ducati Lenovo Team	Ducati Desmosedici	M	F: Soft/R: Medium	28	42m 14.886s 107.4mph/172.8km/h
2	**Fabio Quartararo**	FRA	20	Monster Energy Yamaha MotoGP	Yamaha YZR-M1	M	F: Hard/R: Medium	28	42m 15.378s
3	**Jack Miller**	AUS	43	Ducati Lenovo Team	Ducati Desmosedici	M	F: Soft/R: Medium	28	42m 17.049s
4	**Luca Marini**	ITA	10	Mooney VR46 Racing Team	Ducati Desmosedici	M	F: Hard/R: Medium	28	42m 23.234s
5	**Johann Zarco**	FRA	5	Prima Pramac Racing	Ducati Desmosedici	M	F: Soft/R: Medium	28	42m 23.707s
6	**Aleix Espargaro**	SPA	41	Aprilia Racing	Aprilia RS-GP	M	F: Hard/R: Soft	28	42m 26.173s
7	**Brad Binder**	RSA	33	Red Bull KTM Factory Racing	KTM RC16	M	F: Hard/R: Medium	28	42m 26.528s
8	**Alex Rins**	SPA	42	Team SUZUKI ECSTAR	Suzuki GSX-RR	M	F: Medium/R: Medium	28	42m 26.666s
9	**Marco Bezzecchi**	ITA	72	Mooney VR46 Racing Team	Ducati Desmosedici	M	F: Hard/R: Soft	28	42m 31.873s
10	**Jorge Martin**	SPA	89	Prima Pramac Racing	Ducati Desmosedici	M	F: Hard/R: Medium	28	42m 32.030s
11	**Fabio Di Giannantonio**	ITA	49	Gresini Racing MotoGP	Ducati Desmosedici	M	F: Soft/R: Medium	28	42m 32.357s
12	**Miguel Oliveira**	POR	88	Red Bull KTM Factory Racing	KTM RC16	M	F: Hard/R: Medium	28	42m 32.921s
13	**Maverick Vinales**	SPA	12	Aprilia Racing	Aprilia RS-GP	M	F: Hard/R: Soft	28	42m 34.898s
14	**Alex Marquez**	SPA	73	LCR Honda CASTROL	Honda RC213V	M	F: Hard/R: Medium	28	42m 41.766s
15	**Andrea Dovizioso**	ITA	4	WithU Yamaha RNF MotoGP Team	Yamaha YZR-M1	M	F: Hard/R: Medium	28	42m 44.630s
16	Pol Espargaro	SPA	44	Repsol Honda Team	Honda RC213V	M	F: Hard/R: Soft	28	42m 45.880s
17	Stefan Bradl	GER	6	Repsol Honda Team	Honda RC213V	M	F: Medium/R: Soft	28	42m 52.846s
18	Raul Fernandez	SPA	25	Tech3 KTM Factory Racing	KTM RC16	M	F: Hard/R: Medium	28	42m 56.968s
19	Lorenzo Savadori	ITA	32	Aprilia Racing	Aprilia RS-GP	M	F: Hard/R: Soft	28	43m 01.552s
20	Remy Gardner	AUS	87	Tech3 KTM Factory Racing	KTM RC16	M	F: Hard/R: Medium	27	43m 03.614s
	Franco Morbidelli	ITA	21	Monster Energy Yamaha MotoGP	Yamaha YZR-M1	M	F: Hard/R: Medium	25	DNF-crash
	Darryn Binder	RSA	40	WithU Yamaha RNF MotoGP Team	Yamaha YZR-M1	M	F: Hard/R: Medium	12	DNF-crash
	Takaaki Nakagami	JPN	30	LCR Honda IDEMITSU	Honda RC213V	M	F: Hard/R: Medium	9	DNF-crash
	Enea Bastianini	ITA	23	Gresini Racing MotoGP	Ducati Desmosedici	M	F: Soft/R: Soft	6	DNF-technical
	Joan Mir	SPA	36	Team SUZUKI ECSTAR	Suzuki GSX-RR	M	F: Hard/R: Medium	0	DNF-crash

Fastest lap: Jorge Martin, on lap 8, 1m 29.854s, 108.2mph/174.2km/h.
Lap record: New layout.
Event maximum speed: Brad Binder, 196.2mph/315.7km/h (free practice).

Qualifying

Weather: Dry
Air Temp: 22° **Humidity:** 63%
Track Temp: 27°

1	Bastianini	1m 28.772s
2	Bagnaia	1m 28.796s
3	Miller	1m 28.881s
4	Martin	1m 28.958s
5	Quartararo	1m 29.003s
6	Zarco	1m 29.046s
7	Vinales	1m 29.135s
8	Mir	1m 29.255s
9	A. Espargaro	1m 29.255s
10	Di Giannantonio	1m 29.336s
11	Rins	1m 29.424s
12	B. Binder	1m 29.536s
	Q1	
13	Marini	1m 29.386s
14	Nakagami	1m 29.390s
15	P. Espargaro	1m 29.475s
16	Morbidelli	1m 29.540s
17	Oliveira	1m 29.613s
18	Bradl	1m 29.809s
19	Dovizioso	1m 30.085s
20	Bezzecchi	1m 30.122s
21	D. Binder	1m 30.328s
22	Gardner	1m 30.397s
23	Fernandez	1m 30.475s
24	Savadori	1m 30.487s
25	A. Marquez	1m 33.653s

Fastest race laps

1	Martin	1m 29.854s
2	Quartararo	1m 29.891s
3	A. Espargaro	1m 29.914s
4	Zarco	1m 29.985s
5	Bagnaia	1m 30.027s
6	Miller	1m 30.055s
7	Marini	1m 30.082s
8	Vinales	1m 30.102s
9	Rins	1m 30.116s
10	Bezzecchi	1m 30.302s
11	Bastianini	1m 30.318s
12	B. Binder	1m 30.330s
13	Di Giannantonio	1m 30.434s
14	Oliveira	1m 30.446s
15	Morbidelli	1m 30.571s
16	D. Binder	1m 30.617s
17	A. Marquez	1m 30.686s
18	Nakagami	1m 30.751s
19	Dovizioso	1m 30.825s
20	P. Espargaro	1m 30.969s
21	Gardner	1m 30.984s
22	Bradl	1m 30.988s
23	Fernandez	1m 31.061s
24	Savadori	1m 31.424s

Championship Points

1	Quartararo	200
2	A. Espargaro	168
3	Bagnaia	156
4	Zarco	125
5	Miller	123
6	Bastianini	118
7	B. Binder	107
8	Rins	92
9	Martin	87
10	Oliveira	85
11	Vinales	85
12	Mir	77
13	Marini	69
14	Bezzecchi	68
15	M. Marquez	60
16	Nakagami	45
17	P. Espargaro	42
18	A. Marquez	29
19	Morbidelli	26
20	Di Giannantonio	23
21	Dovizioso	11
22	D. Binder	10
23	Gardner	9
24	Fernandez	5

Constructor Points

1	Ducati	296
2	Yamaha	200
3	Aprilia	185
4	KTM	140
5	Suzuki	118
6	Honda	90

Grid order	1	2	3	4	5	6	7	8	9	10	11	12	13	14	15	16	17	18	19	20	21	22	23	24	25	26	27	28	·
23 BASTIANINI	63	63	63	63	63	63	63	63	63	63	63	63	63	63	63	63	63	63	63	63	63	63	63	63	63	63	63	63	1
63 BAGNAIA	23	23	23	43	43	43	43	43	43	43	43	43	43	43	43	43	43	43	43	43	43	43	43	43	20	20	20	20	2
43 MILLER	43	43	43	89	89	89	89	89	89	89	89	89	89	89	89	89	20	20	20	20	20	20	20	20	43	43	43	43	3
89 MARTIN	89	89	89	23	23	20	20	20	20	20	20	20	20	20	20	20	89	89	89	89	89	89	89	89	89	89	89	10	4
20 QUARTARARO	12	12	12	12	20	41	41	41	41	41	41	41	41	41	41	41	41	41	41	41	10	10	10	10	10	10	10	5	5
5 ZARCO	20	20	20	20	41	12	12	12	12	12	12	12	12	10	10	10	10	10	10	10	41	41	41	41	5	5	5	41	6
12 VINALES	10	41	41	41	5	10	10	10	10	10	10	10	10	12	12	12	12	12	5	5	5	5	5	5	41	41	41	33	7
36 MIR	41	5	5	5	12	5	5	5	5	5	5	5	5	5	5	5	5	5	42	42	42	42	42	42	42	33	33	42	8
41 A. ESPARGARO	5	10	10	10	10	42	42	42	42	42	42	42	42	42	42	42	42	42	12	33	33	33	33	33	33	42	42	72	9
49 DI GIANNANTONIO	42	42	42	42	42	33	33	33	33	33	33	33	33	33	33	33	33	33	33	12	12	12	12	12	12	72	72	89	10
42 RINS	33	33	33	33	33	49	49	49	49	49	49	49	49	49	49	49	49	72	72	72	72	72	72	72	72	12	49	49	11
33 B.BINDER	49	40	49	49	49	72	72	72	72	72	72	72	72	72	72	72	72	49	49	49	49	49	49	49	49	49	88	88	12
10 MARINI	40	49	40	40	40	40	40	40	88	88	88	88	88	88	88	88	88	88	88	88	88	88	88	88	88	88	12	12	13
30 NAKAGAMI	88	88	88	72	72	88	88	88	40	40	40	21	21	21	21	21	21	21	21	21	21	21	21	21	73	73	73	73	14
44 P. ESPARGARO	30	21	72	88	88	21	21	21	21	21	21	40	73	73	73	73	73	73	73	73	73	73	73	73	4	4	4	4	15
21 MORBIDELLI	21	72	21	21	21	73	73	73	73	73	73	73	44	44	44	44	44	4	4	4	4	4	4	4	44	44	44	44	
88 OLIVEIRA	73	73	73	73	73	30	30	30	30	44	44	44	6	4	4	4	4	44	44	44	44	44	44	44	6	6	6	6	
6 BRADL	6	30	30	30	30	44	44	44	44	6	6	6	4	6	6	6	6	6	6	6	6	6	6	6	25	25	25	25	
4 DOVIZIOSO	44	44	44	44	44	6	6	6	6	4	4	4	25	25	25	25	25	25	25	25	25	25	25	25	32	32	32	32	
72 BEZZECCHI	72	6	6	6	6	25	25	25	25	25	25	25	32	32	32	32	32	32	32	32	32	32	32	32	*87*	*87*	*87*		
40 D.BINDER	4	4	4	4	25	4	4	4	4	32	32	32	*87*	*87*	*87*	*87*	*87*	*87*	*87*	*87*	*87*	*87*	*87*	*87*	*21*				
87 GARDNER	25	25	25	25	87	32	32	32	32	*87*	*87*	*87*																	
25 FERNANDEZ	87	87	87	87	4	23	*87*	*87*	*87*																				
32 SAVADORI	32	32	32	32	32	*87*																							
73 A. MARQUEZ																													

23 Pit stop *87 Lapped rider*

Moto2

RACE DISTANCE: 25 laps, 67.543 miles/108.700km · RACE WEATHER: Dry (air 20°, humidity 62%, track 22°)

Pos.	Rider	Nat.	No.	Entrant	Machine	Laps	Time & Speed
1	**Ai Ogura**	JPN	79	IDEMITSU Honda Team Asia	Kalex	25	39m 30.070s 102.6mph/165.1km/h
2	**Somkiat Chantra**	THA	35	IDEMITSU Honda Team Asia	Kalex	25	39m 30.243s
3	**Jake Dixon**	GBR	96	Zinia GASGAS Aspar Team	Kalex	25	39m 37.924s
4	**Pedro Acosta**	SPA	51	Red Bull KTM Ajo	Kalex	25	39m 38.030s
5	**Augusto Fernandez**	SPA	37	Red Bull KTM Ajo	Kalex	25	39m 38.107s
6	**Aron Canet**	SPA	40	Flexbox HP40	Kalex	25	39m 39.471s
7	**Alonso Lopez**	SPA	21	CAG Speed Up	Boscoscuro	25	39m 43.065s
8	**Marcel Schrotter**	GER	23	Liqui Moly Intact GP	Kalex	25	39m 48.324s
9	**Albert Arenas**	SPA	75	Zinia GASGAS Aspar Team	Kalex	25	39m 50.731s
10	**Jeremy Alcoba**	SPA	52	Liqui Moly Intact GP	Kalex	25	39m 52.297s
11	**Jorge Navarro**	SPA	9	Flexbox HP40	Kalex	25	39m 53.513s
12	**Barry Baltus**	BEL	7	RW Racing GP	Kalex	25	39m 55.863s
13	**Cameron Beaubier**	USA	6	American Racing	Kalex	25	39m 57.858s
14	**Joe Roberts**	USA	16	Italtrans Racing Team	Kalex	25	39m 57.979s
15	**Bo Bendsneyder**	NED	64	Pertamina Mandalika SAG Team	Kalex	25	39m 58.417s
16	Niccolo Antonelli	ITA	28	Mooney VR46 Racing Team	Kalex	25	40m 04.681s
17	Senna Agius	AUS	8	Elf Marc VDS Racing Team	Kalex	25	40m 04.998s
18	Zonta van den Goorbergh	NED	84	RW Racing GP	Kalex	25	40m 06.384s
19	Marcos Ramirez	SPA	42	MV Agusta Forward Racing	MV Agusta	25	40m 14.907s
20	Simone Corsi	ITA	24	MV Agusta Forward Racing	MV Agusta	25	40m 18.672s
21	Rory Skinner	GBR	33	American Racing	Kalex	25	40m 18.884s
22	Taiga Hada	JPN	29	Pertamina Mandalika SAG Team	Kalex	25	40m 29.274s
	Fermin Aldeguer	SPA	54	CAG Speed Up	Boscoscuro	20	DNF-crash
	Celestino Vietti	ITA	13	Mooney VR46 Racing Team	Kalex	18	DNF-crash
	Lorenzo Dalla Porta	ITA	19	Italtrans Racing Team	Kalex	17	DNF-crash
	Tony Arbolino	ITA	14	Elf Marc VDS Racing Team	Kalex	17	DNF-crash
	Filip Salac	CZE	12	Gresini Racing Moto2	Kalex	10	DNF-crash
	Manuel Gonzalez	SPA	18	Yamaha VR46 Master Camp Team	Kalex	6	DNF-crash
	Keminth Kubo	THA	81	Yamaha VR46 Master Camp Team	Kalex	5	DNF-crash
	Sean Dylan Kelly	USA	4	American Racing	Kalex	5	DNF-crash
	Alessandro Zaccone	ITA	61	Gresini Racing Moto2	Kalex	1	DNF-crash

Fastest lap: Celestino Vietti, on lap 14, 1m 34.073s, 103.3mph/166.3km/h.

Lap record: New layout

Event maximum speed: Jorge Navarro, 164.5mph/264.7km/h (free practice).

Qualifying

Weather: Dry

Air: 21° **Humidity:** 59% **Track:** 27°

Pos.	Rider	Time
1	Ogura	1m 33.933s
2	Lopez	1m 33.981s
3	Fernandez	1m 34.101s
4	Dixon	1m 34.104s
5	Chantra	1m 34.105s
6	Acosta	1m 34.126s
7	Vietti	1m 34.170s
8	Schrotter	1m 34.245s
9	Arenas	1m 34.254s
10	Dalla Porta	1m 34.257s
11	Beaubier	1m 34.382s
12	Aldeguer	1m 34.421s
13	Canet	1m 34.445s
14	Salac	1m 34.516s
15	Arbolino	1m 34.602s
16	Bendsneyder	1m 34.655s
17	Navarro	1m 34.692s
18	Baltus	1m 34.800s
	Q1	
19	Alcoba	1m 34.619s
20	Roberts	1m 34.655s
21	Agius	1m 34.938s
22	Ramirez	1m 34.996s
23	Zaccone	1m 35.007s
24	VD Goorbergh	1m 35.117s
25	Antonelli	1m 35.122s
26	Gonzalez	1m 35.205s
27	Corsi	1m 35.206s
28	Kubo	1m 35.301s
29	Kelly	1m 35.651s
30	Hada	1m 35.721s
31	Skinner	1m 35.899s

Fastest race laps

Pos.	Rider	Time
1	Vietti	1m 34.073s
2	Chantra	1m 34.281s
3	Ogura	1m 34.316s
4	Acosta	1m 34.392s
5	Lopez	1m 34.491s
6	Dixon	1m 34.526s
7	Canet	1m 34.555s
8	Fernandez	1m 34.557s
9	Arenas	1m 34.699s
10	Aldeguer	1m 34.737s
11	Dalla Porta	1m 34.813s
12	Arbolino	1m 34.817s
13	Schrotter	1m 34.858s
14	Salac	1m 34.886s
15	Beaubier	1m 34.973s
16	Navarro	1m 35.012s
17	Baltus	1m 35.021s
18	Gonzalez	1m 35.104s
19	Alcoba	1m 35.154s
20	Bendsneyder	1m 35.175s
21	Roberts	1m 35.238s
22	Agius	1m 35.259s
23	Ramirez	1m 35.325s
24	Antonelli	1m 35.327s
25	VD Goorbergh	1m 35.546s
26	Corsi	1m 35.758s
27	Kubo	1m 35.847s
28	Hada	1m 36.029s
29	Skinner	1m 36.060s
30	Kelly	1m 36.209s

Championship Points

Pos.	Rider	Points
1	Ogura	183
2	Fernandez	182
3	Vietti	156
4	Canet	137
5	Roberts	108
6	Arbolino	108
7	Dixon	108
8	Schrotter	96
9	Chantra	92
10	Acosta	88
11	Navarro	75
12	Lopez	64
13	Bendsneyder	62
14	Arenas	52
15	Lowes	51
16	Gonzalez	44
17	Beaubier	43
18	Alcoba	41
19	Aldeguer	38
20	Salac	21
21	Baltus	20
22	Dalla Porta	10
23	Manzi	9
24	Fenati	7
25	Rodrigo	6
26	Zaccone	6
27	Ramirez	5
28	Kubo	4
29	Kelly	3
30	Pasini	1

Constructor Points

Pos.	Constructor	Points
1	Kalex	325
2	Boscoscuro	86
3	MV Agusta	5

Moto3

17 laps, 62.324 miles/100.300km · RACE WEATHER: Dry (air 20°, humidity 52%, track 37°)

Pos.	Rider	Nat.	No.	Entrant	Machine	Laps	Time & Speed
1	**Ayumu Sasaki**	JPN	71	Sterilgarda Husqvarna Max	Husqvarna	23	39m 03.516s 95.4mph/153.6km/h
2	**Tatsuki Suzuki**	JPN	24	Leopard Racing	Honda	23	39m 03.580s
3	**David Munoz**	SPA	44	BOE Motorsports	KTM	23	39m 03.808s
4	**Deniz Oncu**	TUR	53	Red Bull KTM Tech3	KTM	23	39m 03.860s
5	**Sergio Garcia**	SPA	11	AutoSolar GASGAS Aspar Team	GASGAS	23	39m 05.969s
6	**Diogo Moreira**	BRA	10	MT Helmets - MSI	KTM	23	39m 06.152s
7	**Izan Guevara**	SPA	28	AutoSolar GASGAS Aspar Team	GASGAS	23	39m 06.590s
8	**Daniel Holgado**	SPA	96	Red Bull KTM Ajo	KTM	23	39m 06.625s
9	**John McPhee**	GBR	17	Sterilgarda Husqvarna Max	Husqvarna	23	39m 10.990s
10	**Kaito Toba**	JPN	27	CIP Green Power	KTM	23	39m 11.229s
11	**Ivan Ortola**	SPA	48	Angeluss MTA Team	KTM	23	39m 11.302s
12	**Dennis Foggia**	ITA	7	Leopard Racing	Honda	23	39m 12.371s
13	**Ryusei Yamanaka**	JPN	6	MT Helmets - MSI	KTM	23	39m 12.468s
14	**Xavier Artigas**	SPA	43	CFMOTO Racing PruestelGP	CFMOTO	23	39m 12.659s
15	**Stefano Nepa**	ITA	82	Angeluss MTA Team	KTM	23	39m 12.776s
16	Lorenzo Fellon	FRA	20	SIC58 Squadra Corse	Honda	23	39m 21.293s
17	Adrian Fernandez	SPA	31	Red Bull KTM Tech3	KTM	23	39m 24.074s
18	Jaume Masia	SPA	5	Red Bull KTM Ajo	KTM	23	39m 24.113s
19	Riccardo Rossi	ITA	54	SIC58 Squadra Corse	Honda	23	39m 24.148s
20	Elia Bartolini	ITA	23	QJMotor Avintia Racing Team	KTM	23	39m 24.175s
21	Scott Ogden	GBR	19	VisionTrack Racing Team	Honda	23	39m 24.254s
22	Joel Kelso	AUS	66	CIP Green Power	KTM	23	39m 31.094s
23	Andrea Migno	ITA	16	Rivacold Snipers Team	Honda	23	39m 34.364s
24	Mario Aji	INA	64	Honda Team Asia	Honda	23	39m 34.948s
25	Taiyo Furusato	JPN	72	Honda Team Asia	Honda	23	39m 35.583s
26	Nicola Fabio Carraro	ITA	9	QJMotor Avintia Racing Team	KTM	23	39m 37.759s
27	Alberto Surra	ITA	67	Rivacold Snipers Team	Honda	23	39m 52.630s
28	Ana Carrasco	SPA	22	BOE Motorsports	KTM	23	39m 52.689s
29	Joshua Whatley	GBR	70	VisionTrack Racing Team	Honda	23	39m 52.958s
	Carlos Tatay	SPA	99	CFMOTO Racing PruestelGP	CFMOTO	9	DNF-crash

Fastest lap: David Munoz, on lap 23, 1m 40.910s, 96.4mph/155.1km/h.

Lap record: New layout.

Event maximum speed: Daniel Holgado, 139.3mph/224.2km/h (race).

Qualifying:

Weather: Dry

Air: 21° **Humidity:** 68% **Track:** 24°

Pos.	Rider	Time
1	Holgado	1m 41.234s
2	Sasaki	1m 41.244s
3	Oncu	1m 41.379s
4	Rossi	1m 41.506s
5	Foggia	1m 41.588s
6	Moreira	1m 41.627s
7	Suzuki	1m 41.638s
8	Guevara	1m 41.642s
9	Toba	1m 41.675s
10	Nepa	1m 41.714s
11	Garcia	1m 41.772s
12	Masia	1m 41.800s
13	Kelso	1m 41.857s
14	Migno	1m 42.025s
15	Yamanaka	1m 42.112s
16	Munoz	1m 42.519s
17	Ogden	1m 42.683s
18	McPhee	1m 42.951s
	Q1	
19	Ortola	1m 42.290s
20	Furusato	1m 42.302s
21	Artigas	1m 42.353s
22	Fernandez	1m 42.510s
23	Fellon	1m 42.749s
24	Tatay	1m 42.871s
25	Aji	1m 42.908s
26	Carraro	1m 42.936s
27	Bartolini	1m 42.969s
28	Whatley	1m 43.644s
29	Surra	1m 43.666s
30	Carrasco	1m 43.736s

Fastest race laps

Pos.	Rider	Time
1	Munoz	1m 40.910s
2	Sasaki	1m 40.995s
3	Oncu	1m 41.083s
4	Suzuki	1m 41.088s
5	McPhee	1m 41.093s
6	Masia	1m 41.166s
7	Holgado	1m 41.217s
8	Moreira	1m 41.224s
9	Ortola	1m 41.280s
10	Guevara	1m 41.317s
11	Garcia	1m 41.322s
12	Yamanaka	1m 41.402s
13	Artigas	1m 41.403s
14	Toba	1m 41.413s
15	Nepa	1m 41.535s
16	Foggia	1m 41.637s
17	Fellon	1m 41.789s
18	Tatay	1m 41.829s
19	Kelso	1m 41.869s
20	Ogden	1m 41.965s
21	Bartolini	1m 42.055s
22	Rossi	1m 42.074s
23	Fernandez	1m 42.088s
24	Carraro	1m 42.107s
25	Migno	1m 42.117s
26	Aji	1m 42.510s
27	Furusato	1m 42.553s
28	Surra	1m 43.111s
29	Carrasco	1m 43.227s
30	Whatley	1m 43.286s

Championship Points

Pos.	Rider	Points
1	Garcia	193
2	Guevara	188
3	Foggia	144
4	Sasaki	138
5	Masia	127
6	Oncu	127
7	Suzuki	114
8	Migno	84
9	Tatay	70
10	Artigas	64
11	Toba	63
12	Yamanaka	62
13	Holgado	56
14	Rossi	54
15	Moreira	54
16	Munoz	48
17	McPhee	40
18	Ortola	38
19	Nepa	30
20	Fernandez	29
21	Bartolini	23
22	Kelso	22
23	Ogden	20
24	Bertelle	16
25	Fellon	11
26	Aji	5

Constructor Points

Pos.	Constructor	Points
1	GASGAS	246
2	Honda	226
3	KTM	210
4	Husqvarna	167
5	CFMOTO	103

Telcowin
alpinestars
withu
YAMAHA
BARRACUDA

FIM WORLD CHAMPIONSHIP · ROUND 14

SAN MARINO GRAND PRIX

MISANO WORLD CIRCUIT MARCO SIMONCELLI

Above: Four in a row. Pecco Bagnaia was on a roll.
Photo: Ducati Corse

Left: "Won't be needing these any more." Andrea Dovizioso throws his gloves to the crowd after his 346th and final grand prix.
Photo: Gold & Goose

Above: **Bagnaia beat Bastianini, but did the Gresini rider hold back on the final lap?**
Photo: Ducati Corse

Top right: **Happiness is… Kazuki Watanabe was drafted in to replace the injured Mir at Suzuki.**
Photo: www.suzuki-racing.com

Above right: **Happiness is (part 2)… Remy Gardner was absorbing his dismissal by KTM.**
Photo: Gold & Goose

Above far right: **Marc Marquez shows off his battle scars.**
Photo: Repsol Honda

Right: **Instant elimination for Zarco, Pirro and Pol Espargaro, who tangled at the first corner.**

Below right: **Ducati wild-card Pirro, prone, was lucky to escape serious injury among the cartwheeling Desmosedicis.**
Photos: Gold & Goose

AFTER 27 laps packed with tension, it was impossible to forget the words of Johann Zarco three days before. Asked whether Ducati had directed their riders to help Bagnaia's title quest, he replied, "Dall'Igna said, 'If you have a chance to win, we don't deny a rider the opportunity. So go for it, but be clever.'"

Were these words going through Bastianini's mind in the final laps, as he bore down on Bagnaia, whose late race-leading speed had splintered a front group of four? How could it be that Bastianini posted fastest lap on the final circuit, despite nearly tailgating his compatriot at Turn Four – a near miss that cost him two-tenths? Had he been holding something back previously, a week after learning of his selection over Jorge Martin for the factory team in 2023? Was there an internal Ducati conspiracy at play? Or was Bagnaia (wearing an ill-advised Dennis Rodman tribute helmet) simply irresistible on the way to his sixth win of the season?

That's what Bastianini said anyway; while Bagnaia's progress seemed to bear it out – he'd suffered a three-place grid penalty for getting in Alex Marquez's way on Friday, but took his sixth win of the year, the first four-in-a-row for Ducati.

Yet only a fortnight later, it would all go the other way…

Bastianini's 2023 elevation, after months of waiting, was at the expense of Martin, who made the most of at least being promised the same latest factory bike, and questioned the need for Ducati to create "a war" between the two riders. He added that he felt Ducati had lost some confidence in his abilities during a shaky season, when he had scored just two podiums in 13 races.

There was a sense, however, that the current title contenders had been making hay while the sun shone – and a cloud was looming on their horizon. Marc Marquez was present at the track, and ready to test on the following Tuesday and Wednesday. He was fast from the outset, ending up 13th overall and top Honda, although he limited himself to relatively short runs on the first day. As important was the impetus he brought to the beleaguered Repsol Honda team, which, as well as conducting aero experiments, had broken its usual exclusive use of in-house technology to test (and subsequently race) a bought-in Kalex aluminium swing-arm in place of their own carbon-fibre unit. Paddock old hands could remember only two previous occasions when Honda had gone shopping for technology: commissioning a chassis for the unsuccessful four-stroke NR500 in 1980 from British company Maxton, and using Girling suspension and a British chassis in the 1960s, after Mike Hailwood famously had flung the Japanese rear shocks into the Suzuka lake.

There was also the significant departure of one of the few riders to have given Marquez a run for his money. After failing to come to any sort of terms with his Yamaha, Andrea Dovizioso said farewell after 346 races. Careful and reliable as well as fast, the three-times MotoGP title-runner had never missed a race through injury. "The weekend was really crazy," he said. "I really didn't expect so many people would support me in a crazy way. I was crying last night [Saturday] with the video [tribute]. My decision to stop here was right, and thank you to Yamaha and the team. When you are not fighting for the championship, it's normal [not to be in the limelight] because you are not so important. But when you decide to retire, all the people look at you in a different way because they start to really focus on what you did and what you are doing." He signed off in some style, finishing 12th for his best result of the year.

Aprilia and its soon-to-be satellite outfit succeeded in signing their first-choice rider line-up, with both Miguel Oliveira and Raul Fernandez confirmed at RNF Aprilia for 2023. Said team manager Massimo Rivola, "I rate Miguel as a top rider, and Raul is a super talent. He didn't do the season he was expecting, but hopefully we can put him in the position to take it out. I think we'll have a very strong mix to fight against eight Ducatis for the championship."

The opposite emotions came from Remy Gardner, still coming to terms with having been dropped. He'd been told on "Saturday afternoon in Austria … I wasn't expecting it to be honest. I've always given 100 per cent and, unfortunately, I don't think it was good enough. They said I was not professional enough. I felt like maybe there's not an appreciation for the world championship I brought them as well … to have only one year in MotoGP breaks my heart." KTM denied that a lack of professionalism was the reason. Motorsport director Pit Beirer said, "I don't know where he got that from. We

are now trying to create the mid-term future, and we just decided it's not okay to go on with Remy."

Gardner had offers to return to Moto2 in 2023, but soon afterwards decided to switch to World Superbikes instead, with the independent GRT Yamaha team.

Dorna released results of a global survey conducted before the summer break, answered by just short of 110,000 fans, at a press briefing distinguished by unsurprising platitudes, for example, "Ninety-two per cent of our fans told us that they are avid followers." (Well, ask a stupid question and you get a stupid answer.) There were some interesting observations about the demographic, with the average age being 36 years and four months, and that 13 per cent of the sample were female, leaving some ground to cover to attract younger supporters and women. Something that wouldn't have been helped by Monday's announcement that MotoGP had signed a memorandum of understanding to race in Saudi Arabia from 2024. The country has a deplorable human rights record, and women's rights there are a constant cause for concern.

Likewise the number of fans at Misano, as a second race in Italy yielded disappointing numbers. On Sunday, 56,981 showed up, compared with 96,212 in 2019, the previous occasion when the circuit had been fully open.

MOTOGP RACE – 27 laps

Miller had headed free practice and also taken pole, leading another Ducati lock-out of all but one of the first seven positions. It was his second career pole, the first in Argentina in 2018.

Above: **Chasing the yellow – Quartararo never could quite catch Marini and the special-paint-job Ducati.**

Top right: **Alonso Lopez wheelies the gaudy Boscoscuro to his first victory in Moto2.**

Above right: **Maverick Vinales took another podium for Aprilia.**

Centre right: **Erstwhile Moto3 championship leader Sergio Garcia heads for the pits after being black-flagged.**

Centre far right: **Australian teenager Harrison Voight was given a wild-card ride on the SIC58 Squadra Corse Honda.**

Right: **Winner Foggia leads Masia, Guevara, Holgado, Oncu and Suzuki in a typical Moto3 chasing game.**

Far right: **Special moment, first-time winner Lopez listens to the Spanish national anthem on the podium.**

Photos: Gold & Goose

Bagnaia was a close second from Bastianini; Bezzecchi (through from Q1) was fourth fastest. But Bagnaia was docked three positions for riding slowly on line in FP1, disturbing Alex Marquez on a fast lap. Thus Bezzecchi took the front row; Vinales and the Aprilia led the second, with Bagnaia alongside, then Zarco. Marini headed row three, and only then came Quartararo and the other title contender, Aleix Espargaro.

Miller led away from Bastianini, with Bagnaia sharply through from row two. Then followed Vinales and Bezzecchi. Espargaro and Quartararo were sixth and eighth, sandwiching Marini.

But it was a messy start. In the first yards, at the first corner, a squeezed Zarco skittled wild-card Pirro and Pol Espargaro. Then on lap two, Miller crashed out of the lead at the tricky Turn Four. Bezzecchi followed suit six turns later, from a highly promising fifth. And having inherited the lead courtesy of Miller's mistake, Bastianini so nearly had the same misfortune at Turn 14 on the same lap, saving a monumental front-end slide on his elbow.

Clearly spooked by the early lack of grip, Bastianini offered little resistance as Bagnaia took over on lap three with a clean pass at Quercia. And sensing the former's troubles, Vinales nabbed second with a surprisingly aggressive move on the young Italian at Turn 14. Now he pressed Bagnaia repeatedly, but the Ducati rider held firm.

Behind them, Marini had made short work of Espargaro on lap two and now joined a lead quartet.

For a while, it appeared that the group might grow. Once Quartararo had fought off Martin early on, then passed Espargaro at Turn 14 on the sixth lap, his fastest lap the seventh time around suggested that he could close the eight-tenths gap. Yet in reality, Bagnaia had been controlling the pace. By lap 15, as he and Vinales exchanged fastest laps, it was clear that Quartararo couldn't live with that pace.

There were indications that Bastianini was in the same boat. While the two leaders posted another round of fastest laps on lap 16, Bastianini lost third for a handful of seconds when he ran wide at Turn Ten. That spurred him on; he immediately repassed Marini into Curvone, and while Bagnaia continued to lower his times up front, Bastianini was a full four-tenths faster on lap 17. At the same time, there were indications that Vinales was short of breath, running wide at Quercia the 19th time around.

Then came Bastianini's late push. A neat move on Vinales at the start of lap 20 left him with six-tenths to make up. With the Aprilia and Marini fading, this was now an all-Italian fight. Bagnaia's own personal best came with four laps to go, but his compatriot was faster still. By the penultimate circuit, there was nothing between them. But for that late mistake, Bastianini might have been close enough through the race's final turns to attempt a clean move.

Vinales was 4.2 seconds adrift for a third podium in four races: happy, but noting how Aprilia still had some way to go to live with Ducati. Marini equalled his career-best fourth from two weeks before, one second behind, doing just enough to hold off Quartararo, who had pushed resolutely to the flag over the closing laps. The Frenchman had "a knife to the throat" all race, he said. The disappointing thing? "I was on the limit with no problem on the bike, and we were still only P5." At least he beat Espargaro by four seconds, the Catalan claiming that this and the Red Bull Ring had been his bogey tracks of the season.

Rins, having climbed through from 12th on the grid, overworking his tyres in the process, survived a run-off and arm-pump for a hard-earned seventh, ahead of Brad Binder and a disappointed Martin. Alex Marquez was a respectable tenth, having passed Oliveira on the last lap as the KTM rider served a long-lap penalty, and the first Honda on an otherwise miserable day: Bradl was 14th, Nakagami up to 15th, having been dropped to the back by the first-corner accident that had eliminated Pol Espargaro.

Some way back, Dovizioso comfortably led Fernandez, Bradl and Nakagami. The remounted Bezzecchi and Miller were 17th and 18th, behind Darryn Binder, but ahead of Gardner, who had also suffered a long-lap penalty. One lap down, Kazuki Watanabe, replacing Mir on the Suzuki, was last. Morbidelli also crashed out.

MOTO2 RACE – 25 laps

From ex-Moto3 rider without a job to Moto2's next hot prospect, Alonso Lopez capped a remarkable 21-month turnaround at Misano. Seven races before, the 20-year-old Spaniard had been controversially put into the Boscoscuro team in place of sacked Italian Romano Fenati – but his exploits on the ex-Speed Up chassis had already put him on the podium at Silverstone. Now, a dominant performance proved that it had been no flash in the pan.

Vietti had qualified on pole, from Arenas and then Lopez; Canet led the second row from Arbolino and Dalla Porta. Title hopefuls Ogura and Fernandez were eighth and ninth on row three, alongside another bright beginner, Aldeguer.

Lopez led away on a first lap during which Dixon crashed (he had fallen also in Q2 to start from 18th on the grid), as well as van den Goorbergh and Kubo, and later the latter's team-mate, Gonzalez – the first on a 12-strong crash list.

Early pressure on the leader came from Arenas and Vietti, before he edged away to be more than a second clear at half-distance. But perhaps it would not be clear cut, with Canet's mid-race pace a cause for concern, after he had dropped early battlers Ogura and Fernandez to close on the tussle for second. His looming threat forced a crucial error from Vietti, who fell for a second race in succession on lap ten at Turn Four.

Once Canet had passed Arenas for second on lap 14, he began working on Lopez's 1.5-second lead. But after edging closer by three-tenths in three laps, Lopez responded to claim a first win for the Boscoscuro chassis since June, 2018, by better than a second. It was also the first win for a non-Kalex since KTM-mounted Binder had won the closing round at Valencia in 2019.

With Canet second, Fernandez finally got the better of Ogura on lap 11 and eventually reeled in Arenas to claim a crucial third with two laps to go.

Ogura was a distant fifth, while Acosta nabbed sixth from Arbolino on the final lap, a second behind the Japanese rider. Chantra had been following Acosta through, but fell short at the finish by a couple of seconds.

Roberts headed Alcoba, a full six seconds down; then came Schrotter, narrowly holding Bendsneyder at bay. Baltus, Beaubier and Zaccona trailed in for the last points, the field much broken up by so many falls, and with only 17 finishers. Victims included Navarro, Salac, Aldeguer (thus avoiding having to take a long-lap), Dalla Porta, Antonelli and Kelly, as well as wild-carding veteran Mattia Pasini, who had qualified tenth and worked his way up to sixth when he fell on lap 13.

Fernandez regained the championship lead by four points from Ogura; Canet (another 37 points adrift) moved past Vietti into third overall.

MOTO3 RACE – 23 laps

Oncu claimed a third pole of the season, ahead of rookies Holgado and Moreiro. Guevara was in the middle of row two, but Garcia on the fifth. Foggia was the first Honda, leading row three.

The start was messy in this class, too: Sasaki taken out on the first lap by Carraro; points leader Garcia running off at the first corner before crashing out of ninth on lap five. His misery was compounded by a black flag, received for rejoining and mixing it with the top ten, albeit one lap down.

By then, Guevara was threatening to break clear, but Foggia, Masia and Oncu fought back, the front quartet out on their own.

Foggia was the smartest, the Italian starting the final lap ahead. A wild move from Oncu at Quercia, which took him from third to second, allowed the Honda man to escape.

Masia eventually got Oncu back to finish second, with Guevara also following through for third.

Four seconds behind, Holgado was fifth, ahead of Suzuki; another five seconds down, Moreira narrowly headed a gang of seven, from Ortola, McPhee, Nepa, Rossi, Munoz and Yamanaka, all over the line within one second. Next up was Australian Kelso, in his second race back from injury, who came through from 30th on the grid to 14th.

Migno and Tatay crashed out, likewise rookie Aji.

Guevara took over the title lead from disqualified team-mate Garcia by 11 points; Foggia's third win was a fillip to his dwindling title chances.

FIM WORLD CHAMPIONSHIP: ROUND 14

GRAN PREMIO GRYFYN DI SAN MARINO E DELLA RIVIERA DI RIMINI

2–4 SEPTEMBER, 2022

MISANO WORLD CIRCUIT

27 laps
Length: 4.226 km / 2.626 miles
Width: 12m

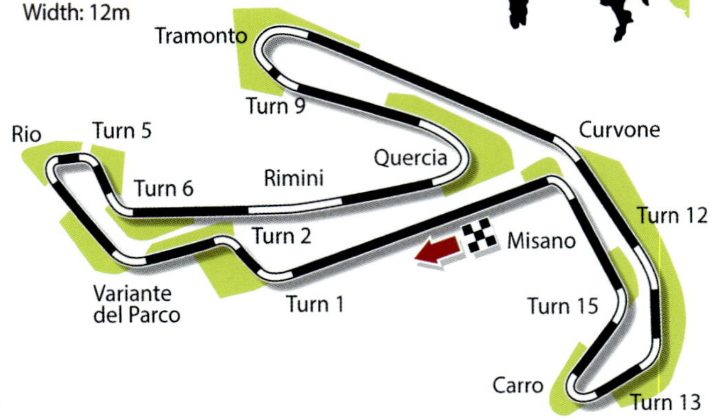

MotoGP

RACE DISTANCE: 27 laps, 70.900 miles/114.102km · RACE WEATHER: Dry (air 27°, humidity 64%, track 42°)

Pos.	Rider	Nat.	No.	Entrant	Machine	Tyres	Race tyre choice	Laps	Time & speed
1	**Francesco Bagnaia**	ITA	63	Ducati Lenovo Team	Ducati Desmosedici	M	F: Hard/R: Medium	27	41m 43.199s 101.9mph/164.0km/h
2	**Enea Bastianini**	ITA	23	Gresini Racing MotoGP	Ducati Desmosedici	M	F: Hard/R: Medium	27	41m 43.233s
3	**Maverick Vinales**	SPA	12	Aprilia Racing	Aprilia RS-GP	M	F: Hard/R: Medium	27	41m 47.411s
4	**Luca Marini**	ITA	10	Mooney VR46 Racing Team	Ducati Desmosedici	M	F: Hard/R: Medium	27	41m 48.482s
5	**Fabio Quartararo**	FRA	20	Monster Energy Yamaha MotoGP	Yamaha YZR-M1	M	F: Hard/R: Medium	27	41m 48.970s
6	**Aleix Espargaro**	SPA	41	Aprilia Racing	Aprilia RS-GP	M	F: Hard/R: Medium	27	41m 53.429s
7	**Alex Rins**	SPA	42	Team SUZUKI ECSTAR	Suzuki GSX-RR	M	F: Hard/R: Medium	27	41m 55.695s
8	**Brad Binder**	RSA	33	Red Bull KTM Factory Racing	KTM RC16	M	F: Hard/R: Medium	27	41m 57.860s
9	**Jorge Martin**	SPA	89	Prima Pramac Racing	Ducati Desmosedici	M	F: Hard/R: Medium	27	42m 00.931s
10	**Alex Marquez**	SPA	73	LCR Honda CASTROL	Honda RC213V	M	F: Hard/R: Medium	27	42m 05.185s
11	**Miguel Oliveira**	POR	88	Red Bull KTM Factory Racing	KTM RC16	M	F: Hard/R: Medium	27	42m 06.884s
12	**Andrea Dovizioso**	ITA	4	WithU Yamaha RNF MotoGP Team	Yamaha YZR-M1	M	F: Hard/R: Medium	27	42m 12.475s
13	**Raul Fernandez**	SPA	25	Tech3 KTM Factory Racing	KTM RC16	M	F: Hard/R: Medium	27	42m 13.632s
14	**Stefan Bradl**	GER	6	Repsol Honda Team	Honda RC213V	M	F: Hard/R: Medium	27	42m 14.967s
15	**Takaaki Nakagami**	JPN	30	LCR Honda IDEMITSU	Honda RC213V	M	F: Hard/R: Medium	27	42m 15.746s
16	Darryn Binder	RSA	40	WithU Yamaha RNF MotoGP Team	Yamaha YZR-M1	M	F: Hard/R: Medium	27	42m 25.056s
17	Marco Bezzecchi	ITA	72	Mooney VR46 Racing Team	Ducati Desmosedici	M	F: Hard/R: Medium	27	42m 33.758s
18	Jack Miller	AUS	43	Ducati Lenovo Team	Ducati Desmosedici	M	F: Hard/R: Medium	27	42m 36.570s
19	Remy Gardner	AUS	87	Tech3 KTM Factory Racing	KTM RC16	M	F: Hard/R: Medium	27	42m 39.812s
20	Fabio Di Giannantonio	ITA	49	Gresini Racing MotoGP	Ducati Desmosedici	M	F: Hard/R: Medium	27	42m 40.503s
21	Kazuki Watanabe	JPN	92	Team SUZUKI ECSTAR	Suzuki GSX-RR	M	F: Medium/R: Medium	26	41m 47.165s
	Franco Morbidelli	ITA	21	Monster Energy Yamaha MotoGP	Yamaha YZR-M1	M	F: Hard/R: Medium	2	DNF-crash
	Johann Zarco	FRA	5	Prima Pramac Racing	Ducati Desmosedici	M	F: Hard/R: Medium	0	DNF-crash
	Michele Pirro	ITA	51	Aruba.it Racing	Ducati Desmosedici	M	F: Hard/R: Medium	0	DNF-crash
	Pol Espargaro	SPA	44	Repsol Honda Team	Honda RC213V	M	F: Hard/R: Medium	0	DNF-crash

Fastest lap: Enea Bastianini, on lap 27, 1m 31.868s, 102.9mph/165.6km/h.
Lap record: Francesco Bagnaia, 1m 32.171s, 102.5mph/165.0km/h (2021).
Event maximum speed: Marco Bezzecchi, 188.0mph/302.5km/h (warm-up).

Qualifying

Weather: Dry
Air Temp: 24° **Humidity:** 69%
Track Temp: 28°

1	Miller	1m 31.899s
2	Bagnaia	1m 31.914s
3	Bastianini	1m 32.014s
4	Bezzecchi	1m 32.048s
5	Vinales	1m 32.118s
6	Zarco	1m 32.169s
7	Marini	1m 32.226s
8	Quartararo	1m 32.246s
9	A. Espargaro	1m 32.577s
10	Oliveira	1m 32.775s
11	Morbidelli	1m 33.351s
12	Rins	1m 33.438s
	Q1	
13	B. Binder	1m 32.600s
14	A. Marquez	1m 32.631s
15	Pirro	1m 32.658s
16	Dovizioso	1m 32.663s
17	P. Espargaro	1m 32.826s
18	Bradl	1m 32.838s
19	D. Binder	1m 33.331s
20	Nakagami	1m 33.484s
21	Watanabe	1m 36.289s
22	Gardner	1m 44.690s
23	Fernandez	1m 46.732s

Fastest race laps

1	Bastianini	1m 31.868s
2	Bagnaia	1m 31.933s
3	Quartararo	1m 32.125s
4	Marini	1m 32.145s
5	Vinales	1m 32.190s
6	Rins	1m 32.398s
7	B. Binder	1m 32.408s
8	A. Espargaro	1m 32.409s
9	Oliveira	1m 32.620s
10	Martin	1m 32.639s
11	Bezzecchi	1m 32.801s
12	Nakagami	1m 32.859s
13	Di Giannantonio	1m 32.887s
14	A. Marquez	1m 32.898s
15	Miller	1m 32.922s
16	Dovizioso	1m 33.068s
17	Bradl	1m 33.126s
18	Fernandez	1m 33.159s
19	D. Binder	1m 33.203s
20	Gardner	1m 33.385s
21	Morbidelli	1m 34.468s
22	Watanabe	1m 35.228s

Championship Points

1	Quartararo	211
2	Bagnaia	181
3	A. Espargaro	178
4	Bastianini	138
5	Zarco	125
6	Miller	123
7	B. Binder	115
8	Vinales	101
9	Rins	101
10	Martin	94
11	Oliveira	90
12	Marini	82
13	Mir	77
14	Bezzecchi	68
15	M. Marquez	60
16	Nakagami	46
17	P. Espargaro	42
18	A. Marquez	35
19	Morbidelli	26
20	Di Giannantonio	23
21	Dovizioso	15
22	D. Binder	10
23	Gardner	9
24	Fernandez	8
25	Bradl	2

Constructor Points

1	Ducati	321
2	Yamaha	211
3	Aprilia	201
4	KTM	148
5	Suzuki	127
6	Honda	96

Grid order	1	2	3	4	5	6	7	8	9	10	11	12	13	14	15	16	17	18	19	20	21	22	23	24	25	26	27	
43 MILLER	43	23	63	63	63	63	63	63	63	63	63	63	63	63	63	63	63	63	63	63	63	63	63	63	63	63	63	1
23 BASTIANINI	23	63	12	12	12	12	12	12	12	12	12	12	12	12	12	12	12	12	12	23	23	23	23	23	23	23	23	2
72 BEZZECCHI	63	12	23	23	23	23	23	23	23	23	23	23	23	23	23	23	23	23	23	12	12	12	12	12	12	12	12	3
12 VINALES	12	10	10	10	10	10	10	10	10	10	10	10	10	10	10	10	10	10	10	10	10	10	10	10	10	10	10	4
63 BAGNAIA	72	41	41	41	41	20	20	20	20	20	20	20	20	20	20	20	20	20	20	20	20	20	20	20	20	20	20	5
5 ZARCO	41	20	20	20	20	41	41	41	41	41	41	41	41	41	41	41	41	41	41	41	41	41	41	41	41	41	41	6
10 MARINI	10	89	89	89	89	89	89	89	89	42	42	89	89	42	42	42	42	42	42	42	42	42	42	42	42	42	42	7
20 QUARTARARO	20	42	42	42	42	42	42	42	42	89	89	42	42	89	89	89	89	89	33	33	33	33	33	33	33	33	33	8
41 A. ESPARGARO	88	88	73	73	73	73	73	73	73	88	88	88	88	88	88	33	33	33	89	89	89	89	89	89	89	89	89	9
88 OLIVEIRA	89	73	88	88	88	88	88	88	88	73	73	33	33	33	33	88	88	88	88	88	88	88	88	88	88	88	73	10
21 MORBIDELLI	42	49	33	33	33	33	33	33	33	33	33	73	73	73	73	73	73	73	73	73	73	73	73	73	73	73	88	11
42 RINS	21	21	4	4	4	4	4	4	4	4	4	4	4	4	4	4	4	4	4	4	4	4	4	4	4	4	4	12
89 MARTIN	73	33	40	40	40	40	40	40	40	25	25	25	25	25	25	25	25	25	25	25	25	25	25	25	25	25	25	13
49 DI GIANNANTONIO	49	4	6	6	6	6	6	25	25	40	40	40	40	40	40	40	40	40	40	40	6	6	6	6	6	6	6	14
33 B.BINDER	33	40	87	87	25	25	25	6	6	6	6	6	6	6	6	6	6	6	6	6	40	30	30	30	30	30	30	15
73 A. MARQUEZ	4	6	25	25	87	87	87	87	87	87	87	87	30	30	30	30	30	30	30	30	30	40	40	40	40	40	40	
51 PIRRO	40	87	30	30	30	30	30	30	30	30	30	30	87	87	87	87	87	87	87	87	87	87	72	72	72	72	72	
4 DOVIZIOSO	87	30	92	92	92	92	92	92	43	43	43	43	43	43	43	43	43	72	72	72	72	72	43	43	43	43	43	
44 P. ESPARGARO	6	25	43	43	43	43	43	43	92	92	72	72	72	72	72	72	72	43	43	43	43	43	87	87	87	87	87	
6 BRADL	30	92	72	72	72	72	72	72	72	72	92	49	49	49	49	49	49	49	49	49	49	49	49	49	49	49	49	
40 D.BINDER	25	43	49	49	49	49	49	49	49	49	49	92	92	92	92	92	92	92	92	92	92	92	92	92	92	*92*		
30 NAKAGAMI	92	72																										
92 WATANABE																												
87 GARDNER																												
25 FERNANDEZ																												

92 Lapped rider

Moto2

RACE DISTANCE: 25 laps, 65.648 miles/105.650km · RACE WEATHER: Dry (air 28°, humidity 60%, track 39°)

Pos.	Rider	Nat.	No.	Entrant	Machine	Laps	Time & Speed
1	**Alonso Lopez**	SPA	21	+Ego Speed Up	Boscoscuro	25	40m 35.332s
							97.0mph/156.1km/h
2	**Aron Canet**	SPA	40	Flexbox HP40	Kalex	25	40m 36.585s
3	**Augusto Fernandez**	SPA	37	Red Bull KTM Ajo	Kalex	25	40m 38.637s
4	**Albert Arenas**	SPA	75	Inde GASGAS Aspar Team	Kalex	25	40m 39.947s
5	**Ai Ogura**	JPN	79	IDEMITSU Honda Team Asia	Kalex	25	40m 44.498s
6	**Pedro Acosta**	SPA	51	Red Bull KTM Ajo	Kalex	25	40m 45.671s
7	**Tony Arbolino**	ITA	14	Elf Marc VDS Racing Team	Kalex	25	40m 45.766s
8	**Somkiat Chantra**	THA	35	IDEMITSU Honda Team Asia	Kalex	25	40m 47.709s
9	**Joe Roberts**	USA	16	Italtrans Racing Team	Kalex	25	40m 53.574s
10	**Jeremy Alcoba**	SPA	52	Liqui Moly Intact GP	Kalex	25	40m 54.892s
11	**Marcel Schrotter**	GER	23	Liqui Moly Intact GP	Kalex	25	41m 03.228s
12	**Bo Bendsneyder**	NED	64	Pertamina Mandalika SAG Team	Kalex	25	41m 03.784s
13	**Barry Baltus**	BEL	7	RW Racing GP	Kalex	25	41m 06.323s
14	**Cameron Beaubier**	USA	6	American Racing	Kalex	25	41m 13.703s
15	**Alessandro Zaccone**	ITA	61	Gresini Racing Moto2	Kalex	25	41m 17.022s
16	Marcos Ramirez	SPA	42	MV Agusta Forward Racing	MV Agusta	25	41m 17.541s
17	Taiga Hada	JPN	29	Pertamina Mandalika SAG Team	Kalex	25	41m 44.506s
	Sean Dylan Kelly	USA	4	American Racing	Kalex	18	DNF-crash
	Celestino Vietti	ITA	13	Mooney VR46 Racing Team	Kalex	14	DNF-crash
	Mattia Pasini	ITA	11	Inde GASGAS Aspar Team	Kalex	12	DNF-crash
	Niccolo Antonelli	ITA	28	Mooney VR46 Racing Team	Kalex	11	DNF-crash
	Simone Corsi	ITA	24	MV Agusta Forward Racing	MV Agusta	9	DNF-ret in pit
	Zonta van den Goorbergh	NED	84	RW Racing GP	Kalex	9	DNF-crash
	Fermin Aldeguer	SPA	54	+Ego Speed Up	Boscoscuro	9	DNF-crash
	Lorenzo Dalla Porta	ITA	19	Italtrans Racing Team	Kalex	6	DNF-crash
	Senna Agius	AUS	8	Elf Marc VDS Racing Team	Kalex	5	DNF-ret in pit
	Jorge Navarro	SPA	9	Flexbox HP40	Kalex	4	DNF-crash
	Filip Salac	CZE	12	Gresini Racing Moto2	Kalex	4	DNF-crash
	Jake Dixon	GBR	96	Inde GASGAS Aspar Team	Kalex	0	DNF-crash
	Manuel Gonzalez	SPA	18	Yamaha VR46 Master Camp Team	Kalex	0	DNF-crash
	Keminth Kubo	THA	81	Yamaha VR46 Master Camp Team	Kalex	0	DNF-crash

Fastest lap: Ai Ogura, on lap 4, 1m 36.867s, 97.6mph/157.0km/h.

Lap record: Augusto Fernandez, 1m 36.182s, 98.2mph/158.1km/h (2021).

Event maximum speed: Tony Arbolino, 157.5mph/253.5km/h (qualifying).

Qualifying

Weather: Dry

Air: 25° **Humidity:** 66% **Track:** 29°

1	Vietti	1m 35.996s
2	Arenas	1m 36.097s
3	Lopez	1m 36.186s
4	Canet	1m 36.373s
5	Arbolino	1m 36.397s
6	Dalla Porta	1m 36.467s
7	Aldeguer	1m 36.482s
8	Ogura	1m 36.489s
9	Fernandez	1m 36.527s
10	Pasini	1m 36.567s
11	Chantra	1m 36.575s
12	Schrotter	1m 36.639s
13	Acosta	1m 36.658s
14	Bendsneyder	1m 36.681s
15	Roberts	1m 36.762s
16	Navarro	1m 36.894s
17	Salac	1m 37.260s
18	Dixon	No Time
	Q1	
19	Gonzalez	1m 36.960s
20	Baltus	1m 37.054s
21	Alcoba	1m 37.066s
22	Zaccone	1m 37.152s
23	Antonelli	1m 37.221s
24	Beaubier	1m 37.481s
25	Agius	1m 37.567s
26	VD Goorbergh	1m 37.826s
27	Ramirez	1m 37.884s
28	Hada	1m 38.018s
29	Kelly	1m 38.435s
30	Corsi	1m 38.523s
31	Kubo	1m 38.588s

Fastest race laps

1	Ogura	1m 36.867s
2	Lopez	1m 36.877s
3	Vietti	1m 36.897s
4	Fernandez	1m 36.900s
5	Canet	1m 36.907s
6	Arenas	1m 36.909s
7	Acosta	1m 36.956s
8	Pasini	1m 37.002s
9	Chantra	1m 37.063s
10	Aldeguer	1m 37.109s
11	Arbolino	1m 37.137s
12	Navarro	1m 37.352s
13	Roberts	1m 37.360s
14	Dalla Porta	1m 37.434s
15	Alcoba	1m 37.453s
16	Schrotter	1m 37.638s
17	Bendsneyder	1m 37.670s
18	Baltus	1m 37.676s
19	Ramirez	1m 37.945s
20	Agius	1m 37.998s
21	Beaubier	1m 38.007s
22	Salac	1m 38.152s
23	Antonelli	1m 38.245s
24	Zaccone	1m 38.263s
25	Corsi	1m 38.324s
26	VD Goorbergh	1m 38.540s
27	Kelly	1m 38.853s
28	Hada	1m 38.948s

Championship Points

1	Fernandez	198
2	Ogura	194
3	Canet	157
4	Vietti	156
5	Arbolino	117
6	Roberts	115
7	Dixon	108
8	Schrotter	101
9	Chantra	100
10	Acosta	98
11	Lopez	89
12	Navarro	75
13	Bendsneyder	66
14	Arenas	65
15	Lowes	51
16	Alcoba	47
17	Beaubier	45
18	Gonzalez	44
19	Aldeguer	38
20	Baltus	23
21	Salac	21
22	Dalla Porta	10
23	Manzi	9
24	Zaccone	7
25	Fenati	7
26	Rodrigo	6
27	Ramirez	5
28	Kubo	4
29	Kelly	3
30	Pasini	1

Constructor Points

1	Kalex	345
2	Boscoscuro	111
3	MV Agusta	5

Moto3

RACE DISTANCE: 23 laps, 60.396 miles/97.198km · RACE WEATHER: Dry (air 27°, humidity 56%, track 33°)

Pos.	Rider	Nat.	No.	Entrant	Machine	Laps	Time & Speed
1	**Dennis Foggia**	ITA	7	Leopard Racing	Honda	23	39m 21.864s
							92.0mph/148.1km/h
2	**Jaume Masia**	SPA	5	Red Bull KTM Ajo	KTM	23	39m 22.153s
3	**Izan Guevara**	SPA	28	Gaviota GASGAS Aspar Team	GASGAS	23	39m 22.198s
4	**Deniz Oncu**	TUR	53	Red Bull KTM Tech3	KTM	23	39m 22.317s
5	**Daniel Holgado**	SPA	96	Red Bull KTM Ajo	KTM	23	39m 26.819s
6	**Tatsuki Suzuki**	JPN	24	Leopard Racing	Honda	23	39m 27.790s
7	**Diogo Moreira**	BRA	10	MT Helmets - MSI	KTM	23	39m 32.866s
8	**Ivan Ortola**	SPA	48	Angeluss MTA Team	KTM	23	39m 33.052s
9	**John McPhee**	GBR	17	Sterilgarda Husqvarna Max	Husqvarna	23	39m 33.247s
10	**Stefano Nepa**	ITA	82	Angeluss MTA Team	KTM	23	39m 33.358s
11	**Riccardo Rossi**	ITA	54	SIC58 Squadra Corse	Honda	23	39m 33.424s
12	**David Munoz**	SPA	44	BOE Motorsports	KTM	23	39m 33.497s
13	**Ryusei Yamanaka**	JPN	6	MT Helmets - MSI	KTM	23	39m 33.749s
14	**Joel Kelso**	AUS	66	CIP Green Power	KTM	23	39m 38.827s
15	**Elia Bartolini**	ITA	23	QJMotor Avintia Racing Team	KTM	23	39m 41.752s
16	Adrian Fernandez	SPA	31	Red Bull KTM Tech3	KTM	23	39m 42.392s
17	Alberto Surra	ITA	67	Rivacold Snipers Team	Honda	23	39m 42.592s
18	Lorenzo Fellon	FRA	20	SIC58 Squadra Corse	Honda	23	39m 42.669s
19	Kaito Toba	JPN	27	CIP Green Power	KTM	23	39m 45.483s
20	Xavier Artigas	SPA	43	CFMOTO Racing PruestelGP	CFMOTO	23	39m 47.420s
21	Taiyo Furusato	JPN	72	Honda Team Asia	Honda	23	39m 57.190s
22	Ana Carrasco	SPA	22	BOE Motorsports	KTM	23	40m 11.854s
23	Harrison Voight	AUS	29	SIC58 Squadra Corse	Honda	23	40m 14.048s
24	Joshua Whatley	GBR	70	VisionTrack Racing Team	Honda	23	40m 18.292s
25	Scott Ogden	GBR	19	VisionTrack Racing Team	Honda	22	40m 26.702s
	Carlos Tatay	SPA	99	CFMOTO Racing PruestelGP	CFMOTO	21	DNF-crash
	Mario Aji	INA	64	Honda Team Asia	Honda	4	DNF-crash
	Andrea Migno	ITA	16	Rivacold Snipers Team	Honda	2	DNF-crash
	Ayumu Sasaki	JPN	71	Sterilgarda Husqvarna Max	Husqvarna	0	DNF-crash
	Nicola Fabio Carraro	ITA	9	QJMotor Avintia Racing Team	KTM	0	DNF-crash
	Sergio Garcia	SPA	11	Gaviota GASGAS Aspar Team	GASGAS	-	DSQ

Fastest lap: Dennis Foggia, on lap 9, 1m 41.710s, 92.9mph/149.5km/h.

Lap record: Romano Fenati, 1m 41.648s, 93.0mph/149.6km/h (2021).

Event maximum speed: Daniel Holgado, 133.1mph/214.2km/h (qualifying)..

Qualifying:

Weather: Dry

Air: 25° **Humidity:** 67% **Track:** 28°

1	Oncu	1m 42.448s
2	Holgado	1m 42.471s
3	Moreira	1m 42.472s
4	Yamanaka	1m 42.488s
5	Guevara	1m 42.609s
6	Tatay	1m 42.626s
7	Foggia	1m 42.652s
8	McPhee	1m 42.657s
9	Migno	1m 42.743s
10	Fernandez	1m 42.810s
11	Masia	1m 42.860s
12	Nepa	1m 42.946s
13	Garcia	1m 43.097s
14	Rossi	1m 43.148s
15	Munoz	1m 43.171s
16	Suzuki	1m 43.316s
17	Sasaki	1m 43.550s
18	Fellon	1m 43.699s
	Q1	
19	Surra	1m 42.932s
20	Carraro	1m 42.968s
21	Bartolini	1m 43.013s
22	Ogden	1m 43.024s
23	Aji	1m 43.228s
24	Toba	1m 43.268s
25	Artigas	1m 43.296s
26	Ortola	1m 43.521s
27	Furusato	1m 43.619s
28	Voight	1m 43.678s
29	Whatley	1m 44.077s
30	Kelso	1m 44.092s
31	Carrasco	1m 44.136

Fastest race laps

1	Foggia	1m 41.710s
2	Masia	1m 41.737s
3	Holgado	1m 41.784s
4	Guevara	1m 41.887s
5	Oncu	1m 41.935s
6	McPhee	1m 42.012s
7	Garcia	1m 42.018s
8	Suzuki	1m 42.019s
9	Nepa	1m 42.062s
10	Moreira	1m 42.133s
11	Rossi	1m 42.153s
12	Munoz	1m 42.158s
13	Bartolini	1m 42.215s
14	Yamanaka	1m 42.216s
15	Fellon	1m 42.242s
16	Tatay	1m 42.302s
17	Ortola	1m 42.307s
18	Kelso	1m 42.311s
19	Artigas	1m 42.359s
20	Surra	1m 42.400s
21	Fernandez	1m 42.670s
22	Toba	1m 42.715s
23	Ogden	1m 42.748s
24	Aji	1m 42.803s
25	Furusato	1m 43.121s
26	Migno	1m 43.447s
27	Voight	1m 43.781s
28	Whatley	1m 44.005s
29	Carrasco	1m 44.026s

Championship Points

1	Guevara	204
2	Garcia	193
3	Foggia	169
4	Masia	147
5	Oncu	140
6	Sasaki	138
7	Suzuki	124
8	Migno	84
9	Tatay	70
10	Holgado	67
11	Yamanaka	65
12	Artigas	64
13	Toba	63
14	Moreira	63
15	Rossi	59
16	Munoz	52
17	McPhee	47
18	Ortola	46
19	Nepa	36
20	Fernandez	29
21	Bartolini	24
22	Kelso	24
23	Ogden	20
24	Bertelle	16
25	Fellon	11
26	Aji	5

Constructor Points

1	GASGAS	262
2	Honda	251
3	KTM	230
4	Husqvarna	174
5	CFMOTO	103

FIM WORLD CHAMPIONSHIP · ROUND 15

ARAGON GRAND PRIX

ARAGON CIRCUIT

Inset, above: Win number four for beaming Bastianini.

Inset, above right: Undone – Quartararo was lucky to escape injury in his hapless early crash.
Photos: Gold & Goose

Inset, right: Future team-mates, deadly rivals. This time Bastianini did not defer to Bagnaia in the battle of the Ducatis.
Photo: Ducati Corse

Inset, left: Ducati wrapped up the constructors' championship.
Photo: Ducati Corse

Main: High plains drifter. Bastianini proved unbeatable.
Photo: Gold & Goose

Above: **Trouble ahead. Marc Marquez runs around the outside in his flying start from 13th to sixth.**
Photo: Repsol Honda

Above right, from top: **Cal Crutchlow was back and finished top Yamaha; Cameron Beaubier announced plans to return to MotoAmerica for 2023; Max Biaggi had to take action against some of his Moto3 team.**

Right: **Pink power. Maria Herrera leaves all-girl Angeluss MTA pit on their Moto3 debut.**
Photos: Gold & Goose

WOULD anyone not expect the return of Marc Marquez to be dramatic? Yet nobody could have predicted exactly how dramatic, and how big the effect on a world championship battle in which he played no particular role, other than as spoiler.

By the end of the afternoon, Quartararo's lead had shrunk to just ten points.

The opening scenes were much as expected. Marc had essayed his RC213V at the Misano tests, and had been the fastest Honda rider taking part. Now, in free practice, he almost immediately executed a trademark miracle save, picking the bike up on knee and elbow after the front wheel had folded and any other rider would have fallen. Then he did fall, in FP3, while striving for the top ten, but narrowly missing out, for Q2. He failed also to make it out of Q1, by the narrowest of margins – almost three-tenths off leader Aleix Espargaro, but a slender 0.066 of a second slower than second-fastest Zarco.

The greater upset came in the race. Very early. Marc took a flying start from 13th on the grid, up to sixth as they accelerated through Turn Three, a right kink after the opening left-right chicane. On the gas, the rear stepped out slightly and he had to check.

Quartararo, right behind, couldn't avoid hitting him as the Honda slowed, and he went sprawling.

Luckily, given the crowded circumstances, nobody ran over him as he slid outwards off the track, though his own bike clobbered him in the chest and caused the zip on his leathers to fail, so he suffered abrasions to his chest and stomach. It could have been much worse. Cold comfort as he contemplated a second no-score in a campaign where the pressure was beginning to tell.

Worse soon followed. Unknown to Marquez, a chunk of Yamaha fairing had lodged in his rear ride-height device, and when he activated it on the exit from Turn Seven, the stricken bike slowed again and veered left. Another clout from behind, this time from LCR Honda rider Nakagami, again in the midst of the swarm. Riders dived right and left, miraculously avoiding the sliding Japanese and his spinning bike. He also escaped serious injury, although significant damage to tendons on the third and fourth fingers of his right hand would require surgery and some missed races.

The endgame of the European season had been a busy weekend, overshadowed by the need for hasty packing of travel cases for a rapid trip to Japan, for the very next weekend, Aragon being the first of three on the trot.

There was no let up in ancillary action either, particularly in the smallest class, where rivalry spilled over into violence and the repeated disciplinary actions of the panel of stewards paled into insignificance. The battle was between Max Biaggi's Sterilgarda Moto3 team mechanics and their former rider, Adrian Fernandez, brother of MotoGP rider Raul. There was already bad blood with the younger sibling, whose combination of histrionics and dourness had alienated the pit staff. Now they were angry because of his persistent following of current rider Ayumu Sasaki in practice, so they jumped in front of him in the pit lane and jammed on his front brake to make sure he didn't do it again. Later in the evening, Fernandez's father sought out a third technician for a confrontation that ended in violence.

Team owner Biaggi was aghast, issuing a public apology on Twitter; in turn, the stewards banned the mechanics from the Australian and Malaysian GPs (it would have been the upcoming Japanese and Thai events, but visa complications would have left Max's team short-staffed).

On a happier note, the advent in Moto3 of racing's first all-women team: the history-making Angeluss MTA squad, backing wild-carding former class regular Maria Herrera, who had scored points in 2015, 2016 and 2017. Five women manned the pits under the management of Aurora Angelucci. Maria was the last finisher, 27th.

Cal Crutchlow was back in place of the departed Dovizioso and joking, "He owes me a significant amount of money," because he'd had to cancel "a holiday with the girls." His

second return from retirement netted championship points (two, for 14th) as top Yamaha rider, a far from shabby 20 seconds down on the win: "I haven't raced for a year, and to me, 20 seconds is a long way … but I lost five of them on the first lap. I'm happy enough."

There was news for 2023 for Rossi's Mooney-sponsored team: both Marini and Bezzecchi would remain, but would be stuck with year-old GP22 Ducatis. This was an upgrade for Bezzecchi, currently riding a GP21, but a miss-hit for Marini. The decision had been taken to save money, being cheaper than the latest up-to-date package.

Moto2's American Racing Team was digesting the news that Cameron Beaubier would return to race in the USA in 2023. He'd been expected to renew for a third season, but instead would return to the MotoAmerica Superbike series, which he had won five times. Beaubier's Moto2 career had been respectable and shown steady improvement, but not fast enough for his liking: "I mainly came over here with the hopes of progressing into MotoGP, and I'm going to be 30 in December. So no matter how good I do next year, I don't see myself getting into MotoGP at 31 years old. I'm okay with that, but I've decided the twilight years of my career would be better spent at home again." Another reason was homesickness: "I didn't realise how much I appreciated racing in the MotoAmerica series and that ability to be home after every race weekend."

More details of 2023's revised format were announced on Saturday, confirming that Friday's MotoGP sessions would be called Practice, rather than Free Practice, with the morning session at 45 minutes plus an hour in the afternoon determining places in Q1 and Q2. Thus Saturday's 30-minute 'FP3' effectively would be untimed. The afternoon sprint race, with bikes restricted to 12 litres of fuel (more than half the 22-litre maximum for a full-length race), would not count towards GP victories in official statistics.

MOTOGP RACE – 23 laps

Bagnaia presided over yet another Ducati front-row lockout, his fifth pole of the year, less than a tenth ahead of teammate Miller and Bastianini. Aleix Espargaro (through from Q1) got among the Desmos to head row two, Zarco (also from Q2) alongside him. Only then, Quartararo, with two Ducatis (Bezzecchi and Martin) taking the next two spots.

If Misano had suggested covert Ducati team orders, this was the opposite.

The race started with two terrifying mid-pack crashes, both unwittingly triggered by the returned Marquez. He'd started brilliantly, up seven positions by Turn Two. His little moment in Turn Three did for Quartararo, sent sprawling on his belly. Rins missed him by inches, running off track in the process.

Four corners later, the second disaster, when his blocked ride-height device sent him veering left. Nakagami hit him and fell off the side of his bike. For a second time in 30 seconds, the pack scattered, again miraculously missing the downed rider and bike. Six riders were forced off track into Turn Eight.

Up front and away from the mayhem, Bagnaia had enjoyed another consummate start, from Miller, Bastianini and Aleix Espargaro. In one turn, Brad Binder had worked miracles to climb from tenth to fifth. Then Espargaro dived under Bastianini in Turn Three, pushing both men wide, letting the KTM through to attack Miller into Turn Five, to sit a barely believable second.

Martin, Zarco and Oliveira had also avoided the carnage to make up a leading octet.

Quartararo's ill fortune became worse when a marshal scootering him back to the pits crashed. On track, meanwhile, Miller moved back into second at the start of lap three. Protected from behind, Bagnaia built up a small, seven-tenths advantage by lap six.

Above: **Sunday man Brad Binder took the KTM from tenth to fourth.**

Top right: **Once Acosta had passed team-mate Fernandez, there was no catching him. Arbolino and Canet give chase.**

Above right: **Aleix Espargaro, between Bagnaia and Bastianini, enjoyed claiming his first podium in seven races.**

Centre right: **Vinales and Crutchlow had a fine scrap over 13th.**

Below right: **Back in the groove after mid-season injury, Pedro Acosta took his second Moto2 win.**

Below far right: **Guevara, Sasaki and Holgado were the class of Moto3.**
Photos: Gold & Goose

But there was a complication. Laid in 2009, the track surface is the oldest on the calendar, and riders were wary of a significant drop in rear tyre performance, and the need to manage the throttle on the notorious long lefts. Thus Bagnaia was too cautious to escape, and that gave Bastianini the chance to recover from his lap-one contretemps with a sharp move on Binder for third at the start of lap four, and then on Miller at Turn 15 on lap six.

Miller's afternoon soon became worse, with Binder repassing him on the following lap, and Espargaro doing the same later on the same lap.

Now Bastianini got to work, leaning heavily on his future team-mate and diving past at the start of lap nine. This was short-lived: a mistake braking for Turn 12 sent the Gresini rider wide and off track, back to second.

Once more, he had to overcome a deficit of close to a second, but as the pair edged clear of the Binder/Espargaro/Miller trio, he reeled in the leader. By lap 17, he was three-tenths behind, then with four laps to go, he was exerting the kind of pressure seen in the late Misano battle.

Passing moves came thick and fast, helped by an apparent top speed advantage. Still, Bagnaia held firm. Until a brilliantly precise move at Turn Seven on the final lap sealed Bastianini's fourth win of the year, four-hundredths clear of Bagnaia's final attempt to regain the 25 points.

Five seconds away, Binder was doing a sterling job of keeping Espargaro and Miller at bay, not least because of an injured right ankle from a fast fall on Saturday. But his own error did for him towards the end: "I tried a different map, but ended up pumping a lot and lost a lot of time." As they started the penultimate lap, the Aprilia got a better drive out of the last corner to take over at Turn One for a welcome return to the podium, in spite of a finger injury from a testing fall and two more tumbles in practice.

Binder "fought like hell" to keep Miller at bay, the Australian six-tenths behind in fifth.

Martin led an all-action quartet disputing sixth, 12 seconds down, with Marini getting the better of Zarco on the last lap. Rins had passed the fading Oliveira to join the group, but could get no further. On the last lap, the latter lost another place to Bezzecchi, but was safely better than a second clear of Alex Marquez.

Vinales, qualified 16th, lost positions in the first-lap tangles and finished an undistinguished 13th, with Crutchlow next, then Pol Espargaro – also slowed early on – who had stolen the final point ahead of Gardner with six laps to go.

MOTO2 RACE – 21 laps

Fernandez's second pole of the season, by better than a tenth from team-mates Arenas and Dixon, put him ahead of his closest title rival, Ogura, who had to come through Q1 to place eighth, flanked by Arbolino and team-mate Chantra on row three. Between them, Lopez, Canet and Acosta made an all-Spanish second row.

At first, it looked as though Fernandez would drive the advantage still further, as he took the lead from Dixon, Canet and Arenas, with Acosta and Ogura in pursuit, only for the Japanese rider to succumb to Arbolino on lap three.

By then, Lopez was long gone, having fallen on the first lap; Arenas also fell out, on lap two.

On the fifth lap, Fernandez had pulled away by 1.8 seconds, but after a slip from Dixon, the pursuit was now led by Acosta, with Canet and a revitalised Arbolino keeping close company. Behind came Dixon and Ogura.

The gap quickly came down. At the end of the ninth lap, Acosta was on his team-mate and effortlessly drafted past him next time down the long back straight. From there, he made his second win look easy, stretching the gap to 2.6 seconds in just his third race since his comeback from injury.

Rather than being able to chase Acosta, Fernandez had to turn his attention to defending second from Canet – without success: his compatriot nabbed a sixth runner-up position of the year on lap 19.

Ogura had been stuck behind Dixon from laps four to 14, by which time Aldeguer and Chantra had joined the pair. Once past, however, Ogura was able to concentrate on catching Arbolino, a job the Italian made much easier with

a slip on lap 15. The Japanese rider was past him with two laps to spare, for a fourth place that meant he lost only three points to Fernandez, some four seconds ahead of him.

By then, Aldeguer had got ahead of Dixon, whose last-lap attempt to regain sixth ended in a crash at Turn 12, leaving Chantra a safe, but now distant seventh.

Navarro had also lost ground and was eighth; likewise, Roberts in ninth. The next battle was for tenth, with Vietti prevailing over a big gang from Beaubier, Dalla Porta, Baltus, Zacconi, Bendsneyer and Marc VDS substitute Senna Agius. The last named missed the point in only his third outing by half a second, in spite of having suffered two long-lap penalties, the first a hangover from the previous round and the second for exceeding track limits. "A top-12 was definitely on the cards today," said the Australian teenager.

Schrotter was another lap-one faller; Alcoba and Gonzales crashed out in the same incident as Arenas. Van den Goorbergh crashed out alone; Kubo and Hada fell together.

Fernandez extended his points lead over Ogura to seven, but Canet's second place gave a boost to his fading hopes, 37 points adrift.

MOTO3 RACE – 19 laps

Starting from a fourth pole of the year, Guevara produced a timely display of control to put daylight between him and his title rivals with a lights-to-flag fourth win. But it wasn't a given for 17 laps, as Sasaki and, for a spell, also rookie Holgado held on.

It was an orderly outing up front, the top three having broken clear by 3.7 seconds by lap seven. Deniz Oncu might have been in the mix, too, but had to pay for a qualifying crash that had left him 13th on the grid. His lap-record rise through the pack to fourth lit up the early running.

Guevara's rhythm was deadly. By lap ten, Holgado had begun to fade, while Sasaki was just about holding on, losing time through the twisty sections, only to regain a handful of tenths in the slipstream on the back straight. On the final lap, the Japanese rider knew the leader wouldn't falter. Guevara won by nine-tenths, with Holgado 6.5 seconds behind for a debut podium. The race time was a stunning 24 seconds faster than 12 months before.

The usual mass brawl was for fifth, the last-lap reshuffle won by Fernandez over Ortola and Munoz, in spite of a long-lap penalty. Positions were a lottery, fifth to 13th all inside half a second, with Massia eighth, then Tatay, McPhee, Artigas, Suzuki and Garcia right behind.

Ogden was 22nd, Whatley crashed out.

An off-form Foggia was 14th, taking the spot from Moreira on the last lap. With him and Garcia claiming just five between them, Guevara's lead extended to 33 points.

FIM WORLD CHAMPIONSHIP: ROUND 15

GRAN PREMIO ANIMOCA BRANDS DE ARAGÓN

16–18 SEPTEMBER, 2022

MOTORLAND ARAGÓN

23 laps
Length: 5.078 km / 3.155 miles
Width: 15m

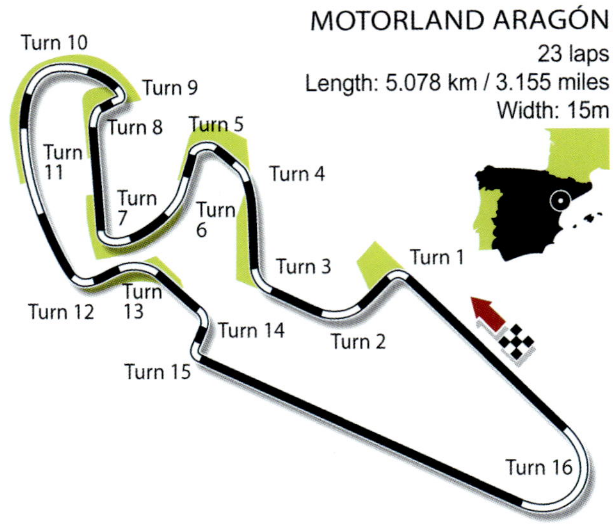

MotoGP

RACE DISTANCE: 23 laps, 72.558 miles/116.771km · RACE WEATHER: Dry (air 23°, humidity 45%, track 40°)

Pos.	Rider	Nat.	No.	Entrant	Machine	Tyres	Race tyre choice	Laps	Time & speed
1	**Enea Bastianini**	ITA	23	Gresini Racing MotoGP	Ducati Desmosedici	M	F: Hard/R: Medium	23	41m 35.462s 104.6mph/168.4km/h
2	**Francesco Bagnaia**	ITA	63	Ducati Lenovo Team	Ducati Desmosedici	M	F: Hard/R: Medium	23	41m 35.504s
3	**Aleix Espargaro**	SPA	41	Aprilia Racing	Aprilia RS-GP	M	F: Hard/R: Medium	23	41m 41.601s
4	**Brad Binder**	RSA	33	Red Bull KTM Factory Racing	KTM RC16	M	F: Hard/R: Medium	23	41m 41.841s
5	**Jack Miller**	AUS	43	Ducati Lenovo Team	Ducati Desmosedici	M	F: Hard/R: Medium	23	41m 42.426s
6	**Jorge Martin**	SPA	89	Prima Pramac Racing	Ducati Desmosedici	M	F: Hard/R: Medium	23	41m 47.492s
7	**Luca Marini**	ITA	10	Mooney VR46 Racing Team	Ducati Desmosedici	M	F: Hard/R: Medium	23	41m 47.936s
8	**Johann Zarco**	FRA	5	Prima Pramac Racing	Ducati Desmosedici	M	F: Hard/R: Medium	23	41m 48.117s
9	**Alex Rins**	SPA	42	Team SUZUKI ECSTAR	Suzuki GSX-RR	M	F: Hard/R: Medium	23	41m 48.164s
10	**Marco Bezzecchi**	ITA	72	Mooney VR46 Racing Team	Ducati Desmosedici	M	F: Hard/R: Medium	23	41m 51.612s
11	**Miguel Oliveira**	POR	88	Red Bull KTM Factory Racing	KTM RC16	M	F: Hard/R: Medium	23	41m 52.533s
12	**Alex Marquez**	SPA	73	LCR Honda CASTROL	Honda RC213V	M	F: Hard/R: Medium	23	41m 53.925s
13	**Maverick Vinales**	SPA	12	Aprilia Racing	Aprilia RS-GP	M	F: Hard/R: Medium	23	41m 54.192s
14	**Cal Crutchlow**	GBR	35	WithU Yamaha RNF MotoGP Team	Yamaha YZR-M1	M	F: Hard/R: Medium	23	41m 55.552s
15	**Pol Espargaro**	SPA	44	Repsol Honda Team	Honda RC213V	M	F: Hard/R: Medium	23	42m 03.050s
16	Remy Gardner	AUS	87	Tech3 KTM Factory Racing	KTM RC16	M	F: Hard/R: Medium	23	42m 04.267s
17	Franco Morbidelli	ITA	21	Monster Energy Yamaha MotoGP	Yamaha YZR-M1	M	F: Hard/R: Medium	23	42m 05.884s
18	Darryn Binder	RSA	40	WithU Yamaha RNF MotoGP Team	Yamaha YZR-M1	M	F: Hard/R: Medium	23	42m 06.792s
19	Fabio Di Giannantonio	ITA	49	Gresini Racing MotoGP	Ducati Desmosedici	M	F: Hard/R: Medium	23	42m 07.057s
20	Raul Fernandez	SPA	25	Tech3 KTM Factory Racing	KTM RC16	M	F: Hard/R: Medium	23	42m 11.622s
	Marc Marquez	SPA	93	Repsol Honda Team	Honda RC213V	M	F: Hard/R: Medium	1	DNF-technical
	Fabio Quartararo	FRA	20	Monster Energy Yamaha MotoGP	Yamaha YZR-M1	M	F: Hard/R: Medium	0	DNF-crash
	Takaaki Nakagami	JPN	30	LCR Honda IDEMITSU	Honda RC213V	M	F: Hard/R: Medium	0	DNF-crash

Fastest lap: Luca Marini, on lap 4, 1m 47.795s, 105.3mph/169.5km/h.
Lap record: Franco Morbidelli, 1m 48.089s, 105.0mph/169.0km/h (2020).
Event maximum speed: Enea Bastianini, 220.0mph/354.1km/h (qualifying).

Qualifying

Weather: Dry
Air Temp: 23° **Humidity:** 43%
Track Temp: 40°

1	Bagnaia	1m 46.069s
2	Miller	1m 46.159s
3	Bastianini	1m 46.313s
4	A. Espargaro	1m 46.590s
5	Zarco	1m 46.646s
6	Quartararo	1m 46.802s
7	Bezzecchi	1m 46.852s
8	Martin	1m 46.911s
9	Rins	1m 46.912s
10	B. Binder	1m 46.924s
11	Oliveira	1m 47.183s
12	Nakagami	1m 47.274s
	Q1	
13	M. Marquez	1m 46.909s
14	Marini	1m 47.056s
15	Di Giannantonio	1m 47.119s
16	Vinales	1m 47.337s
17	A. Marquez	1m 47.489s
18	P. Espargaro	1m 47.511s
19	Crutchlow	1m 47.541s
20	Morbidelli	1m 47.651s
21	Fernandez	1m 47.671s
22	Gardner	1m 47.847s
23	D. Binder	1m 49.309s

Fastest race laps

1	Marini	1m 47.795s
2	Bastianini	1m 47.929s
3	Rins	1m 48.011s
4	A. Espargaro	1m 48.036s
5	Bagnaia	1m 48.076s
6	B. Binder	1m 48.092s
7	Miller	1m 48.142s
8	Martin	1m 48.166s
9	A. Marquez	1m 48.221s
10	Bezzecchi	1m 48.222s
11	Zarco	1m 48.321s
12	P. Espargaro	1m 48.376s
13	Crutchlow	1m 48.398s
14	Oliveira	1m 48.435s
15	Vinales	1m 48.436s
16	Fernandez	1m 48.505s
17	D. Binder	1m 48.565s
18	Gardner	1m 48.586s
19	Di Giannantonio	1m 48.733s
20	Morbidelli	1m 48.755s

Championship Points

1	Quartararo	211
2	Bagnaia	201
3	A. Espargaro	194
4	Bastianini	163
5	Miller	134
6	Zarco	133
7	B. Binder	128
8	Rins	108
9	Martin	104
10	Vinales	104
11	Oliveira	95
12	Marini	91
13	Mir	77
14	Bezzecchi	74
15	M. Marquez	60
16	Nakagami	46
17	P. Espargaro	43
18	A. Marquez	39
19	Morbidelli	26
20	Di Giannantonio	23
21	Dovizioso	15
22	D. Binder	10
23	Gardner	9
24	Fernandez	8
25	Bradl	2
26	Crutchlow	2

Constructor Points

1	Ducati	346
2	Aprilia	217
3	Yamaha	213
4	KTM	161
5	Suzuki	134
6	Honda	100

	Grid order	1	2	3	4	5	6	7	8	9	10	11	12	13	14	15	16	17	18	19	20	21	22	23	
63	BAGNAIA	63	63	63	63	63	63	63	63	63	63	63	63	63	63	63	63	63	63	63	63	63	63	23	1
43	MILLER	33	33	43	43	43	23	23	23	23	23	23	23	23	23	23	23	23	23	23	23	23	23	63	2
23	BASTIANINI	43	43	33	23	23	43	33	33	33	33	33	33	33	33	33	33	33	33	33	33	33	41	41	3
41	A. ESPARGARO	23	23	23	33	33	33	41	41	41	41	41	41	41	41	41	41	41	41	41	41	41	33	33	4
5	ZARCO	41	41	41	41	41	41	43	43	43	43	43	43	43	43	43	43	43	43	43	43	43	43	43	5
20	QUARTARARO	89	89	89	89	89	89	89	89	89	89	89	89	89	89	89	89	89	89	89	89	89	89	89	6
72	BEZZECCHI	5	5	5	5	5	5	5	5	5	5	5	5	5	5	5	5	5	5	5	5	5	10	10	7
89	MARTIN	88	88	88	88	88	88	88	88	10	10	10	10	10	10	10	10	10	10	10	10	10	5	5	8
42	RINS	10	10	10	10	10	10	10	10	88	88	88	88	88	88	88	88	42	42	42	42	42	42	42	9
33	B.BINDER	72	72	73	73	73	73	73	73	73	73	73	73	73	73	42	42	88	88	88	88	88	88	72	10
88	OLIVEIRA	73	73	35	35	35	72	72	72	72	42	42	42	42	42	73	73	73	73	73	72	72	72	88	11
30	NAKAGAMI	35	35	72	72	72	35	35	35	42	72	72	72	72	72	72	72	72	72	72	73	73	73	73	12
93	M. MARQUEZ	87	87	87	87	42	42	42	42	35	35	35	35	35	35	35	12	12	12	35	12	12	12	12	13
10	MARINI	44	44	44	42	87	87	87	87	87	87	87	12	12	12	12	35	35	35	12	35	35	35	35	14
49	DI GIANNANTONIO	40	40	42	44	44	44	44	44	44	44	12	87	87	87	87	87	87	44	44	44	44	44	44	15
12	VINALES	42	42	40	40	40	40	40	40	12	12	44	44	44	44	44	44	44	87	87	87	87	87	87	
73	A. MARQUEZ	12	25	25	25	25	12	12	12	40	40	40	25	25	49	49	49	49	49	49	49	21	21	21	
44	P. ESPARGARO	49	49	49	12	12	25	25	25	25	25	25	40	40	21	21	21	21	21	21	21	49	49	40	
35	CRUTCHLOW	25	12	12	49	49	49	49	49	49	49	49	49	49	40	40	40	40	40	40	40	40	40	49	
21	MORBIDELLI	21	21	21	21	21	21	21	21	21	21	21	21	21	25	25	25	25	25	25	25	25	25	25	
25	FERNANDEZ	93																							
87	GARDNER																								
40	D.BINDER																								

93 Pit stop

Moto2

RACE DISTANCE: 21 laps, 66.249 miles/106.617km · RACE WEATHER: Dry (air 21°, humidity 46%, track 35°)

Pos.	Rider	Nat.	No.	Entrant	Machine	Laps	Time & Speed
1	**Pedro Acosta**	SPA	51	Red Bull KTM Ajo	Kalex	21	39m 35.337s
							100.4mph/161.5km/h
2	**Aron Canet**	SPA	40	Flexbox HP40	Kalex	21	39m 37.949s
3	**Augusto Fernandez**	SPA	37	Red Bull KTM Ajo	Kalex	21	39m 39.136s
4	**Ai Ogura**	JPN	79	IDEMITSU Honda Team Asia	Kalex	21	39m 43.073s
5	**Tony Arbolino**	ITA	14	Elf Marc VDS Racing Team	Kalex	21	39m 43.140s
6	**Fermin Aldeguer**	SPA	54	CAG Speed Up	Boscoscuro	21	39m 43.957s
7	**Somkiat Chantra**	THA	35	IDEMITSU Honda Team Asia	Kalex	21	39m 50.230s
8	**Jorge Navarro**	SPA	9	Flexbox HP40	Kalex	21	39m 55.351s
9	**Joe Roberts**	USA	16	Italtrans Racing Team	Kalex	21	40m 02.095s
10	**Celestino Vietti**	ITA	13	Mooney VR46 Racing Team	Kalex	21	40m 06.697s
11	**Cameron Beaubier**	USA	6	American Racing	Kalex	21	40m 06.838s
12	**Lorenzo Dalla Porta**	ITA	19	Italtrans Racing Team	Kalex	21	40m 07.213s
13	**Barry Baltus**	BEL	7	RW Racing GP	Kalex	21	40m 07.289s
14	**Alessandro Zaccone**	ITA	61	Gresini Racing Moto2	Kalex	21	40m 07.515s
15	**Bo Bendsneyder**	NED	64	Pertamina Mandalika SAG Team	Kalex	21	40m 08.232s
16	Senna Agius	AUS	8	Elf Marc VDS Racing Team	Kalex	21	40m 08.733s
17	Filip Salac	CZE	12	Gresini Racing Moto2	Kalex	21	40m 18.335s
18	Marcos Ramirez	SPA	42	MV Agusta Forward Racing	MV Agusta	21	40m 20.651s
19	Simone Corsi	ITA	24	MV Agusta Forward Racing	MV Agusta	21	40m 25.425s
20	Niccolo Antonelli	ITA	28	Mooney VR46 Racing Team	Kalex	21	40m 28.719s
21	Sean Dylan Kelly	USA	4	American Racing	Kalex	21	40m 37.836s
	Jake Dixon	GBR	96	Shimoko GASGAS Aspar Team	Kalex	20	DNF-crash
	Keminth Kubo	THA	81	Yamaha VR46 Master Camp Team	Kalex	16	DNF-crash
	Taiga Hada	JPN	29	Pertamina Mandalika SAG Team	Kalex	16	DNF-crash
	Zonta van den Goorbergh	NED	84	RW Racing GP	Kalex	6	DNF-crash
	Albert Arenas	SPA	75	Shimoko GASGAS Aspar Team	Kalex	1	DNF-crash
	Manuel Gonzalez	SPA	18	Yamaha VR46 Master Camp Team	Kalex	1	DNF-crash
	Jeremy Alcoba	SPA	52	Liqui Moly Intact GP	Kalex	1	DNF-crash
	Alonso Lopez	SPA	21	CAG Speed Up	Boscoscuro	0	DNF-crash
	Marcel Schrotter	GER	23	Liqui Moly Intact GP	Kalex	0	DNF-crash

Fastest lap: Pedro Acosta, on lap 6, 1m 52.484s, 100.9mph/162.4km/h.

Lap record: Sam Lowes, 1m 51.730s, 101.6mph/163.5km/h (2020).

Event maximum speed: Jorge Navarro, 181.4mph/292.0km/h (free practice).

Qualifying

Weather: Dry

Air: 24° **Humidity:** 39% **Track:** 42°

1	Fernandez	1m 51.888s
2	Arenas	1m 52.012s
3	Dixon	1m 52.179s
4	Lopez	1m 52.270s
5	Canet	1m 52.274s
6	Acosta	1m 52.280s
7	Arbolino	1m 52.289s
8	Ogura	1m 52.397s
9	Chantra	1m 52.475s
10	Roberts	1m 52.576s
11	Aldeguer	1m 52.807s
12	Salac	1m 52.872s
13	Navarro	1m 52.883s
14	Gonzalez	1m 52.967s
15	Beaubier	1m 53.002s
16	Bendsneyder	1m 53.404s
17	Vietti	1m 53.481s
18	Zaccone	1m 54.042s
	Q1	
19	Baltus	1m 52.834s
20	Dalla Porta	1m 52.887s
21	Agius	1m 52.941s
22	Schrotter	1m 53.045s
23	VD Goorbergh	1m 53.243s
24	Corsi	1m 53.364s
25	Antonelli	1m 53.450s
26	Ramirez	1m 53.487s
27	Alcoba	1m 53.500s
28	Hada	1m 53.954s
29	Kubo	1m 53.959s
30	Kelly	1m 54.115s

Fastest race laps

1	Acosta	1m 52.484s
2	Fernandez	1m 52.574s
3	Canet	1m 52.591s
4	Arbolino	1m 52.627s
5	Aldeguer	1m 52.699s
6	Chantra	1m 52.723s
7	Ogura	1m 52.807s
8	Roberts	1m 52.898s
9	Navarro	1m 52.959s
10	Dixon	1m 53.133s
11	Baltus	1m 53.158s
12	Dalla Porta	1m 53.360s
13	Beaubier	1m 53.532s
14	Bendsneyder	1m 53.608s
15	Agius	1m 53.622s
16	Vietti	1m 53.724s
17	Salac	1m 53.748s
18	Zaccone	1m 53.785s
19	Ramirez	1m 54.072s
20	VD Goorbergh	1m 54.322s
21	Kubo	1m 54.524s
22	Hada	1m 54.603s
23	Corsi	1m 54.625s
24	Antonelli	1m 54.706s
25	Kelly	1m 54.947s

Championship Points

1	Fernandez	214
2	Ogura	207
3	Canet	177
4	Vietti	162
5	Arbolino	128
6	Acosta	123
7	Roberts	122
8	Chantra	109
9	Dixon	108
10	Schrotter	101
11	Lopez	89
12	Navarro	83
13	Bendsneyder	67
14	Arenas	65
15	Lowes	51
16	Beaubier	50
17	Aldeguer	48
18	Alcoba	47
19	Gonzalez	44
20	Baltus	26
21	Salac	21
22	Dalla Porta	14
23	Manzi	9
24	Zaccone	9
25	Fenati	7
26	Rodrigo	6
27	Ramirez	5
28	Kubo	4
29	Kelly	3
30	Pasini	1

Constructor Points

1	Kalex	370
2	Boscoscuro	121
3	MV Agusta	5

Moto3

RACE DISTANCE: 19 laps, 59.939 miles/96.463km · RACE WEATHER: Dry (air 19°, humidity 52%, track 26°)

Pos.	Rider	Nat.	No.	Entrant	Machine	Laps	Time & Speed
1	**Izan Guevara**	SPA	28	Autosolar GASGAS Aspar Team	GASGAS	19	37m 29.944s
							95.9mph/154.3km/h
2	**Ayumu Sasaki**	JPN	71	Sterilgarda Husqvarna Max	Husqvarna	19	37m 30.901s
3	**Daniel Holgado**	SPA	96	Red Bull KTM Ajo	KTM	19	37m 36.480s
4	**Deniz Oncu**	TUR	53	Red Bull KTM Tech3	KTM	19	37m 42.850s
5	**Adrian Fernandez**	SPA	31	Red Bull KTM Tech3	KTM	19	37m 46.639s
6	**Ivan Ortola**	SPA	48	Angeluss MTA Team	KTM	19	37m 46.665s
7	**David Munoz**	SPA	44	BOE Motorsports	KTM	19	37m 46.799s
8	**Jaume Masia**	SPA	5	Red Bull KTM Ajo	KTM	19	37m 46.905s
9	**Carlos Tatay**	SPA	99	CFMOTO Racing PruestelGP	CFMOTO	19	37m 46.992s
10	**John McPhee**	GBR	17	Sterilgarda Husqvarna Max	Husqvarna	19	37m 47.015s
11	**Xavier Artigas**	SPA	43	CFMOTO Racing PruestelGP	CFMOTO	19	37m 47.080s
12	**Tatsuki Suzuki**	JPN	24	Leopard Racing	Honda	19	37m 47.111s
13	**Sergio Garcia**	SPA	11	Autosolar GASGAS Aspar Team	GASGAS	19	37m 47.161s
14	**Dennis Foggia**	ITA	7	Leopard Racing	Honda	19	37m 48.027s
15	**Diogo Moreira**	BRA	10	MT Helmets - MSI	KTM	19	37m 53.386s
16	Riccardo Rossi	ITA	54	SIC58 Squadra Corse	Honda	19	37m 55.581s
17	Taiyo Furusato	JPN	72	Honda Team Asia	Honda	19	37m 58.632s
18	Andrea Migno	ITA	16	Rivacold Snipers Team	Honda	19	38m 01.379s
19	Stefano Nepa	ITA	82	Angeluss MTA Team	KTM	19	38m 01.469s
20	Elia Bartolini	ITA	23	QJMotor Avintia Racing Team	KTM	19	38m 01.536s
21	Joel Kelso	AUS	66	CIP Green Power	KTM	19	38m 01.543s
22	Scott Ogden	GBR	19	VisionTrack Racing Team	Honda	19	38m 01.934s
23	Kaito Toba	JPN	27	CIP Green Power	KTM	19	38m 04.359s
24	Mario Aji	INA	64	Honda Team Asia	Honda	19	38m 04.691s
25	Ana Carrasco	SPA	22	BOE Motorsports	KTM	19	38m 30.571s
26	Alessandro Morosi	ITA	91	MT Helmets - MSI	KTM	19	38m 53.489s
27	Maria Herrera	SPA	69	Angeluss MTA Team	KTM	19	38m 53.552s
	Ryusei Yamanaka	JPN	6	MT Helmets - MSI	KTM	12	DNF-crash
	Lorenzo Fellon	FRA	20	SIC58 Squadra Corse	Honda	1	DNF-crash
	Nicola Fabio Carraro	ITA	9	QJMotor Avintia Racing Team	KTM	1	DNF-crash
	Joshua Whatley	GBR	70	VisionTrack Racing Team	Honda	0	DNF-crash

Fastest lap: Deniz Oncu, on lap 4, 1m 57.896s, 96.3mph/155.0km/h.

Lap record: Sergio Garcia, 1m 57.976s, 96.3mph/154.9km/h (2020).

Event maximum speed: Ivan Ortola, 153.7mph/247.3km/h (free practice).

Qualifying:

Weather: Dry

Air: 21° **Humidity:** 50% **Track:** 36°

1	Guevara	1m 57.868s
2	Sasaki	1m 57.963s
3	Holgado	1m 58.037s
4	Suzuki	1m 58.271s
5	McPhee	1m 58.296s
6	Foggia	1m 58.363s
7	Ortola	1m 58.404s
8	Masia	1m 58.407s
9	Nepa	1m 58.548s
10	Artigas	1m 58.675s
11	Tatay	1m 58.756s
12	Garcia	1m 58.875s
13	Oncu	1m 59.034s
14	Furusato	1m 59.195s
15	Fernandez	1m 59.229s
16	Munoz	1m 59.281s
17	Moreira	No Time
18	Rossi	No Time
	Q1	
19	Migno	1m 59.146s
20	Toba	1m 59.221s
21	Yamanaka	1m 59.221s
22	Kelso	1m 59.369s
23	Ogden	1m 59.415s
24	Fellon	1m 59.468s
25	Aji	2m 00.091s
26	Whatley	2m 00.298s
27	Carrasco	2m 00.361s
28	Bartolini	2m 00.892s
29	Herrera	2m 01.456s
30	Carraro	2m 01.938s
	Morosi	No Time

Fastest race laps

1	Oncu	1m 57.896s
2	Sasaki	1m 57.967s
3	Holgado	1m 57.977s
4	Guevara	1m 57.998s
5	Moreira	1m 58.037s
6	McPhee	1m 58.111s
7	Suzuki	1m 58.203s
8	Munoz	1m 58.212s
9	Ortola	1m 58.259s
10	Fernandez	1m 58.266s
11	Garcia	1m 58.365s
12	Masia	1m 58.389s
13	Artigas	1m 58.456s
14	Tatay	1m 58.565s
15	Kelso	1m 58.622s
16	Foggia	1m 58.663s
17	Rossi	1m 58.859s
18	Bartolini	1m 58.932s
19	Ogden	1m 59.025s
20	Toba	1m 59.152s
21	Furusato	1m 59.197s
22	Migno	1m 59.223s
23	Aji	1m 59.295s
24	Nepa	1m 59.436s
25	Yamanaka	2m 00.099s
26	Carrasco	2m 00.493s
27	Morosi	2m 01.398s
28	Herrera	2m 01.427s

Championship Points

1	Guevara	229
2	Garcia	196
3	Foggia	171
4	Sasaki	158
5	Masia	155
6	Oncu	153
7	Suzuki	128
8	Migno	84
9	Holgado	83
10	Tatay	77
11	Artigas	69
12	Yamanaka	65
13	Moreira	64
14	Toba	63
15	Munoz	61
16	Rossi	59
17	Ortola	56
18	McPhee	53
19	Fernandez	40
20	Nepa	36
21	Bartolini	24
22	Kelso	24
23	Ogden	20
24	Bertelle	16
25	Fellon	11
26	Aji	5

Constructor Points

1	GASGAS	287
2	Honda	255
3	KTM	246
4	Husqvarna	194
5	CFMOTO	110

agv
Lenovo
FRECCIAROSSA
Lenovo
CARRERA
FRECCIAROSSA
Lenovo
CARRERA
DAIKO
Lenovo

Main: Jack Miller rode "the race of my life".

Inset: To the victor, the spoils.
Photos: Ducati Corse

FIM WORLD CHAMPIONSHIP · ROUND 16

JAPANESE GRAND PRIX

TWIN RING MOTEGI

Above: Race-day brought welcome sunshine. Pole-sitter Marc Marquez and Brad Binder dispute Turn One.

Top right: Marquez splashed his way to his 63rd pole for his 150th MotoGP start.

Above right: Bad weather and a truncated schedule left little time to prepare for the dry race.

Centre right: 'Bunny ears' looked friendlier than dinosaur spines for the Suzuki's tailpiece.

Centre far right: Aprilia's Aleix Espargaro sits on the grid before his team's costly error, which ruined a race he had expected to win.

Photos: Gold & Goose

Right: Miller outbrakes Martin around the outside at his favourite passing point.

Photo: Ducati Corse

FOR a third race in a row, the Bagnaia/Bastianini Ducati situation took centre stage. Should there be team orders? Were there team orders? In this case, Bagnaia had got back in front of Bastianini, but arguably their battle had discomposed the supposedly senior rider.

If so, was this the cause of his headlong blunder on the last lap, falling off in a half-hearted attempt to pass Quartararo at the notorious Turn Four? Instead of losing one point to his title rival, he lost eight, potentially crucial in an increasingly tight battle. And as a fifth race crash under pressure, it further undermined his reputation as a cool head. Nobody had ever won a title in a season with five zero scores.

The controversy almost, but not quite, overshadowed team-mate Jack Miller's magnificent start-to-finish victory – he rode "out of my skin" in the race of his life. And Marc Marquez's first full race back, to a fighting fourth place from pole position.

It was a let-off for Quartararo, who extended his lead, and doubly so because of a strange affliction that meant likely podium finisher Aleix Espargaro also failed to score. With fuel consumption a concern here, riders made the sighting lap with a fuel-saving map, which limited revs to around 5,000rpm – but the Aprilia engineers forgot to disable it on Espargaro's machine on the grid. That became clear on the warm-up lap, and he hastily entered the pits to switch to his second machine for a pit-lane start, sacrificing his row-two qualifying position. The number-two machine was fitted with a soft-compound rear tyre, not his preferred medium, which limited his recovery to 16th, but he was philosophical: "They made a big mistake, a huge mistake." Was this down to fatigue in the middle of an exhaustive schedule? "I'm tired, everybody's tired," he said. "But we are humans, so we are a team, and I will try to win in Thailand." What would he have done without this mishap? "Win, 100 per cent," was the response.

With five days to travel halfway around the world, a revised schedule reduced practice time, with just one session for each class on Friday afternoon, instead of two over the whole day. Then foul weather, courtesy of category-one typhoon Nanmadol, disrupted it still further, with a resoundingly wet Saturday cutting Moto2 qualifying in half when the track became unrideable, causing MotoGP's afternoon FP3 to be abandoned. It was touch and go whether the wet qualifying would make it before the light faded.

Since there had been no race at this track since 2019, everybody was left desperately short of dry set-up time at a tricky circuit of stop-and-go extremes. The race lap record was narrowly beaten, but Miller's 1m 45.198s was still 1.4 seconds off Jorge Lorenzo's all-time best lap, set on a Yamaha in 2015. A more telling measurement was that the race time was 12 seconds faster than in 2019, and it afforded an opportunity to measure how MotoGP machines had evolved over three years.

Advanced aerodynamics and ride-height devices on every bike (in 2019, only Jack Miller was using one) made the track a different proposition. Marquez summed it up neatly. "The track has become narrower and shorter," he said, adding that he was using the acceleration-friendly rear lowering system five times on each lap.

The biggest difference over three years had come to Aprilia. Aleix Espargaro was amazed at the changes he had made to attack the Japanese venue. "[Look at] the measurements," he said. "It's like a motocross bike and MotoGP. The '19 bike was super-high, the engine position was super-high. Now, it's another bike, longer with aerodynamics. It's another bike. The power delivery is a lot higher. But you're able to use it. The torque is different, the aerodynamics. This track was the third worst on the calendar where the wheelie was a problem. Now we're not even half of this. And with more power. It's crazy. I use a different gear in five corners. I did in

three places in first gear and I will go second. In one place, I did second and I will go third. We changed some gear ratios by close to 20km/h."

Suzuki introduced its own new aero, aping Ducati's rear-seat 'stegosaurus' fins with a much cuddlier version resembling a pair of floppy bunny ears. With factory tester Takuya Tsuda replacing the injured Mir, they had been intended for him to try, but as soon as Alex Rins heard about this unexpected development, he "went running to the Japanese guys and said, 'Let's give it to me to try.'" They took a little persuading, but the Spaniard approved. "Comparing the first to the second run, I was able to brake a little bit harder," he said.

A full-blown disaster was narrowly avoided on Thursday evening when the Marc VDS garage went up in smoke as teams were leaving the track. During a heavy rain shower, water had seeped into the pit and on to a starter motor, which short-circuited and triggered an electrical fire. Aprilia, whose garage was next door, sounded the alarm, and the blaze was soon extinguished by track security and the local fire service. Fortunately, the pit contents, including bikes and spares, were rescued. Suzuki's MotoGP team, also next door, helped the clean up and rebuild. Returned Marc VDS rider Sam Lowes said, "We have to say thanks to Suzuki. Without them, stopping the fire early would've been difficult. In the end, there wasn't big damage." They had also stayed on to reset the pit. "This is what makes you proud of MotoGP. You don't even know some of the other people, and they did a big job to help us when they didn't need to." It did beg the question: what would have happened if the fire had broken out late at night, when all the other teams had gone home?

Finally, some more wisdom from Marquez, commenting on the friendliness between the riders at the pre-event press conference, often a stultifying "How pleased are you/how hard will you try?" experience. Bagnaia, Quartararo and Espargaro said it was because of their respect for one another. Marquez responded that it reminded him of his fight for the title with Dovizioso: "We got along well, with smiles, but the tension was noticeable. The good feeling that exists now is because we have not yet experienced a real melee, last lap. When I am in that situation, I play the cards differently."

MOTOGP RACE – 24 laps

Grippy Michelin wet tyres and his undimmed flair had put Marquez on pole position for the first time in 1,071 days – the last occasion had been at the same circuit in 2019. The conditions made things slightly unexpected: Zarco had come through from Q1 to place second, then Brad Binder, the KTM rider's first time on the front row.

Vinales led row two from Martin and Aleix Espargaro; Miller headed the third. Title contenders Quartararo, Bagnaia and Bastianini were effectively ruled out of podium contention after qualifying ninth, 12th and 15th; the misfortunate Nakagami, determined to give the home fans a show, in spite of severe pain in his right hand after surgery to repair tendons in his third and fourth fingers, was last.

With dry track time limited to 95 minutes before the race and ten of the full-time riders MotoGP rookies at this track, they were still working on corner lines and braking points in the early laps. One such, Binder, nonetheless managed to get the jump off the line to lead Martin, Marquez and Oliveira into the first U-bend. Vinales was fifth, ahead of Miller; Quartararo stranded in ninth, behind Zarco and Marini; Bagnaia 12th, just ahead of Bastianini.

Martin, also a beginner, coolly outbraked the KTM into Turn Seven. However, it was Miller's Ducati that caught the eye as he followed a Turn Five lunge on Vinales with his candidate for overtake of the season, passing both Oliveira and Marquez into Turn 11 at the bottom of the plunge down the hill.

The sharp downhill right was again the scene of quick-fire Miller moves on Binder (lap two) and Martin (lap three)

Above: **A welcome podium return after six races away for Pramac's Jorge Martin.**

Top right: **Bagnaia trudges away after his late-race fall.**

Above right: **Tattoo You. Aaron Canet's Moto2 championship chances slipped away.**

Above far right: **Quartararo shows the injuries sustained at Aragon.**

Right: **Ai Ogura leads the three-way Moto2 battle from Lopez and Fernandez.**

Below right: **Sasaki (71) leads Guevara (28), Masia (5) and Foggia.**

Below far right: **Ogura's victory brought him to within two points of title rival Fernandez.**

Photos: Gold & Goose

to take the lead for the first time since Misano. This time, he was on a different plane. Martin hung in his shadow for four laps, but Miller's choice of the hard rear started to tell over his rival's medium. He posted fastest laps on the third, fourth, fifth and ninth laps to open up an advantage of three seconds on lap ten. From there, he cruised home, eventually winning by 3.4 seconds.

Martin seemed well placed for a comfortable second, with almost two seconds in hand over the battling KTMs and Marc Marquez, but on lap ten he was on the defensive. After an instructive period behind Oliveira, Binder had got to grips with the hard rear compound he was trying for the first time all weekend. Gradually, he reeled in a wheel-spinning Martin before an expert last-lap move secured second.

Almost four seconds down came an entertaining scrap for fourth. Past Quartararo on lap five and Vinales on lap 14 with smart moves at Turn One, and gaining a place from a series of Zarco mistakes on lap six, Marini joined Marquez and Oliveira for the closing laps. By then, Marquez (using the new Kalex aluminium swing-arm) had dispelled thoughts that he wasn't physically fit enough for full distance, moving by Oliveira at Turn Nine three laps from the flag. It was enough for fourth, a fine effort in his 150th MotoGP race, considering he was also nursing Michelin's softest rear. Marini's last-gasp Turn 11 pass on Oliveira wasn't enough for fifth, as the Portuguese rider responded by lunging under him into the following left.

A second behind, the fight for seventh was given extra weight by three title contenders being in the thick of it. Quartararo was shadowing Vinales, but unable to get close enough to attempt a pass, while Bastianini and Bagnaia lurked behind. Much like Misano and Aragon, there were grimaces in the factory Ducati box as Bastianini barged his 2023 team-mate wide at Turn Ten on lap ten. But Bagnaia found his second wind to repass at Turn 12 with four laps left.

Now he was inching up to his rival and had his eye set not only on Quartararo, but also Vinales ahead of him. "Even one extra point can be important," he said later. But he misjudged his move on Quartararo at Turn Four on the final lap and was left mockingly applauding his careless fifth DNF of the year.

Vinales hung on for seventh, Quartararo and Bastianini close behind. Three seconds away, Bezzecchi held off Zarco; then the Hondas of Pol Espargaro and Alex Marquez were followed by Morbidelli, his first points in four races, and just two-tenths ahead of substitute team-mate Crutchlow. Aleix Espargaro was a disheartening six seconds behind.

Honda wild-card Tetsuta Nagashima crashed out, likewise Darryn Binder. Alex Rins pitted with a slow puncture, while second Suzuki rider Takuya Tsuda's bike burst into flames dramatically on track, fortunately without leaking any fluids.

MOTO2 RACE – 22 laps

Q2 was just under way when the rain redoubled, and redoubled again. The red flags came out after five minutes, and after a delay of more than one-and-a-half hours, the remaining nine minutes and 37 seconds of the session went ahead, the track still streaming, but at least rideable.

Canet took pole, ahead of Aldeguer and Dixon; Arbolino, wet specialist Chantra and Salac filled row two. Title rivals Fernandez and Ogura (enjoying huge crowd support) were 11th and 13th, on the fourth and fifth rows.

Aldeguer got the jump, but Canet was past at Turn Two and blazed away into a commanding lead, approaching two seconds at the end of lap three. At this point, Aldeguer had slipped off out of second and Chantra was leading the chase, clear of the pursuit, where Arbolino was bickering with Ogura, who had made a brilliant start. Lopez was with them, and Dixon, while Beaubier was dropping away, having just lost seventh to Fernandez.

But on the following lap, Canet blew his chance of a long awaited first win, tucking the front at Turn Nine.

Lopez took over up front on lap seven, with an inspired Ogura also displacing his team-mate, Chantra, for second. Arbolino was still with them, while on lap eight, Fernandez had got ahead of Dixon and was working on closing the gap.

Arbolino would soon run into arm-pump issues, ceding

third to Fernandez on lap 12 and continuing to lose ground. Chantra was also suffering grip problems and losing places.

Ogura's move on Lopez came at the far twisty section on lap 13, and fastest lap so far meant that immediately he put a bit of daylight between them. Three laps later, the closing Fernandez got past Lopez, and it was between the title contenders. But by then, Ogura had built a 1.8-second lead, and though Fernandez set fastest laps on the 17th and 18th, Ogura was able to match his pace and held on to take his third win of the year by better than a second.

Six seconds back, Lopez fended off a late and spirited charge by Dixon. Chantra and Arbolino followed, just managing to keep Acosta seventh. He had qualified 18th and finished the first lap 14th before moving through steadily.

He left Arenas in eighth, with Bendsneyder a lone ninth and Salac narrowly securing tenth on the last lap, ahead of Beaubier, Roberts and Schrotter. Navarro had crashed out just ahead of them with three laps to go. Zaccone, Antonelli, Alcoba and, for a second time, Canet also crashed out, but importantly also early title leader Vietti, out of 15th, his championship chances over.

It was now a two-horse and two-point race between Fernandez and Ogura, with Canet also effectively out of it.

MOTO3 RACE – 20 laps

Suzuki led a rain-affected front row, with British rookie Scott Ogden alongside in second, then Garcia. Foggia was fifth, points leader Guevara ninth. What ensued was a pivotal encounter for the crown, as Guevara scored a fifth win in customary style, stretching his lead over Garcia to 45 points, after the older rider could only manage fourth.

Guevara's Sunday began badly with a terrifying warm-up collision, when he ran into the back of McPhee's Husqvarna at speed, which destroyed his bike. Unaccountably, the FIM stewards found no fault with what looked like an extraordinarily careless and dangerous piece of riding.

Garcia led away, but was soon outshone by his team-mate as Guevara picked off eight positions to lead at the end of the first lap. By the fourth, it was clear that Garcia couldn't run with the leaders, and after Suzuki high-sided out on lap five, Sasaki, Foggia and Masia formed a lead quartet.

Sasaki made most of the running until Guevara grabbed control on lap 16, then pulled the group apart with his usual late pace. Only Masia appeared capable of matching him, but no sooner had he got into second than he crashed out at Turn 12 with just over three laps to go. Foggia took over second, but was powerless to stop Guevara from sweeping to victory by half a second. Sasaki was third, 1.7 seconds back.

Garcia salvaged fourth from an intense four-way fight that included rookies Munoz and Moreira, and McPhee. Yamanaka, Migno and Rossi completed the top ten in a close trio; Oncu had suffered painful hand injuries in a morning warm-up crash, but preserved his perfect points record in 15th. On the dry track, first-timer Ogden faded to 20th.

FIM WORLD CHAMPIONSHIP: ROUND 16

MOTUL GRAND PRIX OF JAPAN

23-25 SEPTEMBER, 2022

MOBILITY RESORT MOTEGI

24 laps
Length: 4.801 km / 2.983 miles
Width: 15m

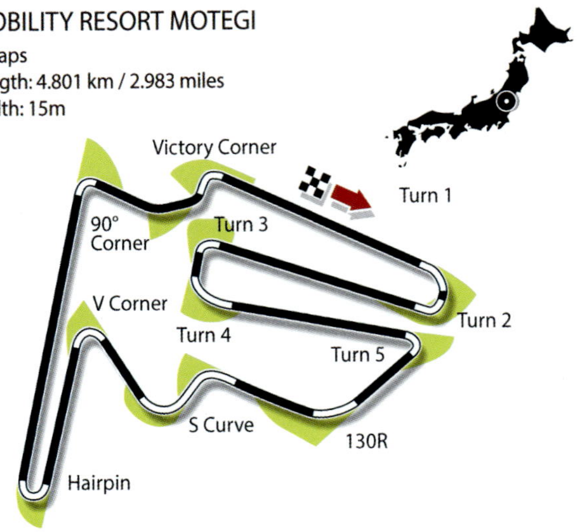

MotoGP

RACE DISTANCE: 24 laps, 71.597 miles/115.224km · RACE WEATHER: Dry (air 22°, humidity 69%, track 38°)

Pos.	Rider	Nat.	No.	Entrant	Machine	Tyres	Race tyre choice	Laps	Time & speed
1	**Jack Miller**	AUS	43	Ducati Lenovo Team	Ducati Desmosedici	M	F: Hard/R: Hard	24	42m 29.174s 101.1mph/162.7km/h
2	**Brad Binder**	RSA	33	Red Bull KTM Factory Racing	KTM RC16	M	F: Hard/R: Hard	24	42m 32.583s
3	**Jorge Martin**	SPA	89	Prima Pramac Racing	Ducati Desmosedici	M	F: Hard/R: Medium	24	42m 33.310s
4	**Marc Marquez**	SPA	93	Repsol Honda Team	Honda RC213V	M	F: Hard/R: Soft	24	42m 36.958s
5	**Miguel Oliveira**	POR	88	Red Bull KTM Factory Racing	KTM RC16	M	F: Hard/R: Hard	24	42m 37.359s
6	**Luca Marini**	ITA	10	Mooney VR46 Racing Team	Ducati Desmosedici	M	F: Hard/R: Hard	24	42m 37.522s
7	**Maverick Vinales**	SPA	12	Aprilia Racing	Aprilia RS-GP	M	F: Hard/R: Medium	24	42m 39.053s
8	**Fabio Quartararo**	FRA	20	Monster Energy Yamaha MotoGP	Yamaha YZR-M1	M	F: Hard/R: Medium	24	42m 39.367s
9	**Enea Bastianini**	ITA	23	Gresini Racing MotoGP	Ducati Desmosedici	M	F: Hard/R: Soft	24	42m 39.492s
10	**Marco Bezzecchi**	ITA	72	Mooney VR46 Racing Team	Ducati Desmosedici	M	F: Hard/R: Hard	24	42m 45.593s
11	**Johann Zarco**	FRA	5	Prima Pramac Racing	Ducati Desmosedici	M	F: Hard/R: Medium	24	42m 45.760s
12	**Pol Espargaro**	SPA	44	Repsol Honda Team	Honda RC213V	M	F: Hard/R: Soft	24	42m 46.630s
13	**Alex Marquez**	SPA	73	LCR Honda CASTROL	Honda RC213V	M	F: Hard/R: Soft	24	42m 47.393s
14	**Franco Morbidelli**	ITA	21	Monster Energy Yamaha MotoGP	Yamaha YZR-M1	M	F: Hard/R: Medium	24	42m 48.186s
15	**Cal Crutchlow**	GBR	35	WithU Yamaha RNF MotoGP Team	Yamaha YZR-M1	M	F: Hard/R: Medium	24	42m 48.375s
16	Aleix Espargaro	SPA	41	Aprilia Racing	Aprilia RS-GP	M	F: Hard/R: Medium	24	42m 54.647s
17	Fabio Di Giannantonio	ITA	49	Gresini Racing MotoGP	Ducati Desmosedici	M	F: Hard/R: Soft	24	42m 56.180s
18	Raul Fernandez	SPA	25	Tech3 KTM Factory Racing	KTM RC16	M	F: Hard/R: Hard	24	42m 58.548s
19	Remy Gardner	AUS	87	Tech3 KTM Factory Racing	KTM RC16	M	F: Hard/R: Hard	24	42m 58.643s
20	Takaaki Nakagami	JPN	30	LCR Honda IDEMITSU	Honda RC213V	M	F: Hard/R: Medium	24	43m 12.468s
	Francesco Bagnaia	ITA	63	Ducati Lenovo Team	Ducati Desmosedici	M	F: Hard/R: Hard	23	DNF-crash
	Alex Rins	SPA	42	Team SUZUKI ECSTAR	Suzuki GSX-RR	M	F: Hard/R: Hard	14	DNF-technical
	Darryn Binder	RSA	40	WithU Yamaha RNF MotoGP Team	Yamaha YZR-M1	M	F: Hard/R: Medium	14	DNF-crash
	Takuya Tsuda	JPN	85	Team SUZUKI ECSTAR	Suzuki GSX-RR	M	F: Hard/R: Medium	11	DNF-technical
	Tetsuta Nagashima	JPN	45	HRC Team	Honda RC213V	M	F: Hard/R: Medium	9	DNF-crash

Fastest lap: Jack Miller, on lap 9, 1m 45.198s, 102.0mph/164.2km/h.
Lap record: Jorge Lorenzo, 1m 45.350s, 101.9mph/164.0km/h (2014).
Event maximum speed: Enea Bastianini, 197.3mph/317.6km/h (race).

Qualifying

Weather: Wet
Air Temp: 22° **Humidity:** 100%
Track Temp: 22°

1	M. Marquez	1m 55.214s
2	Zarco	1m 55.422s
3	B. Binder	1m 55.537s
4	Vinales	1m 55.620s
5	Martin	1m 55.686s
6	A. Espargaro	1m 55.771s
7	Miller	1m 55.784s
8	Oliveira	1m 55.895s
9	Quartararo	1m 56.326s
10	Marini	1m 56.354s
11	P. Espargaro	1m 57.354s
12	Bagnaia	1m 57.373s
	Q1	
13	Bezzecchi	1m 55.934s
14	Morbidelli	1m 56.006s
15	Bastianini	1m 56.130s
16	Di Giannantonio	1m 56.432s
17	A. Marquez	1m 56.578s
18	Rins	1m 56.656s
19	Nagashima	1m 57.229s
20	Gardner	1m 57.288s
21	Tsuda	1m 57.787s
22	Fernandez	1m 57.827s
23	Crutchlow	1m 58.115s
24	D. Binder	1m 58.292s
25	Nakagami	1m 58.717s

Fastest race laps

1	Miller	1m 45.198s
2	Martin	1m 45.424s
3	Bagnaia	1m 45.616s
4	Oliveira	1m 45.669s
5	B. Binder	1m 45.745s
6	Marini	1m 45.842s
7	M. Marquez	1m 45.930s
8	Vinales	1m 45.937s
9	Quartararo	1m 45.939s
10	Bastianini	1m 45.993s
11	Rins	1m 46.015s
12	Bezzecchi	1m 46.023s
13	Crutchlow	1m 46.025s
14	Zarco	1m 46.036s
15	A. Espargaro	1m 46.090s
16	A. Marquez	1m 46.144s
17	P. Espargaro	1m 46.213s
18	Morbidelli	1m 46.232s
19	Di Giannantonio	1m 46.449s
20	D. Binder	1m 46.558s
21	Fernandez	1m 46.563s
22	Nakagami	1m 46.579s
23	Gardner	1m 46.721s
24	Nagashima	1m 46.769s
25	Tsuda	1m 48.082s

Championship Points

1	Quartararo	219
2	Bagnaia	201
3	A. Espargaro	194
4	Bastianini	170
5	Miller	159
6	B. Binder	148
7	Zarco	138
8	Martin	120
9	Vinales	113
10	Rins	108
11	Oliveira	106
12	Marini	101
13	Bezzecchi	80
14	Mir	77
15	M. Marquez	73
16	P. Espargaro	47
17	Nakagami	46
18	A. Marquez	42
19	Morbidelli	28
20	Di Giannantonio	23
21	Dovizioso	15
22	D. Binder	10
23	Gardner	9
24	Fernandez	8
25	Crutchlow	3
26	Bradl	2

Constructor Points

1	Ducati	371
2	Aprilia	226
3	Yamaha	221
4	KTM	181
5	Suzuki	134
6	Honda	113

Grid order	1	2	3	4	5	6	7	8	9	10	11	12	13	14	15	16	17	18	19	20	21	22	23	24	
93 M. MARQUEZ	89	89	43	43	43	43	43	43	43	43	43	43	43	43	43	43	43	43	43	43	43	43	43	43	1
5 ZARCO	33	43	89	89	89	89	89	89	89	89	89	89	89	89	89	89	89	89	89	89	89	89	89	33	2
33 B.BINDER	43	33	33	33	88	88	88	88	33	33	33	33	33	33	33	33	33	33	33	33	33	33	33	89	3
12 VINALES	88	88	88	88	33	33	33	33	88	88	88	88	88	88	88	88	88	88	88	88	88	93	93	93	4
89 MARTIN	93	93	93	93	93	93	93	93	93	93	93	93	93	93	93	93	93	93	93	93	93	88	88	88	5
41 A. ESPARGARO	12	12	12	12	12	12	12	12	12	12	12	12	12	10	10	10	10	10	10	10	10	10	10	10	6
43 MILLER	5	5	5	5	5	10	10	10	10	10	10	10	10	12	12	12	12	12	12	12	12	12	12	12	7
88 OLIVEIRA	10	20	20	20	10	20	20	20	20	20	20	20	20	20	20	20	20	20	20	20	20	20	20	20	8
20 QUARTARARO	20	44	10	10	20	44	44	44	44	44	23	23	23	23	23	23	23	23	23	63	63	63	63	23	9
10 MARINI	44	10	44	44	44	63	63	63	23	23	44	63	63	63	63	63	63	63	63	23	23	23	23	72	10
44 P. ESPARGARO	42	63	63	63	63	23	23	23	63	63	63	72	72	72	72	72	72	72	72	72	72	72	72	5	11
63 BAGNAIA	63	42	23	23	23	72	72	72	72	72	72	44	44	44	44	44	44	44	44	5	5	5	5	44	12
72 BEZZECCHI	23	23	72	72	72	5	5	73	73	73	73	5	5	5	5	5	5	5	5	44	44	44	44	73	13
21 MORBIDELLI	73	72	42	73	73	73	73	5	5	5	5	73	73	73	73	73	73	73	73	73	73	73	73	21	14
23 BASTIANINI	72	73	73	42	21	42	21	21	42	42	21	21	21	21	21	21	21	21	21	21	21	21	21	35	15
49 DI GIANNANTONIO	21	21	21	21	42	21	42	42	21	21	42	49	49	35	35	35	35	35	35	35	35	35	35	41	
73 A. MARQUEZ	40	40	40	40	40	49	49	49	49	49	49	35	35	49	49	49	49	49	49	49	41	41	41	49	
42 RINS	87	87	87	49	49	40	40	40	35	35	35	40	40	25	41	41	41	41	41	41	49	49	49	25	
45 NAGASHIMA	49	49	49	87	87	35	35	35	40	40	40	42	25	41	25	25	25	25	25	25	25	25	25	87	
87 GARDNER	30	30	35	35	35	87	87	87	87	87	87	25	42	87	87	87	87	87	87	87	87	87	87	30	
85 TSUDA	35	35	25	25	25	25	25	25	25	25	25	41	41	42	30	30	30	30	30	30	30	30	30		
25 FERNANDEZ	25	25	30	30	30	30	30	30	41	41	41	87	87	30											
35 CRUTCHLOW	45	45	45	45	45	41	41	41	30	30	30	30	30	40											
40 D.BINDER	85	85	41	41	41	45	45	45	45	85	85														
30 NAKAGAMI	41	41	85	85	85	85	85	85	85																

42 Pit stop

Moto2

RACE DISTANCE: 22 laps, 65.630 miles/105.622km · RACE WEATHER: Dry (air 23°, humidity 66%, track 41°)

Pos.	Rider	Nat.	No.	Entrant	Machine	Laps	Time & Speed
1	**Ai Ogura**	JPN	79	IDEMITSU Honda Team Asia	Kalex	22	40m 56.269s
							96.2mph/154.8km/h
2	**Augusto Fernandez**	SPA	37	Red Bull KTM Ajo	Kalex	22	40m 57.461s
3	**Alonso Lopez**	SPA	21	Beta Tools Speed Up	Boscoscuro	22	41m 03.437s
4	**Jake Dixon**	GBR	96	Shimoko GASGAS Aspar Team	Kalex	22	41m 03.866s
5	**Somkiat Chantra**	THA	35	IDEMITSU Honda Team Asia	Kalex	22	41m 08.524s
6	**Tony Arbolino**	ITA	14	Elf Marc VDS Racing Team	Kalex	22	41m 10.458s
7	**Pedro Acosta**	SPA	51	Red Bull KTM Ajo	Kalex	22	41m 10.789s
8	**Albert Arenas**	SPA	75	Shimoko GASGAS Aspar Team	Kalex	22	41m 14.679s
9	**Bo Bendsneyder**	NED	64	Pertamina Mandalika SAG Team	Kalex	22	41m 16.667s
10	**Filip Salac**	CZE	12	Gresini Racing Moto2	Kalex	22	41m 19.409s
11	**Cameron Beaubier**	USA	6	American Racing	Kalex	22	41m 19.873s
12	**Joe Roberts**	USA	16	Italtrans Racing Team	Kalex	22	41m 20.002s
13	**Marcel Schrotter**	GER	23	Liqui Moly Intact GP	Kalex	22	41m 20.440s
14	**Barry Baltus**	BEL	7	RW Racing GP	Kalex	22	41m 30.064s
15	**Lorenzo Dalla Porta**	ITA	19	Italtrans Racing Team	Kalex	22	41m 31.817s
16	Zonta van den Goorbergh	NED	84	RW Racing GP	Kalex	22	41m 36.275s
17	Taiga Hada	JPN	29	Pertamina Mandalika SAG Team	Kalex	22	41m 38.765s
18	Keminth Kubo	THA	81	Yamaha VR46 Master Camp	Kalex	22	41m 42.761s
19	Sean Dylan Kelly	USA	4	American Racing	Kalex	22	41m 45.395s
20	Marcos Ramirez	SPA	42	MV Agusta Forward Racing	MV Agusta	22	42m 06.023s
	Jeremy Alcoba	SPA	52	Liqui Moly Intact GP	Kalex	21	DNF-crash
	Jorge Navarro	SPA	9	Flexbox HP40	Kalex	20	DNF-crash
	Niccolo Antonelli	ITA	28	Mooney VR46 Racing Team	Kalex	15	DNF-crash
	Aron Canet	SPA	40	Flexbox HP40	Kalex	15	DNF-crash
	Celestino Vietti	ITA	13	Mooney VR46 Racing Team	Kalex	7	DNF-crash
	Simone Corsi	ITA	24	MV Agusta Forward Racing	MV Agusta	5	DNF-technical
	Alessandro Zaccone	ITA	61	Gresini Racing Moto2	Kalex	5	DNF-crash
	Fermin Aldeguer	SPA	54	Beta Tools Speed Up	Boscoscuro	2	DNF-crash
	Manuel Gonzalez	SPA	18	Yamaha VR46 Master Camp Team	Kalex	0	DNS

Fastest lap: Augusto Fernandez, on lap 18, 1m 50.801s, 96.9mph/155.9km/h.

Lap record: Franco Morbidelli, 1m 50.788s, 96.9mph/156.0km/h (2016).

Event maximum speed: Ai Ogura, 164.0mph/264.0km/h (race).

Qualifying

Weather: Wet

Air: 23° **Humidity:** 88% **Track:** 21°

1	Canet	2m 04.939s
2	Dixon	2m 05.669s
3	Arbolino	2m 05.891s
4	Chantra	2m 06.111s
5	Salac	2m 06.123s
6	Aldeguer	2m 06.311s
7	Navarro	2m 06.468s
8	Beaubier	2m 06.680s
9	Kubo	2m 06.785s
10	Baltus	2m 07.119s
11	Fernandez	2m 07.348s
12	Lopez	2m 07.443s
13	Ogura	2m 07.697s
14	Roberts	2m 07.764s
15	Bendsneyder	2m 07.831s
16	VD Goorbergh	2m 08.284s
17	Arenas	2m 08.634s
18	Acosta	2m 09.394s
	Q1	
19	Canet	2m 05.543s
20	Baltus	2m 05.734s
21	Kubo	2m 06.501s
22	Beaubier	2m 06.513s
23	Dalla Porta	2m 06.790s
24	Hada	2m 07.002s
25	Schrotter	2m 07.087s
26	Vietti	2m 07.114s
27	Zaccone	2m 07.296s
28	Lowes	2m 07.423s
29	Kelly	2m 08.067s
30	Antonelli	2m 08.684s
31	Ramirez	2m 09.131s
32	Corsi	2m 09.950s
33	Alcoba	2m 10.530s
	Gonzalez	No Time

Fastest race laps

1	Fernandez	1m 50.801s
2	Ogura	1m 50.861s
3	Dixon	1m 51.048s
4	Lopez	1m 51.092s
5	Canet	1m 51.121s
6	Chantra	1m 51.132s
7	Acosta	1m 51.179s
8	Arbolino	1m 51.218s
9	Aldeguer	1m 51.404s
10	Beaubier	1m 51.788s
11	Bendsneyder	1m 51.803s
12	Arenas	1m 51.820s
13	Schrotter	1m 51.932s
14	Roberts	1m 51.943s
15	Navarro	1m 51.946s
16	Salac	1m 52.008s
17	Vietti	1m 52.033s
18	Alcoba	1m 52.154s
19	Baltus	1m 52.294s
20	Dalla Porta	1m 52.336s
21	Hada	1m 52.377s
22	Antonelli	1m 52.405s
23	VD Goorbergh	1m 52.428s
24	Kubo	1m 52.813s
25	Kelly	1m 52.840s
26	Zaccone	1m 53.057s
27	Ramirez	1m 53.067s
28	Corsi	1m 53.298s

Championship Points

1	Fernandez	234
2	Ogura	232
3	Canet	177
4	Vietti	162
5	Arbolino	138
6	Acosta	132
7	Roberts	126
8	Dixon	121
9	Chantra	120
10	Lopez	105
11	Schrotter	104
12	Navarro	83
13	Bendsneyder	74
14	Arenas	73
15	Beaubier	55
16	Lowes	51
17	Aldeguer	48
18	Alcoba	47
19	Gonzalez	44
20	Baltus	28
21	Salac	27
22	Dalla Porta	15
23	Manzi	9
24	Zaccone	9
25	Fenati	7
26	Rodrigo	6
27	Ramirez	5
28	Kubo	4
29	Kelly	3
30	Pasini	1

Constructor Points

1	Kalex	395
2	Boscoscuro	137
3	MV Agusta	5

Moto3

RACE DISTANCE: 20 laps, 59.664 miles/96.020km · RACE WEATHER: Dry (air 23°, humidity 66%, track 40°)

Pos.	Rider	Nat.	No.	Entrant	Machine	Laps	Time & Speed
1	**Izan Guevara**	SPA	28	Autosolar GASGAS Aspar Team	GASGAS	20	39m 26.526s
							90.7mph/146.0km/h
2	**Dennis Foggia**	ITA	7	Leopard Racing	Honda	20	39m 27.119s
3	**Ayumu Sasaki**	JPN	71	Sterilgarda Husqvarna Max	Husqvarna	20	39m 28.267s
4	**Sergio Garcia**	SPA	11	Autosolar GASGAS Aspar Team	GASGAS	20	39m 35.864s
5	**David Munoz**	SPA	44	BOE Motorsports	KTM	20	39m 35.940s
6	**Diogo Moreira**	BRA	10	MT Helmets - MSI	KTM	20	39m 36.269s
7	**John McPhee**	GBR	17	Sterilgarda Husqvarna Max	Husqvarna	20	39m 36.341s
8	**Ryusei Yamanaka**	JPN	6	MT Helmets - MSI	KTM	20	39m 42.016s
9	**Andrea Migno**	ITA	16	Rivacold Snipers Team	Honda	20	39m 42.099s
10	**Riccardo Rossi**	ITA	54	SIC58 Squadra Corse	Honda	20	39m 42.213s
11	**Xavier Artigas**	SPA	43	CFMOTO Racing PruestelGP	CFMOTO	20	39m 48.549s
12	**Stefano Nepa**	ITA	82	Angeluss MTA Team	KTM	20	39m 49.182s
13	**Ivan Ortola**	SPA	48	Angeluss MTA Team	KTM	20	39m 49.440s
14	**Taiyo Furusato**	JPN	72	Honda Team Asia	Honda	20	39m 50.945s
15	**Deniz Oncu**	TUR	53	Red Bull KTM Tech3	KTM	20	39m 56.894s
16	Elia Bartolini	ITA	23	QJMotor Avintia Racing Team	KTM	20	40m 11.596s
17	Mario Aji	INA	64	Honda Team Asia	Honda	20	40m 11.725s
18	Adrian Fernandez	SPA	31	Red Bull KTM Tech3	KTM	20	40m 15.057s
19	Ana Carrasco	SPA	22	BOE Motorsports	KTM	20	40m 19.785s
20	Scott Ogden	GBR	19	VisionTrack Racing Team	Honda	20	40m 32.582s
21	Kaito Toba	JPN	27	CIP Green Power	KTM	17	40m 38.734s
	Jaume Masia	SPA	5	Red Bull KTM Ajo	KTM	16	DNF-crash
	Lorenzo Fellon	FRA	20	SIC58 Squadra Corse	Honda	9	DNF-crash
	Nicola Fabio Carraro	ITA	9	QJMotor Avintia Racing Team	KTM	6	DNF-crash
	Tatsuki Suzuki	JPN	24	Leopard Racing	Honda	4	DNF-crash
	Daniel Holgado	SPA	96	Red Bull KTM Ajo	KTM	3	DNF-crash
	Kanta Hamada	JPN	34	Rivacold Snipers Team	Honda	3	DNF-crash
	Carlos Tatay	SPA	99	CFMOTO Racing PruestelGP	CFMOTO	0	DNF-crash
	Joel Kelso	AUS	66	CIP Green Power	KTM	0	DNF-crash
	Joshua Whatley	GBR	70	VisionTrack Racing Team	Honda	0	DNF-crash

Fastest lap: Jaume Masia, on lap 7, 1m 57.360s, 91.5mph/147.2km/h.

Lap record: Alex Marquez, 1m 57.112s, 91.7mph/147.5km/h (2014).

Event maximum speed: David Munoz, 139.5mph/224.5km/h (warm-up).

Qualifying:

Weather: Wet

Air: 23° **Humidity:** 92% **Track:** 22°

1	Suzuki	2m 11.246s
2	Ogden	2m 11.568s
3	Garcia	2m 11.788s
4	Sasaki	2m 11.942s
5	Foggia	2m 12.015s
6	Migno	2m 12.038s
7	Rossi	2m 12.120s
8	Oncu	2m 12.124s
9	Guevara	2m 12.155s
10	Masia	2m 12.229s
11	Tatay	2m 12.505s
12	McPhee	2m 12.993s
13	Fellon	2m 13.109s
14	Fernandez	2m 13.686s
15	Moreira	2m 14.078s
16	Munoz	2m 14.856s
17	Yamanaka	2m 15.706s
18	Toba	2m 15.837s
	Q1	
19	Furusato	2m 12.749s
20	Ortola	2m 13.081s
21	Holgado	2m 13.237s
22	Kelso	2m 13.393s
23	Artigas	2m 13.447s
24	Whatley	2m 13.755s
25	Nepa	2m 13.775s
26	Bartolini	2m 13.985s
27	Hamada	2m 14.027s
28	Aji	2m 14.763s
29	Carraro	2m 15.402s
30	Carrasco	2m 20.016s

Fastest race laps

1	Masia	1m 57.360s
2	Foggia	1m 57.379s
3	Sasaki	1m 57.462s
4	Guevara	1m 57.483s
5	Suzuki	1m 57.512s
6	McPhee	1m 57.636s
7	Moreira	1m 57.687s
8	Garcia	1m 57.797s
9	Munoz	1m 57.852s
10	Rossi	1m 57.862s
11	Migno	1m 58.008s
12	Fernandez	1m 58.009s
13	Yamanaka	1m 58.064s
14	Holgado	1m 58.107s
15	Ortola	1m 58.233s
16	Nepa	1m 58.494s
17	Ogden	1m 58.503s
18	Furusato	1m 58.503s
19	Oncu	1m 58.560s
20	Artigas	1m 58.562s
21	Fellon	1m 58.693s
22	Toba	1m 58.720s
23	Bartolini	1m 59.034s
24	Aji	1m 59.062s
25	Carrasco	1m 59.826s
26	Carraro	1m 59.932s
27	Hamada	2m 00.189s

Championship Points

1	Guevara	254
2	Garcia	209
3	Foggia	191
4	Sasaki	174
5	Masia	155
6	Oncu	154
7	Suzuki	128
8	Migno	91
9	Holgado	83
10	Tatay	77
11	Artigas	74
12	Moreira	74
13	Yamanaka	73
14	Munoz	72
15	Rossi	65
16	Toba	63
17	McPhee	62
18	Ortola	59
19	Nepa	40
20	Fernandez	40
21	Bartolini	24
22	Kelso	24
23	Ogden	20
24	Bertelle	16
25	Fellon	11
26	Aji	5
27	Furusato	2

Constructor Points

1	GASGAS	312
2	Honda	275
3	KTM	257
4	Husqvarna	210
5	CFMOTO	115

Right: Monsoon master Miguel – Oliveira confirms his victory to the KTM team.

Below: From the middle of the grid to the front of a tricky race, it was his second such win of the year.

Photos: Gold & Goose

FIM WORLD CHAMPIONSHIP · ROUND 17

THAI GRAND PRIX

BURIRAM CIRCUIT

SHARK
Red Bull
88
KTM
KTM

Above: The Moto2 race begins in rapidly worsening conditions.

Top right: Pole first-timer, rookie Marco Bezzecchi was the tenth rider to top qualifying in the year so far.

Above right: 'Gentleman Johann' – Zarco settled for fourth, in the background a relieved Gigi Dall'Igna wipes his brow.

Above far right: Self-styled Thailand holidaymaker Danilo Petrucci was a popular one-time Suzuki rider.

Right: Out of sorts and out of the points. Quartararo was mired in a lowly battle with Darryn Binder, Crutchlow, Pol Espargaro and Di Giannantonio.

Below right: A collective groan greeted Thai star Chantra's lap-two crash out of the Moto2 lead.

Photos: Gold & Goose

WHAT a difference a week makes. Throw in some wild weather, undo a reputation or two, and a world champion's defence is laid bare – from domination to desperation in one wet afternoon.

Quartararo endured a horror-show Sunday on the return to Buriram after two years away, struggling in a significantly delayed, but only slightly shortened race from the second row of the grid to a desperate and pointless 17th. A lead of 91 points over Bagnaia eight races before was whittled down to two points with three races remaining, after the Italian enjoyed a slightly assisted ride to a podium return. After the race, the Frenchman didn't even speak to his team, let alone TV broadcasters or the media, storming out of his pit before leaving the track.

It was left to temporary stable-mate Crutchlow to assess the problem: front tyre pressure, again, so the bike wouldn't turn, he said. While he blamed team tactics, factory team manager Massimo Meregalli was puzzled: "It's difficult to judge until we speak with Fabio. This race was a gamble, because all the sessions were dry, the race wet. But it was the same in Indonesia, and we performed well. Here, the opposite."

Something else was similar to Indonesia, however – a brilliant race by Miguel Oliveira, who took over the lead from fellow wet specialist Miller and held firm on a decidedly tricky circuit. Miller was comfortably clear of Bagnaia, with no need to consider his team-mate's championship position. There was a bonus, though, for all of the top three.

In the latter stages, Zarco had been catching up in great strides, setting five fastest laps in a row and dealing with Marquez – who had been harrying Bagnaia for third – with five laps to go. He had every chance of taking Bagnaia, and possibly also Miller and Oliveira. But he had Ducati's Dall'Igna's words in mind, as well as his continued status in the satellite team: "Since many races now, Ducati doesn't want to deny a victory to a rider. But for other positions, if we can calculate a little bit, they will be thankful." So he held back his attack. After the race, Dall'Igna described his actions as "gentlemanly".

It was a conclusion of a thoroughly messed-up Sunday. Rain had been expected, but mainly had stayed away during practice and qualifying, and also for the Moto3 race, which ran on time to full length.

Moto2 lined up on the grid on slicks for the 13:20 start, but then the weather took over. Some five minutes before the warm-up lap, rain was reported from the further reaches of the circuit, and as the clock ticked down and the grid stayed dry, heavy and very local downpours soaked other parts of the track. This triggered 'Wet Race' signs and the 'Rain on the Grid' procedure: five minutes to change tyres, the start delayed by eventually 12 minutes, and the race distance cut from 24 to 16 laps.

The gods were not finished, however. Heavy rain was hitting more of the circuit as they got under way and soon began falling everywhere, with highly challenging visibility making it difficult to see the growing pools of standing water. Pole-starter and home hero Chantra was an early victim, crashing out of the lead to break his heart and those of a dedicated grandstand full of fans; the survivors soldiered on in increasingly dire conditions. Until after eight laps, the red flags were waved.

A five-lap restart was scheduled for just after 14:00, but with conditions no better, eventually it was called off and half-points awarded for the first attempt.

Now the MotoGP race was in jeopardy, but after an anxious hour of further storms and squalls, it was able to start 57 minutes late, and cut by one lap. And it ran all the way to the end.

Not without tension. Visibility was a major concern on the high-speed run from Turn Two to Three, and there was standing water between Turns Three and Four. It made for scary early laps. "Nobody could see," said Crutchlow, stranded in the pack. "People were shutting the throttle in fifth gear in the straight. Just ridiculous. To me, it was way over the limit to race."

Danilo Petrucci, dropped by Ducati at the end of 2020 and by KTM at the end of 2021, was back to replace the

still unfit Joan Mir on the Suzuki. Since then, he'd ridden the Dakar rally for KTM, winning a stage and finishing 32nd, and raced a Ducati to second overall in the MotoAmerica Superbike series. He had had little time to prepare. "I got the call before the race last Sunday in Alabama, when I was still fighting for the [MotoAmerica] title," he explained. "So I said, 'Let me think about it,' because I'm retired now and the race in Thailand was tough when I was fully fit. Now I'm an old man, it will be even tougher!" The lure was too great, but the task rather daunting: he qualified 24th and finished 20th. But, "This is a vacation for me, and nice to be here and see all of you. I don't think a rider has come from the Dakar back to MotoGP."

The provisional 2023 calendar was released on Friday, with a few surprises among the 21 rounds, including two new venues in two new countries. The Sokol International Racetrack was slated to host the first ever Kazakhstan GP in July, with the inaugural Indian GP scheduled for late September at the Buddh International Circuit, both subject to homologation. Aragon had been dropped, the on-again/off-again Finnish round was absent and Qatar moved from the first race to the penultimate, in November. The season would end with an exhausting overseas run, where races in India, Japan, Indonesia, Australia, Thailand, Malaysia, Qatar and Valencia would be held across just ten weeks.

Aleix Espargaro was one not enamoured with the idea of 42 races (sprint races included) in 2023. "To do three consecutive races twice so far from home will be very demanding physically and mentally, and with the sprint races and the new tracks," he said.

MOTOGP RACE – 25 laps (shortened)

Bezzecchi was a record tenth pole qualifier of the year, his first, with a new track record. The long straights favoured Ducati, with six of the top seven, Quartararo the interloper in fourth. He was behind Martin and Bagnaia, alongside Zarco and Bastianini. Miller led row three from Marc Marquez, the Honda rider saying, "I start to play with the bike, to slide on the left corners, to shake on the braking points."

First time on wet tyres all weekend was a step into the unknown, and the race was not even one corner old when Bezzecchi went elbow to elbow with Martin and both ran off track. Knowing visibility on the long run to Turn Three would be an issue, the Italian kept it pinned, rejoining in front of Bagnaia, Miller and Marquez. Martin slotted in next, ahead of Marini, Oliveira, Bastianini and Zarco.

It was difficult to pick out Quartararo among the murk. He dropped 13 places in four corners – contact with Miller in Turn One, and a wrong line through Turn Four. Two sectors into the race, and he was 17th.

At the start of lap three, Bezzecchi was notified to drop a position for showing no disadvantage after running off. Soon there was another incident. Making good on his promise to risk everything, Aleix Espargaro rose from 13th to 11th on lap one, then tried too hard too soon, clattering into Brad Binder while grappling for tenth and pushing the South African off track. That earned him a long-lap penalty, which he served on lap ten, dropping to 14th.

Eventually, Bezzecchi ceded the lead to Miller on the fourth lap, after the Australian had nicked second from Bagnaia at Turn Three on the third. Oliveira was one danger-man, Marini another. With Marquez cautious early on, both got by on the second lap. Martin was next, Oliveira passing him for fourth at Turn Nine on lap three, Marini at Turn Three on lap four, but a crash six turns later ended his hopes. It was his first DNF in 35 MotoGP races.

Oliveira's surge continued. A neat move at Turn 12 on lap five took him past Bagnaia; he eased under Bezzecchi, who would begin to fade, 20 seconds later on the exit of Turn Three. And after harrying Miller with an unsuccessful lunge at Turn 12 (lap eight), he finally made it stick on lap 14 with a clean move at the track's final turn. Trading fastest

Above: **Spray-bound and struggling, Pol Espargaro, Darryn Binder, Crutchlow and Di Giannantonio peer ahead past the pits.**
Photo: Gold & Goose

Top right: **Marc Marquez couldn't hold off the charging Zarco, but the Frenchman politely stopped in fourth.**
Photo: Repsol Honda

Above right: **Halfway there – Tony Arbolino overcame Filip Salac to win the eight-lap Moto2 race.**

Centre right: **A second podium visit for Riccardo Rossi in Moto3 (*left*); a first for Filip Salac in Moto2.**

Right: **Sergio Garcia slides out on lap one; his assailant, Adrian Fernandez, goes flying.**

Far right: **Foggia, here leading Sasaki, Munoz, Rossi, Moreira and Masia, was dominant in Moto3.**
Photos: Gold & Goose

laps, the pair moved clear of Bagnaia and Marquez by 1.8 seconds.

As Bezzecchi and Martin faded behind, Alex Marquez, liberated from his Honda's intractability by the conditions, had climbed from 20th to fifth, and Zarco to sixth.

Now the Frenchman started coming into his own, his 13th lap the fastest of the race so far. Soon he was past Alex, posting four straight fastest laps from lap 16 to 19. From 2.5 seconds off fourth on lap 12, he was on the closely engaged Bagnaia and Marquez with five laps to go. Such was his speed that the 2.7 seconds to Oliveira and the still pressing Miller up front didn't appear such a long shot. His Turn Nine barge on Marquez on lap 21 appeared to signal that he still felt a maiden premier-class win was within reach, but thereafter discretion prevailed, and he didn't once attempt a pass on Bagnaia.

Up front, the lap had two halves for Oliveira and Miller. Thanks to his braking prowess into Turn Three, the Australian could close right up on the KTM by the second sector. Yet Oliveira's agility through sectors three and four gave him just enough of a buffer to stay clear. Miller still managed to close a 1.1-second lead down to 0.5 of a second by the penultimate lap, however. And by the last lap, "I threw caution to the wind," said the Australian. "I had a dig through sector three, but I had a moment." That settled it in Oliveira's favour by seven-tenths.

Bagnaia held on to third for his eighth podium of the year. In fifth, Marc Marquez was just 2.9 seconds off the win. Bastianini had risen consistently to sixth, 13s away, while Vinales passed Alex Marquez and Martin – struggling on the drying track – for seventh on the final lap. Also on the last lap, Brad Binder got by both Aleix Espargaro and Morbidelli for tenth, with the Aprilia rider 11th, but Morbidelli dropped one more place behind Rins for exceeding track limits. Pol Espargaro and a distant Fernandez wrapped up the points; Quartararo was another four seconds away, behind Bezzecchi. Gardner crashed out, the only non-finisher.

MOTO2 RACE – 8 laps (shortened)

This should have been Chantra's triumphant homecoming. The previous time at this track, he had scored a first top-ten. Now the signs were better, after he had taken a first pole ahead of Arbolino and team-mate Ogura. Vietti had come through from Q1 to lead the second row from Lopez and Dixon, with narrow points-leader Fernandez eighth.

The omens improved once the race finally started in the rain, and the Thai rider – who had claimed his only GP win in similar conditions in Indonesia – seized the lead and was pulling clear. Until the fourth corner of lap two, when he hit standing water and crashed.

A chaotic race had been preceded by chaotic scenes on the grid, the scheduled 24-lapper being delayed and cut to 16 laps as rain fell on parts of the circuit. The start came 12 minutes late. Arenas and Gonzales had been wheeled off for failing to change tyres in time, to start from the back of the grid, while Dalla Porta elected to start from the pit lane on slicks, a long-shot gamble that was never going to work.

The first lap was fraught. Ogura led Arbolino into the first corner, but ran wide; Chantra came bursting past the pair of them, followed by Lopez. Ogura survived a big wobble out of Turn Two, while fast-starting Beaubier pushed through to second, only to high-side out at Turn Four.

Chantra led by 1.2 seconds at the end of lap one, but suffered a high-side at Turn Four, which put him out, to the audible groans of the crowd. That left Lopez ahead of Canet, Dixon and Czech rider Filip Salac, up from 12th on the grid.

Conditions were dismal, visibility horrendous. Those with less to lose decided to risk it all. Salac was one of them, rising to the lead by lap five, with Arbolino also charging back after ending the first lap ninth. Title contenders Ogura and Fernandez veered to the side of caution, circulating in sixth and seventh.

A mistake by Salac entering Turn Three on lap eight allowed Arbolino through to lead. By now, the conditions had

deteriorated still further, the pack slithering through incipient lakelets at various points.

Eventually, Arbolino's lead at the end of lap eight gave him a win – or half a win. The red flags came out during lap nine and another delay followed, with a further heavy shower as riders exited the pit lane for a five-lap restart.

In the end, the race was abandoned, with half-points for the lap-eight order. Arbolino took a second win of the year, ahead of Salac, Canet, Dixon, Lopez, Ogura and Fernandez, the Japanese rider gaining half a point on the Spaniard to sit 1.5 points adrift.

Roberts and second Thai rider Keminth Kubo completed the top ten; then came Vietti, Kelly, Baltus, Hada, Arenas and Schrotter, who wrapped up the points. Acosta missed out by two seconds.

Aldeguer crashed out on lap two, Alcoba a little later; slick-shod Dalla Porta retired.

MOTO3 RACE – 22 laps

Foggia took a third pole of the season (and of his career) with a new record lap, and made a mockery of the belief that the circuit's layout would not lend itself to an escape act. At the same time, with Guevara having (for him) an off-day in fifth, it revived the tiniest inkling of the Italian's title chances.

Foggia grabbed the initiative early and led every lap bar one. A small error while braking for the final turn had caused him to run off and momentarily cede the lead to his race-long pursuer, Sasaki.

An early lead group of six also included Rossi, Masia, and rookies Moreira and Munoz until Foggia's pace broke them apart. Only Sasaki and Rossi stayed the pace, but it was barely a contest, with Foggia's fourth win of the year achieved by 1.5 seconds, while Sasaki withstood a last-corner lunge from Rossi.

The other three were swallowed up by a pursuit gang. Eventually, Stefano Nepa bagged a career-best fourth, ahead of Guevara, through from his year's-worst 11th on the grid. Moreira, Migno, Masia, Munoz and Yamanaka were close. Holgado led the next brawl from recovering Australian Kelso, Tatay, Artigas, Ogden, Fellon and Oncu, Ogden the last in the points. Oncu had suffered two long-lap penalties and was demoted one position.

It was another rotten day for early title-leader Garcia, wiped out at the final turn on the first lap. He remounted at the back, hoping for a red flag and a restart, but finally retired after his own long-lap penalty.

FIM WORLD CHAMPIONSHIP: ROUND 17

OR THAILAND GRAND PRIX

30 SEPTEMBER–2 OCTOBER, 2022

CHANG INTERNATIONAL CIRCUIT

26 laps
Length: 4.600km. / 2.830 miles
Width: 12m

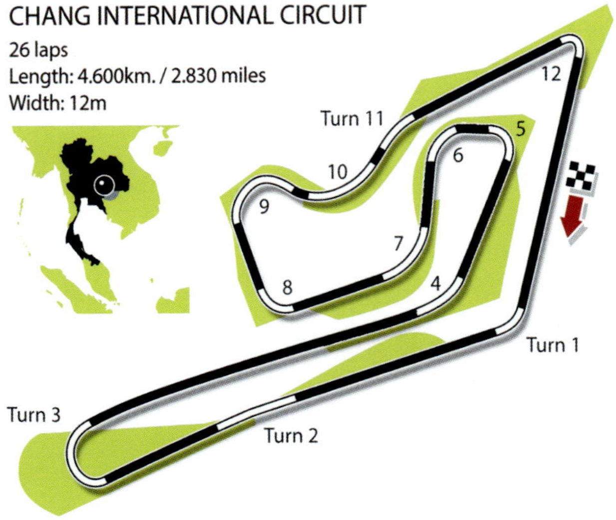

MotoGP RACE DISTANCE: 25 laps, 70.743 miles/113.850km · RACE WEATHER: Wet (air 27°, humidity 85%, track 29°)

Pos.	Rider	Nat.	No.	Entrant	Machine	Tyres	Race tyre choice	Laps	Time & speed
1	**Miguel Oliveira**	POR	88	Red Bull KTM Factory Racing	KTM RC16	M	F: Med Wet/R: Med Wet	25	41m 44.503s 101.7mph/163.6km/h
2	**Jack Miller**	AUS	43	Ducati Lenovo Team	Ducati Desmosedici	M	F: Med Wet/R: Med Wet	25	41m 45.233s
3	**Francesco Bagnaia**	ITA	63	Ducati Lenovo Team	Ducati Desmosedici	M	F: Med Wet/R: Med Wet	25	41m 46.471s
4	**Johann Zarco**	FRA	5	Prima Pramac Racing	Ducati Desmosedici	M	F: Med Wet/R: Med Wet	25	41m 46.993s
5	**Marc Marquez**	SPA	93	Repsol Honda Team	Honda RC213V	M	F: Med Wet/R: Med Wet	25	41m 47.461s
6	**Enea Bastianini**	ITA	23	Gresini Racing MotoGP	Ducati Desmosedici	M	F: Med Wet/R: Med Wet	25	41m 57.760s
7	**Maverick Vinales**	SPA	12	Aprilia Racing	Aprilia RS-GP	M	F: Med Wet/R: Med Wet	25	41m 59.069s
8	**Alex Marquez**	SPA	73	LCR Honda CASTROL	Honda RC213V	M	F: Med Wet/R: Med Wet	25	41m 59.364s
9	**Jorge Martin**	SPA	89	Prima Pramac Racing	Ducati Desmosedici	M	F: Med Wet/R: Med Wet	25	41m 59.868s
10	**Brad Binder**	RSA	33	Red Bull KTM Factory Racing	KTM RC16	M	F: Med Wet/R: Med Wet	25	42m 02.600s
11	**Aleix Espargaro**	SPA	41	Aprilia Racing	Aprilia RS-GP	M	F: Med Wet/R: Med Wet	25	42m 03.544s
12	**Alex Rins**	SPA	42	Team SUZUKI ECSTAR	Suzuki GSX-RR	M	F: Med Wet/R: Med Wet	25	42m 04.162s
13	**Franco Morbidelli**	ITA	21	Monster Energy Yamaha MotoGP	Yamaha YZR-M1	M	F: Med Wet/R: Med Wet	25	42m 06.942s
14	**Pol Espargaro**	SPA	44	Repsol Honda Team	Honda RC213V	M	F: Med Wet/R: Med Wet	25	42m 08.149s
15	**Raul Fernandez**	SPA	25	Tech3 KTM Factory Racing	KTM RC16	M	F: Med Wet/R: Med Wet	25	42m 14.986s
16	Marco Bezzecchi	ITA	72	Mooney VR46 Racing Team	Ducati Desmosedici	M	F: Med Wet/R: Med Wet	25	42m 17.969s
17	Fabio Quartararo	FRA	20	Monster Energy Yamaha MotoGP	Yamaha YZR-M1	M	F: Med Wet/R: Med Wet	25	42m 18.575s
18	Fabio Di Giannantonio	ITA	49	Gresini Racing MotoGP	Ducati Desmosedici	M	F: Med Wet/R: Med Wet	25	42m 20.706s
19	Cal Crutchlow	GBR	35	WithU Yamaha RNF MotoGP Team	Yamaha YZR-M1	M	F: Med Wet/R: Med Wet	25	42m 21.035s
20	Danilo Petrucci	ITA	9	Team SUZUKI ECSTAR	Suzuki GSX-RR	M	F: Med Wet/R: Med Wet	25	42m 27.011s
21	Darryn Binder	RSA	40	WithU Yamaha RNF MotoGP Team	Yamaha YZR-M1	M	F: Med Wet/R: Med Wet	25	42m 34.495s
22	Tetsuta Nagashima	JPN	45	LCR Honda IDEMITSU	Honda RC213V	M	F: Med Wet/R: Soft Wet	25	42m 35.849s
23	Luca Marini	ITA	10	Mooney VR46 Racing Team	Ducati Desmosedici	M	F: Med Wet/R: Med Wet	23	42m 37.685s
	Remy Gardner	AUS	87	Tech3 KTM Factory Racing	KTM RC16	M	F: Med Wet/R: Med Wet	11	DNF-crash

Fastest lap: Johann Zarco, on lap 19, 1m 38.941s, 102.9mph/165.6km/h.
Lap record: Marc Marquez, 1m 30.904s, 112.0mph/180.3km/h (2019).
Event maximum speed: Enea Bastianini, 209.7mph/337.5km/h (warm-up).

Qualifying

Weather: Dry
Air Temp: 30° **Humidity:** 72%
Track Temp: 43°

1	Bezzecchi	1m 29.671s
2	Martin	1m 29.692s
3	Bagnaia	1m 29.775s
4	Quartararo	1m 29.909s
5	Zarco	1m 29.963s
6	Bastianini	1m 29.988s
7	Miller	1m 30.106s
8	M. Marquez	1m 30.133s
9	Marini	1m 30.214s
10	Rins	1m 30.337s
11	Oliveira	1m 30.485s
12	B. Binder	1m 30.542s
	Q1	
13	A. Espargaro	1m 30.202s
14	Morbidelli	1m 30.528s
15	Crutchlow	1m 30.542s
16	Fernandez	1m 30.566s
17	Vinales	1m 30.578s
18	Gardner	1m 30.602s
19	P. Espargaro	1m 30.641s
20	A. Marquez	1m 30.692s
21	Di Giannantonio	1m 30.794s
22	Nagashima	1m 31.331s
23	D. Binder	1m 31.356s
24	Petrucci	1m 31.604s

Fastest race laps

1	Zarco	1m 38.941s
2	M. Marquez	1m 39.448s
3	Marini	1m 39.475s
4	Oliveira	1m 39.537s
5	Bagnaia	1m 39.566s
6	Miller	1m 39.732s
7	Vinales	1m 39.770s
8	A. Espargaro	1m 39.821s
9	B. Binder	1m 39.884s
10	Bastianini	1m 39.899s
11	Morbidelli	1m 39.963s
12	A. Marquez	1m 39.991s
13	P. Espargaro	1m 40.054s
14	Rins	1m 40.069s
15	Martin	1m 40.159s
16	Fernandez	1m 40.317s
17	Bezzecchi	1m 40.478s
18	Crutchlow	1m 40.585s
19	Quartararo	1m 40.637s
20	Gardner	1m 40.654s
21	Petrucci	1m 40.721s
22	Di Giannantonio	1m 40.795s
23	Nagashima	1m 41.185s
24	D. Binder	1m 41.236s

Championship Points

1	Quartararo	219
2	Bagnaia	217
3	A. Espargaro	199
4	Bastianini	180
5	Miller	179
6	B. Binder	154
7	Zarco	151
8	Oliveira	131
9	Martin	127
10	Vinales	122
11	Rins	112
12	Marini	101
13	M. Marquez	84
14	Bezzecchi	80
15	Mir	77
16	A. Marquez	50
17	P. Espargaro	49
18	Nakagami	46
19	Morbidelli	31
20	Di Giannantonio	23
21	Dovizioso	15
22	D. Binder	10
23	Gardner	9
24	Fernandez	9
25	Crutchlow	3
26	Bradl	2

Constructor Points

1	Ducati	391
2	Aprilia	235
3	Yamaha	224
4	KTM	206
5	Suzuki	138
6	Honda	124

Grid order	1	2	3	4	5	6	7	8	9	10	11	12	13	14	15	16	17	18	19	20	21	22	23	24	25	
72 BEZZECCHI	72	72	72	43	43	43	43	43	43	43	43	43	43	88	88	88	88	88	88	88	88	88	88	88	88	1
89 MARTIN	63	63	43	72	72	88	88	88	88	88	88	88	88	43	43	43	43	43	43	43	43	43	43	43	43	2
63 BAGNAIA	43	43	63	63	88	63	63	63	63	63	63	63	63	63	63	63	63	63	63	63	63	63	63	63	63	3
20 QUARTARARO	89	89	88	88	63	93	93	93	93	93	93	93	93	93	93	93	93	93	93	93	5	5	5	5	5	4
5 ZARCO	93	88	89	93	93	72	72	72	73	73	73	73	73	73	5	5	5	5	5	5	93	93	93	93	93	5
23 BASTIANINI	10	10	10	89	89	89	73	73	5	5	5	5	5	5	73	73	73	73	73	73	73	73	23	23	23	6
43 MILLER	88	93	93	5	5	73	89	5	72	89	89	89	89	89	89	23	23	23	23	23	23	23	73	73	12	7
93 M. MARQUEZ	23	5	5	73	73	5	5	89	89	72	23	23	23	23	23	89	89	89	89	89	89	89	89	89	73	8
10 MARINI	5	23	73	23	23	23	23	23	23	23	72	21	21	21	21	21	21	21	21	12	12	12	12	12	89	9
42 RINS	33	73	23	41	25	25	41	41	41	21	21	72	12	12	12	12	12	12	12	21	21	21	21	41	33	10
88 OLIVEIRA	41	41	41	25	41	41	25	25	25	25	25	12	33	33	33	33	41	41	41	41	41	41	41	21	41	11
33 B.BINDER	25	87	25	87	21	21	21	21	21	33	12	25	41	41	41	41	33	33	33	33	33	33	33	33	21	12
41 A. ESPARGARO	21	25	87	21	87	87	87	87	33	12	33	33	72	25	42	42	42	42	42	42	42	42	42	42	42	13
21 MORBIDELLI	73	21	21	33	33	33	33	33	42	41	41	41	25	42	25	44	44	44	44	44	44	44	44	44	44	14
35 CRUTCHLOW	87	33	33	42	42	42	42	42	87	42	42	42	42	44	44	25	25	25	25	25	25	25	25	25	25	15
25 FERNANDEZ	42	20	42	20	12	12	12	12	12	87	44	44	44	72	72	72	72	72	72	72	72	72	72	72	72	
12 VINALES	20	42	20	12	20	44	44	44	44	44	87	35	35	35	35	35	35	35	35	35	35	20	20	20	20	
87 GARDNER	44	40	40	40	40	20	20	20	35	35	35	20	20	20	20	20	20	20	20	20	20	35	35	35	49	
44 P. ESPARGARO	40	44	35	35	35	40	35	35	20	20	20	49	49	49	49	49	49	49	49	49	49	49	49	49	35	
73 A. MARQUEZ	49	35	12	44	44	35	40	49	49	49	49	9	9	9	9	9	9	9	9	9	9	9	9	9	9	
49 DI GIANNANTONIO	35	12	44	49	49	49	49	40	9	9	9	40	40	40	40	40	40	40	40	40	40	40	40	40	40	
45 NAGASHIMA	12	49	49	9	9	9	9	9	40	40	40	45	45	45	45	45	45	45	45	45	45	45	45	45	45	
40 D.BINDER	9	9	9	45	45	45	45	45	45	45	45	*10*	*10*	*10*	*10*	*10*	*10*	*10*	*10*	*10*	*10*	*10*	*10*			
9 PETRUCCI	45	45	45	*10*	*10*	*10*	*10*	*10*	*10*	*10*	*10*															
30 NAKAGAMI																										

10 Lapped rider

Moto2

8 laps, 22.638 miles/36.432km · RACE WEATHER: Wet (air 26°, humidity 90%, track 37°)

Pos.	Rider	Nat.	No.	Entrant	Machine	Laps	Time & Speed
1	**Tony Arbolino**	ITA	14	Elf Marc VDS Racing Team	Kalex	8	15m 10.854s
							89.4mph/143.9km/h
2	**Filip Salac**	CZE	12	Gresini Racing Moto2	Kalex	8	15m 11.105s
3	**Aron Canet**	SPA	40	Flexbox HP40	Kalex	8	15m 13.966s
4	**Jake Dixon**	GBR	96	Inde GASGAS Aspar Team	Kalex	8	15m 14.122s
5	**Alonso Lopez**	SPA	21	Beta Tools Speed Up	Boscoscuro	8	15m 14.991s
6	**Ai Ogura**	JPN	79	IDEMITSU Honda Team Asia	Kalex	8	15m 16.569s
7	**Augusto Fernandez**	SPA	37	Red Bull KTM Ajo	Kalex	8	15m 20.716s
8	**Joe Roberts**	USA	16	Italtrans Racing Team	Kalex	7	13m 26.089s
9	**Keminth Kubo**	THA	81	Yamaha VR46 Master Camp Team	Kalex	7	13m 32.823s
10	**Celestino Vietti**	ITA	13	Mooney VR46 Racing Team	Kalex	7	13m 33.461s
11	**Sean Dylan Kelly**	USA	4	American Racing	Kalex	7	13m 33.647s
12	**Barry Baltus**	BEL	7	RW Racing GP	Kalex	7	13m 33.747s
13	**Taiga Hada**	JPN	29	Pertamina Mandalika SAG Team	Kalex	7	13m 35.299s
14	**Albert Arenas**	SPA	75	Inde GASGAS Aspar Team	Kalex	7	13m 35.654s
15	**Marcel Schrotter**	GER	23	Liqui Moly Intact GP	Kalex	7	13m 37.462s
16	Pedro Acosta	SPA	51	Red Bull KTM Ajo	Kalex	7	13m 39.553s
17	Zonta van den Goorbergh	NED	84	RW Racing GP	Kalex	7	13m 39.829s
18	Bo Bendsneyder	NED	64	Pertamina Mandalika SAG Team	Kalex	7	13m 42.782s
19	Sam Lowes	GBR	22	Elf Marc VDS Racing Team	Kalex	7	13m 50.757s
20	Jorge Navarro	SPA	9	Flexbox HP40	Kalex	7	13m 54.198s
21	Alessandro Zaccone	ITA	61	Gresini Racing Moto2	Kalex	7	14m 06.811s
22	Niccolo Antonelli	ITA	28	Mooney VR46 Racing Team	Kalex	7	14m 09.745s
23	Marcos Ramirez	SPA	42	MV Agusta Forward Racing	MV Agusta	7	14m 22.979s
24	Simone Corsi	ITA	24	MV Agusta Forward Racing	MV Agusta	7	14m 23.406s
25	Manuel Gonzalez	SPA	18	Yamaha VR46 Master Camp Team	Kalex	6	13m 51.945s
	Lorenzo Dalla Porta	ITA	19	Italtrans Racing Team	Kalex	5	DNF-crash
	Jeremy Alcoba	SPA	52	Liqui Moly Intact GP	Kalex	4	DNF-crash
	Somkiat Chantra	THA	35	IDEMITSU Honda Team Asia	Kalex	1	DNF-crash
	Fermin Aldeguer	SPA	54	Beta Tools Speed Up	Boscoscuro	1	DNF-crash
	Cameron Beaubier	USA	6	American Racing	Kalex	0	DNF-crash

Fastest lap: Tony Arbolino, on lap 7, 1m 52.003s, 90.9mph/146.3km/h.

Lap record: Luca Marini, 1m 36.097s, 106.0mph/170.6km/h (2019).

Event maximum speed: Marcel Schrotter, 176.1mph/283.4km/h (free practice).

Qualifying

Weather: Dry

Air: 29° **Humidity:** 73% **Track:** 45°

1	Chantra	1m 35.625s
2	Arbolino	1m 35.710s
3	Ogura	1m 35.889s
4	Acosta	1m 35.956s
5	Vietti	1m 35.973s
6	Lopez	1m 35.987s
7	Dixon	1m 36.106s
8	Fernandez	1m 36.130s
9	Navarro	1m 36.264s
10	Gonzalez	1m 36.316s
11	Beaubier	1m 36.558s
12	Salac	1m 36.672s
13	Bendsneyder	1m 36.809s
14	Alcoba	1m 36.843s
15	Arenas	1m 36.914s
16	Kubo	1m 37.360s
17	Roberts	1m 38.065s
18	Canet	No Time
	Q1	
19	Lowes	1m 36.360s
20	Dalla Porta	1m 36.474s
21	Aldeguer	1m 36.507s
22	Schrotter	1m 36.567s
23	Baltus	1m 36.732s
24	VD Goorbergh	1m 36.816s
25	Zaccone	1m 36.869s
26	Kelly	1m 37.074s
27	Ramirez	1m 37.206s
28	Antonelli	1m 37.264s
29	Hada	1m 37.279s
	Corsi	No Time

Fastest race laps

1	Arbolino	1m 52.003s
2	Salac	1m 52.644s
3	Lopez	1m 52.942s
4	Ogura	1m 53.052s
5	Dixon	1m 53.240s
6	Fernandez	1m 53.380s
7	Vietti	1m 53.489s
8	Canet	1m 53.492s
9	Kubo	1m 54.305s
10	Schrotter	1m 54.338s
11	Roberts	1m 54.346s
12	Hada	1m 54.359s
13	Kelly	1m 54.666s
14	Baltus	1m 54.745s
15	Acosta	1m 54.949s
16	Bendsneyder	1m 55.062s
17	Arenas	1m 55.265s
18	Lowes	1m 55.585s
19	VD Goorbergh	1m 55.749s
20	Navarro	1m 57.382s
21	Gonzalez	1m 57.565s
22	Zaccone	1m 58.137s
23	Antonelli	1m 58.256s
24	Alcoba	1m 58.703s
25	Corsi	1m 59.273s
26	Ramirez	1m 59.915s
27	Dalla Porta	2m 10.506s

Championship Points

1	Fernandez	238.5
2	Ogura	237
3	Canet	185
4	Vietti	165
5	Arbolino	150.5
6	Acosta	132
7	Roberts	130
8	Dixon	127.5
9	Chantra	120
10	Lopez	110.5
11	Schrotter	104.5
12	Navarro	83
13	Arenas	74
14	Bendsneyder	74
15	Beaubier	55
16	Lowes	51
17	Aldeguer	48
18	Alcoba	47
19	Gonzalez	44
20	Salac	37
21	Baltus	30
22	Dalla Porta	15
23	Manzi	9
24	Zaccone	9
25	Kubo	7.5
26	Fenati	7
27	Rodrigo	6
28	Kelly	5.5
29	Ramirez	5
30	Hada	1.5
31	Pasini	1

Constructor Points

1	Kalex	407.5
2	Boscoscuro	142.5
3	MV Agusta	5

Moto3

RACE DISTANCE: 22 laps, 62.254 miles/100.188km · RACE WEATHER: Dry (air 25°, humidity 94%, track 38°)

Pos.	Rider	Nat.	No.	Entrant	Machine	Laps	Time & Speed
1	**Dennis Foggia**	ITA	7	Leopard Racing	Honda	22	37m 52.331s
							98.6mph/158.7km/h
2	**Ayumu Sasaki**	JPN	71	Sterilgarda Husqvarna Max	Husqvarna	22	37m 53.855s
3	**Riccardo Rossi**	ITA	54	SIC58 Squadra Corse	Honda	22	37m 55.135s
4	**Stefano Nepa**	ITA	82	Angeluss MTA Team	KTM	22	38m 01.745s
5	**Izan Guevara**	SPA	28	Gaviota GASGAS Aspar Team	GASGAS	22	38m 01.858s
6	**Diogo Moreira**	BRA	10	MT Helmets - MSI	KTM	22	38m 02.302s
7	**Andrea Migno**	ITA	16	Rivacold Snipers Team	Honda	22	38m 01.941s
8	**Jaume Masia**	SPA	5	Red Bull KTM Ajo	KTM	22	38m 02.364s
9	**David Munoz**	SPA	44	BOE Motorsports	KTM	22	38m 02.377s
10	**Ryusei Yamanaka**	JPN	6	MT Helmets - MSI	KTM	22	38m 02.419s
11	**Daniel Holgado**	SPA	96	Red Bull KTM Ajo	KTM	22	38m 06.902s
12	**Joel Kelso**	AUS	66	CIP Green Power	KTM	22	38m 15.763s
13	**Carlos Tatay**	SPA	99	CFMOTO Racing PruestelGP	CFMOTO	22	38m 16.094s
14	**Xavier Artigas**	SPA	43	CFMOTO Racing PruestelGP	CFMOTO	22	38m 16.173s
15	**Scott Ogden**	GBR	19	VisionTrack Racing Team	Honda	22	38m 16.199s
16	Lorenzo Fellon	FRA	20	SIC58 Squadra Corse	Honda	22	38m 16.563s
17	Deniz Oncu	TUR	53	Red Bull KTM Tech3	KTM	22	38m 16.386s
18	Elia Bartolini	ITA	23	QJMotor Avintia Racing Team	KTM	22	38m 32.423s
19	Vicente Perez	SPA	21	Rivacold Snipers Team	Honda	22	38m 32.425s
20	Ivan Ortola	SPA	48	Angeluss MTA Team	KTM	22	38m 32.559s
21	Mario Aji	INA	64	Honda Team Asia	Honda	22	38m 32.697s
22	Ana Carrasco	SPA	22	BOE Motorsports	KTM	22	38m 36.207s
23	Joshua Whatley	GBR	70	VisionTrack Racing Team	Honda	22	38m 40.811s
24	Nicola Fabio Carraro	ITA	9	QJMotor Avintia Racing Team	KTM	22	38m 47.078s
25	Taiyo Furusato	JPN	72	Honda Team Asia	Honda	19	39m 15.754s
	Sergio Garcia	SPA	11	Gaviota GASGAS Aspar Team	GASGAS	14	DNF-crash
	Tatsuki Suzuki	JPN	24	Leopard Racing	Honda	7	DNF-technical
	John McPhee	GBR	17	Sterilgarda Husqvarna Max	Husqvarna	7	DNF-crash
	Kaito Toba	JPN	27	CIP Green Power	KTM	1	DNF-crash
	Adrian Fernandez	SPA	31	Red Bull KTM Tech3	KTM	0	DNF-crash

Fastest lap: Jaume Masia, on lap 5, 1m 42.530s, 99.3mph/159.8km/h.

Lap record: Dennis Foggia, 1m 42.963s, 98.9mph/159.2km/h (2018).

Event maximum speed: Diogo Moreira, 148.4mph/238.9km/h (race).

Qualifying:

Weather: Dry

Air: 28° **Humidity:** 77% **Track:** 45°

	Foggia	1m 42.077s
2	Masia	1m 42.369s
3	Sasaki	1m 42.486s
4	Nepa	1m 42.531s
5	Moreira	1m 42.716s
6	Holgado	1m 42.740s
7	Rossi	1m 42.847s
8	McPhee	1m 42.906s
9	Yamanaka	1m 42.986s
10	Munoz	1m 43.031s
11	Guevara	1m 43.047s
12	Kelso	1m 43.129s
13	Furusato	1m 43.167s
14	Migno	1m 43.221s
15	Fellon	1m 43.387s
16	Oncu	1m 43.407s
17	Toba	1m 43.824s
18	Suzuki	1m 44.167s
	Q1	
19	Fernandez	1m 43.134s
20	Garcia	1m 43.140s
21	Bartolini	1m 43.215s
22	Ogden	1m 43.253s
23	Tatay	1m 43.408s
24	Artigas	1m 43.573s
25	Ortola	1m 43.760s
26	Perez	1m 43.829s
27	Whatley	1m 43.982s
28	Carrasco	1m 44.062s
29	Aji	1m 44.920s
30	Carraro	2m 05.528s

Fastest race laps

1	Masia	1m 42.530s
2	Suzuki	1m 42.538s
3	Munoz	1m 42.660s
4	Yamanaka	1m 42.787s
5	Nepa	1m 42.787s
6	Moreira	1m 42.837s
7	Holgado	1m 42.860s
8	Guevara	1m 42.873s
9	Migno	1m 42.928s
10	McPhee	1m 42.949s
11	Artigas	1m 43.130s
12	Tatay	1m 43.190s
13	Ogden	1m 43.258s
14	Fellon	1m 43.292s
15	Kelso	1m 43.311s
16	Garcia	1m 43.416s
17	Oncu	1m 43.542s
18	Ortola	1m 43.586s
19	Perez	1m 43.838s
20	Bartolini	1m 43.952s
21	Aji	1m 44.117s
22	Carrasco	1m 44.144s
23	Whatley	1m 44.194s
24	Fabio	1m 44.251s

Championship Points

1	Guevara	265
2	Foggia	216
3	Garcia	209
4	Sasaki	194
5	Masia	163
6	Oncu	154
7	Suzuki	128
8	Migno	100
9	Holgado	88
10	Moreira	84
11	Rossi	81
12	Tatay	80
13	Munoz	79
14	Yamanaka	79
15	Artigas	76
16	Toba	63
17	McPhee	62
18	Ortola	59
19	Nepa	53
20	Fernandez	40
21	Kelso	28
22	Bartolini	24
23	Ogden	21
24	Bertelle	16
25	Fellon	11
26	Aji	5
27	Furusato	2

Constructor Points

1	GASGAS	323
2	Honda	300
3	KTM	270
4	Husqvarna	230
5	CFMOTO	118

FIM WORLD CHAMPIONSHIP · ROUND 18

AUSTRALIAN GRAND PRIX

PHILLIP ISLAND CIRCUIT

Inset, left: The order of Miller's boot was adopted by Marquez, Rins and Bagnaia.

Inset, far left: Guevara wrapped up the Moto3 title. Rider coach Julian Simon, 2009 125 champion, joined the party.

Inset, centre: Marco Bezzecchi shows joy unbounded after securing Rookie of the Year in MotoGP.
Photos: Gold & Goose

Main: Great track, great weather, great race. Rins, Bagnaia, Marquez, Martin and Marini provided the spectacle.
Photo: www.suzuki -racing.com

Above: **On top form, Alex Rins climbed through to claim a surprise Suzuki win.**
Photo: www.suzuki-racing.com

Right: **Miller and Ducati prepare for a race that would end abruptly.**
Photo: Ducati Corse

SOME races, some racetracks, are particularly blessed by the gods of speed and competition. After 1,085 days away from Phillip Island, every passing lap reminded us of just how badly it had been missed.

This was an Australian classic, the entire MotoGP field engaged in all-out war. From 24 names jostling up front, the lead group was eventually whittled down to ten. Then Alex Rins gave the contest the final twist it deserved, claiming the most unexpected of wins, Suzuki's 96th, but not last, in a seven-bike lead group covered by just 0.884 of a second.

As impressive as the numbers on the time sheets were (5.9 seconds covered the top ten, displacing Silverstone as the second closest in history), they don't tell the full story of 40 minutes and 50 seconds of pure entertainment. Riders were bunched up by the need to limit rear tyre wear around the long, open turns and overtaking was incessant, with more than 60 position changes among the leading four. In a highly competitive field, this might even have been the best yet contest at the seaside venue.

Another meltdown for Quartararo meant that he wasn't part of it, while a completely innocent crash also took out Miller, ironically at the corner that had been rechristened in his honour the day before. With Bagnaia taking the benefit and the lead on points, the championship took another step to match the race for closeness.

Aleix Espargaro also lost some ground, finishing ninth after confidently predicting a challenge for victory. Overly conservative electronic settings had hindered his late speed. "I had no acceleration," he explained. "The bike was cutting a lot of power for some reason. We knew the tyre would drop, but if you analyse the pace of everybody at the end, they dropped about half a second. We dropped one second or even more. The last three races, we proved that we are not together as a team, not at the level to fight for this title. We conceded many points."

In turn, Quartararo rejected the notion that he is weak in high-pressure situations after scoring just eight points from the previous four races. He made two critical mistakes. The first, at Turn Four, dropped him from seventh to 22nd; the second, at Turn Two, resulted in him crashing out. There were reminders of 2020, when he had arrived at the penultimate triple-header leading the title fight, but eventually had slipped to eighth overall. That was different, he said, "2020 was mentally and technically, and now I don't feel mentally like overthinking too much. Just trying to do my best, I'm overriding a little bit, and the risk of a mistake is really close. That's what happened today."

Marc Marquez, less than two-tenths away from a comeback win, was continuing testing at pace for 2023. Due to his enforced six-race absence, he had yet to use his one allocated aero update. After sampling some revisions at the Misano test, he tried further evolutions on the Friday at Phillip Island. His Honda featured Ducati-like side pods as well as fins on his seat unit, which again resembled Bologna's innovation. "We already tried this kind of concept in Misano and I felt some positive points," he said, "but we decided not to homologate it then because like this, Honda had the chance to keep working and have another evolution that I received here." There were, he continued, "some positives and some negatives."

The same was true of the legendary circuit. Along with its fabulous long, open bends and stunning sea views, Phillip Island had gained notoriety for another aspect: wildlife. Seagulls were a constant menace, but in 2022 there was more. A wallaby ran across the track in front of Aleix Espargaro during FP1, while both Moto3 FP3 and Moto2 qualifying were red-flagged prematurely due to Cape Barren geese nonchalantly crossing the track. The riders brought up the matter in Friday's Safety Commission meeting. "At the beginning, everybody was laughing because I understand it could be

fun. But it was very dangerous. We asked for them to close a bit better the track [with higher perimeter fencing]," said the shaken Espargaro.

The Turn Four hairpin, formerly Honda Corner, was renamed 'Miller Corner' in a ceremony on Saturday. An almost sheepish Jack felt that he didn't deserve the honour: "It's an amazing gesture. I'm definitely not worthy of it, but I'll take it. For them to recognise what I do for motorcycle racing ... I love everything about this sport, and it shows. If you can be a nice guy and go fast from time to time, then it definitely pays off."

A new communications system was mooted after tricky conditions on Friday were "on the limit" due to high winds, according to Luca Marini. Riders suggested in the Safety Commission that the best way to signal when conditions are too bad to continue riding would be to communicate to Race Direction via a button on their handlebar. The Italian explained, "If it's on the limit riding, for IRTA, Dorna or Race Direction, when they need to take this kind of decision, it's not an easy job for them, because they are not on track. They are here, and from here you don't feel the wind. So we are asking them to have a button to push and maybe if, say, 80 per cent push this button, also in a race, they can have a red flag."

Suzuki's imminent withdrawal had taken everyone by surprise. Now, with two races left, they had another one – the test team and rider Takuya Tsuda would try a handful of new parts before the Valencia race. Joan Mir and Alex Rins were astonished by the news. "They will test before Malaysia," said an exasperated Rins, "a totally new fairing and completely different to what we are using here, with a different intake and different wings. If you ask me why, then I have no idea, it makes no sense. But let them spend the money."

After his surprise victory, Rins referred to Suzuki's imminent departure again. "This one is for all the team," he said. "For the ones that got contracts for next year and the ones that didn't."

MOTOGP RACE - 27 laps

Very close qualifying presaged a very close race, the top dozen inside less than a second, rival bikes for once among the Ducatis. Martin led the front row from Marquez's Honda and Bagnaia; Aleix Espargaro's Aprilia headed row two from Quartararo's Yamaha and Zarco's Ducati, through from Q1. Miller was on row three, with winner Rins (also from Q1) leading row four.

Martin set the early pace as he led Marquez – the only man on Michelin's soft rear tyre compound – through Turn One from the three title contenders, with Bagnaia third after his start device had failed to engage. A mistake through Turn Three dropped Quartararo behind Espargaro. Following, Marini, Alex Marquez, Miller and Rins were in the thick of it.

Initially, Martin and Marquez appeared capable of breaking the group, enjoying a rare seven-tenths advantage. But there were flashbacks to Motegi with Miller on the move, using his braking prowess into Turn Ten to pass Marini for sixth on lap two, then Espargaro for fifth the next time around. Soon he was nibbling at Bagnaia at the same place, succeeding on the fifth lap, having failed on the fourth. But then the baton of 'danger man' was passed to Rins, a lowly 11th on lap three. The Spaniard was irresistible into Turn Two, picking off Espargaro (lap six), Miller (lap seven) and Bagnaia (lap eight) on the cut-back from Turn One.

At the other end of the spectrum, Zarco was 18th after issues with his start device; even worse, Bastianini was 21st on lap two, flustered by his airbag going off after hitting a major bump early on.

Quartararo never looked comfortable. He was shuffled back to seventh when a massive shake on entry to Miller Corner forced him to lift to avoid the others ahead. He ran off and rejoined 22nd, his chances ruined. Then he crashed running into the Southern Loop on the 11th lap, compounding a third disastrous race out of four.

Then more drama at Turn Four, where Alex Marquez

Above: **Alex Marquez skittles out luckless Miller at the corner that bears his name.**
Photo: John Morris-MPIX

Above right: **Marquez just missed the win, but celebrated his 100th podium and Honda's first of the 2022 season.**
Photo: Repsol Honda

Right: **Four-way fight in Moto3. Garcia (11) leads eventual winner Guevara (28), followed by Sasaki (half hidden) and Oncu.**

Below right: **Moto2 rising star Lopez overcame a penalty for another fine win. Acosta and Dixon flanked him on the podium.**
Photos: Gold & Goose

smashed into Miller, taking both down and ending the Australian's slender title hopes for good. "I was mid-corner, just about to get on the gas when I got a front wheel to the middle of my spine," he said. Of the championship: "Aleix and Bastianini didn't get too many points today, so my main goal is to try and beat those guys."

That incident gave the lead eight – Martin, Marquez, Rins, Bagnaia, Bezzecchi, Aleix Espargaro, Brad Binder and Marini – a head start. And how they went at it. The overtaking was incessant, with Rins first grabbing the initiative on lap 14, again into Turn Two, then Three, to his advantage over Martin, who was quickly shuffled behind Marquez and Bagnaia. Then it was the Italian's turn to lead on lap 15, using the Ducati's top speed to breeze past the Suzuki into Turn One. By then, Zarco and Bastianini had recovered brilliantly to make this a lead group of ten.

Soon, however, the early efforts of Zarco and Binder would tell as they dropped away. Espargaro was the same, ruing the Aprilia's power-sapping electronics. Now there were seven.

Ducati's chances looked more than promising when Bezzecchi – enjoying his best ride to date – fought past both Marquez and Rins on the main straight on lap 21, to provide back-up to Bagnaia, who was struggling with front-tyre wear.

But both the Suzuki and Honda men knew that fighting two Ducatis wasn't possible, but one certainly was. With three to go, Rins moved under Bezzecchi at Turn Three, and Marquez immediately followed suit at the next corner. Then the pair duly doubled up on Bagnaia at the Southern Loop the final time around. First Rins outbraked the Ducati on entry, then Marquez barged him off line with the most opportune of moves.

It was all set up for a Marquez victory lunge at Turn Ten, but by then, he was running on empty. Rins took Suzuki's first victory in two years by 0.186 of a second; Marquez claimed second and a 100th premier-class podium.

Bagnaia led a Ducati sextet home a further tenth back, Bezzecchi, Bastianini, Marini and Martin flashing by the line in the blink of an eye. Zarco was a colossal three seconds back in eighth, with Espargaro and Binder behind, mechanical issues and tyre wear their downfall.

Pol Espargaro was a lone 11th; then Oliveira led Crutchlow and the still-close Darryn Binder, the top two Yamahas; Gardner took the last point after earlier running tenth before suffering tyre drop-off. Team-mate Fernandez seized 16th from the fading Vinales on the last lap. Mir had dropped to 18th, citing major tyre pressure problems due to a faulty gauge. Morbidelli also crashed out.

MOTO2 RACE – 25 laps

Kalex rival Boscoscuro chassis again showed strongly in a topsy-turvy race, where title leader and current favourite Augusto Fernandez crashed out while challenger Ai Ogura, badly off form and not even in the top ten, took the points lead.

The Japanese rider had been out of sorts throughout practice, qualifying 13th on the fifth row, alongside Dixon, for once also off the pace.

Up front, first-timer Aldeguer took a second pole and third front row of the year, ahead of Fernandez's Kalex, with Boscoscuro team-mate Lopez third. Arbolino, Canet and Vietti were behind.

Lopez was burdened with a long-lap penalty after knocking Vietti off in qualifying – less costly at this track than at other circuits, being a short run around the outside of Turn Four, but still an obstacle to be overcome. He did that resoundingly as he sped to a second victory in four races. The Boscoscuro chassis allowed him to use Dunlop's hard front tyre, while the Kalexes struggled to do so.

The Spaniard seized the lead from Arbolino on lap one and had stretched it to 2.6 seconds by the time he took his penalty on lap four. He still rejoined with 1.5 seconds in hand. From there, it was a cruise, and he won by 3.5 seconds.

In the early stages, there was a lively scrap for second. Arbolino was holding Fernandez and Acosta at bay, only to tuck the front at the Hayshed on the seventh lap. From there, puzzlingly, Acosta overtook his championship-leading team-mate on lap nine, before Fernandez inexplicably tucked the front at the Southern Loop on lap 16. For Ogura, languishing outside the top ten, it was like a get-out-of-jail-free card.

That left Acosta clear to collect second, with Dixon coming through strongly to third from the fifth row. Aldeguer held off fellow rookies Gonzalez and Alcoba, and Beaubier for fourth. Chantra was a couple of seconds adrift, while a fading Canet was ninth.

Tenth went to Bendsneyder, who had caught and passed Ogura mid-race, the Japanese only just safe from Lowes in 12th. Ogura was a massive 32 seconds behind the winner,

but five points were enough to regain the championship lead from no-score Fernandez by just 3.5 points.

Schrotter won a battle for 13th from Arenas and Hada; there were only 17 finishers, with a long crash list.

As well as Arbolino and Fernandez at the front, Salac, Kubo, Antonelli, Vietti and Baltus crashed; Roberts retired with technical issues.

The worst crash was between Navarro and veteran Corsi, the former being stretchered away with a broken femur. Both were out of the next GP, and Navarro for the rest of the year. The Spaniard's team-mate, Zonta van den Goorbergh, was also out for two races after breaking his wrist in FP1.

MOTO3 RACE – 23 laps

Sasaki claimed a second pole of the year ahead of Garcia and Ortola; Guevara led row three. KTMs were in control, teenage Japanese rookie Taiyo Furusato the top Honda in tenth, Foggia 12th.

The race was run in blustery conditions, with not a Honda in sight. In the closing moments, Guevara demonstrated his ice-cold precision to seal the World Championship, edging clear of a frenetic quartet to win by three-tenths.

An earlier shower had left wet patches, but you'd not have known from Garcia's early speed, as he took a half-second lead from Sasaki, Guevara, fast-starting Oncu, inspired Australian Kelso, plus Moreira, McPhee and Nepa. Four laps on, they'd closed up. Then Kelso grazed Nepa exiting Miller Corner and, together with McPhee and Moreira, they lost touch.

It all came down to the final lap. They were inseparable exiting Turn One, but Guevara edged under Oncu for the lead in the Southern Loop. The Turk was left to defend second place from Garcia, leaving Guevara to take another flawless finale.

Oncu was three-tenths back, with Garcia and Sasaki in close attendance. Another seven seconds down, Nepa just managed to edge McPhee for fifth, with Moreira and Kelso right behind.

Almost ten seconds adrift, Foggia narrowly led a five-bike pack, while Rossi was awarded tenth ahead of Munoz in a video finish.

Furusato was taken out early on by Holgado; Ogden and Suzuki were among a number of others to crash out.

Guevara's 290 points put him out of reach of Garcia (225), who took over second from Foggia by two points.

FIM WORLD CHAMPIONSHIP: ROUND 18

ANIMOCA BRANDS AUSTRALIAN MOTORCYCLE GRAND PRIX

14–16 OCTOBER, 2022

PHILLIP ISLAND

27 laps
Length: 4.448 km / 2.764 miles
Width: 13m

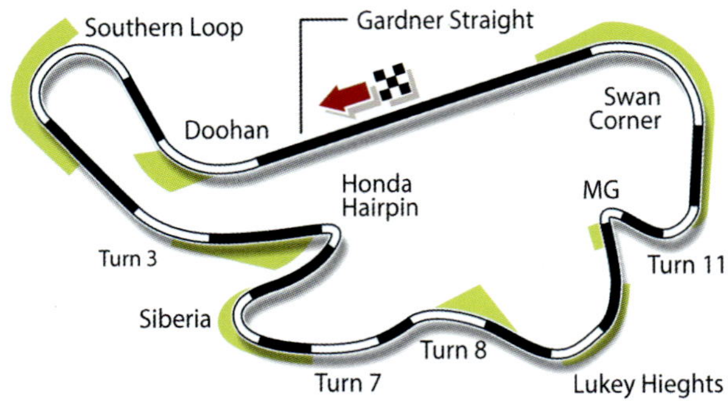

MotoGP RACE DISTANCE: 27 laps, 74.624 miles/120.096km · RACE WEATHER: Dry (air 14°, humidity 61%, track 35°)

Pos.	Rider	Nat.	No.	Entrant	Machine	Tyres	Race tyre choice	Laps	Time & speed
1	**Alex Rins**	SPA	42	Team SUZUKI ECSTAR	Suzuki GSX-RR	M	F: Medium/R: Hard	27	40m 50.654s 109.6mph/176.4km/h
2	**Marc Marquez**	SPA	93	Repsol Honda Team	Honda RC213V	M	F: Hard/R: Soft	27	40m 50.840s
3	**Francesco Bagnaia**	ITA	63	Ducati Lenovo Team	Ducati Desmosedici	M	F: Medium/R: Hard	27	40m 50.878s
4	**Marco Bezzecchi**	ITA	72	Mooney VR46 Racing Team	Ducati Desmosedici	M	F: Medium/R: Hard	27	40m 51.188s
5	**Enea Bastianini**	ITA	23	Gresini Racing MotoGP	Ducati Desmosedici	M	F: Hard/R: Hard	27	40m 51.211s
6	**Luca Marini**	ITA	10	Mooney VR46 Racing Team	Ducati Desmosedici	M	F: Medium/R: Hard	27	40m 51.342s
7	**Jorge Martin**	SPA	89	Prima Pramac Racing	Ducati Desmosedici	M	F: Hard/R: Hard	27	40m 51.538s
8	**Johann Zarco**	FRA	5	Prima Pramac Racing	Ducati Desmosedici	M	F: Medium/R: Hard	27	40m 53.795s
9	**Aleix Espargaro**	SPA	41	Aprilia Racing	Aprilia RS-GP	M	F: Medium/R: Hard	27	40m 55.202s
10	**Brad Binder**	RSA	33	Red Bull KTM Factory Racing	KTM RC16	M	F: Hard/R: Hard	27	40m 56.594s
11	**Pol Espargaro**	SPA	44	Repsol Honda Team	Honda RC213V	M	F: Hard/R: Medium	27	41m 01.702s
12	**Miguel Oliveira**	POR	88	Red Bull KTM Factory Racing	KTM RC16	M	F: Hard/R: Hard	27	41m 04.260s
13	**Cal Crutchlow**	GBR	35	WithU Yamaha RNF MotoGP Team	Yamaha YZR-M1	M	F: Hard/R: Medium	27	41m 04.544s
14	**Darryn Binder**	RSA	40	WithU Yamaha RNF MotoGP Team	Yamaha YZR-M1	M	F: Medium/R: Hard	27	41m 05.180s
15	**Remy Gardner**	AUS	87	Tech3 KTM Factory Racing	KTM RC16	M	F: Medium/R: Hard	27	41m 10.124s
16	Raul Fernandez	SPA	25	Tech3 KTM Factory Racing	KTM RC16	M	F: Hard/R: Hard	27	41m 11.299s
17	Maverick Vinales	SPA	12	Aprilia Racing	Aprilia RS-GP	M	F: Medium/R: Hard	27	41m 12.821s
18	Joan Mir	SPA	36	Team SUZUKI ECSTAR	Suzuki GSX-RR	M	F: Medium/R: Hard	27	41m 14.143s
19	Tetsuta Nagashima	JPN	45	LCR Honda IDEMITSU	Honda RC213V	M	F: Medium/R: Medium	27	41m 30.272s
20	Fabio Di Giannantonio	ITA	49	Gresini Racing MotoGP	Ducati Desmosedici	M	F: Medium/R: Hard	27	41m 30.287s
	Franco Morbidelli	ITA	21	Monster Energy Yamaha MotoGP	Yamaha YZR-M1	M	F: Hard/R: Hard	21	DNF-crash
	Fabio Quartararo	FRA	20	Monster Energy Yamaha MotoGP	Yamaha YZR-M1	M	F: Medium/R: Hard	10	DNF-crash
	Jack Miller	AUS	43	Ducati Lenovo Team	Ducati Desmosedici	M	F: Medium/R: Medium	8	DNF-crash
	Alex Marquez	SPA	73	LCR Honda CASTROL	Honda RC213V	M	F: Medium/R: Hard	8	DNF-crash

Fastest lap: Johann Zarco, on lap 13, 1m 29.622s, 111.0mph/178.6km/h.
Lap record: Marc Marquez, 1m 28.108s, 112.9mph/181.7km/h (2013).
Event maximum speed: Enea Bastianini, 209.7mph/337.5km/h (warm-up).

Qualifying

Weather: Dry
Air Temp: 16° **Humidity:** 58%
Track Temp: 30°

1	Martin	1m 27.767s
2	M. Marquez	1m 27.780s
3	Bagnaia	1m 27.953s
4	A. Espargaro	1m 27.957s
5	Quartararo	1m 27.973s
6	Zarco	1m 28.007s
7	Marini	1m 28.029s
8	Miller	1m 28.116s
9	Bezzecchi	1m 28.185s
10	Rins	1m 28.541s
11	A. Marquez	1m 28.733s
12	Vinales	1m 28.765s
	Q1	
13	P. Espargaro	1m 28.392s
14	Mir	1m 28.492s
15	Bastianini	1m 28.647s
16	B. Binder	1m 28.652s
17	Crutchlow	1m 28.677s
18	D. Binder	1m 28.760s
19	Gardner	1m 28.820s
20	Di Giannantonio	1m 28.830s
21	Oliveira	1m 28.859s
22	Fernandez	1m 28.966s
23	Morbidelli	1m 29.146s
24	Nagashima	1m 29.624s

Fastest race laps

1	Zarco	1m 29.622s
2	A. Espargaro	1m 29.793s
3	Bezzecchi	1m 29.796s
4	A. Marquez	1m 29.805s
5	Rins	1m 29.850s
6	Bastianini	1m 29.880s
7	B. Binder	1m 29.901s
8	Marini	1m 29.903s
9	Quartararo	1m 30.019s
10	Miller	1m 30.060s
11	Oliveira	1m 30.089s
12	Martin	1m 30.092s
13	Bagnaia	1m 30.096s
14	Fernandez	1m 30.106s
15	M. Marquez	1m 30.117s
16	Vinales	1m 30.140s
17	Gardner	1m 30.145s
18	D. Binder	1m 30.211s
19	P. Espargaro	1m 30.256s
20	Mir	1m 30.284s
21	Morbidelli	1m 30.306s
22	Crutchlow	1m 30.349s
23	Di Giannantonio	1m 30.687s
24	Nagashima	1m 31.049s

Championship Points

1	Bagnaia	233
2	Quartararo	219
3	A. Espargaro	206
4	Bastianini	191
5	Miller	179
6	B. Binder	160
7	Zarco	159
8	Rins	137
9	Martin	136
10	Oliveira	135
11	Vinales	122
12	Marini	111
13	M. Marquez	104
14	Bezzecchi	93
15	Mir	77
16	P. Espargaro	54
17	A. Marquez	50
18	Nakagami	46
19	Morbidelli	31
20	Di Giannantonio	23
21	Dovizioso	15
22	D. Binder	12
23	Gardner	10
24	Fernandez	9
25	Crutchlow	6
26	Bradl	2

Constructor Points

1	Ducati	407
2	Aprilia	242
3	Yamaha	227
4	KTM	212
5	Suzuki	163
6	Honda	144

Grid order	1	2	3	4	5	6	7	8	9	10	11	12	13	14	15	16	17	18	19	20	21	22	23	24	25	26	27	·
89 MARTIN	89	89	89	89	89	89	89	89	89	89	89	89	89	42	63	63	63	63	63	42	63	63	63	63	63	63	42	1
93 M. MARQUEZ	93	93	93	93	93	93	93	93	93	93	42	42	42	63	93	93	42	42	42	63	72	72	72	72	42	42	93	2
63 BAGNAIA	63	63	63	63	43	63	63	42	42	42	93	93	93	93	42	42	93	89	93	72	93	42	42	42	93	93	63	3
41 A. ESPARGARO	41	41	43	43	63	43	42	63	63	63	63	63	63	72	72	72	89	93	72	93	42	89	93	93	72	72	72	4
20 QUARTARARO	20	20	41	41	41	42	43	43	41	41	72	72	72	89	89	89	72	72	89	89	89	93	10	10	10	10	23	5
5 ZARCO	10	43	20	10	42	41	41	41	72	72	41	41	41	41	41	41	41	41	10	10	10	10	89	89	89	89	10	6
10 MARINI	73	10	10	36	73	10	10	10	33	33	33	33	33	33	33	33	33	33	41	23	41	23	23	23	23	23	89	7
43 MILLER	43	73	36	42	10	72	72	72	10	10	10	10	10	10	10	10	10	10	33	41	23	41	33	41	5	5	5	8
72 BEZZECCHI	42	36	73	73	36	73	73	73	12	12	12	12	5	5	5	23	23	23	23	5	5	5	41	5	41	41	41	9
42 RINS	44	42	72	72	72	36	33	33	87	87	87	5	12	12	23	5	5	5	5	33	33	33	5	33	33	33	33	10
73 A. MARQUEZ	72	12	42	12	33	33	36	36	36	36	5	23	23	23	12	12	12	12	12	12	44	44	44	44	44	44	44	11
12 VINALES	36	72	12	33	12	12	12	12	5	5	23	87	87	44	44	44	44	44	44	44	12	35	35	35	35	35	88	12
44 P. ESPARGARO	12	44	33	44	44	87	87	87	44	23	36	36	44	87	87	87	36	36	35	35	35	40	40	40	40	88	35	13
36 MIR	40	33	44	87	87	44	44	44	23	44	44	44	36	36	36	36	87	35	36	40	40	88	88	88	88	40	40	14
23 BASTIANINI	33	40	87	40	40	5	5	5	20	20	40	40	35	35	35	35	35	40	40	36	88	12	12	12	87	87	87	15
33 B.BINDER	87	87	40	5	5	23	23	23	40	40	35	35	40	40	40	40	40	87	87	87	87	87	87	87	12	12	25	
35 CRUTCHLOW	23	23	49	23	23	40	40	40	35	35	21	88	88	88	88	88	88	88	88	88	36	36	36	36	36	25	12	
40 D.BINDER	5	5	5	49	35	35	35	35	21	21	25	21	25	21	21	25	25	25	25	25	21	25	25	25	25	36	36	
87 GARDNER	49	49	35	35	20	20	20	20	25	25	88	25	21	25	25	21	21	21	21	21	25	49	49	49	49	49	45	
49 DI GIANNANTONIO	35	25	23	25	25	25	21	21	88	88	45	45	45	45	45	45	45	45	45	45	49	45	45	45	45	45	49	
25 FERNANDEZ	25	35	25	21	21	21	25	25	45	45	49	49	49	49	49	49	49	49	49	49	45							
21 MORBIDELLI	45	88	21	20	88	88	88	88	49	49																		
45 NAGASHIMA	88	45	45	88	45	45	45	45																				
88 OLIVEIRA	21	21	88	45	49	49	49	49																				

21 Pit stop

Moto2

RACE DISTANCE: 25 laps, 69.096 miles/111.200km · RACE WEATHER: Dry (air 14°, humidity 61%, track 26°)

Pos.	Rider	Nat.	No.	Entrant	Machine	Laps	Time & Speed
1	**Alonso Lopez**	SPA	21	Beta Tools Speed Up	Boscoscuro	25	39m 14.947s
							89.4mph/143.9km/h
2	**Pedro Acosta**	SPA	51	Red Bull KTM Ajo	Kalex	25	39m 18.503s
3	**Jake Dixon**	GBR	96	Inde GASGAS Aspar Team	Kalex	25	39m 24.530s
4	**Fermin Aldeguer**	SPA	54	Beta Tools Speed Up	Boscoscuro	25	39m 30.692s
5	**Manuel Gonzalez**	SPA	18	Yamaha VR46 Master Camp Team	Kalex	25	39m 30.722s
6	**Jeremy Alcoba**	SPA	52	Liqui Moly Intact GP	Kalex	25	39m 30.839s
7	**Cameron Beaubier**	USA	6	American Racing	Kalex	25	39m 30.981s
8	**Somkiat Chantra**	THA	35	IDEMITSU Honda Team Asia	Kalex	25	39m 32.896s
9	**Aron Canet**	SPA	40	Flexbox HP40	Kalex	25	39m 39.764s
10	**Bo Bendsneyder**	NED	64	Pertamina Mandalika SAG Team	Kalex	25	39m 45.599s
11	**Ai Ogura**	JPN	79	IDEMITSU Honda Team Asia	Kalex	25	39m 47.928s
12	**Sam Lowes**	GBR	22	Elf Marc VDS Racing Team	Kalex	25	39m 49.354s
13	**Marcel Schrotter**	GER	23	Liqui Moly Intact GP	Kalex	25	40m 02.531s
14	**Albert Arenas**	SPA	75	Inde GASGAS Aspar Team	Kalex	25	40m 02.555s
15	**Taiga Hada**	JPN	29	Pertamina Mandalika SAG Team	Kalex	25	40m 02.975s
16	Alessandro Zaccone	ITA	61	Gresini Racing Moto2	Kalex	25	40m 08.774s
17	Marcos Ramirez	SPA	42	MV Agusta Forward Racing	MV Agusta	25	40m 09.303s
18	Sean Dylan Kelly	USA	4	American Racing	Kalex	25	40m 09.584s
	Joe Roberts	USA	16	Italtrans Racing Team	Kalex	23	DNF-technical
	Barry Baltus	BEL	7	RW Racing GP	Kalex	17	DNF-crash
	Augusto Fernandez	SPA	37	Red Bull KTM Ajo	Kalex	15	DNF-crash
	Celestino Vietti	ITA	13	Mooney VR46 Racing Team	Kalex	12	DNF-crash
	Filip Salac	CZE	12	Gresini Racing Moto2	Kalex	10	DNF-crash
	Keminth Kubo	THA	81	Yamaha VR46 Master Camp Team	Kalex	10	DNF-crash
	Niccolo Antonelli	ITA	28	Mooney VR46 Racing Team	Kalex	10	DNF-crash
	Lorenzo Dalla Porta	ITA	19	Italtrans Racing Team	Kalex	8	DNF-ret in pit
	Tony Arbolino	ITA	14	Elf Marc VDS Racing Team	Kalex	6	DNF-crash
	Simone Corsi	ITA	24	MV Agusta Forward Racing	MV Agusta	3	DNF-crash
	Jorge Navarro	SPA	9	Flexbox HP40	Kalex	3	DNF-crash

Fastest lap: Alonso Lopez, on lap 3, 1m 33.030s, 106.9mph/172.1km/h.

Lap record: Thomas Luthi, 1m 32.609s, 107.4mph/172.9km/h (2019).

Event maximum speed: Cameron Beaubier, 186.5mph/300.1km/h (free practice).

Qualifying

Weather: Dry

Air: 17° **Humidity:** 57% **Track:** 29°

	Rider	Time
1	Aldeguer	1m 32.233s
2	Fernandez	1m 32.306s
3	Lopez	1m 32.543s
4	Arbolino	1m 32.721s
5	Canet	1m 32.837s
6	Vietti	1m 32.858s
7	Gonzalez	1m 32.858s
8	Acosta	1m 32.872s
9	Alcoba	1m 32.946s
10	Salac	1m 32.970s
11	Beaubier	1m 33.006s
12	Lowes	1m 33.040s
13	Ogura	1m 33.067s
14	Dixon	1m 33.241s
15	Roberts	1m 33.284s
16	Chantra	1m 33.299s
17	Bendsneyder	1m 33.328s
18	Dalla Porta	1m 34.152s
	Q1	
19	Arenas	1m 33.598s
20	Schrotter	1m 33.599s
21	Kelly	1m 33.774s
22	Ramirez	1m 33.922s
23	Corsi	1m 34.011s
24	Navarro	1m 34.031s
25	Baltus	1m 34.461s
26	Kubo	1m 34.501s
27	Antonelli	1m 34.600s
28	Zaccone	1m 34.607s
29	Hada	1m 35.082s

Fastest race laps

	Rider	Time
1	Lopez	1m 33.030s
2	Acosta	1m 33.531s
3	Salac	1m 33.567s
4	Alcoba	1m 33.663s
5	Fernandez	1m 33.670s
6	Dixon	1m 33.670s
7	Beaubier	1m 33.715s
8	Arbolino	1m 33.741s
9	Aldeguer	1m 33.889s
10	Vietti	1m 33.913s
11	Gonzalez	1m 33.975s
12	Canet	1m 33.979s
13	Roberts	1m 34.008s
14	Chantra	1m 34.044s
15	Bendsneyder	1m 34.461s
16	Ogura	1m 34.574s
17	Dalla Porta	1m 34.765s
18	Lowes	1m 34.826s
19	Schrotter	1m 34.929s
20	Arenas	1m 34.963s
21	Baltus	1m 35.129s
22	Hada	1m 35.163s
23	Zaccone	1m 35.174s
24	Ramirez	1m 35.190s
25	Kelly	1m 35.281s
26	Navarro	1m 35.367s
27	Antonelli	1m 35.516s
28	Kubo	1m 35.546s
29	Corsi	1m 35.556s

Championship Points

	Rider	Points
1	Ogura	242
2	Fernandez	238.5
3	Canet	192
4	Vietti	165
5	Acosta	152
6	Arbolino	150.5
7	Dixon	143.5
8	Lopez	135.5
9	Roberts	130
10	Chantra	128
11	Schrotter	107.5
12	Navarro	83
13	Bendsneyder	80
14	Arenas	76
15	Beaubier	64
16	Aldeguer	61
17	Alcoba	57
18	Lowes	55
19	Gonzalez	55
20	Salac	37
21	Baltus	30
22	Dalla Porta	15
23	Manzi	9
24	Zaccone	9
25	Kubo	7.5
26	Fenati	7
27	Rodrigo	6
28	Kelly	5.5
29	Ramirez	5
30	Hada	2.5
31	Pasini	1

Constructor Points

	Constructor	Points
1	Kalex	427.5
2	Boscoscuro	167.5
3	MV Agusta	5

Moto3

RACE DISTANCE: 23 laps, 63.569 miles/102.304km · RACE WEATHER: Dry (air 14°, humidity 62%, track 24°)

Pos.	Rider	Nat.	No.	Entrant	Machine	Laps	Time & Speed
1	**Izan Guevara**	SPA	28	Gaviota GASGAS Aspar Team	GASGAS	23	37m 38.762s
							101.3mph/163.0km/h
2	**Deniz Oncu**	TUR	53	Red Bull KTM Tech3	KTM	23	37m 39.107s
3	**Sergio Garcia**	SPA	11	Gaviota GASGAS Aspar Team	GASGAS	23	37m 39.222s
4	**Ayumu Sasaki**	JPN	71	Sterilgarda Husqvarna Max	Husqvarna	23	37m 39.322s
5	**Stefano Nepa**	ITA	82	Angeluss MTA Team	KTM	23	37m 46.190s
6	**John McPhee**	GBR	17	Sterilgarda Husqvarna Max	Husqvarna	23	37m 46.258s
7	**Diogo Moreira**	BRA	10	MT Helmets - MSI	KTM	23	37m 46.336s
8	**Joel Kelso**	AUS	66	CIP Green Power	KTM	23	37m 46.337s
9	**Dennis Foggia**	ITA	7	Leopard Racing	Honda	23	37m 55.556s
10	**Riccardo Rossi**	ITA	54	SIC58 Squadra Corse	Honda	23	37m 55.593s
11	**David Munoz**	SPA	44	BOE Motorsports	KTM	23	37m 55.828s
12	**Carlos Tatay**	SPA	99	CFMOTO Racing PruestelGP	CFMOTO	23	37m 56.530s
13	**Ivan Ortola**	SPA	48	Angeluss MTA Team	KTM	23	37m 56.646s
14	**Xavier Artigas**	SPA	43	CFMOTO Racing PruestelGP	CFMOTO	23	38m 00.116s
15	**Jaume Masia**	SPA	5	Red Bull KTM Ajo	KTM	23	38m 01.176s
16	Andrea Migno	ITA	16	Rivacold Snipers Team	Honda	23	38m 18.857s
17	Kaito Toba	JPN	27	CIP Green Power	KTM	23	38m 20.561s
18	Adrian Fernandez	SPA	31	Red Bull KTM Tech3	KTM	23	38m 20.588s
19	Lorenzo Fellon	FRA	20	SIC58 Squadra Corse	Honda	23	38m 20.590s
20	Elia Bartolini	ITA	23	QJMotor Avintia Racing Team	KTM	23	38m 20.599s
21	Joshua Whatley	GBR	70	VisionTrack Racing Team	Honda	23	38m 20.708s
22	Nicola Fabio Carraro	ITA	9	QJMotor Avintia Racing Team	KTM	23	38m 20.768s
23	Ana Carrasco	SPA	22	BOE Motorsports	KTM	23	38m 21.515s
24	Alberto Surra	ITA	67	Rivacold Snipers Team	Honda	23	38m 33.402s
	Ryusei Yamanaka	JPN	6	MT Helmets - MSI	KTM	22	DNF-crash
	Mario Aji	INA	64	Honda Team Asia	Honda	21	DNF-crash
	Tatsuki Suzuki	JPN	24	Leopard Racing	Honda	18	DNF-crash
	Scott Ogden	GBR	19	VisionTrack Racing Team	Honda	12	DNF-crash
	Daniel Holgado	SPA	96	Red Bull KTM Ajo	KTM	2	DNF-crash
	Taiyo Furusato	JPN	72	Honda Team Asia	Honda	2	DNF-crash

Fastest lap: John McPhee, on lap 8, 1m 36.886s, 102.7mph/165.2km/h.

Lap record: Jack Miller, 1m 36.302s, 103.3mph/166.2km/h (2014).

Event maximum speed: Scott Ogden, 156.6mph/252.0km/h (race).

Qualifying:

Weather: Dry

Air: 15° **Humidity:** 60% **Track:** 28°

	Rider	Time
1	Sasaki	1m 35.854s
2	Garcia	1m 36.041s
3	Ortola	1m 36.579s
4	Tatay	1m 36.671s
5	Moreira	1m 36.680s
6	Nepa	1m 36.690s
7	Guevara	1m 36.774s
8	Oncu	1m 36.796s
9	Masia	1m 36.852s
10	Furusato	1m 36.978s
11	Munoz	1m 37.021s
12	Foggia	1m 37.023s
13	Holgado	1m 37.030s
14	Kelso	1m 37.031s
15	Fernandez	1m 37.107s
16	McPhee	1m 37.271s
17	Toba	1m 37.418s
18	Suzuki	No Time
	Q1	
19	Ogden	1m 37.495s
20	Yamanaka	1m 37.502s
21	Rossi	1m 37.694s
22	Fellon	1m 37.801s
23	Migno	1m 37.852s
24	Artigas	1m 37.864s
25	Surra	1m 37.933s
26	Carrasco	1m 38.128s
27	Carraro	1m 38.267s
28	Aji	1m 38.287s
29	Whatley	1m 38.359s
30	Bartolini	1m 38.431s

Fastest race laps

	Rider	Time
1	McPhee	1m 36.886s
2	Sasaki	1m 36.923s
3	Kelso	1m 37.045s
4	Oncu	1m 37.061s
5	Guevara	1m 37.107s
6	Garcia	1m 37.157s
7	Nepa	1m 37.178s
8	Moreira	1m 37.270s
9	Yamanaka	1m 37.294s
10	Rossi	1m 37.509s
11	Masia	1m 37.546s
12	Munoz	1m 37.559s
13	Tatay	1m 37.580s
14	Foggia	1m 37.667s
15	Suzuki	1m 37.709s
16	Artigas	1m 37.715s
17	Ortola	1m 37.758s
18	Bartolini	1m 38.603s
19	Surra	1m 38.607s
20	Carrasco	1m 38.624s
21	Whatley	1m 38.648s
22	Fernandez	1m 38.671s
23	Toba	1m 38.757s
24	Migno	1m 38.784s
25	Furusato	1m 38.808s
26	Ogden	1m 38.866s
27	Aji	1m 38.918s
28	Fabio	1m 38.964s
29	Fellon	1m 39.070s
30	Holgado	1m 39.091s

Championship Points

	Rider	Points
1	Guevara	290
2	Garcia	225
3	Foggia	223
4	Sasaki	207
5	Oncu	174
6	Masia	164
7	Suzuki	128
8	Migno	100
9	Moreira	93
10	Holgado	88
11	Rossi	87
12	Munoz	84
13	Tatay	84
14	Yamanaka	79
15	Artigas	78
16	McPhee	72
17	Nepa	64
18	Toba	63
19	Ortola	62
20	Fernandez	40
21	Kelso	36
22	Bartolini	24
23	Ogden	21
24	Bertelle	16
25	Fellon	11
26	Aji	5
27	Furusato	2

Constructor Points

	Constructor	Points
1	GASGAS	348
2	Honda	307
3	KTM	290
4	Husqvarna	243
5	CFMOTO	122

FIM WORLD CHAMPIONSHIP · ROUND 19

MALAYSIAN GRAND PRIX

SEPANG CIRCUIT

Inset, above: Advantage Bagnaia. A philosophical Quartararo had only a slim home of retaining his title.

Main: Red Bull-sponsored riders and teams led the way in a minute of applause for the late Dietrich Mateschitz.

Photos: Gold & Goose

PETRONAS
DUCATI

Above: **Discretion the better part of valour? 'The Beast' gave Bagnaia an uncomfortable afternoon.**

Top right: **Crestfallen Ogura takes a ride back to the pits, his title hopes in tatters after his last-lap crash.**

Above right: **Quartararo's broken finger didn't show, and didn't slow him down.**

Right: **Run for cover. A marshal clambers to safety as race leader Jorge Martin crashes out.**

Photos: Gold & Goose

DUCATI'S team-orders dilemma received full public exposure at Sepang. While Bagnaia had regained a fragile lead over frequent assailant Bastianini at around two-thirds-distance, the situation was rendered more complicated by fast rookie Bezzecchi challenging Quartararo in third. This offered a chance of sealing the title if Bagnaia won, and it triggered pit-wall discussions among Ducati managers Davide Tardozzi, Paolo Ciabatti and Gigi Dall'Igna.

Post-race explanations told of how this all became irrelevant, as Bezzecchi faded slightly in the closing stages, so no instruction (or would it have been a heavily loaded request) was given to Bastianini to back off from attacking the leader; and even more irrelevant when Bagnaia managed to hold his future team-mate at bay by around a quarter of a second.

Speculation continued, however, not only as to whether 'The Beast' would have obeyed, but also whether he had voluntarily ceded first place anyway. He soon contradicted that. Asked directly if he had intended to win on the last lap, putting his own interests ahead of Ducati's, he gave a mischievous grin. "Yes," he said. "You know me." Had a clean pass offered itself, he would have taken it.

Circumstances and Bagnaia's determination had defused the situation it seemed, yet later in the evening, there were reports of a flare-up between redoubtable paddock stalwart Carlo Pernat, Bastianini's personal manager, and Ducati sporting director Paolo Ciabatti, the latter expressing dismay at the rider's attitude. This suggested salty times to come when Bastianini joins the factory team for 2023.

With one more race of 2022 remaining, however, that would have to wait. In the meantime, Quartararo's return to the podium – for the first time in six races and only the second time in nine – would prolong the agony for the two remaining candidates for the crown. Bagnaia left Sepang with a 23-point lead and needed only to finish 14th in Valencia if Quartararo were to win. But he would need to finish, and he hadn't been able to do that at five races so far.

Meanwhile, Quartararo was in playful mood, consciously trying to recapture the fun of racing after a difficult spell. On Friday, he cheekily stole a photographer's camera in the pit, then completed an extravagantly smoky rolling burnout at the end of FP2. His mood was tested on Saturday, however, when he broke the middle finger of his left hand in a fast crash in FP4, and he qualified only 12th. But he rode like a champion for Sunday's return to the podium, saying that the injury had not been a major hindrance, except when engaging the rear ride-height device: "It's a track where you use it a lot, but with the medicine and the adrenaline, it was not a problem."

In the main, the weather stayed benign – if enervating sweaty heat can be regarded as such – except on Friday, when the ever threatening tropical downpour hit with a vengeance during Moto2 FP2, bringing out red flags. The track remained unrideable, and everyone waited in the pits while the safety car splashed around through deep standing water. Eventually, proceedings resumed, and with the unusual running order putting MotoGP practice last, it was delayed by some 45 minutes, the track remaining wet. Rather surprisingly, that left Cal Crutchlow fastest of the day and put extra emphasis on Saturday morning's FP3 for qualifying.

Rain spots threatened late in that session, too, causing a cautious Franco Morbidelli to slow just at the wrong time, baulking both Bagnaia and Marc Marquez on their late fast laps. As a result, Morbidelli reinforced his reputation as the most punished rider in the class, earning a double long-lap penalty that he admitted was justified. He was less sanguine about a further penalty in the race, when he was docked three seconds and dropped one position for a barging pass on Aleix Espargaro on the last lap: "If I cannot make an overtake in the second-last corner where there is a shed-load of space and I have a bike that cannot overtake on the straight ... I feel the scale is not right. We need some dialogue with the people making the decisions."

Meanwhile, Bagnaia and Marquez were condemned to rare runs in Q1 after losing their best laps. They led that session, at the expense of Brad Binder and Miller, and Marquez again managed an astounding qualifying lap (stunning even his own team) to start from the front row, while Bagnaia was down on row three. But their fortunes were reversed in one of Honda's toughest races of the season, with Marquez dropping to seventh. "I feel a slow bike all weekend, then you are pushing more in the corners," he explained. "For a single lap, you can do it. For a race distance, you're pushing more the tyres, and in the end, I had zero grip."

With the next best Hondas 14th (Pol Espargaro) and 17th (Alex Marquez), team boss Puig admitted, "We are struggling here, with a lack of power, a lack of grip. We don't really understand how Marc put those laps together to be so competitive. We're talking about a super rider."

Joan Mir suffered a disappointing end to the season, after climbing to a strong fifth from 11th on the grid by lap 12, only to drop back rapidly to an eventual last place. The reason: an unexpectedly severe bout of arm-pump that meant "I lost all the strength in my right arm and I couldn't understand the brake pressure I was using." He was left contemplating corrective surgery during the winter break.

Few people could have been as disappointed as Moto2's erstwhile points leader Ai Ogura who, the week before, had taken the benefit when his title rival, Augusto Fernandez, had crashed out.

Ogura had qualified on pole and was a strong second in the race, while Fernandez laboured in fifth. Then, on the last lap, a headstrong dive under long-time leader Arbolino was a lunge too far. He lost the front, and it was his turn to throw away 20 secure points. His usual impassive mood was tested, as he explained: "For me, to finish second wasn't enough to arrive with a comfortable advantage at Valencia. I needed to win. In the end, I crashed. But that's racing. Sometimes it happens."

MOTOGP RACE – 20 laps

Another pole (his fourth) and another record for Martin, almost half a second quicker than Bastianini, and Marc Marquez – a near-miraculous third man on row one, after coming through Q1 with an equally transcendental performance.

Bezzecchi, Rins and Marini filled row two, with Morbidelli a best-of-the-year seventh ahead of Vinales and Bagnaia.

Martin's launch was flawless, leading away, but it was only average compared to Bagnaia's wonderful run off the line, surging from ninth to second into the first corner. "My best ever start," he called it.

Quartararo's effort was almost as impressive, as he slotted into sixth, behind Bastianini, Marc Marquez and Morbidelli. By Turn Nine, the Frenchman's team-mate had moved aside, providing a buffer in front of Suzuki pair Mir and Rins, and Bezzecchi.

At first, Marquez was mixing it with the leading Ducatis. In reality, he was just hanging on. As the Martin/Bagnaia/Bastianini axis edged clear, he was soon back in Quartararo's range. The Yamaha rider moved by decisively at the first corner on lap five. Now he was three seconds behind the leading trio.

From there, Marquez was defending as Bezzecchi and Brad Binder joined the Suzukis behind, with Morbidelli dropping from sixth to tenth on lap four, after taking the first of two long-lap penalties.

Up front, Martin was pushing. He was a full four-tenths quicker than Bagnaia on lap five, stretching his lead to 1.2 seconds. But no sooner had he switched engine map to break his pursuers than he was on his backside, having tucked the front at Turn Five on lap seven. Suddenly, Bagnaia clinching the title was a very real possibility. If only Bezzecchi – now past Marquez and the two Suzukis – could home in on Quartararo, 1.6 seconds ahead. And if only Bastianini would give the leader some space.

Above: **Chasing the leaders, Quartararo heads Mir and Morbidelli, who had moved aside to let his team-mate past on lap one.**
Photo: Monster Energy Yamaha

Top right: **Another strong ride from Bezzecchi netted fourth place for the VR46 rookie.**

Above right: **Ogura briefly leads Arbolino in their Moto2 duel.**

Right: **Chantra ends up underneath Acosta following their crash at the second corner.**

Below right: **John McPhee cools down after his epic ride from 22nd on the grid to victory.**

Below far right: **McPhee snatched the win in the six-rider, last-corner shuffle. Sasaki, Garcia, Masia, Moreira and Foggia were the losers.**
Photos: Gold & Goose

But the Gresini Ducati rider refused to relent. On the tenth lap, he dived under the championship leader at Turn Four to lead for the first time. And with Bezzecchi slashing the deficit to Quartararo to just three-tenths by the 14th lap, Ducati's bosses were faced with a dilemma. If Bezzecchi went third, a Bagnaia triumph would seal the crown. Surely, it would be foolish not to take advantage of this open goal?

Tense discussions between Paolo Ciabatti, Davide Tardozzi and Gigi Dall'Igna established that if Bezzecchi gained third, they would ask Bastianini to cede.

But it soon became clear that this was a different Quartararo from the one who had folded so spectacularly in Australia. On lap 14, not only was he putting visible space ahead of the tiring Bezzecchi, but also he was reeling in the lead duo. Bagnaia was all too aware and pressed to retake the lead, feigning a pass on Bastianini at Turns Nine and 14, before getting it done decisively at the track's final hairpin.

Still Quartararo gained. The gap was down to 1.6 seconds on lap 15, the Frenchman riding out of his skin, with Bezzecchi 1.2 seconds behind. This was the Yamaha's ceiling, however, with Bagnaia doing enough to ensure space remained behind the leading pair.

But who would win? A front-end moment for Bastianini through Turn 14 on lap 17 put half a second between first and second. But a lap later, he was back on Bagnaia's tail. A repeat of Aragon was on the cards as he pushed and probed on the final lap, coming within inches of taking them both down at Turn Nine. But Bagnaia just held on for the most important victory of his career, only two-tenths separating them at the flag, securing the teams' championship for Lenovo Ducati.

Quartararo was a brilliant third, 2.7 seconds behind and a similar distance ahead of Bezzecchi. Too little, too late? But he could do no more. Rins took a solid fifth, seven seconds behind; Miller recovered from a dire first lap (17th after being boxed at the first corner) to pip Marc Marquez for sixth on the last lap.

Mir had faded with arm-pump to 19th, leaving Binder to eighth. Zarco was a meek ninth, Aleix Espargaro, tenth, even though Morbidelli had crossed the line ahead, but he was penalised for his aggressive last-lap overtake.

Crutchlow made the points again, narrowly ahead of Oliveira and Pol Espargaro in 12th; Fernandez took the last point, with Vinales three seconds adrift, but clear of a desultory battle between Alex Marquez and Gardner.

Darryn Binder, Di Giannantonio and Nakagami-substitute Nagashima crashed out; Marini retired with a seized-on launch-control system, his first non-finish in two years of racing in MotoGP.

MOTO2 RACE – 18 laps

It was beginning to look as though no one actually wanted to win the Moto2 World Championship. For the second race in succession, the leader in the standings crashed out of a potentially decisive position, handing the initiative back to their rival. At Sepang, it was Ogura's turn to do something beyond comprehension, with a maximum-risk failed overtake on Arbolino for the lead on the final lap.

Ogura had been on fine form throughout, leading free practice, then claiming pole ahead of Arbolino, albeit by less than a tenth. Canet was third; Dixon led row two from the increasingly impressive Gonzalez and Fernandez. Chantra, Acosta and Beaubier were behind, with double-winner Lopez the first non-Kalex in tenth.

Arbolino was on blazing form, leading into the first corner, pursued by Ogura, Dixon and Chantra. By the end of the lap, Lopez was ahead of Dixon, and next time around Gonzalez also. Chantra had fallen after touching Dixon's back wheel in the second corner, taking Acosta down with him.

The leading pair soon stretched away, better than two seconds ahead of Lopez by lap five, and more than five clear by half-distance.

With Fernandez out of touch behind Dixon in fifth, Ogura wouldn't let Arbolino rest. First, he moved past with a neat move in Turn One on lap 13, only to run wide there next time around.

They settled again for the remaining laps, and it seemed as though the Japanese would be satisfied with second and a championship lead of 12.5 points. They started the final lap with Arbolino 0.495 of a second clear and appearing safe. But Ogura's usual racecraft deserted him, and while his Turn Nine lunge put him in front for a few yards, the front tucked and he was down. It was an inexplicable way to relinquish control of the title and hand Arbolino a third win of the year.

For his part, Fernandez had been pushing Dixon hard, nosing ahead several times and leading him over the line with three laps to go. But the Briton responded aggressively to every attempt, while the action resulted in them closing up on Lopez and Gonzalez for a four-way fight for what would soon become second place. As Gonzalez faded and Lopez edged clear, Dixon held on for a sixth podium of the year, with Fernandez pleased to regain the title lead.

Schrotter had escaped his group for a lone sixth, leaving Beaubier to outpace Canet, who narrowly held off Alcoba and Aldeguer to complete the top ten.

American Kelly was alone, three places out of the points. Early points leader Vietti's dire second half of the season ended with another crash, his fifth non-finish in seven races. Acosta remounted only to crash again, and Roberts suffered a second consecutive retirement with mechanical problems.

MOTO3 RACE – 17 laps

In his last season after reaching the age limit, John McPhee capped the most unlikely of comebacks with a thrilling last-gasp win in an epic six-rider shootout. He'd been 22nd on the grid and on the verge of walking out on his team on Saturday. On Sunday, he fought through to sit fifth with just two corners remaining.

Then, as Masia, Foggia, Sasaki and Garcia jostled for the lead through Turns 12 and 13, McPhee launched an outrageous four-in-one move into Turn 14 to take the lead. From there, a cut-back on Sasaki, who had outbraked him into the final turn, sealed a fourth career victory, with Garcia third.

Earlier, two scarily narrow escapes had marked a scrappy race. First, Stefano Nepa high-sided out of the lead group at Turn Nine, with a rider behind running over (and breaking) his left leg. Then new champion Guevara tagged Sasaki's back wheel out of the final hairpin on lap 13 and went careering off track at speed, managing to regain control on the wet grass to avoid hitting the pit wall.

That left the top five plus Moreira to fight over the final lap. Foggia (who had led four laps) appeared strong and in control mid-lap, but he was bamboozled in the brawl. The final-turn sort-out had Masia fourth, Moreira fifth and Foggia a frustrated sixth.

Holgado managed to retain control of the next group, from Yamanaka, Ortola, Oncu and Artigas, seventh to 11th inside a second.

Front-running Suzuki and Rossi crashed out, likewise Ogden and Furusato; Whatley was a distant last after starting from the pit lane plus five seconds, for having exceeded the engine allowance.

Guevara was champion, but second in the standings was still open, Garcia eight points ahead of Foggia, Sasaki another four behind.

FIM WORLD CHAMPIONSHIP: ROUND 19

PETRONAS GRAND PRIX OF MALAYSIA

21-23 OCTOBER, 2022

SEPANG INTERNATIONAL CIRCUIT

20 laps
Length: 5.548 km / 3.447 miles
Width: 16 m

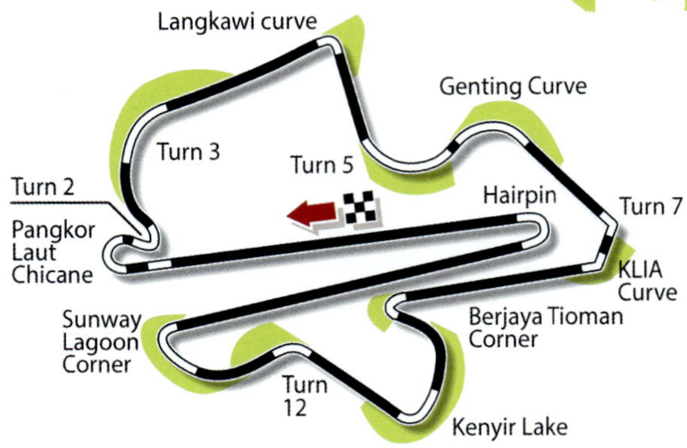

MotoGP

RACE DISTANCE: 20 laps, 68.885 miles/110.860km · RACE WEATHER: Dry (air 31°, humidity 57%, track 38°)

Pos.	Rider	Nat.	No.	Entrant	Machine	Tyres	Race tyre choice	Laps	Time & speed
1	**Francesco Bagnaia**	ITA	63	Ducati Lenovo Team	Ducati Desmosedici	M	F: Medium/R: Soft	20	40m 14.332s 102.7mph/165.3km/h
2	**Enea Bastianini**	ITA	23	Gresini Racing MotoGP	Ducati Desmosedici	M	F: Medium/R: Soft	20	40m 14.602s
3	**Fabio Quartararo**	FRA	20	Monster Energy Yamaha MotoGP	Yamaha YZR-M1	M	F: Medium/R: Soft	20	40m 17.105s
4	**Marco Bezzecchi**	ITA	72	Mooney VR46 Racing Team	Ducati Desmosedici	M	F: Medium/R: Soft	20	40m 19.778s
5	**Alex Rins**	SPA	42	Team SUZUKI ECSTAR	Suzuki GSX-RR	M	F: Medium/R: Soft	20	40m 26.255s
6	**Jack Miller**	AUS	43	Ducati Lenovo Team	Ducati Desmosedici	M	F: Medium/R: Soft	20	40m 27.804s
7	**Marc Marquez**	SPA	93	Repsol Honda Team	Honda RC213V	M	F: Medium/R: Soft	20	40m 28.636s
8	**Brad Binder**	RSA	33	Red Bull KTM Factory Racing	KTM RC16	M	F: Medium/R: Soft	20	40m 31.137s
9	**Johann Zarco**	FRA	5	Prima Pramac Racing	Ducati Desmosedici	M	F: Medium/R: Soft	20	40m 32.690s
10	**Aleix Espargaro**	SPA	41	Aprilia Racing	Aprilia RS-GP	M	F: Medium/R: Soft	20	40m 35.923s
11	**Franco Morbidelli**	ITA	21	Monster Energy Yamaha MotoGP	Yamaha YZR-M1	M	F: Medium/R: Soft	20	40m 37.567s
12	**Cal Crutchlow**	GBR	35	WithU Yamaha RNF MotoGP Team	Yamaha YZR-M1	M	F: Medium/R: Soft	20	40m 38.973s
13	**Miguel Oliveira**	POR	88	Red Bull KTM Factory Racing	KTM RC16	M	F: Medium/R: Soft	20	40m 39.250s
14	**Pol Espargaro**	SPA	44	Repsol Honda Team	Honda RC213V	M	F: Medium/R: Soft	20	40m 39.918s
15	**Raul Fernandez**	SPA	25	Tech3 KTM Factory Racing	KTM RC16	M	F: Medium/R: Soft	20	40m 41.371s
16	Maverick Vinales	SPA	12	Aprilia Racing	Aprilia RS-GP	M	F: Medium/R: Soft	20	40m 44.759s
17	Alex Marquez	SPA	73	LCR Honda CASTROL	Honda RC213V	M	F: Medium/R: Soft	20	40m 47.654s
18	Remy Gardner	AUS	87	Tech3 KTM Factory Racing	KTM RC16	M	F: Medium/R: Soft	20	40m 48.023s
19	Joan Mir	SPA	36	Team SUZUKI ECSTAR	Suzuki GSX-RR	M	F: Medium/R: Soft	20	40m 56.170s
	Darryn Binder	RSA	40	WithU Yamaha RNF MotoGP Team	Yamaha YZR-M1	M	F: Medium/R: Soft	10	DNF-crash
	Fabio Di Giannantonio	ITA	49	Gresini Racing MotoGP	Ducati Desmosedici	M	F: Medium/R: Soft	10	DNF-crash
	Jorge Martin	SPA	89	Prima Pramac Racing	Ducati Desmosedici	M	F: Medium/R: Soft	6	DNF-crash
	Tetsuta Nagashima	JPN	45	LCR Honda IDEMITSU	Honda RC213V	M	F: Medium/R: Soft	4	DNF-crash
	Luca Marini	ITA	10	Mooney VR46 Racing Team	Ducati Desmosedici	M	F: Medium/R: Soft	1	DNF-technical

Fastest lap: Jorge Martin, on lap 2, 1m 59.634s, 103.6mph/166.7km/h.
Lap record: Valentino Rossi, 1m 59.661s, 103.6mph/166.7km/h (2019).
Event maximum speed: Enea Bastianini, 209.0mph/336.4km/h (qualifying).

Qualifying

Weather: Dry
Air Temp: 33° **Humidity:** 54%
Track Temp: 45°

1	Martin	1m 57.790s
2	Bastianini	1m 58.246s
3	M. Marquez	1m 58.454s
4	Bezzecchi	1m 58.490s
5	Rins	1m 58.575s
6	Marini	1m 58.579s
7	Morbidelli	1m 58.654s
8	Vinales	1m 58.766s
9	Bagnaia	1m 58.862s
10	A. Espargaro	1m 58.935s
11	Mir	1m 59.145s
12	Quartararo	1m 59.215s
	Q1	
13	B. Binder	1m 59.053s
14	Miller	1m 59.064s
15	Crutchlow	1m 59.256s
16	Di Giannantonio	1m 59.278s
17	P. Espargaro	1m 59.363s
18	Zarco	1m 59.690s
19	Oliveira	1m 59.699s
20	Gardner	1m 59.803s
21	A. Marquez	2m 00.008s
22	Fernandez	2m 00.077s
23	Nagashima	2m 00.803s
24	D. Binder	2m 10.717s

Fastest race laps

1	Martin	1m 59.634s
2	Bastianini	1m 59.686s
3	Bagnaia	1m 59.703s
4	M. Marquez	1m 59.969s
5	Morbidelli	1m 59.983s
6	Bezzecchi	2m 00.003s
7	Rins	2m 00.120s
8	Mir	2m 00.142s
9	Quartararo	2m 00.145s
10	B. Binder	2m 00.146s
11	Zarco	2m 00.391s
12	Miller	2m 00.392s
13	Oliveira	2m 00.552s
14	Fernandez	2m 00.638s
15	D. Binder	2m 00.681s
16	A. Espargaro	2m 00.704s
17	Crutchlow	2m 00.782s
18	Vinales	2m 00.865s
19	A. Marquez	2m 00.880s
20	P. Espargaro	2m 01.046s
21	Di Giannantonio	2m 01.052s
22	Gardner	2m 01.109s
23	Nagashima	2m 01.679s

Championship Points

1	Bagnaia	258
2	Quartararo	235
3	A. Espargaro	212
4	Bastianini	211
5	Miller	189
6	B. Binder	168
7	Zarco	166
8	Rins	148
9	Oliveira	138
10	Martin	136
11	Vinales	122
12	M. Marquez	113
13	Marini	111
14	Bezzecchi	106
15	Mir	77
16	P. Espargaro	56
17	A. Marquez	50
18	Nakagami	46
19	Morbidelli	36
20	Di Giannantonio	23
21	Dovizioso	15
22	D. Binder	12
23	Gardner	10
24	Crutchlow	10
25	Fernandez	10
26	Bradl	2

Constructor Points

1	Ducati	432
2	Aprilia	248
3	Yamaha	243
4	KTM	220
5	Suzuki	174
6	Honda	153

	Grid order	1	2	3	4	5	6	7	8	9	10	11	12	13	14	15	16	17	18	19	20	
89	MARTIN	89	89	89	89	89	89	63	63	63	63	23	23	23	63	63	63	63	63	63	63	1
23	BASTIANINI	63	63	63	63	63	63	23	23	23	23	63	63	63	23	23	23	23	23	23	23	2
93	M. MARQUEZ	23	23	23	23	23	23	20	20	20	20	20	20	20	20	20	20	20	20	20	20	3
72	BEZZECCHI	93	93	93	93	20	20	93	72	72	72	72	72	72	72	72	72	72	72	72	72	4
42	RINS	20	20	20	20	93	93	72	93	36	36	36	36	42	42	42	42	42	42	42	42	5
10	MARINI	36	21	21	36	36	36	36	36	93	93	42	42	93	93	93	93	93	93	93	43	6
21	MORBIDELLI	21	36	36	42	42	72	42	42	42	42	93	93	36	36	33	43	43	43	43	93	7
12	VINALES	42	42	42	72	72	42	33	33	33	33	33	33	33	33	43	33	33	33	33	33	8
63	BAGNAIA	41	33	33	33	33	33	88	88	88	43	43	43	43	43	36	36	5	5	5	5	9
41	A. ESPARGARO	33	72	72	21	21	88	43	43	43	88	5	5	5	5	5	5	41	41	41	21	10
36	MIR	72	41	40	40	40	40	5	5	5	5	41	41	41	41	41	41	36	21	21	41	11
20	QUARTARARO	40	40	88	88	88	43	40	41	41	41	88	88	12	21	21	21	21	12	35	35	12
33	B.BINDER	88	88	35	35	43	41	41	40	12	12	12	12	88	88	12	12	12	35	88	88	13
43	MILLER	35	35	41	43	35	21	21	12	40	21	21	21	21	12	88	88	88	88	12	44	14
35	CRUTCHLOW	44	43	43	41	41	5	12	21	21	35	35	35	35	35	35	35	35	44	44	25	15
49	DI GIANNANTONIO	49	44	44	5	5	35	35	35	35	40	44	44	44	44	44	44	44	25	25	12	
5	ZARCO	43	49	5	44	44	12	44	44	44	44	25	25	25	25	25	25	25	87	73	73	
88	OLIVEIRA	73	73	49	49	12	44	49	49	49	49	87	87	87	87	87	87	87	73	87	87	
87	GARDNER	12	12	73	12	49	49	25	25	25	25	73	73	73	73	73	73	73	36	36	36	
44	P. ESPARGARO	87	5	12	87	87	25	87	87	87	87											
73	A. MARQUEZ	5	87	87	25	25	87	73	73	73	73											
25	FERNANDEZ	25	25	25	73	73	73															
45	NAGASHIMA	45	45	45	45																	
40	D.BINDER	10																				

10 Pit stop

Moto2

RACE DISTANCE: 18 laps, 61.997 miles/99.774km · RACE WEATHER: Dry (air 31°, humidity 59%, track 38°)

Pos.	Rider	Nat.	No.	Entrant	Machine	Laps	Time & Speed
1	**Tony Arbolino**	ITA	14	Elf Marc VDS Racing Team	Kalex	18	38m 25.233s 96.8mph/155.8km/h
2	**Alonso Lopez**	SPA	21	Beta Tools Speed Up	Boscoscuro	18	38m 36.644s
3	**Jake Dixon**	GBR	96	Inde GASGAS Aspar Team	Kalex	18	38m 37.035s
4	**Augusto Fernandez**	SPA	37	Red Bull KTM Ajo	Kalex	18	38m 38.439s
5	**Manuel Gonzalez**	SPA	18	Yamaha VR46 Master Camp Team	Kalex	18	38m 40.003s
6	**Marcel Schrotter**	GER	23	Liqui Moly Intact GP	Kalex	18	38m 42.399s
7	**Cameron Beaubier**	USA	6	American Racing	Kalex	18	38m 45.455s
8	**Aron Canet**	SPA	40	Flexbox HP40	Kalex	18	38m 49.512s
9	**Jeremy Alcoba**	SPA	52	Liqui Moly Intact GP	Kalex	18	38m 49.640s
10	**Fermin Aldeguer**	SPA	54	Beta Tools Speed Up	Boscoscuro	18	38m 49.715s
11	**Filip Salac**	CZE	12	Gresini Racing Moto2	Kalex	18	38m 55.869s
12	**Lorenzo Dalla Porta**	ITA	19	Italtrans Racing Team	Kalex	18	38m 58.828s
13	**Albert Arenas**	SPA	75	Inde GASGAS Aspar Team	Kalex	18	38m 59.681s
14	**Bo Bendsneyder**	NED	64	Pertamina Mandalika SAG Team	Kalex	18	39m 00.160s
15	**Taiga Hada**	JPN	29	Pertamina Mandalika SAG Team	Kalex	18	39m 08.990s
16	Keminth Kubo	THA	81	Yamaha VR46 Master Camp Team	Kalex	18	39m 10.173s
17	Marcos Ramirez	SPA	42	MV Agusta Forward Racing	MV Agusta	18	39m 10.415s
18	Sean Dylan Kelly	USA	4	American Racing	Kalex	18	39m 14.051s
19	Kasma Daniel	MAL	27	Petronas MIE Racing RW	Kalex	18	39m 18.354s
20	Borja Gomez	SPA	72	Flexbox HP40	Kalex	18	39m 19.698s
21	Niccolo Antonelli	ITA	28	Mooney VR46 Racing Team	Kalex	18	39m 20.045s
22	Azroy Anuar	MAL	20	Petronas MIE Racing RW	Kalex	18	39m 20.918s
	Ai Ogura	JPN	79	IDEMITSU Honda Team Asia	Kalex	17	DNF-crash
	Pedro Acosta	SPA	51	Red Bull KTM Ajo	Kalex	9	DNF-crash
	Alessandro Zaccone	ITA	61	Gresini Racing Moto2	Kalex	9	DNF-ret in pit
	Joe Roberts	USA	16	Italtrans Racing Team	Kalex	8	DNF-ret in pit
	Celestino Vietti	ITA	13	Mooney VR46 Racing Team	Kalex	5	DNF-crash
	Somkiat Chantra	THA	35	IDEMITSU Honda Team Asia	Kalex	1	DNF-crash
	David Sanchis	SPA	98	MV Agusta Forward Racing	MV Agusta	0	DNF-crash

Fastest lap: Tony Arbolino, on lap 5, 2m 7.132s, 97.5mph/156.9km/h.

Lap record: Alex Marquez, 2m 5.860s, 98.5mph/158.5km/h (2019).

Event maximum speed: Jeremy Alcoba, 173.4mph/279.0km/h (free practice).

Qualifying

Weather: Dry

Air: 32° **Humidity:** 60% **Track:** 46°

1	Ogura	2m 06.405s
2	Arbolino	2m 06.488s
3	Canet	2m 06.652s
4	Dixon	2m 06.701s
5	Gonzalez	2m 06.705s
6	Fernandez	2m 06.738s
7	Chantra	2m 06.896s
8	Acosta	2m 06.934s
9	Beaubier	2m 06.950s
10	Lopez	2m 06.952s
11	Roberts	2m 07.011s
12	Bendsneyder	2m 07.096s
13	Arenas	2m 07.181s
14	Schrotter	2m 07.203s
15	Dalla Porta	2m 07.281s
16	Aldeguer	2m 07.535s
17	Antonelli	2m 08.148s
18	Salac	No Time
	Q1	
19	Alcoba	2m 07.679s
20	Vietti	2m 07.711s
21	Ramirez	2m 07.893s
22	Hada	2m 08.055s
23	Kubo	2m 08.148s
24	Sanchis	2m 08.350s
25	Kelly	2m 08.440s
26	Gomez	2m 08.525s
27	Zaccone	2m 08.686s
28	Anuar	2m 08.738s
29	Daniel	2m 09.641s

Fastest race laps

1	Arbolino	2m 07.132s
2	Ogura	2m 07.236s
3	Gonzalez	2m 07.510s
4	Lopez	2m 07.585s
5	Acosta	2m 07.699s
6	Fernandez	2m 07.854s
7	Dixon	2m 07.889s
8	Beaubier	2m 07.983s
9	Aldeguer	2m 08.269s
10	Canet	2m 08.296s
11	Schrotter	2m 08.308s
12	Salac	2m 08.357s
13	Vietti	2m 08.536s
14	Alcoba	2m 08.613s
15	Roberts	2m 08.619s
16	Dalla Porta	2m 08.817s
17	Hada	2m 09.002s
18	Arenas	2m 09.052s
19	Bendsneyder	2m 09.064s
20	Kubo	2m 09.218s
21	Ramirez	2m 09.569s
22	Gomez	2m 09.636s
23	Daniel	2m 09.813s
24	Kelly	2m 09.869s
25	Antonelli	2m 09.940s
26	Zaccone	2m 10.022s
27	Anuar	2m 10.338s

Championship Points

1	Fernandez	251.5
2	Ogura	242
3	Canet	200
4	Arbolino	175.5
5	Vietti	165
6	Dixon	159.5
7	Lopez	155.5
8	Acosta	152
9	Roberts	130
10	Chantra	128
11	Schrotter	117.5
12	Navarro	83
13	Bendsneyder	82
14	Arenas	79
15	Beaubier	73
16	Aldeguer	67
17	Gonzalez	66
18	Alcoba	64
19	Lowes	55
20	Salac	42
21	Baltus	30
22	Dalla Porta	19
23	Manzi	9
24	Zaccone	9
25	Kubo	7.5
26	Fenati	7
27	Rodrigo	6
28	Kelly	5.5
29	Ramirez	5
30	Hada	3.5
31	Pasini	1

Constructor Points

1	Kalex	452.5
2	Boscoscuro	187.5
3	MV Agusta	5

Moto3

RACE DISTANCE: 17 laps, 58.552 miles/94.231km · RACE WEATHER: Dry (air 31°, humidity 59%, track 36°)

Pos.	Rider	Nat.	No.	Entrant	Machine	Laps	Time & Speed
1	**John McPhee**	GBR	17	Sterilgarda Husqvarna Max	Husqvarna	17	38m 04.589s 92.2mph/148.4km/h
2	**Ayumu Sasaki**	JPN	71	Sterilgarda Husqvarna Max	Husqvarna	17	38m 04.637s
3	**Sergio Garcia**	SPA	11	Gaviota GASGAS Aspar Team	GASGAS	17	38m 04.735s
4	**Jaume Masia**	SPA	5	Red Bull KTM Ajo	KTM	17	38m 04.834s
5	**Diogo Moreira**	BRA	10	MT Helmets - MSI	KTM	17	38m 04.908s
6	**Dennis Foggia**	ITA	7	Leopard Racing	Honda	17	38m 04.960s
7	**Daniel Holgado**	SPA	96	Red Bull KTM Ajo	KTM	17	38m 10.406s
8	**Ryusei Yamanaka**	JPN	6	MT Helmets - MSI	KTM	17	38m 10.623s
9	**Ivan Ortola**	SPA	48	Angeluss MTA Team	KTM	17	38m 10.819s
10	**Deniz Oncu**	TUR	53	Red Bull KTM Tech3	KTM	17	38m 11.321s
11	**Xavier Artigas**	SPA	43	CFMOTO Racing PruestelGP	CFMOTO	17	38m 11.378s
12	**Izan Guevara**	SPA	28	Gaviota GASGAS Aspar Team	GASGAS	17	38m 13.737s
13	**Elia Bartolini**	ITA	23	QJMotor Avintia Racing Team	KTM	17	38m 18.005s
14	**Andrea Migno**	ITA	16	Rivacold Snipers Team	Honda	17	38m 18.271s
15	**Adrian Fernandez**	SPA	31	Red Bull KTM Tech3	KTM	17	38m 19.248s
16	Syarifuddin Azman	MAL	63	VisionTrack Racing Team	Honda	17	38m 19.401s
17	Kaito Toba	JPN	27	CIP Green Power	KTM	17	38m 19.579s
18	Joel Kelso	AUS	66	CIP Green Power	KTM	17	38m 25.119s
19	Lorenzo Fellon	FRA	20	SIC58 Squadra Corse	Honda	17	38m 32.829s
20	Nicola Fabio Carraro	ITA	9	QJMotor Avintia Racing Team	KTM	17	38m 32.874s
21	Mario Aji	INA	64	Honda Team Asia	Honda	17	38m 47.644s
22	Ana Carrasco	SPA	22	BOE Motorsports	KTM	17	38m 47.839s
23	Joshua Whatley	GBR	70	VisionTrack Racing Team	Honda	17	38m 58.699s
	Taiyo Furusato	JPN	72	Honda Team Asia	Honda	15	DNF-crash
	Riccardo Rossi	ITA	54	SIC58 Squadra Corse	Honda	12	DNF-crash
	Carlos Tatay	SPA	99	CFMOTO Racing PruestelGP	CFMOTO	12	DNF-ret in pit
	Alberto Surra	ITA	67	Rivacold Snipers Team	Honda	8	DNF-crash
	Tatsuki Suzuki	JPN	24	Leopard Racing	Honda	4	DNF-crash
	David Munoz	SPA	44	BOE Motorsports	KTM	3	DNF-crash
	Stefano Nepa	ITA	82	Angeluss MTA Team	KTM	1	DNF-crash
	Scott Ogden	GBR	19	VisionTrack Racing Team	Honda	1	DNF-crash

Fastest lap: Ayumu Sasaki, on lap 3, 2m 12.671s, 93.5mph/150.4km/h.

Lap record: Adam Norrodin, 2m 12.775s, 93.3mph/150.2km/h (2017).

Event maximum speed: Scott Ogden, 156.6mph/252.0km/h (race).

Qualifying:

Weather: Dry

Air: 31° **Humidity:** 63% **Track:** 40°

1	Foggia	2m 11.411s
2	Guevara	2m 11.635s
3	Garcia	2m 11.674s
4	Masia	2m 11.751s
5	Holgado	2m 11.836s
6	Migno	2m 11.843s
7	Sasaki	2m 11.907s
8	Suzuki	2m 11.934s
9	Rossi	2m 11.960s
10	Munoz	2m 12.051s
11	Moreira	2m 12.136s
12	Nepa	2m 12.403s
13	Yamanaka	2m 12.432s
14	Ortola	2m 12.441s
15	Furusato	2m 12.517s
16	Kelso	2m 12.612s
17	Tatay	2m 13.362s
18	Toba	2m 13.662s
	Q1	
19	Fernandez	2m 12.944s
20	Artigas	2m 13.091s
21	Azman	2m 13.240s
22	McPhee	2m 13.241s
23	Carraro	2m 13.403s
24	Bartolini	2m 13.444s
25	Oncu	2m 13.471s
26	Surra	2m 13.585s
27	Fellon	2m 14.031s
28	Carrasco	2m 14.260s
29	Aji	2m 14.802s
30	Ogden	2m 15.019s
	Whatley	No Time.

Fastest race laps

1	Sasaki	2m 12.671s
2	Holgado	2m 12.962s
3	Rossi	2m 12.980s
4	Guevara	2m 13.048s
5	Masia	2m 13.054s
6	Moreira	2m 13.183s
7	Foggia	2m 13.208s
8	McPhee	2m 13.273s
9	Ortola	2m 13.321s
10	Munoz	2m 13.378s
11	Migno	2m 13.395s
12	Yamanaka	2m 13.399s
13	Garcia	2m 13.449s
14	Artigas	2m 13.501s
15	Oncu	2m 13.586s
16	Bartolini	2m 13.621s
17	Fernandez	2m 13.784s
18	Furusato	2m 13.814s
19	Toba	2m 13.870s
20	Tatay	2m 13.875s
21	Azman	2m 13.886s
22	Suzuki	2m 13.937s
23	Kelso	2m 13.963s
24	Carraro	2m 14.015s
25	Fellon	2m 14.141s
26	Surra	2m 14.991s
27	Aji	2m 15.256s
28	Carrasco	2m 15.471s
29	Whatley	2m 15.951s

Championship Points

1	Guevara	294
2	Garcia	241
3	Foggia	233
4	Sasaki	227
5	Oncu	180
6	Masia	177
7	Suzuki	128
8	Moreira	104
9	Migno	102
10	McPhee	97
11	Holgado	97
12	Rossi	87
13	Yamanaka	87
14	Munoz	84
15	Tatay	84
16	Artigas	83
17	Ortola	69
18	Nepa	64
19	Toba	63
20	Fernandez	41
21	Kelso	36
22	Bartolini	27
23	Ogden	21
24	Bertelle	16
25	Fellon	11
26	Aji	5
27	Furusato	2

Constructor Points

1	GASGAS	364
2	Honda	317
3	KTM	303
4	Husqvarna	268
5	CFMOTO	127

FIM WORLD CHAMPIONSHIP · ROUND 20

VALENCIA GRAND PRIX

VALENCIA CIRCUIT

Inset: Top-step farewell – Alex Rins made Suzuki say goodbye with a 97th win.

Main: Rins was untouchable from flag to flag. Martin, Miller, Marquez and Quartararo strive to keep him in sight.

Photos: Gold & Goose

Above: "Ninety-nine per cent negative". The outgoing champion collects his thoughts as the monitor covers Bagnaia's celebrations.
Photo: Monster Energy Yamaha

Right: Former world champion (and riders' choice) Franco Uncini bowed out from his role as safety officer.

Below right: Tome Alfonso Ezpeleta (and management choice) would take over.

Far right: Jorge Martin and Brad Binder enjoyed their battle for second place.
Photos: Gold & Goose

THE end of the longest ever season brought the climax to a battle of great variety, and in an entirely appropriate manner. It was the 20th time that the premier-class title had been decided at the final race, and tension was preserved almost throughout.

For Pecco Bagnaia, after a faltering and erratic start to his campaign, it was a tense, but tame ride to ninth. He only needed to get to the flag no lower than 14th. This he did, to become Ducati's only second champion, 15 years after Casey Stoner, and to secure the Bologna marque's first triple title since that year. In fact, a quadruple title, in a steamroller season, after Bezzecchi had already added the informal rookie championship to the riders', constructors' and teams' crowns.

Pecco had maintained a calm mien throughout the weekend, which was not echoed within his garage, according to departing team-mate Jack Miller: "Those guys were wound up like one of those toys – you wind it up until it stops."

For defender and early points leader Fabio Quartararo, the task was simpler. He had to win and hope that his rival suffered misfortune. He carried it with remarkable good cheer. "Why would I be nervous?" he asked. "I have nothing to lose." Once again, he rode to and beyond the limits of his Yamaha; once again, it was not enough.

After the race, Quartararo's good cheer evaporated for a while: "Of course I was emotional. I'm a fighter. I'm a winner, so the next 15 minutes after the race were tough. But it's finished. We need to make a new chapter. Even if now I see 99 per cent of negatives, the one per cent positive is the next four months, to work for the next race. I will have even more hunger for 2023."

The duel for the crown did detract somewhat from the poignancy of the last race of 2022, and also the last race for the small, tightly-knit Suzuki team – which the blue bike won in convincing style. It was Alex Rins's second of the year, and second in the last three races.

If anything was needed to underline the incomprehensibility of Suzuki's decision to quit (at least inside the paddock and among bike racing fans worldwide), this was it. Rins's Phillip Island win might have been ascribed to the track's fast and flowing nature playing to the Suzuki's sweet-handling strength while minimising its relatively average acceleration, at least compared with Ducati. But Valencia's ultra-compact Ricardo Tormo circuit is the exact opposite: tight and tadgy. Here was a demonstration of just what a good all-rounder the GSX-RR could be.

Rins admitted to having been tearful on the grid, his last moment with his faithful pit crew, as well as after the race: "So many emotions came to me." Team-mate Mir, with sixth his own best result since before the summer break, was asked what he imagined Suzuki's board members were thinking as they watched the race: "I don't know if they will be regretting it, and maybe they want to invest in other things. But to me, the image we are giving here in MotoGP – a beautiful bike, a beautiful team – I think that no publicity campaign can give what we are giving here."

Some might have thought the win a trifle lucky, for had the race been a couple of laps longer, it might have had a different winner. After a year when development, for KTM, had seemed to move at glacial pace, they had brought a new chassis. Binder found some negatives, but importantly improved drive out of the corners, long a weakness. Combined with his dismay at the first season since 2017 without a single win, this added to his usual Sunday impetus for another trademark late-race gallop. That produced two consecutive fastest laps (on the 12th and 13th) on a run through from seventh to second, less than four-tenths adrift.

The result moved him to within one point of Miller (who crashed out) for fifth overall, but more significantly moved KTM ahead of Aprilia to second in the teams' championship, after a dire weekend for the Italian squad, which had started the season so strongly. A double non-finish – fuel-pump problems (Espargaro) and an undisclosed engine issue (Vinales) – also dropped Espargaro to fourth behind Bastianini in the riders' championship, and Aprilia to third behind Yamaha in the constructors'.

The retirement of Franco Uncini as safety officer marked the end of an era, while his replacement raised eyebrows, and triggered fresh allegations of nepotism and cronyism on the

part of Dorna boss Carmelo Ezpeleta. This followed a similar reaction to the news a month before that, in 2023, the long-serving paddock medical facility, the Italian Clinica Mobile founded by Dr Claudio Costa, would be replaced after more than 40 years by Spanish healthcare providers Quironsalud, which already sponsored MotoGP's own medical team.

Uncini's replacement, per Dorna's official press release, was Spaniard Bartolome Alfonso, whose past experience included senior roles at Dorna and as timekeeping co-ordinator for the FIM, management at both Aragon and Losail circuits, and development of the new circuit in Kazakhstan, due to join the calendar in 2023. At the same time, his partner, Tamara Matko, was set to be appointed to the FIM stewards' panel headed by Freddie Spencer.

Rather coyly, the official release omitted his full name, which by Spanish custom adds the mother's maiden name at the end. In this case, that suffix is 'Ezpeleta', for he is Carmelo's nephew. Originally, Uncini had been nominated by the riders in the 1990s, but today's riders stopped short of criticism, with several pointing out that this latest Ezpeleta was experienced in track construction and management, and at least should be given a chance.

The aforementioned stewards had some unusual cases to deliberate, in addition to the routine of three grid places for slow riding in practice (Nakagami), a long-lap for ignoring a yellow flag (Moreira), and a double long-lap, deferred until the following season, for disobeying marshals and then a black flag (Vietti). Marco Bezzecchi was hit with a 1,000-euro fine for abusing a marshal he had deemed to be too slow in responding when his bike caught fire after a crash in FP3 (he apologised later and they made up), while Moto3 combatants Masia and Toba were given pit-lane starts plus long-laps for coming to blows by the trackside after colliding in FP3.

MOTOGP RACE – 27 laps

Martin's third pole in a row was his fifth of the year, equalling Bagnaia. Marc Marquez put in another jaw-dropper to slot into second, with Miller third. Quartararo led row two from Rins, who had come through from Q1; Bagnaia was in the middle of row three.

Rins launched past the four ahead to lead into Turn One, a position he would hold to the flag. Martin slotted into second ahead of Miller, Marquez and Quartararo, taking a wide line around Turns One and Two. Bagnaia was at his most assertive early on, gaining two spots to sit sixth, while Binder, forced wide at Turn One, was already hovering impatiently in seventh.

Then came a flurry of activity. First, Marquez dived under Miller at Turn Six. The Australian fought back two corners later, but he ran marginally wide and Quartararo was able to push through.

The Australian sought revenge. Entering Turn Two the second time around, it was Quartararo on the receiving end of a hard pass and his turn to lift to avoid contact. A temporarily opportunistic Bagnaia also lunged through, hitting the Yamaha, which broke off the Ducati's right winglet. Then the two contenders went at it, exchanging fifth through Turns Four, Six and Eight, somehow avoiding further contact along the way. By the time Quartararo passed his rival for good at Turn Six two laps later, he was 1.6 seconds off Miller ahead.

The squabbling had allowed Rins, Martin and Marquez to stretch clear, with Miller scrambling to regain a footing. Three laps on, and he had succeeded, signalling the intention of ending his Ducati career on a high with a neat Turn One move on Marquez. And despite the eight-times champion's best efforts to retaliate, it was clear that his RC213V wasn't

Above: **Red-carpet treatment: Ducati's second champion after a 15-year wait takes the applause of team boss Paolo Ciabatti.**
Photo: Ducati Corse

Top right: **Close behind fellow Rossi protégé and training companion Bagnaia, Morbidelli and Bezzecchi battled over ninth.**
Photo: Gold & Goose

Above right: **Quartararo deposes Bagnaia after a brief, but dramatic early skirmish.**
Photo: Monster Energy Yamaha

Right: **Pedro Acosta took the Moto2 win, team-mate Fernandez the title.**

Below right: **Once again, Guevara denied Oncu the long-awaited win after a thrilling Moto3 duel.**

Below far right: **Golden boy. Fernandez had some blingy leathers ready for the podium.**
Photos: Gold & Goose

up to the job. It ended with a crash at Turn Eight on the tenth lap.

There were further echoes of Sepang, with Quartararo working miracles to regain lost ground on the lead quartet. He soon had company, Binder disposing of the nervy Bagnaia on lap nine to latch on to his slipstream. With the lead Yamaha gaining on the trio at the front, there remained a glimmer of a chance for an unlikely title triumph, not least as Bagnaia was causing a log-jam in sixth. On lap 13, Mir was easily past; four laps later, also Oliveira, Bagnaia putting up no resistance.

Now it was Marini behind, but instead of staying there to protect his stablemate, he also eased by on lap 19. At this rate, a drop out of the top ten didn't seem completely out of the question, with Bastianini a couple of tenths behind.

Out front, Rins had eked out eight-tenths on Martin by lap 17, while Quartararo was 1.5 seconds behind in fourth, half a second off Miller. Yet now Binder was the danger man, able to brake later once the fuel load lightened. He posted fastest laps on the 12th and 13th to make it a lead group of five. The sideways South African made short work of Quartararo on lap 18, then Miller on lap 23, with a ruthlessly accurate pass at Turn Two. Miller's chances of a dream Ducati farewell came to nothing moments later, as he tucked the front through Turn Ten. At least, that meant his team-mate had gained another place.

With four laps to go, it was clear that only a disaster would derail Bagnaia. Despite gaining a spot after Miller's crash, Quartararo's deficit to Rins was up to two seconds. And he had nothing for Binder, who was edging closer to the front. On lap 26, he took second, diving under Martin with an exquisite Turn Four pass. Rins began the season's final lap seven-tenths clear, and he was kept honest until the end, with Binder having slashed that to less than four-tenths at the flag. Martin completed the podium with a heartening performance after a troubled campaign.

Quartararo just fell short in fourth, 1.9 seconds off Rins – a snapshot of his season as a whole. Oliveira rallied for a fine fifth, ahead of Mir, the pair another five seconds down. Marini was seventh, trailed by Bastianini, who eventually had been let past by Bagnaia on lap 23. The new champion resisted late pressure from compatriot Morbidelli and started celebrating as he crossed the line.

Bezzecchi was a lone 11th; Fernandez got the better of his trio, with Gardner regaining 13th from Nakagami on the last lap. Di Giannantonio took the last point, with Crutchlow and Alex Marquez one minute and one lap behind respectively, both having fallen and remounted. Pol Espargaro and Zarco also crashed; both Aprilias retired.

MOTO2 RACE – 25 laps

The fight for the Moto2 title might have been overshadowed, but it was no less tense and compelling than that in MotoGP. All season long, Ai Ogura had been reliably racking up points, including three wins. His only no-score had been in Portugal, as one of many victims of the early multiple crash.

Then, at the previous round, in Malaysia, while poised for a worthwhile, though not title-winning, second place, he'd risked it all to win and crashed on the last lap.

Rival Augusto Fernandez had taken a little while to get going, then undermined his four wins with an unforced crash in Australia. He might have been thought lucky to have arrived at the final round leading by 9.5 points. If Ogura were to win, he had to finish at least third.

It was finely balanced.

Lopez, often a late-season spoiler, put his Boscoscuro on pole for the first time, with Acosta second, ahead of team-mate Fernandez. Arbolino, also strong in the latter races and through from Q1, led Ogura and Roberts on row two.

Ogura attacked from the start, while Fernandez was flustered. By lap two, the Japanese rider appeared the man more likely, as he slotted into second, behind Arbolino and ahead of Lopez. Acosta was next, then Fernandez, who later described the first eight laps as a nightmare.

Soon, Acosta began pressing Ogura, who was already riding above and beyond. Entering Turn Eight on the eighth lap, the Japanese rider tucked the front for a second race in a row, for a spectacular end-over-end crash.

The tension was over and Fernandez's title won. The Spaniard, bound for MotoGP in 2023, was visibly relieved and settled into an ordinary race.

Lopez had already crashed out on lap four, and by lap 12, both Ajo bikes were past Arbolino, formation flying out front.

In the end, it was an untroubled run to a fine one-two, with Acosta leading his senior team-mate by better than a second. Arbolino had dropped to almost ten seconds away in third, relieved with six laps to go when Aron Canet crashed out after closing threateningly. Canet had already done enough, however, to secure third in the championship.

He had left Aldeguer behind, but fourth equalled his best result of the year, comfortably ahead of Arenas, Gonzalez and Dixon, who had recovered well from 23rd on lap two. But Acosta's win meant that he pushed Dixon from fifth to sixth overall.

Alcoba was along behind, then impressive Australian teenager Senna Agius (substituting again for Sam Lowes) got the better of Schrotter in the German's last GP.

Cameron Beaubier's early bid for a first podium in his last grand prix came to an end when he crashed out of fourth, just after setting fastest lap and taking the position from Fernandez on lap six. Others to swell a long crash list included Chantra, Vietti, Antonelli, and veterans Simone Corsi (also his last GP) and Mattia Pasini, back this time to replace the injured Barry Baltus.

MOTO3 RACE – 23 laps

New champion Guevara's fifth pole of the year presaged a race in which the Moto2-bound teenager demonstrated exactly why he had wrapped up this championship with two races to spare. He kept his cool expertly in a tight last-lap fight with Oncu for his seventh win of the season.

As so often, Guevara's performance had the hallmarks of classic Jorge Lorenzo. He took the holeshot and stretched the pack from the front on the very first lap. Initially, Oncu, Garcia and Ortola were the only men who could go with him. Soon, it was only Oncu as the pair streaked clear.

Aside from Oncu disposing of something loose on his fairing on lap ten, it was clear that this would come down to a final showdown. And the young Turk made good, diving under Guevara to lead for the first time at Turn Eight on the last lap. He nearly pulled off a smash-and-grab win, but when braking for the final Turn 14, he was slightly off line and overly defensive. Sensing this, Guevara ran in wide for a better exit, easing alongside to win by just 0.062 of a second.

Garcia was six seconds behind, third place enough to clinch second in the championship. A further seven seconds away came a huge freight train, led by Foggia, Sasaki, Fernandez, Munoz and Moreira, who had taken his long-lap penalty early and only dropped from fifth to seventh.

Ogden, Furusato, Rossi and Artigas crashed out; ever-winless Oncu had the consolation of the only lap record of the day, set on lap two.

FIM WORLD CHAMPIONSHIP: ROUND 20

GRAN PREMIO MOTUL DE LA COMUNITAT VALENCIANA

4–6 NOVEMBER, 2022

CIRCUITO DE LA COMUNITAT VALENCIANA

27 laps
Length: 4.005 km / 2.489 miles
Width: 12m

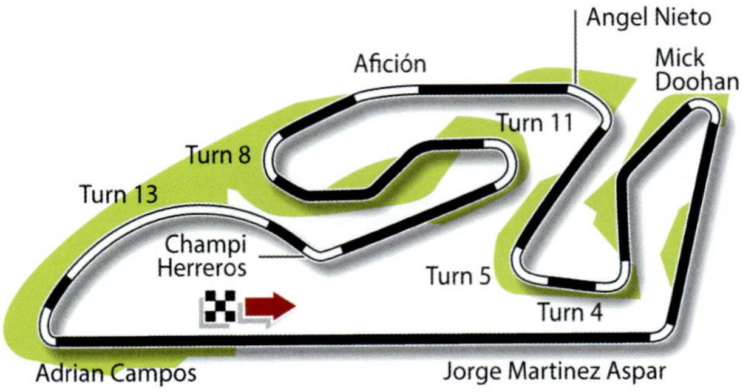

MotoGP

RACE DISTANCE: 27 laps, 67.192 miles/108.135km · RACE WEATHER: Dry (air 27°, humidity 18%, track 32°)

Pos.	Rider	Nat.	No.	Entrant	Machine	Tyres	Race tyre choice	Laps	Time & speed
1	**Alex Rins**	SPA	42	Team SUZUKI ECSTAR	Suzuki GSX-RR	M	F: Hard/R: Medium	27	41m 22.250s
									97.4mph/156.8km/h
2	**Brad Binder**	RSA	33	Red Bull KTM Factory Racing	KTM RC16	M	F: Hard/R: Medium	27	41m 22.646s
3	**Jorge Martin**	SPA	89	Prima Pramac Racing	Ducati Desmosedici	M	F: Hard/R: Medium	27	41m 23.309s
4	**Fabio Quartararo**	FRA	20	Monster Energy Yamaha MotoGP	Yamaha YZR-M1	M	F: Hard/R: Medium	27	41m 24.161s
5	**Miguel Oliveira**	POR	88	Red Bull KTM Factory Racing	KTM RC16	M	F: Hard/R: Medium	27	41m 29.372s
6	**Joan Mir**	SPA	36	Team SUZUKI ECSTAR	Suzuki GSX-RR	M	F: Hard/R: Medium	27	41m 29.985s
7	**Luca Marini**	ITA	10	Mooney VR46 Racing Team	Ducati Desmosedici	M	F: Hard/R: Medium	27	41m 30.774s
8	**Enea Bastianini**	ITA	23	Gresini Racing MotoGP	Ducati Desmosedici	M	F: Hard/R: Medium	27	41m 34.288s
9	**Francesco Bagnaia**	ITA	63	Ducati Lenovo Team	Ducati Desmosedici	M	F: Hard/R: Medium	27	41m 36.691s
10	**Franco Morbidelli**	ITA	21	Monster Energy Yamaha MotoGP	Yamaha YZR-M1	M	F: Hard/R: Medium	27	41m 36.926s
11	**Marco Bezzecchi**	ITA	72	Mooney VR46 Racing Team	Ducati Desmosedici	M	F: Hard/R: Medium	27	41m 39.905s
12	**Raul Fernandez**	SPA	25	Tech3 KTM Factory Racing	KTM RC16	M	F: Hard/R: Medium	27	41m 47.120s
13	**Remy Gardner**	AUS	87	Tech3 KTM Factory Racing	KTM RC16	M	F: Hard/R: Medium	27	41m 48.796s
14	**Takaaki Nakagami**	JPN	30	LCR Honda IDEMITSU	Honda RC213V	M	F: Hard/R: Soft	27	41m 48.860s
15	**Fabio Di Giannantonio**	ITA	49	Gresini Racing MotoGP	Ducati Desmosedici	M	F: Hard/R: Medium	27	41m 54.069s
16	Cal Crutchlow	GBR	35	WithU Yamaha RNF MotoGP Team	Yamaha YZR-M1	M	F: Hard/R: Medium	27	42m 51.120s
17	Alex Marquez	SPA	73	LCR Honda CASTROL	Honda RC213V	M	F: Hard/R: Soft	26	42m 07.305s
	Jack Miller	AUS	43	Ducati Lenovo Team	Ducati Desmosedici	M	F: Hard/R: Medium	22	DNF-crash
	Johann Zarco	FRA	5	Prima Pramac Racing	Ducati Desmosedici	M	F: Hard/R: Medium	15	DNF-crash
	Maverick Vinales	SPA	12	Aprilia Racing	Aprilia RS-GP	M	F: Hard/R: Medium	15	DNF-technical
	Marc Marquez	SPA	93	Repsol Honda Team	Honda RC213V	M	F: Hard/R: Medium	9	DNF-crash
	Pol Espargaro	SPA	44	Repsol Honda Team	Honda RC213V	M	F: Hard/R: Medium	4	DNF-crash
	Darryn Binder	RSA	40	WithU Yamaha RNF MotoGP Team	Yamaha YZR-M1	M	F: Hard/R: Medium	4	DNF-crash
	Aleix Espargaro	SPA	41	Aprilia Racing	Aprilia RS-GP	M	F: Hard/R: Medium	3	DNF-technical

Fastest lap: Brad Binder, on lap 13, 1m 31.192s, 98.2mph/158.1km/h.
Lap record: Francesco Bagnaia, 1m 31.042s, 98.4mph/158.3km/h (2021).
Event maximum speed: Enea Bastianini, 209.4mph/337.0km/h (race)..

Qualifying

Weather: Dry
Air Temp: 25° **Humidity:** 18%
Track Temp: 31°

1	Martin	1m 29.621s
2	M. Marquez	1m 29.826s
3	Miller	1m 29.834s
4	Quartararo	1m 29.900s
5	Rins	1m 29.940s
6	Vinales	1m 29.955s
7	B. Binder	1m 30.039s
8	Bagnaia	1m 30.049s
9	Zarco	1m 30.102s
10	A. Espargaro	1m 30.124s
11	Marini	1m 30.143s
12	Mir	1m 30.241s
	Q1	
13	Bastianini	1m 30.193s
14	Oliveira	1m 30.236s
15	A. Marquez	1m 30.453s
16	Morbidelli	1m 30.504s
17	Crutchlow	1m 30.548s
18	Bezzecchi	1m 30.588s
19	Di Giannantonio	1m 30.695s
20	Gardner	1m 30.804s
21	Nakagami	1m 30.830s
22	P. Espargaro	1m 30.936s
23	Fernandez	1m 31.676s
24	D. Binder	1m 31.989s

Fastest race laps

1	B. Binder	1m 31.192s
2	Martin	1m 31.294s
3	Rins	1m 31.345s
4	Miller	1m 31.381s
5	Quartararo	1m 31.410s
6	M. Marquez	1m 31.419s
7	Marini	1m 31.568s
8	Vinales	1m 31.663s
9	Bastianini	1m 31.687s
10	Mir	1m 31.688s
11	Oliveira	1m 31.693s
12	Zarco	1m 31.695s
13	Bagnaia	1m 31.701s
14	Bezzecchi	1m 31.722s
15	Morbidelli	1m 31.794s
16	P. Espargaro	1m 31.923s
17	Crutchlow	1m 32.013s
18	Fernandez	1m 32.023s
19	Di Giannantonio	1m 32.041s
20	A. Marquez	1m 32.179s
21	Gardner	1m 32.197s
22	Nakagami	1m 32.234s
23	D. Binder	1m 32.465s
24	A. Espargaro	1m 36.052s

Championship Points

1	Bagnaia	265
2	Quartararo	248
3	Bastianini	219
4	A. Espargaro	212
5	Miller	189
6	B. Binder	188
7	Rins	173
8	Zarco	166
9	Martin	152
10	Oliveira	149
11	Vinales	122
12	Marini	120
13	M. Marquez	113
14	Bezzecchi	111
15	Mir	87
16	P. Espargaro	56
17	A. Marquez	50
18	Nakagami	48
19	Morbidelli	42
20	Di Giannantonio	24
21	Dovizioso	15
22	Fernandez	14
23	Gardner	13
24	D. Binder	12
25	Crutchlow	10
26	Bradl	2

Constructor Points

1	Ducati	448
2	Yamaha	256
3	Aprilia	248
4	KTM	240
5	Suzuki	199
6	Honda	155

Grid order	1	2	3	4	5	6	7	8	9	10	11	12	13	14	15	16	17	18	19	20	21	22	23	24	25	26	27	•
89 MARTIN	42	42	42	42	42	42	42	42	42	42	42	42	42	42	42	42	42	42	42	42	42	42	42	42	42	42	42	1
93 M. MARQUEZ	89	89	89	89	89	89	89	89	89	89	89	89	89	89	89	89	89	89	89	89	89	89	89	89	89	33	33	2
43 MILLER	93	93	93	93	93	43	43	43	43	43	43	43	43	43	43	43	43	43	43	43	43	43	33	33	33	89	89	3
20 QUARTARARO	20	43	43	43	43	93	93	93	93	20	20	20	20	20	20	20	20	33	33	33	33	33	20	20	20	20	20	4
42 RINS	43	63	63	20	20	20	20	20	20	33	33	33	33	33	33	33	33	20	20	20	20	20	36	36	36	88	88	5
12 VINALES	63	20	20	63	63	63	63	63	33	63	63	63	36	36	36	36	36	36	36	36	36	36	88	88	88	36	36	6
33 B.BINDER	33	33	33	33	33	33	33	33	63	36	36	36	63	63	63	63	88	88	88	88	88	88	10	10	10	10	10	7
63 BAGNAIA	5	5	5	5	5	36	36	36	36	88	88	88	88	88	88	88	63	63	10	10	10	10	23	23	23	23	23	8
5 ZARCO	10	36	36	36	36	5	5	5	88	10	10	10	10	10	10	10	10	10	63	63	63	23	63	63	63	63	63	9
41 A. ESPARGARO	12	88	88	88	88	88	88	88	10	23	23	23	23	23	23	23	23	23	23	23	23	63	21	21	21	21	21	10
10 MARINI	36	10	10	10	10	10	10	10	23	5	5	5	5	5	5	21	21	21	21	21	21	21	72	72	72	72	72	11
36 MIR	73	12	12	23	23	23	23	23	5	72	72	72	21	21	21	72	72	72	72	72	72	72	25	25	25	25	25	12
23 BASTIANINI	88	73	23	21	21	21	21	21	72	21	21	21	72	72	72	87	25	25	25	25	25	25	87	87	30	30	87	13
88 OLIVEIRA	41	23	73	73	73	73	72	72	21	87	87	87	87	87	87	25	87	87	87	87	87	87	30	30	87	87	30	14
73 A. MARQUEZ	23	21	21	87	87	87	87	87	87	49	49	49	25	25	25	49	49	49	30	30	30	30	49	49	49	49	49	15
21 MORBIDELLI	21	35	87	12	72	72	49	49	49	25	25	25	49	49	49	30	30	30	49	49	49	49	35	35	35	35	35	
35 CRUTCHLOW	35	87	35	72	12	35	25	25	25	30	30	30	30	30	30	35	35	35	35	35	35	35	*73*	*73*	*73*	*73*		
72 BEZZECCHI	25	25	72	35	35	49	30	30	30	12	12	12	12	12	12	*73*	*73*	*73*	*73*	*73*	*73*	*73*						
49 DI GIANNANTONIO	44	72	25	44	49	25	12	12	12	35	35	35	35	35	35													
87 GARDNER	87	44	44	49	25	30	35	35	35	*73*	*73*	*73*	*73*	*73*	*73*													
44 P. ESPARGARO	72	49	49	25	30	12	73	*73*	*73*																			
25 FERNANDEZ	30	30	30	30																								
40 D.BINDER	49	40	40	40																								
30 NAKAGAMI	40	41	41																									

41 Pit stop *73 Lapped rider*

Moto2

RACE DISTANCE: 25 laps, 62.215 miles/100.125km · RACE WEATHER: Dry (air 22°, humidity 29%, track 27°)

Pos.	Rider	Nat.	No.	Entrant	Machine	Laps	Time & Speed
1	**Pedro Acosta**	SPA	51	Red Bull KTM Ajo	Kalex	25	39m 52.413s
							93.6mph/150.6km/h
2	**Augusto Fernandez**	SPA	37	Red Bull KTM Ajo	Kalex	25	39m 53.645s
3	**Tony Arbolino**	ITA	14	Elf Marc VDS Racing Team	Kalex	25	40m 02.576s
4	**Fermin Aldeguer**	SPA	54	Beta Tools Speed Up	Boscoscuro	25	40m 06.820s
5	**Albert Arenas**	SPA	75	Inde GASGAS Aspar Team	Kalex	25	40m 11.317s
6	**Manuel Gonzalez**	SPA	18	Yamaha VR46 Master Camp Team	Kalex	25	40m 12.967s
7	**Jake Dixon**	GBR	96	Inde GASGAS Aspar Team	Kalex	25	40m 13.657s
8	**Jeremy Alcoba**	SPA	52	Liqui Moly Intact GP	Kalex	25	40m 18.281s
9	**Senna Agius**	AUS	8	Elf Marc VDS Racing Team	Kalex	25	40m 26.176s
10	**Marcel Schrotter**	GER	23	Liqui Moly Intact GP	Kalex	25	40m 27.530s
11	**Bo Bendsneyder**	NED	64	Pertamina Mandalika SAG Team	Kalex	25	40m 28.011s
12	**Borja Gomez**	SPA	72	Flexbox HP40	Kalex	25	40m 28.749s
13	**Filip Salac**	CZE	12	Gresini Racing Moto2	Kalex	25	40m 31.355s
14	**Lorenzo Dalla Porta**	ITA	19	Italtrans Racing Team	Kalex	25	40m 34.123s
15	**Joe Roberts**	USA	16	Italtrans Racing Team	Kalex	25	40m 37.651s
16	Alessandro Zaccone	ITA	61	Gresini Racing Moto2	Kalex	25	40m 44.240s
17	Keminth Kubo	THA	81	Yamaha VR46 Master Camp Team	Kalex	25	40m 45.297s
18	Sean Dylan Kelly	USA	4	American Racing	Kalex	25	40m 45.522s
19	Alex Escrig	SPA	17	MV Agusta Forward Racing	MV Agusta	25	40m 47.592s
20	Marcos Ramirez	SPA	42	MV Agusta Forward Racing	MV Agusta	25	40m 48.040s
21	Zonta van den Goorbergh	NED	84	RW Racing GP	Kalex	25	40m 56.317s
22	Taiga Hada	JPN	29	Pertamina Mandalika SAG Team	Kalex	23	41m 08.999s
	Aron Canet	SPA	40	Flexbox HP40	Kalex	19	DNF-crash
	Mattia Pasini	ITA	11	RW Racing GP	Kalex	18	DNF-crash
	Somkiat Chantra	THA	35	IDEMITSU Honda Team Asia	Kalex	14	DNF-crash
	Niccolo Antonelli	ITA	28	Mooney VR46 Racing Team	Kalex	14	DNF-crash
	Ai Ogura	JPN	79	IDEMITSU Honda Team Asia	Kalex	7	DNF-crash
	Celestino Vietti	ITA	13	Mooney VR46 Racing Team	Kalex	7	DNF-crash
	Cameron Beaubier	USA	6	American Racing	Kalex	5	DNF-crash
	Alonso Lopez	SPA	21	Beta Tools Speed Up	Boscoscuro	3	DNF-crash
	Simone Corsi	ITA	24	MV Agusta Forward Racing	MV Agusta	0	DNF-crash

Fastest lap: Cameron Beaubier, on lap 3, 1m 34.850s, 94.4mph/152.0km/h.
Lap record: Thomas Luthi, 1m 34.820s, 94.4mph/152.0km/h (2019).
Event maximum speed: Jeremy Alcoba, 172.9mph/278.3km/h (free practice).

Qualifying

Weather: Dry
Air: 25° **Humidity:** 16% **Track:** 30°

1	Lopez	1m 34.314s
2	Acosta	1m 34.315s
3	Fernandez	1m 34.481s
4	Arbolino	1m 34.583s
5	Ogura	1m 34.665s
6	Roberts	1m 34.674s
7	Canet	1m 34.765s
8	Aldeguer	1m 34.771s
9	Vietti	1m 34.773s
10	Dalla Porta	1m 34.866s
11	Arenas	1m 34.875s
12	Chantra	1m 34.907s
13	Beaubier	1m 34.920s
14	Gonzalez	1m 34.928s
15	Dixon	1m 34.976s
16	Salac	1m 35.138s
17	Pasini	1m 35.139s
18	Alcoba	1m 35.258s
	Q1	
19	Agius	1m 35.076s
20	Bendsneyder	1m 35.080s
21	Gomez	1m 35.109s
22	Schrotter	1m 35.165s
23	Zaccone	1m 35.282s
24	Escrig	1m 35.409s
25	Hada	1m 35.474s
26	Corsi	1m 35.631s
27	Kelly	1m 35.737s
28	Kubo	1m 35.823s
29	Ramirez	1m 35.910s
30	VD Goorbergh	1m 35.956s
31	Antonelli	1m 36.160s

Fastest race laps

1	Beaubier	1m 34.850s
2	Acosta	1m 34.950s
3	Arbolino	1m 35.156s
4	Canet	1m 35.176s
5	Ogura	1m 35.209s
6	Fernandez	1m 35.281s
7	Lopez	1m 35.586s
8	Aldeguer	1m 35.652s
9	Chantra	1m 35.707s
10	Arenas	1m 35.728s
11	Gonzalez	1m 35.741s
12	Vietti	1m 35.753s
13	Dixon	1m 35.778s
14	Salac	1m 35.872s
15	Alcoba	1m 35.998s
16	Pasini	1m 36.013s
17	Agius	1m 36.069s
18	Hada	1m 36.125s
19	Schrotter	1m 36.162s
20	Roberts	1m 36.201s
21	Gomez	1m 36.217s
22	Bendsneyder	1m 36.286s
23	Escrig	1m 36.363s
24	Dalla Porta	1m 36.537s
25	Zaccone	1m 36.910s
26	Kubo	1m 36.912s
27	Kelly	1m 37.014s
28	VD Goorbergh	1m 37.044s
29	Ramirez	1m 37.104s
30	Antonelli	1m 37.264s

Championship Points

1	Fernandez	271.5
2	Ogura	242
3	Canet	200
4	Arbolino	191.5
5	Acosta	177
6	Dixon	168.5
7	Vietti	165
8	Lopez	155.5
9	Roberts	131
10	Chantra	128
11	Schrotter	123.5
12	Arenas	90
13	Bendsneyder	87
14	Navarro	83
15	Aldeguer	80
16	Gonzalez	76
17	Beaubier	73
18	Alcoba	72
19	Lowes	55
20	Salac	45
21	Baltus	30
22	Dalla Porta	21
23	Manzi	9
24	Zaccone	9
25	Kubo	7.5
26	Agius	7
27	Fenati	7
28	Rodrigo	6
29	Kelly	5.5
30	Ramirez	5
31	Gomez	4
32	Hada	3.5
33	Pasini	1

Constructor Points

1	Kalex	477.5
2	Boscoscuro	200.5
3	MV Agusta	5

Moto3

RACE DISTANCE: 23 laps, 57.238 miles/92.115km · RACE WEATHER: Dry (air 22°, humidity 28%, track 27°)

Pos.	Rider	Nat.	No.	Entrant	Machine	Laps	Time & Speed
1	**Izan Guevara**	SPA	28	Valresa GASGAS Aspar Team	GASGAS	23	38m 10.406s
							89.9mph/144.7km/h
2	**Deniz Oncu**	TUR	53	Red Bull KTM Tech3	KTM	23	38m 10.468s
3	**Sergio Garcia**	SPA	11	Valresa GASGAS Aspar Team	GASGAS	23	38m 16.963s
4	**Dennis Foggia**	ITA	7	Leopard Racing	Honda	23	38m 24.539s
5	**Ayumu Sasaki**	JPN	71	Sterilgarda Husqvarna Max	Husqvarna	23	38m 24.980s
6	**Adrian Fernandez**	SPA	31	Red Bull KTM Tech3	KTM	23	38m 25.082s
7	**David Munoz**	SPA	44	BOE Motorsports	KTM	23	38m 25.295s
8	**Diogo Moreira**	BRA	10	MT Helmets - MSI	KTM	23	38m 25.454s
9	**Ryusei Yamanaka**	JPN	6	MT Helmets - MSI	KTM	23	38m 25.694s
10	**Daniel Holgado**	SPA	96	Red Bull KTM Ajo	KTM	23	38m 25.846s
11	**John McPhee**	GBR	17	Sterilgarda Husqvarna Max	Husqvarna	23	38m 25.939s
12	**Ivan Ortola**	SPA	48	Angeluss MTA Team	KTM	23	38m 26.024s
13	**Carlos Tatay**	SPA	99	CFMOTO Racing PruestelGP	CFMOTO	23	38m 26.183s
14	**Tatsuki Suzuki**	JPN	24	Leopard Racing	Honda	23	38m 38.899s
15	**Andrea Migno**	ITA	16	Rivacold Snipers Team	Honda	23	38m 38.909s
16	Nicola Fabio Carraro	ITA	9	QJMotor Avintia Racing Team	KTM	23	38m 38.951s
17	Elia Bartolini	ITA	23	QJMotor Avintia Racing Team	KTM	23	38m 39.224s
18	David Salvador	SPA	38	Angeluss MTA Team	KTM	23	38m 39.566s
19	Filippo Farioli	ITA	77	GASGAS Aspar Team	GASGAS	23	38m 39.808s
20	Lorenzo Fellon	FRA	20	SIC58 Squadra Corse	Honda	23	38m 39.860s
21	Joel Kelso	AUS	66	CIP Green Power	KTM	23	38m 42.321s
22	Jaume Masia	SPA	5	Red Bull KTM Ajo	KTM	23	38m 46.888s
23	Xavier Artigas	SPA	43	CFMOTO Racing PruestelGP	CFMOTO	23	38m 46.932s
24	Kaito Toba	JPN	27	CIP Green Power	KTM	23	38m 47.157s
25	David Almansa	SPA	95	Finetwork Team BOE Motorsports	KTM	23	38m 52.497s
26	Joshua Whatley	GBR	70	VisionTrack Racing Team	Honda	23	39m 00.421s
27	Mario Aji	INA	64	Honda Team Asia	Honda	23	39m 00.562s
28	Ana Carrasco	SPA	22	BOE Motorsports	KTM	23	39m 07.686s
29	Alberto Surra	ITA	67	Rivacold Snipers Team	Honda	23	39m 07.766s
	Scott Ogden	GBR	19	VisionTrack Racing Team	Honda	15	DNF-crash
	Taiyo Furusato	JPN	72	Honda Team Asia	Honda	14	DNF-crash
	Riccardo Rossi	ITA	54	SIC58 Squadra Corse	Honda	8	DNF-crash

Fastest lap: Deniz Oncu, on lap 2, 1m 38.790s, 90.7mph/145.9km/h.
Lap record: Sergio Garcia, 1m 38.858s, 90.6mph/145.8km/h (2020).
Event maximum speed: David Salvador, 147.3mph/237.1km/h (race).

Qualifying:

Weather: Dry
Air: 22° **Humidity:** 21% **Track:** 30°

1	Guevara	1m 38.479s
2	Oncu	1m 38.525s
3	Garcia	1m 38.654s
4	Moreira	1m 38.697s
5	Sasaki	1m 38.761s
6	Ortola	1m 38.797s
7	Foggia	1m 38.856s
8	Suzuki	1m 38.875s
9	Yamanaka	1m 38.927s
10	McPhee	1m 38.949s
11	Masia	1m 39.016s
12	Rossi	1m 39.018s
13	Salvador	1m 39.021s
14	Munoz	1m 39.039s
15	Holgado	1m 39.146s
16	Artigas	1m 39.167s
17	Tatay	1m 39.262s
18	Carraro	1m 39.307s
	Q1	
19	Kelso	1m 39.486s
20	Farioli	1m 39.513s
21	Bartolini	1m 39.579s
22	Almansa	1m 39.626s
23	Fellon	1m 39.781s
24	Migno	1m 39.788s
25	Toba	1m 39.836s
26	Fernandez	1m 39.958s
27	Ogden	1m 40.049s
28	Surra	1m 40.064s
29	Furusato	1m 40.191s
30	Aji	1m 40.498s
31	Whatley	1m 40.735s
32	Carrasco	1m 41.384s
	Whatley	No Time

Fastest race laps

1	Oncu	1m 38.790s
2	Guevara	1m 38.826s
3	Garcia	1m 38.878s
4	Ortola	1m 38.913s
5	Moreira	1m 38.918s
6	Munoz	1m 38.956s
7	Artigas	1m 39.148s
8	Yamanaka	1m 39.242s
9	Rossi	1m 39.257s
10	Holgado	1m 39.268s
11	McPhee	1m 39.303s
12	Foggia	1m 39.342s
13	Suzuki	1m 39.389s
14	Sasaki	1m 39.389s
15	Fernandez	1m 39.396s
16	Tatay	1m 39.416s
17	Kelso	1m 39.437s
18	Salvador	1m 39.487s
19	Carraro	1m 39.619s
20	Fellon	1m 39.751s
21	Masia	1m 39.796s
22	Migno	1m 39.853s
23	Toba	1m 39.857s
24	Bartolini	1m 39.890s
25	Farioli	1m 39.905s
26	Almansa	1m 40.027s
27	Ogden	1m 40.051s
28	Furusato	1m 40.064s
29	Aji	1m 40.084s
30	Surra	1m 40.585s
31	Whatley	1m 40.797s
32	Carrasco	1m 40.962s
29	Whatley	2m 15.951s

Championship Points

1	Guevara	319
2	Garcia	257
3	Foggia	246
4	Sasaki	238
5	Oncu	200
6	Masia	177
7	Suzuki	130
8	Moreira	112
9	Migno	103
10	Holgado	103
11	McPhee	102
12	Yamanaka	94
13	Munoz	93
14	Rossi	87
15	Tatay	87
16	Artigas	83
17	Ortola	73
18	Nepa	64
19	Toba	63
20	Fernandez	51
21	Kelso	36
22	Bartolini	27
23	Ogden	21
24	Bertelle	16
25	Fellon	11
26	Aji	5
27	Furusato	2

Constructor Points

1	GASGAS	389
2	Honda	330
3	KTM	323
4	Husqvarna	279
5	CFMOTO	130

2022 FIM MotoGP™ WORLD CHAMPIONS

WORLD CHAMPIONSHIP POINTS 2022

Compiled by PETER McLAREN

MotoGP – Riders

Position	Rider	Nationality	Machine	Qatar	Indonesia	Argentina	United States	Portugal	Spain	France	Italy	Catalunya	Germany	Netherlands	Great Britain	Austria	San Marino	Aragon	Japan	Thailand	Australia	Malaysia	Valencia	**Points total**
1	**Francesco Bagnaia**	ITA	Ducati	-	1	11	11	8	25	-	25	-	-	25	25	25	25	20	-	16	16	25	7	**265**
2	**Fabio Quartararo**	FRA	Yamaha	7	20	8	9	25	20	13	20	25	25	-	8	20	11	-	8	0	-	16	13	**248**
3	**Enea Bastianini**	ITA	Ducati	25	5	6	25	-	8	25	-	-	6	5	13	-	20	25	7	10	11	20	8	**219**
4	**Aleix Espargaro**	SPA	Aprilia	13	7	25	5	16	16	16	16	11	13	13	7	10	10	16	0	5	7	6	-	**212**
5	**Jack Miller**	AUS	Ducati	-	13	2	16	-	11	20	1	2	16	10	16	16	0	11	25	20	-	10	-	**189**
6	**Brad Binder**	RSA	KTM	20	8	10	4	-	6	8	9	8	9	11	5	9	8	13	20	6	6	8	20	**188**
7	**Alex Rins**	SPA	Suzuki	9	11	16	20	13	0	-	-	-	-	6	9	8	9	7	-	4	25	11	25	**173**
8	**Johann Zarco**	FRA	Ducati	8	16	-	7	20	-	11	13	16	20	3	-	11	-	8	5	13	8	7	-	**166**
9	**Jorge Martin**	SPA	Ducati	-	-	20	8	-	0	-	3	20	10	9	11	6	7	10	16	7	9	-	16	**152**
10	**Miguel Oliveira**	POR	KTM	-	25	3	0	11	4	-	7	7	7	7	10	4	5	5	11	25	4	3	11	**149**
11	**Maverick Vinales**	SPA	Aprilia	4	0	9	6	6	2	6	4	9	-	16	20	3	16	3	9	9	0	0	-	**122**
12	**Luca Marini**	ITA	Ducati	3	2	5	0	4	0	7	10	10	11	0	4	13	13	9	10	0	10	-	9	**120**
13	**Marc Marquez**	SPA	Honda	11	-	-	10	10	13	10	6	-	-	-	-	-	-	-	13	11	20	9	-	**113**
14	**Marco Bezzecchi**	ITA	Ducati	-	0	7	-	1	7	4	11	-	5	20	6	7	0	6	6	0	13	13	5	**111**
15	**Joan Mir**	SPA	Suzuki	10	10	13	13	-	10	-	-	13	-	8	-	-	-	-	-	-	0	0	10	**87**
16	**Pol Espargaro**	SPA	Honda	16	4	-	3	7	5	5	-	0	-	-	2	0	-	1	4	2	5	2	-	**56**
17	**Alex Marquez**	SPA	Honda	-	3	1	-	9	3	2	2	6	-	1	0	2	6	4	3	8	-	0	0	**50**
18	**Takaaki Nakagami**	JPN	Honda	6	0	4	2	0	9	9	8	-	-	4	3	-	1	-	0	-	-	-	2	**48**
19	**Franco Morbidelli**	ITA	Yamaha	5	9	-	0	3	1	1	0	3	3	-	1	-	-	0	2	3	-	5	6	**42**
20	**Fabio Di Giannantonio**	ITA	Ducati	0	0	-	0	-	0	3	5	-	8	2	0	5	0	0	0	0	0	-	1	**24**
21	**Andrea Dovizioso**	ITA	Yamaha	2	-	0	1	5	0	0	0	-	2	0	0	1	4	-	-	-	-	-	-	**15**
22	**Raul Fernandez**	SPA	KTM	0	0	0	0	-	-	-	0	1	4	-	0	0	3	0	0	1	0	1	4	**14**
23	**Remy Gardner**	AUS	KTM	1	0	0	0	2	0	-	0	5	1	0	0	0	0	0	0	-	1	0	3	**13**
24	**Darryn Binder**	RSA	Yamaha	0	6	0	0	0	-	0	0	4	-	-	0	-	0	0	-	0	2	-	-	**12**
25	**Cal Crutchlow**	GBR	Yamaha	-	-	-	-	-	-	-	-	-	-	-	-	-	-	2	1	0	3	4	0	**10**
26	**Stefan Bradl**	GER	Honda	-	-	0	-	-	-	-	-	-	0	0	0	0	2	-	-	-	-	-	-	**2**
27	**Michele Pirro**	ITA	Ducati	-	-	-	-	-	-	-	0	0	-	-	-	-	-	-	-	-	-	-	-	**0**
28	**Lorenzo Savadori**	ITA	Aprilia	-	-	-	-	-	0	-	0	-	-	0	-	0	-	-	-	-	-	-	-	**0**
29	**Tetsuta Nagashima**	JPN	Honda	-	-	-	-	-	-	-	-	-	-	-	-	-	-	-	-	0	0	-	-	**0**
30	**Danilo Petrucci**	ITA	Suzuki	-	-	-	-	-	-	-	-	-	-	-	-	-	-	-	-	0	-	-	-	**0**
31	**Kazuki Watanabe**	JPN	Suzuki	-	-	-	-	-	-	-	-	-	-	-	-	-	0	-	-	-	-	-	-	**0**
32	**Takuya Tsuda**	JPN	Suzuki	-	-	-	-	-	-	-	-	-	-	-	-	-	-	-	-	-	-	-	-	**0**

MotoGP - Teams

Position	Team	Qatar	Indonesia	Argentina	United States	Portugal	Spain	France	Italy	Catalunya	Germany	Netherlands	Great Britain	Austria	San Marino	Aragon	Japan	Thailand	Australia	Malaysia	Valencia	**Points total**
1	**Ducati Lenovo Team**	-	14	13	27	8	36	20	26	2	16	35	41	41	25	31	25	36	16	35	7	**454**
2	**Red Bull KTM Factory Racing**	20	33	13	4	11	10	8	16	15	16	18	15	13	13	18	31	31	10	11	31	**337**
3	**Aprilia Racing**	17	7	34	11	22	18	22	20	20	13	29	27	13	26	19	9	14	7	6	-	**334**
4	**Prima Pramac Racing**	8	16	20	15	20	-	11	16	36	30	12	11	17	7	18	21	20	17	7	16	**318**
5	**Monster Energy Yamaha MotoGP**	12	29	8	9	28	21	14	20	28	28	-	9	20	11	-	10	3	-	21	19	**290**
6	**Team SUZUKI ECSTAR**	19	21	29	33	13	10	-	-	13	-	14	9	8	9	7	-	4	25	11	35	**260**
7	**Gresini Racing MotoGP**	25	5	6	25	-	8	28	5	-	14	7	13	5	20	25	7	10	11	20	9	**243**
8	**Mooney VR46 Racing Team**	3	2	12	-	5	7	11	21	10	16	20	10	20	13	15	16	-	23	13	14	**231**
9	**Repsol Honda Team**	27	4	-	13	17	18	15	6	-	-	-	2	-	2	1	17	13	25	11	-	**171**
10	**LCR Honda**	6	3	5	2	9	12	11	10	6	-	5	3	2	7	4	3	8	-	-	2	**98**
11	**WithU Yamaha RNF MotoGP Team**	2	6	-	1	5	-	-	-	4	2	-	-	1	4	2	1	-	5	4	-	**37**
12	**Tech3 KTM Factory Racing**	1	-	-	-	2	-	-	-	6	5	-	-	-	3	-	-	1	1	1	7	**27**

Moto2

Position	Rider	Nationality	Machine	Qatar	Indonesia	Argentina	United States	Portugal	Spain	France	Italy	Catalunya	Germany	Netherlands	Great Britain	Austria	San Marino	Aragon	Japan	Thailand	Australia	Malaysia	Valencia	Points total
1	**Augusto Fernandez**	SPA	Kalex	13	11	-	7	-	13	25	11	16	25	25	25	11	16	16	20	4.5	-	13	20	**271.5**
2	**Ai Ogura**	JPN	Kalex	10	10	16	20	-	25	11	16	9	8	20	13	25	11	13	25	5	5	-	-	**242**
3	**Aron Canet**	SPA	Kalex	20	16	13	-	-	20	20	-	20	7	-	11	10	20	20	-	8	7	8	-	**200**
4	**Tony Arbolino**	ITA	Kalex	11	8	10	25	-	16	-	13	6	6	9	4	-	9	11	10	12.5	-	25	16	**191.5**
5	**Pedro Acosta**	SPA	Kalex	4	7	9	-	-	0	-	25	10	20	-	-	13	10	25	9	0	20	-	25	**177**
6	**Jake Dixon**	GBR	Kalex	5	-	11	16	-	-	0	10	13	5	16	16	16	-	-	13	6.5	16	16	9	**168.5**
7	**Celestino Vietti**	ITA	Kalex	25	20	25	-	20	10	8	-	25	-	13	10	-	-	6	-	3	-	-	-	**165**
8	**Alonso Lopez**	SPA	Boscoscuro	-	-	-	-	-	-	-	8	8	9	10	20	9	25	-	16	5.5	25	20	-	**155.5**
9	**Joe Roberts**	USA	Kalex	8	5	3	8	25	8	9	20	-	3	8	9	2	7	7	4	4	-	-	1	**131**
10	**Somkiat Chantra**	THA	Kalex	-	25	20	-	-	-	16	-	4	1	3	3	20	8	9	11	-	8	-	-	**128**
11	**Marcel Schrotter**	GER	Kalex	6	0	4	13	13	11	10	7	11	13	-	-	8	5	-	3	0.5	3	10	6	**123.5**
12	**Albert Arenas**	SPA	Kalex	3	6	8	5	-	7	0	6	-	10	-	-	7	13	-	8	1	2	3	11	**90**
13	**Bo Bendsneyder**	NED	Kalex	0	1	7	9	8	9	2	5	3	0	11	6	1	4	1	7	0	6	2	5	**87**
14	**Jorge Navarro**	SPA	Kalex	9	3	-	11	16	6	7	4	2	-	4	8	5	-	8	-	0	-	-	-	**83**
15	**Fermin Aldeguer**	SPA	Boscoscuro	0	9	-	-	9	-	-	2	1	11	5	1	-	-	10	-	-	13	6	13	**80**
16	**Manuel Gonzalez**	SPA	Kalex	0	0	2	3	11	0	5	0	7	4	7	5	-	-	-	-	0	11	11	10	**76**
17	**Cameron Beaubier**	USA	Kalex	7	4	5	-	-	-	13	9	-	2	-	-	3	2	5	5	-	9	9	-	**73**
18	**Jeremy Alcoba**	SPA	Kalex	2	2	0	10	10	4	3	0	0	0	2	2	6	6	-	-	-	10	7	8	**72**
19	**Sam Lowes**	GBR	Kalex	16	13	6	-	-	-	-	-	-	16	-	-	-	-	-	-	0	4	-	-	**55**
20	**Filip Salac**	CZE	Kalex	-	0	-	2	2	0	1	3	-	-	6	7	-	-	0	6	10	-	5	3	**45**
21	**Barry Baltus**	BEL	Kalex	-	-	-	6	7	2	-	0	0	-	1	0	4	3	3	2	2	-	-	-	**30**
22	**Lorenzo Dalla Porta**	ITA	Kalex	-	0	-	0	-	1	4	-	5	-	0	0	-	-	4	1	-	-	4	2	**21**
23	**Stefano Manzi**	ITA	Kalex	-	-	-	-	-	3	6	-	0	-	-	-	-	-	-	-	-	-	-	-	**9**
24	**Alessandro Zaccone**	ITA	Kalex	0	0	-	-	1	5	0	0	-	0	-	0	-	1	2	-	0	0	-	0	**9**
25	**Keminth Kubo**	THA	Kalex	0	-	0	-	4	-	-	0	-	-	0	0	-	-	-	0	3.5	-	0	0	**7.5**
26	**Senna Agius**	AUS	Kalex	-	-	-	-	-	-	-	-	-	-	-	-	0	-	0	-	-	-	-	7	**7**
27	**Romano Fenati**	ITA	Boscoscuro	1	0	0	1	5	-	-	-	-	-	-	-	-	-	-	-	-	-	-	-	**7**
28	**Gabriel Rodrigo**	ARG	Kalex	0	0	-	-	6	0	-	-	-	-	-	-	-	-	-	-	-	-	-	-	**6**
29	**Sean Dylan Kelly**	USA	Kalex	0	-	-	0	3	0	0	0	0	0	0	0	-	-	0	0	2.5	0	0	0	**5.5**
30	**Marcos Ramirez**	SPA	MV Agusta	0	0	1	4	-	-	-	-	0	-	0	-	0	0	0	0	0	0	0	0	**5**
31	**Borja Gomez**	SPA	Kalex	-	-	-	-	-	-	-	-	-	-	-	-	-	-	-	-	-	-	0	4	**4**
32	**Taiga Hada**	JPN	Kalex	-	-	-	-	-	-	-	-	-	-	-	-	0	0	-	0	1.5	1	1	0	**3.5**
33	**Mattia Pasini**	ITA	Kalex	-	-	-	-	-	-	-	1	-	-	-	-	-	-	-	-	-	-	-	-	**1**
34	**Zonta van den Goorbergh**	NED	Kalex	0	0	-	-	-	0	0	0	0	0	0	-	0	-	-	0	0	-	-	0	**0**
35	**Simone Corsi**	ITA	MV Agusta	0	-	0	-	-	0	0	-	0	-	0	0	0	-	0	-	0	-	-	-	**0**
36	**Niccolo Antonelli**	ITA	Kalex	0	0	-	-	-	0	-	0	0	-	-	0	0	-	0	-	0	-	0	-	**0**
37	**Alex Escrig**	SPA	MV Agusta	-	-	-	-	-	-	-	-	-	-	-	-	-	-	-	-	-	-	-	0	**0**
38	**Kasma Daniel**	MAL	Kalex	-	-	-	-	-	-	-	-	-	-	-	-	-	-	-	-	-	-	0	-	**0**
39	**Rory Skinner**	GBR	Kalex	-	-	-	-	-	-	-	-	-	-	-	0	0	-	-	-	-	-	-	-	**0**
40	**Alex Toledo**	SPA	Kalex	-	-	-	-	-	-	-	-	-	0	0	-	-	-	-	-	-	-	-	-	**0**
41	**Azroy Anuar**	MAL	Kalex	-	-	-	-	-	-	-	-	-	-	-	-	-	-	-	-	-	-	0	-	**0**
42	**Piotr Biesiekirski**	POL	Kalex	-	-	-	-	-	-	-	-	0	-	-	0	-	-	-	-	-	-	-	-	**0**
43	**David Sanchis**	SPA	MV Agusta	-	-	-	-	-	-	-	-	-	-	-	-	-	-	-	-	-	-	-	-	**0**

Photos: Gold & Goose

Moto3

Position	Rider	Nationality	Machine	Qatar	Indonesia	Argentina	United States	Portugal	Spain	France	Italy	Catalunya	Germany	Netherlands	Great Britain	Austria	San Marino	Aragon	Japan	Thailand	Australia	Malaysia	Valencia	Points total
1	**Izan Guevara**	SPA	GASGAS	8	20	-	9	11	25	16	20	25	25	20	-	9	16	25	25	11	25	4	25	**319**
2	**Sergio Garcia**	SPA	GASGAS	20	13	25	-	25	20	9	25	13	16	16	-	11	-	3	13	-	16	16	16	**257**
3	**Dennis Foggia**	ITA	Honda	9	25	20	20	8	0	13	-	-	20	-	25	4	25	2	20	25	7	10	13	**246**
4	**Ayumu Sasaki**	JPN	Husqvarna	-	-	16	13	16	10	20	-	-	13	25	-	25	-	20	16	20	13	20	11	**238**
5	**Deniz Oncu**	TUR	KTM	13	11	2	11	13	13	7	1	11	9	7	16	13	13	13	1	0	20	6	20	**200**
6	**Jaume Masia**	SPA	KTM	-	9	-	25	20	16	25	0	8	4	-	20	0	20	8	-	8	1	13	0	**177**
7	**Tatsuki Suzuki**	JPN	Honda	-	6	11	6	4	-	11	16	16	11	13	-	20	10	4	-	-	-	-	2	**130**
8	**Diogo Moreira**	BRA	KTM	10	-	10	-	6	6	2	-	-	0	0	10	10	9	1	10	10	9	11	8	**112**
9	**Andrea Migno**	ITA	Honda	25	-	-	16	9	2	6	13	-	5	1	7	0	-	0	7	9	0	2	1	**103**
10	**Daniel Holgado**	SPA	KTM	0	7	9	-	-	7	5	-	-	10	10	-	8	11	16	-	5	-	9	6	**103**
11	**John McPhee**	GBR	Husqvarna	11	-	-	-	-	-	4	-	9	0	-	9	7	7	6	9	-	10	25	5	**102**
12	**Ryusei Yamanaka**	JPN	KTM	7	5	4	0	0	8	8	11	0	-	8	8	3	3	-	8	6	-	8	7	**94**
13	**David Munoz**	SPA	KTM	-	-	-	-	-	-	-	5	20	7	-	-	16	4	9	11	7	5	-	9	**93**
14	**Riccardo Rossi**	ITA	Honda	4	0	13	7	5	-	3	10	5	-	5	2	0	5	0	6	16	6	-	-	**87**
15	**Carlos Tatay**	SPA	CFMOTO	-	16	8	8	10	-	10	0	10	-	2	6	-	-	7	-	3	4	-	3	**87**
16	**Xavier Artigas**	SPA	CFMOTO	6	10	-	10	0	11	-	0	6	3	11	5	2	0	5	5	2	2	5	0	**83**
17	**Ivan Ortola**	SPA	KTM	5	-	1	5	-	3	0	9	0	6	4	-	5	8	10	3	0	3	7	4	**73**
18	**Stefano Nepa**	ITA	KTM	3	-	0	3	1	1	0	-	0	1	9	11	1	6	0	4	13	11	-	-	**64**
19	**Kaito Toba**	JPN	KTM	16	4	7	-	0	9	1	0	1	0	6	13	6	0	0	0	-	0	0	0	**63**
20	**Adrian Fernandez**	SPA	KTM	2	-	3	2	-	-	0	6	7	8	-	1	0	0	11	0	-	0	1	10	**51**
21	**Joel Kelso**	AUS	KTM	1	0	6	0	7	-	-	4	4	-	-	-	0	2	0	-	4	8	0	0	**36**
22	**Elia Bartolini**	ITA	KTM	0	8	5	0	0	0	0	8	0	2	-	0	0	1	0	0	0	0	3	0	**27**
23	**Scott Ogden**	GBR	Honda	-	3	-	4	3	4	-	-	2	-	-	4	0	0	0	0	1	-	-	-	**21**
24	**Matteo Bertelle**	ITA	KTM	0	1	0	-	0	5	0	7	3	-	-	-	-	-	-	-	-	-	-	-	**16**
25	**Lorenzo Fellon**	FRA	Honda	-	0	0	1	2	-	0	2	0	0	3	3	0	0	-	-	0	0	0	0	**11**
26	**Mario Aji**	INA	Honda	0	2	0	0	0	0	0	3	-	0	0	0	0	-	0	0	0	-	0	0	**5**
27	**Taiyo Furusato**	JPN	Honda	-	-	0	0	0	0	0	0	-	0	0	0	0	0	0	2	0	-	-	-	**2**
28	**Syarifuddin Azman**	MAL	Honda	-	-	-	-	0	0	-	-	0	-	-	-	-	-	-	-	-	-	0	-	**0**
29	**Nicola Fabio Carraro**	ITA	KTM	-	-	-	-	-	-	-	-	-	-	-	0	0	-	-	-	0	0	0	0	**0**
30	**Alberto Surra**	ITA	Honda	-	-	0	-	-	-	-	-	-	0	0	0	0	0	-	-	-	0	-	0	**0**
31	**David Salvador**	SPA	Husqvarna/KTM	-	-	-	0	0	0	-	-	-	-	-	-	-	-	-	-	-	-	-	0	**0**
32	**Ana Carrasco**	SPA	KTM	0	0	-	0	0	0	0	0	0	0	0	0	0	0	0	0	0	0	0	0	**0**
33	**Filippo Farioli**	ITA	GASGAS	-	-	-	-	-	-	-	-	-	-	-	-	-	-	-	-	-	-	-	0	**0**
34	**Vicente Perez**	SPA	Honda	-	-	-	-	-	-	-	-	-	-	-	-	-	-	-	-	0	-	-	-	**0**
35	**Luca Lunetta**	ITA	KTM	-	-	-	-	-	-	-	-	-	-	0	-	-	-	-	-	-	-	-	-	**0**
36	**Joshua Whatley**	GBR	Honda	0	0	0	-	0	-	0	0	-	-	0	0	0	0	-	-	0	0	0	0	**0**
37	**Gerard Riu Male**	SPA	KTM	0	0	0	0	0	0	0	-	-	-	-	-	-	-	-	-	-	-	-	-	**0**
38	**Jose Antonio Rueda**	SPA	Honda	-	-	-	-	-	-	0	-	-	-	-	-	-	-	-	-	-	-	-	-	**0**
39	**Marc Garcia**	SPA	KTM	-	-	-	-	-	-	-	-	-	-	-	0	-	-	-	-	-	-	-	-	**0**
40	**Harrison Voight**	AUS	Honda	-	-	-	-	-	-	-	-	-	-	-	-	-	0	-	-	-	-	-	-	**0**
41	**David Almansa**	SPA	KTM	-	-	-	-	-	-	-	-	-	-	-	-	-	-	-	-	-	-	-	0	**0**
42	**Alessandro Morosi**	ITA	KTM	-	-	-	-	-	-	-	-	-	-	-	-	-	-	0	-	-	-	-	-	**0**
43	**Maria Herrera**	SPA	KTM	-	-	-	-	-	-	-	-	-	-	-	-	-	-	0	-	-	-	-	-	**0**
44	**David Alonso**	COL	GASGAS	-	-	-	-	0	-	-	-	-	-	-	-	-	-	-	-	-	-	-	-	**0**
45	**Marcos Uriarte**	SPA	Honda	-	-	-	-	-	-	-	-	-	-	-	-	-	-	-	-	-	-	-	-	**0**
46	**Kanta Hamada**	JPN	Honda	-	-	-	-	-	-	-	-	-	-	-	-	-	-	-	-	-	-	-	-	**0**

2022 MotoE WORLD CUP REVIEW

RE-ENERGISED AEGERTER POWERS UP

By OLLIE BARSTOW

Above: **Consistent strength brought redemption for Dominique Aegerter, after he had lost the Cup in 2021 on a penalty.**

Top right: **Eric Granado was the main challenger, claiming four wins from 12 races.**

Above right: **A first victory after four years – Mattia Casadei leads in France.**

Right: **Matteo Ferrari won at home in Misano, one of three in the season.**
Photos: Gold & Goose

MOTORCYCLE racing has come a long way in the 16 years since 2022 MotoE World Cup Champion Dominique Aegerter began his international career. From the fizz of his initial two-stroke 125GP machines to the whine of the advanced technology of his electric MotoE bike, much like the sport itself, his career has matured through eras of evolutionary progress.

Runner-up to Jordi Torres in MotoE in 2021 – due to a controversial finale, during which his provisional title win was overturned by a penalty – Aegerter went one better in 2022. The feat consolidated a prosperous 12 months, during which the Swiss rider also landed top prize in the 2021 WorldSSP Championship.

In its fourth year on the grand prix bill, MotoE established its status as a value-added, emissions-free spectacle, to complement the MotoGP headliners. Although a 'heretical' one-make, production-based formula, it had made steps towards shaking off its reputation as a poor relation, proving that you don't need fossil fuels and long races to produce exciting action.

This was the final season for the sturdy and reliable Energica Ego, a heavyweight machine that, while a touch compromised by its humble roadgoing origins, had helped MotoE to achieve competitive racing.

Season four was rolled out over an expanded six-round, 12-race schedule, with 18 riders across 11 teams. Torres headed the roll call, the amiable Spaniard eyeing a third consecutive riders' title. He was joined in the Pons Racing 40 outfit by Mattia Casadei, one of only a handful of riders to switch teams over the winter. Others were Eric Granado, who moved to LCR from One Energy Racing, and Kevin Zannoni, who went from LCR to take up Casadei's vacant seat at Ongetta SIC58.

Elsewhere, inaugural MotoE champion Matteo Ferrari remained with Felo Gresini alongside rookie Alessio Finello; Hikari Okubo entered into a second season with Ajo Motorsport; newcomer Marc Alcoba joined Maria Herrera at Aspar; and Miquel Pons stuck with LCR.

Tech3 E-Racing welcomed back Hector Garzo from Moto2, joined by teenage CEV European Superstock 600 champion Alex Escrig. WorldSBK podium finisher Xavi Fores and Kevin Manfredi debuted with Pramac, while Andorran racer Xavier Cardelus remained with Avintia.

Finally, RNF Racing put its faith in the experienced pairing of ex-MotoGP racers Niccolo Canepa and Bradley Smith – two founding members of MotoE's inaugural season returning for 2022, although injuries would be a blight on the latter's campaign.

Sunny Jerez raised the curtain with hallmark competitive, down-to-the-wire action, plus a few actual marks and

scratches, setting the tone for the year ahead. A fresh qualifying format ditched the 'one lap, one chance' E-Pole in favour of more engaging MotoGP-style Q1/Q2 sessions.

Both went the way of Granado, the Brazilian, one of only four riders to have competed in every MotoE race to date, kicking off his bid for a first title. After picking his way to the front of a pack chasing early leader Casadei, he pounced at the final turn prior to starting the last lap and succeeded in creating an Energica-sized gap to overtake. The closely-following Pons simply ploughed into the Italian in an attempt to follow through.

While the heavy thump sent Casadei to the asphalt and Garzo through the gravel trap, Granado remained clear to complete the final lap and take victory from Aegerter, the Swiss racer having benefited from the dramas ahead. Pons crossed the line third, but a long-lap-equivalent three-second penalty elevated Ferrari to the podium.

Granado completed the double with another late attack in the second race, rising from third to first on the final lap at the expense of Pons and Aegerter.

Pons had led going into the last lap, but Aegerter's lunge into Turn One simply sent him wide on the exit, inviting both his rival and closely-following Granado back through to track Pons on to the back straight before slipstreaming past. Pons settled for second; Casadei snatched third from Aegerter at the last turn, consigning him to one of only two finishes off the podium all season.

If round one was all about one MotoE veteran, Granado, then round two belonged to another. Casadei, who had contested every season so far, finally ended his long wait for a maiden victory at Le Mans. After seven podium finishes, his eighth took him to the top step after repelling the late advances of a determined Kevin Zannoni.

The Italian might have considered a more committed lunge into the final turn but for his maiden MotoE podium being on the line, so it was a cruel twist of fate when his caution resulted in him folding the front and crashing. His exit metres from the finish line promoted Aegerter to second, followed by Hikari Okubo, the Japanese rider notching up his first MotoE podium.

Granado could only manage seventh after losing time circumventing a midfield tangle that led to defending champion Torres falling in the pack at Turn Three, to be struck by both Canepa and Fores. The outcome was a broken fibula, the ensuing absence from Mugello all but nixing any aspirations of a third straight title.

Torres's injury was a painful contrast to his 2021 MotoE sparring partner, Aegerter, whose positive start to the season took a further step forward with victory in race two. That denied Casadei a double. The Pons rider had converted his pole position into a comfortable advantage initially, but a wily Aegerter hunted him down and pounced in the closing stages of the race.

RNF's Canepa prevailed in a tight fight with Zannoni for third, the experienced Italian beating his younger countryman to a first MotoE podium. Behind Zannoni, Granado ceded the points lead to Aegerter with his run to fifth, the Swiss rider opening an eight-point advantage.

The 2021 runner-up maintained the momentum during round three, the series' first visit to iconic Mugello, Aegerter inaugurating MotoE's Tuscan debut with a skilfully attained second victory of the season in race one.

With its famed 1.1km home straight, Mugello is considered a high-speed test of mettle for any rider. Aegerter's steely nerves on the brakes made the difference as he lunged from fourth to first into Turn One before escaping to the flag.

He was tailed home by Ferrari, while Granado inherited third when Andrea Mantovani was disqualified for a technical infringement. He had been standing in at RNF for Smith, who had been injured in a first-lap crash at the Le Mans 24-hour race.

Race two raised the tempo further as an eight-strong pack

shuffled the leading positions to the flag. Ferrari kept his cool for his first win of the year, ahead of a dead heat for second between Aegerter and Alcoba. With the latter demoted for a yellow-flag infringement, however, Aegerter took the spot, with Pons duly inheriting third. A similar penalty for Granado consigned him to eighth.

Three rounds down, and three to go. Aegerter's lead over Granado had grown to 29 points, while Ferrari's win had put him just one point adrift. Casadei and Pons completed the top five.

Aegerter pushed on during round four at Assen with a third win of the season. Taking the fight to Casadei as they entered the final lap, Aegerter had suffered an out-of-the-seat moment, which appeared to give his rival the upper hand, but the Swiss rider was back on his tail into the last turns. Sweeping around the outside at Ramshoek, he scurried up the inside into the final chicane, taming his bucking bike to head a blanket finish ahead of Granado and Casadei in third, the trio covered by just 0.081 of a second.

In race two, Granado returned to the top step after his third win of the season, giving his faltering title ambitions a timely boost. A fortuitous overtake for the lead on Casadei had put him in the right place at the right time when red flags appeared under rainy skies, although a half-points discount softened the impact to second-place finisher Aegerter, now with a 31.5-point advantage.

Aegerter was in 'match point' position going into the penultimate round at the Red Bull Ring, but Granado regained the initiative with a double victory. Again, fortune favoured the Brazilian when Casadei fell from the lead and out of race one at the penultimate bend. He went on to complete the double with an assured fifth win of the season, to take the title fight down to the wire.

Aegerter also gained from Casadei's blunder, inheriting second in race one. He was lucky just to get to the flag in race two, however, after lap-one contact almost knocked him off his bike. A gritty fight back, culminating in a last-corner pass for third, ensured an eighth straight podium. He had a 17.5-point lead heading to Misano.

That had been the scene of his title-dashing tangle with

Torres a year earlier, when he had arrived as the chaser. Now he was the target for Granado's long shot.

Aegerter needed only a modest brace of results to secure the crown, but in the end, it was all but decided three laps into the first race when Granado low-sided at Turn 14. Aegerter kept it neat to the flag, crossing the line second and clinching the title with one race to spare.

It was a redemptive outcome for both Aegerter and Dynavolt Intact GP following their finale *faux pas* of the previous year, when joy had turned to despair in just a few seconds. After a campaign built on sheer consistency, Aegerter's fourth place in race two kept his 100 per cent finishing record intact.

Granado sealed the runner-up spot for a career-best MotoE finish, while Ferrari and Casadei – the only other riders to top the podium in 2022 – added a victory each to their tallies in Misano to conclude their campaigns in third and fourth respectively.

Pons completed the overall top five, ahead of Okubo and Canepa, the trio emerging as the only other riders to pick up scraps of podium results outside a steadfast top quartet. Tech3 duo Garzo and Escrig ended the season eighth and ninth, the latter top rookie, while Zannoni rounded out the top ten.

The 2023 season begins a new era, when the Energica Ego is retired in favour of a grid of all-new dedicated electric racing bikes, developed and supplied by Ducati. New from the ground up, the leaner, more honed prototypes will be brought into line with MotoE's grand prix counterparts, thus earning the series official World Championship status for the first time, after spending four years as the MotoGP series' only World Cup.

Left: **Four podium finishes put Miquel Pons fifth overall.**

Below left: **Japanese rider Hikari Okubo was back for a second season with Ajo Motorsport.**

Far left: **Silent, but deadly – Aegerter (77) leads Matteo Ferrari, Niccolo Canepa (7), Eric Granado (51) and Kevin Zannone (21) in typically close action.**

Below: **Assen, and Ferrari leads Granado, eventual winner Aegerter, Casadei, Pons and Alcoba.**

Photos: Gold & Goose

ROOKIE RUEDA'S RESISTANCE

Yet another precociously talented Spaniard emerged from the Red Bull melting pot. PETER CLIFFORD followed a titanic teenaged struggle...

Above: Jose Rueda leads title rival Collin Veijer, Casey O'Gorman (67), Filippo Farioli (77) and the pack.

Top right: Max Quiles (27) took three wins and finished third overall.

Above right: Teenage titans – champion Rueda (_left_) was pushed all the way by Dutchman Collin Veijer, with three wins apiece.

Right: Veijer heads Rueda, Salmela, Piqueras, Lunetta (58) and Marcus Ruda (69).

Photos: Red Bull Content Pool/Gold & Goose

BREATHTAKING battles built another classic season, and Jose Rueda countered Collin Veijer's skill and determination with a calm, seasoned brilliance that denied his youth. The Spaniard had turned 17 a week before the final of the Red Bull MotoGP Rookies Cup, and he put in the perfect weekend to protect his points lead and take the Cup in his debut season.

Veijer leapt to prominence in his third season, the Dutch 17-year-old matching Rueda's three wins and pushing him all the way. Both fought a massed opposition in every race; it was never a private duel, and usually eight or ten KTMs swapped places up front.

Over the 14 races, wins went to Max Quiles (three), Angel Piqueras (two), Tatchakorn Buasri, Rico Salmela and Luca Lunetta (one each). Others, like Filippo Farioli, Harrison Voight and Casey O'Gorman, were always challenging, but just missed the top step.

It had started in April, when the Portimao pre-season test had been exactly that, very testing, with enough wind and rain to prepare the Rookies for anything the year was likely to throw at them. There was also sufficient dry running that riders and machinery were well in tune for the first event of the season, at the same venue nine days later.

The weather continued wet through Friday, and two first-year Rookies were quickest. Piqueras took pole by almost a second over fellow Spaniard Quiles. Fifteen-year-old Australian Voight completed the front row.

The new guys were already up to speed, and race one was further proof. Rueda had qualified only 13th, but he rode a brilliant debut race to claim victory. The 16-year-old Spaniard seized an early lead; compatriot Piqueras was on his tail by the penultimate lap, but when he forced his RC250 R into a sudden change of direction, it snapped sideways and he was off. Rueda was left with a nine-second advantage over O'Gorman and Veijer. Voight, Buasri and Gabin Planques followed on after a thrilling race-long battle with multiple place changes at every turn.

In race two, 17-year-old Veijer won from 12th on the grid. Rueda had crossed the line first, but had exceeded track limits at the final turn and therefore was docked a place. Irishman O'Gorman (14) added another podium with third, missing the win by 0.004 of a second.

The battle for the lead left Voight a little frustrated with another fourth place; Rico Salmela, the diminutive 14-year-old Finn, delivered a storming ride to claim fifth ahead of Buasri, the 21-year-old Thai who had done a good bit of the leading.

Veijer hadn't seen Rueda stray on to the green, and "out of the last corner, Casey passed me a little bit, and then I got Jose's slipstream and got back ahead of him. I didn't know I'd won, but I could see that the big screen was showing me riding around, and I wondered," he laughed.

To Jerez for round two, and it was clear that everyone was likely to be chasing Seville local Rueda, who added pole position to his points lead. He had only a small pace advantage over Farioli, just 0.054 of a second slower, but the 17-year-old Italian was penalised three grid places for speeding in the pit lane. In the middle of the front row instead was fellow Italian Lunetta (16), with Voight alongside.

It was another intense contest, and a very impressive ride from Rueda, who had to battle for every millimetre. He took victory by just 0.018 of a second over Piqueras. Veijer was a close third.

Having won the first three races, Rueda was on a roll, but there was nothing easy about race four, one of the truly great Rookies Cup battles. It was won by Quiles, who had no

idea how he had finished in front. The Spaniard had jumped out of the 12-rider lead pack with a couple of laps to go, put in two sensational tours and led Lunetta across the line in a photo finish.

Veijer was third across the stripe, but was demoted a position, giving Rueda third and reversing the last-lap drama in Portugal. Rueda's points advantage stretched to 16 over Veijer, with O'Gorman a further 12 behind.

Quiles could not explain his victory: "I was at the back of the group because I wasn't feeling good on the bike. Then, in the last two laps, I don't know what happened. I went crazy and I overtook in one lap nine of them."

The Italian GP round was next, at fabulous Mugello – a great challenge and the perfect place for local heroes. Farioli slapped down the gauntlet with a sensational final two laps to take pole, ahead of Spaniard Piqueras and fellow Italian Lunetta, who had been circulating alone without the benefit of any slipstream.

It was all set for a perfect action Saturday... and then it rained. The wet and treacherous circuit produced a race of attrition. Just finishing was an achievement. Quiles showed himself the master of the most challenging situation to take a superb win, keeping his head while those around, and mostly in front of him, were losing theirs. Second was Buasri, with Salmela holding off Piqueras for third. O'Gorman and 16-year-old New Zealander Cormac Buchanan had both led, but fell dramatically.

Sunday was sunny, for a great race. On the last lap, on the run to the flag, Veijer flicked out of the slipstream of Farioli's KTM, willing his identical RC250 R alongside and ahead as the pair led a pack of 13 rookies across the Mugello finish line, covered by just two seconds – a masterly performance. Third went to Buasri by just a thousandth of a second over 15-year-old Briton Eddie O'Shea.

Rueda had finished 11th and sixth in Italy, and now headed the Cup table by just five points going north for his first visit to the Sachsenring. But if his confidence was shaken, he didn't show it, claiming pole from Farioli. O'Shea completed the front row; Veijer was 11th.

Above: Thailand's Tatchakorn Buasri took a first win in Austria.

Top: Diminutive 14-year-old Finn Rico Salmela (27) prevailed in a blanket finish at Aragon.

Above right: Quiles celebrates victory at Misano.

Above far right: Identikit racers await the fray at Misano.

Right: Angel Piqueras (18), leading Soma Gorbe, took two wins to finish fourth, just five points behind Quiles.

Below right: Italian rider Luca Lunetti closed his season with a win in Valencia.

Photos: Red Bull Content Pool/Gold & Goose

Rueda carried his confidence into race one, leaving the chasing pack well behind. The thrills came ten seconds adrift, with a swarming 15-rider battle, eventually won by Australian Voight over Lunetta.

It is useless to predict anything in the Rookies Cup, and Rueda's dominance did not carry through to Sunday. A race-long battle came down to the most incredible final two corners and a mass finish, with victory for Piqueras over Veijer and Farioli. Just six-tenths covered the first seven over the finish line. Rueda, Salmela, Quiles and Voight might equally well have been on the podium.

Victory was particularly sweet for Piqueras, as the 15-year-old had slid off early in race one.

Veijer was sensational, passing Rueda, who had defended a narrow advantage right from the first lap, into Turn One on the final lap. That set up a fabulous finale, with Veijer being passed on the run down to the final two corners, and Farioli making the most audacious overtake into the penultimate left-hander.

With the season reaching its second half, it was time for Spielberg in Styria, in the south of Austria, and the dauntingly fast Red Bull Ring.

Piqueras claimed pole ahead of fellow Spaniard Quiles, Buasri completing the front row. Points leader Rueda was down in tenth, but he said he was not troubled. Arch rival Veijer was fourth fastest and ready to fight for the win.

Track first-timer Piqueras was full of confidence, and true to his word, he took the win, but he had to fight for every centimetre and was swallowed up several times by the pack of more that ten riders, often four abreast into every turn. The race was decided on the run to the line. Buasri ran wide and Piqueras stole the drive. Points leader Rueda flashed across the line third, but Buasri had exceeded track limits at that final corner and thus was demoted a place.

Fourth went to Veijer, who had taken the lead with four laps to go, only to be passed in the final laps.

Race two was every bit as exciting. Buasri rode another brilliant 17 laps, and this time the Thai took his first victory, as Quiles had clipped the green with the wheels of his KTM on the exit to the last corner and was dropped a place. Saturday winner Piqueras was third, narrowly getting the better of Rueda; Veijer took fifth after a late-race battle with 17-year-old Spaniard Marcos Ruda.

With four races remaining, there were still nine riders with a mathematical chance of winning the Cup. But the favourites were certainly Rueda and Veijer. Nineteen points separated them, with Piqueras a further 36 behind.

Rueda stamped his authority on Motorland Aragon qualifying by six-tenths and started the weekend as favourite. Lunetta and Farioli completed the front row for Italy; arch rival Veijer took the middle of row two, just behind Voight and ahead of Buchanan.

Every racing thrill imaginable was packed into 15 laps of race one, with the top four split by six-hundredths of a second at the finish.

Rueda led Quiles towards the line, but both were passed in the final metres by Salmela for the Finn's first win. Veijer was fourth; a single second covered the first nine.

Sunday was as thrilling, and lanky Dutchman Veijer crawled under the paintwork of his KTM, just managing to better Spaniards Quiles and Piqueras through the final corner. Although Piqueras arrived ahead, he was dropped one place for exceeding track limits on the final lap, gifting second to Quiles.

It had been an even closer finish, half a second covering the top nine, three seconds the top 13. Saturday winner Salmela slid off unhurt on the final lap, and Veijer was tied with Rueda on three wins for the season. Each had only been outside the top six once.

Crucially, points leader Rueda had finished sixth, just 0.183 of a second behind Veijer. That narrow margin represented 15 points, leaving Rueda just 11 ahead going into the final round, seven weeks later in Valencia.

With the days shortening and time running out, the Cup would be decided over the last two races.

Piqueras, O'Gorman and Quiles lined up on the front row for race one. Crucially, Rueda and Veijer sat on row two, joined by Lunetta.

The race was an intense struggle from first lap to last, with the front row swapping the lead between them, just

ahead of Veijer and Rueda. Lunetta was in the closely following pack, along with Salmela and Ruda as the first eight pulled away. Only in the closing stages did Lunetta challenge for the lead, but he made it stick and was brilliant at the final corner where the race was decided.

"I've wanted this win for a long time," beamed Lunetta, in his third year in the Cup.

Spaniards Piqueras and Quiles joined the Italian on the podium, while Rueda extended his advantage to 15 by finishing fourth to Veijer's seventh.

Rueda had the Cup to lose in the final. He needed only to shadow Veijer, and he did that even more effectively than he had done in race one. The pair ran in the lead pack, and the Spaniard made sure of the title.

At the front of that group, the racing was far less controlled. It came down to Quiles putting in a perfect final lap of the season to claim victory over arch rival Piqueras, with Saturday winner Lunetta third.

It was an eight-man battle all the way, but seventh was sufficient for Rueda to secure the championship, with Veijer just ahead, but 14 points behind, after a struggle throughout the 14-race season.

Irishman O'Gorman had slid off while battling for the lead with seven laps to go.

Rueda had stuck to his plan for the final two races: "I had the points lead and a strategy this weekend, and it worked. I knew that as long as I ran behind Collin, I would take it. Especially today, it made sense just to follow that.

"It's been an incredible year and result for my family, and all those who support me. It is very special to be the first rider to win the Junior World Championship and the Rookies Cup. I could not wish for a better season," he concluded. While not the most loquacious of teenagers, he was always ready with a beaming smile and content to express himself on track.

He would head to the Moto3 World Championship, chasing the success of other Cup graduates. During 2022, ex-Rookies passed the 150th GP win marker, and by the end of the year, Moto3 rookie Izan Guevara had scored the tenth world championship for a former Red Bull Rookie.

WORLD SUPERBIKE CHAMPIONSHIP

NEW FOR OLD IN '22

By GORDON RITCHIE

THE Superbike World Championship almost threw off the last vestiges of Covid in 2022, but the threat of the virus was still there. The new normal was pretty much like many previous normals, but with added spice in the bantamweight form of Alvaro Bautista. His big talent was back on the most monstrous device in the paddock – Gigi Dall'Igna's road-legal fire-breathing V4R dragon.

To say that the early WorldSBK rounds were like watching a three-way mobile cage-fighting tournament viewed at triple fast-forward speeds is not quite hyperbolic enough.

In 2021, we had had two true championship contenders, from two manufacturers. In 2022, we had three riders who were helmet and shoulders above the rest, representing three competitive manufacturers. Thanks to the 'super-concession' rules that had been long discussed, and which suddenly appeared before the season's end, Honda and BMW might play catch-up sooner rather than later in 2023, as they have talented riders and good teams, too.

In the end, there was only one champion, as there always is. He was the one with the slightest physical stature, but who stood over the final six rounds like a colossus.

After the first six race weekends, it could have been anybody's year from among the top trio, despite the Ducati's evident speed and acceleration. After the summer break, however, all roads led to Bologna.

It took a lot to beat Rea and Kawasaki, and Razgatlioglu and Yamaha. In the end, it took the biggest power output allied to the lightest rider, with the widest experience, on the highest-revving bike with the lowest number of crashes and technical issues during races.

Many of the tracks with big straight sections – Magny-Cours, Barcelona, Portimao, Villicum – were on the calendar after the summer break, skewing the results just when the ideal championship scenario would have been a closing of the gap between the big three as we neared the final round, not an expansion of it.

The fight for the WorldSBK championship in 2022 was actual-

Ready for the off. Far-flung territories, including Argentina, were welcomed back to the WorldSBK calendar.
Photo: Gold & Goose

ly much closer than Bautista's eventual taming of his rivals one round early would have led us to believe. There were needless no-scores or low scores by his rivals, through set-up imperfections, tech failures or simple over-exuberance.

It was always going to be tight out front, and the championship would have definitely gone to the final round had it not been for all the points left behind by the clash at Assen between Rea and Razgatlioglu, the latter's tech fail in Misano, Rea's race-one fall in Magny-Cours and a similar issue for Razgatlioglu while leading that same race, and, to cap it all, Toprak committing that uncharacteristic and simply bizarre first-lap error in Argentina.

Compared to Bautista's single self-caused DNF (Donington) and another that was not his fault (Magny-Cours), any and all of those relatively few errors from his rivals amounted to profligacy.

In the WorldSSP championship, the tech revolution to take the championship back to the streets worked out almost perfectly, with the next-generation bikes all taking their chance to shine. Two out of the three 'rookie' bikes won races, even against well-sorted and race-focused Yamaha R6 four-cylinders and the still win-capable Kawasaki.

In 2022, WorldSSP300 also returned to sanity, with half the number of entrants, no two-stage qualifying heats and soon also age limits. That did not prevent the loss of Victor Steeman to an accident that could have happened to any rider in any class, but the loss of a young life again, after Dean Berta Vinales's passing in 2021, shook the whole scene to the core.

But life can and does go on in a world that accepts risk as a workplace reality in every on-track session.

On balance, it was a year when people fell in love with World-SBK once again, even if the production-derived championship still thrives one level down in the hierarchy of two-wheeled motorsport, peeking out from shadow of the more exotic MotoGP.

The immediate future, after what will be a very short winter break, appears to promise even closer competition in 2023, especially if there is any massaging of the balancing rules in the meantime. But they'd better be quick.

Photo: Gold & Goose

CHAMPION PROFILE: ALVARO BAUTISTA

THE PRODIGAL SON...

By GORDON RITCHIE

EVEN midway through the season, any one of three experienced WorldSBK riders was in realistic contention to carve his name into the riders' championship trophy. It was a season of two halves for Alvaro Bautista, just like 2019, and also not at all like 2019. This time, he won it, and in almost flawless fashion.

Back in his first Ducati WorldSBK season, he also had the smallest build and fewest kilos to haul around. Plus the highest-revving and most specialised race-replica road bike imaginable. In the minus column, almost no experience of his new class, Pirelli tyres, half the WorldSBK circuits and Ducati's sometimes 'unique' factory rider motivational approaches.

In the end, 2019 became nightmarish for Bautista, Ducati and Aruba – the last being much more than the team's title sponsor. It became so bad that even before season's end, he had taken HRC's offer of a lead role in their new Fireblade WorldSBK project, which some thought would be immediately competitive and others said would be no good. No good for a serious World Championship attempt anyway.

The latter thinking was correct. Honda struggled for two full seasons with the impact of Covid and a bike probably developed more to run on Bridgestone tyres in the Suzuka 8 Hours than on Pirellis in WorldSBK.

Why are we speaking about two semi-disastrous Honda seasons for Bautista rather than the most recent glory-laden one with Ducati? Because the man himself cites those two campaigns, of riding on the edge of crashes and straying into gravel traps with little warning, as much more of a motivation to succeed in 2022 than the scarring second half of the 2019 Ducati season.

In the end, Honda admitted unwillingly that the otherwise fabulously engineered CBR100RR-R SP, no matter how conventionally UJM (Universal Japanese Motorcycle) it was in its outward design, needed help in WorldSBK. They did this by pushing for what would be called 'super-concessions'. By then, however, Bautista, Ducati and Aruba had mended their once burned bridges and had almost got the job done that they all really needed to do. Maybe by just letting him and his pit crew get on with on with it, weekend by weekend.

At Mandalika, it was as though everybody in Ducati's bright red uniforms had held their breath all year and finally could breathe freely again.

Bautista was simply revelling in a package that allowed him to compete at even the previous 'bad' tracks. He could, of course, overtake at will using his bike's main asset: that V4 engine, a rev-monster with some MotoGP shapes thrown into the design.

It says a lot about the prowess of Toprak Razgatlioglu and Jonathan Rea that they were able to compete as well as they did for as long as they did, but in the end, Bautista became champ with a round to spare.

He was Ducati's missing prodigal link after all.

The intense debates about relative competitiveness of a tiny rider and that big red rocket-ship raged – sometimes literally – all year. But he made so few mistakes, and his bike proved sufficiently capable of winning even on the twisty circuits.

Cold analysis says that Bautista's rivals, both flesh and metal, left far too many points in the pit garage, in the hay bales or on the recovery truck to apply the kind of pressure that partly had been his undoing in 2019.

It's easy to forget that Bautista was already an FIM world champion, in the 125cc class way back in 2006, but he is the first modern-day WorldSBK champion who can fairly be described as a fully-fledged MotoGP product since Sylvain Guintoli in 2014.

He is the first Spaniard and first Ducati rider to win the championship since Carlos Checa in 2011. Yes, 2011.

How did we go so long without a Ducati WorldSBK champion in the upstart series that had rebirthed Ducati as a great dominant racing marque all those decades ago?

There are lots of reasons, but let's not forget the fact that only Bautista was able get this level of consistent performance from the V4R. If it had been just about that aspect of relative machine performance, he would have been fighting with Michael Ruben Rinaldi, not Razgatlioglu and Rea.

In the 2022 season, all associated with Ducati could stand tall again because the biggest prizes of all went to the original WorldSBK reds and Alvaro Bautista, a deserving champion in his 37th year.

He might be small in stature, but he's a Superbike giant now.

2022 TEAMS & RIDERS

By GORDON RITCHIE

BMW

BMW Motorrad WorldSBK Team

British rider **Scott Redding (29)** lined up alongside Dutchman **Michael van der Mark** (28) in the official BMW team.

Shaun Muir led the UK-based SMR staff and logistics; Marc Bongers was in control of the factory BMW Motorrad side once more.

With van der Mark often out through injury, **Illia Mykhalchyk** (26) rode at Aragon, Misano and Donington, and **Peter Hickman** (35) at Most.

Bonovo Action BMW

Eugene Laverty (36) had his final WorldSBK season before moving into a future-proofing managerial role with the same team in 2023. A challenging final year offered some personal highlights, like best Independent rider in Argentina.

Loris Baz (29) was welcomed back to WorldSBK as a full-timer after a year in MotoAmerica and a few high-profile Ducati rides as a replacement for the injured Chaz Davies.

Bonovo was effectively a fully supported Independent team. Only Yamaha rivalled the close relationship that existed between this main satellite team and the full factory effort.

B-MAX Racing Team

The M1000RR-equipped team ran CIV rider **Gabriele Ruiu** (21) at his home round at Misano.

Rohac & Fejta Motoracing BMW

Michal Prasek (31) raced at home in Most, adding some local interest.

FHO Racing BMW

Peter Hickman (35) rode at Donington for his own team, between his BSB and TT commitments, giving the locals another point of nationalistic focus.

DUCATI

Aruba.it Racing – Ducati World Superbike Team

Michael Ruben Rinaldi (26) had a new team-mate in **Alvaro Bautista** (36) in the official Ducati factory effort, managed by Serafino Foti.

Aruba was more like a management partner than a major sponsor, with the involvement of owner Stefano Cecconi.

Marco Zambenedetti was again technical controller for the overall Ducati effort, pulling the tech strings from inside Ducati Corse.

Bautista's prodigal return was a gamble for all, one that had seemed impossible after they had fallen out so publicly when he left to join Honda in 2020. Once large helpings of humble pie had been eaten by all, communal glory followed as a just dessert.

Barni Spark Racing Team Ducati

Sanmarinese rider **Luca Bernardi** (21) moved up to WorldSBK in 2022, but was out of the team from Villicum onwards, his place taken by former Barni privateer podium runner **Xavi Fores** (37).

Team GO Eleven Ducati

Philipp Oettl (26) made a more than respectable privateer entry after two years on a Kawasaki WorldSSP bike. He was replaced – literally overnight – by super-sub Xavi Fores at Estoril after the German rider suffered an early injury.

MotoCorsa Racing Ducati

Axel Bassani (23) came back for seconds and secured some strong results again. He did not quite get the factory Ducati ride for 2023, but he remains a talented and fearless rider, and headed the Independent riders' rankings on merit. He would ride for the same team again in 2023.

HONDA

Team HRC Honda

Season three for the direct HRC factory effort was a year of evolution and revolution. **Iker Lecuona** (22) and fellow long-time MotoGP paddock companion **Xavi Vierge** (25) brought a fresh perspective, but the same up-and-down results as their predecessors.

Based in Barcelona, the team had direct support from Japan in all things, and thus was a true factory team.

Honda test rider **Tetsuta Nagashima** (30) subbed for the injured Lecuona at the final round, in impressive fashion.

MIE Racing Honda Team

Leandro Mercado (30) was not on as competitive a Honda and found it all very difficult, no matter what he tried.

Malaysian **Hafizh Syaharin** (28) was a new WorldSBK face, another from the MotoGP paddock, but he found it tough on the second-string privateer Honda. He was replaced at Villicum by Chilean rider **Maximilian Scheib** (27), due to Covid-19.

KAWASAKI

Kawasaki Racing Team

Six-times champion **Jonathan Rea** (35) pushed as hard as he could to stay in contention for the championship, but with a bike that was both venerable and restricted below its true performance capabilities, it appeared to be the hard work the results suggested. Although still one of the true big three riders, he found that a fully fit **Alex Lowes** (32) had even improved enough to challenge him at times.

Once again, Guim Roda was team manager of the Provec Racing side of the overall KRT effort.

Kawasaki Puccetti Racing

Lucas Mahias (33) came back for a second WorldSSP year, but it was a frustrating season on a bike that had had its teeth drawn in privateer mode some time before, because of too much factory-team success.

Former MotoGP rider and Barni Ducati rider **Tito Rabat** (33) joined for the Misano round while Mahias was injured, in a season marked by occasional falls and brighter patches from the French rider.

TPR Team Pedercini Racing Kawasaki

Supposed full-season rider **Loris Cresson** (23) lasted one round before being replaced at Assen (and subsequently Donington and Portimao) by veteran **Leon Haslam** (39). **Alessandro Delbianco** (25), **Isaac Vinales** (29), **Marco Solorza** (34), **Ryan Vickers** (23), **Oscar Guitierrez** (23) and finally proven WorldSSP talent **Kyle Smith** (31) all took part in another season-long game of swaps and survival for WorldSBK fixture Lucio Pedercini's squad.

Orelac Racing VerdNatura Kawasaki

Oliver Konig (20) was a curve ball as a lone rider with a privateer team, but he stuck to his task and appeared to be enjoying every minute of an intense experience.

YAMAHA

Pata Yamaha With Brixx WorldSBK Team

After becoming champion in 2021, **Toprak Razgatlioglu** (26) came out of his shell and started to revel in being the focus of attention, while keeping his genuine nice-guy character intact. Too often outgunned by Bautista and Ducati, he also won some races that perhaps he had no right to, in his own exuberant hard-braking fashion.

Andrea Locatelli (26) came back for a second time, riding the only other true factory bike in an almost subdued, but effective manner.

Andrea Dosoli was responsible for the Yamaha techical and strategy side from HQ in Italy; Paul Denning's UK-based Crescent Racing took care of bike preparation and logistics.

GRT Yamaha WorldSBK

Garrett Gerloff (27) had a final season riding for Yamaha's *de facto* second team, and was one of the few in the class beyond the 'Big Three' to reach podium standard. Although a strong rider, he was too inconsistent, and a change of team for 2023 could do him a power of good.

Kohta Nozane (27) had another lacklustre year, despite his radical riding style.

GIL Motorsport Yamaha Racing

Christophe Ponsson (26) had another season, and a tough one at that, with his privateer Yamaha team.

IXS-YART

Marvin Fritz (29) raced for his own (usually Endurance World Championship) team at Portimao, and as a substitute rider with Yamaha Motoxracing WSBK Team at Estoril.

Yamaha Motoxracing WorldSBK Team

A former top Superstock rider from the past, **Roberto Tamburini** (31) was almost a European constant for the new WorldSBK Yamaha team, except for Estoril, where Marvin Fritz took over the ride.

McAMS Yamaha

Injury meant that 2021 BSB champion **Tarran Mackenzie** (27) only enjoyed one wild-card ride, having an up-and-down weekend at this level in his first fully fit weekend for months after suffering an early-season ankle injury.

Attack Performance Yamaha Racing

Jake Gagne (29) won the MotoAmerica title, and shortly afterwards, he and his very own team flew to Portimao for a one-off wild-card race with their own bike, boosted by help from Yamaha.

Jonathan Rea

Alvaro Bautista

Toprak Razgatlioglu

Andrea Locatelli

Alex Lowes

Michael Ruben Rinaldi

Scott Redding

Axel Bassani

Iker Lecuona

Xavi Vierge

Garrett Gerloff

Philipp Oettl

Lucas Mahias

Loris Baz

Michael van der Mark

Xavi Fores

Roberto Tamburini

Eugene Laverty

THE SUPERBIKES OF 2022 by Gordon Ritchie

DUCATI PANIGALE V4R

DUCATI PANIGALE V4R

BACK for a fourth full WorldSBK season, the only V4 featured a lightly uprated engine and slightly changed gearbox ratios. Head porting and minor exhaust modification gave more power, but in particular, the goal during the off-season was to maintain similar top power to previous iterations while providing better driveablilty for the riders. The rest of the engine was basically the same as in 2021, primarily because the technical regulations demand so many stock parts.

Ducati tested a new swing-arm in the winter, and it was ready for the start of the season. This was the most important and visible change on the chassis side.

Going from a taller lead rider to a shorter one required some ergonomic changes, which led to a redesign of the fuel tank. At the beginning of each race, with a full fuel load, the 2022 bike had a lower centre of gravity than the previous version. The complicated new alloy tank allowed riders to move around more easily on the bike, to tuck themselves in more closely on the straights and to be better balanced through the longer turns. All sizes of rider felt an improvement from the new ergonomics package.

ECU strategies were constantly in development, and because of the freedom in WorldSBK compared to the locked-in control software of MotoGP, Ducati could use the series to develop software and transfer it to roadgoing machines.

Ducati denied that having a very small and light lead rider was an advantage across the board, and they encountered challenges during the winter when trying to get the bike to work in the twisties with Bautista, rather than a rider like Redding, for example. Conversely, it made things simpler for overall development, as Rinaldi is also at the smaller end of the rider scale.

Ducati had done a lot of work with technical partners Brembo on their braking systems, with the 2022 caliper performance the best so far. Work was still needed on discs, however. Ducati concentrates more on optimising the calibration between master and slave cylinders, rather than worrying about the newest materials, as this is what gives the rider the best feel.

They also had a close working relationship with Öhlins, running the Swedish company's 46mm RVP25/30 front forks and RSP50 rear shock.

The Marelli MLE ECU had a limited number of inputs by regulation, but Ducati used 100 per cent of the ECU's potential and processing power.

With a radical 81 x 48.5mm bore and stroke, the 90-degree V4 breathes through elliptical throttle bodies, equivalent to a 54mm diameter. Ride-by-wire signals from the ECU determine the final opening of the butterfly valves.

The V4R breathes out via an Akrapovic 4-into-2, all-titanium exhaust.

The bike has a claimed peak power at 235bhp at more than 16,000 rpm. It could rev even higher, but the balancing rules do not allow it.

BMW M1000RR

IN its second year, the M1000RR fielded the same 80 x 49.7mm bore-and-stroke engine as before, but with more work completed on the cylinder head over the winter. Porting and camshaft changes were the main update allowed in the concession rules between 2021 and 2022, creating the new engine spec. A broader torque range and more top-end power were claimed.

The camshafts were splined along their length to allow the use of BMW's shift-cam technology. A higher-lift cam lobe is used at high rpm, when a solenoid moves the camshaft outers sideways on their splines to engage the more radical cam lobe on the next engine rotation. Broader torque is always a benefit for riders with such an over-square engine, but the BMW was still one of the more peaky units in the WorldSBK paddock.

The Akrapovic exhaust was modified for this latest engine upgrade and stayed in place all season.

Externally, the bodywork was the same, in what had always been a silhouette class in this regard, but there was a change in design for the fuel tank and subframe to lower the centre of gravity, as well as the seat. This was partly due to having riders as tall as Redding and Baz. Even Laverty's bike featured these mods, with seat foam changes to suit his shorter frame.

There were several changes in the chassis package, with even a late-season modification for one of the engine hangers, to promote chassis flex. This previously outlawed move was permitted by the early introduction of the super-concession rules, due to come into effect formally in 2023.

Before that, changes in the chassis and swing-arm, offering greater stiffness in certain areas, were introduced early in the year. The swing-arm was completely new, from Kalex.

BMW used PVM wheels, the new 2022 designs being intended to maximise the relationship between weight and stiffness, to create more feel. Öhlins provided suspension, with an RVP50 rear shock and the longest option of RVP25/34 front forks.

The Nissin brakes underwent several upgrades throughout the season. BMW went from six-pot calipers to four-pot, depending on rider preference, but also there were technical improvements to the materials. Barcelona, and other tracks with seriously heavy braking sections, required the use of the thicker and larger-diameter discs.

Braking was a hot topic in 2022, with limits on prices of components and steel brakes in general resulting in them operating on the edge of current permitted technology. Ever increasing machine performance means greater heat build-up in the braking phase, and BMW had an entire range of caliper-cooling ducts for different circuits.

BMW staunchly defended the relatively free electronics in WorldSBK, and their Bosch-based in-house system in particular. This was under continuous development to control the claimed 230bhp engine output at "more than 14,000 rpm".

HONDA CBR1000RR-R SP

THE Fireblade, in its latest overall design, had featured some big facts and figures since it first arrived in WorldSBK trim in 2020, looking to lean heavily on HRC's decades-long MotoGP tech experience. The 54mm-diameter throttle bodies were very close to the cylinder head, and the engine had an 81mm bore.

BMW M1000RR

YAMAHA YZF-R1

KAWASAKI NINJA ZX-10RR

HONDA CBR1000RR-RS-P

The Akrapovic 'stubby' exhaust design was new and came in two stages, one at the beginning of the season, the other at its mid-point.

It was always one of the fastest bikes, thanks to a relatively low-inertia engine, but the chassis needed most work to provide the two rookie riders with enough feedback on the limit to ride with confidence, yet still allow the bike to turn quickly. Electronics were particularly important in controlling corner entry.

The Honda's continued inability to perform consistently on Pirelli tyres (after being largely developed on Bridgestones for the Suzuka 8 Hours, it appears), together with perhaps some initial chassis geometry imperfections in the original homologation, eventually led to an early adoption of the super-concessions rule, starting at Portimao.

From then on, the permitted range of adjustments in the headstock and rear swing-arm pivot point were extended beyond the previous limits. The final cure for the current homologation was to machine the chassis to move the headstock position (not the headstock angle, the entire position of the headstock) further forward. More machining also dropped the rear swing-arm pivot point, and both improvements were made in time for the penultimate round in Mandalika.

At the beginning of the year, HRC made the surprise decision to change not only their brake suppliers, but also their suspension suppliers.

They went from Brembo to Nissin brake calipers and attendant Yutaka discs, trying several possibilities and combinations before the start of the year. Once the best caliper body had been chosen, it remained in place for the season.

The suspension change for 2022 was a big call, rekindling an old HRC partnership with Showa. They had been – almost – *de facto* KRT suppliers until 2022, so the adoption by Honda made things more even in the endless Showa vs Öhlins tech struggle in WorldSBK.

The Hondas ran on OZ wheels, new for 2022.

Honda also played with fork top-yoke development, but in general, both riders followed the same basic vector with chassis development. There was also a new swing-arm, and a rear linkage set-up.

The Barcelona-based team probably had the least to do in respect of development, with new parts coming from Japan only after they had been thoroughly tested.

KAWASAKI NINJA ZX-10RR

KAWASAKI'S relatively long-stroke, 76 x 55mm engine could produce more power and revs than the balancing rev limits allowed, but in the hands of the right rider, it was still a race-winning package. The big old engine was still limited to a ceiling of 14,600rpm by regulation.

The big Ninja was a multiple championship-winning base package, but regulatory help might be needed in the near future to keep it that way.

Akira, the French engine tuning company, was a key partner for Kawasaki's relatively small race department. Estimates are that Akira did around 80 per cent of the engine development, and Kawasaki the rest. The Akrapovic exhaust system was the same as that used in 2021.

The days of factories making a major new model for the street are long gone, of course, but the impending Euro 6 emission regulations might be just the excuse Kawasaki needs to truly re-homologate their engine, to stay in straight-line contention from 2024.

A modified rear swing-arm and other chassis changes were made to allow for the latest generation of more grippy rear tyres. Having struggled with rear grip in higher track temperatures, Kawasaki concentrated on hot-weather tests throughout the season.

There were some occasional braking gremlins, for Rea in particular, but in terms of suspension, there were real improvements to the internals of the Showa front forks. That was of the most profound benefit in braking. Kawasaki knew that they had to find something to take on Razgatlioglu, one of the all-time great brakers. In the first half of the season, Rea noticed that on occasions he could win the braking battles – he had had no chance in 2021.

In terms of the chassis, there was more focus on the rear of the ZX-10RR in the second half of the year, and some strengthening of the swing-arm to help during corner entry phases.

The latest version of 2021's Marchesini wheels, and now OZ wheels, was adopted.

Kawasaki was yet another manufacturer running the almost ubiquitous Marelli MRE ECU unit. It's possible that they suffered by not having the same overall breadth of electronics experience as those manufacturers who still compete in MotoGP, even though the rules are more liberal in WorldSBK.

YAMAHA YZF-R1

UNCHANGED in homologation from 2021, that season's championship-winning YZF-R1 was improved in three main areas. One of these was the performance of the 79mm-bore engine – an attempt to rectify a top-speed disadvantage. Yamaha would not provide any details of how this increase in power had been achieved, but it came with a revised design of Akrapovic exhaust. Although it worked, since everyone else had made their own genuine improvements, it could be seen as a kind of pyrrhic victory.

Another area was an improved level of mechanical traction out of the corners, after too much spinning in the previous year. New suspension linkages and overall geometry were massaged to improve grip, and after that, a lot of effort was put into fine-tuning the electronic traction control.

The third and final major winter development improved the ergonomics and aerodynamics. A different seat, tank and subframe were the obvious aspects of the changes, with the time-honoured trick of altering the seat padding depending on rider preference. The ergonomic improvements helped braking and improved the aerodynamic cross-section.

The Marchesini wheels were as per 2021, but the Öhlins front fork settings were different. There were options of rear swing-arm, but all the riders used the same version.

In the previous few seasons, increasingly, Yamaha development had been done in Europe, but on the engine side, the team received good support from Japan. With things like electronics, there is greater independence from the home factory.

SUPERBIKE WORLD CHAMPIONSHIP

ARAGON

ROUND 1 · SPAIN

Above: The big three started the season as they meant to go on.
Photo: Gold & Goose

Top left: False dawn? Rea over-hauled Bautista to win the first race of the season.
Photo: Ducati Corse

Left: Bautista's first win came in race two.

Right: A race-two freight train – Gerloff chased by Laverty, Baz, Mykhalchyk, sideways Redding and Bernardi.
Photos: Gold & Goose

Above: **Rea earned the bouquet in race one, but was twice usurped by Bautista on Sunday.**

Left: **MotoGP refugee Iker Lecuona made a promising sixth-place debut on the factory Honda.**

Below: **Ukranian Illia Mykhalchyk replaced injured Dutchman van der Mark on the BMW, and claimed a first-race top-ten.**

Photos: Gold & Goose

THE Motorland Aragon opener to the 2022 Motul FIM Superbike World Championship followed a very chilly official test on the preceding Monday and Tuesday. It was obvious that there would be three main challengers for glory at the opening round, finally held in improving dry conditions, when the real battle began.

On the new SCQ Pirelli rear tyre, designed for more than one flying lap in Superpole (and maybe even the ten-lap sprint races at some tracks), 2021 world champion Toprak Razgatlioglu set a new lap record of 1m 48.267s in Superpole qualifying. He was followed at similarly strong pace by Ducati's pint-sized prodigal son, Alvaro Bautista, with recently deposed six-times champion Jonathan Rea, on the ageing, but adaptable Kawasaki, third.

As expected, those three riders dominated the podiums, so kudos to Michael Ruben Rinaldi on the other factory Ducati. He was a thorn in the side of each of the top three, especially Rea and Razgatlioglu.

The Turkish rider had to use all the tricks at his disposal, and no small amount of elbow grease, to ease Rinaldi out of the podium places on more than one occasion at key moments.

Three fourths for Rinaldi took him from depressed after official testing to merely angry after missing out on a podium – as any real racer would be.

The first race victory went to Rea, who delivered one of his masterclasses by keeping the plainly faster Bautista and V4R combination within sight after each main-straight, top-speed no-contest, repassing firmly through the twistier sections.

Leading at the time, Bautista came so close to falling as he exited the final curve under power on lap ten, not long after he and Rea had ambushed Razgatlioglu into the final turn.

In a fantastic finish, Rea demonstrated more determination and final-corner agility to cut inside on the long last left-hander to win by just 0.090 of a second. There were top-four fireworks from start to finish, and eight official changes of lead across the finish line.

In the Tissot Superpole Race on Sunday morning, as ever over ten laps, Bautista got his chance to really spread the Panigale's winglets. To great effect, winning by 5.141 seconds from Rea, with Razgatlioglu again third, almost a second behind Rea. The Yamaha and Kawasaki riders had touched hard and very early in the race, helping Bautista to escape.

Rinaldi passed both of the most recent world champions when they outbraked themselves, but Rea didn't allow the other Ducati to escape, and finally Razgatlioglu pushed Rinaldi wide as they touched on the final turn, to take third.

Race two was over as a contest for Rea and Razgatlioglu once Bautista took to the clean air out front, denied him in race one by Rea's wiles. Rinaldi's over-late braking into T1 caused him and the following Rea to run wide, allowing Bautista more breathing space out in front.

Once again, new lap record holder Razgatlioglu (1m 49.375s in the Superpole race) did not have enough front tyre grip and confidence to ride with his usual extravagant braking style for full race distance. However, three podiums at a previous Yamaha black-hole circuit were strong results in the circumstances.

Behind the podium fights, Iker Lecuona and Xavi Vierge, the two new rookie HRC Honda riders fresh from the GP paddock, made positive headlines. They left their home race fifth and sixth in the points table. Impressive, and clearly new assets for a championship turning 35 years old.

BMW had a disaster of sorts, with Michael van der Mark missing after suffering a right lower leg spiral fracture. New superstar signing Scott Redding left Spain with one point, for 15th in race one.

SUPERBIKE WORLD CHAMPIONSHIP

ASSEN

ROUND 2 · NETHERLANDS

Left, from top: Czech rookie Oliver Konig; a heroic, but hobbling van der Mark; Leon Haslam was drafted into the Pedercini squad.

Far left: Race one kicks off in front of a large Assen crowd.

Below far left: Razgatlioglu and Rea collide...

Bottom far left: ...and end the race in the gravel.
Photos: Gold & Goose

Below centre left: Revived Lecuona gave HRC an early podium.
Photo: HRC

Below: Andrea Locatelli inherited a distant second on Sunday morning.

Bottom: Roberto Tamburini took points in both feature races.

Below right: Rinaldi falls to earth in race one.
Photos: Gold & Goose

DING-DING, round two, but it took until the third and final race of the weekend for old on-track rivals Jonathan Rea and Toprak Razgatlioglu to get into a bout of consequential fairing 'fisticuffs'.

Assen opened its historic doors fully for the first time since Covid arrived and upset the global order. A pleasingly large Sunday crowd witnessed some wonderful kinetic dramas played out around the flat Dutch field that remains so much more than the sum of its regularly nipped, tucked and resculpted parts.

The Friday and Saturday crowds were also reasonable, eagerly waiting to watch more racing history being made. What most had really come to see was a miracle – the small matter of home hero Michael van der Mark back on his official BMW just weeks after suffering a serious fracture to his lower right leg.

Sure enough, he made a convincing orthopaedic Lazarus as he hobbled in, was cleared to race, then scored gutsy points.

A big practice fall for Eugene Laverty on his Bonovo BMW meant that he was forced to miss the Assen races altogether. Meanwhile, a pre-race fall-out between Team Pedercini Kawasaki and rider Loris Cresson resulted in him being dropped, with Leon Haslam stepping in at the last minute.

Razgatlioglu took his second pole of the year on the new SCQ tyre. His 1m 32.934s was the first WorldSBK lap under 1m 33s and was nearly half a second faster than resurgent KRT rider Alex Lowes in second place. Rea was alongside in third, Bautista fifth.

Race one started with Razgatlioglu leading and then Andrea Locatelli. Rea was soon into second, however, and then the lead at the start of lap four.

Lowes's prospects ended in a DNF, after an off-track excursion by Locatelli fired a stone into the Kawasaki's oil pump.

Up front, Rea and Razgatlioglu swapped places, with the threat of Bautista catching the leading slipstream made real before half-distance. Rea was aggressive in his defence when Bautista finally passed him, and with Razgatlioglu just a full second behind, too far back to challenge, Kawasaki's leading man won by 0.103 of a second from Ducati's prodigal son.

Sunday's Tissot Superpole race was held over only nine laps after wild-card rider Gabriele Ruiu was forced to vacate the grid on his Bmax Racing BMW, which delayed the start.

Razgatlioglu scored the holeshot, but Bautista took the lead just as Rea made it a leading trio. Again, it was a two-rider fight that Rea would win from Bautista on the last lap. It was his 115th career WorldSBK win and his 100th for Kawasaki.

Eventually, Bautista was 'pinged' for grazing the green track limits at the final chicane, however, and he was banished into third place by the stewards, to Razgatlioglu's benefit.

In the final race of the weekend, Kohta Nozane crashed out on his GRT Yamaha on lap one. Team-mate Garrett Gerloff tagged Rea's bike shortly afterwards, but we had to wait for lap six, and a small mistake with amplifying consequences, for the real drama.

Running a little wide at the T1 apex and then using the rumble strips to recover on the exit, Razgatlioglu rejoined the asphalt at exactly the same point in space and time that Rea had in mind to complete his opportunistic inside pass. They clashed, crashed, and neither could restart.

Bautista finally took a clear, dominant win from Locatelli, making an exaggerated last-lap show of staring at the final-corner green paint and giving it a very wide berth. And third on the podium? No less than WorldSBK rookie and MotoGP reject Iker Lecuona, on the revamped full-factory HRC Honda Fireblade. In only his sixth WorldSBK race, he had even led for a while after the Rea/Razgatlioglu incident.

Assen always delivers, if not what at least two championship contenders had wanted on this occasion.

SUPERBIKE WORLD CHAMPIONSHIP

ESTORIL

ROUND 3 · PORTUGAL

Above: Bautista breaks clear of Lowes, Lecuona and the pack in pursuit of Razgatlioglu during the first race.

Left: Razgatlioglu's Yamaha team brass – Paul Denning and crew chief Phil Marron.

Right: Double point scores for GRT Yamaha's Kohta Nozane.

Below: Rea and Razgatlioglu keep close company.

Photos: Gold & Goose

Above: **Only tenth, but Baz was still top Independent rider in race one.**

Left: **Still no wins for double runner-up Toprak.**

Below: **Xavi Fores scored across all three races.**

Bottom: **Ducati rider coach Chaz Davies and double winner Bautista enjoy another podium moment.**

Below right: **Lowes struggled manfully with his Kawasaki.**

Photos: Gold & Goose

FROM north to southwest Europe, WorldSBK's third step back into a more regular calendar took place at the circuit of Estoril. Updates to its level of run-off safety had been enough to bring the circuit near Lisbon back into the WorldSBK fold for a third straight year. That gave Jonathan Rea and Toprak Razgatlioglu some benefit, as they had ridden their current bikes there before. However, it was the first time for the 2019 retread combo of Alvaro Bautista and the Ducati.

Rea had the best race prep of all, winning his first Superpole of the year, while both he and Razgatlioglu smashed the old track best. Rea's 1m 35.346s was just 0.091 of a second better than Razgatlioglu, but Bautista was still third on the grid.

A small surge in BMW fortune, after a post-Assen test for Scott Redding, put him fourth in Superpole.

Once again, the Estoril racing was fireball hot between the top three.

In the first race, over 21 laps, Razgatlioglu had a handy lead after he and Bautista had capitalised on Rea's grip issues. Toprak did everything humanly possible to keep Bautista behind him in the final sector, but on the last-corner exit the Turk's hopes of his first 2022 race win were slammed into reverse. A clever choice of line, to maximise drive on the exit, and the peerlessly high-revving Ducati fired the diminutive Bautista into the lead.

The champ shook his head in frustration as Bautista blew past. The margin of victory was only 0.126 of a second, all gained on the run to the finish line.

Rea was 4.835 seconds back, enduring a dissatisfying podium.

The second points-scoring opportunity of the weekend was the Superpole race on Sunday morning, held after early morning rainfall. With damp patches and a final wide dry line, it appeared that Razgatlioglu had it covered again – until Rea put in the fastest lap of the race with one to go. He was still over 0.7 of a second back, so something drastic had to happen – and it did.

Entering Turn Nine, Toprak turned left into the tight chicane, only for his front end to fold completely. A combination of extraordinary riding skill, a well-placed elbow slider and the simple determination to ride out the slide allowed him to regain grip from both tyres – and to witness Rea scoot past with inches to spare.

Instantly regaining his composure, Razgatlioglu continued to compete all the way. He got to within 0.174 of a second of Rea, but had been foiled once again by a dramatic late plot twist.

Razgatlioglu only finished third in the final Estoril race, officially race two, leaving him nine races in without a win.

Rea, chasing Bautista's decent late lead, once more set the fastest lap on the penultimate tour. His pressure was relentless, almost causing him to run into the back of Bautista in the first few corners. He duly made a pass into T7, but Bautista cut back under to lead on the exit.

At the Turn Nine chicane, the site of his winning pass on Razgatlioglu in the morning, Rea dived inside and held Bautista wide, creating an instant and significant time gap.

Dreaming of a repeat of Saturday's drag-race triumph, Bautista nearly got his wish when Rea suffered a huge rear slide on the very apex of the final corner. As Razgatlioglu had done in race one, Rea rode into and through his potential disaster, and was rewarded with enough drive and buffer zone to take his second astounding Sunday win.

The real winners, however, were the fans, by now drunk on three jolting shots of last-lap adrenaline.

SUPERBIKE WORLD CHAMPIONSHIP

MISANO

ROUND 4 · ITALY

Above: Rea congratulates winner Razgatlioglu after the Superpole race.
Photo: Gold & Goose

Top: Bautista takes the narrow road to *parc fermé* after his clear win in race two.
Photo: Ducati Corse

Above right: Follow my leader in Superpole. Razgatlioglu, Rea, Bautista and Locatelli head the squabbling Lowes and Rinaldi.

Right: Bautista and Rea dispute the lead in race one, while Razgatlioglu's race is coming to an end.
Photos: Gold & Goose

Above: Rossi, with Bezzecchi and Bagnaia, was at their local track for the race.

Left: Tito Rabat made a one-off appearance in place of injured Mahia on the Puccetti Kawasaki.

Below left: Luca Bernardi was thrice in the points on the BARNI Ducati.
Photos: Gold & Goose

Bottom: Xavi Vierge took a best-of-the-season fifth in race one.
Photo: HRC

Below right: Michael Ruben Rinaldi and Alvaro Bautista were third and first in both main races.
Photo: Gold & Goose

IT would be nearly impossible to replicate the gladiatorial entertainment that had energised the preceding rounds, yet Misano's slightly more sanitised levels of on-track action still had thrilling passes and tricks in the tales of the unexpected. The enthusiasm of the crowd and the perennial joy of racing near the sea, immersed in the crucible of an Italian summer, made the Adriatic weekend blissful.

There was torrential pre-weekend rain, of course, caused by all that coastal humidity, but for the races, it was all heat and dust-ups.

Valentino Rossi, a regular visitor in the past, was even trackside at one stage, watching his home WorldSBK round.

For riders, sometimes home advantage can count for nothing when it comes to results, especially in this case, when the lead Ducati rider was Spanish, not Italian. In reality, Bautista's V4-R – revving into falsetto territory compared to most others – knew its way around Misano under his experienced guidance to take a new track best of 1m 33.328s in Superpole qualifying.

It was Bautista's first pole since October, 2019, when he had been fastest pre-race at Villicum. A pre-race trophy also garnered aboard a Ducati. His projected race pace was worryingly good for his rivals, but in race one, it was still winless 2021 champion Razgatlioglu who gained the holeshot.

The top three in the series formed an early leading trio, with Rinaldi and Bassani chasing hard. Rea took the lead, trying to create a gap, but Bautista was ready to make a decisive move into the super-fast Curvone. Rea, initially startled, held his ground in second for a time, but Bautista eased out to win by over five seconds.

With seven of the 21 laps to go, Razgatliolgu had to pull over exiting the final corner: his bike stopped after a fault developed in its charging circuit – right in front of the pits for all to see. His 2022 winless streak now ran to ten.

Bautista took a new lap record on lap 18, despite the hot asphalt, running one of the two development SCX Pirelli rears. He had now won at least one race in all four early rounds.

The final place on the podium went to Rinaldi, by over two seconds from the battling Bassani.

In Sunday's ten-lap Superpole race, Razgatlioglu had new machine settings and a resurrected ability to win, which he did by 2.087 seconds from Bautista. Rea was a distant third; rookie Vierge won an intra-HRC battle for fourth place; Lecuona was fifth.

Razgatlioglu had broken Saturday's lap record with a 1m 33.722s on lap five, a lightning pace that would survive the weekend intact. The unspoken relief emanating from the Turk after his first 2022 win was palpable, given how heavy the crown had clearly been weighing on him. That said, Bautista was still the ultra-light favourite for the full-distance race two.

The race itself provided some superb early action, but once Bautista had broken Razgatlioglu up front, he was able to ease his way to a margin of victory of more than seven seconds.

Again, Rinaldi was in particularly effective form at home, staying with the top three all the way. A very fast crash at the Curvone caused Vierge to fall, injuring his hand.

For the first time in 2022, Rea did not get a podium place in a race he finished, as Rinaldi had got the better of him by 3.782 seconds – helped by Rea's unexpected lack of grip.

Rinaldi, who stopped out on track to throw his gloves into the crowd, had ridden as if his factory career had depended on it, which in some ways it probably did.

Heat, crowded paddocks, Ducati doing a double in Italy, and Toprak on a top step. Some level of normality had been resumed.

SUPERBIKE WORLD CHAMPIONSHIP

DONINGTON

ROUND 5 · GREAT BRITAIN

Above: Bassani and Rinaldi lock horns in race one.

Top: Lots of sunshine and lots of fans for a fine British round.

Right: Only human after all. Bautista dropped his Ducati in race one.

Centre right: Lowes and Redding enjoyed a good scrap for the race-one podium.

Photos: Gold & Goose

Above: **After winning the first two races, Toprak prepares to do it again on Sunday afternoon.**

Left: **Alex Lowes celebrates his year's first podium.**

Below right: **Tarran Mackenzie was a wild-card draw for the fans, and he made the points twice.**

Photos: Gold & Goose

IN 2021, the backdrop to the WorldSBK weekend at Donington had been the tail end of the Covid pandemic and the European Championship football competition, in which host country England narrowly lost the final to Italy. For 2022, there were no real Covid restrictions, while the long hot summer provided race conditions that were almost too good.

Across all three races, Toprak Razgatlioglu was also too good, because – spoiler alert – he won all of them.

He didn't sport a new watch for being fastest in Superpole qualifying, however, as Rea further overloaded his shelf of timepieces at a record pace of 1m 26.080s. He had the common decency to kick himself (just a little) for not quite setting a 1m 25s... That he was fully 0.273 of a second ahead of the next best rider, yet only one of four to beat the previous track best, made it a bit special all the same.

In race one on Saturday, Razgatlioglu claimed an early lead that he would not surrender for all 23 laps around the most schizophrenic track layout on the WorldSBK calendar.

Rea was in early trouble when he and team-mate Lowes tried to pass Razgatlioglu into the Foggy Esses. His rear wheel kicked sideways, putting him off his perfect entry line and losing him four places across the finish line on lap one.

By then, Razgatlioglu was gone.

Bautista slotted into second, and Rea took until lap eight to get past the lead Ducati rider. On lap 14, Bautista was second again, but one lap later, he fell at the infamous Goddards, the final hairpin, for his first DNF of the year.

Rea ended up more than six seconds down on Razgatlioglu, but over three seconds up on team-mate Lowes, who earned his first podium of the year.

In Sunday's ten-lap Superpole race, Bautista got to the finish, but scored his first off-podium points since returning to the Ducati fold. Once again, Razgatlioglu was untouchable after the early exchanges, setting a new lap record of 1m 26.767s on lap three.

Rea was second again, while in a profound turnaround since round one's disaster, Redding converted a fourth-place grid spot into his first BMW podium, a full second ahead of Bautista.

Razgatlioglu had won the title without ever having taken a trio of wins on any individual weekend. This was another career milestone, thanks to his effusive style and granite-hard determination in race two.

For a time, there had been an engaging tussle between the championship's big three. The reigning champion finally beat Bautista by 1.102 seconds, however, and Rea by 2.615.

After missing the opportunity to wild-card at Assen, due to a tricky early-season ankle injury, 2021 BSB champion Tarran Mackenzie joined FHO BMW Racing's Peter Hickman as a local wild-card. No podium heroics, of course, given the gulf between world and national competition levels, but it was a welcome echo of years gone by.

Mackenzie finished 14th in race one, crashed into Vierge in the Superpole race (earning a five-place grid penalty for the finale) and then took another championship point for 15th in race two. He said that it had been the first weekend he had felt 100 per cent fit since his ankle injury. Hickman went 22-16-19 in the races.

The local fans still had a lot to be thankful for, given the excellent entertainment and glorious summer weather. In reality, WorldSBK and Donington rights holders MSV were even more pleased to see an official attendance figure of over 50,000.

SUPERBIKE WORLD CHAMPIONSHIP

MOST

ROUND 6 · CZECH REPUBLIC

Above: Podium-bound Redding escapes from Locatelli in race one.

Top: The three usual suspects power away in race one.

Right: BMW team owner Shaun Muir and rider Redding celebrate their first podium together.

Above right: Rea takes a detour after running off in the Superpole race. He recovered to take second.

Photos: Gold & Goose

Left: Razgatlioglu took the win on Sunday morning and celebrated with a trademark stoppie.

Below left: Ex-rider Leon Camier manages the Honda factory team.
Photos: Gold & Goose

Below: The Hondas of MIE Racing pair Syahrin and Mercado picked up points in race two.
Photo: MIE Racing Team

Bottom: A thousand and counting. Ducati marked another Superbike milestone.
Photo: Ducati Corse

Below right: A Continental outing for team owner Faye Ho and Peter Hickman, in place of the still-injured van der Mark and in the points, too.
Photo: Ducati Photo: Gold & Goose

EVERYONE who entered the weekend at Most knew that psychology mattered almost as much as points, given that there would be a long break in the season right after the sound and fury of the Czech round had abated. Some would be grinning; those who had had a bad time would be hurting for weeks.

After the championship fight had closed up at Donington, the anticipation was more than eager, it was electric. In Superpole qualifying, Rea scored yet again, taking another new track best for his collection with a 1m 30.947s.

Not the most modern of circuits, Most did feature some improvements, although there was more work to do in respect of safety enhancements in some places. The risks were a talking point for some, and with race one featuring spots (but not lots) of rain, those prepared to ignore the evidence clinging to their visors would make some instant gains.

Race one was close from the start – so close that Rea collided with the rear tyre of Razgatlioglu in the resurfaced, hyper-tight first chicane. No real harm done, they continued harrying each other.

As the drops of water arrived, first Rea and then Bautista bounced leader Razgatlioglu back to third place.

Bautista used his primary weapons – good corner exit drive and titanically better straight-line speed – to take the lead on lap ten. He enjoyed a small advantage, while Rea and Razgatlioglu battled behind so much that Redding was able to close, then pass Razgatlioglu for third and Rea for second.

Rea's pace slipped near the end due to braking issues, so Razgatlioglu naturally outbraked him, then made a hard pass on Redding into the fast Turn 13. Run off track in the manoeuvre, Redding was verbosely unimpressed.

Rea also had a go at Redding on the very last lap, but ran wide, leaving the finishing order Bautista, Razgatlioglu, Redding and Rea. Another contentious epic all round.

On a sunny Sunday morning, Razgatlioglu took the holeshot in the Superpole race. With Bautista eventually a safe third and team-mate Rinaldi just behind him, the ten-lap mini-title fight was between the two recent WorldSBK champions, Rea and Razgatlioglu.

Fighting for supremacy under braking into Turn One on the last lap, the Kawasaki rider performed a small miracle to pass the king of the stoppie, only for Razgatlioglu to power past on the improbable inside at the fast Turn Four.

The Turk dangled a leg out in Turn 15, but Rea, already going for the inside pass, could not avoid it, tapped his heel... and ran wide, although upright, through the gravel for second.

In the final race, Razgatlioglu took the lead at the first turn, with Bautista soon behind. Rea was close to Rinaldi when the latter fell on lap four going into Turn One, but escaped the incident to move up to third.

Bautista screamed past Razgatlioglu on the straight with 17 laps to go, only to run off, rejoining via the slip road.

Then a leading, fighting, warring melee of top three championship rivals formed. It was a sight and fight to behold.

Ducati power did for Rea's chances of victory with just under half a race to go, and then Razgatlioglu passed Rea to leave him third. Bautista was picked off and finally Razgatlioglu pushed on consistently enough to win by 0.756 of a second.

Top Independent rider Bassani left Most with a trio of excellent fifth places, and more kudos from his peers and the fans.

Yamaha reached 100 WorldSBK race wins over the Czech weekend, and Ducati 1,000 WorldSBK podiums. But, most importantly, Bautista made up ground that he had lost at Donington to sit on a 31-point summer-break margin over Rea and 38 ahead of Razgatlioglu.

SUPERBIKE WORLD CHAMPIONSHIP

MAGNY-COURS

ROUND 7 · FRANCE

Top: Rea and Bautista collide on the second lap of race two.

Above: Bautista paid the price.

Above right: Second on Saturday proved to be a season's best for Scott Redding.

Right: Toprak got the better of Bautista in the sprint race.

Photos: Gold & Goose

THE restart of the season was peculiar in some ways, not least because when it came to Tissot Superpole qualifying, Jonathan Rea and Toprak Razgatlioglu stopped the clock with exactly the same 1m 36.124s time showing on the display. It had never been done before, but Rea took the best grid spot anyway, as his next best lap was faster than his rival's.

This Magny-Cours weekend, like the previous year's, would end in rancour and recrimination, but on this occasion, more than green trackside paint would have been grazed.

The racing itself actually started in mind-boggling style for the two championship contenders. In the Saturday opener, Rea was right with Razgatlioglu early on until his front wheel sensor clipped the infamously high final chicane kerb, which caused him to lose the front and crash. To paraphrase a famous racing saying, it was also possible not to hit the kerb. He finished 24th, scoring no points.

His misfortune was not quite mirrored by Razgatlioglu, but soon after, he endured enough of a rear-end kick when his tyre made contact with the local *terroir* at Turn 13 that he also ran off, toppling over rather than crashing. He got going again and rode as only he can to 11th.

The silver lining for Bautista in his two main rivals' clouds was the chance to run clear and win, from the once more fully competitive Scott Redding. Third place went to privateer princeling Axel Bassani, from a resurgent Alex Lowes.

The Superpole race, run on an even sunnier Sunday morning, was a shuffle of 2022's big three playing cards, with Razgatlioglu winning and Bautista battling with Rea for second, getting the job done with a final overtake into the last chicane. It was a mini-epic of the ten-lap WorldSBK race meme.

Race two was where the real shouting of the weekend would begin, after another potential cliffhanger from the leaders resulted in green-on-red contact that knocked off Bautista, who was unable to restart.

Rea had positioned himself inside Bautista at Turn 13, but was a bit too hot, and just before the point of contact – depending on your point of view – either simply fouled up, or leant over and hit Bautista deliberately, or realised that he had misjudged his braking and braced himself with his elbow for the inevitable contact with Bautista.

Ducati, in the form of Bautista's verbal incandescence and a surprise gate-crashing of the post-race media debrief by normally cool and quiet tech chief Marco Zambenedetti, made their corporate feelings plain. Rea's long-lap penalty – and a finishing place of fifth – was nowhere near the punishment that would assuage the Aruba crew's anger and indignation.

Rea admitted that it had been his fault and offered his apologies, but he made it clear that there had been no bad intent on his behalf. Race Direction took no further action beyond that long-lap penalty.

Before those bitter final comments, there was the small matter of completing the second full-distance race. It was won by Razgatlioglu, from a visibly relieved Rinaldi. We did not know it for sure, but his second place might well have saved his factory position for 2023, especially as he beat the still potent Bassani to a higher podium step.

Lowes claimed his third fourth place of the weekend. Although not what he would have preferred, it was still much better than some of his early-season disappointments.

After all the splintered carbon-fibre and shattered fraternity of near equals in *parc fermé*, Bautista's boom-and-bust weekend resulted in him leaving France still in a clear lead in the championship, but with double race winner Razgatlioglu closing in after that incident in race two.

Above: Under pressure? Rinaldi made his point verbally, and later on the podium.

Top: Bassani enhanced his growing reputation with two third places.

Above centre: Razgatlioglu and Rea shared identical lap times in Superpole.

Right: Redding mixes it with the big boys at the start of race one.

Photos: Gold & Goose

SUPERBIKE WORLD CHAMPIONSHIP

CATALUNYA

ROUND 8 · SPAIN

Above: Spanish rider Oscar Gutierrez was the latest to try his luck on the Pedercini Kawasaki.

Right: Surprise fastest qualifier Iker Lecuona claimed Honda's first pole since 2016.
Photos: Gold & Goose

Top: Bautista takes charge of race one. Rea is back in the pack, ahead of Redding after running wide.
Photo: Ducati Corse

WITH a vast main straight and enough track width to allow even a smaller rider like Bautista to hustle his big red powerhouse around, the now classic Barcelona layout was always going to provide real potential for him to score strongly. He was also hyper-motivated to win after the 'incident' at Magny-Cours.

In the end, however, it was another Spanish rider in red who earned the best grid spot in Superpole. Iker Lecuona took Bautista's old HRC Honda to pole position, proving that a million laps of any track (from a previous career and recent tests) can help even a rookie find pace that is missing elsewhere.

Having a similarly powerful and high-revving engine to the Ducati also didn't hurt on the big main straight in front of that iconic curved grandstand. In any case, it was all deeply memorable, and it took some pressure off the official HRC effort, with its HQ located nearby. A first Honda pole since 2016.

With Bautista only fifth in Superpole qualifying, and Rea starting third, was there a chance that he could also make his slower, but well-proven Kawasaki fly for real in the races?

It would have been nice, especially at this, his KRT squad's literal home round. He could also have done with a couple of wins at least, but once again there would be no victory. Nor for Razgatlioglu, who had qualified eighth.

In the opening race, the six-times champion had run wide at T1 and suddenly was down in eighth. He had to summon up all his pace and experience to get back up to second with four laps remaining.

Out front, Bautista had already made the race his, especially after Razgatlioglu had faded from the lead to an eventual fifth.

Behind Bautista and Rea at the flag, there was a new podium name for 2022. Garrett Gerloff scored third at the track where he had taken his first ever top-three finish in 2020. After a rough season, at least now he had one bronze Texan star to brighten it up.

The Superpole race on Sunday morning was held in warm conditions, on a generally hot weekend, with race one's tyre-drop issues supposedly less problematic over ten laps.

Once again, Bautista was untouchable, while Rea had to pass his own teammate, Lowes (who didn't put up too much of a fight, finally), to make sure he would get second. Perhaps it is not surprising that a six-times champion would be unhappy with second place, but an inherited runner-up position, with Bautista stretching out another few points on him, was surely unpalatable for Rea.

Razgatlioglu's fourth place in the ten-lapper was even more unpleasant for the 2021 world champion, now watching the points just slip away.

The final race of the weekend emphasised just how potent a well-set-up V4R Ducati had been since 2019, as Rinaldi rode strongly to secure second.

Obviously, Bautista won again.

Razgatlioglu was unable to clamber any higher than the third step of the podium, losing not five, but nine points to Bautista in a single contest. Rea was fourth. He had suffered from a false neutral at a bad time, then found another Ducati thorn in his side, and on his preferred line, for much of the latter part of the race. He was over ten seconds from Bautista.

Catalunya was a Ducati playground right enough, but a sweatshop of emotional and sometimes physical pain for others.

Lowes and Redding, both on recent upward trajectories, were fallers in race two.

This had the feel of a pivotal weekend, especially as the points gaps between the top three suddenly appeared a bit overstretched by Bautista's beautifully woven triple crown.

Above: Oettl leads Vierge and Redding in their fight for the middling points in Sunday's sprint race.
Photos: Gold & Goose

Top: As easy as 1-2-3. Ducati took first and second in race two, Bautista all three wins.
Photo: Ducati Corse

Above centre: Yamaha's Garrett Gerloff claimed his sole podium of the season.

Right: Teams prepare for the Superpole race in front of an almost empty grandstand.
Photos: Gold & Goose

SUPERBIKE WORLD CHAMPIONSHIP

PORTIMAO

ROUND 9 · PORTUGAL

Above: Bautista, Razgatlioglu and Rea ride the crest in race two.

Right: Eugene Laverty announced his impending retirement.

Centre right: Andrea Locatelli kept scoring points to place one ahead of Alex Lowes in the championship.

Below right: Baz, Gerloff and Oettl disputed ninth in race two.

Below centre right: Two wins for Toprak kept his recovery hopes alive.

Photos: Gold & Goose

Far right: Bautista, Bassani and Lowes in close combat.

Photo: Ducati Corse

Above: **WorldSBK appetiser? Jake Gagne, 2022 MotoAmerica champion, made the trip with his crew, scoring a point for their trouble.**

Top: **Wheel to wheel, Bautista and Razgatlioglu battled it out.**

Left: **Marvin Fritz was back for a second Portuguese outing, on the IXS Yamaha.**

Photos: Gold & Goose

EVEN if Portimao did feature a downward-sloping runway of a main straight, it also offered a hillside assault course fit for only the brave and agile. Razgatlioglu proved the point by jumping his factory R1 for over 20m at the top of the hill between T8 and T9. Just for fun in practice, and for the inevitable fan-friendly pictures, of course.

Bautista would almost come to grief there in a real race, suffering a proper, if short-lived, tank-slapper and proving that Portimao at full combat speed is pretty near the white knuckle for even the best riders.

The nature of the track does seem suited to sweeter handling bikes, but that big straight, and the fact that a long right-hander with a downhill section provides a high-speed approach, still allowed the Ducati riders to pop past their rivals at will into Turn One. It also made the non-Ducati riders almost have to repass every single lap, or risk being dropped during the next power-sapping rolling drag race back to Turn One.

The good news for the neutrals, wise or lucky enough to get some sunshine alongside one of the best holiday race weekends of the year, was that both Rea and Razgatlioglu had performed well at the track, with the former actually the unofficial King of Portimao's podium ceremonies.

Surely, we could expect some real action for race wins this time around.

Again, in 2022, it was a different story, as the second half of the year was proving not to be quite as even a fight as it had been in the first half.

In Superpole, once again, Rea was unstoppable, well into the 1m 39s along with three others, and leading them all away in the first two races.

Razgatlioglu took the honours in race one, from Bautista and Rea. He had passed Rea into T1 as Bautista was working his way through the other top five riders. He'd had to work hard to pass Bassani, then zapped past Rea on the straight with four to go. Rea could only shake his head in disbelief, but then the Ducati ran wide, momentarily losing second place.

Razgatlioglu made use of his leading position to keep going for the opening-race win, from Bautista and Rea. Bassani was fourth, showing the Ducati's strength again as he kept Lowes behind him.

In the ten-lap Superpole race, there was a repeat of the race-one top three, after Razgatlioglu rode one of his very best races ever to keep Bautista behind at the line. Rea was just outgunned in third, pushed on by team-mate Lowes in fourth. To the surprise of many, Razgatlioglu's braking prowess was the undoing of Bautista's fast, but flighty Ducati masterplan for the second time in two Portimao races.

In the final race, Bautista ultimately showed that he had enough pace and set-up on his side, even though his bike appeared to be a handful at times. This was the race in which he suffered that scary tank-slapper, but far from unsettling him, it seemed to perk him up.

Bassani crashed out, his first fall of the year.

Rea and Razgatlioglu swapped the race-two lead, until Bautista came past on the straight, passing each on consecutive laps.

It seemed all over, but Razgatlioglu managed to get back ahead with seven laps to go. Temporarily. Once in clean air again, Bautista eased away to win by over two seconds, with Rea a further two seconds down in third.

Rinaldi and Lowes completed the top five; Lecuona crashed out.

At the end of the European races, it seemed almost inevitable that Bautista was about to collect more than just hefty air miles as we headed off to the final three flyaways.

SUPERBIKE WORLD CHAMPIONSHIP

VILLICUM

ROUND 10 · ARGENTINA

Above: Bautista blasts down the double-dip straight towards the finish line.
Photo: Ducati Corse

Right: No stopping me now. Bautista points the way to the title after his race-one win.

Far right: Picture worth a thousand words… Razgatlioglu and Rea chew their cheeks as Bautista exults in his second South American win.

Top right: Rinaldi enjoys some shade on the scorching hot grid.

Above centre right: Bassani and Rea battled for second in race one.

Below right: A message to Didi from Toprak and his team.

Below centre right: Eugene Laverty enjoyed the limelight as race two's top Independent rider.

Far right: Ready to rumble – Rea, Lowes, Redding and the rest await the start of race two.
Photos: Gold & Goose

THE return to San Juan Villicum meant long and complicated journeys for all, so the racing had to be worth it, right? At times, it really was, even though the hot asphalt tested everyone, although at least it delivered almost consistent track conditions to help find a set-up.

Superpole, in both qualifying and race modes, would be the personal property of Toprak Razgatlioglu, the tall Turk first pummelling the previous best at the dusty, but surprisingly grippy high-desert circuit. His qualifying 'win' was outstanding, even though he was not too far ahead of Rea and Bautista, who joined him on the front row.

All of Razgatlioglu's good work in qualifying was undone, however, after just one run down the kilometre-long back straight, as Bautista went past and held track position inside the strange T8/T9 double-left 'squiggle'.

Razgatlioglu's desperation to put Bautista behind him resulted in him losing his famed depth perception (or simply his judgement) as he entered T9 on an impossible inside line. He braked on the dusty off-line area and immediately lost the front.

His slithering bike so nearly collected Bautista as it sped past his Ducati on its side. In taking avoiding action, the Spaniard lost several places.

An amazingly dramatic start, but there was many a heady slug left in this bottle of motorised Malbec. Rea led for a time, but Bautista was in attacking mood, and once he was out front, he was well away, winning by five seconds as he took the plaudits from his ecstatic team on the last-lap run down the unique 'double-drop' main straight.

Rea was second, and Bassani third. The latter had acted as a massive high-speed obstacle to the former as he tried to reach clean air in his pursuit of the fleeing Bautista. Lecuona, a newbie at the complicated Villicum circuit, was a strong fourth.

Rea might have been the favourite for the Superpole race after taking the lead (even Bautista said so later), but in missing a gear down the last drop into the braking zone for T1, he ran wide, allowing Razgatlioglu and Bautista through to fight for the win.

Rea came back so hard that probably he would have had the winning pace without his very public mishap, but the man-to-man fight out front was one of the best races of the year.

Bautista held the late advantage, but Razgatlioglu made a block pass in the final corners and took the win. The top three were covered by less than a second, an echo of some early-season jousts.

In the final race of the weekend, Rinaldi took the lead, but as in the Superpole race, albeit at Turn Ten this time, Rea ran wide and had to reboot well inside the chasing pack.

Bautista overtook Lowes for second, then swiftly Rinaldi for the lead. The only realistic threat to his race-two supremacy, Razgatlioglu, eased past Rinaldi into the first turn on lap five.

Axel Bassani caused Loris Baz to crash out, and the perfectly understandable single-finger salute the latter gave landed him with a 1,000-euro fine. Bassani finished 20th after an eventual ride-through for missing a second long-lap penalty.

Razgatliolgu could not counter Bautista's pure repetitive pace, finishing over 3.3 seconds back.

Rea made a pass on Lowes for third, but he was almost ten seconds down after yet another mishap while trying to stay in contention.

Overall, it was like 2019 all over again, except much worse for Bautista's rivals. This time, there was a higher level of competence and confidence emanating from the Ducati garage, not an attenuating one.

Bautista was now over 80 points clear of Razgatlioglu and almost 100 up on Rea, with two rounds to run.

SUPERBIKE WORLD CHAMPIONSHIP

MANDALIKA

ROUND 11 · INDONESIA

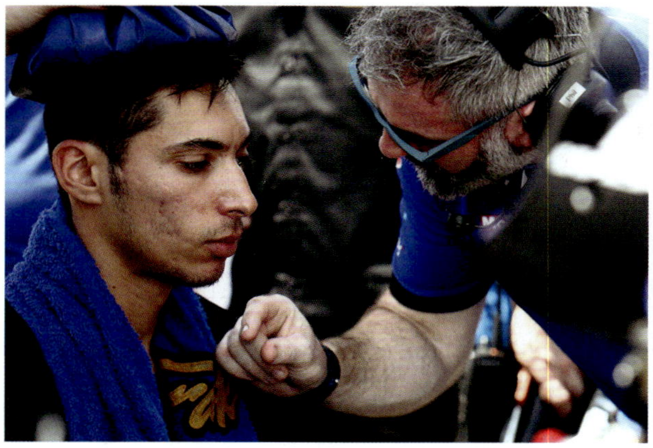

BEACHES, sunshine and motorbike racing always make a nice combination for the fans. They duly turned up at Mandalika in some numbers, but only on Sunday.

Spoiler alert… They came just in time to see Ducati's Spanish star, Alvaro Bautista, win the championship he really should have nailed to his parlour wall in 2019. Better late than never.

The hot favourite coming to the overheated Mandalika round (regularly over 60°C on the asphalt), Bautista and his rivals were met by the challenge of a very dirty and slippery track surface. Thankfully, there was no rain. Not during the sessions at least, even though it was verging on torrential at other times.

The track relaying job looked incredibly well done, smooth and shining like a diamond through the dust, but it had only been completed two weeks before the start of the race weekend, with predictably poor initial results. More gripes than grip were offered on Friday.

Once the early action of the riders had done its work, the track was rubbered-in well enough for Toprak Razgatlioglu to go over a second faster than even Jonathan Rea, smashing the existing track best in Superpole qualifying.

He was heavily tipped to excel in the races, even by his closest rivals, which was good news for the neutrals and Bautista's only realistic championship rival, Razgatlioglu. Rea was almost 100 points behind Bautista before kick-off.

In the opening 21-lap race, Razgatlioglu won by over four seconds from Bautista and a significant 12 seconds or so from Rea. He had too much pace and commitment for everybody, but Bautista had too much pace and champion-elect desire to give up too easily. Rea was third, fighting fading rear grip.

After the Superpole race on Sunday morning, one new champ was crowned, but not quite another. Axel Bassani became the new top Independent rider for the year on his Motocorsa V4R, thanks to his fifth place.

Bautista finished fourth and was still just shy of a championship-winning celebration, even though he was less than two seconds behind Razgatlioglu, who was busy taking his second Mandalika race win. Rea was runner-up by less than half a second, while a relatively resurgent official Yamaha rider, Andrea Locatelli, placed third.

Razgatlioglu claimed the new race lap record with a 1m 36.163s as the new track surface gradually began to play ball, developing an ever widening racing line.

At the start of race two, all would be decided in favour of Bautista if he finished on the podium, even if Razgatlioglu won the race. And that is exactly what he did, strongly, claiming a triple crown of Indonesian race victories, new track records and a Superpole trophy. A perfect weekend, if not a quite a perfect season this time around.

In a way, it was fitting that Sunday afternoon's race, which would crown Bautista the champion, would be led, at some point, by all three of the main championship rivals.

Rea, still winless since Estoril in the spring, led for five laps. Then Razgatlioglu took over, before Bautista was in front for two. Razgatlioglu was so determined to take a second trio of wins, however, that he made perfect use of his effective bike set-up to lead the last six laps and finish 1.230 seconds up on Bautista. Rea was third.

The arithmetic was now unchallengeable for Bautista. He became the first Spanish champion since Carlos Checa, and the first Ducati champion since… also Carlos Checa, back in 2011.

Bautista also became the first Ducati V4 world champion, and a most unlikely prodigal, having left under a cloud after only a single yin and yang 2019 season.

He was pushed all the way – and sometimes literally more than all the way – by Razgatlioglu and Rea during this classic racing year, which still had one round left before the short winter break.

Above: **Axel Bassani did enough to ensure that he became 2022's top Independent rider.**

Top: **Clincher. Bautista got the better of Rea in race two.**

Above left: **Blinged-up Bautista is decked in championship gold.**

Left: **Razgatlioglu leads team-mate Locatelli out of the heat haze in race one.**

Centre far left: **A strong weekend for Locatelli brought a podium in the Superpole race.**

Below far left: **Keeping a cool head. Razgatlioglu takes instructions on Sunday morning. The Turk took all three races.**
Photos: Gold & Goose

Right: **Mandalika's podium takes the role of Indianapolis's yard of bricks for the new champion.**
Photo: Ducati Corse

SUPERBIKE WORLD CHAMPIONSHIP

PHILLIP ISLAND

ROUND 12 · AUSTRALIA

Above: Gerloff narrowly leads Vierge and van der Mark in race-one.

Left: The two Troys – Australian WorldSBK legends Corser and Bayliss were on hand.

Below left: Alex Lowes beat Locatelli each time, but narrowly failed to catch him on points.

Far left: Bautista's gamble to start Superpole on slicks paid off.

Bottom left: Race one kicked off with the field on full wets – and then it dried out.

Below: Rea and Bautista jousted in race two before its early finish.

Bottom: Tetsuta Nagashima was an impressive substitute for Lecuona on the Honda.

Below right: Applause for Bautista after two more wins.

Photos: Gold & Goose

ANY racing return to Phillip Island was going to be welcomed by the riders, teams and support staff who make WorldSBK happen. The circuit itself, and Australia in general, is a cool place to spend some time during the European winter.

A bit too cool this time, as it transpired.

Unfortunately, the Australian spring decided to imitate the northern European autumn/winter in all regards, with heavy rains, surprisingly cold temperatures, unpredictably high winds and generally sky-borne misery allied to a very poor sense of timing.

Luckily for the plucky fans who braved the elements just a month after MotoGP had kickstarted PI's global racing life following the global pandemic, the racing was just as wild and unpredictable as the weather,

This was no dead rubber, in spite of almost all of the titles having been sorted out already.

This was the 'Big Three' looking to get one over on each other to keep their racing wrath warm in the winter months, to demonstrate mastery of a track that is unique and awe-inspiring in what it takes to win there. All three riders had won races at PI in the past, but with the weather closing in, even Rea's solidly fast laps on Friday were a guarantee of nothing come the races.

Just before race one, and just after a wet FP3, new champion Bautista won the enthusiastic game of 'pass the best lap time' in Superpole qualifying. During his final run on SCO race tyres (no Qs or even SCX soft race options at the worst circuit for tyre wear), he dropped below the 1m 30s mark with a 1m 29.815s.

Come race one, which would have no fewer than seven different leading riders, the race was declared wet, and almost everyone showed up on the grid with full wet tyres.

This being PI, the wind and occasional cracks of sunshine ensured that the track dried out quickly, so an unofficial flag-to-flag race, from wet to dry, was the result.

The question was, when to come in? Rea and the following Razgatlioglu timed it just right, by not staying out on full wets for too long.

The former's pit stop was bang on the pit-lane intervention time (the minimum time any rider can spend in the pit lane, to make sure wheel changes are not too rushed), but Razgatlioglu's crew hit an unexpected problem when fitting a wheel and he lost over five seconds.

He would never make them up, and Rea took a teamwork win – his first victory since round three in May. Razgatlioglu was second and Alex Lowes third. Bautista was fifth, nearly 20 seconds back.

The Superpole race, delayed by yet another heavy fall of rain, provided a straight race with no tyre changes. The kink in the competition this time was Bautista, who opted for slick tyres when almost everyone else was using a combination of a wet front and intermediate rear.

Bautista's experience of Phillip Island from his MotoGP days left his team scratching their heads, but fitting slicks and selecting a dry set-up anyway. Indeed, the track did dry quickly. Thus leading duo Razgatlioglu and Rea were caught and passed comprehensively, the final top three being Bautista, Razgatlioglu and Rea.

The final race of the 2022 season got under way on schedule, but at a relatively late 16:00. The early fight for the leading places was particularly intense, as the riders had dry conditions to run on for a full 22-lap race.

Or not, as it transpired. It had just begun to spit with rain again when Eugene Laverty, in his final WorldSBK race, crashed and was struck by the following rider. With Laverty lying trackside and injured, the red flag was thrown to halt the race on 17 laps, with Bautista just ahead of Rea and Lowes to form the final podium of 2022. Razgatlioglu was fourth.

2022 WORLD SUPERBIKE CHAMPIONSHIP RESULTS

Compiled by Peter McLaren

Round 1 ARAGON, Spain · 8–10 April, 2022 · 3.155-mile/5.077km circuit

Race 1: 18 laps, 56.785 miles/91.386km
Weather: Dry · Track 28°C · Air 16°C
Time of race: 33m 13.308s
Average speed: 102.555mph/165.047km/h

Pos.	Rider	Nat.	No.	Entrant	Machine	Time & Gap	Laps
1	**Jonathan Rea**	GBR	65	Kawasaki Racing Team WorldSBK	Kawasaki ZX-10RR		18
2	**Alvaro Bautista**	ESP	19	Aruba.it Racing - Ducati	Ducati Panigale V4R	0.090s	18
3	**Toprak Razgatlioglu**	TUR	1	Pata Yamaha with Brixx WorldSBK	Yamaha YZF R1	5.416s	18
4	**Michael Rinaldi**	ITA	21	Aruba.it Racing - Ducati	Ducati Panigale V4R	10.272s	18
5	**Andrea Locatelli**	ITA	55	Pata Yamaha with Brixx WorldSBK	Yamaha YZF R1	15.767s	18
6	**Iker Lecuona**	ESP	7	Team HRC	Honda CBR1000 RR-R	18.760s	18
7	**Xavi Vierge**	ESP	97	Team HRC	Honda CBR1000 RR-R	21.521s	18
8	**Illia Mykhalchyk**	UKR	37	BMW Motorrad WorldSBK Team	BMW M1000RR	21.605s	18
9	**Garrett Gerloff**	USA	31	GYTR GRT Yamaha WorldSBK Team	Yamaha YZF R1	21.946s	18
10	**Eugene Laverty**	IRL	50	Bonovo Action BMW	BMW M1000RR	25.346s	18
11	**Loris Baz**	FRA	76	Bonovo Action BMW	BMW M1000RR	25.927s	18
12	**Luca Bernardi**	SMR	29	BARNI Spark Racing Team	Ducati Panigale V4R	28.460s	18
13	**Philipp Oettl**	GER	5	Team Goeleven	Ducati Panigale V4R	28.728s	18
14	**Lucas Mahias**	FRA	44	Kawasaki Puccetti Racing	Kawasaki ZX-10RR	29.117s	18
15	**Scott Redding**	GBR	45	BMW Motorrad WorldSBK Team	BMW M1000RR	29.637s	18
16	Axel Bassani	ITA	47	Motocorsa Racing	Ducati Panigale V4R	30.861s	18
17	Roberto Tamburini	ITA	2	Yamaha Motoxracing WorldSBK Team	Yamaha YZF R1	31.463s	18
18	Kohta Nozane	JPN	3	GYTR GRT Yamaha WorldSBK Team	Yamaha YZF R1	33.158s	18
19	Christophe Ponsson	FRA	23	Gil Motor Sport-Yamaha	Yamaha YZF R1	53.223s	18
20	Leandro Mercado	ARG	36	MIE Racing Honda Team	Honda CBR1000 RR-R	56.013s	18
21	Hafizh Syahrin	MAS	35	MIE Racing Honda Team	Honda CBR1000 RR-R	58.036s	18
22	Oliver Konig	CZE	52	Orelac Racing Verdnatura	Kawasaki ZX-10RR	1m 08.037s	18
23	Loris Cresson	BEL	84	TPR Team Pedercini Racing	Kawasaki ZX-10RR	1m 16.388s	18
	Alex Lowes	GBR	22	Kawasaki Racing Team WorldSBK	Kawasaki ZX-10RR	DNF	6
	Gabriele Ruiu	ITA	16	Bmax Racing	BMW M1000RR	DNF	4

Fastest race lap: Razgatlioglu on lap 3, 1m 50.025s, 103.22mph/166.12km/h.
Lap record: Rea, 1m 49.62s, 103.60mph/166.73km/h (2020).

Superpole: 10 laps, 31.547 miles/50.770km
Weather: Dry · Track 22°C · Air 13°C
Time of race: 18m 19.201s
Average speed: 103.320mph/166.277km/h

Pos.	Rider	Time & Gap	Laps
1	**Alvaro Bautista**		10
2	**Jonathan Rea**	5.141s	10
3	**Toprak Razgatlioglu**	6.008s	10
4	**Michael Rinaldi**	6.067s	10
5	**Andrea Locatelli**	7.532s	10
6	**Alex Lowes**	7.623s	10
7	**Axel Bassani**	8.801s	10
8	**Iker Lecuona**	10.127s	10
9	**Xavi Vierge**	11.414s	10
10	Garrett Gerloff	11.476s	10
11	Eugene Laverty	13.795s	10
12	Scott Redding	15.408s	10
13	Loris Baz	15.564s	10
14	Lucas Mahias	18.529s	10
15	Roberto Tamburini	22.786s	10
16	Philipp Oettl	22.818s	10
17	Luca Bernardi	24.011s	10
18	Kohta Nozane	25.367s	10
19	Gabriele Ruiu	32.598s	10
20	Leandro Mercado	32.661s	10
21	Christophe Ponsson	35.858s	10
22	Hafizh Syahrin	36.631s	10
23	Oliver Konig	37.920s	10
24	Loris Cresson	37.980s	10
	Illia Mykhalchyk	DNF	4

Fastest race lap: Razgatlioglu on lap 2, 1m 49.375s, 103.84mph/167.11km/h.

Race 2: 18 laps, 56.785 miles/91.386km
Weather: Dry · Track 36°C · Air 20°C
Time of race: 33m 17.081s
Average speed: 102.362mph/164.735km/h

Pos.	Rider	Time & Gap	Laps
1	**Alvaro Bautista**		18
2	**Jonathan Rea**	4.393s	18
3	**Toprak Razgatlioglu**	6.223s	18
4	**Michael Rinaldi**	8.817s	18
5	**Alex Lowes**	12.247s	18
6	**Axel Bassani**	15.775s	18
7	**Loris Baz**	23.925s	18
8	**Xavi Vierge**	24.790s	18
9	**Garrett Gerloff**	25.406s	18
10	**Iker Lecuona**	25.570s	18
11	**Lucas Mahias**	27.641s	18
12	**Eugene Laverty**	28.867s	18
13	**Philipp Oettl**	29.325s	18
14	**Roberto Tamburini**	29.555s	18
15	**Illia Mykhalchyk**	31.843s	18
16	Luca Bernardi	43.246s	18
17	Gabriele Ruiu	45.734s	18
18	Christophe Ponsson	46.349s	18
19	Andrea Locatelli	55.354s	18
20	Hafizh Syahrin	59.398s	18
21	Leandro Mercado	1m 01.009s	18
22	Oliver Konig	1m 07.061s	18
23	Loris Cresson	1m 18.230s	18
	Kohta Nozane	DNF	13
	Scott Redding	DNF	11

Fastest race lap: Lowes on lap 3, 1m 50.334s, 102.93mph/165.65km/h.

Superpole

1, Razgatlioglu 1m 48.267s; 2, Bautista 1m 48.273s; 3, Rea 1m 48.476s; 4, Rinaldi 1m 48.755s; 5, Lowes 1m 48.986s; 6, Locatelli 1m 48.998s; 7, Lecuona 1m 49.329s; 8, Mykhalchyk 1m 49.447s; 9, Bassani 1m 49.454s; 10, Baz 1m 49.469s; 11, Gerloff 1m 49.541s; 12, Oettl 1m 49.636s; 13, Vierge 1m 49.655s; 14, Laverty 1m 49.659s; 15, Tamburini 1m 49.729s; 16, Redding 1m 49.758s; 17, Mahias 1m 50.081s; 18, Bernardi 1m 50.114s; 19, Nozane 1m 51.098s; 20, Ruiu 1m 51.255s; 21, Ponsson 1m 51.522s; 22, Mercado 1m 51.689s; 23, Syahrin 1m 52.012s; 24, Cresson 1m 52.650s; 25, Konig 1m 52.839s.

Points

1, Bautista 57; 2, Rea 54; 3, Razgatlioglu 39; 4, Rinaldi 32; 5, Lecuona 18; 6, Vierge 18; 7, Locatelli 16; 8, Lowes 15; 9, Baz 14; 10, Gerloff 14; 11, Bassani 13; 12, Laverty 10; 13, Mykhalchyk 9; 14, Mahias 7; 15, Oettl 6; 16, Bernardi 4; 17, Tamburini 2; 18, Redding 1.

Round 2 ASSEN, The Netherlands · 22–24 April, 2022 · 2.822-mile/4.542km circuit

Race 1: 21 laps, 59.268 miles/95.382km
Weather: Dry · Track 29°C · Air 18°C
Time of race: 33m 22.865s
Average speed: 106.529mph/171.442km/h

Pos.	Rider	Nat.	No.	Entrant	Machine	Time & Gap	Laps
1	**Jonathan Rea**	GBR	65	Kawasaki Racing Team WorldSBK	Kawasaki ZX-10RR		21
2	**Alvaro Bautista**	ESP	19	Aruba.it Racing - Ducati	Ducati Panigale V4R	0.103s	21
3	**Toprak Razgatlioglu**	TUR	1	Pata Yamaha with Brixx WorldSBK	Yamaha YZF R1	1.014s	21
4	**Andrea Locatelli**	ITA	55	Pata Yamaha with Brixx WorldSBK	Yamaha YZF R1	9.712s	21
5	**Iker Lecuona**	ESP	7	Team HRC	Honda CBR1000 RR-R	17.451s	21
6	**Loris Baz**	FRA	76	Bonovo Action BMW	BMW M1000RR	17.983s	21
7	**Philipp Oettl**	GER	5	Team Goeleven	Ducati Panigale V4R	22.002s	21
8	**Garrett Gerloff**	USA	31	GYTR GRT Yamaha WorldSBK Team	Yamaha YZF R1	24.545s	21
9	**Scott Redding**	GBR	45	BMW Motorrad WorldSBK Team	BMW M1000RR	25.118s	21
10	**Axel Bassani**	ITA	47	Motocorsa Racing	Ducati Panigale V4R	26.938s	21
11	**Xavi Vierge**	ESP	97	Team HRC	Honda CBR1000 RR-R	35.566s	21
12	**Christophe Ponsson**	FRA	23	Gil Motor Sport-Yamaha	Yamaha YZF R1	41.901s	21
13	**Michael van der Mark**	NED	60	BMW Motorrad WorldSBK Team	BMW M1000RR	41.967s	21
14	**Roberto Tamburini**	ITA	2	Yamaha Motoxracing WorldSBK Team	Yamaha YZF R1	42.014s	21
15	**Lucas Mahias**	FRA	44	Kawasaki Puccetti Racing	Kawasaki ZX-10RR	45.699s	21
16	Leon Haslam	GBR	91	TPR Team Pedercini Racing	Kawasaki ZX-10RR	45.882s	21
17	Kohta Nozane	JPN	3	GYTR GRT Yamaha WorldSBK Team	Yamaha YZF R1	45.972s	21
18	Luca Bernardi	SMR	29	BARNI Spark Racing Team	Ducati Panigale V4R	47.975s	21
19	Leandro Mercado	ARG	36	MIE Racing Honda Team	Honda CBR1000 RR-R	48.144s	21
20	Hafizh Syahrin	MAS	35	MIE Racing Honda Team	Honda CBR1000 RR-R	58.169s	21
21	Oliver Konig	CZE	52	Orelac Racing Verdnatura	Kawasaki ZX-10RR	1m 12.087s	21
	Michael Rinaldi	ITA	21	Aruba.it Racing - Ducati	Ducati Panigale V4R	DNF	16
	Alex Lowes	GBR	22	Kawasaki Racing Team WorldSBK	Kawasaki ZX-10RR	DNF	11
	Gabriele Ruiu	ITA	16	Bmax Racing	BMW M1000RR	DNF	7

Fastest race lap: Rea on lap 2, 1m 34.535s, 107.47mph/172.96km/h.
Lap record: Bautista, 1m 34.564s, 107.44mph/172.91km/h (2019).

Superpole: 9 laps, 25.400 miles/40.878km
Weather: Dry · Track 21°C · Air 13°C
Time of race: 14m 10.648s
Average speed: 107.496mph/172.998km/h

Pos.	Rider	Time & Gap	Laps
1	**Jonathan Rea**		9
2	**Toprak Razgatlioglu**	0.267s	9
3	**Alvaro Bautista**	0.300s	9
4	**Andrea Locatelli**	6.959s	9
5	**Iker Lecuona**	11.997s	9
6	**Loris Baz**	12.953s	9
7	**Garrett Gerloff**	13.410s	9
8	**Michael Rinaldi**	13.512s	9
9	**Axel Bassani**	13.567s	9
10	Philipp Oettl	13.871s	9
11	Scott Redding	14.239s	9
12	Xavi Vierge	16.491s	9
13	Lucas Mahias	16.800s	9
14	Kohta Nozane	18.989s	9
15	Michael van der Mark	20.625s	9
16	Roberto Tamburini	21.463s	9
17	Leon Haslam	23.762s	9
18	Leandro Mercado	23.998s	9
19	Christophe Ponsson	24.207s	9
20	Luca Bernardi	25.949s	9
21	Gabriele Ruiu	33.209s	9
22	Hafizh Syahrin	33.519s	9
23	Oliver Konig	33.717s	9
	Alex Lowes	DNF	8

Fastest race lap: Bautista on lap 2, 1m 33.62s, 108.52mph/174.65km/h.

Race 2: 21 laps, 59.268 miles/95.382km
Weather: Dry · Track 26°C · Air 14°C
Time of race: 33m 20.602s
Average speed: 106.650mph/171.636km/h

Pos.	Rider	Time & Gap	Laps
1	**Alvaro Bautista**		21
2	**Andrea Locatelli**	8.770s	21
3	**Iker Lecuona**	11.580s	21
4	**Alex Lowes**	13.329s	21
5	**Scott Redding**	14.672s	21
6	**Axel Bassani**	17.490s	21
7	**Michael Rinaldi**	23.374s	21
8	**Michael van der Mark**	28.511s	21
9	**Xavi Vierge**	29.067s	21
10	**Lucas Mahias**	29.434s	21
11	**Roberto Tamburini**	36.810s	21
12	**Christophe Ponsson**	36.814s	21
13	**Leon Haslam**	37.000s	21
14	**Luca Bernardi**	38.862s	21
15	**Leandro Mercado**	41.674s	21
16	Gabriele Ruiu	51.252s	21
17	Hafizh Syahrin	51.382s	21
18	Oliver Konig	1m 10.088s	21
	Toprak Razgatlioglu	DNF	5
	Jonathan Rea	DNF	5
	Philipp Oettl	DNF	1
	Loris Baz	DNF	1
	Garrett Gerloff	DNF	1
	Kohta Nozane	DNF	0

Fastest race lap: Rea on lap 3, 1m 34.093s, 107.98mph/173.78km/h.

Superpole

1, Razgatlioglu 1m 32.934s; 2, Lowes 1m 33.412s; 3, Rea 1m 33.621s; 4, Locatelli 1m 33.888s; 5, Bautista 1m 34.018s; 6, Gerloff 1m 34.175s; 7, Baz 1m 34.453s; 8, Lecuona 1m 34.543s; 9, Bassani 1m 34.666s; 10, Mahias 1m 34.702s; 11, Oettl 1m 35.018s; 12, Rinaldi 1m 35.045s; 13, Redding 1m 35.047s; 14, Vierge 1m 35.199s; 15, Van der Mark 1m 35.206s; 16, Nozane 1m 35.215s; 17, Haslam 1m 35.590s; 18, Ruiu 1m 35.761s; 19, Mercado 1m 35.956s; 20, Ponsson 1m 36.000s; 21, Syahrin 1m 36.553s; 22, Tamburini 1m 36.634s; 23, Konig 1m 37.027s; 24, Bernardi No Time.

Points

1, Bautista 109; 2, Rea 91; 3, Razgatlioglu 64; 4, Locatelli 55; 5, Lecuona 50; 6, Rinaldi 43; 7, Bassani 30; 8, Vierge 30; 9, Lowes 28; 10, Baz 28; 11, Gerloff 25; 12, Redding 19; 13, Oettl 15; 14, Mahias 14; 15, Van der Mark 11; 16, Laverty 10; 17, Mykhalchyk 9; 18, Tamburini 9; 19, Ponsson 8; 20, Bernardi 6; 21, Haslam 3; 22, Mercado 1.

Round 3 ESTORIL, Portugal · 20–22 May, 2022 · 2.599-mile/4.182km circuit

Race 1: 21 laps, 54.570 miles/87.822km
Weather: Dry · Track 32°C · Air 19°C
Time of race: 33m 58.478s
Average speed: 96.372mph/155.096km/h

Pos.	Rider	Nat.	No.	Entrant	Machine	Time & Gap	Laps
1	**Alvaro Bautista**	ESP	19	Aruba.it Racing - Ducati	Ducati Panigale V4R		21
2	**Toprak Razgatlioglu**	TUR	1	Pata Yamaha with Brixx WorldSBK	Yamaha YZF R1	0.126s	21
3	**Jonathan Rea**	GBR	65	Kawasaki Racing Team WorldSBK	Kawasaki ZX-10RR	4.835s	21
4	**Andrea Locatelli**	ITA	55	Pata Yamaha with Brixx WorldSBK	Yamaha YZF R1	17.079s	21
5	**Xavi Vierge**	ESP	97	Team HRC	Honda CBR1000 RR-R	19.107s	21
6	**Iker Lecuona**	ESP	7	Team HRC	Honda CBR1000 RR-R	19.215s	21
7	**Alex Lowes**	GBR	22	Kawasaki Racing Team WorldSBK	Kawasaki ZX-10RR	21.956s	21
8	**Scott Redding**	GBR	45	BMW Motorrad WorldSBK Team	BMW M1000RR	23.090s	21
9	**Michael Rinaldi**	ITA	21	Aruba.it Racing - Ducati	Ducati Panigale V4R	24.104s	21
10	**Loris Baz**	FRA	76	Bonovo Action BMW	BMW M1000RR	25.212s	21
11	**Xavi Fores**	ESP	12	Team Goeleven	Ducati Panigale V4R	27.516s	21
12	**Axel Bassani**	ITA	47	Motocorsa Racing	Ducati Panigale V4R	30.686s	21
13	**Luca Bernardi**	SMR	29	BARNI Spark Racing Team	Ducati Panigale V4R	39.599s	21
14	**Kohta Nozane**	JPN	3	GYTR GRT Yamaha WorldSBK Team	Yamaha YZF R1	39.643s	21
15	**Eugene Laverty**	IRL	50	Bonovo Action BMW	BMW M1000RR	41.735s	21
16	Marvin Fritz	GER	17	Yamaha Motoxracing WorldSBK Team	Yamaha YZF R1	41.854s	21
17	Lucas Mahias	FRA	44	Kawasaki Puccetti Racing	Kawasaki ZX-10RR	42.790s	21
18	Christophe Ponsson	FRA	23	Gil Motor Sport-Yamaha	Yamaha YZF R1	50.082s	21
19	Hafizh Syahrin	MAS	35	MIE Racing Honda Team	Honda CBR1000 RR-R	1m 08.940s	21
20	Oliver Konig	CZE	52	Orelac Racing Verdnatura	Kawasaki ZX-10RR	1m 08.979s	21
21	Isaac Vinales	ESP	32	TPR Team Pedercini Racing	Kawasaki ZX-10RR	2 Laps	19
	Leandro Mercado	ARG	36	MIE Racing Honda Team	Honda CBR1000 RR-R	DNF	0

Fastest race lap: Rea on lap 4, 1m 36.204s, 97.24mph/156.49km/h.
Lap record: Razgatlioglu, 1m 36.594s, 96.85mph/155.86km/h (2020).

Superpole: 10 laps, 25.986 miles/41.820km
Weather: Wet · Track 22°C · Air 18°C
Time of race: 16m 21.784s
Average speed: 95.284mph/153.345km/h

Pos.	Rider	Time & Gap	Laps
1	**Jonathan Rea**		10
2	**Toprak Razgatlioglu**	0.174s	10
3	**Alvaro Bautista**	4.925s	10
4	**Iker Lecuona**	7.050s	10
5	**Andrea Locatelli**	8.240s	10
6	**Alex Lowes**	8.684s	10
7	**Scott Redding**	10.293s	10
8	**Michael Rinaldi**	29.516s	10
9	**Xavi Fores**	29.541s	10
10	Axel Bassani	32.114s	10
11	Kohta Nozane	32.141s	10
12	Christophe Ponsson	52.258s	10
13	Isaac Vinales	53.209s	10
14	Leandro Mercado	55.481s	10
15	Luca Bernardi	1m 06.281s	10
16	Hafizh Syahrin	1m 07.723s	10
17	Oliver Konig	1m 07.758s	10
	Eugene Laverty	DNF	4
	Loris Baz	DNF	3
	Xavi Vierge	DNF	1
	Marvin Fritz	DNF	0
	Lucas Mahias	DNF	0

Fastest race lap: Rea on lap 9, 1m 36.801s, 96.64mph/155.53km/h..

Race 2: 21 laps, 54.570 miles/87.822km
Weather: Dry · Track 29°C · Air 18°C
Time of race: 34m 10.420s
Average speed: 95.810mph/154.192km/h

Pos.	Rider	Time & Gap	Laps
1	**Jonathan Rea**		21
2	**Alvaro Bautista**	0.194s	21
3	**Toprak Razgatlioglu**	4.350s	21
4	**Alex Lowes**	7.125s	21
5	**Andrea Locatelli**	8.232s	21
6	**Iker Lecuona**	8.309s	21
7	**Axel Bassani**	10.865s	21
8	**Michael Rinaldi**	16.082s	21
9	**Xavi Vierge**	18.292s	21
10	**Xavi Fores**	18.412s	21
11	**Scott Redding**	19.758s	21
12	**Loris Baz**	25.193s	21
13	**Kohta Nozane**	27.753s	21
14	**Eugene Laverty**	38.391s	21
15	**Luca Bernardi**	38.424s	21
16	Christophe Ponsson	41.541s	21
17	Marvin Fritz	42.555s	21
18	Leandro Mercado	49.775s	21
19	Hafizh Syahrin	51.353s	21
20	Oliver Konig	1m 14.141s	21
	Isaac Vinales	DNF	5

Fastest race lap: Rea on lap 20, 1m 36.919s, 96.52mph/155.34km/h.

Superpole

1, Rea 1m 35.346s; 2, Razgatlioglu 1m 35.437s; 3, Bautista 1m 35.963s; 4, Redding 1m 35.979s; 5, Locatelli 1m 36.198s; 6, Rinaldi 1m 36.236s; 7, Lecuona 1m 36.433s; 8, Lowes 1m 36.538s; 9, Laverty 1m 36.659s; 10, Mahias 1m 36.674s; 11, Vierge 1m 36.747s; 12, Baz 1m 36.755s; 13, Nozane 1m 36.980s; 14, Bassani 1m 37.015s; 15, Bernardi 1m 37.105s; 16, Fritz 1m 37.124s; 17, Fores 1m 37.521s; 18, Ponsson 1m 37.775s; 19, Mercado 1m 37.867s; 20, Syahrin 1m 38.065s; 21, Vinales 1m 38.436s; 22, Konig 1m 38.709s.

Points

1, Bautista 161; 2, Rea 144; 3, Razgatlioglu 109; 4, Locatelli 84; 5, Lecuona 76; 6, Rinaldi 60; 7, Lowes 54; 8, Vierge 48; 9, Bassani 43; 10, Baz 38; 11, Redding 35; 12, Gerloff 25; 13, Oettl 15; 14, Mahias 14; 15, Laverty 13; 16, Fores 12; 17, Van der Mark 11; 18, Bernardi 10; 19, Mykhalchyk 9; 20, Tamburini 9; 21, Ponsson 8; 22, Nozane 5; 23, Haslam 3; 24, Mercado 1.

Round 4 MISANO, Italy · 10–12 June, 2022 · 2.626-mile/4.226km circuit

Race 1: 21 laps, 55.144 miles/88.746km
Weather: Dry · Track 44°C · Air 26°C
Time of race: 33m 14.661s
Average speed: 99.525mph/160.170km/h

Pos.	Rider	Nat.	No.	Entrant	Machine	Time & Gap	Laps
1	**Alvaro Bautista**	ESP	19	Aruba.it Racing - Ducati	Ducati Panigale V4R		21
2	**Jonathan Rea**	GBR	65	Kawasaki Racing Team WorldSBK	Kawasaki ZX-10RR	0.126s	21
3	**Michael Rinaldi**	ITA	21	Aruba.it Racing - Ducati	Ducati Panigale V4R	4.835s	21
4	**Axel Bassani**	ITA	47	Motocorsa Racing	Ducati Panigale V4R	17.079s	21
5	**Alex Lowes**	GBR	22	Kawasaki Racing Team WorldSBK	Kawasaki ZX-10RR	19.107s	21
6	**Andrea Locatelli**	ITA	55	Pata Yamaha with Brixx WorldSBK	Yamaha YZF R1	19.215s	21
7	**Xavi Vierge**	ESP	97	Team HRC	Honda CBR1000 RR-R	21.956s	21
8	**Garrett Gerloff**	USA	31	GYTR GRT Yamaha WorldSBK Team	Yamaha YZF R1	23.090s	21
9	**Iker Lecuona**	ESP	7	Team HRC	Honda CBR1000 RR-R	24.104s	21
10	**Scott Redding**	GBR	45	BMW Motorrad WorldSBK Team	BMW M1000RR	25.212s	21
11	**Roberto Tamburini**	ITA	2	Yamaha Motoxracing WorldSBK Team	Yamaha YZF R1	27.516s	21
12	**Kohta Nozane**	JPN	3	GYTR GRT Yamaha WorldSBK Team	Yamaha YZF R1	30.686s	21
13	**Eugene Laverty**	IRL	50	Bonovo Action BMW	BMW M1000RR	39.599s	21
14	**Luca Bernardi**	SMR	29	BARNI Spark Racing Team	Ducati Panigale V4R	39.643s	21
15	**Loris Baz**	FRA	76	Bonovo Action BMW	BMW M1000RR	41.735s	21
16	Tito Rabat	ESP	53	Kawasaki Puccetti Racing	Kawasaki ZX-10RR	41.854s	21
17	Hafizh Syahrin	MAS	35	MIE Racing Honda Team	Honda CBR1000 RR-R	42.790s	21
18	Illia Mykhalchyk	UKR	37	BMW Motorrad WorldSBK Team	BMW M1000RR	50.082s	21
19	Leandro Mercado	ARG	36	MIE Racing Honda Team	Honda CBR1000 RR-R	1m 08.940s	21
20	Oliver Konig	CZE	52	Orelac Racing Verdnatura	Kawasaki ZX-10RR	1m 08.979s	21
	Toprak Razgatlioglu	TUR	1	Pata Yamaha with Brixx WorldSBK	Yamaha YZF R1	DNF	13
	Gabriele Ruiu	ITA	16	Bmax Racing	BMW M1000RR	DNF	11
	Philipp Oettl	GER	5	Team Goeleven	Ducati Panigale V4R	DNF	4
	Christophe Ponsson	FRA	23	Gil Motor Sport-Yamaha	Yamaha YZF R1	DNF	2
	Alessandro Delbianco	ITA	25	TPR Team Pedercini Racing	Kawasaki ZX-10RR	DNF	0

Fastest race lap: Bautista on lap 18, 1m 34.221s, 100.33mph/161.47km/h.
Lap record: Rinaldi, 1m 34.356s, 100.19mph/161.24km/h (2021).

Superpole: 10 laps, 26.259 miles/42.260km
Weather: Dry · Track 39°C · Air 27°C
Time of race: 15m 46.121s
Average speed: 99.916mph/160.800km/h

Pos.	Rider	Time & Gap	Laps
1	**Toprak Razgatlioglu**		10
2	**Alvaro Bautista**	2.087s	10
3	**Jonathan Rea**	4.975s	10
4	**Xavi Vierge**	5.903s	10
5	**Iker Lecuona**	7.197s	10
6	**Andrea Locatelli**	8.476s	10
7	**Axel Bassani**	8.749s	10
8	**Alex Lowes**	9.383s	10
9	**Garrett Gerloff**	9.566s	10
10	Michael Rinaldi	12.303s	10
11	Scott Redding	12.400s	10
12	Eugene Laverty	19.399s	10
13	Hafizh Syahrin	21.834s	10
14	Luca Bernardi	22.000s	10
15	Illia Mykhalchyk	24.547s	10
16	Tito Rabat	25.000s	10
17	Roberto Tamburini	26.420s	10
18	Gabriele Ruiu	28.132s	10
19	Leandro Mercado	28.479s	10
20	Oliver Konig	2 Laps	8
	Kohta Nozane	DNF	9
	Philipp Oettl	DNF	6
	Loris Baz	DNF	5
	Alessandro Delbianco	DNF	0

Fastest race lap: Razgatlioglu on lap 5, 1m 33.722s, 100.87mph/162.33km/h.

Race 2: 21 laps, 55.144 miles/88.746km
Weather: Dry · Track 45°C · Air 28°C
Time of race: 33m 12.030s
Average speed: 99.657mph/160.382km/h

Pos.	Rider	Time & Gap	Laps
1	**Alvaro Bautista**		21
2	**Toprak Razgatlioglu**	7.194s	21
3	**Michael Rinaldi**	11.119s	21
4	**Jonathan Rea**	14.901s	21
5	**Iker Lecuona**	18.774s	21
6	**Andrea Locatelli**	20.217s	21
7	**Axel Bassani**	21.149s	21
8	**Alex Lowes**	23.533s	21
9	**Scott Redding**	29.638s	21
10	**Loris Baz**	38.831s	21
11	**Philipp Oettl**	40.881s	21
12	**Roberto Tamburini**	41.588s	21
13	**Luca Bernardi**	43.353s	21
14	**Eugene Laverty**	43.833s	21
15	**Illia Mykhalchyk**	43.889s	21
16	Kohta Nozane	44.697s	21
17	Tito Rabat	49.375s	21
18	Leandro Mercado	1m 02.448s	21
19	Oliver Konig	1m 22.808s	21
	Xavi Vierge	DNF	11
	Hafizh Syahrin	DNF	7
	Alessandro Delbianco	DNF	7
	Gabriele Ruiu	DNF	3
	Garrett Gerloff	DNF	2

Fastest race lap: Bautista on lap 8, 1m 34.255s, 100.30mph/161.41km/h.

Superpole

1, Bautista 1m 33.328s; 2, Razgatlioglu 1m 33.465s; 3, Rea 1m 33.518s; 4, Lowes 1m 33.669s; 5, Rinaldi 1m 33.674s; 6, Locatelli 1m 33.949s; 7, Vierge 1m 33.991s; 8, Lecuona 1m 33.999s; 9, Redding 1m 34.039s; 10, Bassani 1m 34.117s; 11, Gerloff 1m 34.514s; 12, Baz 1m 34.520s; 13, Oettl 1m 34.530s; 14, Tamburini 1m 34.654s; 15, Nozane 1m 34.939s; 16, Ponsson 1m 34.994s; 17, Laverty 1m 35.265s; 18, Syahrin 1m 35.315s; 19, Rabat 1m 35.420s; 20, Ruiu 1m 35.462s; 21, Bernardi 1m 35.614s; 22, Mercado 1m 35.746s; 23, Mykhalchyk 1m 35.813s; 24, Konig 1m 36.209s; 25, Delbianco 1m 36.494s.

Points

1, Bautista 220; 2, Rea 184; 3, Razgatlioglu 141; 4, Locatelli 108; 5, Lecuona 99; 6, Rinaldi 92; 7, Lowes 75; 8, Bassani 68; 9, Vierge 63; 10, Redding 48; 11, Baz 45; 12, Gerloff 34; 13, Oettl 20; 14, Laverty 18; 15, Tamburini 18; 16, Bernardi 15; 17, Mahias 14; 18, Fores 12; 19, Van der Mark 11; 20, Mykhalchyk 10; 21, Nozane 9; 22, Ponsson 8; 23, Haslam 3; 24, Mercado 1.

Round 5 DONINGTON PARK, UK · 15–17 July, 2022 · 2.500-mile/4.023km circuit

Race 1: 23 laps, 57.495 miles/92.529km
Weather: Dry · Track 42°C · Air 24°C
Time of race: 33m 46.954s
Average speed: 102.114mph/164.337km/h

Pos.	Rider	Nat.	No.	Entrant	Machine	Time & Gap	Laps
1	**Toprak Razgatlioglu**	TUR	1	Pata Yamaha with Brixx WorldSBK	Yamaha YZF R1		23
2	**Jonathan Rea**	GBR	65	Kawasaki Racing Team WorldSBK	Kawasaki ZX-10RR	6.397s	23
3	**Alex Lowes**	GBR	22	Kawasaki Racing Team WorldSBK	Kawasaki ZX-10RR	9.499s	23
4	**Scott Redding**	GBR	45	BMW Motorrad WorldSBK Team	BMW M1000RR	11.515s	23
5	**Axel Bassani**	ITA	47	Motocorsa Racing	Ducati Panigale V4R	12.820s	23
6	**Michael Rinaldi**	ITA	21	Aruba.it Racing - Ducati	Ducati Panigale V4R	14.482s	23
7	**Garrett Gerloff**	USA	31	GYTR GRT Yamaha WorldSBK Team	Yamaha YZF R1	17.127s	23
8	**Iker Lecuona**	ESP	7	Team HRC	Honda CBR1000 RR-R	17.438s	23
9	**Loris Baz**	FRA	76	Bonovo Action BMW	BMW M1000RR	24.903s	23
10	**Andrea Locatelli**	ITA	55	Pata Yamaha with Brixx WorldSBK	Yamaha YZF R1	28.498s	23
11	**Philipp Oettl**	GER	5	Team Goeleven	Ducati Panigale V4R	31.467s	23
12	**Lucas Mahias**	FRA	44	Kawasaki Puccetti Racing	Kawasaki ZX-10RR	33.514s	23
13	**Xavi Vierge**	ESP	97	Team HRC	Honda CBR1000 RR-R	33.647s	23
14	**Tarran Mackenzie**	GBR	95	McAMS Yamaha	Yamaha YZF R1	34.870s	23
15	**Leon Haslam**	GBR	91	TPR Team Pedercini Racing	Kawasaki ZX-10RR	44.961s	23
16	Illia Mykhalchyk	UKR	37	BMW Motorrad WorldSBK Team	BMW M1000RR	45.205s	23
17	Hafizh Syahrin	MAS	35	MIE Racing Honda Team	Honda CBR1000 RR-R	52.808s	23
18	Luca Bernardi	SMR	29	BARNI Spark Racing Team	Ducati Panigale V4R	53.315s	23
19	Kohta Nozane	JPN	3	GYTR GRT Yamaha WorldSBK Team	Yamaha YZF R1	54.779s	23
20	Eugene Laverty	IRL	50	Bonovo Action BMW	BMW M1000RR	55.987s	23
21	Roberto Tamburini	ITA	2	Yamaha Motoxracing WorldSBK Team	Yamaha YZF R1	56.072s	23
22	Peter Hickman	GBR	10	FHO Racing	BMW M1000RR	1m 00.554s	23
23	Oliver Konig	CZE	52	Orelac Racing Verdnatura	Kawasaki ZX-10RR	1m 07.239s	23
	Alvaro Bautista	ESP	19	Aruba.it Racing - Ducati	Ducati Panigale V4R	DNF	16
	Christophe Ponsson	FRA	23	Gil Motor Sport-Yamaha	Yamaha YZF R1	DNF	13
	Leandro Mercado	ARG	36	MIE Racing Honda Team		DNF	6

Fastest race lap: Rea on lap 4, 1m 27.263s, 102.94mph/165.67km/h.
Lap record: Rea, 1m 27.166s, 103.47mph/166.52km/h (2019).

Superpole: 10 laps, 24.998 miles/40.230km
Weather: Dry · Track 36°C · Air 26°C
Time of race: 14m 35.464s
Average speed: 102.793mph/165.430km/h

Pos.	Rider	Time & Gap	Laps
1	**Toprak Razgatlioglu**		10
2	**Jonathan Rea**	1.089s	10
3	**Scott Redding**	3.889s	10
4	**Alvaro Bautista**	4.970s	10
5	**Alex Lowes**	5.244s	10
6	**Michael Rinaldi**	6.282s	10
7	**Iker Lecuona**	8.665s	10
8	**Andrea Locatelli**	10.445s	10
9	**Loris Baz**	10.802s	10
10	Garrett Gerloff	12.491s	10
11	Philipp Oettl	12.558s	10
12	Axel Bassani	18.053s	10
13	Leon Haslam	21.933s	10
14	Lucas Mahias	24.090s	10
15	Xavi Vierge	24.540s	10
16	Peter Hickman	26.834s	10
17	Kohta Nozane	27.400s	10
18	Illia Mykhalchyk	27.958s	10
19	Hafizh Syahrin	29.595s	10
20	Leandro Mercado	29.653s	10
21	Roberto Tamburini	30.394s	10
22	Luca Bernardi	30.658s	10
23	Eugene Laverty	30.681s	10
24	Oliver Konig	32.678s	10
	Tarran Mackenzie	DNF	4

Fastest race lap: Razgatlioglu on lap 3, 1m 26.767s, 103.25mph/166.16km/h.

Race 2: 23 laps, 57.495 miles/92.529km
Weather: Dry · Track 41°C · Air 29°C
Time of race: 33m 48.407s
Average speed: 102.042mph/164.220km/h

Pos.	Rider	Time & Gap	Laps
1	**Toprak Razgatlioglu**		23
2	**Alvaro Bautista**	1.102s	23
3	**Jonathan Rea**	2.615s	23
4	**Michael Rinaldi**	5.067s	23
5	**Scott Redding**	8.256s	23
6	**Alex Lowes**	10.114s	23
7	**Axel Bassani**	13.422s	23
8	**Andrea Locatelli**	15.514s	23
9	**Loris Baz**	23.119s	23
10	**Iker Lecuona**	23.512s	23
11	**Garrett Gerloff**	23.596s	23
12	**Philipp Oettl**	24.142s	23
13	**Xavi Vierge**	24.896s	23
14	**Lucas Mahias**	32.872s	23
15	**Tarran Mackenzie**	33.356s	23
16	Luca Bernardi	44.719s	23
17	Leandro Mercado	51.052s	23
18	Kohta Nozane	52.320s	23
19	Peter Hickman	52.457s	23
20	Hafizh Syahrin	57.785s	23
21	Roberto Tamburini	58.338s	23
22	Oliver Konig	1m 03.669s	23
	Eugene Laverty	DNF	19
	Leon Haslam	DNF	7
	Illia Mykhalchyk	DNF	2

Fastest race lap: Bautista on lap 3, 1m 27.644s, 102.81mph/165.46km/h.

Superpole

1, Rea 1m 26.080s; 2, Lowes 1m 26.353s; 3, Razgatlioglu 1m 26.506s; 4, Redding 1m 26.514s; 5, Bautista 1m 26.736s; 6, Rinaldi 1m 27.011s; 7, Lecuona 1m 27.038s; 8, Gerloff 1m 27.100s; 9, Locatelli 1m 27.191s; 10, Bassani 1m 27.206s; 11, Oettl 1m 27.336s; 12, Mahias 1m 27.390s; 13, Mackenzie 1m 27.670s; 14, Baz 1m 27.711s; 15, Haslam 1m 27.806s; 16, Vierge 1m 27.861s; 17, Mercado 1m 27.929s; 18, Mykhalchyk 1m 27.957s; 19, Tamburini 1m 28.025s; 20, Laverty 1m 28.048s; 21, Syahrin 1m 28.141s; 22, Hickman 1m 28.378s; 23, Nozane 1m 28.617s; 24, Ponsson 1m 28.935s; 25, Konig 1m 29.011s.

Points

1, Bautista 246; 2, Rea 229; 3, Razgatlioglu 203; 4, Locatelli 124; 5, Rinaldi 119; 6, Lecuona 116; 7, Lowes 106; 8, Bassani 88; 9, Redding 79; 10, Vierge 69; 11, Baz 60; 12, Gerloff 48; 13, Oettl 29; 14, Mahias 20; 15, Laverty 18; 16, Tamburini 18; 17, Bernardi 15; 18, Fores 12; 19, Van der Mark 11; 20, Mykhalchyk 10; 21, Nozane 9; 22, Ponsson 8; 23, Haslam 4; 24, Mackenzie 3; 25, Mercado 1.

Round 6 MOST, Czech Republic · 29–31 July, 2022 · 2.617-mile/4.212km circuit

Race 1: 22 laps, 57.579 miles/92.664km
Weather: Dry · Track 25°C · Air 19°C
Time of race: 34m 0.965s
Average speed: 101.561mph/163.447km/h

Pos.	Rider	Nat.	No.	Entrant	Machine	Time & Gap	Laps
1	**Alvaro Bautista**	ESP	19	Aruba.it Racing - Ducati	Ducati Panigale V4R		22
2	**Toprak Razgatlioglu**	TUR	1	Pata Yamaha with Brixx WorldSBK	Yamaha YZF R1	2.109s	22
3	**Scott Redding**	GBR	45	BMW Motorrad WorldSBK Team	BMW M1000RR	2.603s	22
4	**Jonathan Rea**	GBR	65	Kawasaki Racing Team WorldSBK	Kawasaki ZX-10RR	2.718s	22
5	**Axel Bassani**	ITA	47	Motocorsa Racing	Ducati Panigale V4R	7.951s	22
6	**Andrea Locatelli**	ITA	55	Pata Yamaha with Brixx WorldSBK	Yamaha YZF R1	9.105s	22
7	**Michael Rinaldi**	ITA	21	Aruba.it Racing - Ducati	Ducati Panigale V4R	12.181s	22
8	**Iker Lecuona**	ESP	7	Team HRC	Honda CBR1000 RR-	12.435s	22
9	**Alex Lowes**	GBR	22	Kawasaki Racing Team WorldSBK	Kawasaki ZX-10RR	13.028s	22
10	**Garrett Gerloff**	USA	31	GYTR GRT Yamaha WorldSBK Team	Yamaha YZF R1	13.119s	22
11	**Loris Baz**	FRA	76	Bonovo Action BMW	BMW M1000RR	17.379s	22
12	**Lucas Mahias**	FRA	44	Kawasaki Puccetti Racing	Kawasaki ZX-10RR	26.631s	22
13	**Philipp Oettl**	GER	5	Team Goeleven	Ducati Panigale V4R	27.364s	22
14	**Luca Bernardi**	SMR	29	BARNI Spark Racing Team	Ducati Panigale V4R	31.278s	22
15	**Xavi Vierge**	ESP	97	Team HRC	Honda CBR1000 RR-	37.260s	22
16	Oliver Konig	CZE	52	Orelac Racing Verdnatura	Kawasaki ZX-10RR	50.854s	22
17	Leandro Mercado	ARG	36	MIE Racing Honda Team	Honda CBR1000 RR-	51.431s	22
18	Kohta Nozane	JPN	3	GYTR GRT Yamaha WorldSBK Team	Yamaha YZF R1	53.058s	22
19	Eugene Laverty	IRL	50	Bonovo Action BMW	BMW M1000RR	58.942s	22
20	Christophe Ponsson	FRA	23	Gil Motor Sport-Yamaha	Yamaha YZF R1	1m 03.366s	22
21	Roberto Tamburini	ITA	2	Yamaha Motoxracing WorldSBK Team	Yamaha YZF R1	1m 03.407s	22
22	Peter Hickman	GBR	10	BMW Motorrad WorldSBK Team	BMW M1000RR	1m 05.450s	22
23	Ryan Vickers	GBR	77	TPR Team Pedercini Racing	Kawasaki ZX-10RR	1m 06.797s	22
	Hafizh Syahrin	MAS	35	MIE Racing Honda Team	Honda CBR1000 RR-R	DNF	20
	Michal Prasek	CZE	6	Rohac & Fejta Motoracing	BMW M1000RR	DNF	16

Fastest race lap: Razgatlioglu on lap 3, 1m 31.936s, 102.10mph/164.32km/h.
Lap record: Rea, 1m 31.996s, 102.06mph/164.25km/h (2021).

Superpole: 10 laps, 26.172 miles/42.120km
Weather: Dry · Track 33°C · Air 25°C
Time of race: 15m 21.996s
Average speed: 102.191mph/164.461km/h

Pos.	Rider	Time & Gap	Laps
1	**Toprak Razgatlioglu**		10
2	**Jonathan Rea**	2.327s	10
3	**Alvaro Bautista**	3.406s	10
4	**Michael Rinaldi**	4.679s	10
5	**Axel Bassani**	7.127s	10
6	**Andrea Locatelli**	8.328s	10
7	**Iker Lecuona**	8.479s	10
8	**Scott Redding**	10.308s	10
9	**Garrett Gerloff**	10.506s	10
10	Xavi Vierge	14.540s	10
11	Loris Baz	14.634s	10
12	Lucas Mahias	14.760s	10
13	Philipp Oettl	15.271s	10
14	Luca Bernardi	18.008s	10
15	Hafizh Syahrin	24.394s	10
16	Kohta Nozane	24.574s	10
17	Leandro Mercado	24.891s	10
18	Eugene Laverty	26.956s	10
19	Peter Hickman	28.649s	10
20	Roberto Tamburini	35.860s	10
21	Michal Prasek	57.426s	10
	Oliver Konig	DNF	8
	Christophe Ponsson	DNF	5
	Alex Lowes	DNF	3
	Ryan Vickers	DNF	2

Fastest race lap: Razgatlioglu on lap 2, 1m 31.18s, 103.15mph/166.00km/h.

Race 2: 22 laps, 57.579 miles/92.664km
Weather: Dry · Track 38°C · Air 27°C
Time of race: 33m 55.494s
Average speed: 101.835mph/163.887km/h

Pos.	Rider	Time & Gap	Laps
1	**Toprak Razgatlioglu**		22
2	**Alvaro Bautista**	0.756s	22
3	**Jonathan Rea**	2.833s	22
4	**Scott Redding**	9.693s	22
5	**Axel Bassani**	11.970s	22
6	**Andrea Locatelli**	17.644s	22
7	**Xavi Vierge**	23.418s	22
8	**Philipp Oettl**	26.436s	22
9	**Lucas Mahias**	27.914s	22
10	**Luca Bernardi**	30.857s	22
11	**Roberto Tamburini**	42.047s	22
12	**Hafizh Syahrin**	45.735s	22
13	**Kohta Nozane**	46.989s	22
14	**Peter Hickman**	47.065s	22
15	**Leandro Mercado**	59.050s	22
16	Oliver Konig	1m 01.271s	22
17	Ryan Vickers	1m 13.958s	22
18	Garrett Gerloff	1m 17.001s	22
	Iker Lecuona	DNF	20
	Christophe Ponsson	DNF	18
	Loris Baz	DNF	4
	Michael Rinaldi	DNF	3
	Michal Prasek	DNS	-

Fastest race lap: Razgatlioglu on lap 20, 1m 31.705s, 102.82mph/165.48km/h.

Superpole

1, Rea 1m 30.947s; 2, Razgatlioglu 1m 31.277s; 3, Rinaldi 1m 31.506s; 4, Bautista 1m 31.567s; 5, Lowes 1m 31.622s; 6, Gerloff 1m 31.627s; 7, Redding 1m 31.684s; 8, Locatelli 1m 31.718s; 9, Bassani 1m 32.051s; 10, Mahias 1m 32.272s; 11, Baz 1m 32.282s; 12, Lecuona 1m 32.359s; 13, Vierge 1m 32.367s; 14, Bernardi 1m 32.396s; 15, Nozane 1m 32.455s; 16, Oettl 1m 32.501s; 17, Tamburini 1m 33.044s; 18, Ponsson 1m 33.266s; 19, Konig 1m 33.286s; 20, Laverty 1m 33.297s; 21, Hickman 1m 33.373s; 22, Syahrin 1m 33.456s; 23, Mercado 1m 33.481s; 24, Vickers 1m 34.049s; 25, Prasek 1m 35.766s.

Points

1, Bautista 298; 2, Rea 267; 3, Razgatlioglu 260; 4, Locatelli 148; 5, Rinaldi 134; 6, Lecuona 127; 7, Bassani 115; 8, Lowes 113; 9, Redding 110; 10, Vierge 79; 11, Baz 65; 12, Gerloff 55; 13, Oettl 40; 14, Mahias 31; 15, Bernardi 23; 16, Tamburini 23; 17, Laverty 18; 18, Fores 12; 19, Nozane 12; 20, Van der Mark 11; 21, Mykhalchyk 10; 22, Ponsson 8; 23, Syahrin 4; 24, Haslam 4; 25, Mackenzie 3; 26, Hickman 2; 27, Mercado 2.

Round 7 MAGNY-COURS, France · 9–11 September, 2022 · 2.741-mile/4.411km circuit

Race 1: 21 laps, 57.558 miles/92.631km
Weather: Dry · Track 29°C · Air 21°C
Time of race: 34m 6.991s
Average speed: 101.561mph/163.447km/h

Pos.	Rider	Nat.	No.	Entrant	Machine	Time & Gap	Laps
1	**Alvaro Bautista**	ESP	19	Aruba.it Racing - Ducati	Ducati Panigale V4R		21
2	**Scott Redding**	GBR	45	BMW Motorrad WorldSBK Team	BMW M1000RR	4.079s	21
3	**Axel Bassani**	ITA	47	Motocorsa Racing	Ducati Panigale V4R	6.751s	21
4	**Alex Lowes**	GBR	22	Kawasaki Racing Team WorldSBK	Kawasaki ZX-10RR	8.531s	21
5	**Garrett Gerloff**	USA	31	GYTR GRT Yamaha WorldSBK Team	Yamaha YZF R1	9.022s	21
6	**Michael Rinaldi**	ITA	21	Aruba.it Racing - Ducati	Ducati Panigale V4R	17.260s	21
7	**Andrea Locatelli**	ITA	55	Pata Yamaha with Brixx WorldSBK	Yamaha YZF R1	20.044s	21
8	**Philipp Oettl**	GER	5	Team Goeleven	Ducati Panigale V4R	20.712s	21
9	**Iker Lecuona**	ESP	7	Team HRC	Honda CBR1000 RR-R	21.583s	21
10	**Lucas Mahias**	FRA	44	Kawasaki Puccetti Racing	Kawasaki ZX-10RR	23.854s	21
11	**Toprak Razgatlioglu**	TUR	1	Pata Yamaha with Brixx WorldSBK	Yamaha YZF R1	26.929s	21
12	**Michael van der Mark**	NED	60	BMW Motorrad WorldSBK Team	BMW M1000RR	27.322s	21
13	**Xavi Vierge**	ESP	97	Team HRC	Honda CBR1000 RR-R	28.639s	21
14	**Loris Baz**	FRA	76	Bonovo Action BMW	BMW M1000RR	37.824s	21
15	**Luca Bernardi**	SMR	29	BARNI Spark Racing Team	Ducati Panigale V4R	38.051s	21
16	Christophe Ponsson	FRA	23	Gil Motor Sport-Yamaha	Yamaha YZF R1	40.505s	21
17	Kohta Nozane	JPN	3	GYTR GRT Yamaha WorldSBK Team	Yamaha YZF R1	40.619s	21
18	Eugene Laverty	IRL	50	Bonovo Action BMW	BMW M1000RR	41.049s	21
19	Roberto Tamburini	ITA	2	Yamaha Motoxracing WorldSBK Team	Yamaha YZF R1	41.743s	21
20	Hafizh Syahrin	MAS	35	MIE Racing Honda Team	Honda CBR1000 RR-R	49.687s	21
21	Leandro Mercado	ARG	36	MIE Racing Honda Team	Honda CBR1000 RR-R	51.725s	21
22	Oliver Konig	CZE	52	Orelac Racing Verdnatura	Kawasaki ZX-10RR	51.964s	21
23	Oscar Gutierrez	ESP	99	TPR Team Pedercini Racing	Kawasaki ZX-10RR	1m 01.857s	21
24	Jonathan Rea	GBR	65	Kawasaki Racing Team WorldSBK	Kawasaki ZX-10RR	1 Lap	20

Fastest race lap: Bautista on lap 12, 1m 36.715s, 102.46mph/164.90km/h.
Lap record: Rea, 1m 36.374s, 102.35mph/164.71km/h (2021).

Superpole: 10 laps, 27.409 miles/44.110km
Weather: Dry · Track 26°C · Air 20°C
Time of race: 16m 7.145s
Average speed: 102.023mph/164.190km/h

Pos.	Rider	Time & Gap	Laps
1	**Toprak Razgatlioglu**		10
2	**Alvaro Bautista**	1.891s	10
3	**Jonathan Rea**	2.040s	10
4	**Alex Lowes**	3.983s	10
5	**Scott Redding**	5.019s	10
6	**Axel Bassani**	5.690s	10
7	**Michael Rinaldi**	6.713s	10
8	**Garrett Gerloff**	11.797s	10
9	**Loris Baz**	12.194s	10
10	Andrea Locatelli	13.092s	10
11	Iker Lecuona	13.794s	10
12	Philipp Oettl	14.285s	10
13	Michael van der Mark	14.413s	10
14	Lucas Mahias	16.345s	10
15	Luca Bernardi	23.491s	10
16	Kohta Nozane	25.030s	10
17	Hafizh Syahrin	26.046s	10
18	Eugene Laverty	28.588s	10
19	Roberto Tamburini	28.675s	10
20	Leandro Mercado	28.837s	10
21	Christophe Ponsson	29.338s	10
22	Oscar Gutierrez	29.476s	10
23	Oliver Konig	34.839s	10
	Xavi Vierge	DNF	4

Fastest race lap: Bautista on lap 3, 1m 36.411s, 101.95mph/164.07km/h.

Race 2: 21 laps, 57.558 miles/92.631km
Weather: Dry · Track 36°C · Air 23°C
Time of race: 34m 4.476s
Average speed: 101.351mph/163.109km/h

Pos.	Rider	Time & Gap	Laps
1	**Toprak Razgatlioglu**		21
2	**Michael Rinaldi**	2.024s	21
3	**Axel Bassani**	4.742s	21
4	**Alex Lowes**	5.084s	21
5	**Jonathan Rea**	10.679s	21
6	**Scott Redding**	11.955s	21
7	**Andrea Locatelli**	15.188s	21
8	**Garrett Gerloff**	15.443s	21
9	**Loris Baz**	16.870s	21
10	**Iker Lecuona**	18.367s	21
11	**Philipp Oettl**	25.740s	21
12	**Lucas Mahias**	33.872s	21
13	**Luca Bernardi**	38.188s	21
14	**Roberto Tamburini**	41.389s	21
15	**Kohta Nozane**	42.657s	21
16	Christophe Ponsson	50.863s	21
17	Oscar Gutierrez	54.487s	21
18	Oliver Konig	1m 04.981s	21
19	Hafizh Syahrin	1m 13.308s	21
	Eugene Laverty	DNF	11
	Xavi Vierge	DNF	9
	Michael van der Mark	DNF	2
	Leandro Mercado	DNF	2
	Alvaro Bautista	DNF	1

Fastest race lap: Razgatlioglu on lap 10, 1m 36.813s, 102.05mph/164.23km/h.

Superpole

1, Rea 1m 36.124s; 2, Razgatlioglu 1m 36.124s; 3, Redding 1m 36.233s; 4, Bautista 1m 36.416s; 5, Gerloff 1m 36.464s; 6, Lowes 1m 36.524s; 7, Rinaldi 1m 36.594s; 8, Bassani 1m 36.629s; 9, Baz 1m 36.630s; 10, Oettl 1m 36.675s; 11, Mahias 1m 36.678s; 12, Locatelli 1m 36.741s; 13, Lecuona 1m 36.892s; 14, Vierge 1m 37.280s; 15, Van der Mark 1m 37.411s; 16, Laverty 1m 37.793s; 17, Nozane 1m 37.830s; 18, Tamburini 1m 37.930s; 19, Ponsson 1m 38.182s; 20, Bernardi 1m 38.337s; 21, Syahrin 1m 38.635s; 22, Mercado 1m 38.804s; 23, Gutierrez 1m 38.934s; 24, Konig 1m 39.204s.

Points

1, Bautista 332; 2, Razgatlioglu 302; 3, Rea 285; 4, Rinaldi 167; 5, Locatelli 166; 6, Bassani 151; 7, Redding 145; 8, Lowes 145; 9, Lecuona 140; 10, Vierge 82; 11, Gerloff 76; 12, Baz 75; 13, Oettl 53; 14, Mahias 41; 15, Bernardi 27; 16, Tamburini 25; 17, Laverty 18; 18, Van der Mark 15; 19, Nozane 13; 20, Fores 12; 21, Mykhalchyk 10; 22, Ponsson 8; 23, Syahrin 4; 24, Haslam 4; 25, Mackenzie 3; 26, Hickman 2; 27, Mercado 2.

Round 8 CATALUNYA, Spain · 23–25 September, 2022 · 2.875-mile/4.627km circuit

Race 1: 20 laps, 57.875 miles/93.140km
Weather: Dry · Track 32°C · Air 22°C
Time of race: 34m 21.395s
Average speed: 101.072mph/162.659km/h

Pos.	Rider	Nat.	No.	Entrant	Machine	Time & Gap	Laps
1	**Alvaro Bautista**	ESP	19	Aruba.it Racing - Ducati	Ducati Panigale V4R		20
2	**Jonathan Rea**	GBR	65	Kawasaki Racing Team WorldSBK	Kawasaki ZX-10RR	8.665s	20
3	**Garrett Gerloff**	USA	31	GYTR GRT Yamaha WorldSBK Team	Yamaha YZF R1	9.289s	20
4	**Michael Rinaldi**	ITA	21	Aruba.it Racing - Ducati	Ducati Panigale V4R	10.783s	20
5	**Toprak Razgatlioglu**	TUR	1	Pata Yamaha with Brixx WorldSBK	Yamaha YZF R1	13.568s	20
6	**Iker Lecuona**	ESP	7	Team HRC	Honda CBR1000 RR-R	13.655s	20
7	**Alex Lowes**	GBR	22	Kawasaki Racing Team WorldSBK	Kawasaki ZX-10RR	14.013s	20
8	**Axel Bassani**	ITA	47	Motocorsa Racing	Ducati Panigale V4R	14.839s	20
9	**Andrea Locatelli**	ITA	55	Pata Yamaha with Brixx WorldSBK	Yamaha YZF R1	29.775s	20
10	**Eugene Laverty**	IRL	50	Bonovo Action BMW	BMW M1000RR	30.094s	20
11	**Loris Baz**	FRA	76	Bonovo Action BMW	BMW M1000RR	30.390s	20
12	**Xavi Vierge**	ESP	97	Team HRC	Honda CBR1000 RR-R	31.755s	20
13	**Roberto Tamburini**	ITA	2	Yamaha Motoxracing WorldSBK Team	Yamaha YZF R1	33.055s	20
14	**Lucas Mahias**	FRA	44	Kawasaki Puccetti Racing	Kawasaki ZX-10RR	35.962s	20
15	**Christophe Ponsson**	FRA	23	Gil Motor Sport-Yamaha	Yamaha YZF R1	37.498s	20
16	Kohta Nozane	JPN	3	GYTR GRT Yamaha WorldSBK Team	Yamaha YZF R1	45.108s	20
17	Oscar Gutierrez	ESP	99	TPR Team Pedercini Racing	Kawasaki ZX-10RR	46.958s	20
18	Leandro Mercado	ARG	36	MIE Racing Honda Team	Honda CBR1000 RR-R	55.315s	20
19	Oliver Konig	CZE	52	Orelac Racing Verdnatura	Kawasaki ZX-10RR	57.534s	20
	Michael van der Mark	NED	60	BMW Motorrad WorldSBK Team	BMW M1000RR	DNF	8
	Scott Redding	GBR	45	BMW Motorrad WorldSBK Team	BMW M1000RR	DNF	2
	Luca Bernardi	SMR	29	BARNI Spark Racing Team	Ducati Panigale V4R	DNF	1
	Philipp Oettl	GER	5	Team Goeleven	Ducati Panigale V4R	DNF	0

Fastest race lap: Bautista on lap 4, 1m 41.823s, 102.22mph/164.50km/h.
Lap record: Razgatlioglu, 1m 41.493s, 103.06mph/165.86km/h (2021).

Superpole: 10 laps, 28.937 miles/46.570km
Weather: Dry · Track 28°C · Air 18°C
Time of race: 16m 59.889s
Average speed: 102.143mph/164.383km/h

Pos.	Rider	Time & Gap	Laps
1	**Alvaro Bautista**		10
2	**Jonathan Rea**	1.185s	10
3	**Alex Lowes**	1.377s	10
4	**Toprak Razgatlioglu**	5.088s	10
5	**Michael Rinaldi**	9.016s	10
6	**Philipp Oettl**	10.506s	10
7	**Xavi Vierge**	10.637s	10
8	**Scott Redding**	10.947s	10
9	**Loris Baz**	14.575s	10
10	Garrett Gerloff	14.601s	10
11	Lucas Mahias	17.326s	10
12	Luca Bernardi	17.644s	10
13	Kohta Nozane	19.942s	10
14	Eugene Laverty	20.672s	10
15	Roberto Tamburini	20.723s	10
16	Axel Bassani	20.886s	10
17	Christophe Ponsson	23.918s	10
18	Oscar Gutierrez	25.744s	10
19	Leandro Mercado	25.759s	10
20	Oliver Konig	37.666s	10
21	Andrea Locatelli	45.370s	10
	Michael van der Mark	DNF	8
	Iker Lecuona	DNF	0

Fastest race lap: Bautista on lap 2, 1m 41.135s, 102.97mph/165.71km/h.

Race 2: 20 laps, 57.875 miles/93.140km
Weather: Dry · Track 39°C · Air 22°C
Time of race: 34m 15.354s
Average speed: 101.369mph/163.137km/h

Pos.	Rider	Time & Gap	Laps
1	**Alvaro Bautista**		20
2	**Michael Rinaldi**	8.103s	20
3	**Toprak Razgatlioglu**	9.090s	20
4	**Jonathan Rea**	10.210s	20
5	**Axel Bassani**	15.677s	20
6	**Xavi Vierge**	20.320s	20
7	**Philipp Oettl**	33.622s	20
8	**Iker Lecuona**	35.008s	20
9	**Loris Baz**	35.092s	20
10	**Roberto Tamburini**	40.108s	20
11	**Luca Bernardi**	42.746s	20
12	**Lucas Mahias**	43.165s	20
13	**Michael van der Mark**	46.197s	20
14	**Eugene Laverty**	46.420s	20
15	**Kohta Nozane**	48.365s	20
16	Andrea Locatelli	50.985s	20
17	Leandro Mercado	54.132s	20
18	Oliver Konig	1m 12.447s	20
	Oscar Gutierrez	DNF	13
	Garrett Gerloff	DNF	11
	Christophe Ponsson	DNF	4
	Alex Lowes	DNF	0
	Scott Redding	DNF	0

Fastest race lap: Bautista on lap 5, 1m 42.181s, 102.36mph/164.74km/h.

Superpole

1, Lecuona 1m 40.766s; 2, Lowes 1m 40.789s; 3, Rea 1m 40.983s; 4, Locatelli 1m 40.991s; 5, Bautista 1m 41.148s; 6, Gerloff 1m 41.208s; 7, Bassani 1m 41.594s; 8, Razgatlioglu 1m 41.638s; 9, Vierge 1m 41.683s; 10, Rinaldi 1m 41.836s; Mahias 1m 41.937s; 12, Oettl 1m 42.028s; 13, Redding 1m 42.038s; 14, Baz 1m 42.384s; 15, Nozane 1m 42.469s; 16, Laverty 1m 42.469s; 17, Bernardi 1m 42.473s; 18, Tamburini 1m 42.509s; 19, Van der Mark 1m 42.916s; 20, Ponsson 1m 43.005s; 21, Gutierrez 1m 43.075s; 22, Konig 1m 43.182s; 23, Mercado 1m 44.128s;

Points

1, Bautista 394; 2, Razgatlioglu 335; 3, Rea 327; 4, Rinaldi 205; 5, Locatelli 173; 6, Bassani 170; 7, Lowes 161; 8, Lecuona 158; 9, Redding 147; 10, Vierge 99; 11, Gerloff 92; 12, Baz 88; 13, Oettl 66; 14, Mahias 47; 15, Tamburini 34; 16, Bernardi 32; 17, Laverty 26; 18, Van der Mark 18; 19, Nozane 14; 20, Fores 12; 21, Mykhalchyk 10; 22, Ponsson 9; 23, Syahrin 4; 24, Haslam 4; 25, Mackenzie 3; 26, Hickman 2; 27, Mercado 2.

Round 9 PORTIMAO, Portugal · 7–9 October, 2022 · 2.853-mile/4.592km circuit

Race 1: 14 laps, 39.947 miles/64.288km
Weather: Dry · Track 43°C · Air 27°C
Time of race: 23m 33.449s
Average speed: 101.743mph/163.739km/h

Pos.	Rider	Nat.	No.	Entrant	Machine	Time & Gap	Laps
1	**Toprak Razgatlioglu**	TUR	1	Pata Yamaha with Brixx WorldSBK	Yamaha YZF R1		14
2	**Alvaro Bautista**	ESP	19	Aruba.it Racing - Ducati	Ducati Panigale V4R	0.657s	14
3	**Jonathan Rea**	GBR	65	Kawasaki Racing Team WorldSBK	Kawasaki ZX-10RR	3.032s	14
4	**Axel Bassani**	ITA	47	Motocorsa Racing	Ducati Panigale V4R	4.471s	14
5	**Alex Lowes**	GBR	22	Kawasaki Racing Team WorldSBK	Kawasaki ZX-10RR	4.562s	14
6	**Andrea Locatelli**	ITA	55	Pata Yamaha with Brixx WorldSBK	Yamaha YZF R1	8.805s	14
7	**Michael Rinaldi**	ITA	21	Aruba.it Racing - Ducati	Ducati Panigale V4R	12.614s	14
8	**Xavi Vierge**	ESP	97	Team HRC	Honda CBR1000 RR-R	17.290s	14
9	**Loris Baz**	FRA	76	Bonovo Action BMW	BMW M1000RR	17.450s	14
10	**Garrett Gerloff**	USA	31	GYTR GRT Yamaha WorldSBK Team	Yamaha YZF R1	17.719s	14
11	**Iker Lecuona**	ESP	7	Team HRC	Honda CBR1000 RR-R	21.391s	14
12	**Philipp Oettl**	GER	5	Team Goeleven	Ducati Panigale V4R	21.628s	14
13	**Lucas Mahias**	FRA	44	Kawasaki Puccetti Racing	Kawasaki ZX-10RR	22.972s	14
14	**Michael van der Mark**	NED	60	BMW Motorrad WorldSBK Team	BMW M1000RR	25.808s	14
15	**Eugene Laverty**	IRL	50	Bonovo Action BMW	BMW M1000RR	29.879s	14
16	Roberto Tamburini	ITA	2	Yamaha Motoxracing WorldSBK Team	Yamaha YZF R1	30.268s	14
17	Luca Bernardi	SMR	29	BARNI Spark Racing Team	Ducati Panigale V4R	30.919s	14
18	Scott Redding	GBR	45	BMW Motorrad WorldSBK Team	BMW M1000RR	33.785s	14
19	Jake Gagne	USA	33	Attack Performance Yamaha Racing	Yamaha YZF R1	34.173s	14
20	Kohta Nozane	JPN	3	GYTR GRT Yamaha WorldSBK Team	Yamaha YZF R1	38.133s	14
21	Marvin Fritz	GER	17	IXS - Yart - Yamaha	Yamaha YZF R1	39.000s	14
22	Christophe Ponsson	FRA	23	Gil Motor Sport-Yamaha	Yamaha YZF R1	41.101s	14
23	Leandro Mercado	ARG	36	MIE Racing Honda Team	Honda CBR1000 RR-R	47.660s	14
24	Oliver Konig	CZE	52	Orelac Racing Verdnatura	Kawasaki ZX-10RR	1m 01.760s	14
	Leon Haslam	GBR	91	TPR Team Pedercini Racing	Kawasaki ZX-10RR	DNF	7
	Hafizh Syahrin	MAS	35	MIE Racing Honda Team		DNF	2

Fastest race lap: Razgatlioglu on lap 3, 1m 40.328s, 102.35mph/164.72km/h.
Lap record: Rea, 1m 41.272s, 101.51mph/163.36km/h (2019).

Superpole: 10 laps, 28.533 miles/45.920km
Weather: Dry · Track 34°C · Air 24°C
Time of race: 16m 45.342s
Average speed: 102.175mph/164.434km/h

Pos.	Rider	Time & Gap	Laps
1	**Toprak Razgatlioglu**		10
2	**Alvaro Bautista**	0.123s	10
3	**Jonathan Rea**	1.434s	10
4	**Alex Lowes**	1.976s	10
5	**Michael Rinaldi**	3.965s	10
6	**Axel Bassani**	5.969s	10
7	**Andrea Locatelli**	6.067s	10
8	**Michael van der Mark**	11.297s	10
9	**Loris Baz**	11.945s	10
10	Xavi Vierge	12.014s	10
11	Philipp Oettl	12.692s	10
12	Iker Lecuona	12.937s	10
13	Scott Redding	15.165s	10
14	Lucas Mahias	18.996s	10
15	Eugene Laverty	20.677s	10
16	Jake Gagne	20.816s	10
17	Marvin Fritz	24.172s	10
18	Luca Bernardi	24.575s	10
19	Leon Haslam	25.909s	10
20	Kohta Nozane	26.206s	10
21	Leandro Mercado	26.421s	10
22	Christophe Ponsson	27.390s	10
23	Hafizh Syahrin	29.711s	10
24	Oliver Konig	45.459s	10
	Garrett Gerloff	DNF	6
	Roberto Tamburini	DNF	5

Fastest race lap: Rea on lap 4, 1m 40.135s, 103.08mph/165.89km/h.

Race 2: 20 laps, 57.067 miles/91.840km
Weather: Dry · Track 42°C · Air 25°C
Time of race: 33m 40.730s
Average speed: 101.666mph/163.616km/h

Pos.	Rider	Time & Gap	Laps
1	**Alvaro Bautista**		20
2	**Toprak Razgatlioglu**	2.256s	20
3	**Jonathan Rea**	4.758s	20
4	**Michael Rinaldi**	7.833s	20
5	**Alex Lowes**	8.406s	20
6	**Andrea Locatelli**	15.191s	20
7	**Scott Redding**	19.661s	20
8	**Xavi Vierge**	20.581s	20
9	**Garrett Gerloff**	20.889s	20
10	**Loris Baz**	23.756s	20
11	**Philipp Oettl**	24.047s	20
12	**Michael van der Mark**	25.749s	20
13	**Luca Bernardi**	29.930s	20
14	**Roberto Tamburini**	31.337s	20
15	**Jake Gagne**	36.203s	20
16	Eugene Laverty	38.719s	20
17	Marvin Fritz	41.026s	20
18	Christophe Ponsson	48.489s	20
19	Hafizh Syahrin	48.591s	20
20	Leandro Mercado	48.727s	20
21	Kohta Nozane	49.505s	20
22	Iker Lecuona	1m 06.148s	20
23	Oliver Konig	1m 13.116s	20
	Axel Bassani	DNF	3
	Leon Haslam	DNF	3
	Lucas Mahias	DNF	1

Fastest race lap: Razgatlioglu on lap 11, 1m 40.497s, 102.49mph/164.94km/h.

Superpole

1, Rea 1m 39.610s; 2, Razgatlioglu 1m 39.772s; 3, Lowes 1m 39.859s; 4, Bautista 1m 39.946s; 5, Locatelli 1m 40.000s; 6, Bassani 1m 40.195s; 7, Baz 1m 40.242s; 8, Redding 1m 40.293s; 9, Rinaldi 1m 40.305s; 10, Lecuona 1m 40.342s; 11, Gerloff 1m 40.497s; 12, Oettl 1m 40.526s; 13, Vierge 1m 40.624s; 14, Tamburini 1m 40.771s; 15, Mahias 1m 40.811s; 16, Gagne 1m 41.161s; 17, Laverty 1m 41.258s; 18, Nozane 1m 41.321s; 19, Bernardi 1m 41.406s; 20, Van der Mark 1m 41.473s; 21, Syahrin 1m 41.741s; 22, Haslam 1m 41.765s; 23, Fritz 1m 41.912s; 24, Mercado 1m 41.982s; 25, Ponsson 1m 42.152s, 26, Konig 1m 43.840s.

Points

1, Bautista 448; 2, Razgatlioglu 392; 3, Rea 366; 4, Rinaldi 232; 5, Locatelli 196; 6, Lowes 189; 7, Bassani 187; 8, Lecuona 163; 9, Redding 156; 10, Vierge 115; 11, Gerloff 105; 12, Baz 102; 13, Oettl 75; 14, Mahias 50; 15, Tamburini 36; 16, Bernardi 35; 17, Laverty 27; 18, Van der Mark 26; 19, Nozane 14; 20, Fores 12; 21, Mykhalchyk 10; 22, Ponsson 9; 23, Syahrin 4; 24, Haslam 4; 25, Mackenzie 3; 26, Hickman 2; 27, Mercado 2; 28, Gagne 1.

Round 10 SAN JUAN VILLICUM, Argentina · 21–23 October, 2022 · 2.657-mile/4.276km circuit

Race 1: 21 laps, 55.797 miles/89.796km
Weather: Dry · Track 49°C · Air 20°C
Time of race: 34m 18.304s
Average speed: 97.589mph/157.054km/h

Pos.	Rider	Nat.	No.	Entrant	Machine	Time & Gap	Laps
1	**Alvaro Bautista**	ESP	19	Aruba.it Racing - Ducati	Ducati Panigale V4R		21
2	**Jonathan Rea**	GBR	65	Kawasaki Racing Team WorldSBK	Kawasaki ZX-10RR	5.141s	21
3	**Axel Bassani**	ITA	47	Motocorsa Racing	Ducati Panigale V4R	6.689s	21
4	**Iker Lecuona**	ESP	7	Team HRC	Honda CBR1000 RR-R	11.917s	21
5	**Michael Rinaldi**	ITA	21	Aruba.it Racing - Ducati	Ducati Panigale V4R	13.882s	21
6	**Alex Lowes**	GBR	22	Kawasaki Racing Team WorldSBK	Kawasaki ZX-10RR	14.507s	21
7	**Scott Redding**	GBR	45	BMW Motorrad WorldSBK Team	BMW M1000RR	18.402s	21
8	**Andrea Locatelli**	ITA	55	Pata Yamaha with Brixx WorldSBK	Yamaha YZF R1	18.869s	21
9	**Xavi Vierge**	ESP	97	Team HRC	Honda CBR1000 RR-R	19.540s	21
10	**Michael van der Mark**	NED	60	BMW Motorrad WorldSBK Team	BMW M1000RR	24.661s	21
11	**Lucas Mahias**	FRA	44	Kawasaki Puccetti Racing	Kawasaki ZX-10RR	31.397s	21
12	**Xavi Fores**	ESP	12	BARNI Spark Racing Team	Ducati Panigale V4R	32.969s	21
13	**Garrett Gerloff**	USA	31	GYTR GRT Yamaha WorldSBK Team	Yamaha YZF R1	35.081s	21
14	**Eugene Laverty**	IRL	50	Bonovo Action BMW	BMW M1000RR	36.961s	21
15	**Toprak Razgatlioglu**	TUR	1	Pata Yamaha with Brixx WorldSBK	Yamaha YZF R1	39.885s	21
16	Loris Baz	FRA	76	Bonovo Action BMW	BMW M1000RR	40.371s	21
17	Philipp Oettl	GER	5	Team Goeleven	Ducati Panigale V4R	44.885s	21
18	Kohta Nozane	JPN	3	GYTR GRT Yamaha WorldSBK Team	Yamaha YZF R1	45.220s	21
19	Oliver Konig	CZE	52	Orelac Racing Verdnatura	Kawasaki ZX-10RR	1m 04.546s	21
20	Maximilian Scheib	CHI	27	MIE Racing Honda Team	Honda CBR1000 RR-R	1m 19.515s	21
21	Marco Solorza	ARG	39	TPR Team Pedercini Racing	Kawasaki ZX-10RR	1m 32.427s	21
	Leandro Mercado	ARG	36	MIE Racing Honda Team	Honda CBR1000 RR-R	DNF	7

Fastest race lap: Bautista on lap 16, 1m 37.389s, 98.57mph/158.63km/h.
Lap record: Redding, 1m 37.345s, 98.39mph/158.34km/h (2021).

Superpole: 10 laps, 26.570 miles/42.760km
Weather: Dry · Track 45°C · Air 22°C
Time of race: 16m 19.266s
Average speed: 97.676mph/157.195km/h

Pos.	Rider	Time & Gap	Laps
1	**Toprak Razgatlioglu**		10
2	**Alvaro Bautista**	0.613s	10
3	**Jonathan Rea**	0.856s	10
4	**Michael Rinaldi**	4.357s	10
5	**Alex Lowes**	5.062s	10
6	**Iker Lecuona**	5.418s	10
7	**Axel Bassani**	8.714s	10
8	**Xavi Vierge**	10.676s	10
9	**Loris Baz**	10.752s	10
10	Andrea Locatelli	10.907s	10
11	Michael van der Mark	12.459s	10
12	Xavi Fores	14.827s	10
13	Garrett Gerloff	15.417s	10
14	Scott Redding	17.709s	10
15	Philipp Oettl	19.308s	10
16	Kohta Nozane	20.627s	10
17	Leandro Mercado	22.760s	10
18	Lucas Mahias	22.958s	10
19	Eugene Laverty	25.234s	10
20	Oliver Konig	26.232s	10
21	Maximilian Scheib	27.217s	10
22	Marco Solorza	46.065s	10

Fastest race lap: Rea on lap 9, 1m 37.277s, 98.46mph/158.45km/h.

Race 2: 21 laps, 55.797 miles/89.796km
Weather: Dry · Track 53°C · Air 28°C
Time of race: 34m 24.501s
Average speed: 97.296mph/156.583km/h

Pos.	Rider	Time & Gap	Laps
1	**Alvaro Bautista**		21
2	**Toprak Razgatlioglu**	3.389s	21
3	**Jonathan Rea**	9.784s	21
4	**Alex Lowes**	11.650s	21
5	**Michael Rinaldi**	15.656s	21
6	**Xavi Vierge**	16.381s	21
7	**Iker Lecuona**	16.584s	21
8	**Andrea Locatelli**	20.401s	21
9	**Scott Redding**	21.420s	21
10	**Michael van der Mark**	22.413s	21
11	**Eugene Laverty**	30.732s	21
12	**Garrett Gerloff**	32.655s	21
13	**Xavi Fores**	34.058s	21
14	**Philipp Oettl**	38.422s	21
15	**Lucas Mahias**	39.869s	21
16	Kohta Nozane	41.107s	21
17	Loris Baz	44.649s	21
18	Oliver Konig	49.119s	21
19	Leandro Mercado	54.421s	21
20	Axel Bassani	1m 06.518s	21
21	Maximilian Scheib	1m 17.049s	21
22	Marco Solorza	1m 37.575s	21

Fastest race lap: Bautista on lap 12, 1m 37.66s, 97.70mph/157.24km/h.

Superpole

1, Razgatlioglu 1m 36.216s; 2, Rea 1m 36.449s; 3, Bautista 1m 36.671s; 4, Lecuona 1m 36.953s; 5, Redding 1m 36.974s; 6, Baz 1m 37.027s; 7, Bassani 1m 37.031s; 8, Rinaldi 1m 37.066s; 9, Lowes 1m 37.122s; 10, Vierge 1m 37.159s; 11, Locatelli 1m 37.347s; 12, Gerloff 1m 37.399s; 13, Mahias 1m 37.634s; 14, Van der Mark 1m 37.770s; 15, Nozane 1m 38.108s; 16, Fores 1m 38.119s; 17, Oettl 1m 38.149s; 18, Laverty 1m 38.153s; 19, Mercado 1m 38.184s; 20, Konig 1m 38.683s; 21, Scheib 1m 39.225s; 22, Solorza 1m 40.750s.

Points

1, Bautista 507; 2, Razgatlioglu 425; 3, Rea 409; 4, Rinaldi 260; 5, Lowes 217; 6, Locatelli 212; 7, Bassani 206; 8, Lecuona 189; 9, Redding 172; 10, Vierge 134; 11, Gerloff 112; 12, Baz 103; 13, Oettl 77; 14, Mahias 56; 15, Van Der Mark 38; 16, Tamburini 36; 17, Bernardi 35; 18, Laverty 34; 19, Fores 19; 20, Nozane 14; 21, Mykhalchyk 10; 22, Ponsson 9; 23, Syahrin 4; 24, Haslam 4; 25, Mackenzie 3; 26, Hickman 2; 27, Mercado 2; 28, Gagne 1; 29.

Round 11 MANDALIKA, Indonesia · 12–13 November, 2022 · 2.672-mile/4.300km circuit

Race 1: 21 laps, 56.123 miles/90.321km
Weather: Dry · Track 58°C · Air 36°C
Time of race: 32m 47.209s
Average speed: 102.705mph/165.288km/h

Pos.	Rider	Nat.	No.	Entrant	Machine	Time & Gap	Laps
1	**Toprak Razgatlioglu**	TUR	1	Pata Yamaha with Brixx WorldSBK	Yamaha YZF R1		21
2	**Alvaro Bautista**	ESP	19	Aruba.it Racing - Ducati	Ducati Panigale V4R	4.324s	21
3	**Jonathan Rea**	GBR	65	Kawasaki Racing Team WorldSBK	Kawasaki ZX-10RR	11.855s	21
4	**Andrea Locatelli**	ITA	55	Pata Yamaha with Brixx WorldSBK	Yamaha YZF R1	19.954s	21
5	**Michael Rinaldi**	ITA	21	Aruba.it Racing - Ducati	Ducati Panigale V4R	23.992s	21
6	**Xavi Vierge**	ESP	97	Team HRC	Honda CBR1000 RR-R	27.114s	21
7	**Garrett Gerloff**	USA	31	GYTR GRT Yamaha WorldSBK Team	Yamaha YZF R1	27.776s	21
8	**Axel Bassani**	ITA	47	Motocorsa Racing	Ducati Panigale V4R	31.015s	21
9	**Alex Lowes**	GBR	22	Kawasaki Racing Team WorldSBK	Kawasaki ZX-10RR	31.363s	21
10	**Loris Baz**	FRA	76	Bonovo Action BMW	BMW M1000RR	39.809s	21
11	**Xavi Fores**	ESP	12	BARNI Spark Racing Team	Ducati Panigale V4R	39.895s	21
12	**Scott Redding**	GBR	45	BMW Motorrad WorldSBK Team	BMW M1000RR	56.317s	21
13	**Hafizh Syahrin**	MAS	35	MIE Racing Honda Team	Honda CBR1000 RR-R	1m 00.618s	21
14	**Eugene Laverty**	IRL	50	Bonovo Action BMW	BMW M1000RR	1m 04.247s	21
15	**Kohta Nozane**	JPN	3	GYTR GRT Yamaha WorldSBK Team	Yamaha YZF R1	1m 05.242s	21
16	Oliver Konig	CZE	52	Orelac Racing Verdnatura	Kawasaki ZX-10RR	1m 06.538s	21
	Michael van der Mark	NED	60	BMW Motorrad WorldSBK Team	BMW M1000RR	DNF	17
	Kyle Smith	GBR	11	TPR Team Pedercini Racing	Kawasaki ZX-10RR	DNF	12
	Leandro Mercado	ARG	36	MIE Racing Honda Team	Honda CBR1000 RR-R	DNF	11
	Philipp Oettl	GER	5	Team Goeleven	Ducati Panigale V4R	DNF	10

Fastest race lap: Razgatlioglu on lap 4, 1m 32.886s, 103.74mph/166.95km/h.
Lap record: Razgatlioglu, 1m 34.288s, 102.00mph/164.16km/h (2021).

Superpole: 10 laps, 26.719 miles/43.000km
Weather: Dry · Track 53°C · Air 34°C
Time of race: 15m 28.792s
Average speed: 103.563mph/166.668km/h

Pos.	Rider	Time & Gap	Laps
1	**Toprak Razgatlioglu**		10
2	**Jonathan Rea**	0.586s	10
3	**Andrea Locatelli**	1.821s	10
4	**Alvaro Bautista**	1.906s	10
5	**Axel Bassani**	4.346s	10
6	**Scott Redding**	5.025s	10
7	**Alex Lowes**	5.686s	10
8	**Michael Rinaldi**	6.142s	10
9	**Xavi Vierge**	7.183s	10
10	Michael van der Mark	9.831s	10
11	Xavi Fores	14.596s	10
12	Loris Baz	16.528s	10
13	Garrett Gerloff	17.355s	10
14	Philipp Oettl	17.902s	10
15	Hafizh Syahrin	21.035s	10
16	Leandro Mercado	22.530s	10
17	Eugene Laverty	22.925s	10
18	Oliver Konig	23.371s	10
19	Kyle Smith	25.329s	10
20	Kohta Nozane	27.729s	10

Fastest race lap: Rea on lap 9, 1m 37.277s, 98.46mph/158.45km/h.

Race 2: 21 laps, 56.110 miles/90.300km
Weather: Dry · Track 61°C · Air 36°C
Time of race: 32m 44.141s
Average speed: 102.841mph/165.507km/h

Pos.	Rider	Time & Gap	Laps
1	**Toprak Razgatlioglu**		21
2	**Alvaro Bautista**	1.230s	21
3	**Jonathan Rea**	2.825s	21
4	**Andrea Locatelli**	7.595s	21
5	**Axel Bassani**	8.205s	21
6	**Scott Redding**	12.478s	21
7	**Xavi Vierge**	15.245s	21
8	**Garrett Gerloff**	17.574s	21
9	**Alex Lowes**	17.976s	21
10	**Michael Rinaldi**	19.698s	21
11	**Xavi Fores**	21.980s	21
12	**Michael van der Mark**	22.218s	21
13	**Loris Baz**	36.192s	21
14	**Hafizh Syahrin**	41.465s	21
15	**Oliver Konig**	44.142s	21
16	Eugene Laverty	45.600s	21
17	Leandro Mercado	50.490s	21
	Kyle Smith	DNF	12
	Kohta Nozane	DNF	10

Fastest race lap: Bautista on lap 12, 1m 37.66s, 97.70mph/157.24km/h.

Superpole

1, Razgatlioglu 1m 31.371s; 2, Rea 1m 32.423s; 3, Locatelli 1m 32.463s; 4, Lowes 1m 32.514s; 5, Bautista 1m 32.823s
6, Bassani 1m 32.936s; 7, Vierge 1m 33.125s; 8, Redding 1m 33.127s; 9, Rinaldi 1m 33.138s; 10, Gerloff 1m 33.208s;
11, Van der Mark 1m 33.364s; 12, Oettl 1m 33.493s; 13, Fores 1m 33.529s; 14, Nozane 1m 33.582s; 15, Baz 1m 33.932s;
16, Syahrin 1m 33.997s; 17, Konig 1m 34.315s; 18, Mercado 1m 34.409s; 19, Smith 1m 34.743s; 20, Laverty 1m 35.208s;
21, Mahias No Time.

Points

1, Bautista 553; 2, Razgatlioglu 487; 3, Rea 450; 4, Rinaldi 279; 5, Locatelli 245; 6, Lowes 234;
7, Bassani 230; 8, Redding 190; 9, Lecuona 189; 10, Vierge 154; 11, Gerloff 129; 12, Baz 112;
13, Oettl 77; 14, Mahias 56; 15, Van der Mark 42; 16, Laverty 36; 17, Tamburini 36; 18, Bernardi 35;
19, Fores 29; 20, Nozane 15; 21, Mykhalchyk 10; 22, Ponsson 9; 23, Syahrin 9; 24, Haslam 4;
25, Mackenzie 3; 26, Hickman 2; 27, Mercado 2; 28, Konig 1; 29, Gagne 1.

Round 12 PHILLIP ISLAND, Australia · 18–20 November, 2022 · 2.762-mile/4.445km circuit

Race 1: 22 laps, 60.764 miles/97.790km
Weather: Wet · Track 22°C · Air 18°C
Time of race: 36m 47.340s
Average speed: 99.101mph/159.488km/h

Pos.	Rider	Nat.	No.	Entrant	Machine	Time & Gap	Laps
1	**Jonathan Rea**	GBR	65	Kawasaki Racing Team WorldSBK	Kawasaki ZX-10RR		22
2	**Toprak Razgatlioglu**	TUR	1	Pata Yamaha with Brixx WorldSBK	Yamaha YZF R1	6.247s	22
3	**Alex Lowes**	GBR	22	Kawasaki Racing Team WorldSBK	Kawasaki ZX-10RR	15.435s	22
4	**Andrea Locatelli**	ITA	55	Pata Yamaha with Brixx WorldSBK	Yamaha YZF R1	18.342s	22
5	**Alvaro Bautista**	ESP	19	Aruba.it Racing - Ducati	Ducati Panigale V4R	19.369s	22
6	**Garrett Gerloff**	USA	31	GYTR GRT Yamaha WorldSBK Team	Yamaha YZF R1	36.235s	22
7	**Axel Bassani**	ITA	47	Motocorsa Racing	Ducati Panigale V4R	37.641s	22
8	**Xavi Vierge**	ESP	97	Team HRC	Honda CBR1000 RR-R	43.137s	22
9	**Loris Baz**	FRA	76	Bonovo Action BMW	BMW M1000RR	57.704s	22
10	**Tetsuta Nagashima**	JPN	49	Team HRC	Honda CBR1000 RR-R	1m 01.086s	22
11	**Michael Rinaldi**	ITA	21	Aruba.it Racing - Ducati	Ducati Panigale V4R	1m 03.075s	22
12	**Kyle Smith**	GBR	11	TPR Team Pedercini Racing	Kawasaki ZX-10RR	1m 06.326s	22
13	**Xavi Fores**	ESP	12	BARNI Spark Racing Team	Ducati Panigale V4R	1m 07.099s	22
14	**Lucas Mahias**	FRA	44	Kawasaki Puccetti Racing	Kawasaki ZX-10RR	1m 08.976s	22
15	**Hafizh Syahrin**	MAS	35	MIE Racing Honda Team	Honda CBR1000 RR-R	1m 12.006s	22
16	Scott Redding	GBR	45	BMW Motorrad WorldSBK Team	BMW M1000RR	1m 12.785s	22
17	Leandro Mercado	ARG	36	MIE Racing Honda Team	Honda CBR1000 RR-R	1m 16.024s	22
18	Eugene Laverty	IRL	50	Bonovo Action BMW	BMW M1000RR	1m 22.552s	22
19	Oliver Konig	CZE	52	Orelac Racing Verdnatura	Kawasaki ZX-10RR	1m 33.661s	22
20	Philipp Oettl	GER	5	Team Goeleven	Ducati Panigale V4R	1 Lap	21
	Michael van der Mark	NED	60	BMW Motorrad WorldSBK Team	BMW M1000RR	DNF	19
	Kohta Nozane	JPN	3	GYTR GRT Yamaha WorldSBK Team	Yamaha YZF R1	DNF	0

Fastest race lap: Lowes on lap 20, 1m 31.847s, 108.27mph/174.25km/h.
Lap record: 1m 34.288s, 102.00mph/164.16km/h (2021)..

Superpole: 10 laps, 27.620 miles/44.450km
Weather: Dry · Track 26°C · Air 15°C
Time of race: 16m 11.935s
Average speed: 102.303mph/164.641km/h

Pos.	Rider	Time & Gap	Laps
1	**Alvaro Bautista**		10
2	**Toprak Razgatlioglu**	3.285s	10
3	**Jonathan Rea**	3.328s	10
4	**Alex Lowes**	6.670s	10
5	**Andrea Locatelli**	9.238s	10
6	**Scott Redding**	9.328s	10
7	**Garrett Gerloff**	12.173s	10
8	**Xavi Vierge**	13.427s	10
9	**Xavi Fores**	17.416s	10
10	Loris Baz	18.069s	10
11	Lucas Mahias	27.298s	10
12	Hafizh Syahrin	29.522s	10
13	Axel Bassani	32.064s	10
14	Leandro Mercado	35.276s	10
15	Eugene Laverty	35.868s	10
16	Philipp Oettl	40.015s	10
17	Kohta Nozane	50.920s	10
18	Kyle Smith	51.281s	10
19	Tetsuta Nagashima	51.701s	10
20	Oliver Konig	1m 03.042s	10
21	Michael van der Mark	1m 11.979s	10
22	Michael Rinaldi	1m 36.397s	10

Fastest race lap: Bautista on lap 8, 1m 32.636s, 107.13mph/172.41km/h.

Race 2: 17 laps, 46.954 miles/75.565km
Weather: Dry · Track 27°C · Air 15°C
Time of race: 27m 8.334s
Average speed: 103.808mph/167.063km/h

Pos.	Rider	Time & Gap	Laps
1	**Alvaro Bautista**		17
2	**Jonathan Rea**	0.357s	17
3	**Alex Lowes**	1 Sector	17
4	**Toprak Razgatlioglu**	1 Sector	17
5	**Andrea Locatelli**	2 Sectors	17
6	**Scott Redding**	2 Sectors	17
7	**Michael Rinaldi**	2 Sectors	17
8	**Philipp Oettl**	2 Sectors	17
9	**Tetsuta Nagashima**	2 Sectors	17
10	**Loris Baz**	3 Sectors	17
11	**Axel Bassani**	3 Sectors	17
12	**Michael van der Mark**	3 Sectors	17
13	**Lucas Mahias**	4 Sectors	17
14	**Oliver Konig**	4 Sectors	17
15	**Leandro Mercado**	4 Sectors	17
16	Kohta Nozane	4 Sectors	17
17	Hafizh Syahrin	4 Sectors	17
18	Kyle Smith	6 Sectors	17
	Eugene Laverty	DNF	17
	Xavi Fores	DNF	17
	Xavi Vierge	DNF	13
	Garrett Gerloff	DNF	0

Fastest race lap: Bautista on lap 7, 1m 30.879s, 109.86mph/176.80km/h.

Superpole

1, Bautista 1m 29.815s; 2, Rea 1m 30.026s; 3, Lowes 1m 30.053s; 4, Razgatlioglu 1m 30.243s; 5, Locatelli 1m 30.580s;
6, Gerloff 1m 30.727s; 7, Oettl 1m 30.963s; 8, Rinaldi 1m 31.106s; 9, Vierge 1m 31.307s; 10, Nagashima 1m 31.339s;
11, Mahias 1m 31.406s; 12, Redding 1m 31.444s; 13, Laverty 1m 31.494s; 14, Bassani 1m 31.613s;
15, Van der Mark 1m 31.738s; 16, Fores 1m 31.767s; 17, Syahrin 1m 32.075s; 18, Baz 1m 32.122s; 19, Nozane 1m 32.270s;
20, Konig 1m 32.909s; 21, Mercado 1m 33.447s; 22, Smith 1m 34.645s.

Points

1, Bautista 601; 2, Razgatlioglu 529; 3, Rea 502; 4, Rinaldi 293; 5, Locatelli 274; 6, Lowes 272; ;
7, Bassani 244; 8, Redding 204; 9, Lecuona 189; 10, Vierge 164; 11, Gerloff 142; 12, Baz 125;
13, Oettl 85; 14, Mahias 61; 15, Van der Mark 46; 16, Laverty 36; 17, Tamburini 36; 18, Bernardi 35;
19, Fores 33; 20, Nozane 15; 21, Nagashima 13; 22, Mykhalchyk 10; 23, Syahrin 10; 24, Ponsson 9;
25, Smith 4; 26, Haslam 4; 27, Konig 3; 28, Mackenzie 3; 29, Mercado 3; 30, Hickman 2; 31, Gagne 1.

2022 WORLD SUPERBIKE POINTS TABLE

Position	Rider	Nationality	Machine	Aragon/1	Aragon/SPole	Aragon/2	Assen/1	Assen/SPole	Assen/2	Estoril/1	Estoril/SPole	Estoril/2	Misano/1	Misano/SPole	Misano/2	Donington/1	Donington/SPole	Donington/2	Most/1	Most/SPole	Most/2	Magny-Cours/1	Magny-Cours/SPole	Magny-Cours/2	Catalunya/1	Catalunya/SPole	Catalunya/2	Portimao/1	Portimao/SPole	Portimao/2	San Juan Villicum/1	San Juan Villicum/SPole	San Juan Villicum/2	Mandalika/1	Mandalika/SPole	Mandalika/2	Phillip Island/1	Phillip Island/SPole	Phillip Island/2	Total Points
1	**Alvaro Bautista**	ESP	Ducati	20	12	25	20	7	25	25	7	20	25	9	25	-	6	20	25	7	20	25	9	-	25	12	25	20	9	25	25	9	25	20	6	20	11	12	25	**601**
2	**Toprak Razgatlioglu**	TUR	Yamaha	16	7	16	16	9	-	20	9	16	-	12	20	25	12	25	20	12	25	5	12	25	11	6	16	25	12	20	1	12	20	25	12	25	20	9	13	**529**
3	**Jonathan Rea**	GBR	Kawasaki	25	9	20	25	12	-	16	12	25	20	7	13	20	9	16	13	9	16	-	7	11	20	9	13	16	7	16	20	7	16	16	9	16	25	7	20	**502**
4	**Michael Ruben Rinaldi**	ITA	Ducati	13	6	13	-	2	9	7	2	8	16	-	16	10	4	13	9	6	-	10	3	20	13	5	20	9	5	13	11	6	11	11	2	6	5	-	9	**293**
5	**Andrea Locatelli**	ITA	Yamaha	11	5	-	13	6	20	13	5	11	10	4	10	6	2	8	10	4	10	9	-	9	7	-	-	10	3	10	8	-	8	13	7	13	13	5	11	**274**
6	**Alex Lowes**	GBR	Kawasaki	-	4	11	-	-	13	9	4	13	11	2	8	16	5	10	7	-	-	13	6	13	9	7	-	11	6	11	10	5	13	7	3	7	16	6	16	**272**
7	**Axel Bassani**	ITA	Ducati	-	3	10	6	1	10	4	-	9	13	3	9	11	-	9	11	5	11	16	4	16	8	-	11	13	4	-	16	3	-	8	5	11	9	-	5	**244**
8	**Scott Redding**	GBR	BMW	1	-	-	7	-	11	8	3	5	6	-	7	13	7	11	16	2	13	20	5	10	-	2	-	-	-	9	9	-	7	4	4	10	-	4	10	**204**
9	**Iker Lecuona**	ESP	Honda	10	2	6	11	5	16	10	6	10	7	5	11	8	3	6	8	3	-	7	-	6	10	-	8	5	-	-	13	4	9	-	-	-	-	-	-	**189**
10	**Xavi Vierge**	ESP	Honda	9	1	8	5	-	7	11	-	7	9	6	-	3	-	3	1	-	9	3	-	-	4	3	10	8	-	8	7	2	10	10	1	9	8	2	-	**164**
11	**Garrett Gerloff**	USA	Yamaha	7	-	7	8	3	-	-	-	-	8	1	-	9	-	5	6	1	-	11	2	8	16	-	-	6	-	7	3	-	4	9	-	8	10	3	-	**142**
12	**Loris Baz**	FRA	BMW	5	-	9	10	4	-	6	-	4	1	-	6	7	1	7	5	-	-	2	1	7	5	1	7	7	1	6	-	1	-	6	-	3	7	-	6	**125**
13	**Philipp Oettl**	GER	Ducati	3	-	3	9	-	-	-	-	-	-	-	5	5	-	4	3	-	8	8	-	5	-	4	9	4	-	5	-	-	2	-	-	-	-	-	8	**85**
14	**Lucas Mahias**	FRA	Kawasaki	2	-	5	1	-	6	-	-	-	-	-	-	4	-	2	4	-	7	6	-	4	2	-	4	3	-	-	5	-	1	-	-	-	2	-	3	**61**
15	**Michael van der Mark**	NED	BMW	-	-	-	3	-	8	-	-	-	-	-	-	-	-	-	-	-	-	4	-	-	-	-	3	2	2	4	6	-	6	-	-	4	-	-	4	**46**
16	**Eugene Laverty**	IRL	BMW	6	-	4	-	-	-	1	-	2	3	-	2	-	-	-	-	-	-	-	-	-	6	-	2	1	-	-	2	-	5	2	-	-	-	-	-	**36**
17	**Roberto Tamburini**	ITA	Yamaha	-	-	2	2	-	5	-	-	-	5	-	4	-	-	-	-	-	5	-	-	2	3	-	6	-	-	2	-	-	-	-	-	-	-	-	-	**36**
18	**Luca Bernardi**	SMR	Ducati	4	-	-	-	-	2	3	-	1	2	-	3	-	-	-	2	-	6	1	-	3	-	-	5	-	-	3	-	-	-	-	-	-	-	-	-	**35**
19	**Xavi Fores**	ESP	Ducati	-	-	-	-	-	-	5	1	6	-	-	-	-	-	-	-	-	-	-	-	-	-	-	-	-	-	-	4	-	3	5	-	5	3	1	-	**33**
20	**Kohta Nozane**	JPN	Yamaha	-	-	-	-	-	-	2	-	3	4	-	-	-	-	-	-	-	3	-	-	1	-	-	1	-	-	-	-	-	-	1	-	-	-	-	-	**15**
21	**Tetsuta Nagashima**	JPN	Honda	-	-	-	-	-	-	-	-	-	-	-	-	-	-	-	-	-	-	-	-	-	-	-	-	-	-	-	-	-	-	-	-	-	6	-	7	**13**
22	**Illia Mykhalchyk**	UKR	BMW	8	-	1	-	-	-	-	-	-	-	-	1	-	-	-	-	-	-	-	-	-	-	-	-	-	-	-	-	-	-	-	-	-	-	-	-	**10**
23	**Hafizh Syahrin**	MAL	Honda	-	-	-	-	-	-	-	-	-	-	-	-	-	-	-	-	-	4	-	-	-	-	-	-	-	-	-	-	-	-	3	-	2	1	-	-	**10**
24	**Christophe Ponsson**	FRA	Yamaha	-	-	-	4	-	4	-	-	-	-	-	-	-	-	-	-	-	-	-	-	-	1	-	-	-	-	-	-	-	-	-	-	-	-	-	-	**9**
25	**Kyle Smith**	GBR	Kawasaki	-	-	-	-	-	-	-	-	-	-	-	-	-	-	-	-	-	-	-	-	-	-	-	-	-	-	-	-	-	-	-	-	-	4	-	-	**4**
26	**Leon Haslam**	GBR	Kawasaki	-	-	-	-	-	3	-	-	-	-	-	-	1	-	-	-	-	-	-	-	-	-	-	-	-	-	-	-	-	-	-	-	-	-	-	-	**4**
27	**Oliver Konig**	CZE	Kawasaki	-	-	-	-	-	-	-	-	-	-	-	-	-	-	-	-	-	-	-	-	-	-	-	-	-	-	-	-	-	-	-	-	1	-	-	2	**3**
28	**Tarran Mackenzie**	GBR	Yamaha	-	-	-	-	-	-	-	-	-	-	-	-	2	-	1	-	-	-	-	-	-	-	-	-	-	-	-	-	-	-	-	-	-	-	-	-	**3**
29	**Leandro Mercado**	ARG	Honda	-	-	-	-	-	1	-	-	-	-	-	-	-	-	-	-	-	1	-	-	-	-	-	-	-	-	-	-	-	-	-	-	-	-	-	1	**3**
30	**Peter Hickman**	GBR	BMW	-	-	-	-	-	-	-	-	-	-	-	-	-	-	-	-	-	2	-	-	-	-	-	-	-	-	-	-	-	-	-	-	-	-	-	-	**2**
31	**Jake Gagne**	USA	Yamaha	-	-	-	-	-	-	-	-	-	-	-	-	-	-	-	-	-	-	-	-	-	-	-	-	-	-	1	-	-	-	-	-	-	-	-	-	**1**

THE NEXT-GENERATION GAME

With three new production-based machines bringing a fresh look to the series, WorldSSP was revitalised for 2022. Even so, Yamaha's established R6 carried Dominique Aegerter to the title. GORDON RITCHIE has the story...

Above: **The main players fight it out at Phillip Island: Aegerter (77) leads Baldassarri (7), Caricasulo (64) and Bulega (11) over Lukey Heights.**

Top right: **Although third in the standings, Can Oncu, leading the Kawasaki challenge, went winless through the season.**
Photos: Gold & Goose

Above right: **Nicolo Bulega was also winless, but eight podiums put his Ducati fourth overall and top new-generation bike.**
Photo: Ducati Corse

Right: **Caricasulo, Aegerter and Baldassarri fill the podium for the Phillip Island final.**
Photo: Gold & Goose

IN 2022, WorldSSP underwent its first significant revolution since it had been promoted to full championship status in 1999. While it didn't quite become an open series, it was certainly a case of run-what-you-find in showrooms and on the street.

Very few territories even sell road-going 600cc Supersport bikes any more, while some are intended only for track use. Something had to be done in a series that had always been production derived. The hordes of Yamaha R6s and the few Ninja ZX-6Rs still racing were potent enough, but really at the end of their development and street-bike lives.

The long-held desire to introduce some fresh models into WorldSSP racing full-time was finally realised, although the challenge was to balance everything from the beginning. An astoundingly complicated set of regulations was finally issued very close to the start of the 2022 season, discussions and simulations having been going on for some time, of course.

It was pretty well matched at the opening round in Motorland Aragon, the existing four-cylinder bikes not having been neutered by the new pretenders, all of which had highly individualised restrictions and freedoms.

Although nothing was perfect, the three next-generation machines, from three different returning manufacturers, demonstrated that they were fairly competitive. All would be given more freedoms before the season wound up to a final release in Australia in November, and that would lead to full race victories for two of them.

The new-for-'22 machines included the 800cc MV Agusta F3 triple, which had been beefed up from its similar-spec 675cc iteration. The scariest prospect for everyone else was the 955cc twin-cylinder Ducati Panigale V2, more than 100cc larger than the first ever WorldSBK Ducati, which had showed up in 1988. The true oddball was the originally fairing-less Triumph Street Triple RR, which was allowed to be fitted with a Daytona 675 full fairing and clip-on handlebars, to go production racing like it was 1969.

Bizarrely, that converted road bike eventually took the first next-generation race win at round nine in Portugal, not the more race-orientated MV or the nearly 1000cc double-barrelled shotgun from Bologna.

A trio of Dominique Aegerter (Ten Kate Racing Yamaha), rookie WorldSSP rider Lorenzo Baldassarri (Evan Bros WorldSSP Yamaha) and early leader Can Oncu (Kawasaki Puccetti Racing) appeared likely to finish in that order in the first race at Motorland Aragon, even after some tight passes and battles, but on the last lap, real drama entered stage left and on to the final straight.

A near crash at the final corner brought about an early candidate for 'save of the season' – Baldassarri, who ploughed the front for a linear acre and then lost the rear just after he had saved the front. His sudden 'moment' forced the closely-following Aegerter to swerve and run wide, leaving the recovered Baldassarri enough of a gap to gas it up on to the straight and win his debut race. Aegerter was second, Oncu third.

In the second Motorland race, Aegerter turned the tables and took the win, from Baldassarri, while Nicolo Beluga (Aruba Racing Ducati) claimed the first next-generation podium for Ducati.

Assen provided a different backdrop, but at his team's local track, Aegerter would go on to win both races. Baldassarri was out of race one, and Glenn van Straalen (EAB Racing Yamaha) took second, with Bulega third. The race was cut short by a red flag just after Aegerter had taken the lead.

The second race gave Aegerter his second win, with Baldassari the runner-up and Oncu third.

Both Estoril races also went to Aegerter. In race one on Saturday, the 2021 champion was clearly ahead of Baldassarri, with Bulega third.

The second race eventually became wet, after everyone had started on slicks in dry conditions. Kyle Smith (VFT Yamaha) was a wild second from 17th on the grid. Baldassarri was third, having won a last-corner fight with Yari Montella (Kawasaki Puccetti Racing) and continuing a positive start to his new racing life.

Misano, in the June heat, was a cauldron for all of Aegerter's potential challengers, and we had two identical podium finishes. Aegerter won from Baldassari from Bulega in each race. 'Balda' had run on to the green paint on the last lap of race two, losing what initially had been his win across the line, promoting Aegerter to victory via the rulebook.

Donington was one of those most treasured of British race weekends, a consistently hot and sunny one, as the English Midlands could have passed for a parched Spanish plain.

At the old flowing circuit, Aegerter again beat Baldassarri for each race, on Saturday and Sunday, but behind the top two, the highly experienced Raffaele de Rosa (Ducati Orelac Racing VerdNatura) had had to wait only five rounds to score his latest podium in the class on what was an all-new bike for him. The race had been red-flagged and restarted, with full points awarded after 12 laps.

In the second race, the more regular early-season Ducati force, Bulega on his official bike, took third. It was nine straight wins for Aegerter by this stage.

However, at Most at the end of July, everything in WorldSSP went topsy-turvey, after a clash between Oncu and Aegerter put the championship's clear leader and others in the gravel at the very tight first chicane.

Aegerter got up, then flopped theatrically to the ground. It was play-acting in an attempt to get a red flag thrown, but initially he was diagnosed with concussion, given the nature of his stand-and-fall routine. When he said that he was fine, the game was up and he was banned from race two for simulating an injury.

A potential 50 points straight down the drain, and a bad way for him to enter the long summer break.

The loss of Aegerter opened opportunities for others on Most's peculiar layout, which features a vast number of quick changes of direction. Baldassari won both races, maximising Aegerter's real pain after his simulated version.

Stefano Manzi (Dynavolt Triumph Street Triple RS) rode with visible brio for the British-owned team. Second in race one morphed into third in race two, so a double podium before the break.

Bulega was second in race two. It was a weekend for weirdness, as 2021's only semi-serious Aegerter challenger, Steven Odendaal (Kallio Racing Yamaha), was third in race one in a one-off stand-in ride – and from 18th on the grid no less.

Magny-Cours rebooted the season in early September, offering even more championship hope to race-one winner Baldassarri, with van Straalen second and Aegerter only third.

A mad second race resulted in a win for Aegerter, while Baldassarri crashed trying to pass him at the hairpin, which allowed Jules Cluzel (GMT94 Yamaha) to finish second at home as his career was winding down to retirement. Third was Bulega.

In Barcelona, a double win and Superpole success went to Aegerter, from Baldassarri and Oncu in race one. In the second race, Oncu was second after Manzi had been demoted to third by a track-limits penalty on the last lap.

Portimao delivered a surprise first-race result, but in reality the signs had been there. Manzi, on the Triumph, won the opening race fair and square, to give the next-generation machines that all-important victory role. Baldassarri placed second, and privateer Federico Caricasulo (Althea Racing Ducati) was third, ahead of Aegerter. In the second race, however, he was the winner once again, after closing down breakaway leader de Rosa. Oncu was third.

A triple treat of flyaway rounds ended the WorldSSP season, with the Argentinian races offering true excitement, despite Aegerter winning both of them. He only just managed to catch and pass long-time leader de Rosa at the flag in the first race, with Ducati coming within a sliver of their first win in the new-look series. Caricasulo had made Aegerter's job easier when he ran wide, gifting the Swiss rider one less overtake and allowing him to catch de Rosa a little earlier.

Caricasulo was second in Villicum's race two, with Bal-

Left: **Steven Odendaal only raced at Most, but took third place.**

Far left: **Dominique domination. Defending champion Aegerter won an astonishing 17 races on his Yamaha.**

Below left: **Yari Montella took Kawasaki's only win of the year at Phillip Island.**

Below far left: **Niki Tuuli scored a victory for MV Agusta at Mandalika.**

Bottom far left: **Triumph rider Stefano Manzi was the first to take a new-generation win, at Portimao.**

Below left: **Popular former champion Jules Cluzel retired at the end of the 2022 season.**

Below: **Tragic SSP300 title runner-up Victor Steeman succumbed to his injuries following a crash in Portugal. The Dutch rider had taken four race wins.**

Bottom: **Alvaro Diaz, his Yamaha leading Hugo de Cancellis's Kawasaki, was a worthy Supersport300 champion.**

Photos: Gold & Goose

dassari – having done his championship hopes no good by finishing ninth in the opener – ending up third after a last-lap sort-out.

The championship was Aegerter's for the taking at Mandalika, and he managed to do it five races early by finishing fourth in the opener.

And what an opening race it was, with Niki Tuuli (MV Agusta Reparto Corse F3 800 RR) suddenly popping up as the Superpole qualifying star on another of the next-generation bikes. After some moments of drama in the first race, he ended up a clear winner, scoring the first race victory for the famous Italian boutique manufacturer and setting another next-generation milestone. Caricasulo took second and Oncu third.

Aegerter, now freed from the short-term shackles of common sense that had kept him off the podium in race one, secured another race win, from Manzi's now serially successful Triumph and Oncu's surprisingly resurgent Kawasaki. The relatively 'old-tech' Kawasaki had seemed like it was going to be in the crosshairs of the next-generation bikes at the beginning of the season, but it was becoming more potent in Oncu's hands, not less.

It is mildly perplexing, therefore, to note that the first Kawasaki rider to win a race in 2022 was his team-mate and front-row qualifier in Australia, Montella. He had been in a leading fight with Superpole winner Caricasulo almost to the end of race one, but the Panigale V2 rider had crashed on the last lap and Montella had taken his first podium with his first win in this category.

Second was Bulega and third, fizzing with understandable frustration, Oncu – doubtless thinking that it should have been him. To add bodywork-injury to the race-one insult, Oncu was hit accidentally on the first lap of the dry Sunday race by Montella, who was given a ride-through penalty.

Normally abnormal WorldSSP service was resumed when Aegerter won the race, his record-setting 17th in a single season, with Caricasulo second and Baldassari third.

Aegerter's 2022 brilliance was almost perfect, save for his mad Most moment. The true rebirth of Ten Kate Racing, on Yamaha machines after decades of winning on Hondas, had occurred in 2021. Two titles in two years, however, underlined just how strongly they had made their comeback.

Bahattin Sofuoglu (MV Agusta Reparto Corse F3 800 RR) won the WorldSSP Challenge title, for riders who race in European rounds only.

FIM Supersport 300 World Championship

Buenos Dias Under A Shadow

THERE was yet another Spanish WorldSSP300 champion, in the shape of Alvaro Diaz (Arco Motor University Team Yamaha), who only really got his spot because former champion Ana Carrasco had moved to Moto3. With so many other former champions or top runners (Huertas, Buis, Booth-Amos, Sofuoglu) heading elsewhere, there would always be more opportunities for many others.

Entry numbers were halved, for safety reasons as well as common sense, but with riders packed in close on relatively low-powered 400cc-ish singles, the risks had already been demonstrated by the loss of Dean Berta Vinales in 2021.

In 2022, the only rider to remain in contention with Diaz right to the end of the season, Victor Steeman (MTM Kawasaki), would succumb to his injuries shortly after the final round, having crashed mid-pack in the Saturday race at Portimao. The weekend was numbing afterwards, but until that point, the eight-round season had been as unpredictable as it had been competitive. Steeman posthumously topped the list of race wins with four.

The first ever WorldSSP300 champion, Marc Garcia, took three wins, new champion Diaz two, as did Matteo Vannucci. Mirko Gennai, Hugo de Cancellis, Samuel Di Sora, Yuta Okaya and Dirk Geiger also won races.

ISLE OF MAN TT

WORTH THE WAIT

Back after a two-year hiatus, the Isle of Man TT mixed tragedy with triumph with its unique traditional grandeur. MICHAEL GUY was there...

WHILE MotoGP, WorldSBK and BSB all continued to run in some guise throughout the global pandemic, the Isle of Man TT was put on ice, making its highly anticipated return in 2022.

The build-up to the event was relentless, with a raft of changes unveiled, the most significant of which meant that for the first time, fans would be able to watch every practice session and race live online for a one-off charge of £14.99. The long-standing commentary team had been given a shake-up, and new TV personalities were drafted in to present a show underlining a whole new era for the 115-year old race.

During the two-year gap since the previous TT in 2019, each of the flagship manufacturers had introduced upgraded models. Lap-record holders BMW unveiled a new M Sport model, complete with wings; Japanese stalwarts Honda finally delivered a new Fireblade with class-leading tech. Kawasaki even had a new ZX-10RR-R, but in truth, this was an evolution, not a revolution, of the bike that had won the 2019 Senior in the hands of Dean Harrison.

The rider line-up was also given a big shake-up. John McGuinness patched up old wounds with Honda, the greatest living TT rider rejoining the official Honda Superbike team after spells with Norton and Kawasaki. His return to the Japanese manufacturer coincided with the 30th anniversary of the Fireblade and his landmark 100th TT start, as well as reaching the age of 50.

While the two fastest TT riders, Peter Hickman and Dean Harrison, remained with their respective BMW and Kawasaki teams, it was all change for Michael Dunlop. He had raced for the Northern Irish Tyco team aboard a BMW in 2019, but the news broke in March that he would ride a Ducati Panigale V4R for multiple BSB title-winning Paul Bird Motorsport.

It seemed a tantalising, yet surprising signing given the strength of character of the two parties involved. Seeing Dunlop on the dominant Ducati at the TT was a mouth-watering proposition, but the deal was over before it began, and the Panigale show bike hastily removed from the stage on the eve of the pre-TT press conference. With no Superbike to ride and the event just weeks away, Dunlop turned to old adversaries Hawk Racing, to ride their BSB Buildbase Suzuki GSXR-1000.

The arrival of high-profile rookies at the TT, or lack of them, had been a concern for organisers in recent years, but Glenn Irwin's TT debut, two years later than planned, made up for that. The multiple-race-winning BSB Honda Superbike rider arrived with a wealth of road racing pedigree, including wins at the Macau GP and a clutch of North West 200 successes. Irwin and McGuinness in the official Honda squad made for a dream team of raw speed, untapped potential and unprecedented experience.

Another Honda rider who arrived at the TT ready to make his mark was Davey Todd. Riding for the proven Padgetts Honda team alongside the fast and experienced Conor Cummins, he had served and passed his road racing apprenticeship, and was the only man able to keep Irwin in sight at the NW200 in the weeks leading up to the TT.

In fact, it was Todd who set the fastest time of 127.49mph during the opening evening of TT practice, ahead of Harrison, Hickman and McGuinness. But Irwin stole the headlines, setting an incredible 122.62mph lap on his first ever session at the formidable circuit. To put his pace into perspective, the previous fastest ever newcomer on day one had been Adam Lyons, who set a first-night best of a 116.450mph lap in 2018.

As the week went on, it didn't take long for the pace to increase, with Hickman setting the first 130mph lap on day two. As he traded places with Harrison, the speeds continued to climb into the 131s and 132s, culminating in Hickman leading out practice week with a 133.22mph best.

SUPERBIKE

With no TT action in 2020 and 2021, there was a buzz like no other on the start-line of the opening Superbike TT. In sunny conditions, huge crowds and an army of TV camera operators lined the Glencrutchery Road ready to catch all the action.

Starting number one on the road and with the full focus of the road racing world upon his shoulders was John McGuinness. This being his 100th TT start in a career that had started way back in 1996, his Fireblade had a special one-off livery. The design featured flashes of gold to match

his special leathers, helmet and boots, and incorporated an image from each of his previous 99 starts.

Renowned faster-starter Dean Harrison appeared as determined as ever to repeat his 2019 Senior TT success. While his team and bike were the same, one significant change for 2022 was a switch to the class-leading Dunlop tyres after a career spent on Metzler.

While Harrison quickly began catching McGuinness, it was man-of-the-moment Davey Todd, starting at number eight, who showed that he had the speed to run at the front. But any advantage was short-lived, as TT benchmark Peter Hickman, historically a slow starter, arrived at Glenn Helen on lap one with a six-tenths lead over Todd, while Harrison was three-tenths further adrift.

Having started number ten, the Gas Monkey by FHO BMW rider had plenty of targets on the horizon, and thanks to a stunning 133.17mph opening lap from a standing start, he enjoyed a 9.3-second lead over Harrison. Padgetts Honda men Conor Cummins and Todd were third and fourth respectively, with Michael Dunlop on his Hawk racing Suzuki rounding out the top five.

On lap two, Hickman extended his advantage to 16.3 seconds with another 133.46mph lap (the fastest of the six-lap race) while slowing down for his first pit stop. A slick stop, backed up by more relentless laps, meant that Hickman went on to record his sixth TT win by a commanding 39.9 seconds. His clear advantage allowed him to manage the race to perfection, doing what he needed to do to stay ahead and make clean calculated passes on the road, knowing that his lead was never under threat.

Arguably, his biggest concern was the possibility of running out of fuel, having spluttered to a halt during Wednesday practice. But breathing space to short-shift during the final laps, combined with tweaked electronics that made the BMW more economical, meant that he suffered no further issues.

With Hickman in control, the battle for second was intense. Early front-runner Todd was forced to retire when his Dunlop rear tyre delaminated on the Sulby Straight. He had been using a cut slick following issues for Dunlop runners with full slicks at the high-speed North West 200. While Hickman had no issues with his tyres, Dunlop subsequently withdrew the cut slick from their allocation, leaving their riders to run the treaded tyre for the remainder of race week.

Despite not having an answer to Hickman, Harrison appeared to be in a safe second, but when Hickman overtook Dunlop on the road, the Northern Irishman was able to tag on to the race leader and, in doing so, claw his way back into contention, reducing Harrison's advantage from 18 seconds to six. Harrison dug deep and responded to the threat to secure the place, 17 seconds ahead of Dunlop at the chequered flag.

Ian Hutchinson secured fourth aboard his Milwaukee BMW, ahead of long-time adversary McGuinness. The latter, who posted a best lap of 129.27mph, narrowly pipped impressive Yamaha privateer Jamie Coward by just 0.438 of a second. Coward beat the high-profile Rich Energy OMG Racing Yamaha squad of James Hiller, and his sixth and final lap of 130.40mph was the fastest ever by a Yamaha.

Glenn Irwin delivered on his undisputed potential by finishing eighth in his first ever TT. By posting a lap of 129.85mph on his own on the final lap, the 32-year-old became the fastest ever newcomer in the history of TT.

Above: **If the caps fit, wear them. Peter Hickman's first of four wins in the week was the Superbike race. Harrison was a happy second, Michael Dunlop pensive after narrowly failing to oust him.**

Above left: **Hickman chasing down the earlier starters to claim his Superbike win.**

Left: **BSB star Glenn Irwin made a record-breaking TT debut.**

Photos: David Collister Photography

SIDECAR – Race One

While victory in the opening Sidecar TT went to race favourites Ben and Tom Birchall aboard their Haith Honda outfit, the race marked a new era for the class, with an array of new talent stepping up to the mark.

With laps being limited during practice week, set-up time was restricted, but the Birchalls were still able to post 119.22mph on lap two to win by 13.989 seconds. The win marked their 11th, and eighth in a row, as they continued to dominate the class on their radical self-engineered outfit, which includes a repositioned engine, dry sump, improved weight distribution and improved aerodynamics.

For many, their win was no surprise, but the lap times they needed to claim victory were. The fight for second made it a true TT classic, with the Manx pairing of Ryan and Callum Crowe (Haven Homes) securing the spot in only their second TT by just 0.11 of a second from Pete Founds and Jevan Walmsley (FHO Racing), after both teams lapped in excess of 118mph on their final circuit.

Ben Birchall said, "For so long, it's been John Holden and Tim Reeves we had to beat, but these lads have come out of nowhere and all credit to them, because I know how hard it is to prepare mentally, physically and mechanically to get to these speeds. They've done it in their second TT, so I've got some battles to come, and I'm looking forward to it."

TT legend Dave Molyneux and Daryl Gibson secured fourth with their KTM 890cc-powered outfit, following rule changes by the organisers to allow bigger-capacity twins to compete against the 600cc four-cylinder machines.

SUPERSPORT – Race One

In what was arguably the race of TT 2022, Michael Dunlop showed why he should never be written off. Outgunned in the big-bike races in recent years by both Hickman and Harrison, he has an affinity with the smaller 600s, but he had to put it all on the line to take victory. Riding the MD Racing Yamaha R6, which he had prepared himself, he was involved in a battle royal with 2018 Supersport TT winner Harrison, riding the DAO Racing Kawasaki ZX-6RR.

Three-lap TT races (shortened by a serious accident) aren't normally won or lost by a handful of seconds, but the first Supersport will go down in history as one of the closest ever. Fighting with Harrison and also Lee Johnston (Ashcourt Racing), Dunlop's lead at the end of lap one, when they came in for the mandatory pit stop, was just 1.8 seconds.

Lap two produced another titanic tussle, and at the start of the final lap, just 0.14 of a second separated Dunlop and Harrison. The final 37.73-mile circuit showed just how bright the fire burns within Dunlop, the 33-year-old setting a 129.475mph lap – a new Supersport record.

"Yeah, to do 129.5mph on a 600 around here, it's rocking on." explained Dunlop. The win increased his tally to 20, making him the third man in history to reach that milestone, with John McGuinness on 23 wins and his own uncle, Joey Dunlop, on 26.

"Aye, 20 wins. It's been good to me. I tell you, I rode hard in that one. It's good to be back. People think I don't have the pace any more, so it's good. The wee 600 was going well, I felt good and we just got on with things," he continued. "They thought I was finished, but there is life in the dog yet."

Although Harrison was disappointed to finish second again, his result was all the more impressive given that he'd swapped back to Metzeler tyres from Dunlops on the morning of the race. True to his understated style, he kept his move quiet, only making the change public when he put on a blue Metzeler cap in the winner's enclosure rather than a yellow Dunlop one.

Hickman, aboard his own K2 Trooper Beer by PHR Performance Triumph, eventually bagged the final spot on the podium after an intense race-long scrap with Yamaha men Lee Johnston and Rich Energy OMG rider James Hillier.

He had to use all his speed and racecraft over the mountain on the final lap to secure third place by 3.5 seconds ahead of Johnston, who was left to lament missing the podium after losing time at the pit stop when his team was unable to close the fuel cap. Johnston's pit-stop time was 8.4 seconds slower than Hickman's. Hillier secured fifth, with Jamie Coward continuing his impressive form in sixth on the Coward Racing Yamaha R6, one place ahead of Manxman Conor Cummins's Padgetts Honda.

Above: **Supersport battle – Hutchinson tails McGuinness and Hickman.**

Top left: **Winner Hickman has caught and is menacing third-place finisher Davey Todd in the Superstock race.**
Photos: David Collister Photography

Above left: **The Birchalls had to work hard to maintain sidecar superiority in race one.**
Photo: David Purves

Right: **Mountain splendour as Hutchinson races the sunset.**

Below right: **Davey Todd was a revelation on the Padgetts Honda.**
Photos: David Collister Photography

SUPERSTOCK

There was an air of inevitability heading in to the RL360 Superstock TT race, given Hickman's form and pace aboard his Gas Monkey by FHO Racing BMW. Demonstrating an unquestionable affinity with the M1000RR, the TT lap record holder secured another flag-to-flag victory, the seventh of his career. In another shortened race, cut from four laps to three, he might have won, but he was pushed hard all the way, especially on the final lap, when he had to dig deep, make key on-the-road passes and set his best lap of 132.274mph.

Ultimately, he secured victory by 12.7 seconds, but unlike the opening two solo races, when his main rivals had been Harrison and Dunlop, this time he had to deal with the resurgent Padgetts Honda pairing of Davey Todd and Conor Cummins. Having suffered the tyre delamination and subsequent knock to his confidence, Todd showed his mental resolve to bounce back strongly and was running second when he came in to make his mandatory pit stop at the end of lap one, closely followed by Harrison. The battle continued to rage, and as it did, Cummins began to make his move, first overhauling Dunlop and then Johnston to move into fourth.

On lap two, Hickman extended his advantage from 9.5 seconds after the pit stop to 15.9 seconds, with Todd now a clear second, having pulled a gap on Harrison. But it was Cummins who emerged as the 'danger man' over the final lap, going head to head with team-mate Todd. It culminated in him overhauling Todd for second after a stunning 133.116mph lap – the fastest ever of his TT career and the fastest ever Honda lap, quicker than John McGuinness's long-standing Fireblade record of 132.701mph, set in the 2015 Senior TT.

"I lost time in the pit stop and then I got held up, so I had to really dig deep on the last two laps," Cummins said. "Incredible, I can't quite get my head round it."

It was a moment of true celebration for Clive Padgett's Honda team. Having had a torrid start to the TT, their turnaround was testament to the desire and passion that flows through the veteran team.

"I'm speechless," Todd said. "The people around me have got me through these past couple of days where my head's maybe not been in the right place, so just honestly so grateful to have them behind me and to now be stood up here on a TT podium is incredible."

Todd was followed home by Dunlop in fourth, with Harrison fifth and Jamie Coward rounding out the top six.

One man expected to shine following his impressive eighth place in the opening Superbike TT was Glenn Irwin. Although more experienced on a full-blown Superbike than a Superstock, unfortunately he opted to retire after experiencing handling issues on his official Honda Racing machine.

SUPERTWINS

Before the start of the Isle of Man TT, Peter Hickman had spoken of his desire to win all six races, with entries in the three big-bike races, two Supersport and the Supertwin TT. With wins in both the Superbike and Superstock races, and third in Supersport, his attention turned to the new-look Supertwin race, where Aprilia had joined the party with their exciting RS660 machine.

Originally, Hickman had planned to run his own Aprilia in the class, but due to the late arrival of the bike and a lack of race components, instead elected to run a Vas Engine Racing Paton – a bike that had enjoyed unprecedented success in the class.

Despite Hickman's outright TT lap record, it was 2019 Lightweight TT winner Michael Dunlop who started as race favourite, due to his clear affinity with the smaller bikes.

From the start, it became clear that Dunlop was the man to beat, but also that Hickman had every intention of taking the fight to the Ulsterman. Dunlop led at the first split at Glen Helen, but by Ballaugh, Hickman had overcome the deficit and held a one-second advantage, with the on-form Jamie Coward aboard the KTS Racing Kawasaki a close third.

By the end of the opening lap, it couldn't have been much closer, with Dunlop leading Hickman by just six-tenths.

Lap two continued in the same vein, the two men never separated by more than a second. Coward's impressive run for the podium ended when his Kawasaki expired at the 11th milestone. That left Aprilia-mounted Johnston, French Paton rider Pierre Yves Bian, Paul Jordan and James Hind battling for the final podium place.

With the battle for supremacy continuing at the front, it was anyone's guess as to who would take the top honours between TT giants Hickman and Dunlop, right until Dunlop slowed at Laurel Bank, restarted and then subsequently was black-flagged due to a loose fuel tank. The 20-times TT winner was clearly furious.

Despite Dunlop being out, Hickman continued to push, setting a 121.293mph lap – the fastest of the race – en route to win number three of the week. The victory, his first in the Supertwin class, meant that Hickman had won TTs in every solo class he had entered – Superbike, Supersport, Superstock, Senior and now Supertwin.

"It's nice because I'm not sure how many people have actually done that," Hickman said. "The race was really close, and to even be close to Michael on a small bike is quite an achievement, because he is super-fast on the little bikes in particular. I never saw more than a second either in front or behind him."

With both Dunlop and Coward out, Lee Johnston recorded his best result of what had been a difficult week, to finish second ahead of Paul Jordan and Hickman's Paton team-mate, Bian.

SUOMY
10
GasMonkey
Weise
MOTUL

SHOEI
1

6

Above: **A Senior moment. Hickman flies towards victory in the delayed main event.**
Photo: David Collister Photography

Left: **Another Dunlop record. His ninth Supersport win made him the most successful in the class. It was his 21st TT victory.**
Photo: David Purves

Far left: **TT great John McGuinness was back with Honda, but unable to repeat his earlier successes.**
Photo: David Collister Photography

SUPERSPORT – Race Two

In a historic day at the Isle of Man, Michael Dunlop became the most successful Supersport rider in history, notching up his ninth victory in the class and, in doing so, securing his second TT win of the week to take his career tally to 21 – just two adrift of John McGuinness.

In another shortened race – run over two laps due to weather-induced schedule changes – Dunlop, aboard his own MD Racing Yamaha, once again fought with TT big hitters Peter Hickman (Trooper Beer PHR Racing Triumph) and Dean Harrison (DAO Racing Kawasaki).

While the race was run in less than ideal weather conditions, with strong winds and damp patches throughout, less than two seconds separated the three men at Glen Helen on the opening lap. As the race progressed, however, Harrison was unable to match the red-hot pace, dropping nearly ten seconds to Dunlop and Hickman, who were split by just over half a second.

Despite encountering traffic, Hickman began to charge, but every time he did, somehow Dunlop managed to respond, increasing his lead with the fastest lap of the race at 128.536mph, to take the win by a relatively comfortable 2.7 seconds.

"I knew it was going to be hard today, being up against Pete and Dean," said Dunlop. "It is good just to be able to prove we can still ride a motorbike. We were fast out of the gate. Everything was mint, and when the bike is good, I am fast, and that is the main thing. I knew the wind would affect me more than it would affect Pete because the triple has torque. Up the mountain, it was horrendous and I knew he would be eating into my lead, and I had to ride a bit harder and give it a bit of a go on the last lap. The pressure was on and even at the end, I didn't know if I had won."

Harrison took third to claim his third podium of the week. In what essentially was a lonely race, he finished ahead of rejuvenated Padgetts Honda rider Davey Todd in fourth. Jamie Coward bounced back from his mechanical failure in the Supertwins race to run at the front, taking fifth with his privateer KTS Racing Yamaha.

SIDECAR – Race Two

The second Sidecar TT of the week had the makings of a classic, with the top three pairings of Ben and Tom Birchall, Peter Founds and Jevan Walmsley, and Ryan and Callum Crowe separated by less than five seconds at the end of the opening lap.

With the majority of the field on lap two, the race was red-flagged following a serious incident at Ago's Leap.

Like the first Sidecar race, the second demonstrated that while the Birchalls remain the TT benchmark, a new breed of young racers is immersed in the class, making its future very bright indeed.

Veteran Dave Molyneux and passenger Daryl Gibson secured fourth with their KTM 890-powered outfit, ahead of Harry Payne and Mark Wilkes in fifth.

SENIOR

The curtain-closing Senior TT, scheduled to run on Friday, had to be postponed due to poor conditions. Although rescheduled for Saturday, there was considerable concern as to whether actually it would be run, due to damp patches around the circuit and high winds battering the island.

When it did finally get under way, nobody could live with the formidable pace and consistency of Peter Hickman's Gas Monkey by FHO Racing BMW. The 35-year-old secured his ninth TT win. In doing so, he became a member of an illustrious group of racers who have won four or more TTs in a week, joining Phillip McCallan (1996), Ian Hutchinson (2010) and Michael Dunlop (2013 and 2014).

Despite another fast start, Hickman trailed Harrison on the DAO Racing Kawasaki by half a second at Glen Helen on the opening lap, but by the time they reached the second checkpoint at Ballaugh, he'd turned the deficit into a 2.4-second lead.

Fast over the mountain and setting a 132.381mph lap from a standing start in far from ideal conditions, Hickman enjoyed an 8.3-second lead by the end of the lap. With Harrison slotting into second, the battle behind was raging as the two Padgetts men, Conor Cummins and Davey Todd, ran ahead of 21-times TT winner Michael Dunlop. Both Cummins and Todd had suffered slow starts to the week due to earlier tyre issues, but as they regained their confidence, Cummins demonstrated why he had been a consistent big-bike TT podium finisher, while Todd reinforced his status as one of the most exciting road racers of his generation.

Lap two continued in the same vein, with Hickman setting the pace. Having started tenth, he was forced to make key on-the-road passes as he caught both Todd and Dunlop. In contrast, Harrison, who had started second, and having soon passed McGuinness, had a clear track in front of him. But he had his own problems, having hit a bird at Handley's on the opening lap. The 150mph impact had broken the screen of his Kawasaki, and covered his helmet and bike in blood and feathers. With insufficient time to change the screen during his pit stop, he was forced to dig deep and ride the remaining 216 miles with severely compromised wind protection.

TT veteran John McGuinness saw his hopes of repeating his top-six finish in the Superbike TT disappear when an uncharacteristic error resulted in him being handed a 30-second time penalty for speeding in the pit lane.

At the end of lap four, Hickman's advantage had increased to 19.3 seconds over Harrison. Needing to take on more fuel, he lost time to his pursuer during the second pit stop, but remained in complete control over the final two laps to win by 16.918 seconds.

An exhausted Harrison finished second, despite also suffering a bird strike, but there was an intense race-long fight between Cummins and Todd for the final place on the podium. On the last lap, the latter had brought the gap down to just half a second, but it was Cummins who excelled over the Mountain to beat his team-mate by 2.8 seconds.

Unable to replicate his Supersport heroics, Dunlop claimed fifth place ahead of James Hillier on the Rich Energy OMG Racing Yamaha. Ian Hutchinson was seventh, trailed home by Jamie Coward, John McGuinness and emerging talent Nathan Harrison, who secured tenth.

Tyre manufacturer Dunlop celebrated a highly successful TT, taking all six solo-class victories, despite running their treaded tyre following issues with their slicks.

A TOTAL of five competitors lost their lives during the event, and a sixth five months later.

Welsh racer MARK PURSLOW (29) was killed during practice week in a crash at Ballagarey. It was his second visit to the TT, and shortly before, he had set a 120mph lap.

French sidecar driver CESAR CHANAL (33) was killed instantly shortly after the start of the opening Sidecar race in a crash at Ago's Leap. His passenger OLIVIER LAVOREL succumbed to serious injuries in October.

Northern Irish veteran of 80 TT starts, DAVEY MORGAN (52), who had finished as high as fifth in the Senior TT in 2006, lost his life in a crash at the 27th Milestone on the final lap of the opening Supersport race.

The second Sidecar race was marred by the tragic deaths of father-and-son team ROGER and BRADLEY STOCKTON (56 and 21) when they crashed at the start of the second lap at Ago's Leap. Roger was an experienced competitor, but it was Bradley's first time at the TT.

SIDECAR WORLD CHAMPIONSHIP

NEW KIDS ON THE BLOCK

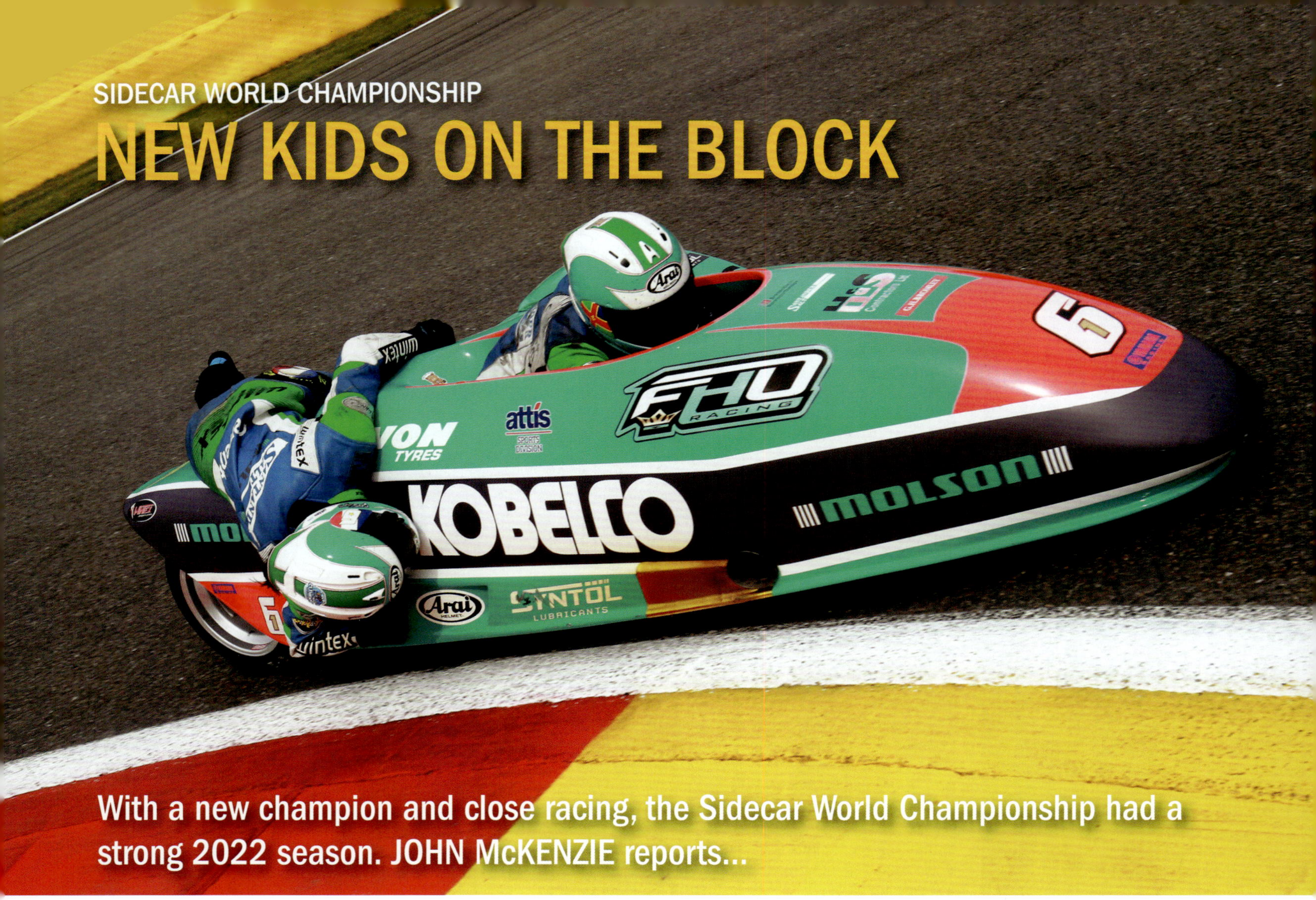

With a new champion and close racing, the Sidecar World Championship had a strong 2022 season. JOHN McKENZIE reports...

WITH 16 races at eight venues, the 2022 season was the longest championship in sidecar history. World champions Markus Schlosser and Marcel Fries, on the Gustoil LCR Yamaha, faced the increasing challenges of 2021 runners-up Todd Ellis and Emmanuelle Clement (Santander Salt LCR Yamaha), multiple world champion Tim Reeves (with Kevin Rousseau), and the ever improving Stephen Kershaw and Ryan Charlwood (Quattro LCR Yamaha). A notable absentee was Pekka Paivarinta, who was recovering from surgery to a shoulder injury.

Round 1 – Le Mans, France

After close qualifying, with less than a second separating the top seven, Reeves made a superb start, with Schlosser starting late from the pit lane after discovering a broken clutch cable.

Ellis, Bennie Streuer, Kershaw and Peugeot battled hard as Schlosser charged through the field. Pole-sitters Harry Payne and Mark Wilkes didn't start after crashing in the second timed practice.

With four laps to go, Ellis took the lead from Reeves and managed to pull out a comfortable three-second gap. Streuer and Peugeot DNF-ed after coming together, benefiting Schlosser. A magnificent effort from the world champion rewarded him with third, after setting fastest lap and slipping past Kershaw on the last lap.

In race two, recovered from injuries and on a borrowed LCR outfit, Payne started from the back of the grid. Reeves, chased by Ellis and Schlosser, inherited the early lead after Wyssen's over-fast start was penalised.

Schlosser harried Reeves, with Ellis right behind, before the Swiss outfit got past and started to pull away, winning by six seconds from Ellis. Reeves was third with a failing sidecar wheel bearing.

Round 2 – Assen, Netherlands

Taking full advantage of pole position, Ellis was away first, pressed hard by Reeves, who took the lead after some close racing. He seemed to be in control, but with seven laps to go, Schlosser had worked through to second, dragging Ellis back to the leader.

At the finish, Schlosser took the flag by 0.622 of a second from Ellis, who posted fastest lap; Reeves was third.

In Sunday's second race, Reeves led away from Ellis, and once again, the two outfits battled to and fro, before Ellis started to pull away. Then Reeves came under pressure from Schlosser, whose efforts gave him the fastest lap. However, he was unable to reel in Ellis, who won by six seconds, putting him top of the table.

Defending champion Schlosser's points lead from the previous day's win had lasted barely 24 hours and would never be regained. Despite four podiums from the first four races, Reeves took no further part in the championship, concentrating on the TT and German championship outings.

Round 3 – Spa Francorchamps, Belgium

With Reeves and Payne absent on the Isle of Man, the sidecars were at the glorious 7km Ardennes circuit for the first time since 1990, when sidecar legend Egbert Streuer had won. Perhaps hoping to emulate that feat, his son, Bennie, shot away to an early lead, but before long, Ellis had squeezed through.

As the pack settled, Ellis was forcing the pace, despite challenges from Streuer and Kershaw, and then from Schlosser as he fought his way tenaciously into second.

Ellis was able to maintain the gap, however, winning by 1.673 seconds from Schlosser after 11 laps. Kershaw, third, took his first podium of the year, with Streuer fourth.

For race two, Streuer again claimed an early lead, but Schlosser had passed him by lap two. Streuer held off Ellis initially, but it soon became a fantastic battle between Ellis and Schlosser, with Ellis winning by 0.321 of a second.

Thirty-two years after Streuer Senior's success, Streuer Junior upheld the family honour with third. But, with a pole, two fastest race laps and a first double win, Ellis forcefully emphasised his fast-growing stature.

Round 4 – Pannoniaring, Hungary

In race one, Ellis led almost from start to finish, with Schlosser on his heels, and briefly in front in a very close race, with Streuer chasing at close quarters for third. Ellis held on to win.

The second race was utterly scintillating, with Ellis, Schlosser, Streuer and Kershaw packed together. Almost inevitably, as Ellis and Schlosser went for the same piece of tarmac, the carbon-fibre fairings kissed, pushing Schlosser wide. Streuer seized the moment and scythed through, and at the next corner, Ellis went wide again, gifting him the lead.

The Dutchman held on under immense pressure to take the flag from Ellis, who beat Schlosser by half a length. It was Streuer's first win since Assen in 2015, and he also claimed fastest lap.

After eight of 16 races, Ellis had a 23-point lead.

Round 5 – Rijeka, Croatia

Blazing sun welcomed the teams for two 18-lap races over the demanding and abrasive circuit, always a tough weekend for the sidecars.

In race one, Ellis streaked away from pole and quickly took command of the race from the front, with

Clement and Ellis

Kershaw and Charlwood

Kershaw and Schlosser chasing hard.

With four laps to go, as Streuer tried an inside line on Kevin Cable, the outfits bumped, and Streuer spun and flipped over. The red flag came out immediately. Streuer was briefly hospitalised and ruled out of the rest of the weekend.

Ellis took the victory with a two-second gap over an ever-improving Kershaw, with Schlosser third.

In Sunday's race, Ellis took the early lead again and dominated. Kershaw and Schlosser were battling for second until a clutch-cable problem slowed the latter, leaving Kershaw free to chase the leader. Somehow, Schlosser managed to find a remedy and started to fight back from seventh.

At the front, Ellis began to slow, pitting on lap nine with a steering problem. He rejoined in an attempt to salvage some points, but was forced to pit again with four laps remaining.

After an eventful race, Kershaw won by some seven seconds from Payne, while Schlosser had forced his way back to third.

Round 6 – Donington Park, Great Britain

In the late afternoon sun, Todd Ellis and Emmanuelle Clement were able to repeat their race-one victory of a year before, despite the best efforts of Schlosser and Kershaw. Fastest qualifier again, Ellis was first into Redgate, and he soon pulled out what seemed to be a commanding lead, but Schlosser and Kershaw pushed hard and were able to make up the gap. At the flag, just 1.1 seconds covered the first three outfits, with Kershaw setting a new lap record.

Race two produced an epic battle between Kershaw and Ellis. The latter led until Kershaw got ahead on lap seven. Schlosser's early challenge faded and he dropped to fourth on lap one after briefly leading, leaving Payne to a lonely third. Eventually, Schlosser retired on lap 12 with a worrying rear-end vibration.

Far left: **Todd Ellis and Emmanuelle Clement won at Spa, one of nine race victories for the championship winning pair in 2022.**
Photos: Mark Walters

The action intensified as Ellis and Kershaw repeatedly swapped the lead. Going into Goddard's for the last time, they were almost side by side. Kershaw just managed to keep the door shut, holding the inside line to get the drive for the last brutal sprint to the flag. He beat Ellis by just three-tenths of a second. Payne was third, more than ten seconds behind.

Round 7 – Oschersleben, Germany

Making a very welcome return was Finnish multiple champion Pekka Paivarinta, who had recovered from his shoulder surgery. Passengered by Ilse de Haas, he qualified fifth and was happy with his progress after missing most of the season.

Ellis was on pole once more as the track dried. Schlosser took the lead, but by lap two, Ellis had demoted him and was in command, with Streuer third, harried by Kershaw.

With torrential rain fast approaching and the entire field on slicks, the race was red-flagged just in time on the 14th lap, with positions to stand as the result. That gave Ellis the win from Schlosser, with Streuer third.

Thankfully, there were blue skies for the second 21-lap race.

Streuer was close behind Schlosser, but the reigning world champion managed to hold position until Ellis joined the fight, pegging Streuer back a place on the second lap. Schlosser and Ellis parried for the lead, and it seemed that the former had it all under control.

With six laps to go, Kershaw was into third, and on lap 17, Ellis saw his chance as they caught the backmarkers. He grabbed the lead, holding on to take his second win of the weekend. Kershaw's growing consistency gave him third.

Round 8 – Estoril, Portugal

IA maximum points score in Germany meant that Ellis and Clement arrived at Estoril on 305, with a 51-point lead over Schlosser. However, the decision to award double points for the final two races meant that the 2021 world champion still had a mathematical chance of retaining his title.

Two weeks previously, Ellis had sewn up the British Championship, and he arrived in Portugal in great form and confident.

Before the race, Schlosser and Fries had announced that they were going to retire from the sport, bringing to an end an illustrious career that stretched back to the two-stroke era in the mid-1990s. They would be looking to finish on a high. A great final weekend of racing was in prospect.

Third in table was Kershaw, on 220 points, who still had an outside chance of the title if the leaders were waylaid by gremlins. Dry practice gave him pole over Schlosser, but it was disaster for unlucky 2015 champion Streuer, who damaged engines in both sessions and, due to a lack of suitable spares, was unable to make the race.

With the morning warm-up's rain blown away and the championship at stake, tensions were high for the first race.

Needing only wins, Schlosser hurtled away, with Kershaw in his wheel tracks. Nevertheless, Ellis had taken the lead by the third corner. Schlosser, demoted to third, bided his time.

As the race progressed, he was able to deliver a masterclass in outbraking. An apparent slight top-speed advantage on the long start/finish straight allowed him to reel in the leading pair, getting alongside before eventually picking off Kershaw and then Ellis. By lap ten, Schlosser was out on his own, gunning the Gustoil outfit to a five-second win and taking a fastest lap in the process. That pegged Ellis's lead to 41 points, with 50 still up for grabs.

With the clouds banished, Schlosser tried to pull a gap again, but he couldn't contain Kershaw, who slipped through on lap three, only for the Swiss to answer back four laps later and start to pull away.

But with just five laps to go, Schlosser spun, allowing Kershaw back into the lead and on to the win with a four-second margin. By way of some consolation, Schlosser posted another fastest lap in his final race.

Meanwhile, Ellis stayed back in third, knowing he'd taken the 2022 World Championship.

It had been an incredible season for 27-year-old Todd Ellis and his 25-year-old French passenger, Emmanuelle Clement. His nine race wins in a season set a new record and, from his debut at the start of 2021, meant that he had an astonishing 27 podium finishes in just 31 World Championship starts. The makings of a legend…

Meanwhile, Kershaw had gained momentum through the season, with three wins in the second half promising a bright future.

The series also said goodbye to Roger Body, whose RKB-F1 organisation had worked tirelessly for the previous few years promoting the British and World Championships. It's no exaggeration to say that without his superhuman efforts, top-level sidecar racing would have faced oblivion. He will be hugely missed. The FIM was considering other offers to take on the arduous duties of managing the series.

Schlosser and Fries lead the pack in Oschersleben.

Photo: Mark Walters

SHARK
BURNELL
WWW.ESKUTA.COM
Bennetts
28
RICH ENERGY
YAMAHA
PIRELLI

2022 BENNETTS BRITISH SUPERBIKE CHAMPIONSHIP REVIEW

OMG - RAY FINALLY SHINES

Bradley Ray had to wait for the Bennetts British Superbike Championship crown. OLLIE BARSTOW charts his march to the top...

Stuart Higgs

Series Director,
Bennetts British Superbike Championship

The 2022 Bennetts British Superbike Championship season has delivered an incredible rollercoaster of emotion, culminating in Bradley Ray sealing the title for himself and the Rich Energy OMG Racing Yamaha team for the first time.

It was another immensely competitive season in Bennetts BSB with ten different race winners, something that we haven't seen in the championship since 2017, not to forget a further three riders who celebrated podium finishes. Fans enjoyed the action both trackside and from home, on Eurosport and free-to-air channel Quest, plus in territories across the globe.

Five different manufacturers claimed race wins this season, notably represented by eight different teams, demonstrating the continued strength of the championship and the level of competition derived from the series technical regulations.

My congratulations to Bradley Ray for his first Bennetts BSB title victory – his performance this season was impressive and I was also delighted for the OMG Racing team who also became title winners for the first time.

We also toast all of our support class champions – Jack Kennedy who has become the most successful rider in the British Supersport Championship with his impressive performances this year, Jack Scott, Johnny Garness, Davey Todd, Max Cook, James McManus, David Shoubridge and Sidecar pairing of Todd Ellis and Emmanuelle Clement.

Of course, when reflecting on the season, we also pay tribute to Chrissy Rouse. He will remain in our memories for his performances on track, including his sensational 2020 Pirelli National Superstock Championship title victory and his character away from it too. An intelligent, personable and hard-working individual who will be missed by us all.

I would also like to recognise the unique skills, professionalism and dedication of our devoted Bennetts BSB medical team and the Herock Racesafe marshals throughout the season.

Finally, I would like to extend thanks to all of our championship partners, led by Bennetts who continue to offer unrivalled experiences at every event to bring you to the heart of the action. My thanks also go to our teams and riders across the classes, and to my series organisation colleagues, who work to ensure the Championship is widely acclaimed around the world.

We now look ahead to the 2023 Championship, which will kick off at Silverstone on 7/8/9 April. We are sure to be in for another sensational season and I thank all of our fans around the world for their continued support both trackside, on social media and across our TV broadcasts.

THEY say that good things come to those who wait. That was certainly the case for 2022 Bennetts British Superbike champion Bradley Ray. The waiting didn't preclude the solid hard graft, steely determination and unwavering commitment required to reach the top. For Ray, this was a wait to find 'the one' – or rather the Yamaha R1 – that would bring out his best and make him an honest champion.

The combination of Ray and the RICH Energy OMG Racing Yamaha R1 was a match made in heaven. A McAMS title-winning 'vintage' from the 2021 BSB season made the bike something old and something blue. Ray's bristling sense of confidence and sharp focus completed his 'something new' for 2022.

His career to that point spoke of never quite having the right bike at the right time. After an eye-catching BSB debut in 2017, his wins and a run to the Title Showdown the following year with Suzuki had the bespectacled, curly-haired youngster shooting towards star status. Then his fortunes and confidence began to fade in 2019, before disappointing campaigns on BMW machinery – first with TAS Racing and then with OMG Racing – yielded only a handful of podiums.

After Ray had spent three seasons toiling in the midfield, while it would have been difficult to find anyone to begrudge him his redemption by the end of 2022, it would have been tougher to find someone to tout him as a would-be runaway title winner at the start of it.

OMG's off-season decision to ditch its lacklustre BMWs after just two seasons in favour of upcycling the surefooted Yamahas that had dominated in 2021, in the hands of McAMS riders Tarran Mackenzie and Jason O'Halloran, was the shrewd investment Ray needed to reward his patience. His 'good things' came thick and fast, with nine wins and 23 podiums, culminating in the most important trophy of them all, his name etched alongside the likes of John Reynolds, Niall Mackenzie, Ryuichi Kiyonari and mentor Shane Byrne.

A big shout-out too to OMG Racing, which, like Ray, achieved its maiden BSB title after only modest success via Suzuki and BMW, hitting the spot with Yamaha.

Ray was paired again with Kyle Ryde, and if OMG flew under the radar of pre-season predictions, there was no disputing the stock of its Yamaha machinery. As a result, it was hard to look beyond factory-backed defending champions McAMS and riders Mackenzie and O'Halloran, a combination so potent it had waltzed to 21 victories in 33 races in 2021.

More than usually, however, predictions were challenged by the depth in rider quality amid a quantity that fluctuated around the 30-strong mark.

Multiple champions Paul Bird Motorsport – aka MCE Ducati – retained Josh Brookes and welcomed back 2013 WorldSBK champion Tom Sykes to BSB, a high-profile return 14 years on from leaving the series for a successful international career.

Runner-up to Mackenzie in 2021, Tommy Bridewell and Moto Rapido's Oxford Racing Ducati stuck together, while Honda Racing retained its Anglo-Japanese triumvirate of Glenn Irwin, Takumi Takahashi and Ryo Mizuno, adding a fourth Fireblade for its National Superstock title-winning protégé Tom Neave.

There was also no change at FS-3 Kawasaki, which paired the experienced Lee Jackson with hot prospect Rory Skinner, while runaway 2018 BSB champion Leon Haslam, like Sykes, back from WorldSBK, joined Lee Hardy Racing's VisionTrack Kawasaki team.

As ever, BMW was well represented at the sharp end, with its factory nominated Synetiq TAS Racing squad fielding an unchanged line-up of Danny Buchan and Andrew Irwin. In addition, FHO Racing dovetailed BSB and Isle of Man TT commitments with Peter Hickman, joined by Ryan Vickers.

Finally, Buildbase Hawk Racing persevered with the ageing Suzuki GSX-R1000R, but secured a coup by signing up 2021 title contender Christian Iddon alongside the retained Danny Kent.

A total of 33 races across 11 triple-header rounds included a trio of Title Showdown events that ultimately would decide the champion. A quasi-equalising points system that affords greater value towards the last three rounds, the Showdown format had been used to great effect by Mackenzie in 2021, overturning a three-figure deficit to team-mate O'Halloran to clinch the title.

However, there was a different reason in 2022 to call on a second chance after a testing accident left him with a fractured ankle days before the start of the season. It was his

Above: **BSB was back and booming, a strong field guaranteeing a close and varied series.**

Opening spread: **A switch to Yamaha gave OMG's Bradley Ray the weapon he needed to win the title.**

Photos: Bryn Willliams

Above: **Strong start. Honda's Glenn Irwin claimed a triple win at the Silverstone opener. He is pressed by Rory Skinner, brother Andrew and the pack.**

Top right: **Former champion Leon Haslam returned, but had little joy apart from a pair of Oulton podiums.**

Above right: **Kyle Ryde won at Donington, but was overshadowed by his Yamaha team-mate, Ray.**

Above far right: **In year two, Rory Skinner never quite claimed a BSB win, but earned a promotion to the Moto2 World Championship.**

Right: **Lee Jackson scored his maiden win at Oulton Park, some eight years after his BSB debut.**

Photos: Bryn Williams

second major off-season injury, and the Silverstone opener and following Oulton Park round raised the curtain without the champion.

This focused attention on the No.2 plate adorning Glenn Irwin's Honda CBR1000RR-R Fireblade, and the Ulsterman snatched the early initiative with a crushing triple victory around Silverstone's short, fast National loop. It was a sibling echo to Honda's blistering start in 2020, when Andrew had taken the spoils. This time, Glenn combined offence and defence against persistent attacks from OMG Yamaha duo Ray and Ryde.

In race one, Irwin held firm against immense pressure from Ryde, the 25-year-old having returned to the scene of his two victories during his 2020 rookie campaign. It was similar come the closing stages of race two, Irwin fighting back from a tardy start to work his way to the front, whereupon Ryde climbed over the back of his Fireblade into the final turns. Changing tactics, the latter squeezed tight alongside Irwin as they rounded Luffield, but a firmly shut door allowed the Ulsterman to hang on to his lead.

Irwin finally got his easy Sunday ride in race three with a more comfortable run, joining an exclusive group of riders to have trebled up on a single BSB weekend. Glenn's brother, Andrew, made it one for the family photo album with his run to third on the Synetiq BMW.

Ray began his season with third in race one and second in race three. A victory might have been in the offing but for an off-line moment at Luffield while leading comfortably in race two. It is telling that he didn't suffer another DNF until after he had sealed the title.

He wouldn't have long to stew over his missed opportunity. He finished what he had started at the next round with a belated return to the top step at Oulton Park. Better still, while it had taken some 135 BSB starts for him to get back to winning ways, he wouldn't have to wait long for the next one either, adding a second victory in race two. He achieved both in emphatic style befitting his burgeoning status, pulling off one of the overtakes of the season in the first race by outfoxing early leader Skinner, whose distracted attempts to resist Ryde simply opened the door for the other OMG Yamaha to sweep past at Old Hall.

Beyond Ray, whose third place in race three allowed him to take the points lead at the expense of Irwin, well short of his Silverstone best, Oulton Park went some way to setting the tone for the season, with a brace of strong results for the FS-3 Kawasaki team courtesy of Skinner and Jackson.

Twenty-year-old Skinner had turned heads during his podium-winning rookie campaign. Now he consolidated his reputation as one of the UK's most compelling young talents by adding to his Silverstone third place with a second at Oulton Park.

However, it was FS-3 Racing team-mate Jackson who netted it in race three. He had been second in race two, and the final race of the weekend allowed him to reel in and overtake both the OMG Yamaha man and Oxford Ducati's Bridewell to claim a celebrated – and long-awaited – maiden BSB victory. That marked a new peak for Jackson, some eight years after his BSB debut, in a slow-burn career split between Superbike and Superstock.

It was also Kawasaki's first BSB win since 2019, and with Haslam third in race two, the Japanese marque enjoyed a strong weekend. Alas, it would prove one of only two podium trips for the 2018 champion in a campaign blighted by set-up issues.

With the pre-season formbook somewhat awry during the openers, round three set a more familiar tone, as O'Halloran and McAMS Yamaha returned to the fore at Donington Park.

Whittled down to just a single bike by Mackenzie's injury, McAMS had struggled to dial in upgrades to its Yamaha R1 at Silverstone and Oulton Park, leaving O'Halloran adrift of the lead fight. At Donington Park, however, he was back to the devastating form that had produced 11 wins in 2021, with victories in races two and three.

He had been a mere 0.038 of a second from a hat trick, but in a first race that had ebbed and flowed between him and the two OMG Yamahas, his determined last-lap dive down the inside of Ryde through the final chicane wasn't quite enough to prevent his rival from scurrying back in front on the cut-back, to win the sprint to the flag in a photo finish.

Ray completed the podium for a Yamaha 1-2-3, but from there on, there was no stopping O'Halloran. Ray was in command for much of race two, his sizeable lead having swelled after Ryde's chase ended abruptly with an off at McLean's. But he was steadily reeled in during the closing stages by O'Halloran and relieved of the win at the Esses.

O'Halloran emphasised his point in race three, keeping a cool head despite initially being bullied down to the lower end of the top ten, before working his way to the front, picking off rivals one by one. Again, Ray had established a comfortable advantage, but after clawing himself into second, it wasn't long before the Australian loomed large in the R1's shadow.

A cheeky overtake into Coppice spooked Ray into surrender. With Jackson in third place, it was an identical podium to race two.

When BSB headed north of the border for its annual blast around the short, undulating Knockhill, the results bore similarities to Donington Park for the most part, O'Halloran scoring two more victories to stimulate his revived title-favourite status. He shared the spoils in Scotland with Ray, who took a third win of the year in race one, from pole position, comfortably leading home O'Halloran and a jubilant Skinner, who had put on a frisky performance on home turf to pull himself back on to the podium ahead of team-mate Jackson.

The Scot was in similarly ebullient form in race two as he scampered into an early lead from Ryde, but hopes of a fairy-tale maiden victory in front of local fans were scuppered by a relentless O'Halloran, who swept through and onwards. Jackson, meanwhile,

Top left: Return of the champion. Relief for Tarran Mackenzie after his first win of the year at Brands Hatch in July.

Above far left: Former double champion Josh Brookes had a season to forget on the MCE Ducati.

Photos: Bryn Williams

Above left: Christian Iddon had an injury hit season on a recalcitrant Suzuki.

Photo: www.suzuki-racing.com

Above: Sizzling August action at Thruxton as the Yamahas of O'Halloran, Ray and Mackenzie lead the pack.

Right: Mackenzie leads Tommy Bridewell and Bradley Ray at Brands Hatch.

Photos: Bryn Williams

prevailed in an entertaining scrap with Skinner, the FS-3 Kawasaki duo completing the podium.

O'Halloran didn't need to work quite so hard for victory in race three, his path smoothed by Skinner crashing out of the lead ahead of him – third-time unlucky. Ray trailed him home to consolidate his otherwise diminishing championship lead, while Jackson's Title Showdown credentials were strengthened on the back of a sixth podium, after capitalising on an error by double BSB champion Brookes. A disappointing outcome for the MCE Ducati rider, it was as close as he would get to the podium during a curiously lacklustre season, with a single top-five en route to missing out on a Showdown berth for the first time in 12 attempts.

There was no ignoring McAMS Yamaha's strengthening momentum come round five at Brands Hatch. They swept the board in all three races, this time with Mackenzie's input.

The reigning champion had endured an arduous recovery process when he had returned at Donington Park, tenth, sixth and eleventh threatening his chances of being inside the top eight at the Showdown cut-off point. At Brands Hatch, his fortunes turned right around. Two wins catapulted him into a provisional top-eight position.

O'Halloran took the spoils in the race-one sprint, eventually outpacing an entertaining scrap between Ray, Mackenzie – evidently enjoying getting his elbows out again – and the interloping Bridewell. In the end, Mackenzie shook out in front of Bridewell and Ray. It was a prelude of what was still to come. In race two, Mackenzie was back to his best with a dominant victory, having seen off Ray early on to lead team-mate O'Halloran home in the first McAMS one-two of the year. Once again, Bridewell was on the podium in third.

There was more history to repeat in race three as Mackenzie and O'Halloran duked it out doggedly. Leaving mere inches between their Yamahas as they slinked through on one another repeatedly, their fight culminated in O'Halloran diving through into Clearways on the final lap, only for Mackenzie to cut back to the inside to nose ahead as they sprinted to the flag.

An eighth consecutive podium was enough for O'Halloran to assume control in the overall standings ahead of Ray, who completed his brace of fourth places in race three behind Irwin. It was the Honda rider's most convincing performance since Silverstone and included a brief foray to the front.

As temperatures continued to rise during the scorching British summer, so did the speeds and intensity of the championship battle at Thruxton's round six. Renowned as the fastest in the UK, the Hampshire circuit delivered a zenith in exhilarating BSB action as the form trio of O'Halloran, Ray and Mackenzie turned up the heat in three sizzling races.

Buoyed by his points lead, O'Halloran added two more trophies to his bulging cabinet, with wins in races one and two, while Mackenzie's success in race three consolidated a second consecutive McAMS Yamaha weekend whitewash.

In race one, O'Halloran was able to escape just enough to reach the flag with less than a second in hand over Mackenzie and Ray, whose attempts to harass the leader were distracted by their own mighty back-and-forth. It culminated in the pair being split in second and third respectively by just 0.003 of a second.

With the soaring temperatures and longer distances of races two and three piling on the punishment for riders and tyres, the trio delivered a masterclass in wheel-to-wheel combat as they ducked and weaved to keep the top of the timing screens flickering like an airport departure board. Whether it was bravery at full throttle through Church or bravery on the anchors into the Club chicane, O'Halloran, Ray and Mackenzie clashed swords at every opportunity.

Race two appeared to be heading the way of Ray as he

netts
YAMAHA

McAMS
1
MONSTER ENERGY
SHOEI
MINT
46
OXFORD
OXFORD

Above: **Thriller at Thruxton – Mackenzie and Ray clash at the last corner, while O'Halloran is at hand to pick up the pieces.**
Photo: Bryn Williams

Top right: **Danny Kent gradually found top-ten form on his Buildbase Suzuki.**
Photo: www.suzuki-racing.com

Above right: **Danny Buchan brought two wins to BMW.**

Right (clockwise): **Lee Jackson, Tarran Mackenzie, Jason O'Halloran, Tommy Bridewell and Glenn Irwin all made the Showdown.**
Photos: Bryn Williams

repelled waves of attack from Mackenzie, while O'Halloran was a touch adrift in third. However, what was presumed to be fading tyres in fact was the opposite, a shrewd move by O'Halloran to let his rubber cool off, which gave him the tools to mount a late assault.

After he had got the better of Mackenzie and then – on the final lap – Ray at Church, a slithering exit on the last run to Club allowed the OMG Yamaha back alongside, just as Mackenzie – benefiting from the 'double bubble' slipstream – scythed past both going into the chicane. A messy entry led to a baulked exit, however, allowing O'Halloran to seize the moment to dip back underneath and nose ahead, to take victory by just 0.079 of a second. Ray was only 0.0165 off the win in third.

It was much the same in race three, albeit with the positions reversed: Mackenzie holding station in front as they entered the final stages, while O'Halloran and Ray slugged it out for second. Eventually, Mackenzie came under attack himself, with Ray leading into the final lap, having drafted both McAMS machines on the run to Club.

With all the bikes squirming as their rear tyres fought the forces being placed on them, Mackenzie and O'Halloran came to blows briefly at Seagrave. That caused the Australian to lose time, giving a clearly struggling Ray some respite out front.

Mackenzie set off in pursuit, slicing down the inside at Club to lead on the run to the final bend. Undeterred, Ray remained in contact as they approached the final corner. He failed to get by on the brakes and focused instead on getting the better exit. Although he did gain momentum, he'd run out of time, Mackenzie ahead by 0.019 of a second.

With two rounds remaining before the cut-off, Mackenzie's win boosted his Showdown chances. O'Halloran – who extended his overall lead – and Ray had done enough to book their spots in good time.

It was on to Cadwell Park for round seven, with just six races remaining to decide which six riders would be joining O'Halloran and Ray in the fight to be crowned 2022 BSB champion. Attention turned to those holding down a provisional spot and those primed for an upset.

Despite being confronted by a three-figure deficit to the two Yamahas out front, FS-3 Kawasaki's Jackson and Skinner remained well placed in third and fourth, as did fifth-place man Irwin, the Ulsterman thankful for the 75 points he had collected in the very first round to shore up his less spectacular results later. Ryde and Mackenzie were sixth and seventh, the two Yamaha riders having converged on points despite the former having struggled in the wake of his race-winning start to the season, while the latter had recovered ground following his injury-hit start.

Heading to Cadwell, Bridewell was eighth, the fans' favourite flying the flag for Ducati as Paul Bird Motorsport faltered with an out-of-form Brookes and Sykes, who was trying hard, but struggling.

Of those looking to usurp one of the eight, Hickman had enjoyed an upturn in form in the wake of his Isle of Man TT success, but an ill-timed technical DNF at Thruxton while en route to a second top-five finish of the weekend had slowed his charge. Buchan, a 2021 Showdown contender, was in a similar situation, the Synetiq BMW rider's hopes having taken a hit in recent rounds. Nevertheless, just as he appeared to be out of contention, his Showdown aspirations were enlivened at Cadwell Park with an extraordinary and unexpected two wins and a podium.

His run to third behind Ray and Skinner in race one was the result of a hefty dose of luck. He had run himself and Sykes off track and down the order with contact at the Hairpin, only for the red flag to fall for a full restart moments later. Jackson had crashed coming off the Mountain, and his Kawasaki had been struck head-on by iForce BMW's Dan Jones. The sickening impact had sent Jones flying over the handlebars, and although he escaped serious injury, he did suffer a broken collarbone.

With the sprint race shortened following a lengthy clean-up operation, Ray prevailed from pole to secure precious podium credits with his first win since Knockhill, while Skin-

ner – fresh from his Moto2 World Championship wild-card debut – moved on to the cusp of Showdown safety with his fifth trip to the podium.

The Bank Holiday Monday, however, was all about Buchan. In race two, he got ahead of Ray early on and held firm out front before a red flag brought the encounter to a premature conclusion, courtesy of Brookes tumbling at the Mountain.

Race three was similar, Buchan seizing the initiative midway around the opening lap before holding off Ray to secure a timely second win of the weekend. This emboldened his Showdown hopes, despite erstwhile nearest contender Bridewell boosting his own bid with a pair of thirds.

Meanwhile, Skinner and Jackson assured their spots in the Showdown. Although the McAMS Yamaha riders had a surprisingly lacklustre weekend, they were safe, with Mackenzie sixth overall behind Irwin. With Bridewell in seventh, Ryde – on the back of another disappointing weekend – found himself suddenly under threat, just 14 points ahead of Buchan with a crucial round eight at Snetterton awaiting.

Above: **Tommy Bridewell's sole win came at Oulton Park in September.**

Top right: **When the pressure began to build, Ray kept his head down and held his nerve.**

Above right: **BMW riders Peter Hickman (*left*) and Andrew Irwin just missed the Showdown, but they shone in the Brands Hatch finale.**

Right: **Returning veteran Tom Sykes used all his Donington Park experience to take two wins.**

Photos: Bryn Williams

On a weekend when indifferent weather marked the shift from summer to autumn, so did the mood among the leading contenders, seemingly conscious that they'd have more to lose than gain should they risk throwing it down the road. This was certainly true for Skinner, whose head-bumping spill in race one ruled him out once concussion had been diagnosed, while O'Halloran, Irwin and Jackson were noticeably playing it safe.

Not so Ray, the OMG Yamaha rider sensing an opportunity to establish a psychological edge before the Showdown by pushing on. He was rewarded with three wins, earning himself a VIP pass into BSB's Hall of Triple-Winning Fame.

The impact should not have been underestimated. At a time when it appeared that McAMS were driving home the Yamaha wedge, rather than accepting his fate, Ray fought right back, two more victories at Snetterton reclaiming the championship lead and, more crucially, also the advantage in terms of podium credits.

Elsewhere, Mackenzie and Ryde's timely podiums in race one all but secured their Title Showdown berths before Bridewell did the same in race two. Although Hickman recovered some ground with a run to second in race three, it wasn't enough to put him into contention.

The Showdown octet was confirmed, with Ray out front from O'Halloran, Jackson and Irwin on the overall leaderboard. Once the points were equalised and the podium credits tallied, the standings took on a different appearance, with Ray up top on 1,061 points, from O'Halloran (1,048), Mackenzie (1,031), Irwin (1,016), Jackson (1,014), Ryde (1,013), Skinner (1,009) and Bridewell (1,008).

With the honours still relatively even, Oulton Park should have marked the beginning of an expected hugely competitive run to the title trophy. Instead, it turned into something of a 'last man standing' exercise on a brutal weekend for three of the eight contenders, which turned the title battle on its head.

To Ray's credit, he was in fine form from the get-go, shrugging off the pressure to kick off the weekend with pole and victory in race one. In the meantime, McAMS Yamaha's title dreams imploded after a series of unfortunate events that would result in both riders leaving Oulton Park without a single point.

O'Halloran's fortunes were dictated by two controversial, yet almost identical, collisions at Druids on the final lap of race one and the first lap of race two. He had appeared destined for a podium in the opening encounter but for a wide sweeping line around the right-hander that was tested by an opportunistic Hickman, whose attempt to snake through led to contact that sent the Australian barrelling out of the race. Hickman carried on to take the flag in fourth behind Ray, Bridewell and Haslam, but later he was excluded altogether.

With the incident still fresh in everyone's minds, O'Halloran then found himself on the receiving end of another collision at Druids, this time at the hands of Bridewell. A second painful exit left him a non-starter in race three, his title aspirations effectively scuppered.

Worse was to follow for team-mate Mackenzie when – after crashing out of race one – a slow fall on his own at Hislop's in race two led to him rolling back on to the track in front of the unsighted Hickman, who couldn't avoid thumping into his leg. A broken femur was the outcome, forcing Mackenzie to relinquish the defence of his BSB crown.

He wasn't the only Showdown rider who had to call time on his season. Skinner was involved in a bizarre collision with Iddon that led to him straddling his rival's Suzuki as they came down, injuring his arm. As a result, he sat out the remaining events to focus on his preparations for joining the Moto2 World Championship in 2023.

With the pathway towards the title clearing, Ray simply needed to keep his nerve in the remaining two races at Oulton Park. He appeared to be on course in race two, but after the second red flag to clear the Skinner/Iddon accident, he struggled with his tyres, allowing a renewed bid from rivals who had benefited from elevated grid slots by virtue of the carnage ahead.

Jackson battled his way through to victory in race two from Bridewell, the Oxford Ducati rider benefiting from the stoppages to negate the ride-through penalty he'd received for the coming-together with O'Halloran; Ray was third.

It was a similar story in race three, with Ray unable to find his groove on the Yamaha en route to fifth place. Instead, Bridewell claimed the honours for his first win of the year, from Irwin and Jackson.

The results left their mark on the overall standings heading to Donington Park. Ray now led Bridewell – who had surged from eighth to second in the standings – Irwin and Jackson, but with a comfortable 40 points in hand.

Back on the full international layout, Ray's rivals arrived armed with renewed belief in a late title charge, but it was the Yamaha rider who had the form to count on as he delivered a pair of gritty podium results – including a win – to end the weekend with one hand and four fingers on the BSB title trophy.

Otherwise, the headlines that weekend belonged to 2013 WorldSBK champion Sykes, who burst from a season spent largely in the midfield with two exemplary wins on the MCE Ducati, which echoed some of his more dominant victories on the international stage over the previous decade.

Sykes led O'Halloran and Hickman in race one, with Ray a cautious fourth, but crucially ahead of Bridewell, Irwin and Jackson. Second behind Sykes, but ahead of Irwin in race two fuelled his title aspirations further, before he resisted the repeated challenge from Irwin in race three to finish ahead of Andrew and Glenn.

With Jackson unable to maintain the tempo of his Oulton Park wins, and O'Halloran needing medical attention for a

third time in little more than a week, after colliding heavily with Sykes in race three, the title battle was whittled down to just Ray, Irwin and Bridewell heading to the season finale at Brands Hatch.

In reality, though, with 66 points to his favour and only a maximum of 75 points available in the final round, Ray simply needed to keep his cool in any one of the three races to reel off a famous title victory. And so it proved. He nervously kept the OMG Yamaha upright to finish fifth in the sprint race, securing the points he needed to be crowned 2022 BSB champion.

Alas, the victory was an altogether sombre occasion for Ray, OMG Racing, Yamaha and the BSB paddock, as it came just days after fellow racer Chrissy Rouse had succumbed to injuries sustained in an accident at the previous Donington Park round (see sidebar). It was a huge shock to the paddock and a sobering reminder of the dangers that remain associated with this sport. The respectful celebrations for the 2020 National Superstock 1000 champion were a reflection of the impact of his loss.

With the title decided, attention turned to the runner-up. That honour went to Irwin after he book-ended both the season and his career as a Honda rider with two more wins at Brands Hatch, the Ulsterman looking ahead to his return to PBM Ducati for 2023.

Bridewell, Irwin's 2023 PBM team-mate, was third overall, while Jackson completed his breakthrough campaign in fourth, from O'Halloran in fifth. Although his results towards the end of the season failed to match those at the start, Ryde made it two OMG Yamahas inside the top six, with the sidelined Mackenzie and Skinner seventh and eighth.

In the fight for BSB Riders' Cup glory, Hickman's race-two win at Brands Hatch gave him the lead over fellow BMW rider Buchan, the Synetiq rider rounding out the top ten.

Elsewhere, WorldSBK exiles Haslam and Sykes concluded their respective seasons in 11th and 12th, ahead of Andrew Irwin, who added three podiums to his tally in the final rounds. Josh Brookes in 14th and Suzuki's Iddon completed the top 15.

Above: Sibling rivalry. Andrew Irwin's BMW leads Glenn Irwin's Honda at Brands Hatch.

Top: Competitors and marshals pay tribute to the late Chrissy Rouse.

Above left: Flame out for Hickman's BMW as he heads for his sole win in the penultimate race.

Left: Trophy in hand, Bradley Ray signals his championship triumph.

Photos: Bryn Williams

CHRISSY ROUSE - 1995–2022

Clive Challinor Motorsport Photography

IT is no exaggeration to describe Chrissy Rouse as one of the most talented figures in BSB, both on and off the track. A multi-skilled racer finally receiving due recognition at the highest levels after years of hard graft, at 26, he had achieved much, yet still had much more to come.

He had made his debut in 2008 in the FAB Racing Series and won the Aprilia Superteen Championship in 2010, appearing in the BSB paddock in 2011 in the 125cc British Championship. He progressed to the Triumph Triple Challenge in 2012, romping to a dominant title win in 2013.

Three years in National Superstock 600 led to the National Superstock 1000 Championship, where he proved a regular front-runner, claiming fourth overall in 2017 and 2019, and taking the title in 2020 with Crowe Performance on a BMW S 1000 RR.

Rouse, who held a degree in mathematics and worked as a university lecturer, achieved his aim of joining BSB with Crowe Performance in 2022. He scored points on several occasions before suffering head injuries in an accident at the start of the third race at Donington Park.

KEITH FARMER - 1987–2022

Clive Challinor Motorsport Photography

November brought a second shock to BSB, with the sudden death of popular former racer Keith Farmer.

A member of a prominent racing family from Northern Ireland, Farmer was champion four times in three different classes between 2011 and 2018, winning the National Superstock 600 title in 2011, the National Superstock 1000 championship in 2012 and 2018, and the 2017 British Supersport crown.

He also rode for several BSB teams including Paul Bird Motorsport, Buildbase Suzuki and TAS Racing, before retiring prematurely in September, 2021, his results hampered by a several injuries and accidents.

At the time, Farmer said, "I count myself extremely lucky to have been given the opportunities to win four British titles." He had enjoyed "ten good years of racing", but cited two relatively big crashes for hastening his retirement.

Keith was cousin to Mark Farmer, the 1992 British Supersport 400 champion, who lost his life on the Isle of Man in 1994.

Father of three, Keith Farmer died suddenly at home of undisclosed causes on 10th November.

Dawn
ashvale
PIRELLI

MACADAM

NITROX

99

Arai
QUATTRO
MACADAM

BSB Support Championships

A COMPREHENSIVE and competitive programme of supporting championships kept the action coming thick and fast between the BSB headline races, offering a chance to catch a glimpse of fresh-faced future stars jostling among esteemed veterans of their various disciplines.

BSB's supporting categories almost stole the show at times in 2022. From the generational mix of Supersport and Superstock classes to MSV's quest to discover Britain's next motorcycling superstar in the Honda Talent Cup, Junior Supersport and Junior Superstock series, the wealth of talent within the domestic ranks remains rich.

After pulling level with the late Karl Harris by winning a third title in 2021, Jack Kennedy established a new **Quattro Plant British Supersport Championship** benchmark in 2022 with an emphatic and record-breaking fourth title. Champion in 2018 and 2019, he had claimed his third crown on Kawasaki machinery, but for 2022 returned to the Yamaha fold with the Mar-Train team. Four wins from four races set the pace early, becoming a steamroller that crushed the competition with one dominant win after another.

With 13 wins and three second-place finishes from 16 races, his was a relentless run of form that wrapped up the title at Snetterton with three rounds to spare, and he curtailed his season early before graduating to BSB for 2023.

Only two riders – Appleyard Macadam Yamaha duo Bradley Perie and Harry Truelove – broke Kennedy's stronghold at the top of the podium while he was around, while Dutchman Jamie van Sikkelerus landed a victory in his absence. Perie prevailed in his intra-team tussle with Truelove to secure a runner-up result that, while distant from Kennedy, was energised by a final tally of seven wins.

Behind third-placed Truelove, Lee Johnston claimed ten podiums for Ashcourt Racing, while van Sikkelerus took fifth for MPM Routz Racing, completing an all-Yamaha top five. Luke Stapleford (Gearlink Kawasaki), Rhys Irwin (Astro JJR Triumph) and Eugene McManus (Completely Motorbikes Affinity Kawasaki) followed in sixth, seventh and eighth respectively as the only other riders to step on the podium in 2022.

The **GP2 Championship**, which runs Moto2 prototypes within British Supersport races, with a separate points system, found a clear champion in Jack Scott. A total of 14 class wins smoothed his run on the One GP2 machine, the Kovara Solutions RS Racing rider proving a nuisance for the Supersport machines at the faster venues, taking the flag first on the road at Thruxton.

Go Racing Chassis Factory duo Cameron Fraser and Harvey Claridge completed the season second and third overall with two wins apiece, while fourth-placed Jake Archer, on the Synergy FTR, was also a double GP2 class winner.

Above: **The Quattro Plant British Supersport race one gets under way at Thruxton.**

Top left: **Jack Kennedy (Yamaha) took his third Supersport championship. Next stop, BSB.**

Above left: **Bradley Perie, on the gas at Oulton, narrowly beat team-mate Harry Truelove to second in the Supersport championship.**

Left: **Truelove wrestles his Yamaha into submission.**

Far left: **Runaway GP2 champion Jack Scott claimed an outright victory at Thruxton.**

Photos: Bryn Williams

Above: **Davey Todd took Pirelli National Superstock honours at his first attempt on the Padgetts Honda.**

Top right: **Billy McConnell leads the applause for rival Todd on the podium at Donington Park.**

Photo: www.suzuki-racing.com

Above right: **Honda-mounted McConnell had the edge in the early races.**

Above far right: **Alex Olson took a win at Thruxton on the FHO Racing BMW.**

Right: **First steps on the official 'Road to MotoGP'. Johnny Garness (14) won 12 of 16 races in the British Talent Cup.**

Far right: **Garness's association with VisionTrack Racing bodes well for the young rider's future.**

Photos: Bryn Williams

As ever, the **Pirelli National Superstock Championship** proved fiercely competitive, with six riders tasting the winner's champagne in their efforts to succeed Honda BSB graduate Tom Neave as champion.

Initially, it appeared that the title trophy would remain within the Neave family after Tom's younger brother, Tim, carved out an early advantage with three wins from five races on the McAMS-backed Edwards Yamaha. Serious injuries suffered in a testing accident left him on the sidelines, however, and the title fight switched to an all-Honda battle between C&L Fairburn Properties Jackson Racing's Billy McConnell and Milenco by Padgetts' Davey Todd.

The experienced McConnell grabbed the initiative to score three wins and establish a healthy lead over Todd at the midpoint of the season. By contrast, the early stages of Todd's title tilt were built on a foundation of consistent results. After six trips to the podium without topping it, he finally stepped up with a victory during round eight at Snetterton. That was the catalyst for him to take control, with three more wins from the next two events, allowing him to surge past McConnell to clinch the title with a round to spare.

Capping off a breakthrough year for the 27-year-old road racing specialist, Todd's short-circuit success came hot on the heels of a maiden podium at the Isle of Man TT and a successful turn at the North West 200.

Alex Olsen won twice on his way to third, the FHO Racing BMW rider ahead of two more Honda riders, Brayden Elliot (CFS Filtration No Bull Racing) and Richard Kerr (AMD Motorsport), who also took turns at the top of the podium en route to fourth and fifth respectively.

Consistent results pushed IN Competition Aprilia's Tom Ward to sixth overall, ahead of Neave, who recovered to seventh on his return from injury. Charlie Nesbitt scored a victory on his way to eighth aboard the VisionTrack Suzuki, one of two wins for the 'Gixxer' after Richard Cooper topped the podium during a one-off guest outing at Brands Hatch with Buildbase Suzuki.

A series that counts BSB front-runner and soon-to-be Moto2 rider Rory Skinner, and Moto3 World Championship contender Scott Ogden among its illustrious title-winning alumni, the **Honda British Talent Cup** is bearing fruit as a breeding ground for the next generation of would-be GP stars. For 2022, there was little doubting Johnny Garness as a name to remember, as the 14-year-old swept to a dominant championship win. Competing with the VisionTrack Academy team, run by Michael Laverty – founder of the VisionTrack Moto3 World Championship outfit – Garness won 12 of the 16 races.

His team-mate, Carter Brown, won twice to secure second ahead of Banks Racing's Harrison Crosby, with Rhys Stephenson (Rocket Racing) and Lucas Brown (SP125/Amphibian Scaffolding) rounding out the top five.

PIRELLI
Bennetts
MILENCO
HONDA
hager

DUNLOP
HONDA
ROAD TO

Left: Junior British Supersport champion Jamie McManus sports the No.1 plate on his Kawasaki.

Far left: McManus shares the podium with team-mate Mikey Hardie, who was title runner-up.

Below far left: Max Cook took nine wins on his Yamaha on the way to the Pirelli Junior Supersport title.

Below: David Shoebridge was champion with 11 wins in the last ever Ducati TriOptions Cup.

Bottom: World sidecar champions Todd Ellis and Emmanuelle Clement also claimed the honours in the British championship.

Photos: Bryn Williams

The **HEL Performance Junior British Supersport Championship with MOTOCOURSE** went down to the wire, with Jamie McManus emerging victorious over fellow Completely Motorbikes Affinity Kawasaki rider Mikey Hardie.

Though five victories en route to the Brands Hatch finale meant that McManus was always well placed, D&P Lovell Kent Racing's Kieran Kent and Symcirrus Motorsport's Charlie Atkins remained within striking distance. In the end, he was saved by a double win for team-mate Hardie, who stole points off McManus's rivals and leapfrogged them to secure the runner-up spot, ahead of Atkins and Kent.

With a stipulation that the top three at the end of the season must move on for the following year, and a roll-call that once included BSB riders Ryan Vickers and Storm Stacey, there is always plenty to play for in the **Pirelli Junior Superstock Championship**. In 2022, the title went to former Junior World Championship racer Max Cook, who took nine wins on the Uggly & Co by Binch Pro Yamaha.

He was comfortably clear of 2020 Honda British Talent Cup champion Franco Bourne, who picked up four victories en route to the runner-up spot aboard the Marvel HCL Motorsport Kawasaki. Dan Brooks (R4R Vision Team Kawasaki), Seth Crump (Seeeeeth Racing Yamaha) and Aaron Silvester (A&J Racing Yamaha) completed the top five.

In the **Ducati TriOptions Cup**, David Shoubridge had the honour of being named its swan-song title winner. Despite a dominant campaign of 11 wins on the RICH Energy bike, he was pushed all the way to a final-round showdown by Tom Tunstall (Motorcycle Race Parts), even though the former BSB rider never topped the podium in 2022. The top five was completed by Trackdemons Racing Powered by HMY's Blaze Baker in third, and JDF Racing duo Max Lofthouse and Adon Davie in fourth and fifth respectively.

With the Ducati TriOptions Cup being absorbed into the British Supersport Championship for 2023, its place on the BSB support bill will be assumed by an intriguing new one-make series, the BMW F 900 R Cup.

Todd Ellis and Emmanuelle Clement reigned supreme in the **Molson Group British Sidecar Championship**, with a dominant 12 wins on the Santander Salt LCR Yamaha, seeing off the challenge from runners-up Sam and Tom Christie (Christie Engineering Services), and third-placed Lewis Blackstock and Paddy Rosney (DHR Express Tyre Services).

Bennetts BSB
BRITISH SUPERBIKES
IN ASSOCIATION WITH PIRELLI

2023

OFFICIAL TESTS

11/12 March	Circuito de Navarra (Spain)
25/26 March	Donington Park GP
28/29 March	Silverstone Nat.
13 April	Oulton Park

RACE EVENTS

7 - 9 April	Silverstone Nat.
29 April - 1 May	Oulton Park
19 - 21 May	Donington Park GP
16 - 18 June	Knockhill
7 - 9 July	Snetterton 300
21 - 23 July	Brands Hatch GP
11 - 13 August	Thruxton
25 - 28 August	Cadwell Park
15 - 17 September	Oulton Park
29 Sept - 1 October	Donington Park Nat.
13 - 15 October	Brands Hatch GP

** Dates are provisional and subject to change*

BRITISHSUPERBIKE
@OFFICIALBSB
OFFICIALBSB
@BRITISHSUPERBIKE
BRITISHSUPERBIKE

FOR EVENT AND TICKET INFORMATION

MSVR MOTORSPORT VISION RACING

WWW.BRITISHSUPERBIKE.COM

A TOUGHER PATH TO THE TITLE

Jake Gagne scored a come-from-behind championship. LARRY LAWRENCE reports...

Above: **Jake Gagne retained his crown, but Ducati's Petrucci made him earn it.**

Top right: **Gagne made a slow start, but a strong finish.**

Above right: **Out of MotoGP, Danilo Petrucci made the most of his American sojourn.**

Right: **Winner first time out. Petrucci leads Petersen, Scholz and Gagne up the hill in round one at the Circuit of The Americas.**

Photos: MotoAmerica/Brian J. Nelson

EARLY in the 2022 MotoAmerica Superbike Championship, it appeared that Jake Gagne's reign would end after just a single season. After the first three races of the ten-round, 20-race series, former MotoGP rider Danilo Petrucci and his factory Warhorse HSBK Racing Ducati NYC Ducati were on a roll, with three straight wins building an impressive points lead. Gagne, meanwhile, was tenth after two DNFs.

After race one at Road Atlanta, defending series champ Gagne had a meagre 16 points, while Petrucci was unbeaten with 75. It looked as if those who had predicted that a solid MotoGP rider would ride roughshod over MotoAmerica regulars were proving prophetic.

Then the tables were turned. Gagne dominated the second leg, while Petrucci's Ducati blew up. Suddenly, it was game on. Gagne left Road Atlanta with a much more manageable 34-point deficit. From that moment, he went on a tear, winning 11 of the next 16 rounds aboard his Fresh N Lean Progressive Yamaha Racing R1, usually in convincing fashion, en route to his second consecutive MotoAmerica Superbike Championship.

The season was not without drama, even late in the summer. Gagne crashed spectacularly out of the lead in Sunday's race at Brainerd (Minnesota), with Petrucci there to pick up the pieces, earning his first victory in three months and reclaiming the series lead. Gagne quickly regained control, however, with a string of three straight victories, but Petrucci kept things interesting with a late-season win in the rain in New Jersey, closing to within four points of Gagne and keeping the fight alive to the final round. In the end, though, after 20 races, it was Gagne by 20 points over Petrucci.

It was another very successful year for Yamaha in MotoAmerica. In addition to Gagne's championship, his Attack Performance Yamaha team-mate, Cameron Petersen, and Westby Racing Yamaha's Mathew Scholtz (both South Africans) made it three Yamaha riders inside the top five.

Another MotoGP refugee, Hector Barbera, riding for the rapidly rising Tytlers Cycle Racing BMW squad, was fifth. The Spaniard claimed a single podium with third at Elkhart Lake, but backed it with a set of solid placings, including several fourths and fifths, and never finished outside the top ten.

New Yorker PJ Jacobsen took sixth overall, 20 points adrift after a slightly more erratic campaign – two podiums at Elkhart Lake and Brainerd, and other strong top-six placings were undermined by several no-scores.

Four riders took race wins: Gagne with 12, then five for Petrucci, Petersen two and Scholtz one. Petrucci was the only first-time winner. Gagne's outstanding campaign took his career total to 29 wins, moving him past Nicky Hayden, Fred Merkel and Ben Spies to sixth on the all-time MotoAmerica/AMA Superbike List, behind Mat Mladin, Josh Hayes, Cameron Beaubier, Miguel Duhamel and Toni Elias.

Circuit of The Americas – 8–10 April

Petrucci's debut was perfect, winning both days of the season-opener at Circuit of The Americas in the MotoAmerica Medallia Superbike class. In his first outing in the series, he set fastest lap as he led Scholtz and Petersen, with Jacobsen and Barbera next, both on BMWs.

Sunday's race produced a larger, 5.1-second margin of victory, but it was the tougher of the two races, the Italian fighting a heated early battle with Scholtz. They traded the lead on several occasions until the South African began having moments that were sketchy enough for him to disengage, to be sure of his second runner-up finish at the opening round.

Gagne was third, salvaging 16 valuable championship points after a miserable weekend. Saturday's race one had been a disaster, his bike having failed to start the race with another engine failure. On Sunday, he rode his back-up bike, but suffered from a lack of track time due to the mechanical ills.

Fortunately, the Petersen side of the team fared better – third on Saturday and fourth on Sunday. He hounded Gagne for the duration, coming up just a tenth behind at the finish.

"Definitely, I have to be happy for this weekend," Petrucci said. "I didn't know what would be my level. The only thing I knew was this track. Fortunately, our bike is really good on braking and maximum speed."

Road Atlanta – 22–24 April

Few would have expected that defender Gagne would not win until the fourth race of the season, but that's how it played out. He notched his first victory in Sunday's race at Michelin Raceway Road Atlanta.

His record was DNF (mechanical), third, DNF (crash), victory. The crash on Saturday had been out of the lead, and zero points combined with Petrucci's third straight win left him 59 points behind.

In his absence, Petrucci beat Scholtz in race one, with Jake Lewis (Vision Wheel M4 ECSTAR Suzuki) taking his only podium of the year in third, 30 seconds adrift.

But Gagne is Gagne, and the eternal positivity never wavered. On Sunday, he dominated from start to finish, despite two red flags, winning by 14.028 seconds over team-mate Petersen, the South African also bouncing back from a Sat-

Above: **Petersen leads Petrucci in race two at a wet Road America.**

Top right: **Matthew Scholtz won at Road America and added eight second places in a strong season.**

Above right: **Winner Petersen and team chassis mechanic Lee Vaughan enjoy the podium at Road America.**

Right: **Scholz (11) momentarily has the edge on Petersen, Petrucci and Gagne as the field blasts off the line at Laguna Seca.**

Photos: MotoAmerica/Brian J. Nelson

urday crash to bring smiles back to the Yamaha camp.

Even better for Gagne, the two riders leading on points failed to finish Sunday's race. Petrucci's Ducati Panigale V4 R blew up on the opening lap of the second restart, while Scholtz crashed, remounted, pitted and finally gave up on the 11th lap.

Virginia International Raceway – 20–22 May

Gagne left Virginia after taking two MotoAmerica Medallia Superbike wins at one of his favourite racetracks, but compared to his crushing performance at VIR in 2021, the margins were much closer – 2.9 seconds on Saturday, 3.2 on Sunday. And he freely admitted that his rivals had gained ground. He also said that he was in favour of that, enjoying the fact that 2022 appeared to be a 180 from the previous year in terms of the speed of his competition.

"There's no such thing as those big eight-second leads any more," Gagne said, post victory. "Every half-tenth or tenth, I'll take it. These guys are all stepping it up this year. I'm excited. I think we're all excited. It's going to be some good battling. As much as I love cruising around at the front, I love battling, too. I love racing these boys."

His race-two win on Sunday completed his perfect weekend. Scholtz finished second in both races, but he wasn't overly upset with his fifth runner-up finish of the year. After all, he'd destroyed his A-bike in a morning warm-up crash, forcing his crew to attempt to replicate the set-up on the second bike.

Petersen was third in race one, Petrucci fourth. The positions were reversed on Sunday, the championship leader crossing the line just 0.020 of a second behind Scholtz. What happened next remains a bit of a mystery, but Petrucci crashed the Panigale V4 R in the fast Turn One after the finish line and suffered a leg laceration that required stitches, missing the podium ceremonies.

The scrap for second had lasted the entire race and featured Scholtz, Petrucci and Petersen, who was dropped in the closing laps to finish 1.5 seconds behind.

With three rounds and six races completed, Petrucci's lead had shrunk to four points over Scholtz; Gagne had vaulted to third, 13 points behind the Italian.

Road America – 3–5 June

Scholtz had finished second in five out of six races so far, but he refused to finish second again. He went head to head with Petrucci on Saturday, coming out on top of a last-lap brawl for his first win of 2022 and the fifth of his career.

Well clear of the battle for third, it came down to the last lap. Petrucci led, but Scholtz had a plan and stuck to it, with a late-braking effort and a block pass into Turn Five. Petrucci tried to get back in the final corner, but it didn't work and Scholtz was able to hold off the Panigale V4 R up the hill by just 0.015 of a second.

Barbera was a season's-best third, narrowly getting the better of Tytler BMW team-mate Jacobsen. Gagne was another six seconds down after a storming ride through the field. He'd tangled with Petrucci on the first lap, run wide and tipped off in the gravel, rejoining in last place.

Petersen had been forced to sit out Saturday's race after a mechanical failure had put him out of the lead. On Sunday, he put that behind him, winning in iffy wet/dry conditions on the four-mile circuit in America's Dairyland. His first of the season was the second of his Superbike career.

It was a good race, with all the top men opting for full rain tyres, but searching for puddles by the end. The battle featured three riders for all eight laps of the shortened race, with Petersen, Jacobsen and Petrucci all taking turns at the front.

Petersen put his head down on the final go-around to win by 1.3 seconds over Jacobsen, the New Yorker just 0.455 of a second ahead of Petrucci.

Ridge Motorsports Park – 24–26 June

Gagne had a perfect weekend in the Pacific Northwest, breaking the lap record while qualifying on pole, then winning both races. If his rivals weren't worried already, they should have been. He appeared to be on the verge of a roll, as during his 17-win 2021 season.

With five rounds (ten races) in the books, he closed to within 11 points of Petrucci, whose second podium of the weekend came from second place on Sunday.

Gagne's team-mate, Petersen, also enjoyed a solid weekend, splitting second- and third-place finishes with Petrucci. Scholtz and Barbera claimed fourth and fifth places in both the races.

Saturday's race was a restarted eight-lapper, after two red flags, one when Jake Lewis crashed in the last corner. Petrucci also fell directly afterwards, but he was able to get his bike back to the pit lane, have the left footrest replaced and make the restart.

Laguna Seca Raceway – 8–10 July

Gagne completed another clean sweep in California on Sunday, taking over the lead of the 2022 title chase.

He nailed the holeshot from third on the front row, put his head down and gapped the field. From there, it was just a matter of putting in quick laps, stretching the lead to four seconds, then maintaining a fast pace to the finish – a signature Gagne race.

Saturday's win was his fourth in a row and seventh of the year as he kicked his season into high gear heading into the second half of the series. Departing Laguna, he led the championship by three points.

Although Sunday's podium was the same as for Saturday's race one, the results were different, with Petrucci turning the tables on Petersen, the pair finishing second and third respectively.

Above: **Race one at a sunny Alabama, and Gagne leads Petersen (45), Scholz (11), Petrucci (9) Jacobsen (66), Lewis (85) and the pack.**

Right: **Josh Hayes (4) disputes the lead with Supersport champion Josh Herrin, while Rocco Landers heads the pursuit at New Jersey.**

Photos: MotoAmerica/Brian J. Nelson

Brainerd International Raceway – 29–31 July

Race one in Minnesota had a familiar feel, with Yamaha team-mates Gagne and Petersen heading Petrucci on the podium; Scholtz was fourth. This time, Jacobsen was fifth.

On Sunday, just when everything seemed to be rolling along nicely for Gagne, his Yamaha YZF-R1 was cartwheeling along the racetrack, steadily destroying itself with every bounce. Fortunately, he escaped uninjured, but his championship points lead took a hit.

Petrucci was the rider who picked up the pieces and reaped the rewards. With his fourth win of the season, and his first since Road Atlanta in April, he moved back to the top of the standings, 253–240, with three rounds and six races remaining.

Petrucci and Petersen had put in quick laps early to maintain pressure on Gagne, and despite a mistake when he was within two seconds, the Italian was keeping that up when the defending champion crashed. Ironically, he said after the race that he was about to abandon trying to keep the pace.

He finished 7.1 seconds ahead of Petersen, the South African earning his 11th podium of the year and his seventh in a row; Jacobsen matched his best finish of the year with his second podium of the season on the Tytlers BMW, the New Yorker, some ten seconds behind Petersen.

Pittsburgh Intl Race Complex – 19–21 August

There are perfect weekends, and then there are perfect weekends. Gagne's weekend at the Pittsburgh International Race Complex was as immaculate at it could be. He didn't put a wheel wrong, and the result was pole position, a new lap record and two victories. And a return to the points lead.

After snatching everything he could on Saturday, he returned on Sunday and did the same thing again. This time, however, the bonus that came with his tenth win of the season and 27th of his career would consign Petrucci to second in the standings.

Gagne stormed away at the start, built a lead and maintained it to the end of the 17-lap race. Behind him, he was inadvertently helped by Scholtz as the South African tore through from sixth on the grid to pass Petrucci for second. That gifted Gagne an extra four championship points.

Scholtz, who was racing with three broken bones in his left wrist, ended up 4.8 seconds behind Gagne and 1.9 seconds ahead of Petrucci.

Earlier, Gagne's team-mate, Petersen, had tussled with Petrucci, but the South African couldn't keep pace and slipped to fourth at the finish. Jacobsen's BMW narrowly beat Rickie Escalante's Suzuki to fifth.

New Jersey Motorsports Park – 9–11 September

Petrucci had been doing a rain dance all year, but it took until the penultimate round of the championship in New Jersey for his wish to come true. But when it did, he took full advantage.

After watching Gagne win Saturday's dry race from Petersen and Scholtz, fourth-placed Petrucci raced away in the rain on Sunday for his fifth and perhaps most important win of the season. With Gagne third, it moved the Italian to within four points, with just one round and two races left to run.

Heavy rain fell prior to the start, leaving no doubt that the field would be using rain tyres, with the distance cut to 14 laps. There was also little doubt that Petrucci would be fast in the conditions, given his MotoGP reputation as a rain-master. And that he was. After slip-sliding around for the duration more capably than the others, he crossed the line with 6.6 seconds in hand.

Scholz was second, the South African also impressing by charging through the field from behind after being relegated to the back of the grid through missing the sighting lap.

Gagne was a cautious third, having little to gain and plenty to lose in the tricky conditions. He stayed out of trouble and gained a spot late in the race when Petersen crashed out of his battle with Scholtz for second. Gagne could also breathe a bit easier when Ashton Yates crashed the Aftercare Hayes Scheibe Racing BMW with two laps to go while hounding the points leader.

Barbera was a distant fourth, with the remounted Petersen a distant fifth, in spite of riding without the use of his left handlebar.

Barber Motorsports Park – 23–25 September

Gagne's victory in Saturday's race, his 12th of the season, earned him 25 points, which, combined with Petrucci finishing third, gave him a 13-point advantage over the Italian going into Sunday's final race of the year.

On Sunday, Gagne finished second to team-mate Petersen, and that earned him a second successive Superbike title. His season had featured 12 wins and 14 total podiums in 20 races – five fewer wins than the previous year.

The race went perfectly for the champion, Petersen leading him for the duration, the pair flying in formation until Gagne backed it down in the final laps. It was Petersen's second win of the season, his third career victory and his first in dry conditions at his favourite track by 3.1 seconds.

Third place went to Jacobsen, who passed Petrucci in the last corner on the last lap – fitting revenge for the New Yorker, who had lost out on third in Saturday's race when Petrucci's jump-start penalty was reversed after the team's appeal was upheld. He beat the Italian to the line by 0.206 of a second.

Gagne's next destination was Portimao, for an exploratory outing in WorldSBK.

Supersport

There was never much doubt that Josh Herrin was going to wrap up the 2022 MotoAmerica Supersport Championship at some point during the eighth round of the series at New Jersey Motorsports Park. However, he wanted to end things early in race one on Saturday, and that's what he did, riding his Warhorse HSBK Racing Ducati NYC Panigale V2 to second place to wrap up the title.

The championship was Herrin's third, after his 2013 AMA Superbike title and his 2016 MotoAmerica Superstock 1000 crown. He closed out the series finale with a ninth victory on a wet-to-drying track.

"It's the best way possible to finish the season, especially when Rocco [Landers] was coming on strong at the end," Herrin said. "Mentally, I think it helps a lot going into next year. You've got six, seven months to sit and think about everything."

Landers did finish strongly. The 17-year-old from Oregon scored four wins and finished runner-up in the championship on a Yamaha. Tyler Scott finished third on a Suzuki, earning nine podiums, including a victory at Road America.

Semi-retired veteran Josh Hayes raced part-time and won three Supersport rounds. Local hero Jason Farrell stunned the series regulars with a win in the second Supersport race at Road America, much to the delight of his home-state Wisconsin crowd.

Right: **With seven wins, Corey Alexander emerged as the Stock 1000 champion.**

Below: **Blake Davis (16) secured the Twins Cup at the final round.**

Bottom: **Junior Cup champion Cody Wyman leads Joseph LiMandri Jr (62), Kayla Yaakov (31), Gus Rodio (96), Max VanDenBrouck (48) and Daniel Lanuza (55) at Laguna Seca.**

Photos: MotoAmerica/Brian J. Nelson

Stock 1000

A few years ago, Corey Alexander thought that he was out of road racing for good. The 2013 AMA Pro SuperSport East champion sat out a couple of years, then tried racing in American Flat Track before returning to MotoAmerica on a limited basis in 2019. He discovered that he still had the talent and the passion to race, so in 2020, he made a return to MotoAmerica full-time. That comeback made his 2022 Stock 1000 Championship even sweeter for the New York-based rider, who ran for Tytlers Cycle/RideHVMC Racing BMW, won seven of the 12 rounds and claimed the title with one round remaining.

"I am delighted to clinch the MotoAmerica Stock 1000 title at NJMP after coming close to it the previous two years," Alexander said at New Jersey.

Hayden Gillim was the only other winner in the series, scoring five victories on his Disrupt Racing Suzuki and finishing a close runner-up in the championship. Travis Wyman finished third for Tytlers Cycle/RideHVMC Racing BMW on the strength of six podium finishes.

Twins Cup

Sixteen-year-old Virginia-based Blake Davis clinched the season championship aboard his N2 Racing/BobbleHeadMoto Yamaha in the season finale at Barber Motorsports Park.

He scored six podiums in the Twins Cup, including three wins. Jody Barry finished second in the series on an Aprilia and had a series-leading four wins. Another Aprilia rider, Anthony Mazziotto, was third with two victories.

Other winners included Yamaha riders Hayden Schultz and Cory Ventura.

Junior Cup

SportbikeTrackGear.com Junior Cup's final race of the season was also the final race of the weekend at Barber Motorsports Park, and Alpha Omega Kawasaki rider Cody Wyman played his cards exactly right with no room for error.

He finished eighth in the race, which was just enough for him to tie on points at the head of the championship with Rodio Racing Kawasaki's Gus Rodio, winner of Sunday's race. Rodio did all he could to wrap up the title with his last-race victory, but he couldn't overcome Wyman's statistical advantage. While tied on points with 285 each, Rodio lagged with three wins; Wyman finished the year with six.

"It's always tough," said Wyman. "All these guys and girls are just absolutely sending it on these 400s. The class has been so good. MotoAmerica did such a good job with the rules. The racing is, I think, the best of the weekend."

The Junior Cup produced five winners through the season. In addition to Wyman and Rodio, Kayla Yaakov (four wins), Joseph LiMandri Jr (two wins) and Max VanDenBrouck (three wins), who finished third, fourth and fifth respectively in the standings, all tasted victory.

MAJOR RESULTS

OTHER CHAMPIONSHIP RACING SERIES WORLDWIDE

Compiled by PETER McLAREN

MOTOAMERICA Superbike Championship

CIRCUIT OF THE AMERICAS, Austin, Texas, 9-10 April
Round 1 (14 Laps, 47.96 miles/77.18km)
Race 1
1 Danilo Petrucci (Ducati); **2** Mathew Scholtz (Yamaha); **3** Cameron Petersen (Yamaha); **4** PJ Jacobsen (BMW); **5** Hector Barbera (BMW); **6** Jake Lewis (Suzuki); **7** Richie Escalante (Suzuki); **8** David Anthony (Suzuki); **9** Travis Wyman (BMW); **10** Corey Alexander (BMW).
Fastest lap: Petrucci, 2m 8.648s, 95.871mph/154.289km/h.

Race 2
1 Danilo Petrucci (Ducati); **2** Mathew Scholtz (Yamaha); **3** Jake Gagne (Yamaha); **4** Cameron Petersen (Yamaha); **5** Richie Escalante (Suzuki); **6** Jake Lewis (Suzuki); **7** Hector Barbera (BMW); **8** Hayden Gillim (Suzuki); **9** Travis Wyman (BMW); **10** Michael Gilbert (Suzuki).
Fastest lap: Petrucci, 2m 9.122s, 95.519mph/153.722km/h.
Championship points: **1** Danilo Petrucci, 50; **2** Mathew Scholtz, 40; **3** Cameron Petersen, 29; **4** Richie Escalante, 20; **5** Jake Lewis, 20; **6** Hector Barbera, 20; **7** Jake Gagne, 16; **8** Travis Wyman, 14; **9** PJ Jacobsen, 13; **10** David Anthony, 13

ROAD ATLANTA, Braselton, Georgia, 23-24 April
Round 2 (19 Laps, 48.45 miles/77.97km)
Race 1
1 Danilo Petrucci (Ducati); **2** Mathew Scholtz (Yamaha); **3** Jake Lewis (Suzuki); **4** Hector Barbera (BMW); **5** Richie Escalante (Suzuki); **6** Kyle Wyman (BMW); **7** Corey Alexander (BMW); **8** Hayden Gillim (Suzuki); **9** Ashton Yates (Honda); **10** Travis Wyman (BMW).
Fastest lap: Petrucci, 1m 23.934s, 109.372mph/176.017km/h.

Race 2
1 Jake Gagne (Yamaha); **2** Cameron Petersen (Yamaha); **3** Kyle Wyman (BMW); **4** Hector Barbera (BMW); **5** Richie Escalante (Suzuki); **6** Corey Alexander (BMW); **7** Ashton Yates (Honda); **8** Travis Wyman (BMW); **9** David Anthony (Suzuki); **10** Geoff May (Honda).
Fastest lap: Gagne, 1m 24.016s, 109.265mph/175.844km/h.
Championship points: **1** Danilo Petrucci, 75; **2** Mathew Scholtz, 60; **3** Cameron Petersen, 49; **4** Hector Barbera, 46; **5** Richie Escalante, 42; **6** Jake Gagne, 41; **7** Jake Lewis, 36; **8** Corey Alexander, 28; **9** Travis Wyman, 28; **10** Kyle Wyman, 26

VIRGINIA INTERNATIONAL RACEWAY, Danville, Virginia, 21-22 May
Round 3 (20 Laps, 45.00 miles/72.42km)
Race 1
1 Jake Gagne (Yamaha); **2** Mathew Scholtz (Yamaha); **3** Cameron Petersen (Yamaha); **4** Danilo Petrucci (Ducati); **5** Jake Lewis (Suzuki); **6** Hector Barbera (BMW); **7** PJ Jacobsen (BMW); **8** Ashton Yates (BMW); **9** Hayden Gillim (Suzuki); **10** Travis Wyman (BMW).
Fastest lap: Petrucci, 1m 24.370s, 96.006mph/154.506km/h.

Race 2
1 Jake Gagne (Yamaha); **2** Mathew Scholtz (Yamaha); **3** Danilo Petrucci (Ducati); **4** Cameron Petersen (Yamaha); **5** PJ Jacobsen (BMW); **6** Richie Escalante (Suzuki); **7** Jake Lewis (Suzuki); **8** Ashton Yates (BMW); **9** Hector Barbera (BMW); **10** Travis Wyman (BMW).
Fastest lap: Gagne, 1m 24.109s, 96.304mph/154.986km/h.
Championship points: **1** Danilo Petrucci, 104; **2** Mathew Scholtz, 100; **3** Jake Gagne, 91; **4** Cameron Petersen, 78; **5** Hector Barbera, 63; **6** Jake Lewis, 56; **7** Richie Escalante, 52 **8** Ashton Yates, 40; **9** Travis Wyman, 40; **10** PJ Jacobsen, 33

ROAD AMERICA, Elkhart Lake, Wisconsin, 4-5 June
Round 4 (12 Laps, 48.00 miles/77.24km)
Race 1
1 Mathew Scholtz (Yamaha); **2** Danilo Petrucci (Ducati); **3** Hector Barbera (BMW); **4** PJ Jacobsen (BMW); **5** Jake Gagne (Yamaha); **6** Jake Lewis (Suzuki); **7** Richie Escalante (Suzuki); **8** Corey Alexander (BMW); **9** Larry Pegram (BMW); **10** Ashton Yates (BMW).
Fastest lap: Gagne, 2m 11.537s, 110.789mph/178.297km/h.

Race 2
1 Cameron Petersen (Yamaha); **2** PJ Jacobsen (BMW); **3** Danilo Petrucci (Ducati); **4** Jake Gagne (Yamaha); **5** Larry Pegram (BMW); **6** Ashton Yates (BMW); **7** Jake Lewis (Suzuki); **8** Mathew Scholtz (Yamaha); **9** Danilo Lewis (BMW); **10** Justin Miest (Kawasaki).
Fastest lap: Petersen, 2m 27.477s, 98.814mph/159.025km/h.
Championship points: **1** Danilo Petrucci, 140; **2** Mathew Scholtz, 133; **3** Jake Gagne, 115; **4** Cameron Petersen, 103; **5** Hector Barbera, 75; **6** Jake Lewis, 75; **7** PJ Jacobsen, 66; **8** Richie Escalante, 62 **9** Ashton Yates, 56; **10** Travis Wyman, 45

THE RIDGE MOTORSPORTS PARK, Shelton, Washington, 25-26 June
Round 5 (16 laps, 40.00 miles/64.37km)
Race 1
(Race shortened to 8 laps due to red flag)
1 Jake Gagne (Yamaha); **2** Cameron Petersen (Yamaha); **3** Danilo Petrucci (Ducati); **4** Mathew Scholtz (Yamaha); **5** Hector Barbera (BMW); **6** Ashton Yates (BMW); **7** Corey Alexander (BMW); **8** Hayden Gillim (Suzuki); **9** Andy DiBrino (Kawasaki); **10** Richie Escalante (Suzuki).
Fastest lap: Gagne, 1m 40.140s, 89.874mph/144.638km/h.

Race 2
1 Jake Gagne (Yamaha); **2** Danilo Petrucci (Ducati); **3** Cameron Petersen (Yamaha); **4** Mathew Scholtz (Yamaha); **5** Hector Barbera (BMW); **6** Richie Escalante (Suzuki); **7** Hayden Gillim (Suzuki); **8** Corey Alexander (BMW); **9** PJ Jacobsen (BMW); **10** David Anthony (Suzuki).
Fastest lap: Gagne, 1m 39.865s, 90.122mph/145.037km/h.
Championship points: **1** Danilo Petrucci, 176; **2** Jake Gagne, 165; **3** Mathew Scholtz, 159; **4** Cameron Petersen, 139; **5** Hector Barbera, 101; **6** Richie Escalante, 78 **7** Jake Lewis, 75; **8** PJ Jacobsen, 73; **9** Ashton Yates, 66; **10** Corey Alexander, 53

LAGUNA SECA RACEWAY, Monterey, California, 9-10 July
Round 6 (20 Laps, 44.76 miles/72.03km)
Race 1
1 Jake Gagne (Yamaha); **2** Cameron Petersen (Yamaha); **3** Danilo Petrucci (Ducati); **4** Richie Escalante (Suzuki); **5** Mathew Scholtz (Yamaha); **6** Hector Barbera (BMW); **7** PJ Jacobsen (BMW); **8** Kyle Wyman (Suzuki); **9** Bryce Prince (Yamaha); **10** Travis Wyman (BMW).
Fastest lap: Gagne, 1m 23.768s, 96.180mph/154.786km/h.

Race 2
1 Jake Gagne (Yamaha); **2** Danilo Petrucci (Ducati); **3** Cameron Petersen (Yamaha); **4** Richie Escalante (Suzuki); **5** Hector Barbera (BMW); **6** PJ Jacobsen (BMW); **7** Kyle Wyman (Suzuki); **8** Travis Wyman (BMW); **9** Corey Alexander (BMW); **10** David Anthony (Suzuki).
Fastest lap: Gagne, 1m 23.443s, 95.555mph/153.780km/h.
Championship points: **1** Jake Gagne, 215; **2** Danilo Petrucci, 212; **3** Cameron Petersen, 175; **4** Mathew Scholtz, 170; **5** Hector Barbera, 122; **6** Richie Escalante, 104 **7** PJ Jacobsen, 92; **8** Jake Lewis, 75; **9** Ashton Yates, 69; **10** Travis Wyman, 64

BRAINERD INTERNATIONAL RACEWAY, Brainerd, Minnesota, 30-31 July
Round 7 (18 Laps, 45.00 miles/72.42km)
Race 1
1 Jake Gagne (Yamaha); **2** Cameron Petersen (Yamaha); **3** Danilo Petrucci (Ducati); **4** Mathew Scholtz (Yamaha); **5** PJ Jacobsen (BMW); **6** Hayden Gillim (Suzuki); **7** Ashton Yates (BMW); **8** Corey Alexander (BMW); **9** Jake Lewis (Suzuki); **10** David Anthony (Suzuki).
Fastest lap: Gagne, 1m 30.573s, 99.367mph/159.915km/h.

Race 2
1 Danilo Petrucci (Ducati); **2** Cameron Petersen (Yamaha); **3** PJ Jacobsen (BMW); **4** Hayden Gillim (Suzuki); **5** Hector Barbera (BMW); **6** Ashton Yates (BMW); **7** Jake Lewis (Suzuki); **8** Andrew Lee (Suzuki); **9** Brandon Paasch (Suzuki); **10** Jeremy Coffey (Suzuki).
Fastest lap: Petrucci, 1m 30.411s, 99.545mph/160.202km/h.
Championship points: **1** Danilo Petrucci, 253; **2** Jake Gagne, 240; **3** Cameron Petersen, 215; **4** Mathew Scholtz, 183; **5** Hector Barbera, 133; **6** PJ Jacobsen, 119; **7** Richie Escalante, 104 **8** Jake Lewis, 91; **9** Ashton Yates, 88; **10** Hayden Gillim, 77

PITTSBURGH INTL RACE COMPLEX, Wampum, Pennsylvania, 20-21 August
Round 8 (17 laps, 47.26 miles/76.06km)
Race 1
1 Jake Gagne (Yamaha); **2** Danilo Petrucci (Ducati); **3** Mathew Scholtz (Yamaha); **4** Cameron Petersen (Yamaha); **5** Jake Lewis (Suzuki); **6** Hayden Gillim (Suzuki); **7** Hector Barbera (BMW); **8** Corey Alexander (BMW); **9** Ashton Yates (BMW); **10** David Anthony (Suzuki).
Fastest lap: Gagne, 1m 40.972s, 98.721mph/158.876km/h.

Race 2
1 Jake Gagne (Yamaha); **2** Mathew Scholtz (Yamaha); **3** Danilo Petrucci (Ducati); **4** Cameron Petersen (Yamaha); **5** PJ Jacobsen (BMW); **6** Richie Escalante (Suzuki); **7** Hayden Gillim (Suzuki); **8** Hector Barbera (BMW); **9** Jake Lewis (Suzuki); **10** Ashton Yates (BMW).
Fastest lap: Gagne, 1m 40.972s, 99.117mph/159.913km/h.
Championship points: **1** Jake Gagne, 290; **2** Danilo Petrucci, 289; **3** Cameron Petersen, 241; **4** Mathew Scholtz, 219; **5** Hector Barbera, 150; **6** PJ Jacobsen, 130; **7** Richie Escalante, 114 **8** Jake Lewis, 109; **9** Ashton Yates, 101; **10** Hayden Gillim, 96

NEW JERSEY MOTORSPORTS PARK, Millville, New Jersey, 10-11 September
Round 9 (17 Laps, 38.25 miles/61.55km)
Race 1
1 Jake Gagne (Yamaha); **2** Cameron Petersen (Yamaha); **3** Mathew Scholtz (Yamaha); **4** Danilo Petrucci (Ducati); **5** PJ Jacobsen (BMW); **6** Hector Barbera (BMW); **7** Hayden Gillim (Suzuki); **8** Ashton Yates (BMW); **9** Jake Lewis (Suzuki); **10** Travis Wyman (BMW).
Fastest lap: Scholtz, 1m 20.796s, 100.252mph/161.339km/h.

Race 2
(Race shortened to 14 laps due to rain)
1 Danilo Petrucci (Ducati); **2** Mathew Scholtz (Yamaha); **3** Jake Gagne (Yamaha); **4** Hector Barbera (BMW); **5** Cameron Petersen (Yamaha); **6** Jake Lewis (Suzuki); **7** Hayden Gillim (Suzuki); **8** David Anthony (Suzuki); **9** Jeremy Coffey (Suzuki); **10** Brandon Paasch (Suzuki).
Fastest lap: Scholtz, 1m 31.698s, 88.333mph/142.158km/h.
Championship points: **1** Jake Gagne, 331; **2** Danilo Petrucci, 327; **3** Cameron Petersen, 272; **4** Mathew Scholtz, 255; **5** Hector Barbera, 173; **6** PJ Jacobsen, 141; **7** Jake Lewis, 126; **8** Richie Escalante, 117 **9** Hayden Gillim, 114 Ashton Yates, 109

BARBER MOTORSPORTS PARK, Birmingham, Alabama, 24-25 September
Round 10 (20 Laps, 47.60 miles/76.60km)
Race 1
1 Jake Gagne (Yamaha); **2** Mathew Scholtz (Yamaha); **3** Danilo Petrucci (Ducati); **4** PJ Jacobsen (BMW); **5** Hector Barbera (BMW); **6** Hayden Gillim (Suzuki); **7** Jake Lewis (Suzuki); **8** Corey Alexander (BMW); **9** Cameron Petersen (Yamaha); **10** David Anthony (Suzuki).
Fastest lap: Gagne, 1m 22.917s, 103.332mph/166.296km/h.

Race 2
1 Cameron Petersen (Yamaha); **2** Jake Gagne (Yamaha); **3** PJ Jacobsen (BMW); **4** Danilo Petrucci (Ducati); **5** Mathew Scholtz (Yamaha); **6** Richie Escalante (Suzuki); **7** Jake Lewis (Suzuki); **8** Hayden Gillim (Suzuki); **9** Kyle Wyman (BMW); **10** Hector Barbera (BMW).
Fastest lap: Gagne, 1m 23.510s, 102.598mph/165.115km/h.

Final 2022 MotoAmerica Superbike Championship Points:

1	Jake Gagne	376
2	Danilo Petrucci	356
3	Cameron Petersen	304
4	Mathew Scholtz	286
5	Hector Barbera	190
6	PJ Jacobsen	170

7 Jake Lewis, 144; **8** Hayden Gillim, 132; **9** Richie Escalante, 127; **10** Ashton Yates, 119.

Final Stock 1000 Championship Points:

1	Corey Alexander	192
2	Hayden Gillim	192
3	Travis Wyman	156
4	Brandon Paasch	137
5	Geoff May	111
6	Andy DiBrino	86

7 Stefano Mesa, 82 ; **8** Hunter Dunham, 81; **9** Ezra Beaubier, 79; **10** Danilo Lewis, 77.

Final Supersport Championship Points:

1	Josh Herrin	387
2	Rocco Landers	281
3	Tyler Scott	229
4	Benjamin Smith	173
5	Luke Power	149
6	Josh Hayes	148

7 Jaret Nassaney, 137; **8** Kevin Olmedo, 114; **9** Samuel Lochoff, 107; **10** Stefano Mesa, 102.

Final Twins Cup Championship Points:

1	Blake Davis	211
2	Jody Barry	191
3	Anthony Mazziotto	191
4	Kaleb De Keyrel	175
5	Hayden Schultz	148
6	Cory Ventura	142

7 Teagg Hobbs, 130; **8** Benjamin Gloddy, 122; **9** Cody Wyman, 88; **10** Dominic Doyle, 69.

Final Junior Cup Championship Points:

1	Cody Wyman	285
2	Gus Rodio	285
3	Kayla Yaakov	277
4	Joseph LiMandri Jr	262
5	Max VanDenBrouck	182
6	Aden Thao	167

7 Avery Dreher, 132; **8** Hayden Bicknese, 116; **9** Chase Black, 106; **10** Owen Williams, 102.

Endurance World Championship

24 HEURES MOTOS, Le Mans Bugatti Circuit, France, 16-17 April 2022
FIM Endurance World Championship, Round 1
840 laps of the 2.600-mile/4.185km circuit, 2184.4 miles/3515.4km
1 Yoshimura SERT Motul: 24h 0m 2.317s.
2 YART - Yamaha Official Team EWC: +1m 45.542s; **3** F.C.C. TSR Honda France: 826 laps; **4** Team 18 Sapeurs Pompiers CMS Motostore: 816 laps; **5** No Limits Motor Team: 816 laps; **6** National Motos Honda: 815 laps; **7** Team 33 Louit April Moto: 813 laps; **8** Team Bolliger Switzerland #8: 812 laps; **9** Pitlane Endurance #86 - JP3: 808 laps; **10** Team LH Racing: 807 laps; **11** Tati Team Beringer Racing: 806 laps; **12** BMRT 3D Maxxess Nevers: 804 laps; **13** Team Univers Racing Motosport #23: 804 laps; **14** Team LRP Poland: 801 laps; **15** ERC Endurance Ducati: 798 laps.
Fastest lap: Yoshimura SERT Motul, 1m 36.195s, 97.31mph/156.6km/h, on lap 564.
Championship points: **1** Yoshimura SERT Motul, 63; **2** YART - Yamaha Official Team EWC, 55; **3** F.C.C. TSR Honda France, 49; **4** Team Bolliger Switzerland #8, 35; **5** Tati Team Beringer Racing, 28; **6** Team LRP Poland, 26.

24H SPA EWC MOTOS, Spa-Francorchamps, Belgium, 4-5 June 2022
FIM Endurance World Championship, Round 2
508 laps of the 4.340-mile/6.985km circuit, 2204.9 miles/3548.4km
1 BMW Motorrad World Endurance Team: 24h 1m 30.088s.
2 Tati Team Beringer Racing: 501 laps; **3** F.C.C. TSR Honda France: 500 laps; **4** Yoshimura SERT Motul: 500 laps; **5** Wójcik Racing Team EWC 77: 497 laps; **6** Viltais Racing Igol: 497 laps; **7** Team Moto Ain: 495 laps; **8** Team LH Racing: 491 laps; **9** Team Bolliger Switzerland #8: 490 laps; **10** Team LRP Poland: 490 laps; **11** Team 18 Sapeurs Pompiers CMS Motostore: 489 laps; **12** OG Motorsport by Sarazin: 488 laps; **13** Team Normandie Motosport: 485 laps; **14** Maco Racing Team: 480 laps; **15** ITeM 17: 479 laps.
Fastest lap: Yoshimura SERT Motul, 2m 21.056s, 110.73mph/178.2km/h, on lap 190.
Championship points: **1** Yoshimura SERT Motul, 106; **2** F.C.C. TSR Honda France, 91; **3** YART - Yamaha Official Team EWC, 76; **4** Tati Team Beringer Racing, 75; **5** BMW Motorrad World Endurance Team, 64; **6** Team Bolliger Switzerland #8, 56.

SUZUKA 8 HOURS, Suzuka, Japan, 7 August 2022
FIM Endurance World Championship, Round 3
214 laps of the 3.617-mile/5.821km circuit, 774.0 miles/1245.7km
1 Team HRC: 8h 2m 9.131s.
2 Kawasaki Racing Team Suzuka 8H: 213 laps; **3** Yoshimura SERT Motul: 212 laps; **4** S-Pulse Dream Racing - ITEC: 210 laps; **5** Toho Racing: 210 laps; **6**

Honda Dream RT Sakurai Honda: 210 laps; **7** YART - Yamaha Official Team EWC: 209 laps; **8** Team ATJ with Japan Post: 208 laps; **9** Team Kodama: 208 laps; **10** F.C.C. TSR Honda France: 208 laps; **11** Honda Asia-Dream Racing with Showa: 208 laps; **12** Goshi Racing: 206 laps; **13** Kawasaki Plaza Racing Team: 205 laps; **14** Sanmei Team Taro Plusone: 204 laps; **15** Webike SRC Kawasaki France: 203 laps.
Fastest lap: Team HRC, 2m 6.934s, 102.53mph/165.0km/h, on lap 113.
Championship points: 1 Yoshimura SERT Motul, 127; **2** F.C.C. TSR Honda France, 104; **3** YART - Yamaha Official Team EWC, 93; **4** Tati Team Beringer Racing, 75; **5** BMW Motorrad World Endurance Team, 64; **6** Team Bolliger Switzerland #8, 56.

BOL D'OR, Paul Ricard Circuit, France, 17-18 September 2022
FIM Endurance World Championship, Round 4. 718 laps of the 3.525-mile/5.673km circuit, 2531.0 miles/4073.2km
1 Viltais Racing Igol: 24h 1m 13.729s.
2 Wójcik Racing Team EWC 77: 717 laps; **3** Webike SRC Kawasaki France: 716 laps; **4** F.C.C. TSR Honda France: 714 laps; **5** ERC Endurance Ducati: 706 laps; **6** Maco Racing Team: 704 laps; **7** RAC41-Chromeburner: 704 laps; **8** BMRT 3D Maxxess Nevers: 702 laps; **9** Team Bolliger Switzerland #8: 702 laps; **10** Pitlane Endurance #86 - JP3: 698 laps; **11** Team LRP Poland: 697 laps; **12** Team Normandie Motosport: 697 laps; **13** No Limits Motor Team: 695 laps; **14** Junior Team LMS Suzuki: 695 laps; **15** Falcon Racing: 693 laps.
Fastest lap: ERC Endurance Ducati, 1m 52.979s, 112.28mph/180.7km/h, on lap 75.

FIM Teams' Endurance World Championship:

1	F.C.C. TSR Honda France	154
2	Yoshimura SERT Motul	130
3	Viltais Racing Igol	114
4	Tati Team Beringer Racing	107
5	Wójcik Racing Team EWC 77	97.5
6	YART - Yamaha Official Team EWC	97

7 Team Bolliger Switzerland #8, 88.5; **8** Webike SRC Kawasaki France, 78; **9** ERC Endurance Ducati, 74.5; **10** Team LRP Poland, 69.5; **11** BMW Motorrad World Endurance Team, 69; **12** Maco Racing Team, 60.5; **13** Team HRC, 35; **14** Motobox Kremer Racing #65, 32.5; **15** Kawasaki Racing Team Suzuka 8H, 28.

MotoE World Cup

Round 1, JEREZ, Spain, 30 April-1 May 2022, 2.748-mile/4.423km circuit
Race 1 (8 laps, 21.987 miles/35.384km)
1 Eric Granado, BRA (Energica), 14m 36.988s, 90.2mph/145.2km/h.
2 Dominique Aegerter, SWI (Energica); **3** Matteo Ferrari, ITA (Energica); **4** Hector Garzo, SPA (Energica); **5** Jordi Torres, SPA (Energica); **6** Hikari Okubo, JPN (Energica); **7** Alex Escrig, SPA (Energica); **8** Miquel Pons, SPA (Energica); **9** Marc Alcoba, SPA (Energica); **10** Lukas Tulovic, GER (Energica); **11** Niccolo Canepa, ITA (Energica); **12** Kevin Zannoni, ITA (Energica); **13** Kevin Manfredi, ITA (Energica); **14** Xavi Fores, SPA (Energica); **15** Maria Herrera, SPA (Energica).
Fastest lap: Hector Garzo, 1m 48.12s, 91.4mph/147.2km/h.

Race 2 (8 laps, 21.987 miles/35.384km)
1 Eric Granado, BRA (Energica), 14m 36.321s, 90.3mph/145.3km/h.
2 Miquel Pons, SPA (Energica); **3** Mattia Casadei, ITA (Energica); **4** Dominique Aegerter, SWI (Energica); **5** Hikari Okubo, JPN (Energica); **6** Matteo Ferrari, ITA (Energica); **7** Jordi Torres, SPA (Energica); **8** Alex Escrig, SPA (Energica); **9** Niccolo Canepa, ITA (Energica); **10** Kevin Manfredi, ITA (Energica); **11** Xavi Fores, SPA (Energica); **12** Lukas Tulovic, GER (Energica); **13** Kevin Zannoni, ITA (Energica); **14** Maria Herrera, SPA (Energica); **15** Alessio Finello, ITA (Energica).
Fastest lap: Eric Granado, 1m 48.185s, 91.4mph/147.1km/h.
Championship points: 1 Granado, 50; **2** Aegerter, 33; **3** Pons, 28; **4** Ferrari, 26; **5** Okubo, 21; **6** Torres, 20.

Round 2, LE MANS, France, 14-15 May 2022, 2.600-mile/4.185km circuit
Race 1 (8 laps, 20.804 miles/ 33.48km)
1 Mattia Casadei, ITA (Energica), 13m 54.984s, 89.7mph/144.3km/h.
2 Dominique Aegerter, SWI (Energica); **3** Hikari Okubo, JPN (Energica); **4** Matteo Ferrari, ITA (Energica); **5** Hector Garzo, SPA (Energica); **6** Miquel Pons, SPA (Energica); **7** Eric Granado, BRA (Energica); **8** Niccolo Canepa, ITA (Energica); **9** Andrea Mantovani, ITA (Energica); **10** Alex Escrig, SPA (Energica); **11** Xavi Cardelus, AND (Energica); **12** Xavi Fores, SPA (Energica); **13** Kevin Manfredi, ITA (Energica); **14** Maria Herrera, SPA (Energica); **15** Alessio Finello, ITA (Energica).
Fastest lap: Mattia Casadei, 1m 43.474s, 90.3mph/145.6km/h.

Race 2 (8 laps, 20.804 miles/33.48km)
1 Dominique Aegerter, SWI (Energica), 13m 56.252s, 89.5mph/144.1km/h.
2 Mattia Casadei, ITA (Energica); **3** Niccolo Canepa, ITA (Energica); **4** Kevin Zannoni, ITA (Energica); **5** Eric Granado, BRA (Energica); **6** Hikari Okubo, JPN (Energica); **7** Matteo Ferrari, ITA (Energica); **8** Hector Garzo, SPA (Energica); **9** Marc Alcoba, SPA (Energica); **10** Miquel Pons, SPA (Energica); **11** Andrea Mantovani, ITA (Energica); **12** Alex Escrig, SPA (Energica); **13** Xavi Fores, SPA (Energica); **14** Xavi Cardelus, AND (Energica); **15** Maria Herrera, SPA (Energica).
Fastest lap: Andrea Mantovani, 1m 43.551s, 90.3mph/145.4km/h.
Championship points: 1 Aegerter, 78; **2** Granado, 70; **3** Casadei, 61; **4** Ferrari, 48; **5** Okubo, 47; **6** Pons, 44.

Round 3, MUGELLO, Italy, 28-29 May 2022, 3.260-mile/5.200km circuit
Race 1 (5 laps, 16.295 miles/26.225km)
1 Dominique Aegerter, SWI (Energica), 10m 10.913s, 96.0mph/154.5km/h.
2 Matteo Ferrari, ITA (Energica); **3** Eric Granado, BRA (Energica); **4** Mattia Casadei, ITA (Energica); **5** Marc Alcoba, SPA (Energica); **6** Niccolo Canepa, ITA (Energica); **7** Miquel Pons, SPA (Energica); **8** Kevin Zannoni, ITA (Energica); **9** Hector Garzo, SPA (Energica); **10** Kevin Manfredi, ITA (Energica); **11** Hikari Okubo, JPN (Energica); **12** Xavi Fores, SPA (Energica); **13** Alessio Finello, ITA (Energica); **14** Alex Escrig, SPA (Energica); **15** Massimo Roccoli ITA (Energica)
Fastest lap: Dominique Aegerter, 1m 58.939s, 98.5mph/158.7km/h.

Race 2 (6 laps, 19.555 miles/31.47km)
1 Matteo Ferrari, ITA (Energica), 12m 4.368s, 97.2mph/156.4km/h.
2 Dominique Aegerter, SWI (Energica); **3** Miquel Pons, SPA (Energica); **4** Andrea Mantovani, ITA (Energica); **5** Kevin Zannoni, ITA (Energica); **6** Niccolo Canepa, ITA (Energica); **7** Marc Alcoba, SPA (Energica); **8** Eric Granado, BRA (Energica); **9** Kevin Manfredi, ITA (Energica); **10** Hector Garzo, SPA (Energica); **11** Massimo Roccoli, ITA (Energica); **12** Xavi Fores, SPA (Energica); **13** Alex Escrig, SPA (Energica); **14** Alessio Finello, ITA (Energica); **15** Maria Herrera, SPA (Energica).
Fastest lap: Dominique Aegerter, 1m 59.068s, 98.5mph/158.5km/h.
Championship points: 1 Aegerter, 123; **2** Granado, 94; **3** Ferrari, 93; **4** Casadei, 74; **5** Pons, 69; **6** Canepa, 56.

Round 4, ASSEN, The Netherlands, 25-26 June 2022, 2.822-mile/4.542km circuit
Race 1 (8 laps, 22.578 miles/36.336km)
1 Dominique Aegerter, SWI (Energica), 13m 55.704s, 96.0mph/156.5km/h.
2 Eric Granado, BRA (Energica); **3** Mattia Casadei, ITA (Energica); **4** Matteo Ferrari, ITA (Energica); **5** Hector Garzo, SPA (Energica); **6** Miquel Pons, SPA (Energica); **7** Niccolo Canepa, ITA (Energica); **8** Bradley Smith, GBR (Energica); **9** Jordi Torres, SPA (Energica); **10** Kevin Zannoni, ITA (Energica); **11** Kevin Manfredi, ITA (Energica); **12** Xavi Fores, SPA (Energica); **13** Hikari Okubo, JPN (Energica); **14** Alex Escrig, SPA (Energica); **15** Maria Herrera, SPA (Energica).
Fastest lap: Eric Granado, 1m 43.086s, 96.8mph/158.6km/h.

Race 2 (3 laps, 8.467 miles/13.626km)
1 Eric Granado, BRA (Energica), 5m 21.094s, 97.2mph/152.7km/h.
2 Dominique Aegerter, SWI (Energica); **3** Mattia Casadei, ITA (Energica); **4** Matteo Ferrari, ITA (Energica); **5** Niccolo Canepa, ITA (Energica); **6** Alex Escrig, SPA (Energica); **7** Kevin Manfredi, ITA (Energica); **8** Maria Herrera, SPA (Energica); **9** Kevin Zannoni, ITA (Energica); **10** Hector Garzo, SPA (Energica); **11** Hikari Okubo, JPN (Energica); **12** Alessio Finello, ITA (Energica); **13** Marc Alcoba, SPA (Energica); **14** Unai Orradre, SPA (Energica); **15** Xavi Fores, SPA (Energica).
Fastest lap: Eric Granado, 1m 44.926s, 96.8mph/155.8km/h.
Championship points: 1 Aegerter, 158; **2** Granado, 126.5; **3** Ferrari, 112.5; **4** Casadei, 98; **5** Pons, 79; **6** Canepa, 70.5.

Round 5, RED BULL RING, Austria, 20-21 August 2022, 2.683-mile/4.318km circuit
Race 1 (7 laps, 18.912 miles/30.436km)
1 Eric Granado, BRA (Energica), 11m 55.313s, 95.1mph/153.1km/h.
2 Dominique Aegerter, SWI (Energica); **3** Miquel Pons, SPA (Energica); **4** Hikari Okubo, JPN (Energica); **5** Hector Garzo, SPA (Energica); **6** Alex Escrig, SPA (Energica); **7** Kevin Zannoni, ITA (Energica); **8** Jordi Torres, SPA (Energica); **9** Xavi Fores, SPA (Energica); **10** Kevin Manfredi, ITA (Energica); **11** Maria Herrera, SPA (Energica); **12** Marc Alcoba, SPA (Energica); **13** Xavi Cardelus, AND (Energica); **14** Matteo Ferrari, ITA (Energica); **15** NA.
Fastest lap: Eric Granado, 1m 41.064s, 96.1mph/154.8km/h.

Race 2 (7 laps, 18.912 miles/30.436km)
1 Eric Granado, BRA (Energica), 11m 54.464s, 95.3mph/153.3km/h.
2 Miquel Pons, SPA (Energica); **3** Dominique Aegerter, SWI (Energica); **4** Mattia Casadei, ITA (Energica); **5** Alex Escrig, SPA (Energica); **6** Xavi Cardelus, AND (Energica); **7** Hikari Okubo, JPN (Energica); **8** Hector Garzo, SPA (Energica); **9** Matteo Ferrari, ITA (Energica); **10** Jordi Torres, SPA (Energica); **11** Kevin Manfredi, ITA (Energica); **12** Niccolo Canepa, ITA (Energica); **13** Kevin Zannoni, ITA (Energica); **14** Maria Herrera, SPA (Energica); **15** Marc Alcoba, SPA (Energica).
Fastest lap: Miquel Pons, 1m 41.163s, 96.1mph/154.7km/h.
Championship points: 1 Aegerter, 194; **2** Granado, 176.5; **3** Ferrari, 121.5; **4** Pons, 115; **5** Casadei, 111; **6** Okubo, 79.5.

Round 6, MISANO, San Marino, 3-4 September 2022, 2.630-mile/4.200km circuit
Race 1 (8 laps, 21.007 miles/33.808km)
1 Mattia Casadei, ITA (Energica), 13m 52.413s, 90.8mph/146.2km/h.
2 Dominique Aegerter, SWI (Energica); **3** Matteo Ferrari, ITA (Energica); **4** Jordi Torres, SPA (Energica); **5** Alex Escrig, SPA (Energica); **6** Niccolo Canepa, ITA (Energica); **7** Hikari Okubo, JPN (Energica); **8** Kevin Manfredi, ITA (Energica); **9** Xavi Cardelus, AND (Energica); **10** Hector Garzo, SPA (Energica); **11** Kevin Zannoni, ITA (Energica); **12** Bradley Smith, GBR (Energica); **13** Marc Alcoba, SPA (Energica); **14** Maria Herrera, SPA (Energica); **15** Xavi Fores, SPA (Energica).
Fastest lap: Matteo Ferrari, 1m 43.212s, 91.8mph/147.4km/h.

Race 2 (8 laps, 21.007 miles/33.808km)
1 Matteo Ferrari, ITA (Energica), 13m 52.553s, 90.8mph/146.1km/h.
2 Mattia Casadei, ITA (Energica); **3** Eric Granado, BRA (Energica); **4** Dominique Aegerter, SWI (Energica); **5** Jordi Torres, SPA (Energica); **6** Niccolo Canepa, ITA (Energica); **7** Miquel Pons, SPA (Energica); **8** Alex Escrig, SPA (Energica); **9** Hikari Okubo, JPN (Energica); **10** Kevin Zannoni, ITA (Energica); **11** Kevin Manfredi, ITA (Energica); **12** Xavi Cardelus, AND (Energica); **13** Marc Alcoba, SPA (Energica); **14** Hector Garzo, SPA (Energica); **15** Xavi Fores, SPA (Energica).
Fastest lap: Matteo Ferrari, 1m 42.904s, 91.8mph/147.8km/h.

Final MotoE World Cup points:

1	Dominique Aegerter	227
2	Eric Granado	192.5
3	Matteo Ferrari	162.5
4	Mattia Casadei	156
5	Miquel Pons	124
6	Hikari Okubo	95.5

7 Niccolo Canepa, 94.5; **8** Hector Garzo, 86; **9** Alex Escrig, 79; **10** Kevin Zannoni, 71.5; **11** Jordi Torres, 65; **12** Kevin Manfredi, 58.5; **13** Marc Alcoba, 46.5; **14** Xavi Fores, 35.5; **15** Xavi Cardelus, 31.

Isle of Man Tourist Trophy Races

ISLE OF MAN TOURIST TROPHY COURSE, 4-11 June 2022, 37.73-mile/60.72km circuit

RST Superbike TT (6 laps, 226.38 miles/364.32km)
1 Peter Hickman (BMW), 1h 43m 58.544s, 130.634mph/210.235km/h.
2 Dean Harrison (Kawasaki), 1h 44m 37.744s; **3** Michael Dunlop (Suzuki), 1h 44m 56.171s; **4** Ian Hutchinson (BMW), 1h 46m 56.628s; **5** John McGuinness (Honda), 1h 47m 7.411s; **6** Jamie Coward (Yamaha), 1h 47m 7.849s; **7** James Hillier (Yamaha), 1h 47m 33.288s; **8** Glenn Irwin (Honda), 1h 47m 40.140s; **9** Shaun Anderson (Suzuki), 1h 48m 29.935s; **10** Dominic Herbertson (BMW), 1h 49m 0.109s; **11** Michael Rutter (BMW), 1h 49m 0.613s; **12** Nathan Harrison (Honda), 1h 50m 5.457s; **13** Rob Hodson (Kawasaki), 1h 50m 20.522s; **14** Craig Neve (BMW), 1h 51m 32.615s; **15** Matt Stevenson (BMW), 1h 51m 42.877s.
Fastest lap: Peter Hickman (BMW), 16m 57.737s, 133.461mph/214.785km/h, on lap 2.
Superbike TT lap record: Dean Harrison (Kawasaki), 16m 50.384s, 134.432mph/216.347km/h (2018).

Monster Energy Supersport TT Race 1 (3 laps, 113.19 miles/182.16km)
1 Michael Dunlop (Yamaha), 53m 31.953s, 126.865mph/204.169km/h.
2 Dean Harrison (Kawasaki), 53m 37.571s; **3** Peter Hickman (Triumph), 54m 7.008s; **4** Lee Johnston (Yamaha), 54m 10.555s; **5** James Hillier (Yamaha), 54m 17.625s; **6** Jamie Coward (Yamaha), 54m 34.848s; **7** Conor Cummins (Honda), 54m 38.641s; **8** Davey Todd (Honda), 55m 10.529s; **9** Dominic Herbertson (Kawasaki), 55m 31.858s; **10** Ian Hutchinson (Yamaha), 55m 35.446s; **11** Paul Jordan (Yamaha), 55m 51.711s; **12** James Hind (Yamaha), 56m 4.044s; **13** Rob Hodson (Yamaha), 56m 15.114s; **14** Michael Sweeney (Yamaha), 56m 15.163s; **15** Mike Browne (Yamaha), 56m 22.431s.
Fastest lap: Michael Dunlop (Yamaha), 17m 29.070s, 129.475mph/208.370km/h, on lap 3.
Supersport lap record: Michael Dunlop (Honda), 17m 31.328s, 129.197mph/207.922km/h (2018).

3wheeling.media Sidecar TT Race 1 (2 laps, 75.46 miles/121.44km)
1 Ben Birchall/Tom Birchall (Honda LCR), 38m 11.339s,
2 Ryan Crowe/Callum Crowe (Honda LCR), 38m 25.328s; **3** Peter Founds/Jevan Walmsley (Honda LCR), 38m 25.440s; **4** Dave Molyneux/Daryl Gibson (DMR 890), 39m 52.553s; **5** Gary Bryan/Philip Hyde (Honda Baker), 40m 21.485s; **6** Conrad Harrison/Andrew Winkle (Honda Bellas), 41m 12.265s; **7** Gary Gibson/Tom Christie (Suzuki Shelbourne), 41m 23.893s; **8** Roger Stockton/Bradley Stockton* (Suzuki LCR), 43m 6.027s; **9** Gordon Shand/Frank Claeys (Shand Suzuki), 43m 21.416s; **10** Bruce Moore/Ashley Moore (Honda Ireson), 43m 32.309s; **11** Andy King/Andrew Sigsworth (Lumley-Ireson Honda), 43m 35.634s; **12** Michael Russell/Freddy Lelubez (Suzuki Shelbourne), 44m 0.233s; **13** Shaun Chandler/Ben Chandler (Honda Baker), 44m 0.726s; **14** Alun Thomas/Kenneth Cole (Honda Ireson), 44m 47.537s; **15** Goulven Crochemore/Marlene Lelubez (Suzuki Shelbourne), h 45m 27.518s.
Fastest lap: Ben Birchall/Tom Birchall (Honda LCR), 18m 59.283s, 119.222mph/191.869km/h, on lap 2.
Sidecar lap record: Ben Birchall/Tom Birchall (Honda), 18m 59.018s, 119.250mph/191.914km/h (2018).

RL360 Superstock TT (3 laps, 113.19 miles/182.16km)
1 Peter Hickman (BMW), 52m 1.236s, 130.552mph/210.103km/h.
2 Conor Cummins (Honda), 52m 13.938s; **3** Davey Todd (Honda), 52m 21.603s; **4** Dean Harrison (Kawasaki), 52m 28.452s; **5** Michael Dunlop (Honda), 52m 40.930s; **6** Jamie Coward (Yamaha), 52m 59.395s; **7** Ian Hutchinson (BMW), 53m 14.021s; **8** Dominic Herbertson (BMW), 53m 37.764s; **9** John McGuinness (Honda), 53m 45.285s; **10** Phillip Crowe (BMW), 53m 58.722s; **11** Nathan Harrison (Honda), 54m 13.069s; **12** Craig Neve (BMW), 54m 15.253s; **13** Michael Rutter (BMW), 54m 24.056s; **14** Brian McCormack (BMW), 54m 36.050s; **15** Paul Jordan (Yamaha), 54m 47.162s.
Fastest lap: Conor Cummins (Honda), 17m 0.375s, 133.116mph/214.229km/h, on lap 3.
Superstock lap record: Peter Hickman (BMW), 16m 50.601s, 134.403mph/216.301km/h (2018).

Bennetts Supertwin TT (3 laps, 113.19 miles/182.16km)
1 Peter Hickman (Paton), 56m 35.517s, 120.006mph/193.131km/h.
2 Lee Johnston (Aprilia), 58m 24.798s; **3** Paul Jordan (Kawasaki), 58m 48.055s; **4** Pierre Yves Bian (Paton), 58m 54.969s; **5** Michael Rutter (Paton), 59m 0.969s; **6** Rob Hodson (Kawasaki), 59m 2.572s; **7** James Hind (Paton), 59m 9.553s; **8** Dominic Herbertson (Kawasaki), 59m 18.285s; **9** Michael Evans (Kawasaki), 59m 52.787s; **10** Xavier Denis (Kawasaki), 1h 0m 19.788s; **11** Barry Furber (Yamaha), 1h 0m 36.002s; **12** Paul Potchy Williams (Kawasaki), 1h 1m 7.319s; **13** Jonathan Perry (Kawasaki), 1h 1m 17.174s; **14** Jonathan Goetschy (Aprilia), 1h 1m 22.012s; **15** Raul Torras Martinez (Aprilia), 1h 1m 49.816s.
Fastest lap: Peter Hickman (Paton), 18m 39.833s, 121.293mph/195.202km/h, on lap 3.
Supertwin (Lightweight) lap record: Michael Dunlop (Paton), 18m 26.543s, 122.750mph/197.547km/h (2018).

Monster Energy Supersport TT Race 2 (2 laps, 75.46 miles/121.44km)
1 Michael Dunlop (Yamaha), 35m 29.154s, 127.589mph/205.335km/h.
2 Peter Hickman (Triumph), 35m 32.452s, **3** Dean Harrison (Kawasaki), 35m 53.800s, **4** Davey Todd (Honda), 36m 11.366s, **5** Jamie Coward (Yamaha), 36m 17.827s, **6** Conor Cummins (Honda), 36m 23.019s, **7** James Hillier (Yamaha), 36m 33.603s, **8** Dominic Herbertson (Kawasaki), 36m 41.569s, **9** Mike Browne (Yamaha), 36m 58.086s, **10** Paul Jordan (Yamaha), 37m 4.354s, **11** James Hind (Yamaha), 37m 5.721s, **12** Rob Hodson (Yamaha), 37m 22.761s, **13** Ian Hutchinson (Yamaha), 37m 32.989s, **14** Michael Evans (Yamaha), 37m 34.921s, **15** Michael Sweeney (Yamaha), 37m 39.223s.
Fastest lap: Michael Dunlop (Yamaha), 17m 36.733s, 128.536mph/206.859km/h, on lap 2.
Supersport lap record: Michael Dunlop (Honda), 17m 31.328s, 129.197mph/207.922km/h (2018).

3wheeling.media Sidecar TT Race 2 (1 lap, 37.73 miles/60.72km)
1 Ben Birchall/Tom Birchall (Honda LCR), 19m 16.699s, 117.427mph/188.980km/h.
2 Peter Founds/Jevan Walmsley (Honda LCR), 19m 19.012s; **3** Ryan Crowe/Callum Crowe (Honda LCR), 19m 21.676s; **4** Dave Molyneux/Daryl Gibson (DMR 890), 20m 9.119s; **5** Harry Payne/Mark Wilkes (Yamaha LCR), 20m 21.851s; **6** Lee Crawford*/Scott Hardie (Suzuki LCR), 20m 22.553s; **7** Paul Leglise/Melanie Farnier (Honda LCR), 20m 23.097s; **8** Gary Bryan/Philip Hyde (Honda Baker), 20m 27.787s; **9** Gary Gibson/Tom Christie (Suzuki Shelbourne), 20m 45.529s; **10** Lewis Blackstock/Patrick Rosney (Honda LCR), 20m 46.707s; **11** Estelle LeBlond/Clement Carre (Suzuki SGR), 20m

58.173s; **12** Wayne Lockey/Matthew Rostron (Honda LCR), 21m 5.485s; **13** Greg Lambert/Ben McBride (Honda LCR), 21m 12.636s; **14** Roger Stockton/Bradley Stockton (Suzuki LCR), 21m 22.213s; **15** John Saunders/James Saunders (Honda Shelbourne), 21m 24.764s,
Fastest lap: Ben Birchall/Tom Birchall (Honda LCR), 19m 16.699s, 117.427mph/188.980km/h, on lap 1.
Sidecar lap record: Ben Birchall/Tom Birchall (Honda), 18m 59.018s, 119.250mph/191.914km/h (2018).

Milwaukee Senior TT (6 laps, 226.38 miles/364.32km)
1 Peter Hickman (BMW), 1h 44m 56.494s, 129.432mph/208.301km/h.
2 Dean Harrison (Kawasaki), 1h 45m 13.412s; **3** Conor Cummins (Honda), 1h 45m 30.099s; **4** Davey Todd (Honda), 1h 45m 32.926s; **5** Michael Dunlop (Suzuki), 1h 47m 15.918s; **6** James Hillier (Yamaha), 1h 47m 26.991s; **7** Ian Hutchinson (BMW), 1h 48m 1.669s; **8** Jamie Coward (Yamaha), 1h 48m 25.506s; **9** John McGuinness (Honda), 1h 48m 35.748s; **10** Nathan Harrison (Honda), 1h 49m 30.139s; **11** Craig Neve (BMW), 1h 49m 53.358s; **12** Shaun Anderson (Suzuki), 1h 50m 4.671s; **13** Phillip Crowe (BMW), 1h 50m 15.352s; **14** Rob Hodson (Kawasaki), 1h 50m 55.674s; **15** Derek Sheils (BMW), 1h 51m 31.650s.
Fastest lap: Peter Hickman (BMW), 17m 4.136s, 132.627mph/213.442km/h, on lap 2.
Senior TT and Outright lap record: Peter Hickman (BMW), 16m 42.778s, 135.452mph/217.989km/h (2018).

British Championships

SILVERSTONE NATIONAL, 15-17 April 2022, 1.640-mile/2.640km circuit
Bennetts British Superbike Championship, Round 1
Race 1 (24 laps, 39.370 miles/63.360km)
1 Glenn Irwin (Honda), 21m 26.803s, 110.14mph/177.25km/h.
2 Kyle Ryde (Yamaha); **3** Bradley Ray (Yamaha); **4** Rory Skinner (Kawasaki); **5** Jason O'Halloran (Yamaha); **6** Andrew Irwin (BMW); **7** Tommy Bridewell (Ducati); **8** Christian Iddon (Suzuki); **9** Lee Jackson (Kawasaki); **10** Danny Buchan (BMW); **11** Peter Hickman (BMW); **12** Tom Sykes (Ducati); **13** Josh Brookes (Ducati); **14** Ryan Vickers (BMW); **15** Tom Neave (Honda).
Fastest lap: Ryde, 53.171s, 111.06mph/178.74km/h.

Race 2 (30 laps, 49.212 miles/79.199km)
1 Glenn Irwin (Honda), 27m 19.420s, 108.60mph/174.77km/h.
2 Kyle Ryde (Yamaha); **3** Rory Skinner (Kawasaki); **4** Lee Jackson (Kawasaki); **5** Andrew Irwin (BMW); **6** Jason O'Halloran (Yamaha); **7** Peter Hickman (BMW); **8** Tommy Bridewell (Ducati); **9** Danny Buchan (BMW); **10** Christian Iddon (Suzuki); **11** Josh Brookes (Ducati); **12** Dan Linfoot (BMW); **13** Ryan Vickers (BMW); **14** Tom Neave (Honda); **15** Leon Haslam (Kawasaki).
Fastest lap: Ray, 53.102s, 111.21mph/178.98km/h.

Race 3 (30 laps, 49.212 miles/79.199km)
1 Glenn Irwin (Honda), 26m 51.061s, 109.57mph/176.34km/h.
2 Bradley Ray (Yamaha); **3** Andrew Irwin (BMW); **4** Rory Skinner (Kawasaki); **5** Jason O'Halloran (Yamaha); **6** Danny Buchan (BMW); **7** Tommy Bridewell (Ducati); **8** Lee Jackson (Kawasaki); **9** Peter Hickman (BMW); **10** Kyle Ryde (Yamaha); **11** Christian Iddon (Suzuki); **12** Tom Neave (Honda); **13** Leon Haslam (Kawasaki); **14** Dan Linfoot (BMW); **15** Danny Kent (Suzuki).
Fastest lap: Buchan, 53.186s, 111.03mph/178.69km/h.
Championship points: **1** Glenn Irwin, 75; **2** Kyle Ryde, 46; **3** Rory Skinner, 42; **4** Andrew Irwin, 37; **5** Bradley Ray, 36; **6** Jason O'Halloran, 32; **7** Lee Jackson, 28; **8** Tommy Bridewell, 26.

Quattro Group British Supersport Championship, Round 1
Race 1 (18 laps, 29.527 miles/47.519km)
1 Jack Kennedy (Yamaha), 16m 50.766s, 105.16mph/169.24km/h.
2 Lee Johnston (Yamaha); **3** Harry Truelove (Yamaha); **4** Jamie van Sikkelerus (Yamaha); **5** Luke Jones (Ducati); **6** Rhys Irwin (Triumph); **7** Eunan McGlinchey (Kawasaki); **8** Cameron Fraser (Chassis Factory); **9** Harvey Claridge (Chassis Factory); **10** Josh Day (Triumph); **11** Max Ingham (Kawasaki); **12** Max Wadsworth (Yamaha); **13** Phil Wakefield (Yamaha); **14** Zak Corderoy (Kawasaki); **15** Harry Rowlings (BER Evo).
Fastest lap: Johnston, 55.677s, 106.07mph/170.70km/h.

Race 2 (25 laps, 41.010 miles/65.999km)
1 Jack Kennedy (Yamaha), 23m 25.554s, 105.04mph/169.05km/h.
2 Lee Johnston (Yamaha); **3** Harry Truelove (Yamaha); **4** Jamie van Sikkelerus (Yamaha); **5** Luke Jones (Ducati); **6** Eunan McGlinchey (Kawasaki); **7** Josh Day (Triumph); **8** Jack Scott (One); **9** Damon Rees (Yamaha); **10** Harvey Claridge (Chassis Factory); **11** Max Ingham (Kawasaki); **12** Caolán Irwin (Yamaha); **13** Phil Wakefield (Yamaha); **14** Jake Archer (FTR); **15** Tomás De Vries (Chassis Factory).
Fastest lap: Perie, 55.739s, 105.95mph/170.51km/h.
Championship points: **1** Jack Kennedy, 50; **2** Lee Johnston, 40; **3** Harry Truelove, 32; **4** Jamie Van, 26; **5** Luke Jones, 22; **6** Eunan McGlinchey, 19.

Honda British Talent Cup, Round 1
Race 1 (22 laps, 36.089 miles/58.08km)
1 Johnny Garness (Honda), 22m 58.844s, 94.22mph/151.63km/h.
2 Harrison Crosby (Honda); **3** Carter Brown (Honda); **4** Kiyano Veijer (Honda); **5** Ryan Hitchcock (Honda); **6** Rhys Stephenson (Honda); **7** Julian Correa (Honda); **8** Peter Willis (Honda); **9** Matthew Ruisbroek (Honda); **10** Clayton Edmunds (Honda); **11** Harrison Dessoy (Honda); **12** Ollie Walker (Honda); **13** Lucas Brown (Honda); **14** Daniel Goodman (Honda); **15** Lucas Hill (Honda).
Fastest lap: C. Brown, 1m 1.652s, 95.79mph/154.15km/h.

Race 2 (22 laps, 36.089 miles/58.08km)
1 Kiyano Veijer (Honda), 22m 50.330s, 94.81mph/152.58km/h.
2 Harrison Crosby (Honda); **3** Julian Correa (Honda); **4** Clayton Edmunds (Honda); **5** Harrison Dessoy (Honda); **6** Matthew Ruisbroek (Honda); **7** Harrison Mackay (Honda); **8** Harley McCabe (Honda); **9** Peter Willis (Honda); **10** Ryan Hitchcock (Honda); **11** Lucas Brown (Honda); **12** Luca Hopkins (Honda); **13** Daniel Goodman (Honda); **14** Ollie Walker (Honda); **15** Bailey Stuart-Campbell (Honda).
Fastest lap: Correa, 1m 1.666s, 95.76mph/154.12km/h.
Championship points: **1** Harrison Crosby, 40; **2** Kiyano Veijer, 38; **3** Johnny Garness, 25; **4** Julian Correa, 25; **5** Clayton Edmunds, 19; **6** Ryan Hitchcock, 17.

OULTON PARK, 30 April-2 May 2022, 2.692-mile/4.332km circuit
Bennetts British Superbike Championship, Round 2
Race 1 (11 laps, 29.612 miles/47.656km)
1 Bradley Ray (Yamaha), 17m 23.862s, 102.12mph/164.35km/h.
2 Rory Skinner (Kawasaki); **3** Kyle Ryde (Yamaha); **4** Josh Brookes (Ducati); **5** Peter Hickman (BMW); **6** Tommy Bridewell (Ducati); **7** Christian Iddon (Suzuki); **8** Jason O'Halloran (Yamaha); **9** Lee Jackson (Kawasaki); **10** Danny Buchan (BMW); **11** Glenn Irwin (Honda); **12** Andrew Irwin (BMW); **13** Leon Haslam (Kawasaki); **14** Ryan Vickers (BMW); **15** Tom Sykes (Ducati).
Fastest lap: Ray, 1m 33.865s, 103.24mph/166.16km/h.

Race 2 (18 laps, 48.456 miles/77.982km)
1 Bradley Ray (Yamaha), 29m 25.084s, 98.83mph/159.05km/h.
2 Lee Jackson (Kawasaki); **3** Leon Haslam (Kawasaki); **4** Kyle Ryde (Yamaha); **5** Rory Skinner (Kawasaki); **6** Jason O'Halloran (Yamaha); **7** Christian Iddon (Suzuki); **8** Peter Hickman (BMW); **9** Glenn Irwin (Honda); **10** Josh Brookes (Ducati); **11** Danny Buchan (BMW); **12** Ryan Vickers (BMW); **13** Tom Sykes (Ducati); **14** Storm Stacey (Kawasaki); **15** Tom Neave (Honda).
Fastest lap: Ray, 1m 33.620s, 103.51mph/166.59km/h.

Race 3 (18 laps, 48.456 miles/77.982km)
1 Lee Jackson (Kawasaki), 29m 30.009s, 98.55mph/158.6km/h.
2 Tommy Bridewell (Ducati); **3** Bradley Ray (Yamaha); **4** Rory Skinner (Kawasaki); **5** Leon Haslam (Kawasaki); **6** Jason O'Halloran (Yamaha); **7** Glenn Irwin (Honda); **8** Josh Brookes (Ducati); **9** Peter Hickman (BMW); **10** Kyle Ryde (Yamaha); **11** Tom Sykes (Ducati); **12** Storm Stacey (Kawasaki); **13** Danny Buchan (BMW); **14** Christian Iddon (Suzuki); **15** Dan Linfoot (BMW).
Fastest lap: Ray, 1m 33.645s, 103.48mph/166.55km/h.
Championship points: **1** Bradley Ray, 102; **2** Glenn Irwin, 96; **3** Rory Skinner, 86; **4** Kyle Ryde, 81; **5** Lee Jackson, 80; **6** Jason O'Halloran, 60; **7** Tommy Bridewell, 56; **8** Peter Hickman, 47.

Quattro Group British Supersport Championship, Round 2
Race 1 (12 laps, 32.304 miles/51.988km)
1 Jack Kennedy (Yamaha), 19m 42.863s, 98.31mph/158.21km/h.
2 Bradley Perie (Yamaha); **3** Lee Johnston (Yamaha); **4** Harry Truelove (Yamaha); **5** Luke Stapleford (Kawasaki); **6** Zak Corderoy (Kawasaki); **7** Eugene McManus (Kawasaki); **8** Luke Jones (Ducati); **9** Jamie van Sikkelerus (Yamaha); **10** Jamie Perrin (Kawasaki); **11** Sam Munro (Yamaha); **12** Jack Scott (One); **13** Caolán Irwin (Yamaha); **14** Cameron Fraser (Chassis Factory); **15** Josh Day (Triumph).
Fastest lap: Johnston, 1m 37.674s, 99.22mph/159.68km/h.

Race 2 (16 laps, 43.072 miles/69.318km)
1 Jack Kennedy (Yamaha), 26m 10.456s, 98.73mph/158.89km/h.
2 Lee Johnston (Yamaha); **3** Bradley Perie (Yamaha); **4** Harry Truelove (Yamaha); **5** Luke Stapleford (Kawasaki); **6** Zak Corderoy (Kawasaki); **7** Jamie van Sikkelerus (Yamaha); **8** Sam Munro (Yamaha); **9** Ian Hutchinson (Yamaha); **10** Jack Scott (One); **11** Josh Day (Triumph); **12** Damon Rees (Yamaha); **13** Caolán Irwin (Yamaha); **14** Cameron Fraser (Chassis Factory); **15** Max Wadsworth (Yamaha).
Fastest lap: Johnston, 1m 37.200s, 99.70mph/160.45km/h.
Championship points: **1** Jack Kennedy, 100; **2** Lee Johnston, 76; **3** Harry Truelove, 58; **4** Jamie van Sikkelerus, 42; **5** Bradley Perie, 36; **6** Luke Jones, 30.

Honda British Talent Cup, Round 2
Race 1 (14 laps, 37.688 miles/60.653km)
1 Johnny Garness (Honda), 25m 44.965s, 87.81mph/141.32km/h.
2 Kiyano Veijer (Honda); **3** Carter Brown (Honda); **4** Harley McCabe (Honda); **5** Harrison Dessoy (Honda); **6** Lucas Brown (Honda); **7** Matthew Ruisbroek (Honda); **8** Ryan Hitchcock (Honda); **9** Harrison Mackay (Honda); **10** Alexander Rowan (Honda); **11** Ollie Walker (Honda); **12** Elijah Banish (Honda); **13** Lucas Hill (Honda); **14** Charlie Huntingford (Honda); **15** Ted Wilkinson (Honda).
Fastest lap: McCabe, 1m 48.706s, 89.15mph/143.47km/h.

Race 2 (14 laps, 37.688 miles/60.653km)
1 Harrison Dessoy (Honda), 25m 29.668s, 88.69mph/142.73km/h.
2 Rhys Stephenson (Honda); **3** Johnny Garness (Honda); **4** Kiyano Veijer (Honda); **5** Matthew Ruisbroek (Honda); **6** Carter Brown (Honda); **7** Bailey Stuart-Campbell (Honda); **8** Julian Correa (Honda); **9** Harley McCabe (Honda); **10** Lucas Brown (Honda); **11** Harrison Mackay (Honda); **12** Luca Hopkins (Honda); **13** Ryan Hitchcock (Honda); **14** Ollie Walker (Honda); **15** Clayton Edmunds (Honda).
Fastest lap: Garness, 1m 47.907s, 89.81mph/144.53km/h.
Championship points: **1** Kiyano Veijer, 71; **2** Johnny Garness, 66; **3** Harrison Dessoy, 52; **4** Carter Brown, 42; **5** Harrison Crosby, 40; **6** Matthew Ruisbroek, 37.

DONINGTON PARK NATIONAL, 20-22 May 2022, 1.979-mile/3.185km circuit
Bennetts British Superbike Championship, Round 3
Race 1 (20 laps, 39.580 miles/63.698km)
1 Kyle Ryde (Yamaha), 22m 9.645s, 107.06mph/172.3km/h.
2 Jason O'Halloran (Yamaha); **3** Bradley Ray (Yamaha); **4** Lee Jackson (Kawasaki); **5** Glenn Irwin (Honda); **6** Christian Iddon (Suzuki); **7** Rory Skinner (Kawasaki); **8** Tommy Bridewell (Ducati); **9** Peter Hickman (BMW); **10** Tarran Mackenzie (Yamaha); **11** Tom Sykes (Ducati); **12** Danny Buchan (BMW); **13** Josh Brookes (Ducati); **14** Chrissy Rouse (BMW); **15** Ryo Mizuno (Honda).
Fastest lap: O'Halloran, 1m 5.928s, 108.06mph/173.91km/h.

Race 2 (26 laps, 51.454 miles/82.807km)
1 Jason O'Halloran (Yamaha), 28m 51.309s, 106.91mph/172.05km/h.
2 Bradley Ray (Yamaha); **3** Lee Jackson (Kawasaki); **4** Peter Hickman (BMW); **5** Leon Haslam (Kawasaki); **6** Tarran Mackenzie (Yamaha); **7** Christian Iddon (Suzuki); **8** Rory Skinner (Kawasaki); **9** Ryan Vickers (BMW); **10** Josh Brookes (Ducati); **11** Tom Sykes (Ducati); **12** Chrissy Rouse (BMW); **13** Danny Buchan (BMW); **14** Andrew Irwin (BMW); **15** Ryo Mizuno (Honda).
Fastest lap: Ryde, 1m 5.723s, 108.40mph/174.45km/h.

Race 3 (26 laps, 51.454 miles/82.807km)
1 Jason O'Halloran (Yamaha), 29m 31.007s, 104.51mph/168.19km/h.
2 Bradley Ray (Yamaha); **3** Lee Jackson (Kawasaki); **4** Rory Skinner (Kawasaki); **5** Kyle Ryde (Yamaha); **6** Christian Iddon (Suzuki); **7** Tom Sykes (Ducati); **8** Josh Brookes (Ducati); **9** Danny Buchan (BMW); **10** Chrissy Rouse (BMW); **11** Tarran Mackenzie (Yamaha); **12** Andrew Irwin (BMW); **13** Ryo Mizuno (Honda); **14** Storm Stacey (Kawasaki); **15** Takumi Takahashi (Honda).
Fastest lap: O'Halloran, 1m 5.810s, 108.26mph/174.22km/h.
Championship points: **1** Bradley Ray, 158; **2** Jason O'Halloran, 130; **3** Lee Jackson, 125; **4** Kyle Ryde, 117; **5** Rory Skinner, 116; **6** Glenn Irwin, 107; **7** Christian Iddon, 68; **8** Peter Hickman, 67.

Quattro Group British Supersport Championship, Round 3
Race 1 (16 laps, 31.664 miles/50.958km)
1 Bradley Perie (Yamaha), 18m 22.275s, 103.29mph/166.23km/h.
2 Jack Kennedy (Yamaha); **3** Harry Truelove (Yamaha); **4** Lee Johnston (Yamaha); **5** Luke Stapleford (Kawasaki); **6** Jack Scott (One); **7** Sam Munro (Yamaha); **8** Jamie Perrin (Kawasaki); **9** Eugene McManus (Kawasaki); **10** Luke Jones (Ducati); **11** Ash Barnes (Yamaha); **12** Damon Rees (Yamaha); **13** Jamie van Sikkelerus (Yamaha); **14** Caolán Irwin (Yamaha); **15** Harvey Claridge (Chassis Factory).
Fastest lap: Perie, 1m 8.299s, 104.31mph/167.87km/h.

Race 2 (24 laps, 47.496 miles/76.437km)
1 Bradley Perie (Yamaha), 27m 34.280s, 103.28mph/166.21km/h.
2 Jack Kennedy (Yamaha); **3** Harry Truelove (Yamaha); **4** Luke Stapleford (Kawasaki); **5** Lee Johnston (Yamaha); **6** Eugene McManus (Kawasaki); **7** Damon Rees (Yamaha); **8** Jack Scott (One); **9** Jamie van Sikkelerus (Yamaha); **10** Luke Jones (Ducati); **11** Sam Munro (Yamaha); **12** Rhys Irwin (Triumph); **13** Caolán Irwin (Yamaha); **14** Cameron Fraser (Chassis Factory); **15** Harvey Claridge (Chassis Factory).
Fastest lap: Kennedy, 1m 8.035s, 104.72mph/168.53km/h.
Championship points: **1** Jack Kennedy, 140; **2** Lee Johnston, 100; **3** Harry Truelove, 90; **4** Bradley Perie, 86; **5** Jamie van Sikkelerus, 54; **6** Luke Stapleford, 46.

Honda British Talent Cup, Round 3
Race 1 (20 laps, 39.580 miles/63.698km)
1 Carter Brown (Honda), 25m 33.384s, 92.83mph/149.4km/h.
2 Johnny Garness (Honda); **3** Harrison Dessoy (Honda); **4** Ryan Hitchcock (Honda); **5** Sullivan Mounsey (Honda); **6** Julian Correa (Honda); **7** Bailey Stuart-Campbell (Honda); **8** Lucas Brown (Honda); **9** Luca Hopkins (Honda); **10** Harrison Crosby (Honda); **11** Clayton Edmunds (Honda); **12** Harrison Mackay (Honda); **13** Daniel Goodman (Honda); **14** Kalvin Kelly (Honda); **15** Ollie Walker (Honda).
Fastest lap: Stephenson, 1m 15.463s, 94.41mph/151.94km/h.

Race 2 (22 laps, 43.538 miles/70.068km)
1 Johnny Garness (Honda), 28m 7.867s, 92.78mph/149.31km/h.
1 Carter Brown (Honda), 28m 7.867s, 92.78mph/149.31km/h.
3 Kiyano Veijer (Honda); **4** Bailey Stuart-Campbell (Honda); **5** Sullivan Mounsey (Honda); **6** Harrison Dessoy (Honda); **7** Ryan Hitchcock (Honda); **8** Julian Correa (Honda); **9** Rhys Stephenson (Honda); **10** Lucas Brown (Honda); **11** Harrison Crosby (Honda); **12** Harrison Mackay (Honda); **13** Luca Hopkins (Honda); **14** Clayton Edmunds (Honda); **15** Daniel Goodman (Honda).
Fastest lap: Mounsey, 1m 15.809s, 93.98mph/151.24km/h.
Championship points: **1** Johnny Garness, 111; **2** Carter Brown, 92; **3** Kiyano Veijer, 87; **4** Harrison Dessoy, 78; **5** Harrison Crosby, 51; **6** Julian Correa, 51.

KNOCKHILL, 17-19 June 2022, 1.268-mile/2.042km circuit
Bennetts British Superbike Championship, Round 4
Race 1 (22 laps, 27.874 miles/44.859km)
1 Bradley Ray (Yamaha), 17m 36.028s, 95.02mph/152.92km/h.
2 Jason O'Halloran (Yamaha); **3** Rory Skinner (Kawasaki); **4** Lee Jackson (Kawasaki); **5** Danny Buchan (BMW); **6** Kyle Ryde (Yamaha); **7** Glenn Irwin (Honda); **8** Tommy Bridewell (Ducati); **9** Storm Stacey (Kawasaki); **10** Josh Brookes (Ducati); **11** Leon Haslam (Kawasaki); **12** Tom Sykes (Ducati); **13** Peter Hickman (BMW); **14** Andrew Irwin (BMW); **15** Ryan Vickers (BMW).
Fastest lap: Ray, 47.434s, 96.15mph/154.74km/h.

Race 2 (30 laps, 38.010 miles/61.171km)
1 Jason O'Halloran (Yamaha), 24m 18.655s, 93.80mph/150.96km/h.
2 Lee Jackson (Kawasaki); **3** Rory Skinner (Kawasaki); **4** Bradley Ray (Yamaha); **5** Tommy Bridewell (Ducati); **6** Josh Brookes (Ducati); **7** Danny Buchan (BMW); **8** Glenn Irwin (Honda); **9** Kyle Ryde (Yamaha); **10** Tarran Mackenzie (Yamaha); **11** Tom Sykes (Ducati); **12** Chrissy Rouse (BMW); **13** Tom Neave (Honda); **14** Danny Kent (Suzuki); **15** Ryo Mizuno (Honda).
Fastest lap: Skinner, 47.126s, 96.78mph/155.76km/h.

Race 3 (30 laps, 38.010 miles/61.171km)
1 Jason O'Halloran (Yamaha), 24m 0.506s, 94.98mph/152.86km/h.
2 Bradley Ray (Yamaha); **3** Lee Jackson (Kawasaki); **4** Danny Buchan (BMW); **5** Tommy Bridewell (Ducati); **6** Glenn Irwin (Honda); **7** Josh Brookes (Ducati); **8** Tarran Mackenzie (Yamaha); **9** Kyle Ryde (Yamaha); **10** Tom Sykes (Ducati); **11** Leon Haslam (Kawasaki); **12** Peter Hickman (BMW); **13** Storm Stacey (Kawasaki); **14** Tom Neave (Honda); **15** Takumi Takahashi (Honda).
Fastest lap: Skinner, 47.485s, 96.05mph/154.58km/h.
Championship points: **1** Bradley Ray, 216; **2** Jason O'Halloran, 200; **3** Lee Jackson, 174; **4** Rory Skinner, 148; **5** Kyle Ryde, 141; **6** Glenn Irwin, 134; **7** Tommy Bridewell, 94; **8** Danny Buchan, 84.

Quattro Group British Supersport Championship, Round 4
Race 1 (18 laps, 22.806 miles/36.703km)
1 Jack Kennedy (Yamaha), 14m 58.157s, 91.40mph/147.09km/h.
2 Luke Stapleford (Kawasaki); **3** Harry Truelove (Yamaha); **4** Bradley Perie (Yamaha); **5** Jamie Perrin (Kawasaki); **6** Korie McGreevy (Chassis Factory); **7** Rhys Irwin (Triumph); **8** Jamie van Sikkelerus (Yamaha); **9** Luke Jones (Ducati); **10** Eugene McManus (Kawasaki); **11** Damon Rees (Yamaha); **12**

Cameron Fraser (Chassis Factory); **13** Barry Burrell (Kramer); **14** Phil Wakefield (Yamaha); **15** Max Ingham (Kawasaki).
Fastest lap: Kennedy, 49.452s, 92.23mph/148.43km/h.

Race 2 (26 laps, 32.942 miles/53.015km)
1 Jack Kennedy (Yamaha), 21m 30.601s, 91.88mph/147.87km/h.
2 Luke Stapleford (Kawasaki); **3** Eugene McManus (Kawasaki); **4** Bradley Perie (Yamaha); **5** Harry Truelove (Yamaha); **6** Korie McGreevy (Chassis Factory); **7** Rhys Irwin (Triumph); **8** Jamie van Sikkelerus (Yamaha); **9** Sam Munro (Yamaha); **10** Jamie Perrin (Kawasaki); **11** Jack Scott (One); **12** Damon Rees (Yamaha); **13** Cameron Fraser (Chassis Factory); **14** Luke Jones (Ducati); **15** Barry Burrell (Kramer).
Fastest lap: Kennedy, 49.211s, 92.68mph/149.16km/h.
Championship points: **1** Jack Kennedy, 190; **2** Harry Truelove, 117; **3** Bradley Perie, 112; **4** Lee Johnston, 100; **5** Luke Stapleford, 86; **6** Jamie van Sikkelerus, 72.

Honda British Talent Cup, Round 4
Race 1 (22 laps, 27.874 miles/44.859km)
1 Evan Belford (Honda), 20m 11.372s, 82.83mph/133.3km/h.
2 Sullivan Mounsey (Honda); **3** Troy Jeffrey (Honda); **4** Bailey Stuart-Campbell (Honda); **5** Kiyano Veijer (Honda); **6** Rhys Stephenson (Honda); **7** Lucas Brown (Honda); **8** Harrison Dessoy (Honda); **9** Julian Correa (Honda); **10** Alexander Rowan (Honda); **11** Ryan Hitchcock (Honda); **12** Harrison Mackay (Honda); **13** Ollie Walker (Honda); **14** Clayton Edmunds (Honda); **15** Kalvin Kelly (Honda).
Fastest lap: Garness, 54.047s, 84.39mph/135.81km/h.

Race 2 (22 laps, 27.874 miles/44.859km)
1 Johnny Garness (Honda), 20m 4.665s, 83.29mph/134.04km/h.
2 Carter Brown (Honda); **3** Troy Jeffrey (Honda); **4** Kiyano Veijer (Honda); **5** Harrison Dessoy (Honda); **6** Rhys Stephenson (Honda); **7** Bailey Stuart-Campbell (Honda); **8** Harrison Crosby (Honda); **9** Lucas Brown (Honda); **10** Harrison Mackay (Honda); **11** Ryan Hitchcock (Honda); **12** Clayton Edmunds (Honda); **13** Alexander Rowan (Honda); **14** Julian Correa (Honda); **15** Filip Surowiak (Honda).
Fastest lap: C. Brown, 53.805s, 84.77mph/136.42km/h.
Championship points: **1** Johnny Garness, 136; **2** Carter Brown, 112; **3** Kiyano Veijer, 111; **4** Harrison Dessoy, 97; **5** Julian Correa, 60; **6** Ryan Hitchcock, 60.

BRANDS HATCH GP, 22-24 July 2022, 2.433-mile/3.916km circuit
Bennetts British Superbike Championship, Round 5
Race 1 (15 laps, 36.495 miles/58.733km)
1 Jason O'Halloran (Yamaha), 21m 26.871s, 102.10mph/164.31km/h.
2 Tarran Mackenzie (Yamaha); **3** Tommy Bridewell (Ducati); **4** Bradley Ray (Yamaha); **5** Kyle Ryde (Yamaha); **6** Josh Brookes (Ducati); **7** Rory Skinner (Kawasaki); **8** Leon Haslam (Kawasaki); **9** Lee Jackson (Kawasaki); **10** Christian Iddon (Suzuki); **11** Peter Hickman (BMW); **12** Danny Kent (Suzuki); **13** Tom Sykes (Ducati); **14** Andrew Irwin (BMW); **15** Josh Owens (Kawasaki).
Fastest lap: Mackenzie, 1m 24.954s, 103.11mph/165.94km/h.

Race 2 (20 laps, 48.660 miles/78.311km)
1 Tarran Mackenzie (Yamaha), 28m 43.344s, 101.66mph/163.61km/h.
2 Jason O'Halloran (Yamaha); **3** Tommy Bridewell (Ducati); **4** Bradley Ray (Yamaha); **5** Leon Haslam (Kawasaki); **6** Rory Skinner (Kawasaki); **7** Kyle Ryde (Yamaha); **8** Tom Sykes (Ducati); **9** Danny Kent (Suzuki); **10** Glenn Irwin (Honda); **11** Tom Neave (Honda); **12** Peter Hickman (BMW); **13** Takumi Takahashi (Honda); **14** Josh Owens (Kawasaki); **15** Danny Buchan (BMW).
Fastest lap: Mackenzie, 1m 25.565s, 102.37mph/164.75km/h.

Race 3 (20 laps, 48.660 miles/78.311km)
1 Tarran Mackenzie (Yamaha), 28m 45.305s, 101.54mph/163.41km/h.
2 Jason O'Halloran (Yamaha); **3** Glenn Irwin (Honda); **4** Bradley Ray (Yamaha); **5** Tommy Bridewell (Ducati); **6** Leon Haslam (Kawasaki); **7** Kyle Ryde (Yamaha); **8** Peter Hickman (BMW); **9** Rory Skinner (Kawasaki); **10** Lee Jackson (Kawasaki); **11** Christian Iddon (Suzuki); **12** Andrew Irwin (BMW); **13** Danny Buchan (BMW); **14** Takumi Takahashi (Honda); **15** Chrissy Rouse (BMW).
Fastest lap: Mackenzie, 1m 25.420s, 102.55mph/165.03km/h.
Championship points: **1** Jason O'Halloran, 265; **2** Bradley Ray, 255; **3** Lee Jackson, 187; **4** Rory Skinner, 174; **5** Kyle Ryde, 170; **6** Glenn Irwin, 156; **7** Tommy Bridewell, 137; **8** Tarran Mackenzie, 105.

Quattro Group British Supersport Championship, Round 5
Race 1 (12 laps, 29.196 miles/46.986km)
1 Jack Kennedy (Yamaha), 17m 45.589s, 98.64mph/158.75km/h.
2 Harry Truelove (Yamaha); **3** Luke Stapleford (Kawasaki); **4** Jack Scott (One); **5** Bradley Perie (Yamaha); **6** Lee Johnston (Yamaha); **7** Mason Law (Triumph); **8** Damon Rees (Yamaha); **9** Korie McGreevy (Chassis Factory); **10** Rhys Irwin (Triumph); **11** Jamie Perrin (Kawasaki); **12** Jamie van Sikkelerus (Yamaha); **13** Ash Barnes (Yamaha); **14** Harvey Claridge (Chassis Factory); **15** Barry Burrell (Kramer).
Fastest lap: Kennedy, 1m 28.103s, 99.42mph/160.01km/h.

Race 2 (18 laps, 43.794 miles/70.48km)
1 Jack Kennedy (Yamaha), 26m 43.734s, 98.31mph/158.21km/h.
2 Luke Stapleford (Kawasaki); **3** Harry Truelove (Yamaha); **4** Bradley Perie (Yamaha); **5** Jack Scott (One); **6** Mason Law (Triumph); **7** Eugene McManus (Kawasaki); **8** Korie McGreevy (Chassis Factory); **9** Damon Rees (Yamaha); **10** Luke Jones (Ducati); **11** Jamie van Sikkelerus (Yamaha); **12** Rhys Irwin (Triumph); **13** Ash Barnes (Yamaha); **14** Harvey Claridge (Chassis Factory); **15** Jake Archer (FTR).
Fastest lap: Kennedy, 1m 28.458s, 99.02mph/159.37km/h.
Championship points: **1** Jack Kennedy, 240; **2** Harry Truelove, 153; **3** Bradley Perie, 138; **4** Luke Stapleford, 122; **5** Lee Johnston, 111; **6** Jamie van Sikkelerus, 85.

Honda British Talent Cup, Round 5
Race 1 (10 laps, 24.330 miles/39.155km)
1 Johnny Garness (Honda), 16m 17.087s, 89.65mph/144.28km/h.
2 Harrison Crosby (Honda); **3** Carter Brown (Honda); **4** Matthew Ruisbroek (Honda); **5** Harrison Dessoy (Honda); **6** Harrison Mackay (Honda); **7** Ryan Hitchcock (Honda); **8** Rhys Stephenson (Honda); **9** Lucas Brown (Honda); **10** Kiyano Veijer (Honda); **11** Julian Correa (Honda); **12** Josh Bannister (Honda); **13** Kalvin Kelly (Honda); **14** Ollie Walker (Honda); **15** Troy Jeffrey (Honda).
Fastest lap: Garness, 1m 36.774s, 90.51mph/145.67km/h.

Race 2 (14 laps, 34.062 miles/54.817km)
1 Johnny Garness (Honda), 22m 4.665s, 89.91mph/144.7km/h.
2 Matthew Ruisbroek (Honda); **3** Evan Belford (Honda); **4** Harrison Crosby (Honda); **5** Ryan Hitchcock (Honda); **6** Kiyano Veijer (Honda); **7** Lucas Brown (Honda); **8** Harrison Mackay (Honda); **9** Rhys Stephenson (Honda); **10** Julian Correa (Honda); **11** Sullivan Mounsey (Honda); **12** Ollie Walker (Honda); **13** Josh Bannister (Honda); **14** Clayton Edmunds (Honda); **15** Alexander Rowan (Honda).
Fastest lap: Garness, 1m 36.497s, 90.77mph/146.09km/h.
Championship points: **1** Johnny Garness, 186; **2** Carter Brown, 128; **3** Kiyano Veijer, 127; **4** Harrison Dessoy, 108; **5** Harrison Crosby, 92; **6** Ryan Hitchcock, 80.

Silverstone MotoGP, 5-7 August 2022, 3.666-mile/5.900km circuit
Honda British Talent Cup, Round 6
Race 1 (11 laps, 40.327 miles/64.900km)
1 Johnny Garness (Honda), 25m 48.317s, 93.70mph/150.80km/h.
2 Rhys Stephenson (Honda); **3** Harley McCabe (Honda); **4** Harrison Dessoy (Honda); **5** Carter Brown (Honda); **6** Lucas Brown (Honda); **7** Matthew Ruisbroek (Honda); **8** Sullivan Mounsey (Honda); **9** Harrison Crosby (Honda); **10** Clayton Edmunds (Honda); **11** Kiyano Veijer (Honda); **12** Julian Correa (Honda); **13** Peter Willis (Honda); **14** Ollie Walker (Honda); **15** Filip Surowiak (Honda).
Fastest lap: Stephenson, 2m 19.831s, 94.30mph/151.80km/h.

Race 2 (11 laps, 40.327 miles/43.071km)
1 Johnny Garness (Honda), 25m 41.626s, 94.14mph/151.50km/h.
2 Rhys Stephenson (Honda); **3** Harley McCabe (Honda); **4** Carter Brown (Honda); **5** Harrison Dessoy (Honda); **6** Clayton Edmunds (Honda); **7** Lucas Brown (Honda); **8** Harrison Crosby (Honda); **9** Julian Correa (Honda); **10** Matthew Ruisbroek (Honda); **11** Peter Willis (Honda); **12** Ollie Walker (Honda); **13** Harrison Mackay (Honda); **14** Evan Belford (Honda); **15** Alexander Rowan (Honda).
Fastest lap: Garness, 2m 18.816s, 95.07mph/153.00km/h.
Championship points: **1** Johnny Garness, 236; **2** Carter Brown, 152; **3** Kiyano Veijer, 132; **4** Harrison Dessoy, 132; **5** Rhys Stephenson, 112. **6** Harrison Crosby, 107.

THRUXTON, 12-14 August 2022, 2.356-mile/3.792km circuit
Bennetts British Superbike Championship, Round 6
Race 1 (15 laps, 35.340 miles/56.874km)
1 Jason O'Halloran (Yamaha), 19m 1.073s, 111.49mph/179.43km/h.
2 Tarran Mackenzie (Yamaha); **3** Bradley Ray (Yamaha); **4** Glenn Irwin (Honda); **5** Peter Hickman (BMW); **6** Lee Jackson (Kawasaki); **7** Rory Skinner (Kawasaki); **8** Leon Haslam (Kawasaki); **9** Tom Sykes (Ducati); **10** Tommy Bridewell (Ducati); **11** Ryan Vickers (BMW); **12** Christian Iddon (Suzuki); **13** Kyle Ryde (Yamaha); **14** Danny Buchan (BMW); **15** Ryo Mizuno (Honda).
Fastest lap: Ray, 1m 15.209s, 112.77mph/181.49km/h.

Race 2 (20 laps, 47.120 miles/75.832km)
1 Jason O'Halloran (Yamaha), 25m 27.217s, 111.07mph/178.75km/h.
2 Tarran Mackenzie (Yamaha); **3** Bradley Ray (Yamaha); **4** Peter Hickman (BMW); **5** Lee Jackson (Kawasaki); **6** Glenn Irwin (Honda); **7** Rory Skinner (Kawasaki); **8** Danny Buchan (BMW); **9** Leon Haslam (Kawasaki); **10** Tommy Bridewell (Ducati); **11** Christian Iddon (Suzuki); **12** Tom Sykes (Ducati); **13** Andrew Irwin (BMW); **14** Ryo Mizuno (Honda); **15** Josh Brookes (Ducati).
Fastest lap: Ray, 1m 15.214s, 112.76mph/181.47km/h.

Race 3 (20 laps, 47.120 miles/75.832km)
1 Tarran Mackenzie (Yamaha), 25m 28.047s, 111.01mph/178.65km/h.
2 Bradley Ray (Yamaha); **3** Jason O'Halloran (Yamaha); **4** Glenn Irwin (Honda); **5** Lee Jackson (Kawasaki); **6** Leon Haslam (Kawasaki); **7** Tommy Bridewell (Ducati); **8** Andrew Irwin (BMW); **9** Rory Skinner (Kawasaki); **10** Tom Sykes (Ducati); **11** Christian Iddon (Suzuki); **12** Ryo Mizuno (Honda); **13** Ryan Vickers (BMW); **14** Takumi Takahashi (Honda); **15** Danny Kent (Suzuki).
Fastest lap: Hickman, 1m 15.478s, 112.37mph/180.84km/h.
Championship points: **1** Jason O'Halloran, 331; **2** Bradley Ray, 307; **3** Lee Jackson, 219; **4** Rory Skinner, 199; **5** Glenn Irwin, 192; **6** Kyle Ryde, 173; **7** Tarran Mackenzie, 170; **8** Tommy Bridewell, 158.

Quattro Group British Supersport Championship, Round 6
Race 1 (12 laps, 28.272 miles/45.499km)
1 Jack Scott (One), 15m 37.297s, 108.58mph/174.74km/h.
2 Jack Kennedy (Yamaha); **3** Bradley Perie (Yamaha); **4** Luke Stapleford (Kawasaki); **5** Eugene McManus (Kawasaki); **6** Harry Truelove (Yamaha); **7** Jamie Perrin (Yamaha); **8** Mason Law (Triumph); **9** Rhys Irwin (Triumph); **10** Lee Johnston (Yamaha); **11** Ash Barnes (Yamaha); **12** Scott Swann (Kawasaki); **13** Korie McGreevy (Chassis Factory); **14** Cameron Fraser (Chassis Factory); **15** Jamie van Sikkelerus (Yamaha).
Fastest lap: Scott, 1m 17.181s, 109.89mph/176.85km/h.

Race 2 (18 laps, 42.408 miles/68.249km)
1 Jack Kennedy (Yamaha), 23m 29.436s, 108.31mph/174.31km/h.
2 Bradley Perie (Yamaha); **3** Jack Scott (One); **4** Luke Stapleford (Kawasaki); **5** Jamie Perrin (Yamaha); **6** Eugene McManus (Kawasaki); **7** Harry Truelove (Yamaha); **8** Lee Johnston (Yamaha); **9** Luke Jones (Ducati); **10** Ash Barnes (Yamaha); **11** Rhys Irwin (Triumph); **12** Scott Swann (Kawasaki); **13** Mason Law (Triumph); **14** Jamie van Sikkelerus (Yamaha); **15** Cameron Fraser (Chassis Factory).
Fastest lap: Kennedy, 1m 17.097s, 110.01mph/177.04km/h.
Championship points: **1** Jack Kennedy, 290; **2** Bradley Perie, 178; **3** Harry Truelove, 174; **4** Luke Stapleford, 154; **5** Lee Johnston, 127; **6** Jamie van Sikkelerus, 92.

Honda British Talent Cup, Round 7
Race 1 (14 laps, 32.984 miles/53.083km)
1 Johnny Garness (Honda), 19m 19.755s, 102.38mph/164.76km/h.
2 Carter Brown (Honda); **3** Rhys Stephenson (Honda); **4** Matthew Ruisbroek (Honda); **5** Harrison Crosby (Honda); **6** Amanuel Brinton (Honda); **7** Evan Belford (Honda); **8** Lucas Brown (Honda); **9** Sullivan Mounsey (Honda); **10** Harrison Mackay (Honda); **11** Clayton Edmunds (Honda); **12** Ryan Hitchcock (Honda); **13** Josh Bannister (Honda); **14** Ollie Walker (Honda); **15** Alexander Rowan (Honda).
Fastest lap: Stephenson, 1m 21.961s, 103.48mph/166.54km/h.

Race 2 (12 laps, 28.272 miles/45.499km)
1 Johnny Garness (Honda), 16m 36.212s, 102.16mph/164.41km/h.
2 Carter Brown (Honda); **3** Evan Belford (Honda); **4** Rhys Stephenson (Honda); **5** Harrison Crosby (Honda); **6** Amanuel Brinton (Honda); **7** Lucas Brown (Honda); **8** Clayton Edmunds (Honda); **9** Harrison Mackay (Honda); **10** Ollie Walker (Honda); **11** Josh Bannister (Honda); **12** Sullivan Mounsey (Honda); **13** Julian Correa (Honda); **14** Harley McCabe (Honda); **15** Daniel Goodman (Honda).
Fastest lap: Garness, 1m 22.140s, 103.25mph/166.17km/h.
Championship points: **1** Johnny Garness, 286; **2** Carter Brown, 192; **3** Rhys Stephenson, 141; **4** Kiyano Veijer, 132; **5** Harrison Dessoy, 132; **6** Harrison Crosby, 129.

CADWELL PARK, 27-29 August 2022, 2.180-mile/3.508km circuit
Bennetts British Superbike Championship, Round 7
Race 1 (12 laps, 26.160 miles/42.100km)
1 Bradley Ray (Yamaha), 17m 21.619s, 90.41mph/145.5km/h.
2 Rory Skinner (Kawasaki); **3** Danny Buchan (BMW); **4** Jason O'Halloran (Yamaha); **5** Tommy Bridewell (Ducati); **6** Peter Hickman (BMW); **7** Andrew Irwin (BMW); **8** Leon Haslam (Kawasaki); **9** Glenn Irwin (Honda); **10** Josh Brookes (Ducati); **11** Tarran Mackenzie (Yamaha); **12** Kyle Ryde (Yamaha); **13** Ryan Vickers (BMW); **14** Tom Neave (Honda); **15** Danny Kent (Suzuki).
Fastest lap: Bridewell, 1m 25.950s, 91.30mph/146.94km/h.

Race 2 (16 laps, 34.880 miles/56.134km)
1 Danny Buchan (BMW), 23m 6.419s, 90.57mph/145.76km/h.
2 Bradley Ray (Yamaha); **3** Tommy Bridewell (Ducati); **4** Leon Haslam (Kawasaki); **5** Rory Skinner (Kawasaki); **6** Andrew Irwin (BMW); **7** Peter Hickman (BMW); **8** Jason O'Halloran (Yamaha); **9** Glenn Irwin (Honda); **10** Tom Sykes (Ducati); **11** Tarran Mackenzie (Yamaha); **12** Christian Iddon (Suzuki); **13** Ryan Vickers (BMW); **14** Lee Jackson (Kawasaki); **15** Kyle Ryde (Yamaha).
Fastest lap: Ray, 1m 25.858s, 91.40mph/147.1km/h.

Race 3 (18 laps, 39.240 miles/63.151km)
1 Danny Buchan (BMW), 25m 59.505s, 90.58mph/145.77km/h.
2 Bradley Ray (Yamaha); **3** Tommy Bridewell (Ducati); **4** Leon Haslam (Kawasaki); **5** Rory Skinner (Kawasaki); **6** Peter Hickman (BMW); **7** Andrew Irwin (BMW); **8** Glenn Irwin (Honda); **9** Jason O'Halloran (Yamaha); **10** Tarran Mackenzie (Yamaha); **11** Josh Brookes (Ducati); **12** Lee Jackson (Kawasaki); **13** Ryan Vickers (BMW); **14** Danny Kent (Suzuki); **15** Takumi Takahashi (Honda).
Fastest lap: Hickman, 1m 25.958s, 91.30mph/146.93km/h.
Championship points: **1** Bradley Ray, 372; **2** Jason O'Halloran, 359; **3** Rory Skinner, 241; **4** Lee Jackson, 225; **5** Glenn Irwin, 214; **6** Tommy Bridewell, 201; **7** Tarran Mackenzie, 186; **8** Kyle Ryde, 178.

Quattro Group British Supersport Championship, Round 7
Race 1 (12 laps, 26.160 miles/42.1km)
1 Harry Truelove (Yamaha), 18m 1.519s, 87.07mph/140.13km/h.
2 Jack Kennedy (Yamaha); **3** Jack Scott (One); **4** Bradley Perie (Yamaha); **5** Eugene McManus (Kawasaki); **6** Luke Stapleford (Kawasaki); **7** Ash Barnes (Yamaha); **8** Luke Jones (Ducati); **9** Jamie Perrin (Yamaha); **10** Damon Rees (Yamaha); **11** Max Ingham (Kawasaki); **12** Tom Toparis (Triumph); **13** Cameron Fraser (Chassis Factory); **14** Barry Burrell (Kramer); **15** Jake Archer (FTR).
Fastest lap: Kennedy, 1m 28.738s, 88.44mph/142.33km/h.

Race 2 (16 laps, 34.880 miles/56.134km)
1 Jack Kennedy (Yamaha), 24m 43.411s, 84.64mph/136.21km/h.
2 Bradley Perie (Yamaha); **3** Jamie van Sikkelerus (Yamaha); **4** Damon Rees (Yamaha); **5** Jamie Perrin (Yamaha); **6** Rhys Irwin (Triumph); **7** Luke Jones (Ducati); **8** Max Ingham (Kawasaki); **9** Ash Barnes (Yamaha); **10** Tom Toparis (Triumph); **11** Cameron Fraser (Chassis Factory); **12** Caolán Irwin (Yamaha); **13** Harry Rowlings (BER Evo); **14** Jake Archer (FTR); **15** Harvey Claridge (Chassis Factory).
Fastest lap: Kennedy, 1m 28.930s, 88.24mph/142.02km/h.
Championship points: **1** Jack Kennedy, 335; **2** Bradley Perie, 214; **3** Harry Truelove, 199; **4** Luke Stapleford, 165; **5** Lee Johnston, 127; **6** Jamie van Sikkelerus, 108.

SNETTERTON, 9-11 September 2022, 2.969-mile/4.778km circuit.
Bennetts British Superbike Championship, Round 8
Race 1 (12 laps, 35.628 miles/57.338km)
1 Bradley Ray (Yamaha), 22m 37.386s, 94.48mph/152.05km/h.
2 Tarran Mackenzie (Yamaha); **3** Kyle Ryde (Yamaha); **4** Christian Iddon (Suzuki); **5** Leon Haslam (Kawasaki); **6** Lee Jackson (Kawasaki); **7** Tom Sykes (Ducati); **8** Peter Hickman (BMW); **9** Glenn Irwin (Honda); **10** Danny Kent (Suzuki); **11** Takumi Takahashi (Honda); **12** Jason O'Halloran (Yamaha); **13** Josh Brookes (Ducati); **14** Tom Neave (Honda); **15** Storm Stacey (Kawasaki).
Fastest lap: Ray, 1m 47.764s, 99.18mph/159.61km/h.

Race 2 (16 laps, 47.504 miles/76.450km)
1 Bradley Ray (Yamaha), 28m 56.976s, 98.45mph/158.44km/h.
2 Tarran Mackenzie (Yamaha); **3** Tommy Bridewell (Ducati); **4** Glenn Irwin (Honda); **5** Peter Hickman (BMW); **6** Kyle Ryde (Yamaha); **7** Danny Buchan (BMW); **8** Lee Jackson (Kawasaki); **9** Jason O'Halloran (Yamaha); **10** Tom Sykes (Ducati); **11** Rory Skinner (Kawasaki); **12** Josh Brookes (Ducati); **13** Storm Stacey (Kawasaki); **14** Tom Neave (Honda); **15** Ryo Mizuno (Honda).
Fastest lap: Mackenzie, 1m 47.079s, 99.81mph/160.63km/h.

Race 3 (16 laps, 47.504 miles/76.450km)
1 Bradley Ray (Yamaha), 29m 40.682s, 96.03mph/154.55km/h.
2 Peter Hickman (BMW); **3** Tarran Mackenzie (Yamaha); **4** Glenn Irwin (Honda); **5** Jason O'Halloran (Yamaha); **6** Leon Haslam (Kawasaki); **7** Tommy Bridewell (Ducati); **8** Kyle Ryde (Yamaha); **9** Andrew Irwin (BMW); **10** Lee Jackson (Kawasaki); **11** Josh Brookes (Ducati); **12** Danny Kent (Suzuki); **13** Tom

Neave (Honda); **14** Ryo Mizuno (Honda); **15** Dean Harrison (Kawasaki).
Fastest lap: Mackenzie, 1m 47.527s, 99.39mph/159.96km/h.
Championship points (start of Showdown): 1 Bradley Ray, 1061; **2** Jason O'Halloran, 1048; **3** Tarran Mackenzie, 1031; **4** Glenn Irwin, 1016; **5** Lee Jackson, 1014; **6** Kyle Ryde, 1013; **7** Rory Skinner, 1009; **8** Tommy Bridewell, 1008.

Quattro Group British Supersport Championship, Round 8
Race 1 (10 laps, 29.690 miles/47.781km)
1 Jack Kennedy (Yamaha), 18m 51.217s, 94.48mph/152.05km/h.
2 Jamie van Sikkelerus (Yamaha); **3** Lee Johnston (Yamaha); **4** Harry Truelove (Yamaha); **5** Jack Scott (One); **6** Luke Jones (Ducati); **7** Luke Stapleford (Kawasaki); **8** Rhys Irwin (Triumph); **9** Tom Toparis (Triumph); **10** Eugene McManus (Kawasaki); **11** Ash Barnes (Yamaha); **12** Damon Rees (Yamaha); **13** Scott Swann (Kawasaki); **14** Cameron Fraser (Chassis Factory); **15** Harvey Claridge (Chassis Factory).
Fastest lap: Kennedy, 1m 52.191s, 95.26mph/153.31km/h.

Race 2 (14 laps, 41.566 miles/66.894km)
1 Jack Kennedy (Yamaha), 26m 16.228s, 94.93mph/152.78km/h.
2 Bradley Perie (Yamaha); **3** Jamie van Sikkelerus (Yamaha); **4** Lee Johnston (Yamaha); **5** Jack Scott (One); **6** Rhys Irwin (Triumph); **7** Luke Stapleford (Kawasaki); **8** Damon Rees (Yamaha); **9** Eugene McManus (Kawasaki); **10** Luke Jones (Ducati); **11** Tom Toparis (Triumph); **12** Ash Barnes (Yamaha); **13** Scott Swann (Kawasaki); **14** Harvey Claridge (Chassis Factory); **15** Harry Rowlings (BER Evo).
Fastest lap: Kennedy, 1m 51.564s, 95.80mph/154.17km/h.
Championship points: 1 Jack Kennedy, 385; **2** Bradley Perie, 234; **3** Harry Truelove, 212; **4** Luke Stapleford, 185; **5** Lee Johnston, 156; **6** Jamie van Sikkelerus, 144.

Honda British Talent Cup, Round 8
Race 1 (12 laps, 35.628 miles/57.338km)
1 Johnny Garness (Honda), 24m 52.804s, 85.91mph/138.26km/h.
2 Rhys Stephenson (Honda); **3** Harrison Crosby (Honda); **4** Lucas Brown (Honda); **5** Filip Surowiak (Honda); **6** Ryan Hitchcock (Honda); **7** Bailey Stuart-Campbell (Honda); **8** Daniel Goodman (Honda); **9** Harley McCabe (Honda); **10** Ollie Walker (Honda); **11** Luca Hopkins (Honda); **12** Evan Belford (Honda); **13** Josh Bannister (Honda); **14** Harrison Mackay (Honda); **15** Sullivan Mounsey (Honda).
Fastest lap: Stephenson, 2m 2.885s, 86.97mph/139.97km/h.

Race 2 (10 laps, 29.690 miles/47.781km)
1 Johnny Garness (Honda), 20m 39.664s, 86.21mph/138.74km/h.
2 Evan Belford (Honda); **3** Harrison Crosby (Honda); **4** Filip Surowiak (Honda); **5** Daniel Goodman (Honda); **6** Harrison Mackay (Honda); **7** Ryan Hitchcock (Honda); **8** Lucas Brown (Honda); **9** Ollie Walker (Honda); **10** Bailey Stuart-Campbell (Honda); **11** Clayton Edmunds (Honda); **12** Luca Hopkins (Honda); **13** Josh Bannister (Honda); **14** Julian Correa (Honda); **15** James Cook (Honda).
Fastest lap: Garness, 2m 2.176s, 87.48mph/140.78km/h.
Championship points: 1 Johnny Garness, 336; **2** Carter Brown, 192; **3** Rhys Stephenson, 161; **4** Harrison Crosby, 161; **5** Kiyano Veijer, 132; **6** Harrison Dessoy, 132.

OULTON PARK, 23-25 September 2022, 2.692-mile/4.332km circuit
Bennetts British Superbike Championship, Round 9
Race 1 (14 laps, 37.688 miles/60.653km)
1 Bradley Ray (Yamaha), 22m 7.589s, 102.19mph/164.46km/h.
2 Tommy Bridewell (Ducati); **3** Leon Haslam (Kawasaki); **4** Glenn Irwin (Honda); **5** Danny Buchan (BMW); **6** Lee Jackson (Kawasaki); **7** Christian Iddon (Suzuki); **8** Rory Skinner (Kawasaki); **9** Kyle Ryde (Yamaha); **10** Josh Brookes (Ducati); **11** Tom Sykes (Ducati); **12** Danny Kent (Suzuki); **13** Tom Neave (Honda); **14** Dean Harrison (Kawasaki); **15** Chrissy Rouse (BMW).
Fastest lap: O'Halloran, 1m 33.884s, 103.22mph/166.12km/h.

Race 2 (7 laps, 18.844 miles/30.326km)
1 Lee Jackson (Kawasaki), 11m 3.517s, 102.24mph/164.54km/h.
2 Tommy Bridewell (Ducati); **3** Bradley Ray (Yamaha); **4** Glenn Irwin (Honda); **5** Danny Buchan (BMW); **6** Leon Haslam (Kawasaki); **7** Tom Sykes (Ducati); **8** Josh Brookes (Ducati); **9** Andrew Irwin (BMW); **10** Peter Hickman (BMW); **11** Storm Stacey (Kawasaki); **12** Danny Kent (Suzuki); **13** Ryan Vickers (BMW); **14** Takumi Takahashi (Honda); **15** Ryo Mizuno (Honda).
Fastest lap: Bridewell, 1m 33.654s, 103.47mph/166.53km/h.

Race 3 (15 laps, 40.380 miles/64.985km)
1 Tommy Bridewell (Ducati), 23m 44.970s, 102.01mph/164.17km/h.
2 Glenn Irwin (Honda); **3** Lee Jackson (Kawasaki); **4** Danny Buchan (BMW); **5** Bradley Ray (Yamaha); **6** Tom Sykes (Ducati); **7** Peter Hickman (BMW); **8** Josh Brookes (Ducati); **9** Kyle Ryde (Yamaha); **10** Danny Kent (Suzuki); **11** Storm Stacey (Kawasaki); **12** Andrew Irwin (BMW); **13** Ryan Vickers (BMW); **14** Leon Haslam (Kawasaki); **15** Dean Harrison (Kawasaki).
Fastest lap: Ray, 1m 33.941s, 103.16mph/166.02km/h.
Championship points: 1 Bradley Ray, 1113; **2** Tommy Bridewell, 1073; **3** Lee Jackson, 1065; **4** Glenn Irwin, 1062; **5** Jason O'Halloran, 1048; **6** Tarran Mackenzie, 1031; **7** Kyle Ryde, 1027; **8** Rory Skinner, 1017.

Quattro Group British Supersport Championship, Round 9
Race 1 (12 laps, 32.304 miles/51.988km)
1 Bradley Perie (Yamaha), 19m 44.642s, 98.16mph/157.97km/h.
2 Harry Truelove (Yamaha); **3** Lee Johnston (Yamaha); **4** Jamie Perrin (Yamaha); **5** Scott Swann (Kawasaki); **6** Damon Rees (Yamaha); **7** Rhys Irwin (Triumph); **8** Jamie van Sikkelerus (Yamaha); **9** Shane Richardson (Triumph); **10** Eugene McManus (Kawasaki); **11** Harvey Claridge (Chassis Factory); **12** Max Wadsworth (Yamaha); **13** Jake Archer (FTR); **14** Cameron Fraser (Chassis Factory); **15** Caolán Irwin (Yamaha).
Fastest lap: Stapleford, 1m 37.618s, 99.27mph/159.77km/h.

Race 2 (12 laps, 32.304 miles/51.988km)
1 Bradley Perie (Yamaha), 19m 41.758s, 98.40mph/158.36km/h.
2 Lee Johnston (Yamaha); **3** Jack Kennedy (Yamaha); **4** Jamie Perrin (Yamaha); **5** Jamie van Sikkelerus (Yamaha); **6** Rhys Irwin (Triumph); **7** Damon Rees (Yamaha); **8** Eugene McManus (Kawasaki); **9** Scott Swann (Kawasaki); **10** Shane Richardson (Triumph); **11** Jack Scott (One); **12** Jake Archer (FTR); **13** Harvey Claridge (Chassis Factory); **14** Ash Barnes (Yamaha); **15** Cameron Fraser (Chassis Factory).
Fastest lap: Kennedy, 1m 37.459s, 99.43mph/160.03km/h.
Championship points: 1 Jack Kennedy, 401; **2** Bradley Perie, 284; **3** Harry Truelove, 232; **4** Lee Johnston, 192; **5** Luke Stapleford, 185; **6** Jamie van Sikkelerus, 163.

DONINGTON PARK INTERNATIONAL, 30 September-2 October 2022, 2.822-mile/4.452km circuit
Bennetts British Superbike Championship, Round 10
Race 1 (15 laps, 37.305 miles/60.037km)
1 Tom Sykes (Ducati), 22m 22.761s, 99.92mph/160.81km/h.
2 Jason O'Halloran (Yamaha); **3** Peter Hickman (BMW); **4** Bradley Ray (Yamaha); **5** Glenn Irwin (Honda); **6** Lee Jackson (Kawasaki); **7** Kyle Ryde (Yamaha); **8** Tommy Bridewell (Ducati); **9** Leon Haslam (Kawasaki); **10** Ryan Vickers (BMW); **11** Josh Brookes (Ducati); **12** Danny Buchan (BMW); **13** Tom Neave (Honda); **14** Takumi Takahashi (Honda); **15** Ryo Mizuno (Honda).
Fastest lap: Hickman, 1m 29.030s, 100.57mph/161.86km/h.

Race 2 (19 laps, 47.253 miles/76.046km)
1 Tom Sykes (Ducati), 28m 17.464s, 100.14mph/161.16km/h.
2 Bradley Ray (Yamaha); **3** Glenn Irwin (Honda); **4** Andrew Irwin (BMW); **5** Lee Jackson (Kawasaki); **6** Tommy Bridewell (Ducati); **7** Jason O'Halloran (Yamaha); **8** Peter Hickman (BMW); **9** Josh Brookes (Ducati); **10** Ryan Vickers (BMW); **11** Kyle Ryde (Yamaha); **12** Danny Buchan (BMW); **13** Charlie Nesbitt (Suzuki); **14** Danny Kent (Suzuki); **15** Takumi Takahashi (Honda).
Fastest lap: Sykes, 1m 28.808s, 100.82mph/162.26km/h.

Race 3 (18 laps, 44.766 miles/72.044km)
1 Bradley Ray (Yamaha), 27m 6.696s, 99.00mph/159.33km/h.
2 Andrew Irwin (BMW); **3** Glenn Irwin (Honda); **4** Tommy Bridewell (Ducati); **5** Danny Buchan (BMW); **6** Kyle Ryde (Yamaha); **7** Lee Jackson (Kawasaki); **8** Ryan Vickers (BMW); **9** Danny Kent (Suzuki); **10** Leon Haslam (Kawasaki); **11** Peter Hickman (BMW); **12** Storm Stacey (Kawasaki); **13** Charlie Nesbitt (Suzuki); **14** Tom Neave (Honda); **15** Takumi Takahashi (Honda).
Fastest lap: Ray, 1m 28.597s, 101.06mph/162.65km/h.
Championship points: 1 Bradley Ray, 1171; **2** Glenn Irwin, 1105; **3** Tommy Bridewell, 1104; **4** Lee Jackson, 1095; **5** Jason O'Halloran, 1077; **6** Kyle Ryde, 1051; **7** Tarran Mackenzie, 1031; **8** Rory Skinner, 1017.

Quattro Group British Supersport Championship, Round 10
Race 1 (12 laps, 29.844 miles/48.029km)
1 Bradley Perie (Yamaha), 18m 36.565s, 96.11mph/154.67km/h.
2 Jamie van Sikkelerus (Yamaha); **3** Lee Johnston (Yamaha); **4** Tom Booth-Amos (Kawasaki); **5** Luke Jones (Ducati); **6** Harry Truelove (Yamaha); **7** Rhys Irwin (Triumph); **8** Damon Rees (Yamaha); **9** Eugene McManus (Kawasaki); **10** Scott Swann (Kawasaki); **11** Shane Richardson (Triumph); **12** Harvey Claridge (Chassis Factory); **13** Caolán Irwin (Yamaha); **14** Ash Barnes (Yamaha); **15** Max Wadsworth (Yamaha).
Fastest lap: Johnston, 1m 31.921s, 97.41mph/156.77km/h.

Race 2 (17 laps, 47.974 miles/77.207km)
1 Jamie van Sikkelerus (Yamaha), 26m 20.333s, 96.23mph/154.87km/h.
2 Harry Truelove (Yamaha); **3** Lee Johnston (Yamaha); **4** Tom Booth-Amos (Kawasaki); **5** Luke Jones (Ducati); **6** Eugene McManus (Kawasaki); **7** Jack Scott (One); **8** Jamie Perrin (Yamaha); **9** Rhys Irwin (Triumph); **10** Damon Rees (Yamaha); **11** Shane Richardson (Triumph); **12** Mason Law (ABM); **13** Caolán Irwin (Yamaha); **14** Max Wadsworth (Yamaha); **15** Jake Archer (FTR).
Fastest lap: van Sikkelerus, 1m 32.107s, 97.21mph/156.45km/h.
Championship points: 1 Jack Kennedy, 401; **2** Bradley Perie, 309; **3** Harry Truelove, 262; **4** Lee Johnston, 224; **5** Jamie van Sikkelerus, 208; **6** Luke Stapleford, 185.

Honda British Talent Cup, Round 9
Race 1 (15 laps, 37.305 miles/60.037km)
1 Evan Belford (Honda), 25m 47.671s, 86.69mph/139.51km/h.
2 Carter Brown (Honda); **3** Harley McCabe (Honda); **4** Lucas Brown (Honda); **5** Harrison Crosby (Honda); **6** Filip Surowiak (Honda); **7** James Cook (Honda); **8** Sullivan Mounsey (Honda); **9** Harrison Dessoy (Honda); **10** Daniel Goodman (Honda); **11** Bailey Stuart-Campbell (Honda); **12** Luca Hopkins (Honda); **13** Charlie Huntingford (Honda); **14** Peter Willis (Honda); **15** Alfie Davidson (Honda).
Fastest lap: Stephenson, 1m 41.839s, 87.92mph/141.50km/h.

Race 2 (12 laps, 29.844 miles/48.029km)
1 Evan Belford (Honda), 20m 56.520s, 85.40mph/137.44km/h.
2 Carter Brown (Honda); **3** Rhys Stephenson (Honda); **4** Sullivan Mounsey (Honda); **5** Lucas Brown (Honda); **6** Harley McCabe (Honda); **7** Harrison Crosby (Honda); **8** Filip Surowiak (Honda); **9** James Cook (Honda); **10** Kiyano Veijer (Honda); **11** Julian Correa (Honda); **12** Harrison Dessoy (Honda); **13** Charlie Huntingford (Honda); **14** Ollie Walker (Honda); **15** Peter Willis (Honda).
Fastest lap: C. Brown, 1m 41.847s, 87.92mph/141.49km/h.
Championship points: 1 Johnny Garness, 336; **2** Carter Brown, 232; **3** Harrison Crosby, 181; **4** Rhys Stephenson, 177; **5** Lucas Brown, 151; **6** Harrison Dessoy, 143.

BRANDS HATCH GP, 14-16 October 2022, 2.433-mile/3.916km circuit.
Bennetts British Superbike Championship, Round 11
Race 1 (16 laps, 38.928 miles/62.649km)
1 Glenn Irwin (Honda), 22m 52.528s, 102.11mph/164.33km/h.
2 Peter Hickman (BMW); **3** Andrew Irwin (BMW); **4** Tommy Bridewell (Ducati); **5** Bradley Ray (Yamaha); **6** Jason O'Halloran (Yamaha); **7** Danny Buchan (BMW); **8** Danny Kent (Suzuki); **9** Kyle Ryde (Yamaha); **10** Tom Sykes (Ducati); **11** Charlie Nesbitt (Suzuki); **12** Josh Owens (Kawasaki); **13** Takumi Takahashi (Honda); **14** Jack Kennedy (Yamaha); **15** Davey Todd (Honda).
Fastest lap: G. Irwin, 1m 25.090s, 102.94mph/165.67km/h.

Race 2 (20 laps, 48.660 miles/78.311km)
1 Peter Hickman (BMW), 28m 41.278s, 101.78mph/163.80km/h.
2 Danny Buchan (BMW); **3** Glenn Irwin (Honda); **4** Kyle Ryde (Yamaha); **5** Tommy Bridewell (Ducati); **6** Danny Kent (Suzuki); **7** Christian Iddon (Suzuki); **8** Charlie Nesbitt (Suzuki); **9** Josh Brookes (Ducati); **10** Tom Sykes (Ducati); **11** Josh Owens (Kawasaki); **12** Dean Harrison (Kawasaki); **13** Takumi Takahashi (Honda); **14** Storm Stacey (Kawasaki); **15** Davey Todd (Honda).
Fastest lap: G. Irwin, 1m 25.458s, 102.50mph/164.96km/h.

Race 3 (20 laps, 48.660 miles/78.311km)
1 Glenn Irwin (Honda), 28m 36.999s, 102.03mph/164.20km/h.
2 Andrew Irwin (BMW); **3** Danny Buchan (BMW); **4** Tommy Bridewell (Ducati); **5** Peter Hickman (BMW); **6** Bradley Ray (Yamaha); **7** Josh Brookes (Ducati); **8** Danny Kent (Suzuki); **9** Christian Iddon (Suzuki); **10** Kyle Ryde (Yamaha); **11** Tom Sykes (Ducati); **12** Charlie Nesbitt (Suzuki); **13** Ryan Vickers (BMW); **14** Josh Owens (Kawasaki); **15** Takumi Takahashi (Honda).
Fastest lap: G. Irwin, 1m 25.126s, 102.90mph/165.6km/h.

Quattro Group British Supersport Championship, Round 11
Race 1 (12 laps, 29.196 miles/46.986km)
1 Bradley Perie (Yamaha), 17m 47.156s, 98.50mph/158.52km/h.
2 Richard Cooper (Yamaha); **3** Rhys Irwin (Triumph); **4** Lee Johnston (Yamaha); **5** Jaimie van Sikkelerus (Yamaha); **6** Damon Rees (Yamaha); **7** Luke Stapleford (Kawasaki); **8** Tom Booth-Amos (Kawasaki); **9** Jamie Perrin (Yamaha); **10** Mason Law (ABM); **11** Max Cook (Yamaha); **12** Eugene McManus (Kawasaki); **13** Scott Swann (Kawasaki); **14** Eunan McGlinchey (Kawasaki); **15** Ash Barnes (Yamaha).
Fastest lap: Truelove, 1m 28.169s, 99.35mph/159.89km/h.

Race 2 (16 laps, 38.928 miles/62.649km)
1 Bradley Perie (Yamaha), 23m 40.186s, 98.68mph/158.81km/h.
2 Lee Johnston (Yamaha); **3** Richard Cooper (Yamaha); **4** Harry Truelove (Yamaha); **5** Tom Booth-Amos (Kawasaki); **6** Jaimie van Sikkelerus (Yamaha); **7** Rhys Irwin (Triumph); **8** Damon Rees (Yamaha); **9** Max Cook (Yamaha); **10** Luke Stapleford (Kawasaki); **11** Mason Law (ABM); **12** Eugene McManus (Kawasaki); **13** Luke Jones (Ducati); **14** Ash Barnes (Yamaha); **15** Max Wadsworth (Yamaha).
Fastest lap: Johnston, 1m 28.049s, 99.48mph/160.11km/h.

Final British Superbike Championship points:

1	Bradley Ray	1192
2	Glenn Irwin	1171
3	Tommy Bridewell	1141
4	Lee Jackson	1095
5	Jason O'Halloran	1087
6	Kyle Ryde	1077

7 Tarran Mackenzie, 1031; **8** Rory Skinner, 1017; **9** Peter Hickman, 283; **10** Danny Buchan, 272; **11** Leon Haslam, 205; **12** Tom Sykes, 187; **13** Andrew Irwin, 181; **14** Josh Brookes, 161; **15** Christian Iddon, 135.

Final British Supersport Championship points:

1	Jack Kennedy	401
2	Bradley Perie	359
3	Harry Truelove	275
4	Lee Johnston	257
5	Jamie van Sikkelerus	229
6	Luke Stapleford	200

7 Rhys Irwin, 155; **8** Eugene McManus, 153; **9** Damon Rees, 145; **10** Luke Jones, 135; **11** Jamie Perrin, 124; **12** Ash Barnes, 73; **13** Max Ingham, 55; **14** Caolán Irwin, 55; **15** Scott Swann, 52.

Final British Talent Cup points:

1	Johnny Garness	336
2	Carter Brown	232
3	Harrison Crosby	181
4	Rhys Stephenson	177
5	Lucas Brown	151
6	Harrison Dessoy	143

7 Evan Belford, 142; **8** Kiyano Veijer, 138; **9** Ryan Hitchcock, 103; **10** Matthew Ruisbroek, 98; **11** Harley McCabe, 95; **12** Julian Correa, 92; **13** Sullivan Mounsey, 88; **14** Harrison Mackay, 85; **15** Bailey Stuart-Campbell, 74.

Supersport World Championship

Round 1, ARAGON, Spain, 8-10 April 2022, 3.155-mile/5.077km circuit
Race 1 (15 laps, 47.321 miles/76.155km)
1 Lorenzo Baldassarri, ITA (Yamaha), 28m 38.988s, 99.101mph/159.488km/h.
2 Dominique Aegerter, SUI (Yamaha); **3** Can Oncu, TUR (Kawasaki); **4** Glenn Van Straalen, NED (Yamaha); **5** Nicolo Bulega, ITA (Ducati); **6** Niki Tuuli, FIN (MV Agusta); **7** Stefano Manzi, ITA (Triumph); **8** Federico Caricasulo, ITA (Ducati); **9** Adrian Huertas, ESP (Kawasaki); **10** Patrick Hobelsberger, GER (Yamaha); **11** Hannes Soomer, EST (Triumph); **12** Bahattin Sofuoglu, TUR (MV Agusta); **13** Thomas Booth-Amos, GBR (Kawasaki); **14** Peter Sebestyen, HUN (Yamaha); **15** Andy Verdoia, FRA (Yamaha).
Fastest lap: Aegerter, SUI (Yamaha), 1m 53.795s, 99.805mph/160.620km/h.

Race 2 (15 laps, 47.321 miles/76.155km)
1 Dominique Aegerter, SUI (Yamaha), 28m 36.096s, 99.268mph/159.757km/h.
2 Lorenzo Baldassarri, ITA (Yamaha); **3** Nicolo Bulega, ITA (Ducati); **4** Glenn Van Straalen, NED (Yamaha); **5** Niki Tuuli, FIN (MV Agusta); **6** Jules Cluzel, FRA (Yamaha); **7** Yari Montella, ITA (Kawasaki); **8** Stefano Manzi, ITA (Triumph); **9** Raffaele De Rosa, ITA (Ducati); **10** Hannes Soomer, EST (Triumph); **11** Adrian Huertas, ESP (Kawasaki); **12** Federico Caricasulo, ITA (Ducati); **13** Patrick Hobelsberger, GER (Yamaha); **14** Bahattin Sofuoglu, TUR (MV Agusta); **15** Thomas Booth-Amos, GBR (Kawasaki).
Fastest lap: Aegerter, SUI (Yamaha), 1m 53.639s, 99.941mph/160.840km/h.
Championship points: 1 Aegerter, 45; **2** Baldassarri, 45; **3** Bulega, 27; **4** Van Straalen, 26; **5** Tuuli, 21; **6** Manzi, 17.

Round 2, ASSEN, The Netherlands, 22-24 April 2022, 2.822-mile/4.542km circuit
Race 1 (13 laps, 39.243 miles/63.156km)
1 Dominique Aegerter, SUI (Yamaha), 22m 54.605s, 102.775mph/165.401km/h.
2 Glenn Van Straalen, NED (Yamaha); **3** Nicolo Bulega, ITA (Ducati); **4** Jules Cluzel, FRA (Yamaha); **5** Federico Caricasulo, ITA (Ducati); **6** Niki Tuuli, FIN (MV Agusta); **7** Hannes Soomer, EST (Triumph); **8** Patrick Hobelsberger, GER (Yamaha); **9** Raffaele De Rosa, ITA (Ducati); **10** Leonardo Taccini, ITA (Yamaha); **11** Adrian Huertas, ESP (Kawasaki); **12** Yari Montella, ITA (Kawasaki); **13** Unai Orradre, ESP

(Yamaha); **14** Oliver Bayliss, AUS (Ducati); **15** Bahattin Sofuoglu, TUR (MV Agusta),
Fastest lap: Aegerter, SUI (Yamaha), 1m 37.926s, 103.757mph/166.980km/h.

Race 2 (18 laps, 50.801 miles/81.756km)
1 Dominique Aegerter, SUI (Yamaha), 29m 35.903s, 102.980mph/165.731km/h.
2 Lorenzo Baldassarri, ITA (Yamaha); **3** Can Oncu, TUR (Kawasaki); **4** Nicolo Bulega, ITA (Ducati); **5** Hannes Soomer, EST (Triumph); **6** Stefano Manzi, ITA (Triumph); **7** Niki Tuuli, FIN (MV Agusta); **8** Kyle Smith, GBR (Yamaha); **9** Yari Montella, ITA (Kawasaki); **10** Bahattin Sofuoglu, TUR (MV Agusta); **11** Oliver Bayliss, AUS (Ducati); **12** Marcel Brenner, SUI (Yamaha); **13** Leonardo Taccini, ITA (Yamaha); **14** Unai Orradre, ESP (Yamaha); **15** Raffaele De Rosa, ITA (Ducati).
Fastest lap: Aegerter, SUI (Yamaha), 1m 37.958s, 103.719mph/166.920km/h.
Championship points: 1 Aegerter, 95; **2** Baldassarri, 65; **3** Bulega, 56; **4** Van Straalen, 46; **5** Tuuli, 40; **6** Oncu, 32.

Round 3, ESTORIL, Portugal, 20-22 May 2022, 2.599-mile/4.182km circuit
Race 1 (18 laps, 46.774 miles/75.276km)
1 Dominique Aegerter, SUI (Yamaha), 30m 18.215s, 92.612mph/149.044km/h.
2 Lorenzo Baldassarri, ITA (Yamaha); **3** Nicolo Bulega, ITA (Ducati); **4** Can Oncu, TUR (Kawasaki); **5** Federico Caricasulo, ITA (Ducati); **6** Yari Montella, ITA (Kawasaki); **7** Glenn Van Straalen, NED (Yamaha); **8** Adrian Huertas, ESP (Kawasaki); **9** Andy Verdoia, FRA (Yamaha); **10** Ondrej Vostatek, CZE (Yamaha); **11** Kyle Smith, GBR (Yamaha); **12** Oliver Bayliss, AUS (Ducati); **13** Simon Jespersen, DEN (Yamaha); **14** Leonardo Taccini, ITA (Yamaha); **15** Marcel Brenner, SUI (Yamaha).
Fastest lap: Aegerter, SUI (Yamaha), 1m 40.058s, 93.492mph/150.460km/h.

Race 2 (18 laps, 46.774 miles/75.276km)
1 Dominique Aegerter, SUI (Yamaha), 30m 52.488s, 90.898mph/146.286km/h.
2 Kyle Smith, GBR (Yamaha); **3** Lorenzo Baldassarri, ITA (Yamaha); **4** Yari Montella, ITA (Kawasaki); **5** Can Oncu, TUR (Kawasaki); **6** Oliver Bayliss, AUS (Ducati); **7** Adrian Huertas, ESP (Kawasaki); **8** Glenn Van Straalen, NED (Yamaha); **9** Tom Edwards, AUS (Yamaha); **10** Ondrej Vostatek, CZE (Yamaha); **11** Luca Ottaviani, ITA (Yamaha); **12** Hannes Soomer, EST (Triumph); **13** Peter Sebestyen, HUN (Yamaha); **14** Bahattin Sofuoglu, TUR (MV Agusta); **15** Benjamin Currie, AUS (Kawasaki).
Fastest lap: Aegerter, SUI (Yamaha), 1m 41.072s, 92.559mph/148.960km/h.
Championship points: 1 Aegerter, 145; **2** Baldassarri, 101; **3** Bulega, 72; **4** Van Straalen, 63; **5** Oncu, 56; **6** Montella, 43.

Round 4, MISANO, Italy, 10-12 June 2022, 2.626-mile/4.226km circuit.
Race 1 (18 laps, 47.266 miles/76.068km)
1 Dominique Aegerter, SUI (Yamaha), 29m 34.863s, 95.872mph/154.291km/h.
2 Lorenzo Baldassarri, ITA (Yamaha); **3** Nicolo Bulega, ITA (Ducati); **4** Can Oncu, TUR (Kawasaki); **5** Stefano Manzi, ITA (Triumph); **6** Yari Montella, ITA (Kawasaki); **7** Jules Cluzel, FRA (Yamaha); **8** Mattia Casadei, ITA (MV Agusta); **9** Marcel Brenner, SUI (Yamaha); **10** Adrian Huertas, ESP (Kawasaki); **11** Hannes Soomer, EST (Triumph); **12** Peter Sebestyen, HUN (Yamaha); **13** Andy Verdoia, FRA (Yamaha); **14** Leonardo Taccini, ITA (Yamaha); **15** Nicholas Spinelli, ITA (Ducati).
Fastest lap: Bulega, ITA (Ducati), 1m 37.765s, 96.692mph/155.610km/h.

Race 2 (18 laps, 47.266 miles/76.068km)
1 Dominique Aegerter, SUI (Yamaha), 29m 33.667s, 95.937mph/154.395km/h.
2 Lorenzo Baldassarri, ITA (Yamaha); **3** Nicolo Bulega, ITA (Ducati); **4** Stefano Manzi, ITA (Triumph); **5** Can Oncu, TUR (Kawasaki); **6** Federico Caricasulo, ITA (Ducati); **7** Yari Montella, ITA (Kawasaki); **8** Mattia Casadei, ITA (MV Agusta); **9** Jules Cluzel, FRA (Yamaha); **10** Raffaele De Rosa, ITA (Ducati); **11** Andy Verdoia, FRA (Yamaha); **12** Hannes Soomer, EST (Triumph); **13** Marcel Brenner, SUI (Yamaha); **14** Peter Sebestyen, HUN (Yamaha); **15** Adrian Huertas, ESP (Kawasaki).
Fastest lap: Bulega, ITA (Ducati), 1m 37.671s, 96.785mph/155.760km/h.
Championship points: 1 Aegerter, 195; **2** Baldassarri, 141; **3** Bulega, 104; **4** Oncu, 80; **5** Van Straalen, 63; **6** Montella, 62.

Round 5, DONINGTON PARK, UK, 15-17 July 2022, 2.500-mile/4.023km circuit
Race 1 (12 laps, 29.997 miles/48.276km)
1 Dominique Aegerter, SUI (Yamaha), 18m 18.408s, 98.315mph/158.223km/h.
2 Lorenzo Baldassarri, ITA (Yamaha); **3** Raffaele De Rosa, ITA (Ducati); **4** Yari Montella, ITA (Kawasaki); **5** Can Oncu, TUR (Kawasaki); **6** Stefano Manzi, ITA (Triumph); **7** Hannes Soomer, EST (Triumph); **8** Andy Verdoia, FRA (Yamaha); **9** Simon Jespersen, DEN (Ducati); **10** Marcel Brenner, SUI (Yamaha); **11** Oliver Bayliss, AUS (Ducati); **12** Mattia Casadei, ITA (MV Agusta); **13** Leonardo Taccini, ITA (Yamaha); **14** Kyle Smith, GBR (Yamaha); **15** Bahattin Sofuoglu, TUR (MV Agusta),
Fastest lap: Baldassarri, ITA (Yamaha), 1m 30.629s, 98.817mph/159.030km/h.

Race 2 (19 laps, 47.496 miles/76.437km)
1 Dominique Aegerter, SUI (Yamaha), 28m 57.352s, 98.417mph/158.387km/h.
2 Lorenzo Baldassarri, ITA (Yamaha); **3** Nicolo Bulega, ITA (Ducati); **4** Federico Caricasulo, ITA (Ducati); **5** Stefano Manzi, ITA (Triumph); **6** Raffaele De Rosa, ITA (Ducati); **7** Adrian Huertas, ESP (Kawasaki); **8** Can Oncu, TUR (Kawasaki); **9** Andy Verdoia, FRA (Yamaha); **10** Simon Jespersen, DEN (Ducati); **11** Mattia Casadei, ITA (MV Agusta); **12** Unai Orradre, ESP (Yamaha); **13** Oliver Bayliss, AUS (Ducati); **14** Isaac Vinales, ESP (Ducati); **15** Leonardo Taccini, ITA (Yamaha).
Fastest lap: Aegerter, SUI (Yamaha), 1m 30.564s, 98.910mph/159.180km/h.
Championship points: 1 Aegerter, 245; **2** Baldassarri, 181; **3** Bulega, 120; **4** Oncu, 99; **5** Montella, 75; **6** Manzi, 72.

Round 6, MOST, Czech Republic, 29-31 July 2022, 2.617-mile/4.212km circuit
Race 1 (19 laps, 49.727 miles/80.028km)
1 Lorenzo Baldassarri, ITA (Yamaha), 30m 23.358s, 98.180mph/158.006km/h.
2 Stefano Manzi, ITA (Triumph); **3** Steven Odendaal, RSA (Yamaha); **4** Valentine Debise, FRA (Yamaha); **5** Glenn Van Straalen, NED (Yamaha); **6** Niki Tuuli, FIN (MV Agusta); **7** Bahattin Sofuoglu, TUR (MV Agusta); **8** Adrian Huertas, ESP (Kawasaki); **9** Nicolo Bulega, ITA (Ducati); **10** Isaac Vinales, ESP (Ducati); **11** Ondrej Vostatek, CZE (Yamaha); **12** Patrick Hobelsberger, GER (Yamaha); **13** Oliver Bayliss, AUS (Ducati); **14** Peter Sebestyen, HUN (Yamaha); **15** Thomas Booth-Amos, GBR (Kawasaki).
Fastest lap: Baldassarri, ITA (Yamaha), 1m 35.112s, 98.953mph/159.425km/h.

Race 2 (15 laps, 39.954 miles/64.300km)
1 Lorenzo Baldassarri, ITA (Yamaha), 24m 26.216s, 98.100mph/157.876km/h.
2 Nicolo Bulega, ITA (Ducati); **3** Stefano Manzi, ITA (Triumph); **4** Can Oncu, TUR (Kawasaki); **5** Bahattin Sofuoglu, TUR (MV Agusta); **6** Federico Caricasulo, ITA (Ducati); **7** Adrian Huertas, ESP (Kawasaki); **8** Valentine Debise, FRA (Yamaha); **9** Hannes Soomer, EST (Triumph); **10** Niki Tuuli, FIN (MV Agusta); **11** Peter Sebestyen, HUN (Yamaha); **12** Andy Verdoia, FRA (Yamaha); **13** Leonardo Taccini, ITA (Yamaha); **14** Marcel Brenner, SUI (Yamaha); **15** Glenn Van Straalen, NED (Yamaha).
Fastest lap: Manzi, ITA (Triumph), 1m 35.218s, 99.090mph/159.470km/h.
Championship points: 1 Aegerter, 245; **2** Baldassarri, 231; **3** Bulega, 147; **4** Oncu, 112; **5** Manzi, 108; **6** Van Straalen, 75.

Round 7, MAGNY-COURS, France, 9-11 September 2022, 2.741-mile/4.411km circuit
Race 1 (12 laps, 32.890 miles/52.932km)
1 Lorenzo Baldassarri, ITA (Yamaha), 20m 51.907s, 94.580mph/152.212km/h.
2 Glenn Van Straalen, NED (Yamaha); **3** Dominique Aegerter, SUI (Yamaha); **4** Can Oncu, TUR (Kawasaki); **5** Yari Montella, ITA (Kawasaki); **6** Niki Tuuli, FIN (MV Agusta); **7** Valentine Debise, FRA (Yamaha); **8** Adrian Huertas, ESP (Kawasaki); **9** Oliver Bayliss, AUS (Ducati); **10** Jules Cluzel, FRA (Yamaha); **11** Nicolo Bulega, ITA (Ducati); **12** Raffaele De Rosa, ITA (Ducati); **13** Peter Sebestyen, HUN (Yamaha); **14** Leonardo Taccini, ITA (Yamaha); **15** Hannes Soomer, EST (Triumph).
Fastest lap: Aegerter, SUI (Yamaha), 1m 40.876s, 97.661mph/157.170km/h.

Race 2 (19 laps, 52.076 miles/83.809km)
1 Dominique Aegerter, SUI (Yamaha), 32m 5.040s, 97.388mph/156.730km/h.
2 Jules Cluzel, FRA (Yamaha); **3** Nicolo Bulega, ITA (Ducati); **4** Valentine Debise, FRA (Yamaha); **5** Lorenzo Baldassarri, ITA (Yamaha); **6** Can Oncu, TUR (Kawasaki); **7** Stefano Manzi, ITA (Triumph); **8** Oliver Bayliss, AUS (Ducati); **9** Federico Caricasulo, ITA (Ducati); **10** Yari Montella, ITA (Kawasaki); **11** Niki Tuuli, FIN (MV Agusta); **12** Adrian Huertas, ESP (Kawasaki); **13** Andy Verdoia, FRA (Yamaha); **14** Raffaele De Rosa, ITA (Ducati); **15** Isaac Vinales, ESP (Ducati).
Fastest lap: Baldassarri, ITA (Yamaha), 1m 40.547s, 97.754mph/157.320km/h.
Championship points: 1 Aegerter, 286; **2** Baldassarri, 267; **3** Bulega, 168; **4** Oncu, 135; **5** Manzi, 117; **6** Van Straalen, 95.

Round 8, CATALUNYA, Spain, 23-25 September 2022, 2.875-mile/4.627km circuit
Race 1 (12 laps, 34.725 miles/55.884km)
1 Dominique Aegerter, SUI (Yamaha), 21m 14.812s, 98.060mph/157.813km/h.
2 Lorenzo Baldassarri, ITA (Yamaha); **3** Can Oncu, TUR (Kawasaki); **4** Federico Caricasulo, ITA (Ducati); **5** Bahattin Sofuoglu, TUR (MV Agusta); **6** Niki Tuuli, FIN (MV Agusta); **7** Adrian Huertas, ESP (Kawasaki); **8** Jules Cluzel, FRA (Yamaha); **9** Glenn Van Straalen, NED (Yamaha); **10** Simon Jespersen, DEN (Yamaha); **11** Leonardo Taccini, ITA (Yamaha); **12** Raffaele De Rosa, ITA (Ducati); **13** Yari Montella, ITA (Kawasaki); **14** Andy Verdoia, FRA (Yamaha); **15** Oliver Bayliss, AUS (Ducati).
Fastest lap: Aegerter, SUI (Yamaha), 1m 45.157s, 98.984mph/159.300km/h.

Race 2 (18 laps, 52.087 miles/83.826km)
1 Dominique Aegerter, SUI (Yamaha), 31m 55.307s, 97.903mph/157.559km/h.
2 Can Oncu, TUR (Kawasaki); **3** Stefano Manzi, ITA (Triumph); **4** Lorenzo Baldassarri, ITA (Yamaha); **5** Niki Tuuli, FIN (MV Agusta); **6** Federico Caricasulo, ITA (Ducati); **7** Bahattin Sofuoglu, TUR (MV Agusta); **8** Yari Montella, ITA (Kawasaki); **9** Leonardo Taccini, ITA (Yamaha); **10** Adrian Huertas, ESP (Kawasaki); **11** Marcel Brenner, SUI (Yamaha); **12** Simon Jespersen, DEN (Yamaha); **13** Hannes Soomer, EST (Triumph); **14** Nicolo Bulega, ITA (Ducati); **15** Jules Cluzel, FRA (Yamaha).
Fastest lap: Aegerter, SUI (Yamaha), 1m 45.386s, 99.320mph/159.840km/h.
Championship points: 1 Aegerter, 336; **2** Baldassarri, 300; **3** Oncu, 171; **4** Bulega, 170; **5** Manzi, 133; **6** Montella, 103.

Round 9, PORTIMAO, Portugal, 7-9 October 2022, 2.853-mile/4.592km circuit
Race 1 (12 laps, 34.240 miles/55.104km)
1 Stefano Manzi, ITA (Triumph), 21m 2.400s, 97.643mph/157.141km/h.
2 Lorenzo Baldassarri, ITA (Yamaha); **3** Federico Caricasulo, ITA (Ducati); **4** Dominique Aegerter, SUI (Yamaha); **5** Niki Tuuli, FIN (MV Agusta); **6** Raffaele De Rosa, ITA (Ducati); **7** Jules Cluzel, FRA (Yamaha); **8** Hannes Soomer, EST (Triumph); **9** Can Oncu, TUR (Kawasaki); **10** Isaac Vinales, ESP (Ducati); **11** Bahattin Sofuoglu, TUR (MV Agusta); **12** Glenn Van Straalen, NED (Yamaha); **13** Yari Montella, ITA (Kawasaki); **14** Peter Sebestyen, HUN (Yamaha); **15** Nicolo Bulega, ITA (Ducati).
Fastest lap: Baldassarri, ITA (Yamaha), 1m 44.436s, 98.736mph/158.900km/h.

Race 2 (17 laps, 48.507 miles/78.064km)
1 Dominique Aegerter, SUI (Yamaha), 29m 46.428s, 97.750mph/157.314km/h.
2 Raffaele De Rosa, ITA (Ducati); **3** Can Oncu, TUR (Kawasaki); **4** Federico Caricasulo, ITA (Ducati); **5** Bahattin Sofuoglu, TUR (MV Agusta); **6** Jules Cluzel, FRA (Yamaha); **7** Lorenzo Baldassarri, ITA (Yamaha); **8** Hannes Soomer, EST (Triumph); **9** Isaac Vinales, ESP (Ducati); **10** Nicolo Bulega, ITA (Ducati); **11** Andy Verdoia, FRA (Yamaha); **12** Simon Jespersen, DEN (Yamaha); **13** Marcel Brenner, SUI (Yamaha); **14** Maximilian Kofler, AUT (Ducati); **15** Ondrej Vostatek, CZE (Yamaha).
Fastest lap: De Rosa, ITA (Ducati), 1m 44.123s, 98.587mph/158.660km/h.
Championship points: 1 Aegerter, 374; **2** Baldassarri, 329; **3** Oncu, 194; **4** Bulega, 177; **5** Manzi, 158; **6** Caricasulo, 126.

Round 10, SAN JUAN VILLICUM, Argentina, 21-23 October 2022, 2.657-mile/4.276km circuit
Race 1 (19 laps, 50.483 miles/81.244km)
1 Dominique Aegerter, SUI (Yamaha), 32m 27.154s, 93.335mph/150.208km/h.
2 Raffaele De Rosa, ITA (Ducati); **3** Federico Caricasulo, ITA (Ducati); **4** Can Oncu, TUR (Kawasaki); **5** Niki Tuuli, FIN (MV Agusta); **6** Jules Cluzel, FRA (Yamaha); **7** Stefano Manzi, ITA (Triumph); **8** Yari Montella, ITA (Kawasaki); **9** Lorenzo Baldassarri, ITA (Yamaha); **10** Hannes Soomer, EST (Triumph); **11** Nicolo Bulega, ITA (Ducati); **12** Peter Sebestyen, HUN (Yamaha); **13** Thomas Booth-Amos, GBR (Kawasaki); **14** Kyle Smith, GBR (Yamaha); **15** Oliver Bayliss, AUS (Ducati).
Fastest lap: De Rosa, ITA (Ducati), 1m 41.693s, 94.281mph/151.730km/h.

Race 2 (19 laps, 50.483 miles/81.244km)
1 Dominique Aegerter, SUI (Yamaha), 32m 34.44s, 92.987mph/149.648km/h.
2 Federico Caricasulo, ITA (Ducati); **3** Lorenzo Baldassarri, ITA (Yamaha); **4** Niki Tuuli, FIN (MV Agusta); **5** Stefano Manzi, ITA (Triumph); **6** Jules Cluzel, FRA (Yamaha); **7** Can Oncu, TUR (Kawasaki); **8** Nicolo Bulega, ITA (Ducati); **9** Andy Verdoia, FRA (Yamaha); **10** Adrian Huertas, ESP (Kawasaki); **11** Glenn Van Straalen, NED (Yamaha); **12** Peter Sebestyen, HUN (Yamaha); **13** Thomas Booth-Amos, GBR (Kawasaki); **14** Ondrej Vostatek, CZE (Yamaha); **15** Marcel Brenner, SUI (Yamaha).
Fastest lap: Aegerter, SUI (Yamaha), 1m 42.186s, 93.473mph/150.430km/h.
Championship points: 1 Aegerter, 424; **2** Baldassarri, 352; **3** Oncu, 216; **4** Bulega, 190; **5** Manzi, 178; **6** Caricasulo, 162.

Round 11, MANDALIKA, Indonesia, 12-13 November 2022, 2.672-mile/4.300km circuit
Race 1 (19 laps, 50.778 miles/81.719km)
1 Niki Tuuli, FIN (MV Agusta), 30m 49.225s, 98.852mph/159.087km/h.
2 Federico Caricasulo, ITA (Ducati); **3** Can Oncu, TUR (Kawasaki); **4** Dominique Aegerter, SUI (Yamaha); **5** Yari Montella, ITA (Kawasaki); **6** Nicolo Bulega, ITA (Ducati); **7** Stefano Manzi, ITA (Triumph); **8** Jules Cluzel, FRA (Yamaha); **9** Raffaele De Rosa, ITA (Ducati); **10** Adrian Huertas, ESP (Kawasaki); **11** Thomas Booth-Amos, GBR (Kawasaki); **12** Andy Verdoia, FRA (Yamaha); **13** Peter Sebestyen, HUN (Yamaha); **14** Oliver Bayliss, AUS (Ducati); **15** Leonardo Taccini, ITA (Yamaha).
Fastest lap: Oncu, TUR (Kawasaki), 1m 36.303s, 99.916mph/160.800km/h.

Race 2 (13 laps, 34.952 miles/56.250km)
1 Dominique Aegerter, SUI (Yamaha), 21m 3.745s, 99.567mph/160.238km/h.
2 Stefano Manzi, ITA (Triumph); **3** Can Oncu, TUR (Kawasaki); **4** Raffaele De Rosa, ITA (Ducati); **5** Yari Montella, ITA (Kawasaki); **6** Nicolo Bulega, ITA (Ducati); **7** Federico Caricasulo, ITA (Ducati); **8** Hannes Soomer, EST (Triumph); **9** Lorenzo Baldassarri, ITA (Yamaha); **10** Jules Cluzel, FRA (Yamaha); **11** Thomas Booth-Amos, GBR (Kawasaki); **12** Adrian Huertas, ESP (Kawasaki); **13** Andy Verdoia, FRA (Yamaha); **14** Oliver Bayliss, AUS (Ducati); **15** Simon Jespersen, DEN (Yamaha).
Fastest lap: Aegerter, SUI (Yamaha), 1m 35.765s, 100.327mph/161.460km/h.
Championship points: 1 Aegerter, 462; **2** Baldassarri, 359; **3** Oncu, 248; **4** Bulega, 210; **5** Manzi, 207; **6** Caricasulo, 191.

Round 12, PHILLIP ISLAND, Australia, 18-20 November 2022, 2.762-mile/4.445km circuit
Race 1 (18 laps, 49.716 miles/80.010km)
1 Yari Montella, ITA (Kawasaki), 32m 2.504s, 93.096mph/149.823km/h.
2 Nicolo Bulega, ITA (Ducati); **3** Can Oncu, TUR (Kawasaki); **4** Lorenzo Baldassarri, ITA (Yamaha); **5** Dominique Aegerter, SUI (Yamaha); **6** Raffaele De Rosa, ITA (Ducati); **7** Federico Caricasulo, ITA (Ducati); **8** Thomas Booth-Amos, GBR (Kawasaki); **9** Simon Jespersen, DEN (Yamaha); **10** Adrian Huertas, ESP (Kawasaki); **11** Glenn Van Straalen, NED (Yamaha); **12** Oliver Bayliss, AUS (Ducati); **13** Peter Sebestyen, HUN (Yamaha); **14** Stefano Manzi, ITA (Triumph); **15** Luca Bernardi, SMR (Ducati).
Fastest lap: Bulega, ITA (Ducati), 1m 45.211s, 95.033mph/152.940km/h.

Race 2 (18 laps, 49.716 miles/80.010km)
1 Dominique Aegerter, SUI (Yamaha), 28m 29.237s, 104.712mph/168.517km/h.
2 Federico Caricasulo, ITA (Ducati); **3** Lorenzo Baldassarri, ITA (Yamaha); **4** Nicolo Bulega, ITA (Ducati); **5** Yari Montella, ITA (Kawasaki); **6** Raffaele De Rosa, ITA (Ducati); **7** Marcel Schroetter, GER (MV Agusta); **8** Oliver Bayliss, AUS (Ducati); **9** Andy Verdoia, FRA (Yamaha); **10** Glenn Van Straalen, NED (Yamaha); **11** Jules Cluzel, FRA (Yamaha); **12** Adrian Huertas, ESP (Kawasaki); **13** Peter Sebestyen, HUN (Yamaha); **14** Simon Jespersen, DEN (Yamaha); **15** Hannes Soomer, EST (Triumph).
Fastest lap: Caricasulo, ITA (Ducati), 1m 33.989s, 105.969mph/170.540km/h.

Final World Supersport Championship points:

1	Dominique Aegerter, SUI	498
2	Lorenzo Baldassarri, ITA	388
3	Can Oncu, TUR	264
4	Nicolo Bulega, ITA	242
5	Federico Caricasulo, ITA	222
6	Stefano Manzi, ITA	209

7 Yari Montella, ITA, 171; **8** Niki Tuuli, FIN, 152; **9** Raffaele De Rosa, ITA, 147; **10** Jules Cluzel, FRA, 132; **11** Glenn Van Straalen, NED, 122; **12** Adrian Huertas, ESP, 120; **13** Hannes Soomer, EST, 95; **14** Bahattin Sofuoglu, TUR, 72; **15** Andy Verdoia, FRA, 66.